FOUNDATIONS OF THE LAW AND ETHICS OF LAWYERING

FOUNDATIONS OF THE LAW AND ETHICS OF LAWYERING

George M. Cohen
Professor of Law
University of Virginia School of Law

Susan P. Koniak
Professor of Law
Boston University School of Law

ISBN: 9781422499450

NOTE TO USERS
To ensure that you are using the latest materials available in this area, please be sure to periodically check the LexisNexis Law School web site for downloadable updates and supplements at www.lexisnexis.com/lawschool.

Editorial Offices
121 Chanlon Rd., New Providence, NJ 07974 (908) 464-6800
201 Mission St., San Francisco, CA 94105-1831 (415) 908-3200
www.lexisnexis.com

(Pub.3349)

To Lauren, Emma, Linda, and Henry,
and for Geoffrey C. Hazard, Jr.,
who showed us the way.

FOUNDATIONS OF LAW SERIES

ROBERTA ROMANO, GENERAL EDITOR

Foundations of Administrative Law
Edited by Peter H. Schuck, Yale Law School

Foundations of Contract Law
Edited by Richard Craswell, Stanford Law School and Alan Schwartz, Yale Law School

Foundations of Corporate Law
Edited by Roberta Romano, Yale Law School

Foundations of Criminal Law
Edited by Leo Katz, Michael S. Moore and Stephen J. Morse, all of the University of Pennsylvania Law School

Foundations of the Economic Approach to Law
Edited by Avery Wiener Katz, Columbia Law School

Foundations of Employment Discrimination Law
Edited by John Donohue, III, Stanford Law School

Foundations of Environmental Law and Policy
Edited by Richard L. Revesz, New York University Law School

Foundations of International Income Taxation
Edited by Michael J. Graetz, Yale Law School

Foundations of Labor Law
*Edited by Samuel Estreicher, New York University Law School
and Stewart J. Schwab, Cornell Law School*

Foundations of the Law and Ethics of Lawyering
*Edited by George M. Cohen, University of Virginia School of Law and
Susan P. Koniak, Boston University School of Law*

Foundations of Tort Law
Edited by Saul Levmore, University of Chicago Law School

CONTENTS

FOUNDATIONS OF THE LAW AND ETHICS OF LAWYERING

*

INTRODUCTION

There are a good number of collections of essays on the legal profession, legal ethics, or, as many prefer to call this subject, professional responsibility. Why another? As believers in the richness of our subject, we are tired of its third-class status as an intellectual lightweight in the law school curriculum. In our view, the law and ethics of lawyering is as intellectually demanding a subject as any in the law school repertoire. This collection is our attempt to convince others that is true.

Scholarship in our field has grown and changed a good deal in recent years. The very definition of the subject has expanded, is still evolving and, as a result, is contested. Traditional essay collections in this field have leaned toward the "ethics as philosophy" school, emphasizing questions such as the dimensions of a lawyer's moral universe and whether lawyers can be good people. We find those questions tired and unsatisfying. Do most lawyers inhabit a simplified moral universe? Probably, but so do most engineers at NASA, corporate executives, doctors, plumbers and grocery store clerks, or so it seems to us. Can lawyers be lawyers and good people? The question strikes us as an affront both to lawyers and to good people, suggesting that the former should be singled out among all modern actors as morally backwards and that the latter is a simple category, achievable almost without effort, provided, that is, that one is not a lawyer. Neither strikes us as true. More to the point, we do not believe these kinds of questions are the ones that students poised to enter the world of practice, legal academics interested in the problems of lawyering, or practitioners looking for theoretical perspectives on their profession, would profit most from thinking about.

The "foundations" we wish to emphasize lie elsewhere. There is law out there that governs the conduct of lawyers. There is a complex ethos (or culture) of lawyering that pulls against that law and competes with it. There are economic forces that influence not only lawyers, clients, and other participants in the legal system, but also the law, ethos, and ultimately the structure of institutions in which lawyers live out their professional lives. There is, in other words, much that law professors and law students, as well as practicing lawyers, can profitably discuss together. And there now exists a sufficient body of academic literature to facilitate such discussion.

1

Other collections of essays on this subject have been relatively light on the law governing lawyers and on the law and economics movement's take on our profession. We focus on both. This collection emphasizes the complex regulatory framework that has developed to govern the conduct of lawyers and draws heavily on the work of law and economics scholars, not because we agree with all of it (we do not), but because it tends to highlight many of the questions that we think have been in the shadows too long and also, let us be frank, because that approach is influential in the legal academy.

Inevitably in books of this type, editors must make difficult choices. We have emphasized depth over breadth, recent articles over older ones, and broadly focused articles over narrowly focused ones. Those looking for all the old "classics" in this field or complete coverage of topics will be disappointed, but those looking for fresh views and a rigor that is often lacking in legal ethics books will, we hope, be energized and as enthusiastic as we are about the work reproduced here. We also hope you will be pleasantly surprised by the length of the excerpts. We include more of the original work than is common in most volumes of this kind because we believe in preserving the voice and views of our authors, and enjoy their work, not just for the major themes, but for the many ancillary insights that would be lost had we wielded our editing knife more bluntly. As a consequence, however, we had to omit many fine articles, some of which we have referenced in the notes.

As for our other editorial contributions, we decided to forego the common practice of writing introductions to each chapter and/or section, summarizing the articles and the topic. Our view is that most people either do not read those or get little from them. And if, as we expect, the main uses of this book will be as a supplement to a Professional Responsibility course or as a main text for an advanced seminar, such introductions are not necessary. Instead, we have focused our energies on the notes following the excerpts, some of which are fairly detailed. We hope these notes will give you some sense of our "take" on the excerpts, as well as the issues we think the excerpts raise, and that they will serve to stimulate rewarding discussion.

It is daunting to be a lawyer and that is, we believe, as it should be. Law is just too important and too powerful—too majestic and too potentially destructive—to expect the lives of its agents to be easy lives. But few things worth doing are easy. Every teacher in this subject already knows that, if not from practicing law, from struggling to make students and colleagues take what they do seriously. To our colleagues, we say we understand, and we have tried to help with this collection. Important as you are, however, you did not come first in our minds when putting this book together. We thought first and most often of the students. To each of them, we say welcome and good luck. We are rooting for you.

We thank all the authors, law reviews, and other publishers for granting us permission to use their work.

We give special thanks to Dianne Johnson for her fine editing work and for the dedication, patience, and good humor she displayed throughout. We also thank Jonathan R. Whitby for his careful proofreading and able research assistance, and Carolyn Smith for her excellent handling of a variety of administrative tasks.

Chapter I: Overview

Who Should Regulate Lawyers?*

DAVID B. WILKINS

. . .

II.   Enforcing Professional Norms: an Overview of the Current Debate

. . .

A.   *The Enforcement Systems*

... [Consider four models of enforcing professional norms]: disciplinary controls, liability controls, institutional controls, and legislative controls. . . .

1.   Disciplinary Controls.—The reference point for this model is the current disciplinary system, in which independent agencies acting under the supervision of state supreme courts investigate and prosecute violations of the rules of professional conduct. The basic structure resembles a criminal prosecution. ... The process is conducted almost exclusively ex post by independent officials. ... These officials are instructed to reach their judgments solely on the basis of the evidence presented at a formal hearing in which the accused lawyer is accorded a full panoply of due process protections. In keeping with the criminal justice analogy, disciplinary agencies primarily focus on punishment and deterrence. Compensation, although allowed under limited circumstances, remains a secondary goal.

* © 1992 The Harvard Law Review Ass'n. Reprinted by permission from 105 Harv.L.Rev. 801 (1992).

2. *Liability Controls.*—Injured clients, and to a limited extent third parties, have traditionally had the right to sue lawyers under a variety of statutory and common law theories. Although bar leaders and others have tried to separate "malpractice" from "discipline," these efforts have been largely unsuccessful....

Like the disciplinary model, liability controls operate on the basis of ex post complaints by injured parties. A victorious claimant, however, is entitled to full compensatory and even punitive damages. Restrictions on the lawyer's right to practice law, on the other hand, are generally not available. Finally, ... trial by jury [is generally available.]

3. *Institutional Controls.*—Lawyers work either directly in, or in the shadow of, state institutions.... For example, rule 11 ... authorizes judges to impose sanctions for certain kinds of litigation-related misconduct.* Similarly, several federal administrative agencies, including the Securities and Exchange Commission (SEC), the Office of Thrift Supervision (OTS) and the Internal Revenue Service (IRS) ... [may] sanction lawyers who do not properly advise their clients about their duties under these regulatory regimes.**

These and similar efforts share a common goal: to locate enforcement authority inside the institutions in which lawyers work. As a result, the structure and operation of any particular system will be primarily a function of the institution within which it is situated. Nevertheless, a few generalizations are useful. First, enforcement authorities are in a position to observe lawyer misconduct directly. A judge, for example, will know if a lawyer has failed to file a pleading. Second, because the enforcement official and the lawyer to be disciplined are involved in a continuing relationship, sanctions can be imposed either immediately or after a separate hearing. Finally, the substantive jurisdiction of these institutional enforcement officials is likely to be confined to

---

* [Editors' note: When this article was written, Federal Rule of Civil Procedure 11 required judges to impose sanctions on lawyers in some circumstances, most notably when the lawyer filed papers with the court that a reasonable investigation would have revealed were not well grounded in fact or were unsupported by law or a good faith argument that existing law should be extended. We refer to this as the 1983 version of Rule 11. Rule 11 has since been amended in a manner that substantially weakens it. Now judges may, but need not, impose sanctions, and lawyers may avoid any sanctions by withdrawing any ungrounded papers that the opposing party discerns and about which she notifies the offending lawyer, provided the papers are withdrawn within the time period prescribed in the rule. Fed.R.Civ.P. 11 (1993).]

** [Editors' note: Although it may have seemed in the early 1990s as if federal administrative agencies were poised to take a more active role in regulating lawyers, that did not happen. Indeed, even after the disclosures of massive corporate fraud in companies like Enron and Worldcom, the SEC's position was that any lawyer involvement was a matter for state bar disciplinary authorities, not the SEC. Congress responded to the SEC's disinterest in lawyer regulation by including a provision in the Sarbanes–Oxley legislation, which was passed to deal with the financial scandals, that required the SEC to get back in the business of regulating the securities bar. See Sarbanes–Oxley Act of 2002, § 307, 15 U.S.C. § 7245; Standards of Professional Conduct for Attorneys Appearing and Practicing Before the Commission in the Representation of an Issuer, 17 C.F.R. Part 205.]

the area in which the institution operates. For example, SEC officials cannot discipline lawyers outside of the securities area.

4. *Legislative Controls.*—Certain public officials and other commentators have proposed a new administrative agency that would have sole responsibility for investigating and prosecuting lawyer misconduct.... [S]uch an agency might be patterned after the agencies that currently regulate doctors ... [or] an agency might adopt procedures utilized by other regulatory agencies, such as the Occupational Safety and Health Administration (OSHA) or the SEC.... [A]uthority and operation [of the agency would] ultimately rest ... [with] the executive or the legislative branch rather than the courts.

. . .

C. The Role of Context

Participants in the various enforcement debates often speak as though their compliance and independence arguments capture universal truths about lawyers, clients, and the state. For example, the ABA's claim that judicially supervised disciplinary agencies should exercise "exclusive" control over the enforcement process implicitly asserts that this form of regulation is the best system for controlling all lawyer misconduct in all contexts.... [But context matters.]   ·

1. *Acknowledging Conflict Within the Lawyer's Role.*—It is axiomatic that lawyers are expected to be both zealous advocates for the interests of their clients and officers of the court. Each of these roles generates distinct professional duties. As an advocate, a lawyer is expected to keep the client informed, safeguard the client's secrets, provide competent and diligent services at a reasonable fee, and abide by the client's wishes concerning the purposes of the attorney-client relationship. As an officer of the court, however, a lawyer should not counsel or assist the client in fraudulent conduct, file frivolous claims or defenses, unreasonably delay litigation, intentionally fail to follow the rules of the tribunal, or unnecessarily embarrass or burden third parties....

. . .

2. *Understanding the Role of the Market.*—... Clients vary widely in their experience and sophistication concerning legal practice. Some clients will hire a lawyer only once in their lifetime. For others, interacting with lawyers is a way of life. Corporations are likely to dominate this latter category....

. . .

III. Compliance Arguments

. . .

A. The Role of Context in the Construction of Costs and Benefits

. . . [E]nforcement officials must try to prevent two categories of professional misconduct. The first, which I call "agency problems," involve cases in which lawyer misconduct primarily injures clients. Common examples include overbilling, allowing the statute of limitations to run, and representing conflicting interests in the same or substantially similar cases. The second, which I call "externality problems" or "strategic behavior," involve cases in which lawyers and clients together impose unjustified harms on third parties or on the legal framework. Common examples include cases in which a lawyer files frivolous pleadings during the course of litigation, knowingly allows her client to present perjured testimony, or assists the client in preparing a false or misleading proxy statement. . . . [T]hese problems may vary according to whether the client is an individual or a corporation. As a result, each enforcement system must be evaluated in terms of its ability to control four categories of lawyer misconduct: individual/agency problems, corporate/agency problems, individual/externality problems, and corporate/externality problems. Figure 2 illustrates this matrix.

Figure 2

Client	Conduct: Agency	Conduct: Externality
Corporation	Corporate/ Agency	Corporate/ Externality
Individual	Individual/ Agency	Individual/ Externality

Whatever compliance gains are achieved in these four quadrants must be balanced against a likely assessment of the costs associated with employing a particular method of control. Three categories of costs are potentially relevant: administrative costs, by which I mean the public costs of operating the enforcement system; participant costs, which represent the costs incurred by lawyers, clients, and other private parties in determining whether a violation has occurred and in fashioning an appropriate sanction; and third party costs, which constitute whatever additional costs the use of a particular enforcement system may impose on public or private actors other than those directly involved in the enforcement process. . . .

. . .

B.   A Comparative Evaluation of Enforcement Systems

1.   The Structural Limitations of Disciplinary Controls.—I begin with disciplinary controls because this is the regulatory structure against which all others are expressly or implicitly compared. Moreover, the ABA continues to insist that a properly functioning disciplinary process can effectively control lawyer misconduct. . . .

(a) Client Reporting Systems Are Unlikely to Control Externality Problems.—The institutional characteristics of disciplinary controls make it unlikely that this system will effectively address externality problems. Given the structural separation of the disciplinary process from the arenas in which lawyers work, disciplinary officials depend on others to generate information about lawyer misconduct. Although judges and lawyers are strongly urged to report misconduct, these knowledgeable parties rarely file complaints.

A cursory examination of the incentives facing lawyers and judges in this context reveals the causes of this deficiency. For lawyers, not only are there no tangible rewards for reporting misconduct, but adversaries who turn in their fellow lawyers also run the risk of inviting a retaliatory response. Moreover, the complex web of embedded controls surrounding many aspects of legal practice makes it possible for a lawyer wishing to sanction another member of the bar to accomplish his goal more effectively through informal controls, [such as filing a retaliatory motion or making sure other lawyers hear about particularly bad behavior.] Although a judge does not face the same adversary system disincentives as a lawyer, she nevertheless may feel that it is not her role to . . . [report misconduct to disciplinary authorities.] Moreover, even if she overcomes this initial resistance, it is likely that she will, like the lawyer, prefer to use the more efficient embedded controls at her disposal to discourage the attorney conduct that most directly implicates her interests.

Given this confluence of incentives and embedded controls facing lawyers and judges, it is not surprising that the vast majority of the complaints coming to the attention of the disciplinary system are filed by clients. These clients, however, have little incentive to report strategic behavior taken on their behalf. Despite its formal breadth, therefore, disciplinary regulation will inevitably focus on agency problems. But even in that area, the system is likely to accomplish much less than it promises.

(b) The Paradox of Agency Problems.—In order to access the benefits of the disciplinary system, a client must first understand that she may have been injured by lawyer misconduct. Paradoxically, clients in

the best position to make this determination are the least likely to bring their complaints to the attention of disciplinary authorities.

As frequent consumers of legal services, corporations have both the resources and the incentive to reduce the information asymmetry that usually exists between lawyers and clients. Thus, many corporations have hired "in house" lawyers to help them identify their legal needs, hire competent outside counsel, and monitor attorney performance. Others have delegated these functions to non-lawyers, [such as insurance company adjusters, accountants, efficiency experts or other consultants.] Access to this kind of sophisticated advice will substantially reduce the incidence of certain kinds of agency problems.

... [For example, d]uring the decade of the seventies, a growing number of corporations began to complain about the rising cost of legal services. Although such complaints are still frequently heard, these sophisticated consumers have undertaken several cost control measures that have made it more difficult for corporate lawyers to "run the meter." Many corporations took a substantial portion of their legal work "inside," which reduced opportunistic pricing by outside firms. More-over, when the decision is made to hire an outside lawyer, corporations can employ their legally sophisticated intermediaries to collect and evaluate reputational information about lawyer competence and trust-worthiness. Outside firms may be asked to submit competitive bids, periodic budgets, detailed records, and obtain prior approval before filing documents or making major strategy decisions....

Finally, these client controls are likely to be reinforced by the structure of relationships inside the corporate law firm. Corporate law-yers are generally paid according to the number of hours worked, which gives them a strong incentive to follow through on their commitments. Lawyers' incentives to keep the client happy also increase as firms move away from lock-step compensation systems toward ones that directly reward lawyers for revenue-generating activities, such as bringing in business or billing more hours. In addition, corporate firms have become increasingly ... bureaucratic. Given that the heightened monitoring capabilities of corporations are likely to make the law firm as a whole more concerned with satisfying client desires, these bureaucratic con-trols help ensure that client directives are followed throughout the organization.

Taken in combination, the embedded controls available to corpora-tions make it more difficult for lawyers to overcharge these sophisticated consumers.... This is not to suggest, however, that corporate lawyers do not commit agency violations. Just as the structure of corporate law practice makes some agency problems less likely to occur, it undoubtedly increases the probability of others. Yet, corporations have little incentive to bring violations to the attention of disciplinary officials.

Conflict-of-interest problems are a typical example. The rules of professional conduct prohibit a lawyer from either simultaneously representing conflicting interests or representing a current client whose interests are adverse to those of a former client in a matter substantially related to the prior representation. The size of the average corporate law firm increases the danger of conflicts problems. Moreover, corporations are in a peculiarly difficult position to detect potential conflicts. At any given time, a large corporation often will have several law firms working on dozens of separate matters. Keeping track of their own work, let alone what other work these firms may be doing, is an extremely time consuming and difficult task. Even sophisticated clients, therefore, may be unable to protect themselves against conflicts.

Yet, when this agency problem became apparent to corporate clients in the mid-seventies, they did not invoke the protection of the disciplinary system. The disciplinary system, with its emphasis on ex post review and punitive sanctions, was not an effective means of accomplishing the objectives of corporate clients. Instead, corporations filed a wave of disqualification motions to prevent their former lawyers from representing clients with conflicting interests. This strategy proved relatively successful, as corporate law firms instituted procedures for preventing these problems from occurring in the first place. . . .

Corporate clients are therefore unlikely to use the disciplinary system, even when they have actually been harmed by lawyer misconduct.[116] Individual clients do not have access to the embedded sanctions available to corporations. Although individuals have a greater incentive to invoke the disciplinary system as a protection against agency problems, they are unlikely to be able to utilize these controls effectively. As "one-shot" participants in the legal marketplace, individual clients are subject to each of the three major information asymmetries that foster agency problems: they do not know what services they need, they do not have access to information that would allow them to predict the quality of the services that a particular lawyer is likely to render, and they do not have a sufficient baseline from which to evaluate the quality of the

---

116. Because corporate clients have so little incentive to report their lawyers, it is not surprising that these lawyers are rarely subject to professional discipline. The number of elite lawyers from major corporate firms who have ever been disciplined is exceedingly small. See, e.g., Deborah L. Rhode, Ethical Perspectives on Legal Practice, 37 Stan. L. Rev. 589, 641 n.168 (1985) (reporting the results of a survey of 125 disciplinary actions in three jurisdictions in which 81% of attorneys sanctioned were solo practitioners and none were members of firms with more than seven lawyers). There is plenty of evidence that disciplinary officials may have discriminated against certain non-elite lawyers in the past. See Jerold S. Auerbach, Unequal Justice: Lawyers and Social Change in Modern America 102–29 (1976) (documenting the bar's discrimination against low status lawyers during the 1920s). However, the growing independence of disciplinary counsel and the current heterogeneity of the bar, see Michael J. Powell, Professional Divestiture: The Cession of Responsibility for Lawyer Discipline, 1986 Am. B. Found. Res. J. 31, 48, cast doubt on the continuing validity of Auerbach's conspiracy theory. If no one reports corporate lawyers to the bar, they will continue to be underrepresented among the lawyers who are sanctioned, regardless of the impartiality of the regulators.

services performed. By relying on client complaints, disciplinary enforcement simply reproduces these market defects.

Overall, the claim that the disciplinary system will effectively enforce professional norms across the entire spectrum of lawyer-client interactions seems quite dubious. The system simply does not address externality problems....

Finally, the administrative costs of [the disciplinary system] ... can be high.... [P]roceedings take place after the fact, [and] enforcement officials must bear all of the costs of investigation, prosecution, and adjudication. Moreover, some of these agencies are chronically underfunded....

. . .

2. Liability Controls: The Costs and Benefits of Using Litigation as Regulation.—As with the disciplinary system, liability controls operate on the basis of ex post complaints by injured parties. Whether these controls can effectively enforce norms of professional conduct depends in the first instance upon which injured parties are likely to sue lawyers and what claims these litigants assert. Traditionally, the range of parties and claims has been narrow.

(a) Reinforcing Agency Controls Through Malpractice Liability.— Liability controls traditionally have been used almost exclusively by injured clients. The results of this limitation are predictable. First, many injured clients are left out of the system because they never discover that they are the victims of malpractice. Second, clients who do sue complain only about agency problems.*** Even with these limitations, however, the structure of liability controls makes it likely that certain claims will be pursued in this system that would not be brought to the attention of disciplinary authorities.

From the perspective of the injured client, the most obvious difference between liability controls and the disciplinary system is that only the former allows for a monetary recovery in excess of whatever fee the client has paid to her lawyer. The chance to recover full compensatory (and perhaps even punitive) damages is obviously a substantial incentive to file suit. The effects of this incentive, however, should not be exaggerated given the large participant costs associated with this form of control. In general, only agency problems that result in large provable damages are likely to be brought into the system. Moreover, litigation against lawyer-defendants is particularly difficult to win. Lawyers are adept at covering their tracks ex ante and fabricating self-interested

---

*** [Editors' note: Because causation and damages are necessary elements of every malpractice case, clients would have great difficulty suing for "externality" problems. When the lawyer harms a third party or injures the legal system on the client's behalf, the client would have difficulty establishing that the lawyer "caused" the harm, as opposed to the client who will often have been "in" on the scheme. Similarly, the client would have difficulty demonstrating "damages."]

reconstructions of the facts ex post. In addition, courts tend to be deferential to the exercise of judgment by lawyers.[131] As a result, despite their desire for compensation, clients with small or difficult to prove claims are unlikely to gain access to the malpractice system. For clients with substantial claims, however, malpractice and other ex post liability schemes are likely to provide an attractive alternative to the disciplinary system.

These advantages might seem particularly appealing to corporate clients, who have both the expertise to discover lawyer misconduct and the resources to minimize the impact of many of the transaction costs normally associated with bringing this kind of claim.[133] In fact, the number of malpractice actions filed by corporate clients remains relatively small. . . .

. . .

Overall, a traditional client-centered liability regime appears likely to replicate the central problems of professional regulation: externality problems are ignored completely, and individual agency violations are substantially underenforced. Moreover, these results can be achieved only at fairly substantial costs to the participants and to society. The picture looks quite different, however, if third parties are given standing to sue.

(b) Controlling Externality Problems Through Third Party Liability.—The growing number of third party suits often raises the kind of externality problems that are unlikely to be brought to the attention of disciplinary authorities. Consider *In re Flight Transportation Corporation Securities Litigation*,[139] a typical example of this kind of litigation. In that case, a class of investors sued a New York law firm. The investors alleged that the firm engaged in a number of false or deceptive practices for its corporate client, including failing to disclose material information in documents prepared on the client's behalf. If true, these allegations would undoubtedly constitute a violation of the law firm's professional duty. It is equally clear, however, that in the absence of this kind of lawsuit such misconduct would fall completely outside of the formal enforcement system. Certainly, the New York firm's client would have no incentive to turn in its alleged partner in crime. Additionally,

---

131.   . . . Juries, on the other hand, are likely to be much less sympathetic toward lawyers.

133.   Some of the indirect costs of filing suit, however, are likely to be more substantial for corporate clients. The danger that confidential information will be revealed during the course of a malpractice suit may pose a significant cost to a corporation involved in a long-term relationship with a single law firm. Indeed, in cases in which the lawyer's malpractice has also damaged third parties—for example, in a case in which the lawyer has negligently drafted a proxy statement used in connection with a securities offering—the risk that defrauded investors will discover that they have a claim against the company itself may very well outweigh any potential monetary gain to be obtained from filing suit against the lawyer.

139.   593 F.Supp. 612 (D. Minn. 1984).

the defrauded investors probably would view the effort involved in helping disciplinary officials "cleanse the profession" as a substantial and not very worthwhile distraction from their main goal of obtaining compensation for their injuries. Allowing them to sue lawyers for their injuries makes this "distraction" coincide with their primary objective.

Moreover, these results are also likely to occur across both hemispheres of legal practice. One of the most striking features of the recent rise in the number of statutory suits against lawyers is the number of blue chip firms whose conduct is being questioned. *In re Flight Transportation Corporation*, for example, involved a leading New York law firm with over 100 lawyers. Because these firms are usually involved in the kind of transactions that pose a significant risk of harming large numbers of consumers or investors, the volume of third party actions involving leading law firms appears destined to increase during the coming decades. At the same time, lawyers in the individual hemisphere have certainly not been immune from such suits. Third party controls have thus proven to be a very democratic form of regulation.[144]

These benefits, however, must be weighed against the administrative and participant costs associated with opening the courts to these kinds of claims. Litigation is notoriously slow and expensive. In addition, the fear of liability may deter lawyers from legitimate as well as illegitimate conduct. This could be a significant cost to both participants and to third parties. For example, the threat of secondary liability for securities fraud may induce lawyers either to overinvest in safety precautions or abandon some classes of clients altogether.... Despite these caveats, the basic point remains: liability controls appear likely to address a broad range of claims that would otherwise fall outside the present disciplinary system.

3. *Institutional Controls: Breaking the Barrier Between Enforcement and Work.*—Institutional controls, such as Rule 11 and the SEC's rule 2(e),**** give enforcement authority to the institutions in which lawyers work. This placement has two important consequences. First, unlike disciplinary regulation, enforcement officials do not need to rely entirely on complaints from injured parties to generate information about lawyer misconduct. Second, the actions taken by interested parties (lawyers, clients, judges, regulators, and adversaries) will be strongly influenced by the background incentives generated by the institution in which the control system is located. Independently, each of these features seems likely to expand the range of conduct coming to the attention of regulatory officials. In combination, however, they are likely to focus these regulatory regimes on certain kinds of externality problems.

144. This form of regulation is democratic in another sense: ultimate decisionmaking authority rests in the hands of the jury. . . .

**** [Editors' Note: Now Rule 102(e), 17 C.F.R. 201.102(e) (1998).]

(a) Situational Monitoring and Adversary Incentives: The Informa-
tion Advantages of Institutional Controls.—In the ordinary course of
litigation, judges extensively observe the lawyers' conduct. Although the
extent of judicial scrutiny should not be exaggerated, a judge will often
be able to form a crude judgment about the lawyers' effort.... A similar
story can be told about enforcement officials at administrative agencies
such as the SEC. In the ordinary course of business, SEC officials review
formal submissions and public documents prepared by lawyers. These
efforts undoubtedly provide some tentative information about lawyer
conduct, such as whether the registration statement was filed on time
and in the proper form or whether the information disclosed in the
offering documents is consistent with the public information available to
investors. Moreover, as part of their normal duties, SEC officials investigate specific market transactions to determine whether the relevant
parties have complied with applicable provisions of the securities laws.
These investigations also produce a significant amount of information
about lawyer conduct. Simply as a result of their participation in an
ongoing process, therefore, trial judges and administrative officials are
likely to uncover information about lawyer misconduct that would escape
the attention of disciplinary officials.

Moreover, because of their stake in the underlying process, these
officials have substantial incentives to act on this information. For
example, in light of the important role that lawyers play in the administration of the securities laws, it is not surprising that the SEC has been
especially vigilant in its investigation and prosecution of lawyers who
have allegedly assisted their clients in circumventing relevant statutory
requirements. It is also not surprising, however, that these same incentives have sometimes led the Commission to engage in what appears
from a compliance perspective to be overzealous enforcement.

. . .

The same point can be made with respect to other participants who
are in a position to observe lawyer misconduct. Given the inherent
limitations of independent observation and investigation, institutional
regulators such as trial judges and SEC officials must rely on other
knowledgeable actors to report instances of professional misconduct. By
making the enforcement process a part of an ongoing system of interactions between these knowledgeable actors and the offending lawyer,
institutional controls increase the incentive for these parties to participate in the regulatory process. Experience with [the tough, 1983, version
of] Rule 11 underscores this conclusion.

Rule 11 [,at least the 1983 version,] offers a number of formal and
informal incentives to lawyers (and their clients) to report misconduct by
their adversaries. Rule 11 specifically states that fee shifting is an
appropriate sanction for violations of the rule.... Moreover, because

Rule 11 operates during the course of litigation, adversaries may gain a number of strategic advantages from reporting lawyer misconduct....

. . .

(b) Agency Problems and the One–Shot Player: The Danger of Reifying Institutional Power.—Each actor in an institutional control system has an agenda. Adversaries in a litigated case want to win on the merits. Trial judges want to dispose of cases efficiently. SEC enforcement officials want to vindicate their ideas about regulatory policy. Moreover, each institution in which such a control system might be located distributes power and information among relevant participants in particular ways. Institutional controls cannot easily escape these preexisting goals and structures. Experience with Rule 11 is again instructive.

. . . Although there is evidence that the rule has influenced the conduct of all attorneys, [other data suggest] . . . that plaintiffs (and their lawyers) are . . . more likely to be the objects of requests for sanctions and to have sanctions imposed . . . [and] that . . . those prosecuting civil rights or employment discrimination claims, are especially likely to be disciplined under the rule.

These results are sadly predictable given the institutional dynamics of this form of control.... As sophisticated repeat players, . . . [institutional defendants] have both a long-range view of the strategic benefits that might result from obtaining Rule 11 sanctions in a particular case and an ability to shoulder the costs of moving for them. At the opposite end of the spectrum, a lawyer for an individual plaintiff operating under a contingent fee agreement can ill afford to invest in strategic maneuvering that, whatever else it accomplishes, will almost certainly increase the cost of ultimately prevailing on the merits....

. . .

4. Legislative Controls: Achieving Efficiency Gains Through Political Accountability.—Underlying the many proposals to transfer some or all of the responsibility for enforcing the rules of professional conduct to a legislatively created enforcement agency is the assertion that politically accountable regulators are likely to be more vigilant in protecting the public than either bar officials or judges.... A given state legislature might choose to enact two quite different kinds of regulatory schemes. The first would simply replace the current disciplinary system with an identical or substantially similar set of institutions under public control. The second would create a proactive agency with broad investigatory and reporting powers similar to OSHA or the SEC....

(a) Political Accountability in the Absence of Structural Change.—In many states, legislatively created administrative agencies have enforcement authority over many professionals, most notably doctors. These agencies are substantially similar to the disciplinary agencies that currently regulate lawyers. Specifically, the typical medical review board is

structurally separated from arenas of professional work, acts almost exclusively on the basis of complaints, and has limited power to impose sanctions other than reprimands, suspensions, and license revocation. As a result, these agencies have encountered many of the same problems that plague the disciplinary system.

. . .

   (b) The Costs of Structural Change.—There are many forms that a legislatively created administrative agency designed to regulate lawyers might take. Consider, for example, a state that decides to create a lawyer regulatory agency modeled after OSHA. An agency following this model would neither depend upon client complaints nor limit its remedial powers to imposing limitations on the professional license. Instead, like OSHA, such an agency would conduct spot inspections of lawyers' offices, interview clients at random, and examine court records and other public documents to discover misconduct by lawyers.[209] To take another example, consider an administrative agency patterned after the SEC. Instead of spot inspections, such an agency might direct lawyers to submit forms certifying that they had complied with relevant professional commands, or it might require a yearly compliance audit to be performed by some certified professional.

   Both the OSHA and the SEC model offer significant enforcement advantages over the current disciplinary system in all four categories of lawyer-client interaction. An active program of spot investigations and random audits would undoubtedly reveal many of the typical agency violations that individual clients (and even corporations) have difficulty detecting on their own. Similarly, detailed reporting requirements and compliance audits should uncover a substantial amount of strategic behavior by even the most sophisticated lawyers and clients.

   The administrative, participant, and third-party costs associated with achieving these goals, however, are likely to be quite high. Most administrative agencies, including OSHA and the SEC, have achieved only partial success at best, although they have generated substantial costs and other unintended consequences. Independent investigation is both time consuming and expensive. Although self-reporting may lower administrative costs, it will impose corresponding costs on lawyers. Because state legislatures have not appropriated sufficient funds to operate the much more limited agencies that currently regulate doctors, the expenditures that would be necessary to make these controls truly effective represent a substantial drawback to the practicality of this enforcement model.

---

209. There are several potential constitutional and statutory impediments to this kind of broad investigatory authority, including the Fourth Amendment and the attorney-client and work product privileges. Although these problems are significant, a combination of client consent and strict confidentiality requirements for regulators would minimize much of their practical significance.

. . .

IV. Independence Arguments

. . .

B. *Independence and Professional Regulation*

. . .

2. *Independent Judgment as Balanced Judgment.*—Those who raise democratic theory objections to particular forms of regulation almost always begin with the example of the criminal defense lawyer. This premise is hardly surprising, given the many powerful arguments for allowing these lawyers maximum autonomy from the state. By vigorously defending the rights of their clients, criminal defense lawyers stand as a bulwark against state power, not just for the accused, but for all who might be accused in the future. A regulatory scheme that seriously interferes with a criminal defense lawyer's willingness or ability to raise every available legal claim would undermine one of the principle values of an independent legal profession.

These insights, however, have a limited impact on the general enforcement questions at issue here. The criminal defense bar represents a very small percentage of the total number of lawyers in America. Although more lawyers represent clients involved in disputes with the government, it is not clear that society has the same stake in providing these claimants with the kind of zealous advocacy that we have come to expect in criminal cases. Nevertheless, the same democratic theory arguments are often used to oppose regulatory measures in this wider context. Even granting his analogy, however, the sweeping claims that are often drawn from this comparison seem strained. . . .

(a) *The Failure of Disciplinary Controls to Correct for Market Inequalities.*— . . . [D]isciplinary controls neither deter externality problems nor effectively prevent individual agency problems. Such compliance failures also undermine the disciplinary system's ability to encourage lawyers to resist market pressures when the relevant norms are ambiguous or in conflict. Consider, for example, the prohibition against frivolous litigation. Even though the prohibition against frivolous claims is a standard fixture of a lawyer's duty to assist the court in securing the efficient administration of justice, lawyers who file frivolous claims or defenses are rarely brought before disciplinary officials. Moreover, the definition of frivolousness is notoriously vague. Thus, the only incentive for lawyers to perform this gatekeeping role comes from their internally generated allegiance to the public aspects of legal practice. Internal motivation, however, is more difficult to maintain in the face of strong client pressure to ignore or minimize the importance of systemic constraints. Corporate clients, with their superior ability to formulate goals and monitor compliance, are in a good position to exert this form of pressure. As a result, corporate lawyers are even less likely to be "independent" in constraining client conduct that violates systemic norms than are lawyers representing individuals, who can exploit the standard information asymmetry to resist or modify their clients' goals. Disciplinary controls do nothing to correct this imbalance.

Nor do these controls promote a defensible vision of independence for lawyers who represent individuals. By condemning only the most flagrant departures from the client service model, the current disciplinary system leaves a regulatory void that may encourage lawyers for individual clients to exploit the indeterminacy of legal rules in ways quite inconsistent with either client or public understandings of professional independence. Sociologists have repeatedly documented instances in which these lawyers have sacrificed the interests of their unsophisticated clients to avoid the powerful embedded controls exerted by colleagues, state officials, or others with whom they share a long-term relationship. Although it is possible that these embedded interests will coincide with a lawyer's independent professional judgment, it is as least at likely that "lawyers may wield a power [they have over individual clients in a manner] that benefits no one so much as themselves."

In short, disciplinary controls do little more than mirror the norms of the marketplace. These norms—and not the idealized vision of the "independent profession"—form the baseline against which we should measure the impact of specific external controls on the norm of professional autonomy.

(b) Balancing the Market Through Enforcement.—Enforcement systems such as third party liability controls and institutional enforcement efforts by the SEC and the IRS are likely to promote rather than undermine independent judgment. By exposing and sanctioning a broad range of externality problems that would otherwise be hidden from view, these systems ensure that lawyers take seriously their duties as officers of the court when advising clients about matters such as regulatory compliance, even when a plausible argument could be made that compliance was not required. The additional check provided by an enforcement system is particularly needed in the corporate sphere, where lawyers are especially prone to undervalue their duties as officers of the court.

. . .

It is possible, however, that these gains might come at the expense of client motivated independence. Each of the forms of external regulation . . . might induce a lawyer to place his own interest in avoiding sanction ahead of his client's interests and thereby undermine client motivated independence. For example, the threat of malpractice liability might make a lawyer reluctant to represent certain clients, such as an individual who previously sued another lawyer for malpractice. . . .

Despite protestations to the contrary, there is very little evidence that corporate lawyers have been unduly "chilled" by these same regulatory measures. Consider, for example, the case of Lord, Bissell & Brook, a leading Chicago corporate firm. In the famous *National Student Marketing* case in the 1970s, the SEC sued Lord, Bissell and alleged that the firm aided and abetted its client's violations of the federal securities laws.[311] This suit was criticized by many leading members of the bar and other commentators on the ground that subjecting lawyers to suits by their adversaries would chill zealous advocacy and deprive corporate clients of the full protection of the law by driving a wedge between lawyer and client. Partially as a result of this widespread outcry, the district judge, who concluded that the attorneys had failed to advise their clients to comply with applicable disclosure requirements, declined to enjoin the lawyers from committing future violations.

Subsequent events support the conclusion that fears of a chilling effect were greatly exaggerated. According to the allegations contained in two lawsuits that Lord, Bissell recently settled for twenty-four million dollars, shortly after the decision in *National Student Marketing*, the firm began aggressively representing National Mortgage Equity Corporation (NMEC), a controversial venture designed to capitalize on the newly emerging market in second mortgages. Whether or not the firm's activities on behalf of this new client violated statutory and common law fraud rules,[315] there is no question that the firm zealously pursued the client's interest. Indeed, according to the deposition testimony of the firm's managing partner, the firm changed virtually none of its practices as a result of the SEC's prosecutions in *National Student Marketing*. Because of the financial and other rewards of a "cutting edge" corporate legal practice, the fear of liability in this context is not sufficient to deter even clearly questionable conduct, let alone legitimate advice that might be made to appear questionable after the fact.

The picture looks quite different, however, from the perspective of the typical individual client trying to convince her lawyer to pursue a marginal but viable claim despite the threat of external sanctions. If the lawyer is operating under a contingent fee agreement, she must weigh the already speculative possibility of winning on the merits and recovering a substantial fee against the danger that she will lose the case and be sanctioned. For these lawyers, sanctions may make an already risky legal practice economically infeasible. If the client is paying by the hour, she will have difficulty determining whether certain actions—such as massive discovery requests, extensive legal research, consulting with experts—are being taken for her benefit or the lawyer's. In either case, the individual client with a plausible legal claim is likely to be the loser.

311. See SEC v. National Student Mktg., 457 F.Supp. 682 (D.D.C.1978).

315. Predictably, the civil actions were settled without any admission of liability by the firm, and the major participants continue to assert that they acted properly. Tim O'Brien, Some Firms Never Learn: Lord, Bissell's Second Escape from Fraud Charges Cost $24 Million—And It Could Happen Again, Am. Law., Oct. 1989, at 65.

Of course, the fear of personal liability will undoubtedly chill some corporate lawyers from pursuing legitimate client projects. Indeed, one can easily imagine a legislatively created administrative agency similar to OSHA adopting a set of procedures—for example, giving administrative officials substantial discretion to disbar lawyers for initiating "frivolous" claims against the state—that would significantly cool the ardor of even the most highly paid and closely monitored corporate advocate.... [T]he risk that the threat of sanctions will chill creative advocacy is a much greater problem for individuals than for corporations. Broad condemnation of external regulatory schemes that focus on corporate conduct, therefore, is unwarranted.

. . .

VI. Conclusion

. . .

Implicit in the many claims about how lawyers should be regulated is the assumption that a single enforcement structure will be appropriate for all lawyers in all contexts. This unitary vision, however, fails to account for the diversity in both the structure of the legal marketplace and society's expectations of the profession....

Notes

1. Wilkins sets up distinctions between agency problems and externality problems, as well as between individual and corporate clients. While these dichotomies are useful, the simplicity that makes them useful can also mask issues. For example, Wilkins points out that corporations do not often sue their lawyers for malpractice, and in a portion of the article we have omitted, argues that because corporate clients are sophisticated and can effectively monitor their lawyers, they should face a higher burden of proof in bringing such cases. But one reason why corporations do not sue their lawyers for malpractice is that there is a second agency problem that Wilkins ignores, namely the agency problem within the corporation. Corporate managers may fail to pursue malpractice claims against the corporation's lawyers for fear that bringing such claims may expose evidence of manager misfeasance. That is, the failure to bring the malpractice action may itself be a breach of the manager's fiduciary duty, or in economic terms, an agency problem. Moreover, if managers use lawyers to commit fraud on third parties, the lawyer's conduct may be *both* an agency problem (harm to the corporate client) *and* an externality problem (harm to third parties). In these situations, new management (or shareholders in a derivative suit) might pursue malpractice claims that the unfaithful managers do not. In the savings and loan crisis, for example, many malpractice suits against corporate counsel were brought by the trustee in bankruptcy of the insolvent corporate client. One question in those cases was whether the wrongs of the former managers would be "imputed" to the trustee, thus barring the malpractice claim. Many courts rejected the imputation claim and allowed the suits to proceed. See, e.g., FDIC v. O'Melveny & Meyers [sic], 61 F.3d 17 (9th Cir.1995)

(reasserting its earlier holding, 969 F.2d 744 (9th Cir.1992), that under California law trustee could sue lawyers for negligence even if the entity's former management might well have been aware of the fraud).

2. Wilkins argues that disqualification motions are superior to discipline as a means of regulating conflicts of interest because the litigation opponent has a strong incentive to raise the conflict question. But is that incentive the right one, especially if the litigation opponent is not the one harmed by the conflict? Courts often express frustration with what they perceive to be strategic disqualification motions. On the other hand, courts often grant such motions. Another problem with relying on disqualification motions to regulate conflicts of interest is the opposite of the first (overenforcement) problem: underenforcement. Litigation opponents might "collude" with each other not to raise conflicts problems, for example through mutual advance waivers. This reciprocity may be good for the litigants, but does not protect the interests of the harmed client who, if not a party, would not be part of the negotiations. What if anything do these problems suggest about the efficacy of disqualification motions as a regulatory mechanism? Note that Wilkins does not consider the liability solution in the context of conflicts of interest. Although such claims are sometimes successfully brought, proving causation can be a big hurdle. In other words, although showing a conflict may not be hard, demonstrating what damages the conflict caused (that might not have been incurred had the relevant lawyer been conflict-free), is often well nigh impossible. Should the causation rules be relaxed in liability claims based on conflicts of interest? Cf. Leubsdorf's proposals for adjusting tort law as applied to lawyers, p. 234.

3. Why is discipline such an ineffective regulatory mechanism for lawyers from large corporate firms? In an omitted footnote, Wilkins argues that corporations have little incentive to report their outside lawyers to disciplinary authorities. Is that a satisfactory explanation? What about the fact that disciplinary authorities are often severely underfunded, a point that Wilkins makes in a different context? Taking on a large law firm would be very expensive. Even if they could afford it, would it be politically feasible? These questions are not merely theoretical. In the recent debate over the SEC's rules governing lawyers, one point that opponents of the regulations made was that states already have disciplinary authority over securities lawyers. But we know of no instance in which a securities lawyer from a large law firm has been charged, no less successfully disciplined, by state bar authorities, notwithstanding the evidence of lawyer misconduct developed in tort suits.

4. The 1983 version of Rule 11, which Wilkins critiques, was substantially revised in 1993. On the surface the 1993 version of the rule expanded the duty of candor, explicitly prohibiting "later advocating" based on a paper filed with a court that violates the rule. But overall the Rule was considerably weakened, in large part due to the concern that it was chilling legitimate advocacy and was being used, many contended in agreement with Wilkins, more against advocates for the dispossessed among us than against lawyers for powerful clients. The 1993 Rule allowed allegations and denials when the lawyer is ignorant of the facts, so long as that ignorance is reasonable at the time of filing. A judge may, but no longer must, impose

sanctions against lawyers who violate the rule. And most important, the new rule includes a "safe harbor" provision. Now, a party who believes the other side's lawyer has violated Rule 11 may not file a Rule 11 motion until it has notified the allegedly offending lawyer and given her an opportunity to withdraw whatever it was that offended the Rule. This gives lawyers one free chance to file in violation of the rule on each paper submitted. Does that make sense? Assuming Wilkins is right about the bad effects of the 1983 version of Rule 11, what should have been done?

5.   When lawyers were sued for reckless (or intentional) involvement in their client's securities fraud, the complaint generally described the lawyer's wrong as aiding and abetting the fraud of the client. In law the general rule is that one who aids (offers substantial help to) the intentional tort (or crime) of another is as culpable as the primary wrongdoer. Although the federal securities laws did not address aiding and abetting liability, the courts had long read into those laws liability for aiding and abetting on the assumption that Congress could not have intended to exempt from civil suit those who aid and abet securities fraud, which is, after all, a crime (a federal statute makes aiding and abetting any federal felony a felony equivalent to the crime aided). All that changed in 1994, when the Supreme Court held in Central Bank of Denver v. First Interstate Bank of Denver, 511 U.S. 164 (1994), that the failure of Congress to state explicitly in the securities laws that aiding and abetting gave rise to a private cause of action meant that no such cause of action could be maintained. Lawyers and accountants everywhere celebrated—one less source of liability, a lot less worry. Congress, however, was on the verge of a major overhaul of the securities laws, which became the Private Securities Litigation Reform Act of 1995. Because the Supreme Court's ruling was statutory, all Congress had to do to restore the old regime was state explicitly what it had not stated explicitly before. Congress said nothing on this matter, which meant the celebrations at law firms and accounting firms across the country could continue. On a closely related question, Congress did speak. The securities laws did not explicitly state that the SEC could bring civil actions against aiders and abettors, just as they had been silent on whether private parties could sue those who facilitated fraud. Under the reasoning of *Central Bank*, the Court, if the question were presented to it, might well bar the SEC from bringing such suits, as it had barred private parties. On this question, Congress stepped in: the SEC could continue to bring aiding and abetting cases, but no longer would reckless aiding suffice to make its case. The agency would have to show the helper acted with the intent to further the fraud. A small, but important change. The result: After the 1995 Act, aiders would be less likely to be sued (no private actions and the SEC has plenty of other work) and less likely to be held accountable for their actions when sued (given the SEC's tougher burden). We obviously think this result is wrong. What arguments can you muster in favor of the changes?

6.   For a recent discussion of the advantages and disadvantages of different institutions for regulating lawyers, with a focus on regulating entry, see Benjamin H. Barton, An Institutional Analysis of Lawyer Regulation: Who Should Control Lawyer Regulation–Courts, Legislatures or the Market? 37 Ga. L. Rev. 1167–1250 (2003).

The Law Between the Bar and the State*
SUSAN P. KONIAK

. . .

The state and the profession have different understandings of the law governing lawyers—they have in effect different "law."[2] The law of lawyering is not inherently more amorphous, contradictory or obtuse than other law. It is not radically uncertain; it is "essentially contested." There is a continuing struggle between the profession and the state over whether the profession's vision of law or the state's will reign. . . .

. . .

II.   The Inadequacy of the Traditional Understanding of the Relationship Between Law and Professional Ethics

As traditionally conceived, the domain of professional ethics begins where the law of the state leaves off. By this I mean that ethics is generally understood to be about obligations above and beyond the requirements of law. . . .[25]

. . .

Professional ethics thus conceived does not compete with state law, nor could it possibly conflict with state law. Professional ethics merely supplements state law, supplying norms to govern conduct that the society at large lacks the necessary expertise to regulate[30] or for which

---

* © 1992 North Carolina Law Review. Reprinted by permission from 70 N.C. L. Rev. 1389 (1992).

2.   This Article uses Robert Cover's rich and original vision of law, which he articulated most fully in Robert M. Cover, The Supreme Court, 1982 Term—Foreward: Nomos and Narrative, 97 Harv. L. Rev. 4 (1983) [hereinafter Cover, Nomos] and developed further in Robert M. Cover, Violence and the Word, 95 Yale L.J. 1601 (1986) [hereinafter Cover, Violence], and Robert M. Cover, Bringing the Messiah Through Law: A Case Study, in Religion, Morality and the Law: Nomos XXX 201 (J. Roland Pennock & John W. Chapman eds., 1988), as a means of understanding the law governing lawyers. Professor Cover died in the summer of 1986. I loved him much and miss him deeply. The magnificence of his vision is still with us. However modest a tribute to my friend and teacher this Article is, it is my sincere hope that it serves at least to bring those unfamiliar with his work to it.

25.   The view that ethics should be about something other than and more than law is exemplified in Stephen Gillers, What We Talked About When We Talked About Ethics: A Critical View of the Model Rules, 46 Ohio St. L.J. 243, 247–48 (1985), an article criticizing the Model Rules of Professional Conduct because, among other things, much of it merely repeats the injunctions of civil and criminal law. "The more [the document traces the commands of civil or criminal law] . . ., the less it can be considered a code of ethics." Id. at 246. "It is [the] extralegal realm that defines ethics." Id. at 248.

30.   The classic sociological understanding of the professions is that society and individual consumers are too lacking in expertise to control or monitor adequately the performance of professionals. At the same time, the larger society and individual consumers are intensely interested in controlling the conduct of professionals because of the high stakes involved in the tasks committed to professionals—high stakes both for the individual client and for the larger society because professional work implicates central social values like justice and the physical well-being of societal members. The professions and society thus "strike a bargain": in exchange for high status, high remuneration, protection from lay

the state's standards are insufficiently exacting. But the traditional understanding of the relationship between professional ethics and law—at least among professionals themselves—goes further than the mere statement that ethics begins where law leaves off. It also includes the notion that it is appropriate for the state to leave substantial areas of conduct in which the profession's own norms govern—i.e., that state law should "leave off" sooner rather than later. The rhetoric of the professions is filled with talk of the "right" of self-regulation, of the "encroachments" by the state into areas of professional control, and of the need to ward off increased state regulation by toughening internal controls.

Insofar as the traditional understanding of the relationship between law and ethics includes an ongoing debate over the extent and nature of the "right" of self-regulation, it exposes the competition between state and group over normative space. But the nature and force of that competition is masked because the traditional understanding asserts that the domain of professional ethics *does* leave off where state law begins. The traditional understanding thus suggests that a consensus exists on the authoritative position of state law where state law exists. It suggests that the professions and the state agree on when the state has spoken, what the state has said, and that the effect of the state pronouncement is to invalidate as a basis of action group norms that are in conflict with state law. These assumptions are central to the traditional understanding of the relationship between law and professional ethics. But they, and consequently the traditional understanding of the relationship between law and professional ethics, are naive and misleading. They are based on a naive positivism about state law, they minimize the richness and power of the group's normative vision, and they conceal the dynamic interplay between state and group norms.

Consider the following example: By 1985 the number of criminal defense lawyers being subpoenaed before grand juries had risen dramatically, and opposition to this practice from individual lawyers and the organized bar was increasing apace. The state was largely unresponsive to the bar's opposition. The courts that had considered the question had rejected the lawyers' claims that client and fee identity were generally privileged from disclosure and that special procedures, such as prior judicial approval, should be required before the government is allowed to subpoena a criminal defense lawyer. While the Justice Department issued guidelines on this subject in 1985, these guidelines provided that such subpoenas could be issued upon a rather modest showing of need by

competition and a significant degree of autonomy from state control, the professions adopt norms designed to protect individual consumers and the public at large, seek to educate members so they will internalize these norms, and monitor compliance with and sanction deviations from such norms. See Dietrich Rueschemeyer, Lawyers and Their Society 13–14 (1973), for a statement of this classic sociological explanation of professional ethics. For a similar explanation of professional ethics from an economist, see Kenneth J. Arrow, The Limits of Organization 36–37 (1974).

the U.S. Attorney's office involved; more important, they provided that the showing of need be made to the Department of Justice itself, not to a court.

The Massachusetts bar then proposed an ethics rule making it unethical for a prosecutor to call a lawyer before a grand jury to testify about a client without prior judicial approval. The Supreme Judicial Court of Massachusetts adopted the rule and the United States District Court for the District of Massachusetts refused to enjoin its operation. The federal government challenged the district court decision, arguing, among other things, that ethics rules should not be used to change grand jury procedures, an area governed by the Federal Rules of Criminal Procedure. In *United States v. Klubock*[41] the United States Court of Appeals for the First Circuit split four-four, leaving in place the district court opinion upholding the rule. In the meantime, courts have continued to hold that special procedures are neither required nor advisable under the Constitution or other law, while state bars, following Massachusetts's lead, have proposed ethics rules that would require such procedures.

In 1988 the American Bar Association passed its second resolution on this issue, which called for even tighter limitations on the government's power to subpoena lawyers to testify before grand juries than those the ABA had originally proposed. The courts, prosecutors and legislatures have remained largely unresponsive to the bar's position. In 1990 the ABA amended the Model Rules of Professional Conduct to require prosecutors to obtain judicial approval before seeking to subpoena a lawyer about her client's affairs and making it unethical for a prosecutor to seek judicial approval unless the information sought is not privileged, it is essential to the investigation, and there is no feasible alternative means to obtain it.[47]

[In *Baylson v. Disciplinary Board of Supreme Court of Pennsylvania*,* however, the Third Circuit held that the Pennsylvania subpoena rule, which had become a local rule of federal district courts by automatic incorporation, could not be enforced against federal prosecutors because its adoption as federal law falls outside the rule-making authority of the district courts and its enforcement as state law violates the Supremacy Clause of the Constitution.]

This example suggests a far more active competition between state and group norms than the traditional understanding suggests . . . ., and . . . it is far from an isolated example of this struggle over law.

. . .

---

41.   832 F.2d 664 (1st Cir.1987) (en banc).

47.   See Model Rules of Professional Conduct Rule 3.8(f) (1991).

* [975 F.2d 102 (3d Cir.1992).]

III.   The Profession's Ethos as Law

Law is more than a collection of rules. Rules require explanation to have meaning. Stories must be told to create even the semblance of a shared understanding of what the rules require. Stories, in turn, demand explanation in the form of a rule—the "point" of the story. . . . But law is not just rules and stories. Rules and stories alone (literature, history), while essential to normative discourse, are to be distinguished from law because they do not license transformations of reality through the use of force. Law does. Law is rules and stories *and* a commitment of human will to change the world that *is* into the world that our rules and stories tell us *ought* to be. This commitment to realize the "ought" distinguishes law from utopian vision, literature, and history. . . .

Law understood as rules, the stories told about the rules, and the commitment to act in accordance with those rules and stories requires no state.[57] A community and the state may share an understanding of what constitutes the operative rule, but if they have radically different understandings of what that rule means (different stories) and each is committed to action based on its understanding, we have two distinct laws.

Why insist on calling each "law"? Normally, we reserve the label "law" for official state pronouncements, relegating the normative visions of communities to the status of "nonlaw" or, at best, advocacy about law. But what we miss by doing so is the force and effect that committed communities with their own vision of law have on state law. State law inevitably changes in the face of action taken in the name of alternative normative visions, even if the change is only to hold that a certain amount of increased state force is justified and will be used to maintain the state's legal vision. The state cannot merely reaffirm its prior law; it must decide what its former understanding means in light of the community's resistance. It must ask itself whether its law means that people who disobey based on their own narrative will go to jail or whether the group's narrative should in some way be incorporated into state law. In other words the state must decide whether and to what extent the state and the group will be reshaped in the struggle. Prior to the committed "disobedience," state law had not confronted these questions and thus did not include the answers. In the face of the "disobedience," it must. And in doing so, state law changes.

. . .

57. Cover, Nomos, supra note 1, at 11. Professor Cover explains:

> The state becomes central in the process not because it is well suited to jurisgenesis [the creation of legal meaning] nor because the cultural processes of giving meaning to normative activity cease in the presence of the state. The state becomes central only because . . . an act of commitment is a central aspect of legal meaning. And violence [as to which the state has an imperfect but important monopoly] is one extremely powerful measure and test of commitment.

Id. at 11 n.30.

... [L]et's take an example from legal ethics. The Tax Reform Act of 1984[60] requires people to report cash payments of $10,000 or more received in their trade or business. The person who received the money must fill in a reporting form, IRS Form 8300, which asks for the paying party's name, address, social security number and occupation and, when applicable, the name of the person on whose behalf the transaction was conducted. In October 1989 the IRS sent letters to 956 lawyers, demanding that they fully complete these forms. The lawyers had submitted incomplete forms, claiming much of the information could not be provided because it was protected by the attorney-client privilege.[64] The vast majority of lawyers receiving the IRS demand letter refused to comply. The IRS then issued ninety summonses to noncomplying lawyers who had reported unusually large cash payments or who had declared multiple instances of cash payments over $10,000. Many, if not most, of the ninety lawyers refused to comply. The government brought a test case in the Southern District of New York to force compliance. The district court ordered the lawyers to comply, holding that nothing in the case justified departing from the general rule that client identity and fee information are not privileged. After the district court ruling and with organized bar support,[68] many of the other ninety lawyers who had received summonses and the other 771 lawyers who did not respond to the IRS demand letter continued to resist.

These lawyers and bar groups claimed that complying with state law (as manifested by the federal statute, the IRS regulations, the IRS activities in applying these rules to lawyers, the long line of court precedents suggesting there is no valid claim of privilege regarding client identity and fee, and the district court opinion) would violate the ethical responsibilities of the lawyers involved. For example, the president of the Criminal Trial Lawyers Association of Northern California urged other lawyers to resist: "There are ethical responsibilities we have as lawyers that foreclose[ ] giving information which may put our clients in jeopardy." On appeal the United States Court of Appeals for the Second Circuit upheld the district court decision, dismissing as "without merit"

60. Tax Reform Act of 1984, Pub. L. No. 98–369, 98 Stat. 685 (1984) (codified as amended at 26 U.S.C. § 6060I (1988)).

64. This claim of privilege was asserted even though courts unanimously have held, in other contexts, that client identity and fee information generally are not protected by the privilege. The courts uniformly describe as rare the circumstances under which client identity and fee information might be privileged information.

68. The organized bar demonstrated its support of these lawyers in various ways. The Association of the Bar of the City of New York, the National Association of Criminal Defense Lawyers and the New York Council of Defense Lawyers filed amicus briefs on behalf of the lawyers.... The American Bar Association communicated to the Justice Department that wholesale enforcement of the federal law would have a devastating effect on the attorney-client relationship.

Perhaps most important for my purposes, several bars have issued ethics opinions stating or strongly suggesting that compliance with the demands of the IRS or similar state revenue agency is unethical, at least in the absence of a court order, and that even when a court order exists, the lawyer may ethically choose not to comply.

the contention that the reporting requirement conflicts with the attorney-client privilege.[72] After this decision, when asked what advice he would give to lawyers in the circuit, the head of the National Association of Criminal Defense Lawyers' "8300 Task Force" commented: "I would say many people subscribe to the notion that you don't violate a confidence until you are ordered to do so by a court." From the context it is obvious he meant *personally* ordered.

. . .

IV.   Two Laws Masquerading as One

. . .

A.   *What We Might Expect to Find*

The legal profession is, by definition, inextricably connected to the state and its laws. The state has the last say over such central matters of group definition as who may be admitted to group membership and who may be excluded. Moreover, the central privilege of membership in the profession is the right to speak to the state on behalf of another in the state's courts. Thus, the profession is dependent on the state for boundary and functional definition, central matters in the normative vision of any community. But the state's nomos is similarly dependent on the profession. To be a lawyer is to have a right to participate in the creation and maintenance of the state's nomos that is denied to other persons in the society.

As an expression of the real interdependence of these two normative worlds, we would expect to find significant areas in which they coincide. Further, . . . the intensity and particular nature of the interdependence of bar and state increase the need of all involved to maintain the myth of a unitary normative system. The idea that the ministers of the state's law are somehow less than faithful to that law is simply too powerful a suggestion to be incorporated easily into either the state's or the bar's normative system. Thus, we would expect to find that each normative world has developed means of masking the existence of the profession's conflicting norms. . . .

B.   *The Hierarchy of Norms*

For the most part, the bar and the state agree on the precepts that are relevant to the law governing lawyers: precepts contained in the Constitution of the United States; the ethics rules as embodied in various codes promulgated by the bar; the common law of lawyering, particularly the attorney-client privilege; and precepts embodied in "other law," including the law of torts, criminal law, securities law and the law of procedure. I say "for the most part" for two reasons. First, the state treats ethics rules as "law" only to the extent that they are (and in

---

72.   United States v. Goldberger & Dubin, P.C., 935 F.2d 501, 504 (2d Cir.1991).

the form in which they are) adopted by the state. On the other hand the bar may treat as law ethics rules adopted by the ABA or a state bar organization but not adopted by the state. Second, the extent to which the bar accepts that precepts of "other law" govern the conduct of lawyers is not clear. Sometimes lawyers and bar groups speak as if lawyers enjoy some form of immunity from the precepts of other law. But, even if we put aside for the moment these two areas of potential disagreement on precepts and assume that the bar and the state are in total agreement on the relevant precepts, the existence of shared precepts indicates a unitary normative system only if the precepts are ordered by each group (the bar and the state) in the same way. They are not. In the bar's *nomos* ethics rules[89] are presumed to control when they conflict with other law, while in the state's *nomos* other law is presumed to control when it conflicts with the ethics rules.

In the state's hierarchy of norms—as it exists in theory—ethics rules occupy a relatively low status. Ethics rules are generally court rules, not legislative, and they are usually state law, not federal law. Those two facts relegate ethics rules to a low status in the state's hierarchy of precepts. First, federal constitutional requirements, including those on procedure, trump all other law. Second, federal law trumps state law. Third, on matters of substantive law, legislation trumps rules adopted by courts. Fourth, on matters of procedure, federal legislation trumps rules adopted by federal courts; and federal rules of procedure adopted pursuant to congressional authorization, such as the Federal Rules of Civil Procedure, trump rules adopted by federal courts, which include ethics rules. And while in many states rules of procedure adopted by a court pursuant to the court's inherent powers (which is how ethics rules are adopted) trump conflicting state legislative pronouncements on procedure, this may be truer in theory than in practice. Finally, federal and state courts often state that the only instances in which they are bound to treat the ethics rules as binding precepts are in disciplinary proceedings against lawyers. Thus, even when the ethics rules purport to speak directly on a matter and are the only existing source of precept on the question, they may be ignored with relative ease so long as the case is not a disciplinary proceeding.

The strongest evidence that the bar's hierarchy of norms differs from the state's is found in the bar narratives that explicate the rules—ethics opinions. . . .

. . .

. . . [Just as] court opinions provide a body of narratives . . . and . . . precepts . . . that are intended to be realized in action[, e]thics opinions

---

89. This is not to say that in the bar's *nomos* each precept in the ethics rules carries equal power to trump other law. The bar is so weakly committed to some rules that they may be said to have taken on the status of "non-law" for the bar, and thus they lack the power to trump other law.

perform a similar function in the bar's *nomos*.... Ethics opinions are also a particularly strong source of evidence of the content of the bar's *nomos* because they generally are not subject to prior state control. They therefore express law to which the bar, but not necessarily the state, is committed.

What do the ethics opinions tell us about the bar's ordering of norms? ...

. . .

[Some e]thics opinions actively and openly encourage disobedience of other law....** [They] provide the strongest evidence that the bar's hierarchy of norms places ethics rules above other state precepts. Such opinions are, however, relatively rare.[128] What is surprising is that they exist at all....

. . .

The bar's understanding that ethics rules trump other law (or qualify it or render it ambiguous) is also evident in its efforts to pass ethics rules or interpret existing rules to stop state action that the courts have held is permitted under other law. Ethics rules that would require prosecutors to get prior judicial approval and demonstrate extreme need before subpoenaing lawyers to testify before grand juries about their clients' affairs are just one example of this. Other examples include ethics rules and ethics opinions prohibiting the disclosure of client fraud

---

** [Editors' Note: State Bar of New Mexico Advisory Op. 1989–2 states:

[T]he intent of the New Mexico Rules of Professional Conduct is that attorney should not reveal exactly what the federal [requirement that a lawyer report the source of a cash payment of $10,000 or more] requires [an] attorney to reveal. Thus, there is a conflict between [the two]. Our Committee does not resolve the conflict, but we [recommend that a lawyer] consistent with the highest ideals of the profession ... may, with the client's consent, agree to "make a good faith effort to determine the validity, scope, meaning or application" of the law at issue [citing a state-court-adopted ethics rule requiring confidentiality]....]

128. Other examples of openly defiant ethics opinions include: Chicago Bar Ass'n, Op. 86–2 (1988) (lawyer would not be condemned for filing a completed IRS form; "however, the better course ... is to file an IRS form that asserts the attorney-client privilege and gives notice ... that information has been withheld"); Ethics Advisory Comm., Nat'l Ass'n of Crim. Def. Lawyers, Formal Op. 89–1 (1989) (stating that lawyer who receives an IRS summons should not disclose client confidences unless a court orders disclosure); State Bar of Ga., Advisory Op. No. 41 (1984) (lawyer should pursue all reasonable avenues of appeal before complying with requests from state agency); State Bar of Wis., Formal Op. E–90–3 (1990) (lawyer should not make disclosure when faced with an IRS summons "unless and until a court, preferably an appellate court, considers the validity of the summons and any judicial enforcement orders in this area and that court's ruling requires such disclosure").

Openly defiant ethics opinions are much more likely to involve certain precepts, such as the rule on confidentiality, than others. For a discussion of the centrality of confidentiality in the bar's nomos, see infra text accompanying notes 159–256. The bar's demonstration of strong commitment to certain precepts in the rules and weak (or negative) commitment to other precepts is another aspect of the bar's hierarchy of norms and is not inconsistent with the general proposition presented here: the bar's hierarchy differs from the state's because the bar presumes that ethics rules (even if only some ethics rules) trump law, which the state considers above the ethics rules.

in connection with the sale or purchase of securities to the Securities and Exchange Commission, purchasers, or stockholders; those prohibiting the simultaneous negotiation of attorneys' fees in civil rights cases;[145] and those prohibiting disclosure of information to the Legal Services Corporation.[146]

. . .

V.   The Centrality of Confidentiality in the Bar's *Nomos*

. . .

The bar texts discussed [above] . . . show that it is confidentiality, and particularly the duty to keep client confidences from the state, more often than any other norm, that triggers the obligation to resist competing state norms and that justifies the passage of ethics rules to "undo" state pronouncements. That the bar deems individual acts of resistance and group efforts to repeal state pronouncements to be appropriate responses to state efforts to secure client confidences reveals the bar's interpretation of the norm—i.e., that it is absolute or nearly absolute.

Confidentiality is a constitutional norm in the bar's *nomos*. By "constitutional norm," I mean a norm so central to group definition (that which constitutes a group) that the group perceives threats to the norm as threats against the group itself—against the group's very existence; that the group sees proposals to change the norm as proposals to change the essence/character/function of the group itself; and consequently that the group feels extreme action in defense of the norm is justified. . . .

. . .

The ethics codes may mask the power of the norm of confidentiality, but the ethics opinions interpreting the codes make it plain. A pattern

---

145.   That the effort to trump state law through ethics opinions largely abated after the Supreme Court's decision in Evans v. Jeff D., 475 U.S. 717 (1986), is not conclusive of the bar's acceptance that state law trumps the ethics rules or the bar's interpretation of those rules. After all, the ethics opinions stood in the face of contrary legal interpretations from lower federal courts. At most, this acquiescence to the Supreme Court's interpretation suggests some limit on the bar's commitment to its alternate vision.

In his dissent in Evans, Justice Brennan invited the bar to use ethics opinions to try to outlaw simultaneous negotiations. Evans, 475 U.S. at 765 (Brennan, J., dissenting). This invitation for the bar to continue its own normative understanding is consistent with Justice Brennan's general approach of inviting alternative normative understandings to counteract the Court's decisions.

146.   As a firm supporter of legal services organizations, this seems like a good place to make explicit that I see the law-generating power of non-state communities as not only descriptive of the world of law around me and inevitable, but also as a good thing. I do not ascribe to all of the bar's vision of law as described in this Article—a point I will come back to in concluding this piece. But the fact that the private bar has a vision that is different from the state is for me a cause for some celebration and not dismay. My celebration comes from the sacred stories that I share with my colleagues at the bar—stories of the danger of unmitigated state power and of the special destiny and history of the profession as protectors of the oppressed and of individual (and, at least in my subcommunity, as protectors of minority group) rights.

emerges in these opinions: rules affirming a duty or the discretion to disclose are either narrowed to the point of near-irrelevance or held to be overridden by rules requiring silence....

. . .

VII. Commitment

> Because the *nomos* is but the process of human action stretched between vision and reality, a legal interpretation cannot be valid if no one is prepared to live by it.[308]

We call the state's normative vision "law" because we know that the state *means* it. It is committed to its interpretation. It is prepared to act, using all the resources of violence at its disposal, if necessary, to enforce its interpretations. Earlier, to justify my use of the word "law" to describe the profession's normative vision, I argued that the profession *means* it too, that it too is committed to its interpretations. If, however, the profession's law diverges from that of the state, how can the profession maintain its commitment, given the state's imperfect monopoly over violence?[311] The answer lies in understanding that commitment is not an all-or-nothing proposition for either the state or the community.[312] ... [A]s we shall see, judges are particularly unlikely to assert their interpretive power or back their interpretations with violence in cases in which their understanding of law diverges from the bar's. The state's commitment is weak. On the other hand, the bar's commitment is relatively strong....

A. *The Weakness of the State's Commitment*

In cases involving the law governing lawyers, the courts show a weak commitment to state law—to the maintenance of a state *nomos*—in two basic ways. First, they are reluctant to create legal meaning and as a consequence create little. Second, they show little inclination to back with violence the legal meaning they do create. Consider the court's decision in *SEC v. National Student Marketing Corp.*[314]

308. Cover, Nomos, supra note 1, at 44 (footnote omitted).

311. To appreciate the importance of the question posed in the text, consider the following quotation:

> Certain efforts to [maintain a separate *nomos*] have a strange, almost doomed character. The state's claims over legal meaning are, at bottom, so closely tied to the state's imperfect monopoly over the domain of violence that the claim of a community to an autonomous meaning must be linked to the community's willingness to live out its meaning in defiance. Outright defiance, guerrilla warfare, and terrorism are, of course, the most direct responses. They are responses, however, that may—as in the United States—be unjustifiable and doomed to failure.

Cover, Nomos, supra note 1, at 52.

312. "Some interpretations are writ in blood and run with a warranty of blood as part of their validating force. Other interpretations carry more conventional limits to what will be hazarded on their behalf." Id. at 46.

314. 457 F.Supp. 682 (D.D.C. 1978).

[In *National Student Marketing* the SEC sought to enjoin several lawyers and their law firms, claiming that they had closed a merger deal knowing that shareholder approval had been obtained on the basis of materially misleading documents]. . . .

. . .

The SEC . . . [had] a complete vision of law—norm, narrative and commitment—that was at odds with the bar's *nomos*. The court's decision showed commitment neither to the law it articulated nor to the court's role as interpreter of law.

. . .

The court agreed with the SEC that the lawyers had violated the securities laws by knowingly and substantially assisting their clients to commit fraud. . . .

. . .

Having articulated [precepts that it is wrong to remain silent and do nothing while assisting clients in a fraudulent securities transaction], however, the court failed to connect them to the lawyers' actions in this case: "[I]t is unnecessary to determine the precise extent of their obligations here, since . . . they took no steps whatsoever to delay the closing. . . . But, at the very least, they were required to speak out [to their clients] at the closing. . . ."

In failing to provide a narrative, in failing to connect norms to the actions of the past, the court showed a weak commitment to its role as creator of legal meaning. The court refused to explain what parts of the world as it exists (represented in this case by the actions of the lawyers) are to be changed by its norms. It thus created little law to project into the future. Was it wrong under state law that the lawyers failed to resign? That they failed to inform officers of the corporate client not present at the meeting? That they failed to inform shareholders or the SEC? Does the law demand that lawyers in the future do any of these things? With the words "at the very least," the court admits that the narrative is incomplete, that state law has more meaning, but it does not assert its power to control that meaning. Instead, it invites the bar to provide that meaning: "The very initiation of this action . . . has provided a necessary and worthwhile impetus for the profession's recognition and assessment of its responsibilities in this area."

. . . By telling a community that it should reconsider its behavior and beliefs in light of state power whether or not the use of that power is legitimate, a court abandons its commitment to a state built on the meaning of shared principles and helps constitute a state built instead on obedience to authority. . . .

. . .

... The court explained its failure to create law by stating that further explication would be "unnecessary [to resolve the case before it]" and that it "must narrow its focus to the present defendants and the charges against them." These statements are allusions to the rule against rendering advisory opinions. . . . The case was before the court to determine whether an injunction was warranted against the defendants. . . . What exactly the lawyers did wrong and the degree to which it was wrong were thus issues directly before the court. The court had to reach for the advisory opinion rule to avoid discussing these issues. This stretch demonstrates the court's weak commitment. The court used the advisory opinion rule in a case where it did not naturally apply, as an excuse not to make law. Moreover, the advisory opinion rule assumes "an ironic cast"[339] in this case: the court's refusal to grant any relief against the defendants, a matter to which we turn next, renders the entire opinion no more than advice.

The court refused to enjoin the lawyers from further violations of the securities laws; it granted the SEC no relief against the defendants. By denying relief, the court showed a weak commitment to the little law it did create and to whatever more the securities laws might mean as applied to lawyers whose clients are engaged in fraud. It refused to back its interpretation with force, and more striking, it explained that force was unnecessary, in part because the defendants were lawyers. The court expressed its confidence that the defendants' "professional responsibilities as attorneys and officers of the court" would lead them to honor the court's interpretation without force.[341] In other words, state law depends on the bar's *nomos* for vindication.

339. Cover, Nomos, supra note 1, at 7. Professor Cover used this phrase to describe the thickness of legal meaning. In his example, it was the Due Process Clause's reference to "life" that had taken on an ironic cast both for opponents of the death penalty and opponents of abortion. Id. When a precept takes on an ironic cast for a community or for the society at large, those who perceive the irony will view the state's invocation of the precept with suspicion. See id.

341. Subsequent events suggest how misguided the court's confidence was and how the court's weak commitment helps the bar maintain its divergent understanding of law:

> According to the allegations contained in two lawsuits that Lord, Bissell [& Brook, the firm involved in *National Student Marketing,*] recently settled for twenty-four million dollars, shortly after the decision in National Student Marketing, the firm began aggressively representing National Mortgage Equity Corporation (NMEC), a controversial venture designed to capitalize on the newly emerging market in second mortgages. . . . [A]ccording to the deposition testimony of the firm's managing partner, the firm changed virtually none of its practices as a result of the SEC's prosecutions in National Student Marketing.

David B. Wilkins, Who Should Regulate Lawyers?, 105 Harv. L. Rev. 801, 870–71 (1992) (citing Tim O'Brien, Some Firms Never Learn: Lord, Bissell's Second Escape from Fraud Charges Cost $24 Million—And It Could Happen Again, Am. Law., Oct. 1989, at 63, 64).

Professor Wilkins uses this example to counter bar arguments that lawyers will be unduly chilled by agency and other state regulations. I agree that *National Student Marketing* is unlikely to "chill" many lawyers, but I disagree that this shows that state regulation is unlikely to "chill" many lawyers. It shows, instead, that state regulation lacking significant commitment is unlikely to "chill" many lawyers.

The court thus implied that the bar's law is somehow stronger and more binding on group members than state law. The power of the bar's law did not trouble the court because in the court's vision the paramount precept for lawyers must be (and therefore for the court is) the obligation to comply with state law. This understanding of the hierarchy of norms contained in the ethics rules is, however, a state understanding. In the bar's *nomos* the duty to comply with other law does not, as we have seen, trump all other norms. . . .

The evidence of weak commitment found in *National Student Marketing* is common in cases involving the law governing lawyers. . . .

. . .

There are numerous other examples of the courts' weak commitment in cases involving the law governing lawyers: cases in which the court refuses to use force to back its interpretation;[369] cases in which the court refuses to create legal meaning;[370] cases using temporary or inherently weak boundary rules; and cases in which the court suggests that the bar's understanding of law controls the court's interpretation.[372]

There are, of course, counter-examples.[373] . . .

369. In In re Carter, [1981 Transfer Binder] Fed. Sec. L. Rep. (CCH) P82,847 (SEC Feb. 28, 1981), the SEC reversed an administrative law judge's decision to suspend two lawyers from practicing before the SEC, holding that while it was "a close judgment" whether the lawyers had aided and abetted securities fraud, id. at 84,167, and while they had acted improperly under the interpretation of rule 2(e) set forth by the SEC in this opinion, id. at 84,169–72, discipline was not appropriate because "generally accepted norms of professional conduct . . . did not . . . unambiguously cover the situation in which [the lawyers] found themselves," id. at 84,173. Notice that the conduct, which the SEC says was not clearly understood by the bar to be improper, is conduct that the SEC finds to be almost enough to constitute criminal activity under the securities laws.

370. See, e.g., Barker v. Henderson, 797 F.2d 490, 497 (7th Cir.1986) (refusing to discuss "[t]he extent to which lawyers . . . should reveal their clients' wrongdoing—and to whom they should reveal," noting that "[t]he professions and the regulatory agencies will debate questions raised by cases such as this one for years to come").

372. See, e.g., United States v. Klubock, 832 F.2d 649, 654 (1st Cir.1987) (en banc) (four judges stating that local court rule adopting bar's understanding of when and how lawyers are to be called before grand juries is valid, despite lack of support in case law or federal procedural rules for such limits on the grand jury, because the "fundamental underlying problem . . . is an ethical one"). Citing bar reports and recommendations, the four judges in Klubock concluded that "[t]he subpoenaing of attorney/witnesses . . . appears to present ethical concerns of a widespread nature." Id. at 657; see also Barker, 797 F.2d at 497 ("[A]n award of damages under the securities laws is not the way to blaze the trail toward improved ethical standards in the legal and accounting professions. . . . The securities law . . . must lag behind changes in ethical and fiduciary standards.").

373. For an example of strong court commitment that also reveals the active clash between the bar's normative vision and the court's, see In re Solerwitz, 848 F.2d 1573 (Fed.Cir.1988), cert. denied, 488 U.S. 1004 (1989). In Solerwitz, despite testimony by three "experts in the field of legal ethics" that the lawyer's conduct was proper, the court held that "clear and convincing evidence [showed] that [the lawyer's] continued course of conduct in filing and maintaining multiple frivolous appeals in the face of this court's orders, notices, instructions, rules, precedents and previous sanctions" was improper and justified a one-year suspension. Id. at 1576, 1578. As for the ethics experts' testimony to the contrary, the court quoted with approval the trial judge's assessment: " '[W]hile based in part on established tenets of the legal profession, [their views] do not fully outline the

. . .

    . . . [D]etecting trends in something as complex as the degree of state commitment is a difficult business, there are many indications that the commitment is increasing.[379] On the other hand, given how pervasive and longstanding the practice of low commitment has been and how sympathetic to the bar's vision many judges are, I would not predict a complete about-face in the immediate future.

B. *The Bar's Commitment: Texts of Resistance*

    Whenever a community resists . . . some . . . law of the state, it necessarily enters into a secondary hermeneutic—the interpretation of the texts of resistance.

    As we have seen, the bar's sacred stories predict a crisis between a lawyer's obligations to her client and the demands of state law put forth by prosecutors, judges and other state actors. . . .[382]

. . .

    . . . It is in [the bar's texts of resistance] that we find the bar's understanding of its obligation to the state and its law. The texts do not deny the obligation; they interpret it. . . .

. . .

    In the bar's texts of resistance, after deciding that something the state calls "law" conflicts with bar law (a question that is resolved in the primary interpretation in the text), the question becomes: is that troublesome thing, which the state calls law, law for purposes of the lawyer's obligation to obey? The first interpretive move is that legislation and regulation conflicting with bar law are not "law" for purposes of this norm. . . .

    While neither legislation nor regulation is law that requires obedience, bar texts emphasize that their nonlaw status is strictly limited to

---

duties of a lawyer. . . .'" Id. at 1577 (quoting trial judge). Specifically, the experts ignored case law upon which the court relied. Id. (citing In re Bithoney, 486 F.2d 319 (1st Cir.1973)).

    379. The Supreme Court's decision in Goldfarb v. Virginia State Bar, 421 U.S. 773, 793 (1975), holding that activities of a mandatory bar association are not exempt from the antitrust laws, may be one of the first and most significant signs of an increased commitment to the role of state law vis-a-vis the profession. Another important sign is the significant erosion in the traditional rule that a lack of privity prevents third parties from suing lawyers for negligence. [Editors' Note: Koniak also cites the 1983 amendments to Fed.R.Civ.P. 11, the Kaye Scholer case (see Weinstein, p. 137), and SEC actions against lawyers. Note that after the article was published, further amendments to Fed.R.Civ.P. 11 cut back on its regulatory bite, see p. 21, note 4, and the SEC (at least until Sarbanes-Oxley) backed off its attempts to discipline lawyers, see p. 41, note 9.]

    382. [Consider William Kunstler's response when] sanctioned under Rule 11 for his conduct in suing state prosecutors for harassing Native American activists. In re Kunstler (Robinson Defense Comm. v. Britt), 914 F.2d 505, 525 (4th Cir.1990). . . . Kunstler . . . said: "I'll tell you this: I'm not going to pay any fine. I'm going to rot in jail if that's what I have to do to dramatize this thing. I think I could do no better thing for my country." Don J. DeBenedictis, Rule 11 Snags Lawyers, 77 A.B.A.J. 16, 17 (1991).

the extent that they conflict with bar law and no further. For example, while client confidentiality, according to the bar, precludes a lawyer from complying with tax law and regulations that require the lawyer to provide the client's name and other identifying information, "confidentiality ... do[es] not relieve the lawyer of the statutory duty to file [the required form]...." It "must still be filed, but the lawyer should insert ... in place of the client's name ... a statement that the lawyer and the client are asserting client confidentiality, the attorney-client privilege and, if applicable, the Fifth and Sixth Amendment privileges."[396] Resistance is to be tailored to contest the "invalid" portion of the legislation or regulation and should not otherwise show disrespect to the state's legislation or regulation.

Moreover, while for the bar neither legislation nor regulation is "law" for purposes of the duty to obey (when they conflict with bar law), bar texts typically distinguish between the two; the obligation to resist regulation is generally greater than the obligation to resist legislation. For example, the Statement of Policy adopted by the ABA House of Delegates on the duties of lawyers to comply with the securities laws states:

> [A]ny principle of law which, except as permitted or required by the [Code of Professional Responsibility], permits or obliges a lawyer to disclose to the S.E.C. otherwise confidential information should be established *only by statute* after full and careful consideration of the public interests involved and should be resisted unless clearly mandated by law.[398]

Implicitly, this suggests that greater resistance is owed to SEC regulations inconsistent with bar law than to legislation, which must be resisted too, but not if "clearly mandated by law." How one decides whether legislation is "clearly mandated by law" is not fully described by this ABA Statement, although a suggestion of the bar's answer is provided in the last paragraph of the opinion, which bemoans the possibility that lawyers would be deterred in the exercise of their responsibilities to their clients by either an "erroneous position of the S.E.C. *or a questionable lower court decision.*" Thus, we may infer that an interpretation of legislation that conflicts with the bar's law and that is supported by only a lower court decision is not "clearly mandated by law."

This brings us to the bar's next interpretive problem, whether court orders and decisions are law that must be obeyed. It is at this point that we may gauge the true nature of the bar's commitment, for at this point the state's use of force may be imminent.... Generally, bar texts of

---

396. Ethics Advisory Comm. of the Nat'l Ass'n of Crim. Def. Lawyers, Formal Op. 89–1 (1989).

398. Statement of Policy Adopted by the American Bar Association Regarding Responsibilities and Liabilities of Lawyers in Advising with Respect to Compliance by Clients with Laws Administered by the Securities and Exchange Commission, reprinted in 61 A.B.A.J. 1085, 1086 (1975) (emphasis added).

resistance allow a lawyer to comply with court orders, but do not require that she do so. For example, the ABA has explained its understanding of the ethics rules as follows:

> If the motion to quash is denied, the lawyer must either testify or run the risk of being held in contempt. . . .
>
> The lawyer has an ethical duty to preserve client confidences and to test any interference with that duty in court. . . .
>
> If a contempt citation is upheld on appeal, however, the lawyer has little choice but to testify or go to jail. Both the Model Rules and the Model Code recognize that a lawyer's ethical duty to preserve client confidences gives way to final court orders.[403]

. . . [W]hile this quote carefully avoids explicitly requiring resistance, the message is clear that a lawyer *should* resist—at least, she should resist a lower court order: ethical duty "gives way" according to the text only after a final court order, and "final court orders" are, according to the quote, orders of an appellate court. Even more telling of the bar's commitment to its law than the strong encouragement to resist lower court orders is the suggestion that bar law "gives way" to appellate orders not because they are legitimate and authoritative interpretations but because the state at this point is *extremely* likely to use force: "the lawyer may have little choice but to testify or go to jail." It is accommodation pure and simple that is being expressed, not concession to the appellate court's role as authoritative interpreter of its law.

The view that it is the state's force and *not* its interpretation or its right to interpret that relieves a lawyer of the obligation to resist appellate orders is also expressed by the bar's understanding of the reach of such orders. Bar texts do not contain any suggestion of an obligation to check controlling precedent in the relevant jurisdiction before deciding whether to comply. Moreover, given the weight of authority on such issues as whether a client's identity or the fees she paid her attorney are privileged, it is clearly the message of these bar texts that court decisions contrary to bar law are to be understood as having decided the question before them and no more. . . .

. . . The efficacy of this move is dependent on the level of the courts' commitment. Courts, after all, have the means to insist that their interpretations are projected into the future: injunctions. But the likelihood of the courts using such a tool against lawyers is remote, given how weakly committed they are to their role when they find themselves at

---

403. Disclosure: Lawyer Subpoenas, [Manual] Laws. Man. on Prof. Conduct (ABA/BNA) 55:1301, 55:1307 (Oct. 25, 1989) (emphasis added) (citations omitted). While I have omitted the citations to court cases in this quotation, I want to point out that the text is scrupulous in its citation of court cases that justify the position of the text. This attention to court cases that justify resistance is typical in the bar's texts of resistance. When, after all, could it be more important to demonstrate loyalty and attention to state law than at the moment that one is claiming to be resisting state law in the name of redeeming state law?

odds with the bar. The bar's commitment, on the other hand, is, as we have just seen, strong. It is the interaction of these two levels of commitment that allows the divergence in normative understanding to continue. . . .

Notes

1. In a part not excerpted here, Koniak acknowledges that the bar and state are not monolithic, but justifies her treatment of the two as if they were by saying that in general the variations among subgroups of the bar tend to converge around the view she ascribes to that entity and the same for the subgroups within the state. Is that overstating the matter? Do the subgroups within the bar and the state defeat her picture of a struggle over normative space?

2. Koniak demonstrates the great power that rhetorical "stories" have over our imaginations. These stories provide useful shorthand devices for thinking about legal issues. The problem is that we often invoke these stories without thinking about how internally consistent they are, how well they fit with each other, and how well they apply to different contexts. Koniak starts with the myths (or "fictions" in Zacharias's terms, see p. 83) of lawyer self-regulation and of ethics being about obligations above and beyond legal requirements. These ideas may seem unrelated at first blush. Koniak's insight is to connect them and show the tension that in fact exists between them. What are we to make of self-regulation or the notion of ethics as about obligations above the law when we consider how laws of general application speak to the behavior of lawyers? The self-regulation ideal encourages us to concentrate on laws that are aimed just at lawyers and thus puts in shadow laws of general application. The ethics-as-above-law concept also places those laws in shadow. But together Koniak claims these two concepts do more, i.e., they provide a basis for challenging other law. How?

3. Koniak also discusses the importance to lawyers of the story that portrays a lawyer as the client's last bastion against an all-powerful government—a story rooted in the paradigm of representing a defendant charged with a crime. This myth provides a moral basis for resisting state law in areas far removed from criminal defense advocacy. As you read through the essays in this book, think about how this story, and the typical tales of self-regulation and ethics-as-above-law, recur. Does Koniak neglect the good purposes that these myths serve? Is it important, for example, that we keep law and ethics separate, resisting her insistence to concentrate on the similarities between them? See also, Koniak's Through the Looking Glass article, p. 287.

4. Most comparisons of ethics and law portray ethics as vague and less powerful than law. For a recent example by a prominent law and economics scholar, see Shavell, Law Versus Morality as Regulators of Conduct, 4 Am. L. & Econ. Rev. 227 (2002). Koniak would say that this commonly repeated and generally accepted understanding is wrong. It rests, she would say, on two mistakes. First, ethics is portrayed as too mushy to matter much by conceiving of it in terms of Kant's moral imperative or some equivalent

measure that insists on locating universal standards, which by definition must be vague and thus susceptible to endless (and every) interpretation. What definition of ethics would Koniak substitute and how does it make ethical standards less indefinite? The second mistake underlying the law-strong, ethics-mushy story, she would say, is in overstating the coercive power of law to affect everyday actions when peer group norms, if at odds with state law, are likely to exert more coercive force. How would an economist describe this second mistake? Is it a mistake?

5. The most recent chapter in the ongoing struggle over IRC § 6050I and IRS Form 8300 is DeGuerin v. US, 214 F.Supp.2d 726 (S.D.Tex.2002). In that case, the court denied a summary judgment motion filed by the defense lawyers challenging the assessment of penalties for "intentional disregard" of the filing requirement. But the court also denied a summary judgment motion by the government to get the lawyers to pay the unpaid part of the penalties. On the attorney-client privilege, the court joined most other courts in holding that a client's identity is normally not privileged, but that a client's identity may be protected from disclosure if its revelation will also reveal the confidential purpose for which the client sought legal advice. The court then found that the lawyers had not presented sufficient evidence to justify the application of the exception. In discussing one of the specific instances of nondisclosure presented, the court said: "The fact that upon disclosure of the ... name the government might have been inclined to initiate an investigation of [that person] ... does not transform the ... name into a privileged communication." Indeed, the court found that in that instance the lawyers had intentionally disregarded the filing requirement, but it left open the possibility that the lawyers might fall under a statutory exception for failure to report that is due to a "reasonable cause," which treasury regulations define in part as exercising that "standard of care that a reasonably prudent person would use under the circumstances in the course of its business in determining its filing obligations." The court said that if the lawyers could show that they had a reasonable belief that specific claims of privilege would apply, the exception would apply.

The relevant state's confidentiality rule allowed a lawyer to disclose confidences when necessary to comply with "other law." The government said that supported its case. The court said that the lawyers, although having presented insufficient evidence thus far to satisfy the statute's exception, presented sufficient evidence to show that a "reasonably prudent attorney ... would not have disclosed his client's name if he believed it was privileged despite [the ethics rule's] authorization to do otherwise. Therefore, even if an attorney might be permitted to disclose his client's name [under the ethics rule], a question of fact remains whether an attorney ... would nevertheless reasonably believe he was ethically prohibited from disclosing the name." How would you analyze this case in light of Koniak's article? What is the court's "rule," "story," and "commitment?" How would you expect lawyers to respond to this case?

6. The Ethics 2000 revisions to the Model Rules added an exception to the duty of confidentiality, similar to the extant state rule just discussed, that permits (but does not require) a lawyer to reveal information to the

extent the lawyer reasonably believes necessary "to comply with other law or a court order." Model Rules of Professional Conduct Rule 1.6(b)(4)(2003). The accompanying comment says:

> Other law may require that a lawyer disclose information about a client. Whether such a law supersedes Rule 1.6 is a question of law beyond the scope of these Rules. When disclosure of information relating to the representation appears to be required by other law, the lawyer must discuss the matter with the client to the extent required by Rule 1.4 [dealing with lawyer-client communication]. If, however, the other law supersedes this Rule and requires disclosure, paragraph (b)(4) permits the lawyer to make such disclosures as are necessary to comply with the law.

> A lawyer may be ordered to reveal information relating to the representation of a client by a court or by another tribunal or governmental entity claiming authority pursuant to other law to compel the disclosure. Absent informed consent of the client to do otherwise, the lawyer should assert on behalf of the client all nonfrivolous claims that the order is not authorized by other law or that the information sought is protected against disclosure by the attorney-client privilege or other law. In the event of an adverse ruling, the lawyer must consult with the client about the possibility of appeal to the extent required by Rule 1.4. Unless review is sought, however, paragraph (b)(4) permits the lawyer to comply with the court's order.

Is this a "text of resistance" by the bar? How would Koniak analyze this rule and the accompanying comments? What does it mean for the legal profession to have an ethics rule that permits, but does not require, compliance with the law? How do you think lawyers will interpret this rule? How might the state respond?

7. Koniak's theory is largely a descriptive one. What are the normative and prescriptive implications of the theory? Is divergence between state law and "bar law" a good thing? If so, should we be doing more to promote it? If not, should we be doing more to curb it? What if the divergence is sometimes good and sometimes bad? How should lawyers, state officials, and others act in a world that has this divergence? How are we to judge which is better when state law and a group's ethic conflict? For a discussion of that last question by Koniak, see When Courts Refuse to Frame the Law and Others Frame it to their Will, 66 S.Calif. L. Rev. 1075, 1109-1113 (1993).

8. Why is confidentiality a "constitutional norm" for the bar? Does it play a less central role for other professions? In agency law?

9. The SEC and the bar are still struggling over regulatory space. Between the mid-1980s and lasting through the start of the new century, the SEC by and large left the field of lawyer regulation, bringing almost no enforcement or disciplinary actions against members of the bar. After Enron's collapse and revelations about other corporate scandals, the SEC showed little interest in getting back into the fray. In response to a letter by a group of law professors, asking the SEC to adopt a rule—which it had proposed but abandoned after bar resistance in the early 1980s—to require

lawyers to report evidence of corporate fraud up the corporate hierarchy until a satisfactory response from the entity was received, the SEC general counsel explained: "There has been a strong view among the bar that these matters are more appropriately addressed by state bar rules, which historically have been the source of professional responsibility requirements for lawyers, and have been overseen by state courts. . . . [T]here are . . . good reasons why consideration of such a significant change in established practice should be undertaken in the context of Congressional legislation, as opposed to agency rulemaking." Congress acted, including in the the Sarbanes–Oxley Act a provision directing the SEC to promulgate rules governing lawyers including a mandatory up-the-ladder reporting rule. The ABA had lobbied against the provision, but lost. It now turned its attention to lobbying the SEC to do as little as possible. At first it looked like the SEC had been emboldened by the legislation, proposing not just an up-the-ladder rule but a rule that would require lawyers to disclose evidence of corporate wrongdoing to the SEC when the lawyer had climbed the ladder as far as it went, i.e., told a company's board of directors, and no satisfactory response to the evidence of wrongdoing had been given. The bar was intent on getting that provision dropped and watering down the standard that triggered the duty to report up-the-ladder too. Thus far the bar seems to have accomplished both aims. The SEC has postponed action on the disclosure to the SEC ("noisy withdrawal") requirement it had proposed (adopting, however, a permissive disclosure rule) and adopted a watered-down version of the reporting-up requirement. The ABA, for its part, changed its model ethics rules in the summer of 2003, approving (after years of rejecting) a rule that would allow (not require) a lawyer to disclose client fraud in which the lawyer's services were used and a rule allowing corporate lawyers to report evidence of corporate lawbreaking outside the corporation when the board refused to act and the lawbreaking seemed especially serious. Reports on the ABA vote emphasized that many ABA House Delegates agreed to support these rule changes in the hope of staving off any further federal regulation (and perhaps with the hope of getting the SEC to resume its laissez faire approach to lawyer regulation). For a fuller description of these events and how they connect to the bar's previous battles with the SEC, see Koniak, When the Hurly–Burly's Done, 103 Columbia L. Rev. 1236 (2003).

10. This latest round of SEC/bar confrontation has given rise to yet another battleground between bar and state over normative space. Although most states had refused to follow the ABA's longstanding position (prior to its about-face in 2003) that lawyers should be prohibited from disclosing evidence of client fraud against third parties or the state (as opposed to fraud on the court, which the ABA required lawyers to reveal in some situations), a minority of states went along with the ABA no-disclosure position. Lawyers in some of these states are now arguing that their state no-disclosure rules mean that lawyers who make disclosure to the SEC under the SEC's permissive disclosure rule would be operating unethically and should be subject to state court sanctions. The Washington state bar has been one of the most aggressive in this movement, prompting the SEC to call upon it to withdraw its rule and its interpretation of that rule, which

threatens lawyers who cooperate with the SEC by making permissive disclosures of client fraud. What does it mean for the SEC to "permit" disclosure? Lawyers argue that federal and state rules that can be read as consistent should be. Thus, if the federal rule permits disclosure but state law prohibits it, these lawyers argue there is no conflict: One can comply with the state rule (keep your mouth shut) without violating the federal rule's permission to do otherwise. Is there anything wrong with that argument?

When Law and Economics Met Professional Responsibility

GEORGE M. COHEN*

I.   Law and Economics as Friend

A.   *A Love Story for the '90s*

... [L]aw and economics scholars have started to turn their attention to the legal regulation of the key areas in legal ethics: prohibited assistance, confidentiality, and conflicts of interest. Their conclusions have ranged from general support of the rules governing lawyers to outright hostility. The goal of this paper is to take stock of the relationship as it now stands and—in true '90s fashion—to offer some therapeutic counseling that may help strengthen the relationship in the future. I have three main observations. First, agency problems take multiple forms. Second, solutions to these problems may be tradeoffs or complements; finding complementary solutions is the key to minimizing agency costs. Third, the legal rules governing lawyers matter a great deal in today's environment. Paying more attention to these traits should bond law and economics with professional responsibility for some time to come.

B.   *Self-Interest: The Tie that Binds*

If we are to discuss the relationship between law and economics and professional responsibility, then the obvious place to start is self-interest, because, at first blush, the two fields take diametrically opposed positions on the topic. For law and economics, the assumption of self-interested behavior is the engine that drives much of the analysis.... On the other hand, for professional responsibility, the working assumption has often been that ethics or professionalism requires lawyers to resist self-interest, and the relevant question has been thought to be simply what the nature of this resistance—that is, the content of ethical behavior—should be.

. . .

... [But] self-interested behavior has always been an important part of the [professional responsibility] picture. First, the existence of ethics rules and other law governing lawyers (as well as all law) presupposes the possibility of self-interested behavior. After all, legal rules are largely the fossilized remains of prior misconduct. Even if most lawyers act ethically most of the time, the assumed few "bad apples" (or, in economic terms, "marginal lawyers") are often motivated by self-interest, especially when the wrongs they commit are for financial gain. And to the extent that professional responsibility serves a regulatory func-

* © 1998 Fordham Law Review. Reprinted by permission from 67 Fordham L. Rev. 273 (1998).

tion, it has always been interested in how the self-interested lawyer acts. We do not deem criminal law or contract law uninteresting simply because most people are law-abiding or honor their contracts.

Second, self-interested behavior may be consistent (or at least not inconsistent) with ethical behavior. The more this is true, the less important the question of "ethical" behavior, defined in contrast to self-interested behavior, becomes. Take, for example, the following ethical "rule": "A lawyer's representation of a client . . . does not constitute an endorsement of the client's political, economic, social or moral views or activities."[22] This rule seems to assume that lawyers are not self-interested because self-interested lawyers would generally prefer more business to less (assuming that controversial clients have the ability to pay).[23] At least to an economist, it seems odd that an ethical rule would be necessary to encourage lawyers to act in their self-interest. Thus, even if the goal of professional responsibility is aspirational, it is useful to identify those situations in which self-interest and ethics are most likely to pull in opposite directions and, where the pull of self-interest is strongest, to know when ethical behavior is likely to be most crucial and most difficult.

Third, lawyer self-interest is not the only type of self-interest relevant for professional responsibility. Clients also may or may not be self-interested and their self-interest may or may not take an extreme form. For example, Justice Holmes's "bad man" theory of law has sometimes been thought applicable to lawyering. If the implication of the theory is that the lawyer should (must? may? does?) view the client as a "bad man," that is, as a self-interested person, then the question is, how bad and under what circumstances? The lawyer may presume that the

---

22. Model Rules of Professional Conduct Rule 1.2(b) (1995). As stated, Model Rules of Professional Conduct Rule 1.2(b) is not really a "rule" at all, but merely a declaration. It could be understood to mean that a lawyer may represent clients with whose views he disagrees; however, unlike other ethics rules formulated as "may" rules—such as Model Rules of Professional Conduct Rules 1.2(c), 1.5(c), 1.6(b), 1.13(c), and 1.16(b)—it is hard to imagine an alternative universe in which the lawyer would be prohibited from representing such clients. Alternatively, the rule could be interpreted to mean that a lawyer should represent clients holding unpopular views or pursuing unpopular causes. This is the reading suggested by the comment. See id. Rule 1.2(d) cmt. [3]. Such a reading would make the rule an aspirational one similar to Model Rules of Professional Conduct Rule 6.1 (pro bono service).

23. One could argue that it might be in a lawyer's self-interest to turn down a controversial client because the representation would upset other clients and potential clients, causing the lawyer to lose business. That argument assumes that clients are not self-interested, that is, they choose lawyers based on whom the lawyers represent rather than the quality of the lawyer's work. Moreover, the argument ignores the possibility that some clients might find it admirable that a lawyer would represent unpopular people because, for example, it demonstrates the lawyer's independence. Even if some lawyers would lose business by representing an unpopular client, it is possible that, consistent with Model Rules of Professional Conduct Rule 1.5(a)(2), a lawyer could charge a premium for representing an unpopular client if such representation were likely to hurt his business. But if the market for lawyers were competitive, it would be unlikely that it would be necessary for unpopular clients to pay such a premium, because they would probably be able to find a lawyer to represent them at market rates.

more "bad" the client, the less the lawyer can lawfully do on his behalf. On the other hand, in some situations, the "bad man" may more likely be the lawyer than the client.

In addition, people with whom clients deal (including other lawyers and government actors) may or may not act in a self-interested way toward those clients. Certainly one of the lawyer's primary—and perhaps most satisfying—roles in both transactional and litigation work is to protect one's client against the (perhaps imagined) self-interested behavior of others. In economic terms, lawyers often advise their clients that they must protect themselves against a "prisoner's dilemma" in which altruistic behavior by the client could lead to disastrous results if the other side behaves in a self-interested way. But what exactly is a lawyer professionally obligated or permitted to presume about the self-interestedness of others? Again, the answers are highly relevant to the nature and extent of ethical conflicts.

The point is that self-interested behavior or its absence should not casually be assumed, but should be justified. Economic analysis, of course, offers a justification, although somewhat circular perhaps because it is itself based on an assumption of self-interested behavior. We should expect to see more self-interested behavior (and less ethical behavior) as the cost of engaging in self-interested behavior decreases or the benefit from such behavior increases. Economic theory can thus help identify the conditions, behavioral patterns, and structures that increase the incentives and opportunities for self-interested behavior.

There are good reasons to think that there has been an increase in self-interested behavior by lawyers, clients, and those with whom clients interact. The key fact is that there has been an increase in competition in the market for legal services, as well as in the markets in which many lawyers' clients operate. The law governing lawyers and clients has also undergone significant change. As a result, this may be a propitious period to study the implications of self-interested behavior for rules governing lawyers.

II. Taking Agency Costs Seriously

The economic theory of agency costs has been expounded and applied extensively in the context of lawyering. My goal in this part is to summarize and critique this model from within the economic framework. The three main critiques of the model are that it: (1) ignores the importance of multiple agency problems; (2) pays insufficient attention to the extent to which proposed solutions to agency problems complement or conflict with each other; and (3) underemphasizes the importance of legal rules given its assumptions.

A. *All in the Family of Agency Problems*

By now, the basic agency theory is well-known. In all principal-agent relationships, there is a divergence of interests because of the separation of ownership (in the principal) and control (in the agent) of productive assets. Because the agent does not reap the full reward from his efforts on the principal's behalf, and because the agent knows more than the principal about what the agent is doing (what economists refer to as "asymmetric information"), the agent has the incentive and opportunity to act—whether alone or in concert with others—in numerous ways that harm the principal's interests. The principal must therefore find ways to control these agency costs. The primary means of control are monitoring, which involves frequent checking up on the agent, and bonding, which involves less frequent checking but large penalties for discovered misbehavior. The many variations on these control mechanisms are usually differentiated by whether the parties themselves, private "third" parties, or government actors are doing the checking and/or the penalizing.

    ... [L]awyers are no different from other professionals in their possession of specialized knowledge that is hard to monitor and evaluate.... [H]owever, ... lawyers are different from ... other professionals in a crucial respect that increases the agency cost temptations for them. Lawyers, because of their knowledge of the legal system, have unique opportunities to do harm to their clients through manipulating the licensed violence of that system. That is not to say that lawyers necessarily can do more harm than others, but rather that the nature of the harm is unique and relevant for addressing the agency cost problems that lawyers face.

    Lawyers' unique ability to do harm is more often recognized in conjunction with a second type of agency cost problem: lawyers colluding with their clients against others....

    . . .

    ... Just as lawyers may act in a self-interested way to use their informational advantage to evade their responsibilities to their clients, they may also act in a self-interested way to use this advantage to help their clients evade their responsibilities toward others....

    Aside from the problems of lawyers acting against their clients' interests and lawyers colluding with their clients against the interests of third parties, there is a third type of "agency problem" that plays a lesser role in professional responsibility and agency law generally, but deserves a brief mention—if only because it is so often ignored. This problem is the collusion of clients and third parties against the lawyer. Although the lawyer generally enjoys an informational advantage over clients and third parties, the lawyer may, in certain circumstances, find himself at a contractual disadvantage. The client and third party (and usually the third party's lawyer), after having received the benefit of the (client's) lawyer's advice, may try to cut the (client's) lawyer out of the deal. Two seemingly unrelated ethics rules address this problem, at least indirectly. The first is the so-called "no contact" rule. Although this rule is ostensibly directed at protecting a client from being taken advantage of by another client's lawyer, it also protects the absent lawyer from being cut out without his knowledge. The other relevant rule is the prohibition of restrictions on the lawyer's right to practice as part of a settlement. The purported purpose of this heavily criticized rule is to make legal services available to more people. But another possible purpose for the rule is to prevent the client and the third party from opportunistically taking advantage of the lawyer by depriving the lawyer of one of the ordinary benefits of representation—future business—at a time when the lawyer might be in a vulnerable bargaining position.

We have not yet exhausted the potential agency problems that exist in legal representation. Agency problems may be compounded by the fact that clients, their lawyers, and third parties may all have agency problems within themselves. The paradigmatic example of agency costs within the client is, of course, the corporate client, which faces agency costs from not only the managers, whose self-interest gave rise to agency theory in the first place, but also from in-house counsel. The problem, however, is broader than that; it includes problems such as: clients who are agents themselves, as with fiduciaries; clients who are represented by agents, as in class actions or unions; or clients who have contractual relationships with insurance companies under which the insurance company provides the lawyer. The paradigmatic agency problem "within the lawyer" is the law firm in which the lawyer practices. Lawyers are agents of their firms as well as of their clients, and difficulty of monitoring poses problems in the lawyer-firm relationship similar to those in the lawyer-client relationship. But again, the problem is broader, for it includes inter-lawyer relationships as well as intra-lawyer (that is, intra-firm) relationships.

These multiple agency problems are mainstays of professional responsibility. If law and economics is to seriously engage professional responsibility, then its practitioners must recognize that they are buying into not simply one relationship, but a whole family. This fact has important practical consequences for economic analysis. First, multiple agency problems complicate matters tremendously. Instead of just a concern with lawyers' acting against their clients' interests, lawyers acting with clients against the interests of third parties, and clients acting with third parties against lawyers, each of these possible agency problems can exist in one of the subsidiary relationships. For example, lawyers may collude with another corporate agent against the corporate client's interest, collude with a corporate client against a corporate agent's interests, or become victimized by a corporate client colluding with its agents against the lawyer. Similarly, a lawyer may collude with aligned lawyers against a client, collude with the client against these aligned lawyers, or become victimized by the client colluding with the aligned lawyers. Second, the interaction among these agency problems may be complex; in particular, attempts to mitigate one agency problem may simultaneously exacerbate another. Economic analysis can play a useful role in helping to develop a sense of judgment about which problems are most significant in any given situation.

B. *Solutions to Agency Problems: Complements of the Firm*

There is no perfect solution to the agency problems described above. All solutions are costly and none completely eliminates all agency problems. The approach of law and economics is to try to identify those solutions that yield the greatest reduction in agency problems at the lowest cost. One way to do this is to compare the effects various solutions might be expected to have on the agency problems discussed above. In doing so, it is useful to distinguish between solutions that create tradeoffs among agency problems and solutions that act as complements by mitigating more than one problem simultaneously.

. . .

In professional responsibility, the most commonly discussed tension is that between the duty the lawyer owes to the client and the duty the lawyer owes to others. Using the economics of agency discussed above, we can recast this tension as a tradeoff between solutions to the lawyer-client agency problem and the lawyer-client collusion problem. Consider the bonding solution to the lawyer-client agency problem, in which some of the lawyer's assets are put at risk of forfeiture in the event that the lawyer acts against the client's interests. The more successful the bonding, and thus the lower the risk of the lawyer-client agency problem arising, the greater the risk that the lawyer-client collusion problem will occur. As a result, the law governing lawyers has always included not only bonding rules, but antibonding rules, better known as rules attempting to promote the lawyer's "independence" from the client. Independence helps solve the lawyer-client collusion problem, but at the expense of exacerbating the lawyer-client agency problem. In general, there is no unique solution to this tradeoff; rather, in evaluating rules one must examine the particular context to see whether it is more important to guard against the lawyer-client agency problem or the lawyer-client collusion problem.

When law and economics met professional responsibility, however, it purported to find a way out of the tradeoff. The trick was to find an institution that simultaneously reduced the risk of the lawyer-client agency problem and the risk of the lawyer-client collusion problem; that is, the solution to one problem must complement rather than exacerbate the solution to the other. The institution economists have identified is the large law firm. The theory is that the law firm protects clients against the lawyer-client agency problem by posting a bond in the form of its reputation for client service and then monitoring the conduct of its member lawyers to prevent forfeiture of the reputational bond. At the same time, the firm protects third parties from lawyer-client collusion by developing client-specific human capital, which makes it costly for the client to switch firms. This lock-in effect gives the law firm sufficient bargaining power to thwart any attempt by the client to wrongfully impose costs on third parties. In the language of antitrust, the legal services offered by law firms present a tying arrangement: if clients want the benefits of monitoring against lawyer-client agency problems, they must accept the tied product of anti-collusion measures.

Though the possibility of a complementary solution, such as the law firm, is quite tempting, it is important to understand the conditions necessary for such a solution to work. If too many celestial bodies must align, then the Age of Aquarius may never arrive, or may be too fleeting to achieve the prophesied results. As a preliminary matter, it is important to note that the law firm solution is procedural rather than substantive; it represents a choice about which institution should resolve the tradeoff rather than identifying how the tradeoff should be resolved. And although the firm solution is common in economics, in the sense that single ownership "eliminates" the problem of conflicting resource uses by internalizing the problem within the firm, in this context the law firm is not playing that role. Thus, the law firm solution depends crucially on how much we really believe the firm can successfully navigate the lawyer-client agency problem and the lawyer-client collusion problem simultaneously. Let us consider the two problems in turn.

The key to the firm as a solution to the lawyer-client agency problem is the effectiveness of the reputational bond. There is no doubt that reputation matters to some degree. Business clients, like most customers, rely on brand name as a proxy for quality that is difficult to assess directly. But there are limits to reputation. For example, for reputational bonding to work, lawyer-client agency problems must be accurately identified and widely publicized, and the reputational bond of potential future business must be large enough that the harm to the law firm's reputational asset from misconduct is commensurate with the social harm the misconduct causes. One would expect, however, that the same information asymmetry that created the lawyer-client agency problems in the first place also makes reputation difficult for clients or the public to assess. Moreover, law firms may be particularly adept at manipulating evidence of agency problems so as to often be able to evade or minimize reputational penalties. As for the information law firms cannot control, it may misrepresent or exaggerate agency problems. In the jargon of law and economics, there will be overinclusion and underinclusion problems in the "enforcement" of the reputational bond.

There are several ways to improve the effectiveness of the reputational bond provided by law firms. One way is to increase the size of the bond by increasing the size of the firm. To the extent that large size puts the firm more at risk, the firm may face something akin to a private punitive damage regime. But law firm size does not guarantee a larger or more effective reputational bond; in fact, size may cut in the opposite direction. Size increases the cost of monitoring—that is, agency problems—within the firm. Relatedly, size makes it difficult for a firm to establish and maintain an ethical "culture" of informal norms rather than formal monitoring and regulation. Size also may make it easier for the firm to explain away misconduct as an aberration and blame it on individual wrongdoers rather than the firm itself, thus reducing the reputational penalty the firm suffers. On the other hand, if large size is effective at increasing the reputational bond, then the bond may create overdeterrence and client opportunism problems well-recognized in punitive damage regimes.

A second way to improve the effectiveness of reputational bonding is to supplement it with additional monitoring to improve the accuracy of the reputational information. That is precisely what many clients have done through the use of in-house counsel. But while in-house counsel may improve client monitoring, it is not clear whether in-house counsel from different companies coordinate their knowledge to the extent necessary to significantly improve the effectiveness of reputational bonding. Moreover, the ability of in-house counsel to monitor outside lawyers is itself limited by the competence and experience of in-house counsel as well as their own self-interest.

Even if the reputational bonding mechanism successfully minimizes lawyer-client agency problems, there nevertheless remains the question of whether the firm simultaneously minimizes lawyer-client collusion problems. A key to the firm's success in this arena is bargaining power, which results from the specific knowledge the firm develops about a client's needs and the firm's quality. But ... once clients become concerned enough about lawyer-client agency problems to increase their monitoring of law firms, the law firm loses the bargaining advantage necessary to resist lawyer-client collusion. Even if bargaining power exists, however, it may not be sufficient to ensure that lawyer-client collusion does not occur. In the first place, the law firm might use the lock-in effect to harm the client rather than to prevent the client from wrongfully harming others. On the other hand, if the law firm decides that the benefit from pleasing the client exceeds the costs it will suffer by colluding with the client against third parties, then the law firm will not be able to resist lawyer-client collusion. Indeed, the very reputational bond that enables the law firm to combat lawyer-client agency problems could be strengthened by a firm's willingness to collude against third parties. This tendency would be exacerbated by agency problems within the client which, interestingly, could result in the complementary solution completely flipping, so that the law firm would wind up engaging or acquiescing in conduct that hurts both the client and third parties simultaneously.

My point is not to disparage law firms or the possibility of complementary solutions, but to suggest that more may be involved in developing such solutions than law and economics scholars have thus far recognized. We now have the makings of a theme. Law and economics has much to offer professional responsibility, from playing out the implications of self-interest to identifying agency problems to recognizing tradeoffs and the potential for complementary solutions. But law and economics also has much to learn, both about when to press the analysis farther than it has done and when to pull back. Relationships are complicated things.

C. Beyond the Shadow of the Rules

Law and economics must pay more attention to the role that legal rules governing lawyers can play in developing solutions to agency problems. In the discussion above, I have provided some examples of how ethics rules and other law governing lawyers attempt to address various agency problems, either directly (through prohibition or punishment of conduct resulting from agency problems) or indirectly (through prohibition of activities that facilitate agency problems). In this section, I suggest two related ways in which legal rules can serve as complementary solutions to agency problems.

First, ethics rules and the law governing lawyers can play the same role as the one discussed in the prior section of this Article relating to law firms. The reason is that the rules define the qualifications for membership in the profession and the scope of acceptable conduct within the profession; in turn, the profession acts, in some sense, as a megafirm. Thus, there are rules designed to protect against both lawyer-client agency problems and lawyer-client collusion problems. More important, however, is that the rules are tied together through regulatory bundling. Thus, clients are legally protected from lawyer-client agency problems, but in return, they must submit to regulation of lawyer-client collusion problems. The market power of the legal profession as a whole allows this tying—or regulatory bundling—to occur because clients will have a difficult time finding a substitute for legal services. . . . [But] as clients find more ways to substitute away from legal services, it becomes more difficult for regulatory bundling to work.

In some sense, this notion is not new at all. Professional responsibility has long recognized the quid pro quo of a limited monopoly for the legal profession in return for an undertaking of various social obligations. What is new in this account is the recognition that there is an inextricable link between the rules intended to solve very different problems, along with a clearer understanding of how that link works. To ignore this link is to miss an important aspect of the regulatory structure of the legal profession.

A second role for legal rules is to complement or facilitate nonlegal solutions to agency problems. Law and economics scholars, in their zest to find private solutions to agency problems, sometimes overlook this role for legal rules, and even find the legal regime hostile to these solutions. For example, legal regulation may enhance reputational effects by publicizing misconduct and providing more accurate information about it than would otherwise exist....

... Legal rules matter. They are the protector of last resort against the excessive pursuit of self-interest. They tie solutions directed at various agency problems together in ways that may reduce tradeoffs. And they are often complementary to nonlegal solutions. Taking agency problems seriously means taking the law governing lawyers seriously.

III. Some Rules of Engagement

Thus far, I have tried to trace and develop the relationship between law and economics and professional responsibility. In this part, I briefly play out some of the themes in a few specific areas that have received recent attention from law and economics scholars.

A. Confidentiality, Legal Advice, and Prohibited Assistance

. . .

... [C]onfidentiality rules are an essential part of agency relation-ships (and agency law) generally because in the absence of such rules, the informational advantage the agent has would enable the agent to use information about the principal to the principal's disadvantage. Applied to the lawyer-client context, the fundamental purpose of confidentiality rules is to help minimize lawyer-client agency costs. Although this point is obvious, it is surprising how often it is neglected in professional responsibility discussions of the duty of confidentiality. Instead, these discussions often focus only on client incentives, rather than lawyer incentives, and they seem to view lawyers as neutral, altruistic, or victims of client manipulation.

This focus on client incentives partly results from the tendency to lump the duty of confidentiality with the attorney-client privilege, which does seem to be more directed to client incentives. But even the attor-ney-client privilege implicates lawyer-client agency problems. Absent the privilege, lawyers' informational advantage over their clients would be magnified: lawyers would be in a much better position than their clients to assess and control the increased legal risks to clients associated with the possibility of lawyer testimony. Although clients would be more reluctant to hire lawyers in the first place, for those who did, this informational asymmetry would give self-interested lawyers a greater ability and incentive to manipulate the creation and presentation of evidence to promote their own interests at the expense of their clients' interests. Thus, the loyal lawyer assumed in most discussions of the attorney-client privilege may be in part a result of the privilege, which helps bond lawyer interest to client interest.

Lawyers may have an interest in characterizing the confidentiality problem as one of client incentives for seeking legal advice rather than lawyer incentives for disloyalty, but law and economics is supposed to be sensitive to self-interested behavior that other approaches overlook. The duty of confidentiality is about lawyer self-interest; in fact, the duty of confidentiality presupposes lawyer self-interest. . . .

. . .

. . . [T]he lawyer-client collusion problem . . . is the biggest problem with confidentiality rules generally. The agency theory discussed above suggests that the duty of confidentiality should not be interpreted so as to facilitate lawyer-client collusion; thus, the duty cannot be absolute. Moreover, lawyer self-interest means that the absence of lawyer-client collusion cannot merely be assumed, but must be actively secured. Yet traditional discussions of lawyer confidentiality often simply assume that lawyers will (altruistically) counsel their clients not to engage in wrongful behavior and that the "ethical moment" occurs when the client says no. In fact, the problem arises when the lawyer sees signals of client misconduct and chooses to ignore those signals rather than act on them. That is the beginning of complicity.

It is also consistent with the self-interest story. The very lawyer self-interest that makes the protection of confidentiality necessary also makes the abuse of confidentiality possible. Confidentiality rules hinder lawyers' ability to use clients' information against them. But by enabling lawyers to get more information about clients, the confidentiality rules give lawyers a leg up on future business. Future business depends on how successful the client is, which, in turn, depends on how many risks the client is willing to take. If clients bear the downside legal risks while lawyers do not, then the lawyers have an incentive to advise or permit clients to take "aggressive" legal positions, which at some point may spill over into criminal or fraudulent acts. If the risky action succeeds, then the lawyer is rewarded; if it fails, then the lawyer does not expect to suffer.[108]

The law of lawyering, as discussed above, recognizes the lawyer-client collusion problem by limiting the confidentiality rules. Lawyer liability to third parties, such as aiding and abetting liability or negligent misrepresentation, is one way of bonding lawyers to their advice (or lack thereof). The crime-fraud exceptions to the attorney-client privilege and the work product doctrine make legal sanctions against client wrongdo-

---

108. Langevoort and Rasmussen worry that transactional lawyers too often overstate legal risks to get more fees. *See* Donald C. Langevoort & Robert K. Rasmussen, Skewing the Results: The Role of Lawyers in Transmitting Legal Rules, 5 S.Cal. Interdisc. L.J. 375, 377 (1997). To the extent that future business is more important than current fees, they may have it exactly backward, depending on how strongly the rules against lawyer-client collusion are enforced. Transactional lawyers' bias is more likely to be in favor of legal advice that permits client activity. If that activity turns out to be legally problematic, lawyers typically argue either that the client was unfairly singled out (in the underenforcement world) or that the client's activity was socially desirable and the law should not be interpreted rigidly to prohibit it (in the overenforcement world). Lawyers have more incentive to overstate legal risks in one-shot transactions, such as real estate closings, wills, divorces, and other consumer transactions.

ing more effective, and so deter lawyers from engaging in the collusive strategy. How effective these limitations are and how far they should extend are matters of great debate, though it is apparent from the legal wreckage that makes up professional responsibility cases that lawyers too often underestimate the import of these limitations. For my purposes, however, three observations will suffice.

First, the confidentiality rules and the limits to those rules represent a good example of the regulatory bundling discussed above. Although clients benefit from confidentiality rules, and the attorney-client privilege and work product doctrine give lawyers market advantages over other groups, these benefits come at a price, namely, the limitations designed to thwart lawyer-client collusion.[109] You have to take the bad with the good. For this to work, however, the "good" has to be good enough for clients and lawyers to buy into the system. . . .

Second, the limits to confidentiality that try to combat lawyer-client collusion are sensitive to economic considerations of when such collusion is likely to occur. For example, many of the recent developments of the law governing lawyers that limits confidentiality have occurred in the context of client insolvency, most notably the savings and loan crisis. Although these developments are often criticized as simply searching for deep pocket defendants, there is an economic explanation. Just as the law of vicarious liability deters principals from reducing their liability bills by hiring insolvent agents, so, too, does the law of lawyering deter lawyers from leeching onto potentially insolvent clients who may be underdeterred by legal sanctions, which inefficiently inflicts costs on third parties. Moreover, the insolvency context is more conducive to the complex client problem of managing agents acting against the entity's best interests.

. . .

B.   Conflicts of Interest

Conflicts of interest rules provide a useful comparison to confidentiality rules, both in the treatment they receive from professional responsibility and from law and economics. First, unlike professional responsibility's justification for confidentiality, which seems almost to assume lawyer altruism, the justifications for conflicts rules seem to assume extreme lawyer self-interest. . . . [For example,] the rules governing vicarious disqualification, that is, extending the conflict beyond the

---

109. Confidentiality rules also may encourage private complementary solutions. In particular, confidentiality rules may encourage greater investigation because clients have less reason to fear that lawyers will use information they discover to their clients' disadvantage. But investigation is a classic tying arrangement: at the time the investigation is conducted, the lawyer does not know whether the information found will be good or bad. Critics of confidentiality rules seem to assume that it is easy for lawyers to suppress bad information, but at least in civil litigation, this is not so given liberal discovery rules. In transactional work, negative information limits the actions lawyers may take on behalf of clients. In both cases, ex ante investigation facilitates ex post policing.

lawyer to the firm, ... establish strict presumptions which assume that lawyers will find it difficult to resist economic temptation....

Even in the conflict of interest context, however, law and economics scholars sometimes downplay agency problems.... [For example, one important issue is the degree to which client consent should be decided to cure a conflicted.] But the situations in which bargaining [over consent] might make sense are also the situations in which the agency problems are likely to be the greatest. Lawyers have an informational advantage in knowing both how much one client is going to be hurt by divulging information and how much the other is going to be helped. Why the client would be willing to trust the lawyer's assessment of these values is not clear.... In some sense, the rules—by restricting waiver— are trying to ensure meaningful or fully informed consent.

Law and economics scholars have also paid insufficient attention to the way the conflict of interest rules and the law of disqualification serve as effective bonding devices. Consider the rules concerning joint representation in a transactional setting. If the relationship between the parties comes unglued, then the lawyer is thereafter generally prohibited from representing either in the same transaction. This rule bonds the lawyer to his judgment regarding the potential for conflict. The lawyer pays a large penalty if conflict in fact occurs. This gives the lawyer an incentive to evaluate carefully ex ante the potential for conflict in joint representation and to avoid biasing this judgment by factoring in the possibility of future work arising out of the subsequent turmoil. A similar justification applies to the general rule that in a successive representation a lawyer may not attack his prior work. Allowing lawyers to do so would weaken the lawyer's bond to his prior work and provide too great an incentive for the lawyer to intentionally or accidentally leave loopholes to preserve the possibility of future work.

. . .

Notes

1. In the hierarchy of legal subjects, legal ethics occupies the academic basement. Law and economics occupies the penthouse suite. We are not suggesting this is how it should be; we are, however, asserting that this is how matters stand today in the legal academy. Why hasn't the law and economics interest in legal ethics boosted the prestige of the latter subject? How could it be that the one subject the ABA requires every law school to teach, legal ethics, is so widely held in contempt—by students and professors (at least professors of other subjects) alike?

2. Cohen discusses the assumption that the rules governing lawyers are a function of self-interest. Flip this around. Do the rules, however they came to be, increase or decrease self-interested behavior by lawyers? One way this might happen is that the rules might influence the types of people who enter the profession. Do the rules governing lawyers (or the lore of the

profession) encourage more self-interested people to become lawyers than altruistic people? Do law schools exacerbate the problem by rewarding excessively self-interested types? By penalizing altruists? Are you too close to the experience to judge?

3. Many people believe that the assumption of self-interested behavior significantly limits the explanatory power of economic analysis. How might the assumption skew observation? Limit the formulation of solutions?

4. Cohen makes the point that law and economics scholars need to take the law of lawyering more seriously. Of course, the same advice might be given to many ethics scholars who ignore the law and concentrate on questions such as, whether lawyers can be good people, and sometimes discuss problems, such as, the limits of acceptable legal advice, with very little mention of the law on the subject. Why do you think that scholars coming from these very different perspectives have trouble keeping "law" in the subject, which so many call "professional responsibility?"

5. Cohen refers to agency law as a possible solution to some of the agency problems involving lawyers. Could agency law answer all the questions of legal ethics? Might it render the ethics rules unnecessary? What problems of legal ethics aren't really "agency" problems? How are lawyers different from other agents?

6. In discussing what he calls the lawyer-client collusion problem of confidentiality, Cohen makes the point that the traditional argument in favor of strict confidentiality, and against a rule of disclosure in the case of client fraud, assumes that the lawyer will act altruistically in dissuading the client from the fraudulent conduct. Another way of putting this point is to think of the lawyer as agent both for the client and for the legal system. As agents of the legal system, lawyers enjoy special privileges and acquire specialized knowledge on the condition that they will not use these privileges and this knowledge to undercut the rule of law and the legal system. Silent acquiescence in client fraud does just that. Lawyers might be inclined to acquiesce because they have a conflict of interest: they are paid by their clients, not the "legal system." Thus, their incentive is to favor client interests. Economic analysts and legal ethicists alike all too often ignore this "agency" problem.

7. For a recent attempt to apply economic principles to explain the ethics rules, see Sean J. Griffith, Ethical Rules and Collective Action: An Economic Analysis of Legal Ethics. 63 U. Pitt. L. Rev. 347–387 (2002).

Rules Lawyers Play By
RICHARD W. PAINTER*

[Introduction]

. . .

... When should rules governing lawyers be immutable (rules that
cannot be changed contractually), and when should they be defaults
(rules that can be changed contractually)? When default rules are used,
should professional responsibility codes emphasize opt-in rules (rules
that apply only if lawyers and clients affirmatively choose them or enter
into a specific arrangement governed by those rules), or opt-out rules
(rules that apply unless lawyers and clients agree otherwise)? Should
professional responsibility codes emphasize majoritarian default rules
(rules that most lawyers and clients would have chosen in hypothetical
ex ante bargaining), or penalty default rules? When should a lawyer not
be governed by clearly defined rules, but instead by more general
standards against which the lawyer's conduct is measured ex post to
ascertain whether her conduct conformed to those standards?

The evolution of professional responsibility rules in the last century
reveals several important trends. First, codes have migrated away from
broad standards and toward clearly defined rules.... Second, when the
subject matter of a rule is particularly controversial, the rule has tended
to remain a standard that is so broad that it is unenforceable, to be a
discretion-laden rule (signified by frequent use of the word "may" in
codes of professional responsibility), or to be phrased in aspirational
language rather than language clearly stating what a lawyer must or
must not do. Third, professional responsibility codes, to some extent,
have moved away from immutable rules toward default rules and opt-in
rules. This change, however, has taken place almost exclusively in rules
governing lawyer conduct that affects clients, but not third parties.
Immutable rules continue to define a lawyer's obligations to nonclients
with whom the lawyer does not have a contractual relationship.

This Article argues that default rules should be used more extensively in professional responsibility codes....

For subjects such as lawyer response to client fraud and to conflicts
within organizations, immutable rules have not worked well, in part
because the rules accommodate so many conflicting viewpoints that they
are ambiguous. Even if these immutable rules are left in place, consensus on additional default rules would enrich codes of professional responsibility. Clients and lawyers who disagree with a default rule—e.g., a rule
that requires a lawyer to report a corporate client's illegal acts to its full
board of directors unless otherwise provided in the client's articles of

* © 2001 New York University Law Review. Reprinted by permission from 76 N.Y.U.L.
Rev. 665 (2001).

organization—could opt out, so long as they do so ex ante, before obligations under the rule arise. An ex ante decision to opt out of a rule or into another rule should give interested third parties ample time to anticipate how the lawyer will respond to various contingencies.

... Reform ... should focus not just on changing the default rules, but also on more clearly defining the opting-out mechanisms and making them easier to use. Finally, the ABA should consider whether encouraging or even requiring law firms to adopt their own codes of professional responsibility would fill gaps in the law and promote meaningful debate within firms about the relative importance of competing ethical principles.

...

I.   The Contractarian Framework

There are three broad categories of professional responsibility rules: rules that protect clients, rules that protect third parties, and rules that protect the legal system. As discussed below, this distinction is often critical for determining where a rule belongs in the contractarian framework. . . .

The first important distinction in contractarian theory is between immutable rules and default rules. An *immutable rule* cannot be changed by contractual agreement. Many professional responsibility rules are immutable—for example, in most jurisdictions, a lawyer cannot negotiate for literary or media rights with a client before the end of a representation, acquire a financial interest in the subject matter of litigation (other than a contingent fee), or commingle client and lawyer funds. Rules that protect third parties or the legal system—for example, the rule prohibiting lawyer assistance of client fraud—are almost always immutable.

...

Another major category of rules is the *default rule*; that is, a rule that may be changed contractually. . . .

... Default rules are particularly attractive if they only allow lawyers to opt for a higher level of professional responsibility than that required by the rule (an *opt-up rule*), although many default rules are *opt-down rules* because they contemplate opting into a lower level of responsibility. *Opt-down default rules* sometimes are coupled with immutable rules requiring that minimum standards be observed.

...

Default rules are usually phrased as *opt-out rules* (i.e., the code states a rule that applies unless the parties opt out). . . . For example, Model Rule 1.7 states that a lawyer may not represent a client having interests adverse to those of an existing client, unless the existing client consents after consultation (an opt-out default rule).

Some rules, however, are *opt-in rules* (i.e., if the parties don't opt in, another rule applies). For example, Model Rule 1.15 requires a lawyer to deliver an accounting for client or third-party funds at the request of the client or third party (if there is no request, the accounting need not be given). . . .

Another important distinction is *when* the contracting parties are allowed to opt out of the default rule or opt into another rule. *Ex ante contracting*, an essential feature of both contract law and corporate law, is completed before all or most of the relevant facts become known. . . . In a lawyer-client relationship, however, a client might not know enough information at the beginning of a representation to fully understand the subject matter of a contract. For this reason, rules that include the term "consent after consultation" sometimes are interpreted to refer only to *ex post contracting*. For example, most conflict waivers are not obtained when the first client retains counsel but when the second client seeks representation. Also, the law in nearly all jurisdictions does not permit a prospective waiver of malpractice liability.

Perhaps ironically, when ex ante contracting is allowed, the contract sometimes is subject to *less* scrutiny than an ex post contract, on the theory that the lawyer is not yet a fiduciary of the client at the time the contract is made. This reduced scrutiny, based on a formalistic determination of exactly when a fiduciary relationship begins, can leave clients exposed to lawyer overreaching early in a representation when clients have access to the least information. Legal fees, for example, are routinely governed by ex ante contracting in retainer agreements that are subject to relatively little judicial scrutiny, although immutable rules at least theoretically limit those fees. . . .

Retainer agreements sometimes also address issues besides the lawyer's fee, such as the scope or objectives of the representation. In some instances, retainer agreements could be used more creatively to devise ex ante solutions to problems that heretofore have been addressed with ex post contracting or immutable rules. At the same time, ex ante contracting is unsettling if the lawyer is contracting for a lower level of responsibility to the client rather than for a higher one, and the client is contracting at a time when she does not know many of the relevant facts

. . .

. . . By choosing a jurisdiction in which to practice, a lawyer chooses a body of rules, but a lawyer cannot choose among the rules of different jurisdictions (for example, by choosing that her Illinois practice be governed by the conflicts rules of New York and the confidentiality rules of New Jersey). Lawyers generally also do not design their own rules, advertise them, and then represent clients willing to agree to the given rules, even though such a system might expand the options available to clients. Lawyer rule choice has obvious pitfalls, particularly if there is

unequal bargaining power or asymmetry of information between lawyers
and clients. On the other hand, expanding lawyer choice would be
appealing in contexts in which individual lawyers have strong philosophical predispositions to play by a particular rule that offers expanded
protection to clients or third parties (usually an opt-up rule).

. . .

. . . [All default rules] fall somewhere on a spectrum between two
other categories: defined rules and standards. *Defined rules* state ex ante
precisely what a lawyer must, may, or may not do. For example, most
jurisdictions provide that an agreement for a contingent fee must be in
writing. . . . *Standards*, by contrast, use subjective language, and rely on
ex post judicial or administrative decisions to determine when specific
conduct meets a standard, and when it does not. For example, most
jurisdictions require that lawyers' fees shall be reasonable. Both the
Model Rules and the Model Code list eight factors for determining
reasonableness, and a large body of highly subjective case law defines
when fees are and are not "reasonable." . . .

[Sometimes] . . . a standard is used because a defined rule's prohibitions might sweep too broadly. Transactions between a lawyer and
client, for example, must be "fully disclosed" and be "fair and reasonable" to the client (a standard), but are not prohibited per se (which
would be a defined rule). . . .

. . .

. . . [As to incentives to comply with the rules, s]ome rules are
legally enforced through discipline, criminal penalties, civil penalties, and
civil suits by clients or third parties. Some rules are enforced more
sporadically, or the penalties are less severe, while other rules are not
enforced at all. Whether or not a rule is legally enforced, it can be
reputationally enforced if breach of the rule is detectable and likely to
harm a lawyer's reputation. . . . An aspirational rule lacks coercive force
of any kind until such time as the bar, clients, or third parties attach
sufficient importance to the rule that reputational capital can be acquired and retained by complying with its terms.

II. Evolution of Rules Within the Contractarian Framework

. . . Although the form of rules is constantly changing, some overall
trends are discernable.

A significant number of rules have shifted from "standards" toward
"defined rules" (although many of them only partially). . . .

. . .

There also has been a trend toward replacing immutable rules with
default rules and opt-in rules. . . .

The Restatement reflects this guarded shift toward a contractarian outlook on the lawyer-client relationship. Section 19 (Agreements Limiting Client or Lawyer Duties) states:

> (1) Subject to other requirements stated in this Restatement, a client and lawyer may agree to limit a duty that a lawyer would otherwise owe to the client if:
>
> > (a) the client is adequately informed and consents; and
> >
> > (b) the terms of the limitation are reasonable in the circumstances.
>
> (2) A lawyer may agree to waive a client's duty to pay or other duty owed to the lawyer.

Although this appears to be a broad endorsement of lawyer-client contracting, the words "subject to other requirements stated in this Restatement" clearly subordinate Section 19 to immutable provisions elsewhere in the Restatement. Comment a to Section 19 explains:

> This section provides default rules that apply when no other, more specific rule of the Restatement applies. Thus, its rules are subject to other provisions, such as those that concern allowing, restricting or forbidding client consent to the disclosure of confidential information, waiver of conflicts of interest, and arbitration of fee disputes. The Section should be applied in view of the prohibition against advance waiver by the client of the lawyer's civil liability.

The Restatement thus recognizes the benefits of contractual freedom, but it is concerned about a lawyer and a client opting down from rules defining the lawyer's responsibilities to the client. The comments and illustrations following Section 19 show that the Restatement drafters are more comfortable with contracts in some areas, such as the scope of a representation, business transactions with clients, resolution of fee disputes, and, to a limited extent, contracts around conflicts rules, than they are with contracts in other areas, such as waiver of legal malpractice claims and disclosure of client confidences. Comment b explains:

> Restrictions on the power of a client to redefine a lawyer's duties are classified as paternalism by some and as necessary protection by others. On the one hand, for some clients the costs of more extensive services may outweigh their benefits. A client might reasonably choose to forgo some of the protection against conflicts of interest, for example, in order to get the help of an especially able or inexpensive lawyer or a lawyer already familiar to the client.
>
> . . .
>
> On the other hand, there are strong reasons for protecting those who entrust vital concerns and confidential information to lawyers. Clients inexperienced in such limitations may well have difficulty understanding important implications of limiting a lawyer's duty. Not every lawyer who will benefit from the limitation can be trusted to explain its costs and benefits fairly.

Concerns about opting down to lower standards of professional conduct also are heightened if the lawyer initially chooses a rule that is then imposed on all the lawyer's clients. Finally, the Restatement encourages arrangements by which the lawyer opts up to increase the lawyer's duties to the client, but it is concerned about situations in which, in doing so, the lawyer opts down from obligations to future clients or to third parties.

. . .

Despite this general, but guarded, shift toward a more contractarian outlook on the lawyer-client relationship both in the Model Rules and in the Restatement, it is important to note that in a few areas the bar has gone in the opposite direction and introduced new immutable (but usually well-defined) rules for situations in which there is likely to be asymmetry of information or unequal bargaining power between lawyers and clients. The Model Code, the Model Rules, and the Restatement all provide that an attorney may not contract with a client for literary or media rights relating to a representation prior to its conclusion. The Canons contain no such specific prohibition. . . .

. . .

A. *Client Conflicts*

Arguably, if lawyers and clients were to bargain for their own rules governing client conflicts, they would agree upon rules substantially similar to the default provisions in the Model Rules (in other words the Model Rules are majoritarian default rules). On the other hand, conflicts rules based on Model Rule 1.7—which prohibits lawyers from concurrently representing clients with adverse interests, even in unrelated matters—may be penalty default rules. In transactional representations in particular, lawyers routinely seek, and are granted, waivers from conflicts after they furnish clients with relevant information about concurrent representations. In one other respect, most conflicts rules are penalty default rules [i.e., a rule that most lawyers and clients would not prefer, which is used to force lawyers to disclose important information to clients when they contract around it]—ambiguous standards for determining whether a matter is "substantially" related or an interest is "adverse" force lawyers to obtain client consent to conflicts even in situations where the conflict prohibitions arguably do not apply. Furthermore, conflicts rules, while default rules, have an immutable component, itself comprised of ambiguous standards[, for example, the requirement of] . . . [informed] consent . . . or (for concurrent conflicts) . . . [the requirement that a] lawyer "reasonably" believe[s] that she . . . [can adequately] represent both clients. Client conflicts thus frequently are litigated [in disqualification motions], and judges often rely upon expert testimony to determine whether or not an impermissible conflict exists.

A principal obstacle to the contractarian paradigm working effectively in this area is that conflicts rules poorly accommodate ex ante
contracting.... Because the words ["informed consent"] ... suggest
that the consenting client should know all, or most, of the relevant facts
about a conflict, advance consents may not ... be enforceable....

Many courts are skeptical of ex ante conflict waivers. Some recent
cases, however, endorse a more flexible approach. Most of these decisions
are not based on straightforward endorsement of advance consent, but
instead on the murkier principle of estoppel, or a finding that confidential information was not conveyed to the lawyer by the client who
consented to the conflict. One ABA Formal Opinion states that it is
permissible for lawyers to seek advance consents in some circumstances.[203] The Opinion, however, makes no promises as to their enforceability.... [T]he Opinion states that "one principle seems certain: No
lawyer can rely with ethical certainty on a prospective waiver of objection to future adverse representations simply because the client has
executed a written document to that effect." Under this approach,
lawyers and clients gain relatively little from including advance consent
terms in their retainer agreements.

. . .

. . . [T]he Model Rules themselves should incorporate a defined rule
that permits advance waivers in some specific instances. First, the Model
Rules should allow a lawyer and a client independently represented by
counsel (including in-house counsel) to make a binding agreement at the
outset of the representation, or at any time during the representation,
with respect to the important elements of a potential conflict:

(i) a definition of who the "client" is in the representation;

(ii) a definition of what is and is not an "adverse" interest;

(iii) the time when a representation ends (after which conflicts are evaluated
as former client conflicts instead of current conflicts);

(iv) a time after termination of a representation when former client conflicts
rules shall cease to apply;

(v) an agreement that conflicts between two current clients shall only be
grounds for disqualification if the matters are "substantially related" (a
criterion usually applied only to former-client conflicts);

(vi) a definition of what is and is not a "substantially related" matter; and

(vii) an agreement whereby the client consents in advance to a specific type
of conflict.

In addition, lawyers and clients should be allowed to agree ex ante that
imputed disqualification of a law firm will be avoided if the lawyers
involved in a matter are screened from any participation in another
matter to which the conflicts rules would otherwise apply. The comment

203. ABA Comm. on Ethics and Prof'l Responsibility, Formal Op. 93–372 (1993)
(Waivers of Future Conflicts of Interest).

to Model Rule 1.10 should state that lawyers and clients can agree ex ante on appropriate screening procedures.

Furthermore, advance waivers should be permitted only when the client is independently represented in the matter by a lawyer, including in-house counsel, who is unaffiliated with the lawyer receiving the consent. In such cases, the advance consent is unlikely to be affected by asymmetry of information or unequal bargaining power between the lawyer and client. . . .

Finally, the comments to Model Rules 1.7 and 1.9 should point out that advance waivers do not allow lawyers to disclose confidential client information in violation of Model Rule 1.6. . . . The comments, however, should . . . state that, once consent is given to a conflicting representation, the client giving consent (and any other complaining third party) will have the burden of producing specific facts establishing that the lawyer has misused confidential information, in order for the lawyer to be disqualified or sanctioned for her conduct. Otherwise, specious claims of misuse of confidential information would eviscerate the advance conflict waiver. . . .

B. *Lawyer Use of Client Information*

The Model Code provides that a lawyer cannot use client information for personal advantage without client consent. The Model Rules only apply this prohibition to uses that disadvantage the client. Model Rule 1.8(b) thus provides that "[a] lawyer shall not use information relating to representation of a client to the disadvantage of the client unless the client consents after consultation. . . ." This default rule is a standard rather than a defined rule because the "disadvantage of the client" element must be evaluated subjectively ex post. . . .

. . . This might be sufficient for disciplinary purposes, but the federal securities laws condition a lawyer's liability for insider trading on the lawyer's breach of a duty to her client, and furthermore require that this breach of duty occur at the time of the trade. . . .

Rather than immerse courts in fact-specific inquiries into whether a lawyer's trades "disadvantaged" her client, or whether the lawyer accounted to her client for the profits from her trades, it would perhaps be better to adopt the Model Code's defined default rule that use of client information for personal profit without permission from the client is prohibited whether or not it harms the client. The client thus would have a defined ex ante entitlement to exclusive use of the information, although the lawyer and client could contract around that entitlement if they wished to do so. . . .

. . . [I]t is conceivable that a majority of clients might not care if their lawyers use confidential information outside of public trading markets for such things as investments in real estate so long as the use does not disadvantage them. They might, however, have strong preferences that their lawyers not use confidential information for securities trades. . . .

. . .

C. *Contractual Restrictions on Practice*

Immutable rules constrain a lawyer's ability to restrict contractually her future practice . . . by becoming an additional party to a settlement agreement of a client. . . . [Such a]greements . . . are quite infrequent for the obvious reason that a lawyer rarely will agree to restrict her future practice in return for a better settlement for a client in a single case. Although there is a relative dearth of commentary on such "three-way" settlement agreements among plaintiffs, defendants, and plaintiffs' counsel, their advantages and disadvantages are worthy of serious consideration.

. . .

. . . [A] lawyer's covenant not to sue a particular person in the future could be an important factor in settlement discussions. Should it be permitted? The traditional argument against such covenants is that future clients who want to sue the same defendant may not be able to find a lawyer who is free to do so. A defendant perhaps even could buy itself immunity from suit by inserting "no sue" clauses in so many settlement agreements that future plaintiffs would have difficulty finding counsel. This argument, however, is not very persuasive because market forces should assure that, as some lawyers retire from suing certain defendants, others will recognize an opportunity, move in, and take their place.

A stronger argument against such covenants is that permitting them creates perverse incentives for a lawyer to file a series of frivolous suits followed by a demand for payment in return for a covenant not to sue on behalf of future clients. Such a lawyer-extortionist probably would insist on structuring the settlement so that she received the bulk of the money paid for the covenant, either by way of a contingent fee or a side payment. Presumably, immutable ethics rules prohibiting frivolous suits and procedural rules sanctioning lawyers for frivolous pleadings would be sufficient to deter such conduct, if Model Rule 5.6(b) were to be liberalized. However, extortion could be discouraged further by barring a lawyer from receiving a fee in connection with a covenant not to sue that is excessively high in proportion to the amount recovered by the lawyer's client (which is not likely to be very high in a frivolous lawsuit). With the extortion temptation thus removed, only rarely would a lawyer agree to an ex ante restriction on the lawyer's future practice.

Occasionally, however, a defendant will offer a high enough price for the covenant not to sue. In such cases, the defendant's motivation is usually not to preclude other plaintiffs from finding counsel but to prevent other plaintiffs from employing a particular lawyer who has acquired valuable information about the subject matter of a case. In effect, the defendant wants the plaintiff's lawyer to contract out of the rule that the lawyer may use information learned in the course of representing the first client in representing subsequent clients so long as the lawyer does not disclose client confidences or disadvantage the first client. The inducement for the lawyer's agreeing to this is a better settlement offer for the first client, who in turn might transfer some of this increased value to the lawyer by paying a higher fee.

Model Rule 5.6, however, effectively transforms the rule that the lawyer may use client information in a subsequent representation into an immutable rule by prohibiting the lawyer from transferring the value of the information back to the first client as part of a three-way settlement agreement. This seems odd in view of the fact that, but for the first client having hired the lawyer, the lawyer would not have had the information, and thus would not be so attractive to future plaintiffs. Another oddity in the existing rules is that the lawyer may realize for herself the value of the first client's information without ever representing another plaintiff simply by selling exclusive use of the information directly to the defendant. The lawyer does this by agreeing to represent the defendant in future similar suits (and thereby disqualifying herself from representing anyone who might sue the defendant in a related matter). She can do so without the first client's consent if the settlement is final and if it removes any lingering adversity between the first client's interests and the defendant's interests. Ironically, in this arrangement the lawyer realizes the entire value of the first client's information by getting paid a retainer from the defendant, and the first client gets next to nothing.

Model Rule 5.6 thus prevents the first client from negotiating with the lawyer and the defendant for a portion of the value of the information, but leaves the lawyer free to sell the information directly to another plaintiff, or to the defendant, as the lawyer sees fit. One advantage of changing Model Rule 5.6 into a default rule—stating that a lawyer's future practice is not restricted by a settlement agreement unless the agreement specifically so provides—is that lawyers would then be allowed to share with their clients some of the value of the information they acquire during the course of a representation.

D. *Disclosure of a Corporate Client's Crime or Fraud*

Courts, bar associations, and regulators often disagree over what a lawyer should do about an impending criminal or fraudulent act by a corporate client. The disagreements are often sharp, in part because rules in this area are immutable (the client generally cannot instruct the lawyer in advance to use a different rule), and in part because secrecy is one of the most controversial topics in the law.

The Model Rules provide that a lawyer may not participate in a client's crime or fraud, but are vague with respect to what a lawyer affirmatively should do to stop or rectify the conduct. A lawyer representing an organizational client simply must act in the "best interests of the organizational client," a standard so broad that it is almost meaningless. The ABA also refuses to impose a defined rule that would require a lawyer for an organization to report illegal acts by its agents to its board of directors.

Federal regulators, such as the OTS and SEC, sometimes impose rules—usually broad standards—on lawyers who "practice before" those agencies. The bar, however, is often hostile to these standards, in part because they can be construed broadly by an agency's administrative law judges. Regulators also inconsistently enforce these standards. At other times, regulators have asked regulated entities to require their lawyers to opt into professional responsibility standards, but the "voluntary" component has done little to appease the bar, and some of these opt-in rules have been rescinded. The ABA has promulgated its own opt-in rules in at least one area that regulators are concerned about—legal opinions. These opt-in rules—many of which are precisely defined in a document known as the "Silverado Accord"—prohibit such practices as rendering a literally accurate opinion on the basis of dubious factual assumptions or in circumstances where the opinion could further an illegal or fraudulent objective. The ABA, however, disfavors opinions containing "negative assurances" about a client's acts. The Silverado Accord states, for example, that it is inappropriate to request an opinion from a lawyer stating that his client is in compliance with all applicable laws.

One approach would be to amend Model Rule 1.13 to include an opt-out default rule requiring a lawyer to report certain acts to a client's full board of directors. For example, such a rule could provide that:

> If measures taken by [an organization's] lawyer fail to prevent an imminent illegal act, or fail to end an ongoing violation of the law, the lawyer shall refer the matter to the highest authority that can act on behalf of the organization with respect to the matter as determined by applicable law and the organization's charter or articles of incorporation.

Corporate clients could opt out of this default rule requiring a report to their directors by stating in their articles of organization that reports of illegal acts and fraud should be made to a body other than the board, such as a compliance committee or the corporation's general counsel. Once such a choice is publicized in the corporation's articles, third parties, such as regulators or investors, could ask the client why it contracted around the default rule.

An even more problematic topic in legal ethics is lawyer disclosure of a client's impending crime or fraud to outside regulatory authorities or to third parties that could be affected by the conduct. The immutable rule in Model Rule 1.6 forbids disclosure[.]* . . . The rule in most states, however, permits, but does not require, a lawyer to disclose client crime or fraud. . . . The Restatement also provides that disclosure is optional but, like the Model Rules and Model Code, provides little specific guidance for lawyers representing organizational clients.

The optional disclosure rule . . . could be changed into a default rule by permitting, and perhaps encouraging, lawyers to contract around it by opting-up and committing themselves ex ante to disclose client fraud or illegal acts outside the organization. This commitment could then be disclosed to third parties, who could adjust their own dealings with the lawyer and the client accordingly. Alternatively, the bar could impose a *penalty default rule.* . . . [R]equiring lawyers for a corporation to report violations of the securities laws to the SEC unless the client's articles of organization provide otherwise, would be such a penalty default rule. The undesirable rule would force the majority of corporations that do not want the rule to specify in their articles exactly what they want the lawyer to do.

. . .

Whether default or immutable rules are used, should disclosure of a corporate client's crime or fraud be governed by defined rules, or by standards? Some criteria, such as whether a lawyer "knows or should know" that a client is embarking on illegal or fraudulent conduct, are intrinsically governed by standards. Hindsight bias on the part of a fact finder may work against the lawyer when these standards are interpreted in cases in which it is not clear whether client conduct was foreseeable. This ambiguity is all the more reason why other aspects of the rule should be more sharply defined. Instead of the current Model Rule 1.13, which gives the lawyer very little guidance on what to do about a crime or fraud, the rule should contain a safe harbor—for example, a rule requiring the lawyer to report to the board of directors but no further.** Whatever rule is chosen, in view of the severe penalties imposed on lawyers who are found to have breached the vague prohibition in Model Rule 1.2(d) against "assisting" a crime or fraud, these situations should be governed as much as possible by defined rules.[286]

* [Editors' Note: The ABA has since changed Model Rule 1.6 to permit disclosure in this situation, in response to the SEC's rules promulgated under the Sarbanes–Oxley Act, which also permit such disclosure.]

** [Editors' Note: The ABA has since changed Model Rule 1.13, also in response to the SEC lawyer rules. The new rule, which has not yet been adopted by any state, requires up-the-ladder reporting in certain situations and also permits disclosure outside the organization.]

286. It is possible that standards would be preferable to defined rules, if courts and agencies would build valuable precedent interpreting the standards as they have in contract and corporate law. A number of factors, however, distinguish the law governing lawyers from contract and corporate law. First, because the underlying issues are so controversial and legal precedent on lawyer liability accumulates relatively slowly, ambiguous standards have stayed ambiguous for a long time. Second, a standard is often construed ex post by an administrative agency—usually the same agency that claims it was misled by the lawyer—and only reviewed by a court on appeal. The ambiguity of the standard,

E.   Race and Sex Discrimination

Race and sex discrimination are areas in which the bar for a long time not only neglected to enact rules of its own, but also resisted efforts by courts to impose immutable rules on lawyers. In the1960s and 1970s, law firms began to comply with antidiscrimination laws, and by the late 1980s local bar associations in a few cities sought to remedy the effects of past discrimination with opt-in rules. Most of these rules establish quantitative hiring "goals," coupled with commitments to facilitate the professional growth and promotion of minority associates. Although the opt-in quantitative goals are usually well defined, the firms' other commitments generally are set forth as standards, and in both instances reputation is used to enforce the chosen rules. Breach cannot legally be penalized. Preservation of the reputational capital that a firm acquires by opting in is the incentive to comply.

. . .

Although substantial numbers of women associates are hired by large law firms, promotion of women associates to partner remains relatively infrequent. Bar associations so far have not used opt-in default rules to address the difficulties women have obtaining partnerships and progressing within partnerships. It is conceivable, however, that firms collectively could agree to opt into policies that enhance the promotional chances of women lawyers (and some men lawyers as well): flexible work schedules, maternity and paternity leaves, nondiscriminatory work assignment policies, mentoring programs, sexual harassment policies, and substitution of flexible partnership promotion policies for rigid up-or-out time tables. Such policies could be agreed upon, even by firms that disfavor numerical goals (which raise the difficult legal and policy issues generally associated with affirmative action). Collective action through ex ante contracting thus could address some problems that firms might be less likely to address on their own[301] and that the bar is unlikely to address with immutable rules.

. . .

F.   Commitment to Work Pro Bono Publico

Under the reign of Henry VII, the lawyer's obligation to work pro bono publico was an immutable rule. In recent times, however, lawyers

coupled with the extraordinary power of the agency, is likely to create an accurate impression on the part of lawyers that the standard is unfair.

301. Presumably, if these policies were efficient, a law firm would have an incentive to adopt them regardless of what other law firms do. However, some policies that discriminate disproportionately against women lawyers may increase firm profits, at least in the short term, and a law firm may be reluctant to change unless other firms also promise to bear the costs of making the same change. Nonpromising firms might thereby gain a cost advantage, but at least the promising firms would not be undercut in cost competition with each other.

have not been required to work for free, although many believe they have a moral obligation to do so.

The ABA and state bar associations have responded to shortages in legal services with aspirational rules. In 1983, the ABA adopted Model Rule 6.1, which states that "[a] lawyer should render public interest legal service," a standard so broad that it had little concrete meaning. In 1993, Model Rule 6.1 shifted toward a defined rule when it was amended to state that "[a] lawyer should aspire to render at least (50) hours of pro bono publico legal services per year." This rule, however, by its own terms, was aspirational, and not legally enforceable. . . .

Another possibility would be an opt-in pro bono rule. Lawyers could be required to make ten-year pro bono commitments ex ante, beginning with the year of their application for admission to the bar (usually the third year of law school). Lawyers could commit zero, 100, 200, or any other number of hours of pro bono services per year over the next ten years. Lawyers could then be disciplined (probably with a fine) for doing less than the amount of work specified in their pro bono commitments. Reputational incentives to make high commitments would be enhanced if the names of bar applicants and their service commitments were publicized. Ten years later, each lawyer would make another commitment for the next ten years, and so on until retirement. High pro bono commitments could then be looked upon favorably when lawyers are selected for prominent positions in bar associations, judicial appointments, and retention by corporate clients that seek to promote pro bono work by their lawyers.[315]

Although it might be desirable to prohibit firms from discriminating against high pro bono lawyers in hiring, it would probably be better to allow both firms and prospective associates to take pro bono commitments into account when making their decisions. New lawyers thus could pick firms based on the pro bono commitments of lawyers already at the firms, and firms that want only low pro bono lawyers could hire them, thereby gaining a low pro bono reputation that might make recruiting new lawyers (and clients) more difficult. Once a lawyer was hired, however, her pro bono commitment would act as an implied covenant in her employment contract that the firm would breach if it later penalized her for meeting the pro bono obligation.

. . .

315. This proposal might work even more effectively if the first pro bono commitment were irrevocably made upon application to law school, considered in law school admissions, and then filed by schools with the bar of the state where each student is admitted after graduation. Indeed, at least one major law school already solicits ex ante public service commitments from applicants by reserving a certain number of slots for students who check a box on the application form requesting a "public interest" law course package. Although future public interest work is not part of the binding commitment, the course package and participation in the School's clinical program apparently are. Public Interest Law and Policy, http://www.law.ucla.edu/students/admissions/AcademicPrograms/Special Programs/PublicInterest.html (last visited Apr. 16, 2001).

Voluntary action within the reputational paradigm, whether in the form of ex ante pro bono commitments or ex post acceptance of pro bono assignments, is most likely to flourish in a regime that requires full disclosure of how much pro bono work lawyers actually do. . . . [R]eputational markets might help address shortages of legal services and thereby avert the more drastic remedy of reinstating the immutable rule of Henry VII.

G. *General Conclusions*

From these examples, . . . some general conclusions can be drawn about which types of rules are appropriate in which circumstances.

Immutable rules that protect clients are appropriate in situations in which clients have insufficient information or bargaining power to protect themselves from lawyer overreaching. Rules prohibiting commingling of client funds are a good example; few honest lawyers would request waiver of these restrictions, so waiver is not allowed. Few honest lawyers would put themselves in a client's will unless they were related to the client, so this also is prohibited. . . .

In other situations, such as waiver of conflicts, default rules are appropriate. Opting out ex ante (before a conflict occurs) would be constructive in many circumstances, but probably should be restricted to clients acting with the advice of independent counsel. A tailored default rule permitting ex ante waiver should apply to these clients, while a default rule permitting only ex post waiver should apply to all other clients. The Model Rules already make a similar distinction by permitting an ex ante agreement limiting a lawyer's malpractice liability only if the client is represented by independent counsel. In yet other situations, default rules should be available to all clients, but subject to immutable rules that remain in place to provide a minimal level of protection. For example, a client can consent in writing to opt out of the default rule that a lawyer may not enter into a business transaction with a client. Neither party, however, can opt out of immutable rules requiring that the lawyer disclose the terms of the transaction to the client in writing, that the client be given an opportunity to seek the advice of independent counsel, and that the transaction be subject to ex post judicial review with respect to whether it was fair and reasonable to the client (an immutable standard).

Immutable rules usually are appropriate when the objective is to protect third parties or the justice system. Whether or not a client or even opposing counsel consents, a lawyer should not be permitted to suborn perjury, misrepresent facts or law to a tribunal, assert a frivolous claim or defense on behalf of a client, or assist a client in a criminal or fraudulent act. However, some immutable rules, such as those prohibiting contractual restrictions on future practice, probably are outdated, given the plentiful supply of lawyers and the advantages that could accrue to clients from greater contractual freedom.

Furthermore, some existing rules already allow a lawyer, acting with the permission of a client, to contract for a higher level of responsibility to third parties. Perhaps in a wider range of areas, such as defining appropriate responses to crime and fraud, a lawyer and client should be permitted to make ex ante undertakings that protect third parties. . . .

Furthermore, tailored rules of all sorts (immutable, default, and opt-in) need to become more common. . . . [Rules t]ailored . . . to particular practice areas also may be easier to draft, easier to muster political support for, and easier to enforce than [rules designed to govern all lawyers] . . .

Other revisions to the Model Rules that have been suggested . . . are statements of "best practices" similar to the ethical considerations of the Model Code. . . . Although the ABA demonstrated its preference for legally-enforced rules when it abandoned the Ethical Considerations in the Model Rules, the Ethical Considerations probably should have been retained. In abandoning the Ethical Considerations, the ABA abandoned a potentially very useful tool for influencing lawyer behavior in areas in which, for whatever reason, a legally-enforced rule is not workable.

III. Law Firm Codes of Professional Responsibility

A logical extension of the contractarian framework is the development of law firm codes of professional responsibility. These codes would be ideal mechanisms for lawyers collectively to select some of their own rules at a more local level than the ABA or state bar associations. Indeed, contractarian solutions to many of the problems discussed above, such as opting in or out of rules for use of client information and disclosure of client fraud, only may be practical if law firms adopt codes of professional responsibility that specifically address these issues.

. . . Many law firms . . . voluntarily have adopted formal policies on issues such as assumption of corporate directorships, new clients and new matters, opinion letters, client conflicts, firm and personal invest-ments, firm audits and client funds, record retention, and representation of depository institutions. Law firms probably should be encouraged, or even required, to integrate these policies into law firm codes of profes-sional responsibility that are then filed with the state bar. Although a lawyer's breach of his firm's code could be considered a breach of state bar rules as well, it is probably best for the bar to leave enforcement to the firms themselves. The bar simply could require that each firm have a code, just as a corporation is required to have articles of incorporation, and then make reasonable efforts to enforce its own code. Codes of professional responsibility would give firms an opportunity not only to consolidate their informal policies into one formal document, but also to specify ex ante what the ethical obligations of their attorneys are in specific types of situations that are not addressed adequately by bar association codes.

Notes

1. Painter demonstrates the wide variety of forms that "default rules" can take. (In fact, the original article includes even more categories.) When the concept becomes so expansive, does it also lose some of its usefulness? Couldn't the categories be expanded still further? For example, suppose lawyers try to "contract around" an "immutable rule" prohibiting covenants not to compete by writing a substitute contract term that discourages competition but does not prohibit it. Or suppose some "immutable" rules are not enforced or are enforced with only mild penalties and so are widely violated. Are those rules defaults too in some sense? On the other side, Painter focuses on some of the costs of "contracting around" but omits others. For example, courts may express a preference for a certain result by viewing with skepticism the voluntariness of, or narrowly construing attempts to, contract around a rule.

2. Painter argues for more default rules. But isn't there a tension between his freedom of contract approach and the problem posed by professionals with specialized expertise? Of course, this is less of a problem with sophisticated business clients, but even they often rely on the expertise of outside counsel.

3. Wouldn't Painter's arguments apply equally to getting legal advice from nonlawyers? Should clients be allowed to agree to "opt in" to whatever licensing scheme they prefer? What other changes in law would be required to make a law license no more than a default rule? For example, would it require abolishing the attorney-client privilege or transforming it to a legal advice privilege? Would that latter option put too much evidence outside the reach of discovery? Be too subject to opportunistic manipulation? More than the attorney-client privilege is now?

4. Competition is certainly a desirable thing, but is competition on as many variables as possible necessarily a desirable thing? Could too many competing standards of behavior lead to inefficiencies?

5. Painter acknowledges that default rules are less defensible when third party rights are at stake. Does he underestimate this problem?

6. Do you find Painter's arguments for changing Model Rule 5.6(b) from an immutable rule to a default rule convincing? Could not covenants not to sue as part of a settlement agreement result from collusion by the plaintiff and defendant against the plaintiff's lawyer? Painter discusses covenants not to bring later suits as all-or-nothing devices, but they can be more nuanced, restricting the plaintiff's lawyer to bring suits asking only for certain relief or to recommend to all future clients a settlement of a certain amount. This can be seen as a form of collusion between the plaintiff's lawyer and the defendant against future clients. It also gives the defendant an incentive to freeze out (by refusing to settle with) plaintiff's lawyers who are not signatories to such deals, in effect steering business to certain

lawyers. Neither Painter nor Silver & Baker, see p. 213, in discussing Model Rule 5.6(b) consider the potential of defendant-sponsored cartels made up of favored plaintiff's lawyers. We have seen enough future practice restrictions of the nuanced form we have just described to suggest this problem may be real.

7. Why should the defendant or the plaintiff "own" information about the defendant that might lead to future lawsuits by the defendant? Couldn't that lead to underdeterrence of harmful conduct by the defendant? Does the fact that the defendant might be willing to circumvent Model Rule 5.6(b) by hiring the plaintiff's lawyer on a retainer mean that Model Rule 5.6(b) is socially harmful? Note that if the intent to circumvent the rule can be shown, discipline may be (and at least in one case, has been) imposed. See Koniak, Are Agreements to Keep Secret Information Learned in Discovery Legal, Illegal or Something in Between?, 30 Hofstra L. Rev. 78 (2002).

8. Do you have a good sense, after reading Painter's article, of when he advises using the various sorts of default rules that he describes? Is there an "I know it when I see it" quality to this part of his argument? Take, for example, a lawyer putting himself in the client's will, which Painter thinks "few honest lawyers" would do. Might not a client be just as interested in reducing his current fee by including his lawyer in his will as he would be in contracting out of some of the other ethics rules? Or take the ban on negotiating for media rights, which Painter seems to support as a good immutable rule. Couldn't "sophisticated" clients be trusted to make reasonable bargains here?

9. Presumably if greater use of default rules were in the interests of the bar, we would see more of them being adopted. Aside from conflicts, though, the bar does not seem to be inclined to move in that direction. Why not? Are there down sides to default rules that Painter neglects?

In Hell There Will Be Lawyers Without Clients or Law [Part I]*

SUSAN P. KONIAK AND **GEORGE M. COHEN**

I. Introduction

More than twenty years ago, moral philosopher Richard Wasserstrom framed the debate in legal ethics by asking two questions.[1] Does the lawyer's duty to zealously represent the client, constrained only by the bounds of the law, render the lawyer "at best systematically amoral and at worst more than occasionally immoral in ... her dealings with the rest of mankind[?]" And is the lawyer's relationship with the client likewise morally tainted in that it generally entails domination by the lawyer over the client rather than mutual respect? Wasserstrom answered both questions affirmatively.[4] Though these questions have preoccupied legal ethics scholars ever since, they are the wrong questions. They were off-base when posed and, if anything, are even more off-base today. The problem with Wasserstrom's questions is that they presuppose individual clients and settled law. The truly troubling questions in legal ethics arise, however, when clients are entities and the law governing these clients and the lawyer's relationship to them is contested. Class actions, the subject of this Essay, raise perhaps the most troubling questions of all.

Wasserstrom wrote in the wake of Watergate. The involvement of so many lawyers in that scandal embarrassed the profession and prompted the American Bar Association ("ABA") to require that all law students receive instruction in legal ethics. The ABA's legal ethics requirement helped spark scholarship in the field, and Wasserstrom's article was one of the first serious entries in what would soon become a burgeoning area of research. Strangely, however, Wasserstrom, who specifically referred to Watergate as an example of lawyer misconduct, and many other legal ethics scholars who followed in his path focused on questions that had little connection to what the lawyers of Watergate infamy did wrong.

The Watergate lawyers did not go wrong because professional ethics condoned all activity on the client's behalf short of actually breaking the law, Wasserstrom's first indictment of legal ethics. They went wrong

---

* © 2001 Hofstra Law Review. Reprinted by permission from 30 Hofstra L. Rev. 129 (2001). Originally published in ETHICS IN PRACTICE edited by Deborah Rhode. © 2000 by Oxford University Press, Inc. Used by permission of Oxford University Press, Inc.

   1. See Richard Wasserstrom, Lawyers as Professionals: Some Moral Issues, 5 Hum. Rts. 1, 1 (1975).

   4. Although Wasserstrom equivocates in answering these questions, his article read in its entirety answers both affirmatively, with an exception. See generally id. When it comes to criminal defense lawyers, Wasserstrom argues that knowing no bounds but the law may be moral. See id. at 6, 12.

because their personal morality condoned even lawbreaking.[10] As for Wasserstrom's second indictment of legal ethics, the domination critique, even if the Watergate lawyers had represented Richard Nixon in his personal capacity, the moral taint in that relationship would surely not have been that the lawyers imposed their will on their client. But even if they could have, none of the Watergate lawyers were representing President Nixon in his personal capacity. Those whose lawbreaking was even arguably undertaken as part of representing a client[13] had clients that the law had created, such as the United States or the Office of the President, and thus had lawyer-client relationships not subject to Wasserstrom's paternalism critique nor amenable to his remedy: a relationship in which the lawyer listened more and dominated less.

The questions articulated by Wasserstrom and accepted by so many legal scholars as central to legal ethics do not fit the patterns of later lawyer scandals any better than they fit Watergate. Just as in Watergate, lawyer involvement in the savings and loan debacle and in the tobacco industry's longstanding pattern of deception involved zealousness not within the bounds of law but outside those bounds. Similarly, all three situations involved not lawyers dominating individual clients but lawyers representing entities and deferring altogether too much, not too little, to dominant individuals acting in the name of those entity-clients. To understand any of this conduct, we need different questions. We need to explore how difficult it is for those trained in law to maintain a belief in its boundaries. Have modern theories of jurisprudence made the notion

---

10. See, e.g., United States v. Haldeman, 559 F.2d 31, 51–52 (D.C. Cir.1976) (per curiam) (affirming conviction of former Attorney General John Mitchell and other top advisors to President Nixon for conspiracy to obstruct justice and perjury); see also United States v. Mardian, 546 F.2d 973, 976 (D.C. Cir.1976) (en banc) (reversing and remanding conspiracy conviction based on error in failing to sever his trial from the others, but noting that Mardian admitted to being "less than honest"); United States v. Barker, 514 F.2d 208, 211 (D.C. Cir.1975) (en banc) (denying motion to withdraw guilty pleas and characterizing appellants as "the foot soldiers of the Watergate Break-in"); United States v. McCord, 509 F.2d 334, 339 (D.C. Cir.1974) (en banc) (affirming conviction for "illegal interception of oral and wire communications," burglary, and conspiracy); United States v. Liddy, 509 F.2d 428, 432 (D.C. Cir.1974) (en banc) (affirming conviction for conspiracy, burglary, and "unlawful endeavor to intercept oral and wire communications").

13. Some of the Watergate lawyers were convicted for acts that were taken by them while acting not as lawyers but in some other capacity. See, e.g., United States v. Chapin, 515 F.2d 1274, 1277 (D.C. Cir.1975). Donald Segretti, although a lawyer, was convicted for activity undertaken by him as a campaign worker, including:

> such disruptive activities as printing and distributing large posters saying "Help Muskie Support Bussing [sic] More Children Now," supposedly distributed by the Mothers Backing Muskie Committee; writing a letter on Citizens for Muskie stationery accusing Senator Jackson of being a homosexual and Senator Humphrey of cavorting with prostitutes at the expense of lobbyists; and putting out a "Humphrey" press release stating that Representative Shirley Chisholm had been committed to a mental institution in the early 1950's after being detained in Richmond, Virginia as a transvestite and that she was still under psychiatric care.

Id. at 1277–78. Dwight L. Chapin, Nixon's Appointments Secretary, was also convicted of lying to the grand jury in their investigation of the "dirty tricks" undertaken by Segretti, Chapin, and others during Nixon's 1972 presidential campaign. See id. at 1277.

that the law has boundaries harder for lawyers to accept? Or was it ever thus? As for the lawyer-client relationship, we need to concentrate more on how that relationship should be structured when the client is an entity. Are the entities that lawyers represent sufficiently similar to support one model of the lawyer-entity relationship—the approach reflected in the ABA Model Rules of Professional Conduct—or are multiple models needed?

. . . .

II. The Complex Relationship Between Lawyers and Law

The traditional approach to legal ethics assumes that the "bounds of the law" are known and focuses on the fact that these boundaries permit much undesirable behavior. From this perspective, the moral dilemma for the lawyer is the conflict between promoting the client's interests within these known bounds and protecting the interests of society against client behavior that is lawful, but harmful. But the premise underlying this dilemma is often false. By assuming that lawyers obey the law and concentrating on what more an ethic should demand of them, the traditional approach has contributed, however unwittingly, to the myth that law, unlike moral philosophy, is simple stuff. Even nonmoralists, such as legal economists, write as if legal rules are fixed in some meaningful sense, which leads them to focus on problems of over- and underdeterrence and to seek "optimal" rules to solve those problems. Like the moralists, the economists thus view the problem of legal advice as stemming from the fact that lawyers will obey the law, but nonetheless may be able to give advice that is socially undesirable.

Yet to accept, without discussion or qualification, that lawyers generally obey the law, one must first believe that for lawyers, if not for everybody, determining what the law demands is relatively easy. One must further believe that, having identified what the law demands, lawyers will determine that obedience is the appropriate course of action. Neither proposition is sustainable. Not only is law more complex than this account suggests, but the relationship between law and lawyers is more complex.

Understanding what the law demands may sometimes be a simple matter: when the light is red, the law demands that you stop. But that is certainly not always so. Lawyers presumably advised Microsoft that the way it was responding to its competitors did not violate the antitrust laws, but the Justice Department's lawyers believed otherwise. Whether or not Microsoft's business practices were legal or illegal was the subject of an intense courtroom battle. There was a final judgment on the matter, but that judgment does not end the difficult questions about the limits of lawful responses to competitors. It is not that there is no law on the matter—antitrust law exists—but its contours are not easy to discern; thus, obedience is no simple task.

Antitrust law is not uniquely uncertain. Uncertainty is inherent in law, if only because lawmakers cannot identify and address all possible problems in advance. Thus, the meaning of a legal rule in a particular situation almost always demands a conscious act of interpretation, the creation of a story about the rule. Stories connect legal rules to facts, and in the process give meaning to both the law and the facts. A court decision, for example, embodies a story that explains what happened; what the law says should have happened; and whether what happened diverges enough from what the law demands to constitute an illegal act.

In counseling clients, lawyers must do more than read legal rules; they must use the stories embodied in court opinions, legislative debates and executive agency pronouncements to assess their client's proposed or past conduct. In assessing whether that conduct is legal or illegal, the lawyer must extrapolate and interpret. After all, the client's conduct will rarely, if ever, be precisely the same as the conduct that has already been ruled on by the courts or specifically contemplated by the legislature in enacting a rule. Thus, the lawyer is required to construct her own story—a story about stories told by others. In doing so, the lawyer in a sense makes law for the client.

To understand the inherent uncertainty of law is to begin to understand the complexity of the lawyer's relationship to law. Lawyers are not only trained to understand that the law's boundaries are uncertain, but they "practice" by constructing stories, thereby helping to shape the law's boundaries. Lawyers are thus a part of, not apart from, the law's boundaries, a fact of which they are all too well aware from their legal training and practice.

This knowledge, however, may lull lawyers into a false belief that law's boundaries either do not exist at all, or do not apply to them. In particular, lawyers may think that there are no constraints on their helping clients to do things that the lawyers imagine are lawful, only to find a court reaching the conclusion that the client's actions were unlawful and, worse yet, that the lawyers should have realized this based on existing law. At some level, of course, lawyers know that the law's limits are real; they affect events. Up close and on a regular basis, lawyers see damages awarded and fines and prison terms imposed in the name of those limits. Good lawyers understand that the ethical practice of law involves lawyers simultaneously shaping legal boundaries and recognizing the real limits to this manipulation. The most significant ethical dilemma for lawyers is therefore not the one traditionally posed by legal ethics scholarship, in which lawyers use their knowledge of certain legal boundaries to assist in legal, though morally questionable, acts. Rather, it is that lawyers sometimes let their awareness of legal uncertainty delude them into thinking that they have more control over constructing legal boundaries than they in fact do. In this sense, the bounds of the law are inextricably intertwined with what lawyers are allowed to do in shaping those bounds.

The recent savings and loan scandal, in which lawyers were forced to pay millions in settlements arising out of their representation of savings and loans that became insolvent, provides a concrete example of this phenomenon. The harsh response of many courts to lawyer conduct in the scandal represents a collective refusal to allow the fuzziness of the law governing corporate fraud to become a rationalization for lawyers' complicity in such fraud. But in many other lawyering contexts—the class action situation we discuss below being the most notable—courts have frequently failed to apply the brakes.

The problem of legal uncertainty casts doubt on a proposition that so many legal ethicists take for granted: lawyers simply obey the law. Legal uncertainty, however, is only one aspect of the complex relationship lawyers have with law, including the law governing lawyers. Not only do lawyers in their role as counselors interpret law for their clients and themselves, but in their roles as advocates and public citizens they also occupy a privileged position in the construction of the legal meaning articulated by courts, and in the construction of the legal rules to which meaning must be attached. In these latter roles, lawyers act in a very public way to help determine just what the "bounds of the law" are.

With respect to judge-made law, lawyers are uniquely empowered by the state to present judges with alternative interpretations of what the law demands. Most of the time, most judges consider the competing legal meanings offered by the lawyers in a case and simply adopt one, albeit generally with some modification, as that court's official interpretation of the law. Although judges are free to invest law with a meaning no lawyer advocated or imagined, they rarely do so. And even when a judge adopts her own interpretation, because lawyers frame the questions courts decide, the lawyers will still have significantly influenced the law-building process, a role that extends far beyond a particular client's case.

The special role lawyers play in constructing law is not limited to courtroom practice. Lawyers still dominate legislatures and other rule-making bodies. In voluntary organizations, most notably the American Law Institute, lawyers draft model statutes, which legislatures often subsequently enact, and purport to codify the common law developed by judges in Restatements (themselves acts of interpretation that often go beyond pure restating), which judges often rely on in later cases. As to the law governing themselves, lawyers in other voluntary organizations, most notably the American Bar Association, draft model ethics rules, which almost every jurisdiction in the country has adopted as law. Although official lawmakers are free to, and often do, modify or (more rarely) reject these proposed statutes, Restatements, and ethics rules, lawyers' influence in promulgating these rules, like their influence in courtroom advocacy, is enormous.

The fact that lawyers occupy a privileged position in the construction of legislative and judicial law complicates lawyers' obedience to the law in at least two ways. First, lawyers, at least when a significant number of them act as a group, occupy a privileged position in constructing new statutes and new interpretations to counter or nullify existing official law. Other groups may propose new law; however, lawyers have a leg up on transforming their proposals into the real thing. This advantage is particularly troubling when lawyers use their privileged status to counter extant law directed at their own conduct.... Second, lawyers may refuse to play their part in the construction of official law, encouraging the maintenance of "free zones" in which the law plays little, if any, role in regulating conduct. This path is the one lawyers have taken in the class action area, as we will discuss shortly. The bar's rhetoric on the right of "self-regulation" can also be understood in this way, as a call for the state to leave most lawyer conduct unregulated by law.

Finally, the lawyer's relationship to law is complicated by the bar's understanding of its obligation to resist the state on behalf of clients and in the name of preserving the independence of the bar itself, an independence that sustains our democracy, at least according to the bar's ethos. If resisting the state is noble, obeying the law may sometimes be wrong. Ethics opinions and commentary to the ethics rules, both promulgated by the bar, reflect a strong sense of noble resistance to official law....

. . .

Lawyers' skepticism about law's limits, their special role in the construction of law, and their ethic of noble resistance to law all help to undermine simplistic assumptions about lawyers living within the bounds of the law. How lawyers understand law, what it means to obey law, and when disobedience to law is justified are subjects that have been pushed off center stage by such simplistic assumptions. Only by concentrating on the many complexities in the lawyer's relationship to law can we adequately understand the lawbreaking that pervades the major lawyer scandals from Watergate to the present, and indeed the nature of law itself.

Notes

1. Richard Wasserstrom's oft-cited article, Lawyers as Professionals: Some Moral Issues, 5 Hum. Rts. 1 (1975), which Koniak & Cohen use as a jumping off point, is excerpted in many ethics readers and textbooks. Koniak & Cohen begin by repeating the questions Wasserstrom saw as central to legal ethics. Why do you think Wasserstrom asked the questions he did? By what criteria do Koniak & Cohen conclude that they are the "wrong" questions?

2. How do the questions that Koniak & Cohen identify in this excerpt differ from the approaches taken by other authors in this collection? For example, Dana, p. 128, asks whether it is possible for lawyers to practice "public service" lawyering. One of our aims in writing this volume is to expand and influence your understanding of what counts as an important

question in legal ethics. As you read through it, consider what other questions strike you as "central" and whether this collection of essays gives you a new view of what the important questions in legal ethics are—a view different from that you may have held before picking up this book.

3.   Do advocates and counselors have a different "relationship to the law?" Are there interpretations of law that are contestable from the point of view of an advocate, but not from the point of view of a counselor?

4.   Koniak & Cohen argue that lawyers may be able to create "free zones" in which law is absent or underdeveloped. They cite class actions as one area in which such free zones exist. Can you think of any others? Consider four possibilities from disparate areas of legal practice: discovery in litigation, prosecutorial discretion (or alternatively the treatment of "enemy combatants" and others accused of terrorist activity), the use of "special purpose entities" by Enron and other corporations, and the development of sophisticated tax shelters. Could any of these areas be considered "free zones?" How are these areas similar to one another? What differences are there among them?

5.   Another example of the complex relationship between lawyers and law is apparent in our reaction to lawyers breaking the law. For example, should we view President Clinton's perjury as more reprehensible than it might otherwise be because he is a lawyer? Should we view the defiance of a federal court order to remove a monument of the Ten Commandments from the Alabama Supreme Court building as more noble or more troubling because the resister was the Chief Justice of that court, not only a lawyer but a judge as well? What if a chief justice of a state court had refused to obey a federal court injunction ordering the return of a fugitive slave? See Robert M. Cover, JUSTICE ACCUSED: ANTI-SLAVERY AND THE JUDICIAL PROCESS (1975) (on the complex and disturbing tendency of some prominent state court judges, who were abolitionists, to be super-strict enforcers of the slave laws, even when there was good legal reason to rule in favor of the slaves).

Confronting Lies, Fictions, and False Paradigms in Legal Ethics Regulation*

FRED C. ZACHARIAS

. . .

III. Examples of Regulatory Fictions

. . . [C]ode drafters, like anyone else, can make mistakes. In referring to lies, delusions, and false assumptions in the ethics codes, this Article focuses on something deeper and more intentional; namely, the tendency of professional regulators to rely on fictions about lawyers, clients, or the way regulation should address the practice of law that skew the resulting regulation.

. . .

. . . [I]f future regulators combine an understanding of false premises in the professional codes with the ability to recognize when the false premises might be undermining existing regulation . . ., the regulators at least will consider adopting more realistic standards of behavior.

A. *Fictions of Symmetry*

The professional codes are replete with what might be called "fictions of·symmetry." . . .

1. *All Lawyers are Competent*

Consider first the unspoken presumption that lawyers are competent, perhaps even equally competent. This finds its way into numerous code provisions, not the least of which is the competence rule itself, Model Rule 1.1. Rule 1.1 states that lawyers unfamiliar with particular areas of law may undertake representation involving those fields if they can make themselves competent. The primary reason for this concession is obvious: it enables lawyers, particularly inexperienced lawyers, to expand their practices. The rule is justified on the basis that lawyers are trained in law school to think like lawyers and that, except in highly specialized fields, lawyers can teach themselves to serve clients as well as the experts do.

No one truly believes this fiction. Specialists undeniably have an advantage over novices. Bringing a new lawyer up to speed, even if possible, adds to a client's expense.

. . .

The questionable assumption that all lawyers are equally competent also underlies code provisions that constrain the ability of lawyers to

* © 2002 by the Arizona Board of Regents. Reprinted by permission from 44 Ariz. L. Rev. 829 (2002).

represent clients on a limited basis. These provisions rely on the faulty premise that clients always are better off receiving full representation from cheaper (but presumably competent or able) lawyers. This approach skews the quality of representation some clients receive and produces other perverse economic effects. And it conflicts with the position of substantive law; contract, tort, and malpractice standards insulate from civil liability lawyers who expressly limit their obligations to clients. This inconsistency between the professional standards and the substantive law ultimately may induce code drafters to confront the counter-factual nature of their assumptions.

2. All Clients are the Same

Perhaps the most clearly false premise in the codes is that all clients are the same (or, at least, should be treated the same for purposes of the rules). Although many of the professional standards focus on the intelligence or state of mind of clients, they do not differentiate among clients. Some rules, for example, require client participation in decisionmaking. Others call for particular types of waivers, assuming that any client who has been informed sufficiently can make intelligent decisions about his or her choices. Yet others forbid lawyers to let clients agree to certain arrangements on the basis that clients are incapable of making the decision or need protection from their lawyers. ·

These rules distinguish sophisticated from unsophisticated or unintelligent clients only at the margins. In doing so, they limit the freedom of some clients to make choices that would benefit them and allow some clients to control decisions that are beyond their capacity to make. The reality is that sophisticated clients—who sometimes even are represented by counsel in their dealings with the lawyer—might need regulatory protection far less than unintelligent or legally unsophisticated clients.

3. All Lawyers and Clients Should be Governed by the Same Rules

The assumptions that all lawyers and all clients are the same have led to perhaps the most dramatic delusion inherent in the modern professional codes; namely, that a single set of rules should apply equally to, and can adequately govern, all legal representation. This premise finds justification only by reference to the notion that lawyers and clients simply could not understand or work with more nuanced professional standards. Yet the premise often leads to bad rules or to situations in which lawyers feel tempted to disobey the rules.

This Article will not catalogue the many situations that fit within this category. But consider the prominent example of matrimonial lawyers bound by the universal obligation of lawyers to be loyal to the client who hires them. May matrimonial lawyers involved in a bitter custody dispute take into account the interests of the unrepresented children? Many matrimonial lawyers will do so even when their clients resist. The nonbinding standards promulgated by the Academy of Matrimonial

Lawyers sanction this approach. Yet because the professional codes in virtually all states decline to differentiate among lawyers, clients, and types of practice, the conduct of these matrimonial attorneys technically is improper.

Adhering to the rigid regulatory approach also has had ramifications in the multidisciplinary practice context. The catalyst for the proposals of the Commission on Multidisciplinary Practice was the desire of large American law firms representing sophisticated global clients to respond to accounting firms' ability to offer an array of legal and nonlegal services. In truth, virtually no one within the ABA code-drafting community wishes to prevent large American firms from competing. Nor does anyone doubt, even in the post-Enron world, that sophisticated multinational corporate clients can protect themselves from the risks of multidisciplinary representation. The opposition to the Multidisciplinary Practice Commission's proposals arose primarily because of the Commission's insistence that the same rules apply to all lawyers. Regulating based on that view necessarily results in regulation that subjects unsophisticated individual clients to the same risks as the multinational law firms' sophisticated clients. Faced with the threat to attorney-client confidentiality if, for example, real estate lawyers are allowed to merge with brokers or the danger that nonlegal associates will come to control individual attorney-client relationships, the ABA's membership has, for now, rejected the Commission's proposals. Never, however, did the Commission or the membership evaluate the need for a uniform rule or truly confront the possibility that the traditional assumption of regulatory symmetry should give way.

4. *The Paradigm of Class Action Representation*

Perhaps the most interesting illustration of the fictions of symmetry—that all lawyers are the same, that all clients are the same, and that all lawyers and clients should be treated alike—involves the regulation of plaintiffs' lawyers in class action litigation. With few exceptions, professional regulation adheres to these false premises and regulates plaintiffs' lawyers and class clients like all others. In reality, however, everyone knows they are distinctive.

Plaintiffs' lawyers tend to be the real parties in interest. They typically bear the costs of the litigation. Class plaintiffs, especially in small-injury consumer class actions, often have little interest in the result and rarely monitor the decisions or fee requests of class counsel.

Recent legal developments are exposing the counter-factual nature of the professional standards in the class action context. In an effort to reduce the expense of legal fees, judges in several cases have auctioned the right to represent a class. The auction procedure relies on the notion that all lawyers are equally competent, but directly calls into question clients' right to choose their own counsel. These recent cases have led the Third Circuit Court of Appeals to commission a task force to study the auction procedure, as well as the even more radical proposal that class claims themselves should be auctioned to lawyers—who would then act as the real parties in interest. The latter approach stands the traditional conceptions of the roles of lawyers and clients on their head.

This Article's point is not to oppose or support the new developments, but rather to note that they will inevitably cause professional regulators to rethink their premises. The judicial innovations introduce market decisionmaking into class action litigation in order to limit fees and to avoid settlements that help lawyers rather than clients. But if, for example, courts end up letting class counsel purchase proprietary interests in class litigation, professional regulators will need to consider whether that right should be extended to all lawyers. Similarly, to the extent courts accept that lawyers, rather than clients, are the driving force behind some litigation, regulators may need to recognize this reality as well. If so, rules governing loyalty, client decisionmaking, and payment of litigation costs would have to be revisited and considered within subcategories of representation.

B. Fictions Relating to the Image of Lawyers

. . .

1. Lawyers are Better than Other Citizens

In recent years, the bar has seemed preoccupied with three common attorney vices: (1) alcohol/substance abuse; (2) sexual relations with clients; and (3) mishandling client funds. Regulation, in the form of new rules and discipline, has multiplied with respect to each vice. Yet the instances of lawyers engaging in the prohibited behavior seem, if anything, to have increased in number.

We shouldn't be surprised. Lawyers are human beings. Faced with the temptations of money, drugs, and sex, some lawyers will succumb.

What do the continuing violations of the professional standards in each of these areas suggest for the bar? First, they suggest that providing a professional standard—even threatening discipline—is unlikely to eliminate the vices. Second, if lawyers are to become more resistant to the temptations in question, they need to be forewarned and educated about the dangers. Finally, experience suggests that a certain number of lawyers will give in to personal and financial incentives, like citizens in all sectors of the community. There is no sense in which lawyers are superior or in which professional self-regulation will take care of the matter.

Facing this reality suggests some significant conclusions for the future of legal regulation. Professional regulators should admit that they cannot control, or at least cannot fully control, lawyers who engage in human misconduct. These lawyers ought to be punished and deterred just like laypersons engaging in such vices. Professional self-regulation should address primarily misbehavior that truly relates to, and affects, the practice of law.

Moreover, instead of intimating that self-regulation addresses the vices, the bar should encourage, when appropriate, the use of civil suits and criminal punishment. Mishandling of client funds typically constitutes conversion or theft. Sex with clients may be rape or assault, as well as a civil breach of fiduciary duties.

At the same time, if the bar exposes lawyers to increased civil and criminal prosecution, future regulation probably should also incorporate enhanced efforts to educate and help lawyers avoid problems. A few jurisdictions have already moved to assist lawyers with substance abuse problems, rather than simply punishing addicted lawyers as persons who have fallen below the standard of the profession's paradigm. Statistics show a dramatic incidence of addiction in the profession, which suggests that a sharper focus on education, in addition to intervention, is appropriate. Likewise, instead of exclusively seeking to punish those who have sexual relationships with clients or who mishandle client funds, regulators should expand their roles to include educational efforts aimed at teaching lawyers why sexual interaction is potentially dangerous and how to avoid trust fund problems.

2.   *Make the Rules and Lawyers Will Follow Them*

Closely related to the wistful assumption that lawyers are especially good citizens is the belief that mere adoption of a professional rule will cause lawyers, at least most lawyers, to follow them. Some rules clearly can serve valid hortatory functions. Nevertheless, code drafters need to regulate more realistically, to take into account lawyers' personal and financial incentives to violate the codes.

The previous section's examples of regulatory prohibitions that lawyers transgress because of human failings illustrate instances that future code drafters probably will confront because of their visible nature. But there are a host of more common professional rules that also highlight the failure of the drafters to face reality. The most potent example is lawyer-reporting rules. Virtually all states' professional codes contain them, but they are rarely enforced and even more rarely followed. Likewise, rules requiring lawyers to give their clients information regarding all important matters, to expedite litigation, to avoid making extrajudicial statements, and to practice full candor towards a tribunal are obeyed largely in the breach, for a variety of reasons relating to the pressures of everyday practice.

Then there are those provisions that regulators know lawyers often disobey because they directly contravene lawyers' financial interests. Regulation barring multijurisdictional practice without a license in each affected state interferes with the practice of national practitioners. If lawyers strictly adhered to the rules against advancing clients money and obtaining proprietary interests in litigation, class action lawyers would not be able to handle most of their cases.

Finally, there are rules the regulators probably hope lawyers will follow, but which the regulators do not or can not enforce even when violations are evident. Violations of advertising rules are routine. Lawyers tend to ignore altogether permissive rules that would permit them to avoid using evidence whose truthfulness they doubt or which authorize, but do not require, disclosure under attorney-client confidentiality rules. Presumably, the code drafters envisioned that lawyers would exercise their discretion under these rules, but lawyers rarely do—in part because lawyers fear that implementing the rules will open them up to competition from less ethical advocates. Yet, because of the rules' equivocal wording, disciplinary agencies cannot enforce compliance and lawyers do not obey their spirit voluntarily.

In light of the actual operation of the codes, one can hardly credit the premise that "if we write a rule, lawyers will follow it." Regulators who do not already know how far reality falls short of this ideal probably are simply closing their eyes to the facts. Yet, the more such rules are violated, and the more frequently that individual states try to enforce the rules—as California began to enforce unauthorized practice rules against out-of-state lawyers through the *Birbrower* case*—the more likely it becomes that the regulators will need to reassess hortatory provisions. That is not to say the codes will, in the future, cease to guide lawyers with respect to conduct that cannot be enforced. It does, however, mean that the future of legal regulation probably will include a greater focus on disciplinary issues and that the recent trend toward "legalization" of the codes will continue.

3. Rules that Improve the Bar's Image Enhance Client Trust

One of the "image" assumptions underlying many code provisions is that forcing lawyers to act in certain ways makes lawyers seem better than other service providers, which in turn enhances client trust in lawyers. The clearest example of this approach is attorney-client confidentiality regulation; clients supposedly trust lawyers more simply because the rules require lawyers to be trustworthy with client confidences. Another prominent example is unauthorized practice of law rules, which posit that lay service providers should be excluded from particular work not only because lawyers are naturally better at providing the services, but also because the professional rules hold lawyers to higher standards of service than nonlawyers.

The flaw inherent in many of these kinds of regulations is that their factual premises regarding the significance of image are incorrect. Re-

---

* [Birbrower, Montalbano, Condon & Frank, P.C. v. Superior Court, 949 P.2d 1 (Cal. 1998).]

cent studies have shown, for example, that clients do not necessarily trust lawyers more than other service providers just because of the existence of legal confidentiality rules....

The increasing availability of empirical evidence and the Multidisciplinary Practice Commission's focus on whether lawyer regulation actually produces performance superior to that of lay service providers herald a fresh look at the validity of the rules' reliance on lawyers' image. Among the likely targets for reconsideration are rules that treat lawyers differently than ordinary businessmen based on the need to preserve the profession's prestige. These include, among others, advertising and solicitation regulation. More substantive regulation, such as the attorney-client confidentiality rules discussed above, also depend on potentially misplaced instrumental assumptions about how clients perceive lawyers and the effect this perception has on representation.

C.   Fictions Relating to the Image of Legal Practice

... Much current professional regulation is devoted to promoting the perception that lawyers, unlike other service providers, serve in a fiduciary capacity for their clients. Another category of regulation focuses on differentiating the practice of law from ordinary business.

Consider a series of rules that cast lawyers as fiduciaries. Only the rules concerning representation of clients with a disability implement fiduciary principles directly. However, all conflict-of-interest rules—including those governing transactions with clients—purport to implement a duty of loyalty. The codes seem to require lawyers to help clients make choices that will benefit themselves. They forbid lawyers to accept certain client decisions that might be against clients' best interests. Similar considerations justify constraints on agreements to limit the scope of representation, advancing money to clients, or acquiring proprietary interests in the subject matter of the litigation. The thrust of the codes' regulation of lawyer dealings with clients is to cast the practice of law as placing the clients' interests first.

In reality, however, the codes are not so clear. They are at least sufficiently ambiguous to allow lawyers to treat the retainer stage of the attorney-client relationship as an arm's length transaction. If lawyers jump through the informational hoops established by the rules, they may accept client decisions that are in the lawyers' interests, but not the client's. Nor do the codes necessarily require lawyers to dissuade clients from making those choices. Likewise, the rules against advancing money may protect lawyers more than clients; it may often be to the clients' advantage to have lawyers finance the litigation. The regulatory paradigm that lawyers always act as fiduciaries thus may be false, or, at least, an overstatement. The tension between reality and the hopeful spirit of the codes may account for both continuing violation and constant amendment of the conflict-of-interest rules.

The codes' attempts to suggest that law is not a business, and therefore should not be regulated like other businesses, are evidenced by a host of provisions. These include advertising and solicitation rules, rules governing the "reasonableness" of fees, rules limiting the ability of lawyers to become executors of wills or gaining other benefits from the clients' property, restrictions on accepting cases in which a lawyer may become a witness, regulation of class counsel, limits on engaging in ancillary businesses, and conflict-of-interest prohibitions. Of course, many of these rules have no teeth. Rightly or wrongly, lawyers have tended either to violate or find ways around most of these restrictions when doing so benefits them. Arguably, the more lawyers engage in business-like activities, such as advertising, the more natural it will become to reconceptualize law as a business for purposes of professional regulation.

The development of the Commission on Multidisciplinary Practice provides an interesting case study. In the multidisciplinary context, the rules that treat lawyers differently from other service providers conflict with the economic interests of large law firms that compete with international accounting firms for business. Since these firms have influence with the ABA, they have, in recent years, been able to force reconsideration of the basic premise that lawyers should be regulated specially. Similarly, the trend towards changes in "anti-screening rules" can be explained by the economic cost that conflict-of-interest regulation limiting the ability of lawyers to change firms (and the ability of firms to hire new lawyers) imposes on lawyers—even though the rules clearly do help assure clients that they can be more secure in the loyalty of lawyers than of other service providers. Seemingly, rules that enforce the counter-factual image that lawyers are not engaging in business as usual find particular resistance within the bar and give rise to the most persistent attempts to reform the codes.

D.   Fictions About the Adversary System

With few exceptions, the professional rules rely upon the paradigm of lawyers advocating the cases of individual clients within an adversary system. This paradigm incorporates at least two sets of faulty assumptions. First, much of the practice of law does not occur within an adversarial litigation setting. Second, the premises that the code drafters attribute to the adversary system sometimes do not hold true.

The first of these criticisms should not need much support. Many types of advice and transactional representation simply do not call for the fierce partisanship that the codes envision. . . .

The second criticism lies at the heart of a controversy that has surrounded professional responsibility regulation since its modern inception. Strict attorney-client confidentiality rules, for example, have fostered more debate than perhaps all other professional rules put together.

Underlying the debate are empirical questions regarding the importance and need for such rules to foster client trust, meaningful attorney-client relationships, and competent representation. Studies have cast doubt on the codes' assumptions that the adversary system requires ultra-strict confidentiality in order to work, which, in turn, has prompted modern regulators to revisit the issues.

Likewise, the Kaye, Scholer incident called into question the codes' paradigm of lawyers as advocates. According to the government's position, lawyers in some contexts must assume other roles and responsibilities, including the responsibility to act for the client in fulfilling the clients' legal obligations. The merits of the government's position in Kaye, Scholer aside, this well-publicized case highlighted the possibility that the codes take too narrow a view of the lawyer's role—that sometimes lawyers should not act in pure advocate's fashion.

Other developments have cast doubt on different assumptions of the adversarial system that the professional codes accept as near gospel. Rule 11 and a series of cases requiring lawyer candor that might be proscribed under attorney-client confidentiality rules seem to contradict the codes' premise that aggressive advocacy and full partisanship maximize the search for truth. The Supreme Court's decision in *Nix v. Whiteside*** similarly called into question the extent to which the adversary system depends on absolute partisanship. Scholars also have questioned the codes' notion that negotiations should be conducted on the basis of an adversarial model—that puffing and following adversarial conventions in negotiations helps produce optimal results for the system; the adversarial approach seems questionable in the negotiations context in the absence of adversarial protections, such as a neutral arbiter.

E.   Fictions of Regulation

. . .

1.   States as the Prime Regulators

In an ideal world, there would be good reasons to rely on states as the regulators of lawyer behavior. States traditionally have taken the lead in this realm. Only states have disciplinary mechanisms readily available. Our federalist society prizes the opportunity for state-to-state experimentation in developing new approaches and in identifying means of enforcement.

But there are signs all around us that this paradigm is unrealistic. Several years ago, I pointed to the increased nationalization of legal practice and suggested problems that might occur if each state actually took seriously its mandate to regulate all lawyers practicing within its jurisdiction. I was castigated for dabbling in unimportant issues and suggesting unrealistic solutions. Yet California's recent *Birbrower* deci-

** [475 U.S. 157 (1986)].

sion, and others, have substantiated my predictions. The new reaction in the literature is that the sky is falling; with the advent of computer technology and cross-state advertising, things will only get worse. Somehow modern regulation will need to confront the question of how national and interstate practice should be monitored, and who should control the substance of the regulation.

The Multidisciplinary Practice Commission highlights the related global phenomenon. States not only must deal with out-of-state practitioners, but also international practice—by foreigners here and our lawyers abroad. It is unlikely that states will be able to address the practice of international law meaningfully on their own. Regulation of practice abroad may infringe on the sovereignty of foreign nations. Local regulation of foreign practice may impinge upon federal commerce power. As a practical matter, regulation of international practice may require federal expertise in negotiating with foreign countries, federal intervention by way of treaty, or simply the broader perspective of federal regulators.

Recent developments also have highlighted the presumptuousness of state regulators' assumption that the federal government will remain on the sidelines with respect to lawyer regulation. The Kaye, Scholer incident was simply one instance in which federal agencies have directly challenged state regulation. In other instances, the Department of Justice has attempted to supercede state regulation of practice by federal lawyers and has claimed a broader power to preempt state regulation. Congress, too, has entered the field. In implementing federal class action rules, federal courts have taken steps that effectively preempt state professional rules governing plaintiffs' counsel. Increased federal judicial intervention in state professional regulation governing criminal litigation also has been recently proposed. The broad assumption that each state can control the conduct of lawyers licensed in that state thus seems passe.

2. The Effectiveness of Professional Discipline

Law students taking the basic professional responsibility course inevitably assume that professional codes are the primary constraint on lawyer conduct. Like the public, untutored students have high expectations for the range of conduct that should be forbidden. And they expect that lawyers who violate the codes will be disciplined; they are horrified when lawyers escape punishment for misbehavior. The bar, hopeful of avoiding regulation by outside institutions, does little to eliminate public misconception about the effectiveness of professional regulation.

In reality, of course, professional discipline is not all it is cracked up to be. The resources of the disciplining bodies are limited. They must choose among the policies of pursuing violations they consider to be the worst, pursuing a random assortment of code violations, or targeting prosecutions that will produce the most general deterrence. They must choose between acting on cases that come to their attention easily or proactively seeking out and investigating violations. In practice, most jurisdictions have focused on lawyer mishandling of client funds, to the exclusion of most other misconduct.

The result is that many rules simply go unenforced or are patently underenforced. The most notable examples include advertising and lawyer reporting rules. But one could safely hazard the assertion that few rules truly are enforced in a way that makes lawyers fear discipline for violating them.

That is not to say that professional rules have no effect. They may guide well-meaning lawyers. They may provide a basis for civil suits or consequences enforceable in judicial proceedings. They may inform lawmakers regarding the bar's vision of appropriate conduct. But it does mean that a public which assumes that professional regulation is all-encompassing both is being misled and inevitably will be disappointed with the product of the regulation.

One cannot point to any groundswell or modern development that will cause the regulators to confront the false premise. There have been a few academic attempts to establish, empirically, the limits of discipline. In the case of individual rules, continued violation may bring about pressure for change. In the end, however, nothing prevents regulators from ignoring the limited effectiveness of professional discipline and the need to address the relationship between discipline and other means of enforcement—except self-interest. . . .

3.   The Primacy of the Professional Codes

The previous section alludes to a broader issue than the limits of professional discipline; namely the limits of professional regulation itself. Implicit in the failure of the codes to admit their own limitations is an assumption that the codes can satisfy the needs of all potential constituencies of the drafters. Lawyers need guidance regarding how to act. The public needs safeguards against misconduct. The court and legal system need tools to arrive at just decisionmaking. Discipliners need rules they can enforce. The codes seem to provide all.

Again, the reality is different. The codes have multiple purposes but, in pursuing various goals, their effectiveness inevitably becomes limited. Providing guidance on a broad variety of issues comes at the expense of providing clear enforceable rules. Providing enforceable rules may cause code drafters to limit client protections, or to avoid providing guidance on broader issues. Simply writing too many rules may undermine the goal of identifying a general role for lawyers to play. As a result, if the various purposes of the codes are to be fulfilled, the codes must rely on other law to help accomplish their goals.

The bar has started to recognize this reality. The publication of the Restatement of the Law Governing Lawyers is an express admission that the professional codes are but a small part of the law that governs, guides, affects, and deters lawyers. The Restatement, however, only attempts to set out existing law. The normative project left for the regulators is to address how the codes and other law should relate and to make clear the purposes and limitations of each set of professional rules.

IV. What Will Happen When We Confront the Faulty Premises of Professional Regulation?

... The Article's only normative conclusion for how regulators should respond is to suggest that they identify the purposes of a particular regulation and that, if they choose to continue to rely on a fiction, they should explicitly determine whether the benefits of a counter-factual approach justify the costs. Although this Article does not presume to predict how the regulators in fact will react, the following sections offer a few speculative notions regarding the changes that we are likely to see.

A. Changes in the Substance of Regulation

... In the end, the tendency to avoid the false paradigms described above—the lies of symmetry, the lies of image, and the like—will result in increasingly nuanced rulemaking that takes into account distinctions among lawyers, clients, and types of practice.

As a result, one might expect the future to encompass an increased emphasis on lawyer specialization, both in licensing and in the professional standards. Some jurisdictions have accepted the ABA's invitation to certify specialists for purposes of legal advertising rules. The regulations, however, typically have not determined who may hold themselves out privately to clients as competent to practice particular kinds of law, or under what circumstances. Nor have the requisite examinations, if any, partaken of the rigor of specialization examinations in non-law fields that seek to insure the competence of practitioners in the specialty.

One also might expect professional rules to differentiate more among clients, lawyers, and the contexts of practice.... There are a variety of ways code drafters might appropriately differentiate among lawyers—both in terms of fields of practice and in terms of the settings in which the lawyers operate. For example, regulators might extend to transactional lawyers (and clients) some leeway to depart from the adversarial ideal and might temper the obligations of in-house counsel with the reality that they often function more like common employees than lawyers with multiple clients.

Finally, greater nuancing may come to include a more realistic focus on what occurs at different stages of representation. The incentives of lawyers at the retainer stage of representation, for example, are different than at later stages; the lawyers' prime interest is to obtain the commission. The regulators therefore cannot rely on lawyers' general sense of obligation to client well-being at the retainer stage and need to spell out the obligations more specifically....

Recognizing the inaccuracy of the traditional image of lawyers and legal practice cannot help but feed into a more economic view of regulation ... that would treat law as a business....

... [I]t seems very likely that future regulators will concede the long-touted unbundling of legal services and open the door to more lay practice. One can also anticipate greater emphasis in the codes on the full provision of information to clients combined with greater deference to client autonomy in decisionmaking with which the regulators might disagree. As the door to lay practice opens, so also will the need for lawyers to compete in the market and to join in economically efficient associations. Regulators will face strong pressure to allow lawyers to merge operations with nonlawyers. To counteract the long-feared adverse impact of such associations on clients, regulators probably will increase regulation in some respects[, for example, by] ... creating incentives for adherence to professional regulation by imposing liability for rule violations on the entire entities through which lawyers practice.

The hallmark of ordinary business regulation is specificity, because legislators and administrators always must be wary of litigation that challenges the right to regulate. The specificity of lawyer regulation has varied, depending on whether the regulators are seeking to set enforceable rules, provide guidance regarding lawyer roles, or accomplish some other function. It would be sad indeed if the regulators ceased to offer guidance even within a structure that lawyers have incentives to obey. Disciplinary agencies may need to conceive of strategies to maximize compliance with the codes. Nevertheless, the trend towards more "legalization" in the codes probably will continue....

The emphasis on specificity and enforceability of some aspects of the codes should make code drafters conscious of the need to maintain the credibility of their less enforceable standards. The more that legal standards are incorporated into the rules, the more lawyers will have to fear their enforcement by other regulators. The more the codes' standards help provide a foundation for civil liability, the more they will deter misconduct....

B.   Changes in the Nature of the Regulators

Perhaps the most inevitable redirection of future regulation will be in who regulates lawyers. We are likely to see more federal involvement in regulation through legislation, administrative regulation, federal court rulemaking, and treaties governing international practice. We also are likely to see states attempting to respond to the nationalization of practice first by flexing their individual muscles, but subsequently by forming compacts with other states in their region regarding lawyer regulation or by moving towards more uniform regulation.

The second likely change is that state regulators may come to recognize their relative insignificance. Sooner or later, the bar will concede that professional self-regulation is but one part of lawyer regulation. Only once this realization sets in can the bar realistically study and consider the interaction between professional standards and alternative regulation—including civil, criminal, and administrative standards and market forces.... [O]ne can envision that future codes will make more specific reference to other law.

C. Changes in Discipline and Disciplinary Process

Of all the movement that one might expect to see in "The Future Structure and Regulation of Law Practice," the greatest probably will be in the design and implementation of the disciplinary process. Significant changes already have occurred in the disciplinary process over the past several decades, with some states totally restructuring their systems. As attention to professional regulation has increased, many states have augmented the resources devoted to prosecuting code violations. The cohesiveness and communication among discipliners in different states also has increased.

But, sadly, many aspects of the disciplinary process remain static. In most jurisdictions, resources are limited. The process usually remains secret until discipline is imposed. Few cases involving discipline are publicly reported and, even when they are, not in sources easily accessible to lawyers.

Moreover, the activities of disciplinary agencies continue to be hidden from public view far more than the actions of other agencies. Few statistics concerning disciplinary agency actions are made public—not even general statistics. Enforcement policies are secret as well. There typically is no process for questioning decisions not to move forward with respect to alleged misconduct. One can guess at the kinds of cases the agencies emphasize based on abstracts reported in local newspapers or bar journals, but such guesses are speculation.

The secret nature of the disciplinary process undermines several aspects of professional regulation. First, the potential for professional discipline lends credibility to the standards in the codes. When, in contrast, lawyers perceive that discipline is unlikely to occur (e.g., because disciplinary actions are not well-publicized), their incentives to obey the codes become muted.

Second, the policies of enforcement bear significantly on the actual drafting of the codes. If, for example, discipliners perceive their function to be maintaining the integrity of the codes by deterring lawyer violations, then a policy of random enforcement of different types of violations would serve deterrence better than simply identifying particular types of violations to pursue. On the other hand, to the extent the discipliners focus on particular violations—for example, mishandling of client funds—the drafters need to write other aspects of the codes in more self-enforcing ways.

Third, the failure to identify either the policies or reality of disciplinary enforcement makes more difficult the task of coordinating discipline with other methods of sanctioning misconduct. . . .

Thus, the twenty-first century should see significant sunshine in the disciplinary process. One might expect changes to be gradual. For example, public pressure to increase discipline of prosecutorial misconduct has always been apparent. As disciplinary agencies move to confront the practical consequences such a focus would have on other cases (e.g. because of resource considerations), they might learn to welcome public involvement in the discussion. Moreover, as new regulators enter the field and states and bar associations begin to reassess their role, discipline becomes part of the package that must be discussed because it involves the highest commitment of resources. . . .

. . . What additional, specific changes in disciplinary focus might one expect?

One is more proactive disciplinary enforcement. . . . Heretofore, discipliners have tended to focus exclusively on cases that come to their attention easily, through complaints by allegedly aggrieved persons. Moreover, if discipliners resolve to coordinate their activities with other enforcement mechanisms, one might also expect a system to develop by which they refer cases to other agencies (e.g., criminal prosecutors) or adopt a policy regarding the priority of discipline and court action in particular types of cases.

Finally, and perhaps most importantly, discipliners eventually will need to define their own roles. One peculiarity of disciplinary decisions in the past has been that sanctions often have been imposed without reference to a clear notion of the purpose of professional discipline. For example, a lawyer's heavy use of alcohol or drugs, in different cases, has been relied upon as grounds for discipline, a mitigating factor, or an excuse. Once professional regulators begin to coordinate discipline with other forms of sanction, the purposes of discipline are likely to become clearer; if client protection becomes the key, punishment might become less important than deterrence notions, but mercy for the human error of lawyers equally irrelevant. . . .

Notes

1. Zacharias argues that the ethics codes are based on a number of fictions and that recognizing this fact might lead to better code drafting. This provocative argument naturally leads to several questions. Are the fictions Zacharias identifies themselves fictions, or perhaps exaggerations? Are the ethics code provisions he identifies really based on those fictions?

And finally, would a more "realistic" perspective necessarily lead to different and/or better rules?

2. One might argue that Zacharias's enterprise is itself based on fiction. It seems to assume that the ethics codes matter to the day-to-day practice of most lawyers. But as he himself recognizes, that is a pretty unlikely description of reality. Should he then be required to start by asking the question to whom and under what circumstances do the ethics rules matter before asking whether the rules themselves are based on fictions or whether (and, if so, how) they should be rewritten? For example, if competence is more effectively regulated by malpractice rules, and conflicts of interest are more effectively regulated by disqualification motions than by ethics rules, see Wilkins, p. 4, then does it make much difference how much fiction is built into the ethics rule formulations? Koniak in The Law Between the Bar and the State writes that the ethics rules diverge from state law for a reason and in predictable patterns, see p. 23. Does her analysis help explain the fictions Zacharias identifies? All of them?

3. Isn't all law "fictional" in Zacharias's terms? Take contract law, for example. Isn't it based on the "fiction" that all contracts and contracting parties are in some meaningful sense the same? Isn't the "reasonable man" of tort law a fiction? Or "equal protection?" Any legal rule requires abstraction from reality to some degree. And many legal rules are based at least in part on empirical presumptions of dubious validity. Are ethics rules more fictional than other law? More fictional in harmful ways?

4. Consider Zacharias's argument that the fiction that all lawyers and clients should be governed by the same rules is justified only by "the notion that lawyers and clients simply could not understand or work with more nuanced professional standards." Is that the only possible justification? What about Cohen's argument on regulatory bundling in When Law and Economics Met Professional Responsibility, p. 44? Or perhaps lawyers find other benefits from uniformity. If it was in the interest of, say, the large law firms to promulgate separate rules for themselves and their clients, wouldn't they have the political clout to do so?

5. One of the fictions Zacharias identifies is that lawyers are better than other citizens at resisting temptations such as drug abuse, sex with clients, or theft of client funds. How do the rules express that? Assuming you find this view in the rules and that it is a fiction, is it wrong for the ethics rules as an aspirational matter to hold lawyers to a higher standard of conduct than other people? Isn't that part of what being a professional means? What if, as a factual matter, lawyers were more prone to alcoholism or doctors more prone to drug abuse. How should a profession's ethics rules deal with that?

6. One of Zacharias's fictions is that lawyers act as fiduciaries of their clients. He argues that this stance is fictional because the ethics rules in many ways allow lawyers to act in their own interests rather than in their clients' interests. One should note, however, the law of agency also contains the "exceptions" Zacharias identifies. For example, fiduciary obligations do not encompass bargaining over the initial contract between agent and

principal. Indeed, most fiduciary obligations are default rules that can be contracted around. See Painter, p. 58. Would Zacharias say agency law is as falsely based as the ethics rules? That the law does not have a concept of fiduciary? Or is his quarrel just that the law should demand of some, including lawyers, more than it now does?

7.   Zacharias does not in his discussion distinguish between the Model Code and Model Rules. Yet at least in some respects, the Model Rules were designed to address some of the fictions he identifies (e.g., it adds rules dealing with transactional lawyering, entity representation, and the responsibilities of managing and subordinate lawyers). Do you sense Zacharias would view the Model Rules as an improvement?

8.   Zacharias engages in mostly descriptive analysis. He does not put forth a normative theory of when, if ever, the use of fictions might be appropriate (other than to suggest in his closing paragraph that regulators identify a regulation's purposes, and engage in some type of cost-benefit analysis before resorting to fictions). Nor does he develop a predictive theory of when we might expect to see fictions used or why they might persist. Can you think of a plausible theory of either type?

9.   There are several types of fictions that are potentially applicable to lawyer regulation, but which Zacharias does not directly address. Two notable, and related, ones are the notion of professionalism and the ideal of self-regulation. How are these related to the fictions identified by Zacharias?

10.   The "fictions of regulation" Zacharias describes had a quite real impact during the debate over the SEC's new rules governing lawyers. Many lawyers—and judges—argued that the SEC should tread lightly, if at all, on regulating in areas that traditionally have been the province of the state ethics codes. Aside from the fact that many lawyers are already subject to some form of federal regulation (a point Zacharias mentions but does not fully elaborate), one point Zacharias neglects is the fact that lawyers from large, corporate firms are almost never disciplined for anything, least of all for assisting in fraudulent transactions of the kind the SEC regulations are concerned with. The disciplinary bodies lack the resources, the expertise and the political clout to bring such disciplinary actions.

11.   What happens if some fictions, or the relaxing of these fictions, conflict with others? For example, Zacharias at one point complains that drafting too many rules that cover too many topics is "fictional" because it undermines clarity and the role of lawyers. But at other times he seems to complain that the rules are too broad in that they sweep within their purview too many disparate problems or types of lawyers or clients. It seems that relieving one type of fiction would exacerbate the other. How should we choose in that situation?

Chapter II:
Legal Limits on Advice and Action

How Far May a Lawyer Go in Assisting a Client in Legally Wrongful Conduct?*

GEOFFREY C. HAZARD, JR.

. . .

. . . The general question to be considered is: How far may a lawyer lawfully go in providing assistance to a client that might enable the client to carry out an act that is to some degree illegal?

. . .

The services that a lawyer can provide cover a wide spectrum, regardless of the client purposes that may be involved. At one end of the spectrum is simply advice as to what the law "is," without specific aid or encouragement to the client. It is not easy to provide advice that is neutral with respect to the purposes implicit in the request for advice. Nevertheless, it is possible to give unsuggestive advice, and doing so is the least instrumental form of assistance that a lawyer can provide a client. At the other end of the spectrum of lawyer assistance is pure instrumentalism—lawyer's physical execution of a purpose that the client would like to realize but cannot or will not actually execute

* © 1981 University of Miami Law Review. Reprinted by permission from 35 U. Miami L. Rev. 669 (1981).

himself. One example would be a lawyer who serves as "bagman" in an illegal payoff for a client who wishes to remain behind the scenes.

At the least instrumental end of the spectrum, the lawyer merely provides the client with an expert definition of the limits of the law, leaving it to the client to consider whether those limits should be transgressed. At the other end of the spectrum, the lawyer personally provides the means without which the client could not achieve the illicit purpose. The law clearly [permits] providing assistance at the least instrumental end of this spectrum. The law clearly prohibits conduct at the other end. But what about forms of conduct that fall within these extremes? ... The questions raised by conduct falling in the middle of the spectrum ... are difficult, and the answers are usually qualified. What advice should the lawyer give about the limits of the law of fraud or breach of fiduciary duty to a client who has fiduciary obligations but shows signs of being self-interested? What about a client who requests his attorney to prepare documents for a transaction whose factual particulars the client refuses to disclose but the lawyer has reason to suspect? What about a client who asks his lawyer to make frequent, but unscheduled, deposits of very large sums of cash in bank accounts bearing fictitious names? In the latter case, what if the city is Miami in 1981, and the client is twenty-four years of age?

. . .

It is rare that the lawyer fully knows a client's purposes or fully anticipates the ways in which the client might make use of the lawyer's services. Indeed, the client himself often does not fully realize his purposes until the moment of choice has come and gone. Furthermore, a lawyer does not learn of a client's purposes in a continuous narrative. Rather, revelation comes in fragments, often beginning in the historical middle rather than at the historical beginning. As the matter unfolds, it may appear to the lawyer that the portents of abuse are strong or weak, clear or ambiguous, firm or wavering. When are these portents sufficiently certain so that the lawyer "knows" that the client intends an illegal objective and is bent on its accomplishment?

It is sometimes suggested that the dilemma is false, because surely a lawyer cannot "know" what a client intends. This suggestion is either disingenuous or absurd. Of course, speaking in terms of radical epistemology, it is true that a lawyer cannot "know" what a client—or anyone else—intends. In these terms it is impossible for a lawyer to "know" anything. Yet the practice of law is based on practical knowledge, that is, practical assessments leading to empirical conclusions which form the basis for irrevocable action. Lawyers certainly possess such practical knowledge. If a lawyer can have practical knowledge of how the purposes of others may affect his client, he can have the same knowledge of how his client's purposes may affect others. It is in that sense that the lawyer can "know" when a client's purpose is illegal. . . .

. . .

The general category embraced by the term "illegality" also includes, beyond the criminal law, various torts. Certain kinds of torts are readily subsumed under the rubric of "illegality." These torts include the civil counterparts of criminal offenses that are *mala in se*: wrongful death by willful unexcused act, physically harmful battery, knowing conversion, and some forms of abuse of process. Other intentional torts, such as piracy of trade secrets or invasion of privacy, can also be included.

On the other hand, it is less apparent why negligence should be regarded as "illegal" conduct even if it results in tort liability. Yet negligence is a violation of the legal standard of reasonable care and is in this sense a violation of law. Suppose, for example, a client asks his lawyer whether compliance with old safety regulations is sufficient, and the lawyer indicates that such compliance would be sufficient because a tenuous argument can be made that new and stricter safety regulations are constitutionally invalid. If someone is injured as a result of the client's noncompliance with the new regulations, is the lawyer chargeable with having materially assisted the client in "illegal conduct"? How would the outcome be affected if that violation also entails criminal sanctions?

. . . We may feel confident about including [torts that are counterparts of serious criminal offenses], but as we move away from this core meaning, the boundaries become increasingly doubtful.

We can also approach the question from a different direction. There is a wide range of client conduct that gives rise to civil liability, but which we would not readily call "illegal" in the present context. Consider, for example, the deliberate default in performance of a contract obligation, the deliberate exercise of dominion and control over property of which another person claims ownership, or the deliberate decision to make a search and seizure of doubtful legality. Should any of these forms of conduct be categorized as "illegal" for the purpose of limiting the client endeavors that a lawyer may further?

The term "illegality" in ordinary legal parlance does not embrace breach of contract or invasion of a property interest [unless tortious conduct is involved]. Yet there are breaches of contract and invasions of personal and property interests that are more flagrant and more harmful than many torts, and indeed more harmful than many regulatory offenses.

. . .

The law of legal ethics . . . specially presupposes the law of torts and of agency. A lawyer in the service of a client is typically an agent. But legal representation is a special kind of agency, involving legally conferred special powers that provide the lawyer with some autonomy from the client in carrying out the agency....

...

In general, the law of agency imposes limits on what an agent may, with legal impunity, do for a principal. Section 343 of the Restatement (Second) of Agency states: "An agent who does an act otherwise a tort is not relieved from liability by the fact that he acted ... on account of the principal, except where he is exercising ... a privilege held by him for the protection of the principal's interests...." As explained in comment b to this section, an agent's act is privileged if "a reasonable belief in the existence of facts causes an act to be privileged, and a command by the principal gives the agent reason to believe in the existence of such facts." Thus, if a client directs his lawyer to commence criminal proceedings against another, and if the lawyer "has reasonable grounds for believing the other guilty of the crime, the [lawyer] is not guilty of malicious prosecution."

Section 348 of the Restatement is also pertinent to the kinds of transactions in which lawyers can be involved. That section provides that "[a]n agent who fraudulently makes representations, uses duress, or knowingly assists in the commission of tortious fraud or duress by his principal or by others is subject to liability in tort to the injured person...." The comments following section 348 make it clear that if a lawyer acts for a client in a transaction that the lawyer knows is founded on misrepresentations, the lawyer acts tortiously.

...

The vital circumstance under the law of agency is therefore not the fact that the actor is an agent, but the existence of facts that render his actions privileged. Applying the law of agency to lawyers, the vital question is what the lawyer knows about the client's endeavor. Using defamation and false arrest as illustrations, comment b to section 343 of the Restatement (Second) of Agency observes that *if* "a reasonable belief in the existence of facts causes an act to be privileged," and *if* what the agent (lawyer) is told by the principal (client) "gives the agent reason to believe in the existence of such facts," then the agent (lawyer) has the privilege that is conferred on innocent actors.

But what if the client's endeavor is *not* one that a "reasonable belief in the existence of facts" will cause to be privileged? For example, in the tort of conversion it is not a defense that the agent reasonably believes that the property was his principal's. This problem is explicitly addressed in section 349 of the Restatement (Second) of Agency: An agent whose acts "would otherwise constitute trespass to or conversion of a chattel is not relieved from liability by the fact that he acts on account of his principal and reasonably, although mistakenly, believes that the principal is entitled to possession of the chattels." Under this rule, what is the situation of a lawyer who advises a client to seize property in possession of a debtor?[4]

The lawyer's knowledge is again the vital question in cases involving misrepresentations in a contract transaction. Under section 348 of the Restatement (Second) of Agency, for example, a lawyer faces liability if he "knowingly assists in the commission of tortious fraud" by his client. If the lawyer proceeds "knowing that the buyer is relying upon the previous misrepresentations by the [client]," then the lawyer is "liable to the same extent as if he had made the previous misrepresentations." [Comment a.] Moreover, if the lawyer "has been given misinformation by a [client], on the strength of which he makes statements to a third person, [and] later discovers the untruth and refrains from taking steps to inform the other party, the [lawyer] is subject to liability if subsequently the other party completes the transaction ... relying in part upon the statements of the [lawyer]." [Comment c.] Under these rules, then, a lawyer would be liable if he discovered on the eve of a closing that the other party had relied on statements by the client that the lawyer knew were false or fraudulently misleading.[5] Such conduct also would seem to be "illegal" within the meaning of DR 7–102(A)(7).

The rules of tort law are similar to the rules of agency, but are cast in terms of "persons acting in concert." That agents and principals act "in concert" is clear as a matter of ordinary usage. Section 343, comment d of the Restatement (Second) of Agency expressly refers to section 876 of the Restatement (Second) of Torts, which is entitled "Persons Acting in Concert." Section 876 provides:

> For harm resulting to a third person from the tortious conduct of another, one is subject to liability if he
>
> > (a) does a tortious act in concert with the other or pursuant to a common design with him, or
> >
> > (b) knows that the other's conduct constitutes a breach of duty and gives substantial assistance or encouragement to the other so to conduct himself. . . .

Advice to a tortfeasor is equivalent to active participation in the tort if the advisor knows that the contemplated act is tortious, and if the advice is a "substantial factor in causing the resulting tort."

. . .

---

4. Flagg Bros., Inc. v. Brooks, 436 U.S. 149 (1978) addresses the situation of a lawyer who advises a client about seizing property in the possession of a debtor. It would seem that if the lawyer "assists" the client, and if the seizure turns out not to be legally privileged, then the lawyer, as well as the client, is prima facie legally responsible. Restatement (Second) of Agency § 343, comment d, says that "[T]he act of the agent may play too small a part to render him legally responsible for the result, or the agent's innocence and purpose may create a privilege for him to act." It is hard to see how the lawyer's role in such a situation is "too small" to count. The comment does not indicate the scope of the privilege that could result in immunity.

5.　. . . [See] SEC v. National Student Marketing Corp., 457 F.Supp. 682 (D.D.C.1978).

Finally, one can look to the principles of complicity expressed in the criminal law for guidance. Section 2.06(1) of the Model Penal Code provides that "[a] person is guilty of an offense if it is committed by his own conduct or by the conduct of another person for which he is legally accountable...." Section 2.06(2)(c) of the Code provides that a person is legally accountable for the conduct of another person if he is an "accomplice of such other person." And section 2.06(3)(a)(ii) provides that an accomplice is one who "aids ... in planning or committing" the offense "with the purpose of promoting or facilitating the commission of the offense." Restating these provisions, a lawyer is guilty of an offense if he aids a client in facilitating conduct that is an offense.

The case law on the question is sparse.... In most of the cases, the lawyer has overtly assisted his client in accomplishing manifestly illegal purposes. Thus, courts have held that it is improper for a lawyer to give advice as to how to commit a crime or fraud or how to conceal criminal or fraudulent acts. These cases beget law that is not hard to formulate. There is less guidance when the conduct is less blatant, but there is enough to point the way. One case, for example, states the test ... as whether "the lawyer conveyed to the client the idea that by adopting a particular course of action [the client] may successfully [accomplish the illegal purpose]?" As to the mode of assistance, courts have held that it is unlawful for a lawyer to negotiate for his client in pursuance of an illegal purpose or to prepare documents to effectuate it. As to the extent of knowledge that will result in complicity, the cases say not only that liability results from actual knowledge of the client's illegal purpose, but also that it results from knowledge of facts that reasonably should excite suspicion.

III

This analysis indicates the dimensions of the lawyer's duty under criminal and civil law to refrain from "assisting" a client in conduct that is "illegal." A lawyer violates that duty if:

(1) The client is engaged in a course of conduct that violates the criminal law or is an intentional violation of a civil obligation, other than failure to perform a contract or failure to sustain a good faith claim to property;

(2) The lawyer has knowledge of the facts sufficient to reasonably discern that the client's course of conduct is such a violation; and

(3) The lawyer facilitates the client's course of conduct either by giving advice that encourages the client to pursue the conduct or indicates how to reduce the risks of detection, or by performing an act that substantially furthers the course of conduct.

Notes

1. How does Hazard's approach to the problem of prohibited assistance differ from Pepper's, p. 109? One way is that Hazard thinks it is difficult

(though possible) to "provide advice that is neutral with respect to the purposes implicit in the request for advice." Pepper seems more sanguine about the possibility. Which position is more persuasive? What steps could you take as a lawyer to ensure that your advice is perceived—by the client now, as well as by third parties later—as "neutral?"

2.   Are the components of Hazard's 3–part test interrelated? When the unlawful conduct in which the client is (or might be) engaging is very serious, should lawyers have to refrain from assisting sooner, i.e., should the law require a relatively lower degree of knowledge or less conduct in aid of the wrong? Should a sliding scale be used for any of the three legs based on proof under one or both of the other legs?

3.   The economic literature on principals and agents tends to focus on trying to align the incentives of the agent with those of the principal. This can be done, for example, by having a contingency fee contract that ties the lawyer's recovery to the fate of the client. Or it can be done by the client's monitoring the lawyer's activities. See, e.g., Cohen, When Law and Economics Met Professional Responsibility, p. 44. The aiding and abetting question is in some sense the mirror image (or more aptly the dark side) of the same problem. Here we do not want the lawyer too closely aligned with the client, and we may try to achieve this by tying the lawyer's fate to the fate of the client or by encouraging the lawyer to monitor the client more. Are there differences between the "upside" agency problem and the "downside" agency problem that suggest different approaches?

4.   What is Hazard's point in demonstrating that similar ideas of aiding and abetting occur in agency law, tort law, regulatory law, and criminal law, as well as legal ethics codes? Perhaps tying these legal concepts together somehow makes it tougher for lawyers to evade the responsibility not to assist in unlawful conduct. For an analysis of similar tactics to control behavior, see Cohen's discussion of regulatory bundling in When Law and Economics Met Professional Responsibility, p. 44. Just as lawyers are forced to take the ethics rules as a package, they must take the entire legal corpus as a package. They can't cherry pick favorable rules and jettison bad ones. If conduct that constitutes aiding and abetting by a lawyer is also unethical and otherwise likely to be a breach of a lawyer's legal duties to the client or others (whether one calls it aiding or abetting or not), why have the organized bar and so many lawyers resisted vehemently the idea of "aiding and abetting" liability? For example, the ABA long resisted permitting disclosure of client fraud, although such disclosure would be an important means of avoiding aiding and abetting liability by helping to refute the inference that a lawyer's actions were intended to (or recklessly did) substantially further the fraud after the lawyer knew or should have known what the client was up to. Many lawyer groups have resisted all past and present efforts of the SEC to punish aiding and abetting and to define the types of conduct necessary to forestall such liability. Lawyers resisted the overturning of *Central Bank of Denver v. First Interstate Bank of Denver*, 511 U.S. 164 (1994), which eliminated private aiding and abetting damage actions under the federal securities laws. In other words, why bother with all that if, as Hazard argues, "aiding" is unethical and in all likelihood otherwise

unlawful, no matter what one calls it? Does Koniak, The Law Between the Bar and the State, p. 23, provide an answer?

5. The knowledge standard is the crucible of aiding and abetting law, lore and struggle. Potential escape hatch and potential clincher to a multi-million dollar damages award (or trip to prison), it offers both promise and damnation, which makes it a battleground. The two polar approaches are the "actual knowledge" standard found in Model Rules of Professional Conduct Rules 1.2(d) and 1.13 and the negligence or "reasonably should have known" standard. Lawyers tend to love the former and to consider the latter an abomination. A simple argument against the lawyer-favored actual knowledge standard is that it encourages lawyers to look the other way, to "know" as little as possible. The usual argument against the negligence standard is that it would in effect impose a costly "duty to investigate," and that it sets too low a bar for tying the lawyer's conduct to the client's. The cases tend to accept a recklessness standard, i.e., "wilful blindness" will get a lawyer in just as much trouble as "actual knowledge." Under the newly adopted SEC rules, a lawyer's duty to avoid acting to help the client's purpose is triggered when a lawyer "becomes aware of evidence of a material violation" by the corporate client or one of its agents. 17 CFR § 205.3(b). The rules then define "evidence of a material violation" to mean "credible evidence, based upon which it would be unreasonable, under the circumstances, for a prudent and competent attorney not to conclude that it is reasonably likely that a material violation has occurred, is ongoing, or is about to occur." Id. § 205.2(e). How is this standard likely to be interpreted by lawyers? By the SEC?

6. When, according to Hazard's test, should a prudent lawyer take special steps to ensure that his actions are not helping the client break the law?

7. Hazard argues that lawyers can have "practical knowledge," which he defines as "practical assessments leading to empirical conclusions which form the basis for irrevocable action." How is a lawyer supposed to make such an assessment? There is inevitably a risk that after the fact, when it turns out the client has engaged in wrongful conduct (or so a jury concludes), a judge or jury will think that the lawyer "must have known"—the so-called "hindsight bias" problem. So one approach suggested by Hazard's formulation is for lawyers to assume that number one in his test is met (the client is engaged in unlawful conduct) and then to consider all the facts known to the lawyer by imagining what a third person would conclude the lawyer (with those facts in hand) would have figured out about the client's conduct. Would that approach chill too much legitimate lawyering activity?

8. A variation on the problem of practical knowledge comes from Hazard's point that knowledge often comes to the lawyer in sequential fragments rather than in one coherent whole. Lawyers may be able to tell themselves persuasive stories about each fragment in isolation, as if they were faced with a series of suspicious smudges on a desk and wiped each one off one at a time. But the whole may add up to more than the individual parts. Thus, although practical knowledge may not entail a duty to investi-

gate, it does, at least, entail a duty to remember and to assimilate fragmentary knowledge. A related point is that different fragments of knowledge may come to several lawyers rather than one. Some have argued that companies may hire a variety of law firms to exploit this diffusion of knowledge. One way the law combats this problem is by "imputing" knowledge from one lawyer to another, as is often done in partnership law. Neither Hazard nor any of the legal doctrines he discusses offers explicit rules on imputation of knowledge. When would such imputation make sense?

Counseling at the Limits of the Law: An Exercise in the Jurisprudence and Ethics of Lawyering*
STEPHEN L. PEPPER

I. Introduction

A. *Summary of the Problem*

. . .

The client often wants or needs to understand what the law is in order to evaluate options and make decisions about his or her life, and the most common function of lawyers (across specializations and areas of practice) is to provide that knowledge. Knowledge of the law, however, is an instrument that can be used to follow the law or to avoid it. Knowing that the speed limit is fifty-five miles per hour on an isolated, rarely patrolled stretch of rural highway will lead some to drive at or below fifty-five, but will lead others to drive at sixty-three miles per hour or faster. Similarly, knowing that the only penalty for engaging in unfair labor practices is back pay and reinstatement for individual harmed employees can lead the employer/client either to avoid such practices or to engage in them intentionally. Knowledge of the law thus is two-edged. When the lawyer is in a situation in which the client may well use the relevant knowledge of the law to violate the law or avoid its norms, what ought the lawyer to do? That question is the subject of this Article.

. . .

Our legal system is premised on the assumption that law is intended to be known or knowable, that law is in its nature public information. The "rule of law" as we understand it requires promulgation. (Consider for a moment the alternative possibility of secret "law.") And one fundamental, well-understood aspect of the lawyer's role is to be the conduit for that promulgation. In a complex legal environment much law cannot be known and acted upon, cannot function as law, without lawyers to make it accessible to those for whom it is relevant. Thus, in our society lawyers are necessary for much of our law to be known, to be functional. The traditional understanding is that lawyers as professionals act for the client's benefit in providing that access to the law. Under this understanding, lawyers do not function as law enforcement officers or as judges of their clients in providing knowledge of the law; the choices to be made concern the client's life and affairs, and they are therefore primarily the client's choices to make.

The limits on the assistance lawyers may provide to their clients have commonly been articulated and thought of as the "bounds of the law." The lawyer may not become an active participant in the client's unlawful activity, and does not have immunity if she becomes an aider

---

* © 1995 Yale Law Journal Co. Reprinted by permission from 104 Yale L.J. 1545 (1995).

and abettor of unlawful conduct. The difficulty arises in deciding whether providing accurate, truthful information about the law—the core function of lawyering—can also be considered active assistance in violation of the law in situations in which the lawyer knows the information may well lead to or facilitate the client's unlawful conduct. The answers or guides to that inquiry are disturbingly unclear. There are no reported cases of civil or criminal liability on the part of the lawyer, or of professional discipline, clearly based only upon providing the client with accurate legal information. On the other hand, the legal limits are not stated in a way to make it clear that providing such advice is within the proper bounds of lawyering. Nor do these limits provide much assistance in knowing when giving the advice is proper and when it is not. And while the case law does not ground liability on such conduct, courts have rarely held or clearly stated that such conduct does not provide a basis for liability. The case law is for the most part silent. Does the client as citizen have an entitlement to knowledge of the law? Or does the lawyer have an ethical or legal obligation not to provide that knowledge when it may facilitate violation of the law or its norms?

. . .

B. A Range of Examples

. . .

Breach of Contract. At one end of the continuum is advice about conduct that most lawyers would not categorize as "unlawful," but to which the law applies a sanction. Advice about breach of contract is the paradigm. The dominant modern understanding of contract law is that one is free to breach a contract, but may thereafter be required to pay compensatory damages. Absent very unusual circumstances, there will be no punishment. Although it is unclear whether the law regards intentional breach of contract as normatively wrong, whether such conduct is "contrary to law," it is clear that the message of the law is that breach of contract is not prohibited. Rather, it is conduct that may entail a cost imposed by the law. Not only do lawyers feel free to give this advice (which may well encourage or facilitate breach of contract), but it would probably be malpractice to fail to give it when relevant to the client's situation or to advise that breach of contract is prohibited by the law.

The Burdens of Civil Litigation. A closely connected example concerns advice about the costs and delays involved in the law's procedures. In counseling the client concerned about the legal consequences of a contemplated breach of contract, should the lawyer inform the client about the substantial burdens imposed upon the person who wants to collect compensatory damages for breach of contract? Should the lawyer inform the client of the three-year delay created by the current docket situation of the relevant court? Should the lawyer inform the client of the evidentiary burdens (or problems) the plaintiff may face in proving existence of the contract, breach, and damages? Should the lawyer inform the client of the probability that these burdens will lead the person to whom he is contractually obligated to accept a substantially discounted amount to settle the claim rather than litigate? If the lawyer concludes that this information will lead the client to breach the contract, should the lawyer refrain from giving the information? Or is it malpractice to fail to give it?

Criminal Conduct Involving Harm to Third Parties. At the other end of the spectrum is legal advice the client may use for clearly criminal conduct involving concrete harm to third parties. The classic example is the client who asks which South American countries have no extradition treaty with the United States covering armed robbery or murder.

Criminal Procedure. What do you advise the lawyer whose childless, middle-aged, male client has just asked whether it is true that police and judges in the community consider children under ten to be incompetent to testify in sexual abuse cases? (Assume it is true.) A more timely example is the defendant in a murder case being informed by the lawyer that the maximum penalty for jury tampering is six months in prison and a $1000 fine. Or imagine the client who consults the lawyer concerning the legality of and penalties for euthanasia. If the facts in the euthanasia situation are sufficiently sympathetic to make the advice relevant, may the lawyer inform the client of the possibilities of prosecutorial discretion and jury nullification?

Examples from the Broad Middle Ground. Assume an Environmental Protection Agency water pollution regulation, widely publicized to relevant industries, prohibiting discharge of ammonia at amounts greater than .050 grams per liter of effluent. The client owns a rural plant that discharges ammonia in its effluent, the removal of which would be very expensive. The lawyer knows from informal sources that: (1) violations of .075 grams per liter or less are ignored because of a limited enforcement budget; and (2) EPA inspection in rural areas is rare, and in such areas enforcement officials usually issue a warning prior to applying sanctions unless the violation is extreme (more than 1.5 grams per liter). Is it appropriate for the lawyer to educate the client concerning these enforcement-related facts even though it may motivate the client to violate the .050 gram limit?

A second, well-known example is the client who wants to file a tax return reporting a favorable outcome based upon an arguable interpretation of the law. The lawyer is confident the IRS would challenge the client's return if it became aware of this interpretation and would be highly likely to succeed in the event of litigation. If that were to occur, the penalties would likely be only the tax due plus interest. The lawyer knows that in the past the audit rate for this type of return has been less than two percent, and knows that this fact is likely to lead this client to take the dubious position on her return. Ought the lawyer to communicate this information to the client?

C. *Law and Lawyering: Predictions, Manipulation, and Norms*

From the perspective of the dominant American understanding of law—taught in the law schools and practiced in the law offices—the enforcement-related facts in the last two examples would be considered part of the "law," and thus appropriate information to convey to an interested client.... Part of the lawyer's job is to take account of and predict as well as possible the way both the written law and the conduct of legal actors will impact on the client's situation.

Often called "legal realism," this view of the law is in fact an amalgam of three major streams of American jurisprudence. First is the positivist understanding of the separation of law and morality. The lawyer sees law more as a set of facts concerning power and limitation than as a norm, an "is" at least as much as an "ought." Second, and connected, this dominant view takes from legal realism the idea that law is at least as much a prediction of what officials with state power will do as it is verbal formulations that provide objectively determinable limits on conduct. The third and most recent stream is the process jurisprudence view, emphasizing law as an instrument of private planning and structuring and deemphasizing law as limit, as adjudication, or as prediction of the outcome of adjudication....

. . .

If the law becomes generally perceived as merely indicating a potential cost, a penalty that one is free to incur and to discount by the probability of its enforcement, then structuring our common life together through law becomes vastly more difficult and requires vastly more resources.... To the extent the client is led to perceive enforcement as a part of law, or, one might say, led to reduce law to the probability of enforcement, the power and effectiveness of the law as written, of the law as norm, has been reduced. Such a conflation of law with enforcement may be the untoward result of legal advice to the client under this "legal realist" view of the law. And the recently dominant jurisprudential trend in the law schools—law and economics—substantially reinforces this effect of legal realism by perceiving legal limits and rules as just another "cost," and clients as "profit maximizers," simply Holmes' "bad man" dressed in modern clothes.

. . .

II. Legal Advice Within the Bounds of the Law: Some Guiding Distinctions

. . .

A. *Desuetude and Laws Rarely Enforced: The Law/No Law Distinction*

From the perspective of law as prediction of what officials with state power will do, legal provisions that have fallen into disuse are not law. Although desuetude is not recognized as a defense to criminal prosecution in this country, judges are not the only legal actors. Prosecutors and police are legal actors with substantial legally authorized discretion. . . . The fact that enforcement does not occur removes the occasion for courts to interpret, apply, or otherwise deal with the legal provision and likewise removes occasions for the legislature to take notice of the law, thus making it less likely that the more traditionally recognized sources of law will modify or remove the provision. . . .

On two dimensions desuetude thus constitutes a form of "law," or at least approaches a kind of promulgation of "no longer law." . . . To the extent this is true, the conduct prohibited by the provision has moved from outside the "bounds of the law" to within that limit, and therefore has become a proper subject for legal advice from the lawyer even though it is advice from which the conduct itself might ensue. . . . [T]he question becomes: Is the decision as to whether this provision is still law to be an educated one made by the citizen (client) in consultation with the lawyer, or is it one to be made unilaterally by the lawyer?

. . .

1. *On the Obligation to Obey the Law, Paternalism, and Lawyer Sophistication*

. . . The extent of the general obligation to obey "the law" seems relevant to the client's choice. If it is, whether or not . . . [a] fornication statute is "law," or the "kind" of law there is such a general obligation to obey, also appears relevant. If the lawyer is supposed to provide access to the law, and if what is "really" the law is sufficiently problematic, then advice about such abstract topics seems appropriate, albeit hard to imagine. The notion that through a lawyer a client ought to have access to a sophisticated understanding of the law leads to the conclusion that the lawyer ought to assist the client in determining to what extent he or she feels obligated to obey law just because it is law, and to what extent the fornication statute counts as law.

. . .

. . . If such counseling is impracticable, or not worth the effort, the lawyer must decide for the client; the lawyer is forced to assume a paternalistic role. . . .

2. *Moving from Unenforced to Rarely Enforced Law*

. . . Probability of enforcement is . . . a continuum, with desuetude occupying one of the extremes. . . .

Consider, for example, the merchant who faces a Sunday closing law that is sometimes, but rarely, enforced. Or imagine the trucker traveling through a western state with a fifty-five-miles-per-hour posted speed limit, and enforcement that occasionally, but only rarely, occurs between fifty-five and sixty-five miles per hour....

. . .

B. The Distinction Between Law as "Cost" and Law as "Prohibition" (the Criminal/Civil Line)

Legal provisions can convey at least three rather different messages. First, the law can tell you that if you want to accomplish x, you will have to do a, b, and c in certain prescribed ways. If you want to create a contract, you will have to have an offer, an acceptance, and consideration.... Second, the law can indicate that some specific conduct will have certain prescribed negative consequences; that some specific conduct creates liability for certain costs or penalties.... A corporation that fails to conduct its business as required by the state of incorporation, by not holding required annual meetings, for example, may forfeit some of the benefits of being a corporation, such as limited liability. Third, the law can indicate that certain conduct is prohibited and will not be tolerated by society. A person who murders or steals will be punished by being forcibly removed from society for some period of time, in part to demonstrate how serious society is about the prohibition and in part to prevent repetition of the violation....

The ethical line for legal advice could be based on ... [these] distinction[s]. Under such a rule or guide, a lawyer could not give legal advice in a context in which that advice is likely to lead to conduct prohibited by law, but such advice could be given in a context in which it is likely to lead to conduct to which the law only attaches a cost or penalty. The distinction between criminal and civil law is traditionally understood as distinguishing the prohibited from the tolerated, the prohibited from the "merely" wrongful.

1. The Ends of the Spectrum

The principal advantage of this distinction lies in its apparent congruence with accepted legal culture and practice at both ends of the range of examples....

Even at the ends of the range the distinction is not without problems, however. Breach of contract can cause serious harm, and our society (and perhaps our law) perceive some level of normative obligation not to breach contracts....

At the other end of the spectrum, the euthanasia example also gives pause. Here we have contemplated murder, ... yet the notion that the client has a "right" to know the law under which her behavior will be judged and the procedures through which that law will be applied does not seem so far-fetched. . . .

2. The Middle Range of the Spectrum

The intuitive appeal of the criminal/civil distinction as applied to limiting lawyer advice about the law is substantially weaker when the examples come from the middle range. In that category, I would include nonobvious or nontraditional crimes, much regulatory law, and torts.

Indiscriminate usage of the criminal sanction creates a problem for drawing our line between civil and criminal wrongs. To the extent that conduct is criminalized when it is not intuitively obvious that the conduct involves a serious moral wrong, the justification for the criminal/civil distinction becomes obscure. . . .

. . .

. . . [I]magine a retailer just within the border of a state with a Sunday closing law, in competition with stores just across the state line, who asks his lawyer about the penalties for remaining open. The lawyer finds out that the penalty is a criminal fine of only twenty-five dollars per Sunday. In such situations, is the message sent by the law that the conduct is prohibited, that it is disfavored and comes with a cost, or some mixture that is difficult to interpret?

This problem is particularly pervasive in major areas of regulatory law administered by agencies. Here much conduct is "prohibited" by law, but the sanction can either be civil or criminal, at the discretion of the administrative agency, and civil enforcement is the norm, with criminal enforcement unusual. . . .

A final problem with the criminal/civil line is contemplated tortious conduct. Nineteenth-century tort opinions speak of negligent conduct not only as wrongful in a strong normative sense, but also often as if it were forbidden. The thrust of the shift in tort thinking over the last eighty years or so has been to drain tort law of much of its normative content, to move away from a focus on the "wrongfulness" of the conduct of defendant and plaintiff and toward allocation of the costs of accidental injury on the bases of compensation, loss spreading, and efficiency. Where the language of the courts once seemed to assimilate tortious conduct to criminal conduct, the language of much torts scholarship and at least some judicial opinions now seems to assimilate tortious conduct to breach of contract. . . . Tortious conduct is not prohibited, but it may, after litigation, result in the imposition of an obligation to pay damages. And thus it would seem that the client is free to commit torts, has a right to commit torts (unless stopped by injunction), and the lawyer has an obligation to educate him about all this if the circumstances make it relevant.[34]

34. This is of course complicated by the possibility of punitive damages. By informing the client of the law, the lawyer might supply the "willfulness" or knowledge element

. . .

3. Counseling: Advice in Addition to the Law

It is important to note, somewhere along this path, that a lawyer is not limited to giving only legal advice, or purely positivistic legal advice unadulterated with other aspects of life. . . . A lawyer can (and should) engage in what has been called a "moral dialogue" with clients who are contemplating wrongful or harmful conduct. Lawyers who give advice about the lawfulness of breach of contract probably ought to be obligated to at least consider also giving advice that the conduct (1) is or may be morally wrong, (2) may cause unjustifiable harm to specific persons, and even—given a perhaps unusual lawyer and client—(3) such conduct if followed generally might be harmful to the fabric of society.

. . .

C. The Law/Enforcement Distinction

Is a distinction between law and enforcement of law the solution to the problem of legal advice that may facilitate unlawful conduct? . . .

Imagine that lawyers have access to a bulletin board behind the counter at the police station with a weekly list of the frequency of patrol of city neighborhoods by day and time. The client, previously represented by a lawyer on burglary charges, wants to know the frequency for Chez Ultra neighborhood, Sunday, 2–4 a.m. Intuitively we know the lawyer ought not to supply this information. The law/enforcement dichotomy provides an explanation. The two-percent audit rate information in our tax return hypothetical appears to be directly analogous under the law/enforcement dichotomy, which would disallow this more generally accepted legal advice. The distinction also provides a plausible answer to the water pollution hypothetical, disallowing any advice beyond the written .050 gram per liter limit.

The law/enforcement distinction is not consistent with the two possibilities previously discussed. Desuetude is a matter of enforcement under this dichotomy, and thus not something the lawyer could communicate to the client. Likewise, the sanction for law violation, whether it be conceived as "cost" or as "prohibition," falls on the "enforcement" side of the dichotomy and would therefore be out of bounds for lawyer

needed for the jury to find a basis for awarding punitive damages. In Grimshaw v. Ford Motor Co., 174 Cal.Rptr. 348 (Ct.App.1981), evidence that Ford used a cost-benefit analysis in its design decision as to where to place the gas tank, and in doing so placed a money valuation on human life, was the basis for a jury award of $125 million in punitive damages (reduced by the trial judge to $3.5 million). Ironically, such a cost-benefit analysis is what the Learned Hand formula indicates a potential defendant ought to consider in determining whether conduct should be avoided because it imposes an "unreasonable risk," and is therefore negligent. And even if the defendant makes an error in the calculation and the conduct is later held to be unreasonable, negligence supports only compensatory, not punitive, damages. . . .

advice. Distinguishing between "law" and "enforcement," while intuitively attractive, thus presents significant difficulties[.] . . .

1. The Problem of Disentangling Civil Law from Enforcement

Imagine being asked to advise a client with a contract or tort problem, but being unable to discuss the nature of the sanctions or the mechanisms of enforcement for breach of contract or for tortious conduct. Could one communicate to the client the nature of contract or tort without telling her how they are enforced; without describing the nature of a civil lawsuit and civil damages? What would the lawyer say? . . .

. . .

Perhaps the example of bankruptcy makes the point most forcefully. What is bankruptcy law other than an elaborate set of procedures dealing with both the enforcement and the extinguishment of debt? If discussion and explanation of these procedures and their consequences is out of bounds for the lawyer, bankruptcy law could not function as intended.

. . .

2. Advice About Legal Procedures in Relation to Contemplated Conduct as Opposed to Pending Litigation

. . . This Article is concerned with the lawyer as adviser, and with how advice about the law influences client behavior. Once the client has acted, however, that concern is no longer relevant. Thus if the law/enforcement distinction is to function at all there is at least one necessary adjunct. The prohibition on advice about enforcement, at least as it is related to civil and criminal procedure, would apply only in regard to advice about contemplated conduct by the client that might entail a legal sanction, and not to pending litigation that involves actions already performed. Litigation is enforcement, and once the client is involved in litigation, legal advice is impossible if it does not deal with enforcement mechanisms and rules. . . .

This distinction, in combination with the impossibility of disentangling civil law from enforcement, yields an additional possibility. . . . As a refinement of the law/enforcement dichotomy, one could educate the client about the nature of contract law but refuse to disclose information about the process of enforcing civil damages. Advice about civil procedure (and its attendant burdens and consequent discounts) would be out of bounds until litigation was pending or contemplated. . . .

Two other, previously explored examples help to illustrate this possibility. First, in the euthanasia situation, the substance of the law of murder (including the grades and defenses) can be communicated without elaborating on criminal procedure. The law/enforcement line as here modified would allow meaningful legal advice about the contemplated conduct and the punishment for law violation, but would rule out the whole area of advice dealing with how that law would be enforced (including prosecutorial discretion and jury nullification).

Second, application of this discrimination to bankruptcy is more difficult, but still conceivable. Consider the person entering into substantial debt, or a course of business involving constant, refinanced debt. Before the debt is undertaken, the client can certainly be advised of the civil nature of the various mechanisms for debt collection, and the various forms of security. But can the client contemplating debt be instructed on the possibilities of bankruptcy? . . .

A large-scale Chapter 11 situation is more problematic under this distinction. The large corporate client with either large products liability exposure or an onerous labor contract might find a Chapter 11 bankruptcy beneficial. But the outcome ("discharge") and the process in such large-scale litigation in a relatively new area of law appear impossible to disentangle. . . .

3. *"Enforcement" of Law: Discovery of Underlying Conduct or the Procedures of Prosecution and Adjudication?*

There is a clear distinction between two senses of "law enforcement." On the one hand this phrase can refer to the process and procedures that will be applied to determine the legal consequences of a particular set of facts. Thus the prosecutor's evaluation of a situation and consequent exercise of discretion as to whether or not to prosecute is an act of law enforcement, as is the police officer's decision as to whether or not to ticket a vehicle going four miles per hour over the speed limit. Similarly, the standard of proof that will be required to show future medical expenses or lost future income in a tort case is an aspect of the enforcement of law between two private parties, as are rules governing the number of persons who will serve on the jury and the rule as to whether lawyers' fees are included in compensatory damages. All of criminal and civil procedure are a part of law enforcement in this sense. On the other hand, "law enforcement" can refer to the discovery of a particular set of facts, which may then be subject to legal evaluation and process. The facts must be known—discovered, gathered, and reported—before the prosecutor can evaluate; the vehicle must be observed and its speed known before the police officer can decide whether or not to ticket. The person who has been injured by the tortious conduct of another must discover at least (1) the identity of the person whose conduct caused the injury, and (2) that the conduct was tortious.

Advice from lawyer to client about "law enforcement" in the first sense is intuitively far more palatable than is advice about law enforcement in the second sense to any lawyer educated in the post-legal realist era. How one's acts will be judged—the procedure of the law—does appear inextricably bound up with the substance of the law. On the other hand, the likelihood that one's conduct will become subject to legal evaluation appears much less a part of the law, although it is certainly part of the administration of the law. Advice about procedure (in the broad sense) may well be relevant to the client who intends to obey the law; advice about discovery is more likely of concern to the client who believes the conduct will be perceived as unlawful.

A possibly attractive alternative for giving content to a distinction between law and enforcement of law for use in limiting advice from lawyer to client is, therefore, to think of enforcement as discovery by government (or a potential civil plaintiff) of the client's conduct, and to prohibit advice concerning it. . . .

Unlike the previous two possibilities, one can imagine lawyers making useful distinctions under the guidance of this alternative, and it thus offers some promise. It would require, however, changes in currently accepted practices. For example, it would appear to prohibit advice about audit frequency in the tax context, advice that many tax practitioners give their clients. . . . In the water pollution hypothetical, the distinction cuts an interesting line. It rules out informing the client that EPA inspection in rural areas is rare, but allows advising that violations of .075 grams per liter or less are ignored. . . .

4. *Intended and Unintended Lax Enforcement*

The water pollution hypothetical raises another problem with distinguishing between enforcement and law. It is possible that a disparity between a written rule and the way it is enforced is intended government policy, and thus amounts to a de facto amendment of the law by a governmental actor with the power to make such a change. On the other hand, it is also possible that the lax enforcement is not a matter of policy, but rather results from unintended circumstances such as budget limits, incompetence, or happenstance.

. . .

If the lawyer knows the reasons for a significant differential between the law-as-written and the law-as-enforced, then the "law/enforcement" distinction might be used in deciding what information to convey to the client. Frequently, however, the lawyer does not know. Absent information, ought the lawyer to assume that such a differential is not substantively based? . . .

In sum, the distinction between law and enforcement has significant intuitive attraction. . . . Our exploration of the possible ways of framing and applying the distinction, however, reveals substantial difficulties. . . .

D. *The Distinction Between Public Information and Private Information*

. . .

. . . Meir Dan–Cohen has suggested that conceptually it is possible and legitimate to have secret law, positing the possibility of different rules (1) to guide the conduct of "the general public," and (2) to guide "officials" judging or administering that same kind of conduct.[53] . . . The rule known by the public—or addressed to the public—would thus be a different rule than that applied by the prosecutors and the courts. The public rule usefully maximizes the deterrence of criminal conduct; the secret rule allows for greater fairness in avoiding punishment for nonculpable conduct. . . . For such differentials to function, there must be what Professor Dan–Cohen refers to as "acoustic separation": what the officials know, the public must not. . . . Significantly for our exploration, Professor Dan–Cohen assumes that information known by a lawyer will be transferred to the client. If the situation is one in which it is foreseeable that clients (potential criminals) will consult a lawyer, under this view it is an inappropriate area for differential rules because communication with a lawyer defeats acoustic separation.

. . .

. . . [T]he public/private guide would focus not upon how or where the lawyer received the information, but on whether it is generally known in the relevant client or lawyer community.

Such a line confirms and helps explain our intuition concerning the behind-the-counter bulletin board in the police station with its information about frequency of police patrols. The "behind-the-counter" aspect of the bulletin board and the fact that it contains information useful to burglars both suggest that the police have no intention of making this information public. To the extent we can identify this aspect of information about enforcement as "law," it is clearly the kind of law for which the lawmaker intends "acoustic separation" to occur.

This public/private distinction also assists us in understanding tax lawyers' willingness to inform clients of the two-percent audit rate under circumstances in which that information may well facilitate unlawful underpayment of tax. Once the audit rate information has been published (by the IRS or someone else), it becomes public information about the way the law will be enforced. As such, it seems unfair for some citizens to have access to it, and others not. The IRS may not have wanted this information published and publicly available, but once known it is hard to suppress. Sophisticated clients can find it for themselves. . . . On the other hand, if one lawyer happened to find the audit guidelines inadvertently left in a conference room by an IRS employee, most lawyers would consider the propriety of that lawyer using the information for clients' benefit, passing it on to clients, or publishing it in an article or service to be questionable. In such a context, the lawyer's conduct approaches misappropriation of private information.

Although not likely to be precise, the public information/private information distinction provides helpful guidance for lawyers. . . .

53. Meir Dan–Cohen, Decision Rules and Conduct Rules: On Acoustic Separation in Criminal Law, 97 Harv. L. Rev. 625, 636–48 (1984).

E. Differentiating Malum in Se from Malum Prohibitum

... The difference between burglary and ... [a] regulatory violation seems to be that the former is clearly wrong in its very nature in addition to being unlawful, and the latter is unlawful, but may or may not be otherwise wrongful.

That difference corresponds to the old distinction between crimes mala in se, wrong in their very nature, and crimes mala prohibita, crimes wrong only because prohibited by positive law. This distinction also helps in understanding our intuitions concerning the criminal/civil dichotomy.... A prohibition on giving the client legal information that might assist in the commission of a crime rings the right chord when the conduct is something we perceive as "really criminal," but strikes quite another note with vast areas of regulatory law. The malum in se/malum prohibitum distinction appears, in older garb, to formulate the difference between law as true prohibition (that is, the identification of conduct not to be tolerated) and law as cost (that is, the identification of conduct to be penalized in some legal fashion, but which the citizen is still free to choose to do).

We have a strong sense that somehow lawyers' ethics must differentiate these two.

Lawyers' ethical rules have already used what appears to be this distinction in one core provision. The ABA Code of Professional Responsibility allows a lawyer to reveal "[t]he intention of his client to commit a crime." In the current ABA Model Rules of Professional Conduct, this has been narrowed to allow disclosure "to prevent the client from committing a criminal act that the lawyer believes is likely to result in imminent death or substantial bodily harm."* Although the organized bar may not have articulated its reasons this way, I suspect that the large and amorphous category of criminal conduct appeared to be too wide an exception to the obligation to keep information learned from the client confidential, and I surmise that no legal classification seemed to do the job better. So the drafters appear to have been forced back upon an old distinction: if what the client is going to do is really wrong, you can reveal it. But that way of putting it is too vague—and too subject to individual interpretations of "really wrong"—to work well as a rule, so an operational definition was used: it is "really wrong" if it is going to kill someone, or hurt someone in a significant, physical way.

An attempt along these lines to translate the malum in se/malum prohibitum distinction into guidance for practicing lawyers in giving legal advice in situations where the client might use it for unlawful conduct could take a narrower or broader form. A narrow rule could be framed to simply track the one on confidentiality quoted above: when it appears likely that the client will use knowledge of the law to facilitate

---

* [Editors' note: Since the publication of this article, the ABA has amended Model Rule 1.6 to broaden this exception.]

unlawful conduct likely to cause death or substantial bodily harm, the lawyer shall not provide that knowledge. Alternatively, a rule could be formulated to track the underlying perception of the "wrong in itself" concept, and apply that concept to a larger area of potential client conduct. Such a rule might state: when it appears more probable than not that the client will use legal information or advice to facilitate conduct that (1) is clearly prohibited by law and (2) involves what is by clear societal consensus a serious and substantial moral wrong, the lawyer shall not provide the client with the legal advice or information.

. . .

. . . Note here that the suggested rules focus upon the results of the particular client conduct at issue, not on the classification of the legal violation or crime. . . .

. . .

. . . A flexible "standard" might be constructed according to which each lawyer must judge under the particular circumstances whether the client's prospective unlawful conduct is "really wrongful" in some fundamental or serious way, or is "merely penalized" in some legal fashion. Thus a client's intentional breach of contract that was likely to bankrupt the business of an innocent, unsophisticated individual might be treated quite differently from an intentional breach that would cost a Fortune 500 company $100,000. . . . The absence of the clear societal consensus that underlies the concepts of malum in se and malum prohibitum would mean that the guidance would be more subjective and contextually determined, but it would still provide the lawyer with a framework for considering the situation and making a decision. Because such a standard would move away both from clear societal consensus and from somewhat more objective lines, it might be that the direction given the lawyer would not be to withhold the legal information. The lawyer might instead be required to provide the information only in tandem with the lawyer's assessment that the conduct not only would be "unlawful" in some sense or other (breach of contract, tortious), but also that it would be "really wrongful," and ought not to occur.

F. Who Initiated Discussion of the Possibly Illegal Conduct: Lawyer or Client?

Many lawyers suggest that the ethical propriety of providing legal information that may lead to conduct contrary to law depends, at least in part, on whether or not the client has asked. Under this line of thought, if the client has requested information about "the law" or legal consequences, the lawyer's primary function is to provide that information. If, however, the client has not asked, providing the information may well amount to the lawyer's suggesting unlawful conduct, and thus would be improper.

. . .

... [Should] it make a determinative difference ... that the client has not asked? Two ... perceptions about the role of the lawyer point in different directions. First, for the lawyer to be the originator of conduct contrary to law certainly doesn't sound right. . . .

The strength of this perception, however, is dependent on all the factors discussed earlier ...: Is the legal provision really "law," or has it been eroded by desuetude or enforcement policy into something society appears not to be very concerned about? Is the conduct really prohibited, or just freighted with a legal cost or penalty? Is the conduct really wrongful, or just legally prohibited?

The second, quite different perception concerns the apparent unfairness of advantaging the more legally sophisticated client over the less knowledgeable client, or of advantaging the less scrupulous client over the more scrupulous one. (I assume here that the less sophisticated or more scrupulous client is less likely to initiate the problematic discussion with the lawyer.) The prime function of lawyers—providing access to the law—suggests that it may not be fair. . . . The person wise enough to ask gains access to the law; the less knowledgeable or curious or sophisticated client does not. Lawyers generally pride themselves on understanding that the client may not be knowledgeable enough about the law to know what he wants or needs. . . .

Just as with the first perception, however, the problem of what counts as "law" to which there should be equal access remains. . . .

G. *Probability that Advice Will Result in Lawful Rather than Unlawful Conduct*

Can we provide guidance to the lawyer based upon the likelihood that the client will use the lawyer's knowledge either to abide by legal norms or to violate them? ... Thus we could create an initial legal guide that suggests that if the lawyer has no reason to foresee that advice may be used to violate the law or a legal norm, she is free to provide the advice. On the opposite side of this guide, we might frame a rule prohibiting the provision of advice when the lawyer knows that the client will use knowledge of the law to violate it.

An effort could be made to further refine such guidance; that is, to find the line somewhere between these two extremes to determine when it is proper or improper to provide the advice. A line oriented toward protecting society's interest in obedience to the law might provide that when there is a substantial possibility that the information will facilitate violation of the law or legal norms, the lawyer ought not provide the information. (A corollary might be that in such a situation the lawyer may communicate further with the client to learn more about the client's intentions or probable actions, but could not provide the information until he or she determined that it was highly unlikely that the information would be used to facilitate conduct contrary to law or legal norms.) A quite different, client-favorable line might say that the lawyer may give such advice—that is, may give the benefit of the doubt to the client—unless it is "very likely" that the client will use the information to violate the law or legal norms. A number of other "in between" variations are possible ("likely," instead of "very likely," for example). Or this approach could operate more like a standard: the more likely it is that the information will be used to violate the law or a legal norm the less appropriate it is for the lawyer to provide it.

Two factors should be considered in relation to this possible approach to limiting lawyers' advice. First, it is likely to be useful only in combination with one or more of the other factors canvassed above....

Second, ... the lawyer's discussion of the legal effect of possible future conduct may itself introduce the possibility of that conduct to the client or otherwise substantially change the likelihood of the client so conducting herself....

. . .

V. Conclusion

I would suggest that the solution to the central problem of this Article consists of a combination of some tentative rules ... with a practical wisdom connected to the roles and tasks of our profession (to the extent it can be developed). The first rule or principle is that the client has a presumptive right to know the law governing his or her situation, understanding "law" in the widely defined contemporary sense. The second rule or principle is that the lawyer has a presumptive moral obligation to engage in a counseling conversation if there is reason to foresee that the client may violate the law or a significant legal or moral norm. When applying these rules, and in determining when and why the presumptions have been overcome, the seven distinctions developed in this Article will be helpful. In addition to that analytic assistance, however, lawyers working their way through these problems ought to be aware that what is necessary to reach a solution is the exercise and development of their own practical wisdom. In such deliberations, reliance on character—on implicit perception and evaluation, on moral habit—is unavoidable. For this reason, in working on the professional ethics of lawyering in the larger sense we—practitioners, teachers, the profession—ought to (1) formulate a set of such tentative rules and principles and (2) work to create a culture that will cultivate a professional practical wisdom for applying them. The dualism here is an effort to suggest the compatibility of a "rights"-oriented perspective, which views the primary job of lawyers as providing clients with access to the law to which they have something resembling a right, with a "virtue"- and "character"-oriented approach to the professional life of the lawyer. We need the rules and principles to protect clients who are often vulnerable or dependent in relation to professionals, and to protect, in turn, third persons who often are vulnerable in relation to the conduct of clients. We need practical wisdom because the rules and principles simply will not be sufficient to deal with the moral questions of lawyering.

Notes

1. Pepper discusses rarely enforced laws as in some sense being not law at all. Isn't the same true of ethics rules, at least as applied to large firm lawyers? Should that affect Pepper's analysis?

2. Pepper discusses the general "right" to breach a contract and argues that the lawyer can generally give advice to do so. Although he notes some of the limits of this right, there are others. For example, bad faith breach of contract, though not generally recognized, does exist in certain areas, most notably insurance law. And courts may take the reason for breach into account in determining the proper level of damages, with the result that some damage measures are more "punitive" than others even if not explicitly so labeled. See Cohen, The Fault Lines in Contract Damages, 80 Va. L. Rev. 1225 (1994). There are then some reasons for breaching a contract that the law, at least to some extent, penalizes. Does this reminder of the thickness of law affect your sense of the appropriate limits on the giving of legal advice? It should help you remember that staying within the law, including the law governing lawyers, requires care and diligence at least as much as it requires good moral character.

3. Compare Pepper's analysis to the Cover framework presented in Koniak, The Law Between the Bar and the State, p. 23. Part of Pepper's point is to confirm the idea, expressed by Cover, that law is made up of stories and commitment as well as rules. The same is true of the law on giving legal advice. Can Pepper's analysis be summed up by saying that a lawyer can give any advice if a "good" story can be told about how the client will use that advice, provided it is reasonable for the lawyer to believe that story?

4. Interestingly, one area of law that Pepper does not discuss extensively is fraud. How would you apply Pepper's categories to analyze the problem of client fraud? He also does not make much of the distinction between individual and entity clients. Does that matter to his argument?

5. Pepper in a number of places refers to the possibility of a malpractice action against lawyers who fail to provide advice that might lead clients to commit illegal acts. As is the case generally in this area, there are few if any reported cases, but is the risk of a malpractice action in such a situation something of a red herring? The Restatement 2d Agency § 411 states: "[O]ne who undertakes to perform service as the agent of another is not liable for failing to perform such service if, at the time of the undertaking or of performance, such service is illegal." If an agent can refuse to perform illegal acts without fear of liability, would it be sensible to hold the agent liable for failing to advise the principal on an illegal route of action the principal might take?

6. Pepper does not mention the rules governing reliance on advice of counsel. Generally, the fact that one relied on a lawyer's advice does not excuse a client from criminal or regulatory liability. Thus, in most of the cases Pepper presents, if the client's conduct was discovered and the client was sued or prosecuted, the client would lose. If the lawyer should have known what the client was up to, why not hold the lawyer liable for damages or discipline too? Then the question would be whether the lawyer was willing to take the same risk he was advising the client to take. If it could not be shown that the client would be liable, the lawyer would not be either. Is Pepper arguing that lawyers should enjoy legal immunity for providing advice even if clients are actually held liable? He seems to suggest as much when he talks about situations in which "formally criminal conduct may well be facilitated, yet most lawyers would think it appropriate to provide the client with information about the law." Is that consistent with Model Rules of Professional Conduct Rule 1.2(d)? What would be the justification for providing lawyers with such immunity?

7. Pepper does not discuss the crime-fraud exception to the attorney-client privilege. Is this relevant to his analysis? If the client is "caught" and prosecuted or sued, and the government or plaintiff presents a prima facie case of client wrongdoing, the attorney may be compelled to testify about lawyer-client communications that furthered the client's crime or fraud. Should this possibility be factored into the analysis of what to tell the client? How?

8. Even if one accepts Pepper's view of the law, how often will it be the case that a lawyer provides "only" advice and *no* other services that can be construed to facilitate the fraud? Consider Hazard's How Far May a Lawyer Go article on this point, see p. 100. Pepper suggests that there are few reported decisions on whether giving "only" advice is lawful because that "is so clearly lawful that cases have not been brought." Is that the only possible explanation? Cases may be brought and settled or not brought because the law is unclear or lawyers don't what any reported decisions on this question. Or maybe lawyers rarely provide "only" nonsuggestive advice on what the law is and then end the representation.

9. In discussing the law on prohibited assistance, Pepper does not discuss the standard of "knowledge" or "intent" (scienter). Yet one of the factors he lists as important is the foreseeability of what the client would do with the advice. If the lawyer intends to further illegal conduct with advice, but the client doesn't commit a crime or is stopped, should the lawyer be subject to discipline or other legal sanction for having provided the advice?

10. Pepper's "solution" to the counseling problem is to encourage lawyers to engage their clients in broader dialogue both about client goals and about the law. This raises several questions. Is such dialogue required? Why should it not be viewed as a kind of quid pro quo in return for the right to provide legal advice? Why don't lawyers do this more often, especially if it would be beneficial to the clients? Is it really because they can't "bill" for it? Or is it because lawyers think they are preserving some kind of "deniability" for themselves in the event the client engages in wrongful conduct? How

would Pepper handle the problem of lawyers and clients who do not want the dialogue, perhaps for self-interested reasons? Once the dialogue has occurred, the lawyer will be in a much better position to "know" what the client intends to do. That is, can a lawyer, after such dialogue, be as passive about how the client will use the advice as a lawyer who has not had the same kind of talk with the client?

11.   There is a tension between Pepper's justification of current legal practice concerning the giving of legal advice and his lamenting how focused on money lawyers seem to be today. If the profession is in such a sorry state, shouldn't we view its norms with skepticism? Might there not be a connection between the views on legal advice Pepper is advocating and the current state of the profession? What kind of connection?

12.   For a critique of some of Pepper's ideas, see Cynthia A. Williams, Corporate Compliance with the Law in an Era of Efficiency, 76 NC L Rev 1265 (1998). See also Holmes, The Path of the Law, 10 Harv. L. Rev. 457 (1897) and the trio of articles in the William & Mary Law Review on a lawyer's duty to obey the law: Simon, Should Lawyers Obey the Law?, 38 Wm. & Mary L. Rev. 217 (1996); Luban, Legal Ideals and Moral Obligations: A Comment on Simon, 38 Wm. & Mary L. Rev. 255 (1996); Wilkins, Why Lawyers Should Have a Prima Facie Duty to Obey the Law, 38 Wm. & Mary L. Rev. 269 (1996).

Business Lawyering and Value Creation for Clients: Environmental Lawyers and the Public Service Model of Lawyering*

DAVID DANA

Much legal scholarship concerns the dichotomy between the lawyer as a business person, whose sole purpose is to maximize the wealth of her clients and hence herself, and the lawyer as a public-minded professional, whose commitments to the public welfare co-exist with, and even may take precedence over, service to the client. In this Article, I explore the professional or (as I will term it) public service model of lawyering in the context of environmental compliance advising. The Article questions that model on two accounts. First, there is little evidence that environmental lawyers aspire to practice a public service version of environmental law. Second, even if some environmental lawyers wish to practice public service environmental law, a number of forces exist that may make it impossible for them to do so, including the content and volume of environmental regulation, the sophistication of environmental clients, and the repeat nature of interactions between regulated entities and environmental regulators.

I. The Client Service and Public Service Models

In one of the dominant models of the private lawyer as counselor, the "client service model," the sole task of the lawyer is to assist the client in maximizing the client's welfare within the constraints of the legal system....

. . .

In a world of unambiguous laws and regulations, immediate detection and vigorous prosecution of every violation, and automatic draconian penalties, the client service and public service models of environmental counseling would be essentially the same—every lawyer simply would inform her clients of plainly applicable requirements. In fact, environmental statutes and regulations often contain ambiguities and inconsistencies, and regulators often remain unaware of arguably unlawful conduct by regulated entities. As a result of both resource limitations and ideological predispositions, regulators sometimes overlook such conduct or fail in their efforts to carry out successful enforcement actions. Even when regulators successfully enforce the law, penalties may be quite modest.

Given these realities, one might expect client service counseling to differ from public service counseling in several fundamental respects. First, client service lawyers might help their clients identify advantageous interpretations of regulatory requirements, and evaluate the likeli-

* © 1995 University of Oregon. Reprinted by permission from 74 Or. L. Rev. 57 (1995).

hood that regulators would accept or reject such interpretations. In the event that regulators rejected those interpretations, client service lawyers might determine the chances of a successful appeal.... Of course, the client service lawyer might advise a client of the possibility that a regulatory agency or a court will reject formally plausible "loopholes" on public purpose grounds. But this advice would not be motivated by the lawyer's commitment to the public purposes animating environmental protection statutes, but rather by a commitment to provide the client with any information that the client might need to maximize its private welfare.

By contrast, a public service lawyer might decline to inform her clients of statutory and regulatory interpretations that she believes are contrary to the public purpose of the statutory or regulatory framework. At a minimum, such a lawyer probably would downplay the attractiveness of those options.

Second, one might expect a client service lawyer to help her clients assess the risk that regulators will discover particular courses of conduct and, assuming they do, the risk that they will bring an enforcement action challenging the conduct. A course of conduct based on a questionable statutory interpretation would appeal more to a client in an environment of little risk of detection and enforcement than in an environment of virtually assured detection and enforcement.

A public service lawyer, by contrast, might believe that clients should act as if regulators will detect and respond to all questionable conduct. Consequently, the public service lawyer might decline to discuss the probabilities of non-detection and non-enforcement, at least where she believes those probabilities to be high. Such a lawyer also might decline to advise clients about means of increasing the likelihood of non-detection, such as immersing an important factual disclosure in the appendix to a mandatory report to a public agency.

Finally, a client service lawyer might assist clients by predicting the magnitude of informal penalties (e.g., loss of regulators' goodwill) and formal civil or criminal penalties that might be imposed at different points in the process. Armed with the client service lawyer's advice, a client would be fairly well-equipped to assess whether the expected benefits of proceeding on the basis of a given statutory or regulatory interpretation exceed the expected costs.

The public service lawyer, on the other hand, might decline to offer a realistic assessment of penalties if she believes that her client, if fully informed, would conclude that the benefits of pursuing a dubious course of conduct outweigh the risks. Such a lawyer might highlight the worst possible outcomes for the client or, at a minimum, might exhort the client that compliance with regulatory requirements is the "right thing to do" regardless of the magnitude of possible penalties.

. . .

II.   The Attitudes and Behavior of Environmental Lawyers

... [W]e know very little at all about regulatory advising in practice. Unlike some aspects of lawyering, such as litigation advocacy, regulatory [indeed, all] counseling occurs in private and under the cover of attorney-client privilege and professional norms that assure confidentiality....

One might suppose that, if any sector of private practice would be characterized by public mindedness, it would be environmental law. In many areas of regulatory law, law students do not strongly identify with the agenda of activist public regulators. As far as I know, aspiring tax lawyers[, for example,] do not generally have greater sympathy for the Internal Revenue Service than for taxpayers.... By contrast, ... anecdotal evidence suggests that many law students study environmental law and plan to enter the field because they regard themselves as environmentalists and, accordingly, hope to take satisfaction in facilitating the protection of the environment.... [S]ome of these students ... [end up in private practice.]

However ... [a]s Karl Llewelyn noted more than fifty years ago, any person's interests and outlook "are shaped in greatest part by what he does.... His sympathies and ethical judgments are determined essentially by the things and the people he works for and with." Consistent with this view, Robert Nelson's study of large firm lawyers in Chicago found that lawyers embrace the values and positions of the clients in their practice area....[36] ....

The only relevant study of environmental lawyers also supports this view. In a 1991 study of environmental law students and practitioners, James Wakefield found that, although a substantial percentage of environmental law students believes that environmental lawyers' primary obligation is to society, environmental practitioners overwhelmingly believe that their primary obligation is to their clients[37]....

A review of the writings of environmental lawyers in practice publications also suggests that environmental lawyers do not take a public service or environmentalist approach in advising clients....

   ...

III.   The Unfavorable Market for Public Service Environmental Law

Even if we assume that some environmental lawyers want to practice public service environmental law, the current market for legal services probably would prevent them from doing so.... [There are] four major obstacles to the practice of public service environmental law:

---

36.   Robert L. Nelson, Ideology, Practice, and Professional Autonomy: Social Values and Client Relationships in the Large Law Firm, 37 Stan.L.Rev. 503, 524 (1985).

37.   James M. Wakefield, Comment, Attitudes, Ideals, and the Practice of Environmental Law, 10 UCLA J. Envtl. L. & Pol'y 169, 197 (1991).

the "fine print" aspect of our environmental statutes; the practical impossibility of full compliance; the sophistication of environmental clients; and the repeat nature of interactions between environmental regulators and regulated entities. . . .

A. Obstacles to the Public Service Environmental Lawyer

1. The Fine Print in Environmental Regulation

. . . The simple fact is that environmental lawyers do not have to work very hard to find "loopholes" that seem to run contrary to the purposes of environmental protection. Interest groups and sympathetic politicians and government officials succeed in inserting clear exemptions and potentially helpful ambiguities in the highly-politicized process of drafting complex environmental legislation and implementing regulations. . . .

2. The Weight of Regulation

The sheer weight of environmental regulation also presents an obstacle to a public service environmental lawyer. In heavily regulated industries, there are so many highly detailed regulations issued by so many different agencies that achieving and maintaining full compliance even with unambiguous regulatory requirements is extremely difficult. . . .

The excess of regulation and the consequent difficulties in achieving full compliance foster a general attitude among businesses that ninety or ninety-five percent compliance is "good enough." A norm or culture of full compliance cannot take hold. In such an environment, the public service lawyer cannot urge compliance with a particular requirement simply because "it is the law," but must instead explain why the expected costs of noncompliance exceed the expected benefits. In other words, the lawyer must engage in the discourse of the client service lawyer.

3. Client Sophistication

If environmental clients were relatively unsophisticated, then they might not insist that their lawyers advise them about fine print opportunities in environmental law and the risks associated with different courses of conduct. Unsophisticated clients might simply accept the lawyer's advice . . . at face value. . . . [But] many environmental clients are, in fact, very sophisticated.

In *The Devolution of the Legal Profession: A Demand Side Perspective*,[46] Ronald Gilson discusses the inverse relationship between the sophistication of clients and the capacity of lawyers to adhere to the public-regarding model of legal professionalism. According to Gilson, the

46. Ronald J. Gilson, The Devolution of the Legal Profession: A Demand Side Perspective, 49 Md.L.Rev. 869 (1990).

legal market at one time was populated by clients who lacked the sophistication necessary to evaluate their legal needs and the quality of different providers of legal services. This lack of sophistication led clients to develop and rely upon long-term, stable relationships with full-service law firms. Because there was little risk that such clients would switch their outside counsel, outside counsel were able to act as "gatekeepers" for the public interest even though their clients, in an ideal world, would have preferred lawyers solely committed to maximizing client welfare. The growth of client sophistication, in turn, has limited lawyers' ability to adhere to the public-regarding model of lawyering . . . .

. . .

4. *The Limited Reputational Market in Environmental Law*

So far, I have implicitly assumed a context in which clients prefer to receive counseling aimed solely at maximizing client welfare. But what about clients who actually want to receive public service advice? If there were a significant number of such clients, a lawyer could adopt a public service stance toward client counseling without, in effect, having to fool or coerce her clients.

. . .

The academic literature suggests one reason that a client might want to retain a lawyer with a reputation solely for giving public service advice: to signal regulators, investors, and the public that the client intends to be environmentally-conscious in deciding how to comply with statutes and regulations. This signal, in turn, might produce material benefits for the client such as friendly (and hence less costly) relations with regulators, money from socially-conscious investment funds, and the patronage of "green" consumers. . . .

It is doubtful, however, that substantial demand exists for the use of private environmental lawyers as reputational intermediaries of this sort. Even assuming lawyers could develop stable reputations as giving only public-minded, environmentally-protective advice, regulators would have no way of knowing that those lawyers' clients would follow the advice. Clients might retain such lawyers as window-dressing and receive more candid guidance elsewhere. . . .

Moreover, in the environmental context, clients may not need to use lawyers as reputational intermediaries because they can independently develop reputations with regulators, investors, and consumers. To understand why this is the case, it is helpful to distinguish between one-time and repeat relationships. The greatest demand for reputational intermediaries exists where parties engage in only a single, non-repeat transaction. . . . By contrast, in ongoing relationships, the parties have historical track records and much greater capacity to play "tit for tat"— to respond to truthfulness or untruthfulness with like behavior.

. . .

B. *Aids to the Public Service Environmental Lawyer*

1. *The Criminalization of Environmental Law*

The recent criminalization of environmental statutory violations may create a demand for legal services that are not aimed solely at maximizing the welfare of corporate clients. Displeased by the notion that corporations may treat even massive civil penalties as simply "a cost of doing business," Congress has classified numerous violations of environmental statutes as felonies. The criminal penalties apply both to corporations and to individual corporate employees. . . .

Although corporations do suffer from criminal convictions, . . . only individuals can be imprisoned. Thus, while it may be welfare-maximizing for a corporation to choose a course of conduct that is associated with a small risk of criminal conviction, it may be welfare-maximizing for an individual corporate employee to reject that course of conduct. . . . When confronted with even a minute risk of imprisonment, [employees] may have little interest in soliciting legal counseling about risks of detection and enforcement. . . .

The actual effects of the criminalization of environmental law, however, are not yet known and may turn out to be limited. Although criminal prosecutions have increased rapidly since the mid–1980s, the penalties for environmental statutory violations are still generally civil, not criminal, and corporate employees presumably are aware of this fact. As a practical matter, the probability of criminal prosecution is quite low when the conduct in question is based on statutory or regulatory interpretations that are formally plausible (albeit not environmentally protective) and that regulators have not yet definitively rejected. . . .

2. *The Threat of Lawyer Liability in the Wake of Kaye, Scholer*

If lawyers routinely were held liable for failing to safeguard the public interest when they counseled clients about environmental compliance, conditions in the market for legal services might change dramatically. . . .

. . .

If the threat of personal liability against environmental lawyers were substantial, it might assist lawyers who aspire to practice a public service version of environmental counseling. In the face of a significant threat of liability, client service lawyers might protect themselves by adopting a more environmentally-conscious, public-minded approach to counseling. Indeed, because the "whole law" principle is quite vague, lawyers could guarantee their protection from liability only by scrupulously avoiding giving advice about anything that conceivably could be characterized as a loophole. Consequently, any competitive pressures in the legal market to provide client service counseling would disappear.

Other scenarios, however, are equally likely. Clients might transfer their business to client service lawyers who are willing to bear a personal liability risk in return for ample fees. The movement in the market, in other words, might simply be from risk-averse client service lawyers to risk-taking client service lawyers. Alternatively, if there are few or no risk-taking client service lawyers, clients might respond by exiting the legal services market altogether. Dissatisfied with the product available in the legal market, businesses might turn to non-lawyers to guide them through environmental regulations.

At any rate, there is no reason to believe that federal or state regulators soon will seek to impose liability on environmental lawyers. . . . Indeed, to my knowledge, no environmental regulator or public prosecutor has successfully targeted "the lawyers" in any environmental civil suit or criminal prosecution.

. . .

Notes

1. Is Dana's dichotomy of "client service" and "public service" lawyering a fair one? Are the interests of the "client" always clear, especially when the client is an entity? And whose conception of the "public interest" counts? Don't lawyers have an ability to influence both client and public interests? Dana carves out of his analysis cases in which the client service and public service models overlap. Might not lawyers have some ability to manipulate how large this area of overlap is? See Gordon, p. 362. Might lawyers practice different types of lawyering in different situations? Lawyers could, for example, operate under a presumption of client service with some exceptions for public service type activity; that is, they may practice client service lawyering at the "macro" level but public service lawyering at the "micro" level. Or lawyers might engage in internal tradeoffs, under which they engage in client service lawyering with respect to particular problems in "exchange" for convincing the client to act in a different area above and beyond what the law strictly requires. Or lawyers might engage in what Dana calls (in an omitted portion of the article) "schizoid" lawyering, in which they practice in a client service way but then advocate public law reforms. Are these alternatives doomed under Dana's analysis?

2. There is, of course, at least one alternative "model" of lawyering, one in which lawyers act in the interests of neither their clients nor the public. We might call this the "self-interested model," best exemplified perhaps by class action lawyers. See e.g., Koniak & Cohen, In Hell [Part II], p. 329. Is self-interested lawyering all there really is? Or if we define self-interest to encompass all or almost all activities that anyone undertakes (on the economists' theory that people act, for the most part, rationally and in their own self-interest) does the idea of self-interest lose some of its interpretive power?

3. Suppose Dana is right that environmental lawyers do not want to practice "public service" lawyering, and could not practice it (and manage to

have clients) even if they did want to. Instead assume these lawyers seek to maximize client welfare "within the constraints of the legal system." Why add, as Dana does, the "constraints of the legal system" to the definition of maximizing client welfare? Are those constraints precise enough and is there enough consensus on what they are to make them a real limit on the maximizing client welfare mode of behavior? See Koniak, The Law Between the Bar and the State, p. 23 (on the difficulties of giving law unitary and stable meaning across communities committed to different world views). Does Dana's analysis have implications more generally for whether lawyers can act ethically, or even lawfully? If we drop "constraints of the legal system" from the client maximizing model as too weak to be much of a constraint, could we substitute "ethical" or "lawful" for "public service" in Dana's arguments? Why assume that lawyers can act ethically or lawfully when their clients do not want them to, if they cannot act in the "public interest" when their clients do not want them to?

4.   What is the relationship between ambiguous and clearly wrongful client conduct? Is client service lawyering likely to lead to illegal or unethical lawyering or unlawful client behavior? Or are there market or other mechanisms in place that preserve the line? What are they? If those mechanisms are weak or non-existent, the implications of Dana's arguments are more serious than the picture he paints. Do you trust the mechanisms designed to keep lawyers within the bounds of law? Why?

5.   Assuming lawyers might want to practice public service lawyering, is Dana unduly pessimistic about their opportunity to do so? What about lawyer-client agency problems? Couldn't public service lawyering be viewed as a form of "positive" employee shirking? For example, Dana's discussion of the differences between public service and client service lawyering focuses on the ability of the public service lawyer to withhold information. Might not lawyers be able to manipulate information on, say, the magnitude and likelihood of liability, by for example exaggerating the cost of collecting such information?

6.   Dana's response to the agency problem is essentially that sophisticated clients are well-equipped to monitor lawyers. That may be true with respect to certain types of activities, such as billing, but can even sophisticated clients really monitor lawyers who "shirk" by engaging in public service lawyering? The complexity of regulation, to which Dana points as hindering public service lawyering, might actually foster it because it makes monitoring harder. If, for example, lawyers focus their energies on researching rules more likely to involve harm to the public and less time on researching rules that are likely to have loopholes in areas where their clients are already "complying," is the client really going to know? Moreover, most of the monitoring by large corporate clients is done by in-house counsel. Who monitors them? Doesn't this simply move the agency problem back one step? What if in-house counsel also want to practice public service lawyering? Although in-house counsel might be expected to toe the company line because of the threat of discharge and close working relationships with management, they may also be in a better position to exploit agency problems within the organization. That is, they may be able to subvert what

they perceive to be managers insufficiently attuned to the corporation's best interests, or corporations insufficiently attuned to the interests of environmentally conscious managers. Is all that too naive, given that one company can watch what others do and fail to do on compliance?

7. Does the empirical data Dana cites support the conclusion that environmental lawyers have no interest in acting as public service lawyers? Consider, for example, whether the behavior of lawyers might vary depending on how small the net benefit to the client was likely to be and how big the net cost to society was? If you were to design a survey of environmental lawyers, what questions would you ask to elicit information on how public service-like they were or client-maximizing?

8. Is environmental law meaningfully different from other areas of corporate practice with respect to lawyers' ability to practice public service lawyering?

Attorney Liability in the Savings and Loan Crisis*
HARRIS WEINSTEIN

I. Introduction

The last four years have seen over 1000 criminal cases and nearly 2000 civil cases arising from the savings and loan crisis. These include more than ninety civil cases brought against lawyers, six of them by my agency, the Office of Thrift Supervision, and the balance by the Federal Deposit Insurance Company (FDIC) and the Resolution Trust Corporation (RTC).

. . .

IV. Kaye Scholer and its Professional Role

. . .

Kaye Scholer was one of many major law firms hired by Charles Keating to represent and advise his enterprises, American Continental Corporation (ACC), a holding company, and Lincoln Savings and Loan, its federally insured subsidiary. I know that most of you have read a lot about Keating, Lincoln, and ACC. What is not widely reported, at least outside of the legal business press, is the large number of lawyers and law firms that Keating from time to time retained. You do read about those that have become defendants. You do not read about those that did not become defendants, and that, too, may some day be an interesting subject for scholarly exploration. Why did some of those law firms become defendants while others did not? . . .

The Notice of Charges against Kaye Scholer—Notice of Charges is what we call a complaint in our administrative tribunal—contained ten claims. Eight were substantive, while two were essentially wrap up charges that synthesized the case in broader terms.

Five of the charges arose from Kaye Scholer's conduct in representing Lincoln during the bank examination process. Here I ought to describe what a bank examination is, because it has rules that are foreign to anyone unfamiliar with bank regulation. As part of the price of federal deposit insurance, a federally insured depository institution—a bank, a savings and loan, a credit union—submits to a regulatory regime. Statute and regulation specifically and unequivocally require that the insured institution make available to its federal regulator every book, record, and individual. Bank examiners, often on an annual basis, come into the institution, review the books and records, and interview the personnel. They then try to make some hardheaded judgments about the quality of the investments on the books, what the institution's real

* © 1993 Board of Trustees of the University of Illinois. Reprinted by permission from 1993 U. Ill. L. Rev. 53.

financial position is, and whether the institution is well and honestly run.

In implementing its authority, the OTS has adopted a regulation that closely resembles in concept and is modeled in language upon Rule 10b–5 of the federal securities laws. That regulation, which applies to the examination process and every other process before the agency other than a formal investigation, requires that anyone making representations to the agency not make any false statements and, more importantly, not make any material omissions. This means that in making statements to the agency, one may not omit any factual matters the omission of which makes the statement misleading in context. Thus, one is forbidden to lie and to make material omissions, and in an examination one is required to provide the agency full access to the books, records, and people.

Kaye Scholer was retained during a bank examination of Lincoln in the middle of 1986. One of the first things Kaye Scholer did was write a letter to the regulators saying, in substance, "You may not ask Lincoln for any information. If you want any information, you must write a letter to our partner in New York City." Our position in the OTS case against Kaye Scholer was that by taking that step, by interposing itself between the Bank Board and the bank, Kaye Scholer assumed the bank's obligations for making the necessary disclosures required by the statute and by our rule.

This point is at the heart of the OTS charges against the firm. Five of the eight specific claims in the case allege that Kaye Scholer made factual representations to the Bank Board that contained either material omissions or misstatements of fact. If you go through our Notice of Charges, you will see that the Notice in these respects is constructed in a specific way. In several instances, the Notice first quotes statements from internal memoranda prepared by Kaye Scholer lawyers who had investigated Lincoln's operations and next quotes a statement made to the Bank Board by Kaye Scholer on behalf of Lincoln. The notice then alleges that Kaye Scholer had material information at odds with the statements that it made to the Bank Board and failed to disclose that material information when it made those statements to the Bank Board. As a result, the notice alleged, the statements made were misleading in context.

For example, the OTS alleged that Kaye Scholer systematically reviewed Lincoln's major loan files over an extended period of months and found a long laundry list of problems in Lincoln's credit risk assessment and loan underwriting. Internal Kaye Scholer files detailed loan by loan what Lincoln was required to do but had not done. Despite this investigation conducted by the firm, however, you will see quoted in the Notice of Charges a series of general statements made by Kaye Scholer to the Bank Board on behalf of Lincoln asserting that, for example, Lincoln "has always undertaken very careful and thorough procedures to analyze the collateral and the borrower." The OTS position was that Kaye Scholer could not make those broad general statements about Lincoln's business practices without at the same time revealing the specific information the law firm had collected from Lincoln's files that impeached those representations.

As I said, allegations of this sort accounted for five of the eight detailed charges in the case. A sixth charge was similar in concept. Kaye Scholer was asked to provide information on the reasons that Lincoln's auditor, Arthur Andersen and Co., had resigned. Kaye Scholer sent to the Bank Board, without comment, Lincoln's securities Form 8–K, which purported to give the reasons for the auditor's resignation. That form stated, among other things, that the auditors' resignation "was not the result of any concern by AA [Arthur Andersen] with [ACC/Lincoln's] operations ... or asset/liability management." The OTS alleged that Kaye Scholer did not disclose, however, that one of its partners had interviewed an Arthur Andersen reviewing partner and had been told that Arthur Andersen had substantial concerns about Lincoln's viability. Those substantial concerns were that Lincoln had a so-called negative spread since its cost of funds and overhead exceeded its income from investments. As a result, Lincoln had to rely on a series of sales of appreciated assets to make up that negative spread.

Not only did a memorandum of that interview exist in Kaye Scholer's files, but about four days before sending the Bank Board the Form 8–K without any comment, that same Kaye Scholer memorandum had been sent to Charles Keating with a letter (also quoted in the Notice of Charges) that said, "[the memorandum] gives some insight into what may have motivated Andersen's decision." The same Kaye Scholer partner who sent that letter to Charles Keating sent the Form 8–K to the Bank Board. OTS charged that the failure to tell us about the interview with the Arthur Andersen partner rendered the law firm's transmission of the Form 8–K to the Bank Board misleading.

Another charge related to Kaye Scholer's retention in 1985 to provide Lincoln with a legal opinion that subsequently was given to the Bank Board and on which Lincoln relied to make many millions of dollars of so-called "direct investments." These direct investments were direct investments by a savings and loan in the equity of a real estate project and thus much riskier than a mortgage loan. In 1985, the Home Loan Bank Board adopted a regulation curtailing the amount of those investments that could be made in the future. The regulation, however, contained a grandfather provision—investments that had been definitively committed as of December 10, 1984, could be made after that date.

Kaye Scholer was engaged to opine on whether certain investments had been committed definitively before that key date of December 10, 1984. One of the issues was whether the board of directors of Lincoln had finally approved those investments before December 10, 1984. Kaye Scholer relied on a series of documents that purported to demonstrate the unanimous consent of the board of directors of Lincoln and that bore dates before December 10, 1984. The Notice alleged that Kaye Scholer had learned, those documents had been prepared in 1985 and were backdated. The OTS position was that Kaye Scholer properly was charged with malpractice for rendering an opinion based on factual assumptions that it knew were incorrect.

The eighth detailed charge against Kaye Scholer involved a mortgage loan that one of its partners had secured from Lincoln. She and her husband had purchased a multi-family building in Manhattan, in which they occupied an apartment. Kaye Scholer represented the partner as borrower at the same time the law firm was doing other work for Lincoln. OTS thought it was ambiguous whether the firm also was representing Lincoln on the specific loan transaction. The loan on its face failed to comply with Bank Board underwriting regulations. For example, OTS alleged that the appraisal showed on its face that the appraiser, who had appraised the property at more than the purchase price, never had visited the property. In addition to not calling that fact to the attention of Lincoln, the Notice alleged that Kaye Scholer failed to perfect Lincoln's security interest in securities that the borrower had posted as additional collateral. The Notice also alleged that the firm's and the partner's participation in that transaction constituted aiding and abetting the regulatory violation of improper underwriting by Lincoln.

Those were the substantive charges. The other two charges were general charges that sought to bring all of these together. In one OTS alleged, for example, that Kaye Scholer violated its fiduciary duty as lawyer to its client, Lincoln. OTS charged that Kaye Scholer had a professional obligation when it learned that officers and directors of Lincoln were engaged in certain unlawful conduct to bring that to the attention of Lincoln's board of directors. Kaye Scholer had not done that.

. . .

V. Discussion of the Professional Issues

A. *Conflict of Interest*

. . .

At Lincoln, you had various law firms dealing simultaneously with the parent corporation, which was not insured, the subsidiary, Lincoln, which was federally insured, and the principal in the enterprise, Mr. Keating, who was an officer of the parent but not of the subsidiary. Who was the client to whom Kaye Scholer owed their professional duties?

Kaye Scholer's client in the representation before the Bank Board was Lincoln. The client was not Charles Keating. It was not the parent company, ACC. The interests of ACC and Keating were not necessarily the same as those of Lincoln. A lawyer in that position must think through whether there is a conflict between the interests of ACC and Keating and the interests of the client that the lawyer is to serve. Was it in Lincoln's interest to make material omissions in submissions to the Bank Board? Was it in Lincoln's interest that the results of Kaye Scholer's investigation were not given to Lincoln's directors, while Lincoln's continued operations generated greater and greater losses? Now, it may have been in ACC's interest, and it might have been in Keating's interest, to conduct the representation in this manner, but was it in Lincoln's? These are among the many issues raised by the OTS Notice of Charges in the Kaye Scholer matter.

How did Lincoln's various law firms resolve these conflicting duties? Perhaps they never did. It is not at all clear that all of Lincoln's law firms recognized the potential for conflict of interest. That may have been a major contributing factor to the claims that a number of firms have faced as a result of their representation of Lincoln.

It was not a unique event in the savings and loan business for lawyers now facing claims either to have failed to distinguish the different interests of parent and subsidiary or, just as importantly, to have failed to recognize that when you represent a corporation, your client is the corporation and not the fellow who is running it or the fellow who controls the stock. Your duty is to represent the interests of the corporate entity. Too many lawyers who have been sued acted as though their duty was to the individual officers of the enterprise rather than to the corporate entity itself.

B. May the Attorney Deceive if the Client Cannot?

Is a lawyer free to lie or to deceive when the client could not do the same thing in the same circumstances without incurring liability? I have yet to hear a coherent argument that says that a lawyer may behave in such a fashion. Our professional rules require us to be honest and to refrain from deceit. Honesty and deceit are not defined with specificity in the literature. Those definitions depend on case by case development.

All agree, I believe, that a lawyer may not lie. Nevertheless, there is disagreement over the lawyer's freedom to deceive by material omissions. I am hard pressed, however, to understand how we can claim that a lawyer is free to deceive a third party when the client could not. If that were the rule, if a lawyer were permitted to do that, what would be left of the liability risked by the client's deception? Any client could overcome that liability simply by hiring a lawyer to do the dirty work for him.

There is another difficulty. The only attempt that I have heard to defend the notion that the lawyer can deceive on the client's behalf rests on the principle of confidentiality and the evidentiary privilege against coerced revelation of certain client communications. The principle of confidentiality and the privilege are not designed to facilitate client deception of third parties. They are intended to promote candid communication between client and lawyer to encourage clients to seek legal advice. The privilege is an absolute barrier to coerced revelation of facts communicated by a client seeking legal help. The privilege, however, does not protect partial revelations of privileged communications structured to deceive. The privilege protects silence, not deceit.

C.   *Intended Illegal Activity of a Client*

Perhaps the most complicated area is the third general area I mentioned. What is a lawyer to do when she finds out that her client is about to do something illegal? Now let me define my terms very carefully. We are not talking about past conduct that has ended, that is, we are not addressing circumstances in which the client has already done something illegal and the illegality is not ongoing. Nor are we talking about an ambiguous situation in which the lawyer in good faith is uncertain whether the conduct would be allowed by the law. Rather, I am talking about a case in which the lawyer has been engaged to give legal advice about an intended future course of conduct and the lawyer reaches the professional judgment that the intended course is illegal.

Let me give you a concrete example. All banks and savings and loans are subject to what is called the loan to one borrower rule. The rule limits the amount that a bank or thrift can loan to a specific borrower. Suppose you are a lawyer who does all the loan closing work for a bank and you are given a loan to close and you know very well from your work with the bank that this loan will place the bank in violation of the loan to one borrower rule with respect to a particular borrower. In that case you have reached a firm, unambiguous conclusion that going forward with this transaction would result in a violation of law. What are you supposed to do?

This question has generated considerable controversy within the bar. Rule 1.13 of the American Bar Association Model Rules of Professional Conduct provides that the lawyer shall proceed in the best interests of the entity and lays out three nonexclusive options for the lawyer. One is to seek a second opinion, one is to try to talk the client out of it, and one is to climb the corporate ladder—go up the chain of command—if need be to the board of directors.

Some would argue that if you induce the client to get a second opinion, and that second opinion agrees with yours, and the client still says "I don't care, I'm going to take the business risk of being caught," you have no need to go further. I disagree. It seems to me you are still in the same position you were at the outset. You have a client who is intending to do something illegal. You had choices A, B, and C, under Rule 1.13. You have tried A, but it did not work; so now you are down to B or C. I would argue that if all else fails, you ultimately need to go up the corporate chain of command to the board of directors, as the highest authority in the client, to try to induce the board to require a change in the intended course of conduct.

Now suppose even that does not succeed. Suppose that you have gone to the board and the client says, "We are still going through with it." Then some additional professional rules come into play.

First, it is clear that you cannot do something as a lawyer that is itself illegal. That is explicit in the Model Rules, and I believe is so in the rules of most states.

If you are engaged in banking work and you help a client implement an illegal scheme, you have committed a violation of law. That is because 12 U.S.C. § 1813 (v) defines a violation to include "any action (alone or with another or others) for or toward causing, bringing about, participating in, counseling, or aiding or abetting" somebody else in violating the law. So if you are doing banking work and you help the client implement an illegal scheme, then you are violating the law, a clear violation of professional ethics.

Suppose, however, in a nonbanking context you are asked to do something that would not itself be illegal, but you know the work would assist your client to implement an illegal scheme. There are those who argue that as a lawyer you may go forward and knowingly assist a client to implement certain illegal activities.

The argument, based on the Model Rules, is as follows. The Rules state that as a lawyer you cannot knowingly assist a client in committing a crime or committing a fraud. Some contend that therefore the Rules inferentially permit a lawyer to assist unlawful conduct so long as the conduct is not criminal or fraudulent. The argument goes inclusio unious, exclusio alterius, a maxim I am sure you all heard during the first week of law school. In other words, if you are interpreting a statute that includes A and B and says nothing of C, the maxim would conclude that the authors of the statute intended to exclude C. What you also learned by the next week of law school is that judges use this maxim when they already have decided what result they want to reach. So, as you can tell, I do not think much of the inclusio-exclusio argument. I think there is another rule of professional conduct that is important and that is the rule I mentioned before that requires lawyers to be honest. The honest lawyer should exist in fact and not as the subject of ironic jokes.

. . .

Let us suppose that you have identified intended illegal conduct and you have protested all the way up to the board of directors. After hearing you out, the board of directors decides to go forward, and you say "I won't participate." The board says, "You are fired," or you say, "I resign."

What do you do next? Are you free or have you even an obligation to report what you know about the intended illegal activity to a third party, either to the intended victim or to an appropriate law enforcement agency? These are among the most difficult and contested questions of all. No issue was more controversial than confidentiality when the ABA was reviewing its rules of professional conduct in the late 1970s and early 1980s.

The ABA Model Rules that resulted embrace only a very limited exception to confidentiality: the lawyer is permitted, but not required, to disclose a client confidence to prevent a criminal act likely to cause death or substantial bodily harm. Is this too protective of client confidences? Most states appear to have concluded it is. Rule 1.6 has been the most frequently amended provision in state enactments of the Rules. Some states permit a lawyer to disclose future crimes likely to cause substantial financial, as well as physical, injury; others follow the ABA Model Code and permit, but do not require, disclosure of a client's intent to commit "any crime;" and still others require disclosure of intended crimes, or intended crimes that will cause serious bodily injury or substantial harm.

The diversity among the state codes indicates that the controversy by and large remains unresolved, although the fate of Model Rule 1.6 in the states suggests that the opportunity for disclosure must extend beyond that recognized by the Model Rules. One lawyer gave this example of the disarray in the rules: If you are in Wilmington, Delaware, confronted by a client's intended fraudulent conduct that will likely cause substantial financial harm, and you practice law also in Pennsylvania and New Jersey, you are subject to three different rules. New Jersey requires disclosure to the proper authorities. Delaware forbids disclosure. Pennsylvania permits but does not require disclosure.

I tend to strike the balance in favor of encouraging candor between lawyer and client. To me, client confidentiality is a principle of utmost importance. In the end, we can do our job as lawyers only if we can have fully candid and open discussions with our clients about their circumstances and their plans. I have great concern about a client's willingness to be open and to consult if he or she cannot be certain that the lawyer will preserve the confidence.

My own view is that the best way to maximize the degree of client compliance with the law is to preserve confidences but also to make clear, both within the profession and to clients and the society at large, that a lawyer may have no role in assisting unlawful conduct. The clients will secure the best legal advice because their lawyer will have access to a fuller picture of the client's circumstances and purposes. The lawyer then will be in the best position to develop a course of action that conforms to the law while advancing the client's interests. The lawyer will have a stronger chance of persuading a client to conform to the law. . . .

Notes

1.   Many articles have been written about the *Kaye Scholer* case. For a sampling, see 66 S. Cal. L. Rev. (1993) (symposium edition on *Kaye Scholer*); Richard W. Painter, Game–Theoretic and Contractarian Paradigms in the Uneasy Relationship between Regulators and Regulatory Lawyers, 65 Fordham L. Rev. 149 (1996); Jonathan R. Macey & Geoffrey P. Miller, Reflections on Professional Responsibility in a Regulatory State, 63 Geo. Wash. L. Rev. 1105 (1995). For a more detailed discussion of the background of the case, see Susan Beck & Michael Orey, They Got What They Deserved, Am. Lawyer, May 1992.

2.   Because Kaye Scholer settled the case before responding to the charges, the OTS allegations were never tested. Some of the arguments that Kaye Scholer might have made were reported in articles published around the time of the settlement. For example, on the allegation that Kaye Scholer misled the regulators about the cause of Arthur Andersen's resignation by omitting negative statements made by Arthur Andersen about Lincoln, the Wall Street Journal reported:

> . . . Kaye Scholer lawyers recount [that] Mr. Fishbein had determined the [Andersen] partner's remarks didn't really contradict the official statement. [Also], the bank board never asked Mr. Fishbein if he had any information that would cast doubt on the official statement. Finally, Mr. Fishbein reasoned, since the regulators theoretically had access to Lincoln's files and advisers, they shouldn't also be entitled to the work product of Lincoln's lawyers. (Regulators say they were denied independent access to the files.)

Amy Stevens & Paulette Thomas, Legal Crisis: How a Big Law Firm Was Brought to Its Knees by Zealous Regulators, Wall St. J., Mar. 13, 1992, A1.

3.   Consider the conflict of interest charge against Kaye Scholer. Did Lincoln and its holding company really have conflicting interests? Don't both organizations have an interest in complying with bank regulations and fiduciary obligations? Didn't the holding company have an interest in making sure the subsidiary complied with the law? If there was a conflict, was it one a client's consent could cure? Who would give that consent?

4.   Is Weinstein's principle—that the lawyer cannot deceive if the client cannot—limited to cases in which the lawyer is acting as sole agent of the client? If not, why does he consider the fact that Kaye Scholer insisted that all requests for information from Lincoln go through the firm so important? If the principle is limited to the sole agent situation, is it stated too broadly? Does the same principle' apply in litigation as in transactional settings?

5.   Despite his defense of his agency's actions in *Kaye Scholer*, Weinstein nevertheless endorses a strict rule on confidentiality on the traditional ground that without such a rule, clients or their agents would be reluctant to talk to lawyers. How does this square with Cole's description of the limita-

tions on the attorney-client privilege, p. 163? Given his first-hand knowledge of lawyer misbehavior, why is Weinstein so convinced that the balance between deterring lawyer assistance in corporate wrongdoing and encouraging client communication should be struck in favor of confidentiality? Isn't it possible that what would *really* make clients not reveal things to their lawyers would be if the lawyers said no to the clients too often? Surely, though, Weinstein and others advocating this position would not argue that lawyers should allow some illegal behavior because otherwise clients might not tell them everything.

Chapter III: Confidentiality

Lawyers and Confidentiality*
DANIEL R. FISCHEL

Confidentiality is the bedrock principle of legal ethics. According to representatives of the legal profession, the duty is nearly absolute. Lawyers who learn information while representing a client are required to maintain secrecy (absent client consent to disclosure), except in the most unusual and extraordinary circumstances. If an attorney obtains information from a client that, if disclosed, would prevent another person from being falsely convicted of murder and sentenced to death, he or she must remain silent, even if the disclosure would not implicate the client in the crime. The same duty of silence remains if the attorney learns of kidnapping plans in a contested child custody case. Attorneys who violate the confidentiality norm are subject to sanctions, including, potentially, disbarment and malpractice suits.

Lawyers are not the only people in society who learn secrets. Friends, partners, relatives, and business associates, among countless others, learn private information, frequently with the express or implied understanding that the information will be kept confidential. No doubt these other groups also face the occasional dilemma of whether to maintain confidentiality or to disclose the information in order to prevent harm to a third party.[5] ... [R]egardless of what nonlawyers would

---

* © 1998 University of Chicago. Reprinted by permission from 65 U. Chi. L. Rev. 1 (1998).

5. The Restatement (Second) of Agency § 395 comment f (1958), for example, provides that an agent is "privileged to reveal information confidentially acquired by him in the course of his agency in the protection of a superior interest of himself or of a third person."

147

do voluntarily, they are subject to compelled disclosure by subpoena and face civil or criminal penalties if they refuse. Not so with attorneys, who are protected from compelled disclosure by the attorney-client privilege.[6]

Why is confidentiality so important? The legal profession has a ready answer—confidentiality is necessary "to encourage full and frank communication between attorneys and their clients."[7] But this standard justification, although repeated endlessly, is empty. Why should "full and frank" communication between attorneys and their clients be encouraged?

Why isn't there a greater need to "encourage" disclosure to the falsely accused defendant or the family of the kidnapped child? And why should communications with attorneys be "encouraged" more than communications with close friends, partners, or relatives? . . .

Another way to ask why encouraging communications with the legal profession is so important is to inquire who benefits from these communications. Stated this way, the question answers itself: confidentiality benefits lawyers because it increases the demand for legal services. The legal profession, not clients or society as a whole, is the primary beneficiary of confidentiality rules.[8]

I. How Confidentiality Rules Benefit Lawyers

While legal codes of ethics are relatively recent (the first American Bar Association ("ABA") code was developed in 1908), the attorney-client privilege has existed for hundreds of years. Initially, the privilege was based on "the oath and the honor of the attorney," who needed to be spared from the unseemly task of having to testify in court. Under this rationale, the privilege belonged to the attorney, not the client. Over time, this status-based justification for special treatment gave way to a candid recognition that the privilege made clients more willing to hire attorneys.

The privilege was particularly valuable in early common law England, when parties to a proceeding were not allowed to testify on their

---

6. The attorney-client privilege is a rule of evidence, not an ethical principle of the organized bar. The privilege allows an attorney to resist compelled disclosure even if relevant to a judicial proceeding. According to John Henry Wigmore's classic formulation, the privilege applies: "(1) Where legal advice of any kind is sought (2) from a professional legal adviser in his capacity as such, (3) the communications relevant to that purpose, (4) made in confidence (5) by the client, (6) are at his instance permanently protected (7) from disclosure by himself or by the legal adviser, (8) except the client waives the protection." John Henry Wigmore, 4 A Treatise on the System of Evidence in Trials at Common Law § 2292 at 3204 (Little, Brown 1905) (emphasis omitted). The privilege is narrower than the ethical duty of confidentiality, which prevents disclosure of all information learned about a client during representation, whether or not the information was communicated to or from the client. See Model Rule 1.6(a).

7. Upjohn Co. v. United States, 449 U.S. 383, 389 (1981).

8. I use the term "confidentiality rules" to refer to the ethical duty of confidentiality, the attorney-client privilege, and the work product doctrine in both civil and criminal contexts. Where appropriate, I discuss the doctrines and contexts separately.

own behalf. Parties could either argue their own cases or hire attorneys to do so for them. As law became more complex—perhaps due to attorneys' efforts—hiring attorneys who specialized in the law became the more attractive option. However, parties who had something to hide would naturally be reluctant to hire attorneys if no confidentiality privilege existed. Because the party could not testify, the negative information would remain secret unless disclosed by someone else, such as the client's attorney. The privilege solved this problem and gave clients with something to hide the incentive to hire attorneys and not risk disclosure....

What is the effect of the privilege now that clients are not only permitted, but required to testify, at least in civil cases? ... Because clients can now be compelled to testify under oath, information known exclusively to them is likely to be revealed, whether or not a privilege exists. At the same time, substantive and procedural rules have become even more complex, making self-representation an unrealistic option in most cases. While attorneys are going to be hired in any event, the legal profession still benefits from confidentiality rules. Sometimes confidentiality rules enable a client to violate a law or regulation and escape detection (and thereby avoid the need to testify). Other times confidentiality rules give lawyers a competitive advantage over other professional groups that operate under different rules. Still other times confidentiality rules enable lawyers to increase their investments in investigation and litigation preparation (with client approval). I expand on these points below.

A. Increased Value of Legal Advice

Confidentiality rules enable clients to obtain the benefit of legal advice without having to bear the cost of disclosing information they would prefer to remain secret. This is particularly true outside the litigation context, where disclosure cannot be compelled. For example, a client who takes an aggressive position on a tax return after receiving legal advice from an attorney on how to minimize the probability of an audit does not want the consultation revealed. The advice is only valuable if it remains secret, because public disclosure by the attorney would increase, not decrease, the probability of an audit. And if an audit does occur, confidentiality is still valuable because it decreases the probability of a more severe sanction, which might be levied if the client's deliberate attempt to evade compliance were revealed. Confidentiality rules, therefore, increase the value of legal advice and hence the demand for lawyers.

B. Substitution Effects

Lawyers offer services that, in certain areas, duplicate those offered by other professionals. Lawyers or accountants can offer tax advice; lawyers or investment bankers can structure defensive tactics in response to a tender offer; lawyers or financial planners can provide estate planning services; lawyers or other investigators can marshal facts from corporate employees in response to a regulatory investigation. Only lawyers, however, can offer the unique advantage that communications with them are privileged. This increases the value of legal advice relative to advice from other professionals, and thus again increases the demand for legal services.

C. Increased Incentives to Investigate

Consider a hypothetical lawsuit between two major corporations. The lawyers for the defendant interview all employees who might have relevant information about the controversy and summarize their findings in written form. The attorney-client privilege protects these notes from disclosure and forces the plaintiff's lawyers to interview these employees a second time. Moreover, the plaintiff's lawyers are prevented from contacting the defendant's employees directly because they are represented by counsel. Contacts are structured and formal, probably through depositions. The defendant's lawyers both prepare employees in advance of any such depositions and are present while questioning occurs. Because they have been interviewed in advance and prepared for anticipated questions, the defendant's employees typically shade their testimony in ways suggested, perhaps subtly, by counsel. And if the employees do not follow "the script" when they are interrogated, the defendant's lawyers can frustrate the examination by making objections or taking breaks to inform a witness how to "improve" his answers to the questions posed. The privilege prevents the plaintiff's lawyers from asking about what was said at the preparation sessions and during conferences in the middle of any actual testimony. As a result, the plaintiff's lawyers will have a difficult time extracting candid responses from the witnesses.

Of course the reverse is also true. The plaintiff's lawyers are able to engage in the identical tactics with the plaintiff's employees to frustrate the factfinding efforts of the defendant. . . .

The work-multiplying effects of the attorney-client privilege for lawyers are exacerbated by the related work product doctrine. This privilege shields from discovery legal research and attorney notes of interviews with nonparty witnesses. As a result, both sets of lawyers must interview the same witnesses and conduct the same research without knowledge of the work being performed by the other side. This duplication merely serves to funnel money from the clients to their attorneys.

Now consider what the situation would be like without privileges (but with discovery). Both sides would have access to whatever the other generated. The need for duplicative work by two sets of lawyers would be correspondingly reduced. Moreover, the recognition that no right to confidentiality existed would affect the client's incentives to have each set of lawyers investigate in the first instance. Parties would be less likely to incur costs for legal services if they knew their adversaries would then be entitled to the same services at no cost. The effect would again be to reduce the demand for legal services.

Subjecting lawyers to investigation would partially offset this effect by creating a new area of discovery, but this in turn would force lawyers to adapt strategically in order to reduce the value of their output to their adversaries. To begin with, fewer lawyers would work on a case. In addition, other more subtle changes would occur: lawyers would cease writing legal memoranda, they would interview witnesses but not take notes, and they would engage in other tactics to raise adversaries' costs of discovering information. This same adaptive behavior, however, would simultaneously reduce the value of legal output to the party bearing the cost of legal services. Interviews are less valuable, for example, if nobody takes notes. Since legal services would be less valuable, fewer services will be demanded and produced. Lawyers would be clear losers if the attorney-client and work product privileges were eliminated.

D. Use of Attorneys to Avoid Discovery

. . .

Assume, for example, a situation in which a company expects to introduce a new product. The company plans to test the product internally before introducing it formally. However, the company is advised by its attorney that any tests performed internally will be discoverable in any future litigation. The company is further advised that the risk of discovery will be minimized if the attorney is retained to hire outside experts to conduct the testing in anticipation of litigation. Any negative results can be hidden; in fact the client never even needs to know the identity of the expert. Positive results, by contrast, can be placed in the client's files. The legal advice itself is confidential under the attorney-client privilege. Because confidentiality facilitates such "creating a record" schemes in anticipation of litigation, it increases the demand for legal services.

E. Avoidance of Personal Sanctions and Negative Publicity

Attorneys face constraints on their behavior deriving from multiple sources, such as ethical rules, agency law, and various bodies of substantive law. Attorneys, for example, cannot knowingly sponsor perjured testimony. The difficulty, of course, is monitoring when an attorney "knows" testimony is perjured. The most direct evidence of perjury is communications between attorneys and their clients, but this is precisely what is difficult to discover because of the privilege.

Similarly, lawyers as agents face personal liability if they knowingly participate in a client's illegal scheme. But again the key determinant of liability is what the attorney "knew" about the scheme. Confidentiality rules create powerful obstacles to the discovery of attorney participation in an unlawful scheme.

. . .

II.   When Confidentiality Imposes Costs on Lawyers

A.   *The Self-Defense Exception*

The proposition that the near-absolute duty of confidentiality benefits lawyers is subject to one major qualification. Sometimes attorneys become embroiled in disputes concerning their performance as agents. Obvious examples include fee disputes and malpractice suits. Other examples involve claims asserted by the government or third parties alleging that attorneys knowingly participated in, or failed to disclose, client wrongdoing. In these situations, lawyers frequently benefit by disclosing confidential information. But this would be impossible if confidentiality obligations were owed to, and could only be waived by, clients. The legal profession has solved this problem by creating a broad "self-defense" exception to the general confidentiality obligations. . . . The juxtaposition of . . . [that] exception [with the ABA's longstanding resistance to an exception that would allow lawyers to reveal ongoing financial frauds even when the client had used the lawyers services, presumably without the lawyer's knowledge, to perpetrate the fraud,] is striking. Lawyers are permitted (but not required) to disclose information to prevent . . . [acts] that are "likely to result in . . . death or substantial bodily harm." Disclosure of past crimes or intent to commit other types of crimes in the future, such as financial fraud, is forbidden. . . .* [In contrast, the self defense exception] permits disclosure to establish any "claim or defense on behalf of the lawyer" in any controversy, civil or criminal, between the lawyer and the client or between the lawyer and a third party relating to his representation of the client.

. . . [T]here . . . [is no] requirement that the lawyer's liberty be at stake, or even that the lawyer be accused of anything criminal. A simple fee dispute with a client is sufficient grounds to disclose confidential information. The lawyer's interest in collecting a fee is apparently a higher priority than . . . helping a distraught family locate an abducted child. Confidentiality means everything in legal ethics unless lawyers lose money, in which case it means nothing.

. . . In one well-known early case, . . . a court held that an attorney seeking to collect a fee could introduce letters written to him by the defendant, his former client, revealing that the defendant "was engaged in leasing buildings for immoral purposes." The court reasoned that the letters proved that the attorney had provided "advice and consultation" services and that the embarrassment to the client resulting from public

---

* [Editors' Note: The ABA has since amended Model Rule 1.6 to permit disclosure of client fraud.]

disclosure was irrelevant. It is not difficult to envision other situations where this so-called "self-defense" exception can be used opportunistically by attorneys who, having obtained sensitive information with a promise of confidentiality, threaten to reveal the information if a client refuses to pay a disputed bill or threatens to expose malpractice.

Of course, the converse situation might also exist if lawyers could never reveal confidential information: clients might attempt to gain an unfair advantage. The client who instructed his lawyer to pursue a particular strategy that turned out poorly could, for example, credibly threaten to blame the lawyer if confidentiality were absolute—but the self defense exception solves this problem. When lawyers are potential victims of confidentiality rules, disclosure is never a problem.

Professional self-interest is even clearer when lawyers invoke the self-defense exception in response to suits brought by third parties. Here, opportunistic behavior by clients is not an issue, but disclosure is permitted anyway. The leading case on this subject is *Meyerhofer v. Empire Fire & Marine Insurance Co.*,[26] where the court held that the disclosure by an attorney defendant, Goldberg, of confidential client information to plaintiffs' counsel was proper in a class action securities fraud suit. Upon receiving the information from the attorney, plaintiffs amended their complaint to include more specific facts and removed the attorney as a defendant. The remaining defendants, including the attorney's client, objected, arguing that the disclosure violated the attorney-client privilege and the ethical duties of confidentiality. The Second Circuit rejected this argument and upheld Goldberg's right to disclose under the self-defense exception:

> The charge, of knowing participation in the filing of a false and misleading registration statement, was a serious one.... The cost in money of simply defending such an action might be very substantial. The damage to [Goldberg's] professional reputation which might be occasioned by the mere pendency of such a charge was an even greater cause for concern.

> Under these circumstances Goldberg had the right to make an appropriate disclosure with respect to his role in the public offering.

Subsequent cases have extended *Meyerhofer*, holding that attorneys can disclose even before being actually named as defendants to avoid the "stigma" of being formally charged.

These concerns about "damage to personal reputation" and "stigma" would be touching, if not so obviously hypocritical.... Encouraging "candid communications" between lawyers and clients always trumps adverse effects on third parties. But the need to encourage candor somehow becomes less important when lawyers' interests are at stake.

---

26.   497 F.2d 1190, 1194–95 (2d Cir.1974).

B.   *Whistle–Blowing and the Fear of Civil and Criminal Liability*

Attorneys' obligations to keep information confidential (other than the self-defense exception) have been steadily expanding in scope in recent decades. More specifically, attorneys' discretion to reveal client wrongdoing—to "blow the whistle" on client misconduct—has been radically curtailed. While the organized bar has justified expanded confidentiality obligations by emphasizing the cardinal importance of client loyalty, there is an alternative, more self-interested explanation. Lawyers have expanded confidentiality obligations to avoid being sued.

Lawyers' discretion to disclose confidential information to protect third parties was initially quite broad. . . . [T]he Canons of Professional [Ethics, the ABA's first set of model ethics rules, included Canon 41]. . . .

Canon 41 [provides]:

> When a lawyer discovers that some fraud or deception has been practiced, which has unjustly imposed upon the court or a party, he should endeavor to rectify it; at first by advising his client, and if his client refuses to forego the advantage thus unjustly gained, he should promptly inform the injured person or his counsel, so that they may take appropriate steps.

These principles were recodified in the revised Code of Professional Responsibility adopted by the ABA in 1969. Disciplinary Rule ("DR") 7–102(B)(1), like the earlier Canon, required a lawyer to rectify fraud by, if necessary, revealing the fraud to third parties.

In 1972, however, whistle-blowing obligations became more than an ethical issue. That year the Securities and Exchange Commission ("SEC") relied on DR 7–102(B)(1) in its complaint in the widely publicized *National Student Marketing* case,[34] asserting that an attorney who knows his client is committing securities fraud must stop the client or, if unable to do so, must disclose the fraud to the SEC. The organized bar predictably denounced the suit. The drafters of the Code of Professional Responsibility certainly did not intend for the legal profession's own ethical rules to be used by third parties to expand theories of liability against lawyers.

Reaction was swift. In 1974, the ABA gutted DR 7–102(B)(1) by amending it to preclude disclosure of client fraud "when the information is protected as a privileged communication." The following year, the ABA defined "privileged communication" to include all "confidences and secrets" learned during a "professional relationship." The duty to disclose was limited to the virtual null set—information learned by an attorney from a third party "but not in connection with his professional relationship with the client."

By 1977, the ABA had decided to produce a new ethics code, partly to clarify lawyers' whistle-blowing obligations. Like the earlier Canons 37 and 41 and DR 7–102(B)(1), the original draft produced by the Kutak

---

34.   SEC v. National Student Marketing Corp., 457 F.Supp. 682 (D.D.C. 1978).

Commission gave attorneys broad discretion to disclose client wrongdoing. Fearful that courts and regulatory agencies would rely on the broad discretion to disclose provided by ethical rules to justify expanding theories of liability against lawyers, however, the ABA rejected the proposed rule. [As originally adopted by the ABA,] ... Rule 1.6 of the Model Rules, which limit[ed] lawyers' discretion to disclose crimes [to those] "likely to result in imminent death or substantial bodily harm," [was] the narrowest standard ever promulgated by the ABA.

The aim of limiting lawyers' exposure is also evident in the official comments to Rule 1.6. If lawyers discover that their services have been used to further a fraudulent scheme, lawyers are instructed by the Rule to withdraw. After withdrawal, lawyers are permitted to provide "notice of the fact of withdrawal, and the lawyer may also withdraw or disaffirm any opinion, document, affirmation or the like." Lawyers, in other words, are not required to stay with a sinking ship. While disclosure to protect third parties is prohibited, lawyers are free to protect themselves by quitting and "disaffirming" their previous work. No provision is made for the return of fees.

Finally, the Model Rules stress that lawyers' failure to disclose, in the few situations where disclosure is permitted, should not create liability. The "exercise of discretion not to disclose information under Rule 1.6 should not be subject to reexamination." And, if there is any remaining doubt that the purpose of ethical duties is to limit, not create, liability, the ABA made clear that the Model Rules "are not designed to be a basis for civil liability.... Nothing in the Rules should be deemed to augment any substantive legal duty of lawyers or the extra-disciplinary consequences of violating such duty." Nor should liability result when ethical rules compel silence but substantive law requires disclosure. "Whether another provision of law supersedes Rule 1.6 is a matter of interpretation beyond the scope of these Rules, but a presumption should exist against such a supersession." According to the ABA, therefore, attorneys should be protected from liability, whether or not they disclose, whether or not they follow ethical rules, and regardless of what substantive law requires. When these rules against whistle-blowing are juxtaposed with the expanded self-defense exception, it is hard to escape the conclusion that confidentiality rules exist to benefit lawyers. Any other effect is coincidental.

. . .

Notes

1. Fischel for the most part does not consider the role of malpractice and third-party liability suits against lawyers. How might such suits affect his analysis?

2. Fischel does not discuss the crime-fraud exception (or other exceptions, such as waiver) to the attorney-client privilege and work product

doctrine. How would he explain the development of these exceptions? Does the existence of the exceptions weaken his arguments?

3. Fischel suggests that plaintiffs' lawyers and defense lawyers are equally able to frustrate their opponents' efforts to find out the truth through tactics like preparing employees for depositions and blocking the opponents' access to employee-witnesses. But this is so only when the plaintiff and defendant are businesses with employees. If one party is an individual and her opponent in litigation is a corporation, the two parties are not equally able to use these tactics. The ethics rules in most states treat some set of corporate employees (how big a set varies depending on the particular "anticontact" rule in force in the state) as if they were "the client" for purposes of determining whether the opposing lawyer may contact those employees without the consent of the corporation's lawyer. See Model Rules of Professional Conduct Rule 4.2. In contrast, lawyers for individual parties to litigation have no right to prevent (or indeed even to be notified of) their opponents' contacts with witnesses critical to their clients' cases. Thus, in litigation between an individual (generally, but not always, in the role of plaintiff) and a corporation (generally, but not always, in the role of defendant), the tactics discussed by Fischel under the heading "Increased Incentives to Investigate," are not equally available. Does that strengthen or weaken Fischel's point?

4. Fischel says: "Confidentiality rules create powerful obstacles to the discovery of attorney participation in an unlawful scheme." In a section of the article we have not reproduced here, Fischel argues that any decrease in lawyer investigation of the facts that might result from a looser (or no) attorney-client privilege would not necessarily result in less reliable outcomes. Clients have enough incentive to produce "good" information, i.e., information that helps them win. What of clients who might not tell their lawyers helpful information because they mistakenly feared it was damning information? See Ronald J. Allen, Mark F. Grady, Daniel D. Polsby, & Michael S. Yashko, A Positive Theory of the Attorney-Client Privilege and the Work Product Doctrine, 19 J.Legal.Stud. 359 (1990). Fischel says confidentiality is not necessary to correct that problem. All the lawyer need do is explain the law to the client and then the client will realize herself that what she feared was damning was actually helpful. Of course, full advice about the law prior to the client confiding could help clients realize what was damning and give them an incentive to lie about some facts or create false evidence. Perhaps the attorney-client privilege is there to encourage confiding *before* instruction about the law to avoid client construction of facts in the light of the law. Does that make sense? Is Fischel suggesting that we substitute full instruction about the law *prior* to client disclosure as a substitute for the privilege? Is that a good trade-off?

5. There is a postscript that needs to be added to Fischel's recounting of the organized bar's longstanding resistance to disclosing client fraud. In the wake of disclosures of large-scale fraud at companies like Enron and Worldcom, Congress, in § 307 of the Sarbanes–Oxley Act of 2002, 15 U.S.C. § 7245 directed the SEC to issue regulations setting out minimum standards of conduct for securities lawyers, including a regulation requiring lawyers to

report evidence of fraud and other serious breaches of fiduciary duties by corporate agents "up the ladder," to the board of directors if necessary, to get the company to investigate the evidence or take other appropriate corrective measures. The SEC proposed an "up the ladder" reporting rule that included a requirement that a lawyer disclose fraud to the SEC via a "noisy withdrawal," if the board of directors did not take appropriate action in response to the lawyer's report of incriminating evidence. The bar fought back, opposing the "report-out" part of the proposed regulations and advocating a fairly high bar as the trigger for reporting up. The SEC retreated, postponing decision on reporting out and adjusting the trigger for reporting up. See 17 C.F.R. § 205. For a discussion of these events, see Koniak, When the Hurly–Burly's Done: The Bar's Struggle with the SEC, 103 Columbia L. Rev. 1236 (2003). See also Roger C. Cramton, Enron and the Corporate Lawyer: A Primer on Legal and Ethical Issues, 58 Bus. Lawyer 143 (2002).

6. Fischel points out the hypocrisy in the ethics rules permitting lawyer disclosure of client confidential information for purposes of self-defense, but prohibiting disclosure in cases of client fraud. (We note that in the summer of 2003, the ABA House of Delegates, in an attempt to stave off the SEC's proposed noisy withdrawal rule, adopted amendments to Model Rules 1.6 and 1.13 that permit the disclosure of client fraud.) A further manifestation of this (now prior) hypocrisy, not discussed by Fischel, is that to justify the prohibition on disclosure of client fraud, lawyers often argue that if a fraud exception to confidentiality were recognized, a lawyer would be forced to warn the client about the exception before the client said something that might later have to be revealed, which would inevitably lead to clients withholding information. But lawyers never seem to make that argument about the self-defense exception. That is, lawyers do not argue that under the existing self-defense exception, a lawyer is obligated to inform his client that the lawyer might reveal the client's information in the event of a later dispute between the client, or a third party, and the lawyer, even though this would seem to have the same incentive effects on the client. Lawyers do not, so far as we know, have such conversations with their clients now. Why not? One possibility, of course, is that they do not think it is necessary for clients to know about this remote possibility. If so, the same argument would seem to apply to a crime-fraud exception. Another possibility is that lawyers do not tell now because that serves their self-interest: the client continues with the representation and provides full information now, and the lawyer remains fully protected in the event of subsequent litigation. In other words, the failure may be an agency problem. Do you think lawyer behavior is likely to change under the newly revised Model Rules 1.6 and 1.13?

7. Interestingly, Fischel, whose scholarship has concentrated on agency problems within corporations, does not discuss the lawyer-client agency problem or the fact that one of agency law's answers to this problem is the duty of confidentiality owed by all agents. Would he advocate abolishing the duty of confidentiality for all agents or only for lawyers?

8.   In a part not reprinted here, Fischel points out that accountants do not have the same privilege that lawyers do (although Congress did adopt a limited accountant-client privilege after the publication of Fischel's article, see 26 U.S.C. § 7525 (1998)), which is a good thing because accountants are concerned about their reputation for truth and honesty. In light of Enron and related scandals, would he still say that honesty and truth-telling are the main reputational concerns of accountants? Might it not be that their bigger reputational concern is the ability to obfuscate truth?

Perjury: The Lawyer's Trilemma*
MONROE H. FREEDMAN

Is it ever proper for a lawyer to present perjured testimony?

One's instinctive response is in the negative. On analysis, however, it becomes apparent that the question is exceedingly perplexing. In at least one situation, that of the criminal defense lawyer, my own answer is in the affirmative.

... As an officer of the court, participating in a search for truth, what is the attorney obligated to do when faced with perjured testimony? That question cannot be answered properly without an appreciation of the fact that the attorney functions in an adversary system of justice which imposes three conflicting obligations upon the advocate. The difficulties presented by these obligations are particularly acute in the criminal defense area because of the presumption of innocence, the burden on the state to prove its case beyond a reasonable doubt, and the right to put the prosecution to its proof.

[The three conflicting obligations of the lawyer in the adversary system are: first, to learn everything the client knows about the case; second, to hold in strictest confidence what the client reveals; and third, to act with candor toward the tribunal.]

As soon as one begins to think about these responsibilities, it becomes apparent that the conscientious attorney is faced with what we may call a trilemma—that is, the lawyer is required to know everything, to keep it in confidence, and to reveal it to the court.

If we recognize that professional responsibility requires that an advocate have full knowledge of every pertinent fact, then the lawyer must seek the truth from the client, not shun it. That means that the attorney will have to dig and pry and cajole, and, even then, the lawyer will not be successful without convincing the client that full disclosure to the lawyer will never result in prejudice to the client by any word or action of the attorney. That is particularly true in the case of the indigent criminal defendant, who meets the lawyer for the first time in the cell block or the rotunda of the jail....

However, the inclination to mislead one's lawyer is not restricted to the indigent or even to the criminal defendant. Randolph Paul has observed a similar phenomenon among a wealthier class in a far more congenial atmosphere. The tax adviser, notes Mr. Paul, will sometimes have to "dynamite the facts of his case out of the unwilling witnesses on his own side—witnesses who are nervous, witnesses who are confused

* © 1975 American Bar Association, Litigation. Reprinted by permission from 1 Litigation 26 (No. 1, Winter 1975). Professor Freedman has considerably expanded and updated his analysis in Freedman & Smith, UNDERSTANDING LEGAL ETHICS, Ch. 6 (2d Ed. 2002) (Matthew Bender).

about their own interest, witnesses who try to be too smart for their own good, and witnesses who subconsciously do not want to understand what has happened despite the fact that they must if they are to testify coherently." Mr. Paul goes on to explain that the truth can be obtained only by persuading the client that it would be a violation of a sacred obligation for the lawyer ever to reveal a client's confidence. Of course, once the lawyer has thus persuaded the client of the obligation of confidentiality, that obligation must be respected scrupulously.

. . .

. . . The Canadian Bar Association, for example, takes an extremely hard line against the presentation of perjury by the client, but it also explicitly requires that the client be put on notice of that fact. Obviously, any other course would be a gross betrayal of the client's trust, since everything else said by the attorney in attempting to obtain complete information about the case would indicate to the client that no information thus obtained would be used to the client's disadvantage.

On the other hand, the inevitable result of the position taken by the Canadian Bar Association would be to caution the client not to be completely candid with the attorney. That, of course, returns us to resolving the trilemma by maintaining confidentiality and candor, but sacrificing complete knowledge. . . .

. . .

. . . I continue to stand with those lawyers who hold that the lawyer's obligation of confidentiality does not permit him to disclose the facts he has learned from his client which form the basis for his conclusion that the client intends to perjure himself. What that means— necessarily, it seems to me—is that, at least the criminal defense attorney, however unwillingly in terms of personal morality, has a professional responsibility as an advocate in an adversary system to examine the perjurious client in the ordinary way and to argue to the jury, as evidence in the case, the testimony presented by the defendant.

Notes

1. Freedman's argument depends on positing three duties—knowing all the facts, keeping confidences, and candor to the court. What about the lawyer's responsibility under the criminal law and under the rules of ethics to refrain from assisting criminal activity? See articles in Chapter II and Model Rules of Professional Conduct Rule 1.16(a) (lawyer's duty to withdraw when continued representation will violate ethical rules or other law). Isn't Freedman's limiting the lawyer's duties to the three he identifies merely an effective rhetorical device, i.e, when one puts two duties on one side and one on the other, it isn't hard to figure out which side wins?

2. Freedman argues that the case for allowing lawyers to present perjured testimony is strongest for criminal defendants. Doesn't Freedman's trilemma apply equally to civil clients as well? Why then does Freedman

draw the distinction? In another part of the article, Freedman argues that "it is simply too much to expect of a human being ... facing loss of liberty and the horrors of imprisonment not to attempt to lie...." Are clients in civil cases really so different?

3. Freedman's article posits (in an omitted portion) a defendant falsely accused of robbery whose truthful testimony about his whereabouts (i.e., that he was near the scene at the time of the crime) might lead the jury to convict him. By positing this case, Freedman presents a scenario in which lying seems not only reasonable, but, perhaps more important, not a clear moral wrong. Is this scenario likely to be the typical one faced by criminal defense lawyers? If, in fact, most criminal defendants perjure themselves for less defensible reasons, does that affect Freedman's argument? Even if Freedman's scenario is common enough, how is it "known," except hypothetically, that the client has been falsely accused? Would it indeed be reasonable for a defendant in this situation to lie?

4. What dangers are there for the innocent defendant who lies and is thought by the fact-finder to have lied? Even if the defendant is morally justified in lying, is the lawyer morally justified in assisting the lie? If morally justified, should the lawyer be ethically required, or merely given the discretion to assist the perjury? Should the lawyer be permitted to assist only those clients whom the lawyer knows/believes/reasonably believes are morally justified in lying? Would it be acceptable for lawyers to "judge" their clients in that way? See Carl M. Selinger, The Perry Mason Perspective and Others: A Critique of Reductionist Thinking about the Ethics of Untruthful Practices by Lawyers for "Innocent" Defendants, 6 Hofstra L. Rev. 631 (1978) (on the moral perspective a rulemaker should adopt in fashioning a rule and how it differs from the moral perspective a lawyer in the situation might be justified in adopting).

5. If Freedman's main concern is the criminal defendant's right to tell her story, why is his argument not one for freeing the criminal defendant from the penalties of perjury or from the requirement of an oath? This path is the one taken in Germany and other countries using nonadversarial legal systems. A related possibility would be to give a criminal defendant the option of testifying under oath or unsworn. What incentives would such a system create for criminal defendants and their lawyers? Under either the no-oath-allowed approach or the option approach, should it be permitted or required for the judge to inform the jury that unsworn testimony, if false, is not subject to punishment?

6. Would Freedman allow, encourage, or require a lawyer to advise his client on the frequency and difficulty of perjury prosecutions, which in fact are rare and difficult to bring and win (Cf. Pepper, p. 109)?

7. If lawyers should (sometimes) help criminal defendants commit perjury, why should they be prohibited from assisting (at least innocent defendants) through other unlawful means? In other words, is there an important distinction between perjury and other crimes that corrupt court processes, such as bribing jurors or witnesses? In a later article, Freedman argued that perjury was distinguishable because crimes like bribery are

clandestine, usually not suspected when committed, and difficult to detect. Perjury, by contrast, takes place in the goldfish bowl of the courtroom, before a skeptical judge and jury, and is subject to immediate impeachment. Also, when perjury is detected by the court, the defendant faces the likelihood of an increased sentence.

> Further, ... the lawyer's knowledge of the client's perjury is usually the direct outcome of lawyer-client communications about the crime that has been charged. Thus, knowledge of the "future crime" of perjury is inextricably interwoven with the crime that is the subject of the representation. A client's announcement of an intent to kill a witness, on the other hand, is a fact that stands separate and apart from communications about the crime that is the subject of the representation....

Monroe H. Freedman, Client Confidences and Client Perjury: Some Unanswered Questions, 136 U. Pa. L. Rev. 1939, 1951 (1988). Are Freedman's distinctions persuasive?

8.   Model Rule 3.3 prohibits lawyers from offering evidence lawyers "know" to be false and requires lawyers who "come to know" of false evidence already presented to take "reasonable remedial measures, including, if necessary, disclosure to the tribunal." Freedman argues that under this rule, lawyers should be ethically obligated to inform clients at the outset of the representation that incriminating facts may have to be revealed to the tribunal, and that therefore the lawyer should advise the client not to be completely candid with the lawyer (e.g., by telling the client not to say whether the client "did it" or not). Suppose the lawyer says, at the outset, the following: "You do not have to testify, but if you do, you may not present false testimony. I cannot help you present false testimony and cannot protect you if you do." Why is this not sufficient? Would it lead to the adverse consequences Freedman predicts?

9.   Is it necessary to give the client any such warning? If the client has no right to expect the lawyers help in conduct that is felonious, why should the lawyer have to bring the subject up? Lawyers, after all, do not warn clients at the outset of the representation that they will not help the client bribe the judge. Is the pervasiveness of lying under oath the difference? Cf. pp. 150-151, note 6. If the urge (or the reality) is actually so pervasive that a blanket warning is appropriate, perhaps perjury is a lot harder to detect and deter than Freedman suggests when he tries to distinguish it from "clandestine" corruptions of court processes.

Revoking Our Privileges:
Federal Law Enforcement's Multi–Front Assault on the Attorney–Client Privilege (And Why it Is Misguided)*

LANCE COLE

. . .

. . . In *Swidler & Berlin v. United States*,[1] the office of Independent Counsel Kenneth W. Starr sought to obtain the handwritten notes taken by Swidler & Berlin attorney James Hamilton during an initial interview with a client, then-Deputy White House Counsel Vincent W. Foster, Jr., shortly before Foster committed suicide.

Two unusual aspects of this case made for a dramatic confrontation between the public interests served by the privilege and the evidentiary costs it imposes by excluding potentially relevant evidence. First, the case involved that most sacred form of attorney work product recording client communications: an attorney's handwritten notes of an initial interview with a client. Second, the information was sought in connection with a criminal investigation of the President of the United States. The combination of these two factors created a test case with a unique juxtaposition of competing public policy interests: those served by the privilege and those presented by allegations of wrongdoing by the country's chief law enforcement officer. Perhaps surprisingly to those who question the importance of the privilege in our modern legal system, the Supreme Court lined up squarely behind the attorney-client privilege.

Read as a whole, the *Swidler & Berlin* opinion reflects an overwhelming reluctance on the part of the Court to accept a change to existing privilege law that would be contrary to the interest of clients and therefore might undermine clients' reliance on the privilege, as well as their willingness to provide their attorneys with full and frank disclosure of relevant information. In rejecting the Independent Counsel's argument for extending "posthumous curtailment of the privilege" beyond cases involving disputes among a deceased client's heirs, the Court emphasized that the rationale for overcoming the privilege in those cases is that doing so furthers the client's intent.

The Court's concern with protecting the interest of the client in maintaining the confidentiality of communications with counsel was most evident in its response to the argument advanced by the Independent Counsel that after the client's death "the interest in determining whether a crime had been committed should trump client confidentiality." Here the Court focused on the concerns a client might have, beyond concern about criminal prosecution, that could cause that client to

* © 2003 Villanova University. Reprinted by permission from 48 Vill. L. Rev. 469 (2003).
1. 524 U.S. 399 (1998).

withhold information from counsel if confidentiality was not assured. The Court identified concerns about "reputation, civil liability [and] possible harm to friends or family as reasons why a client might withhold information." The Court was unwilling to accept the risk that clients' willingness to confide in counsel would be impaired, even if the exception to the privilege applied only in criminal cases.

The *Swidler & Berlin* Court also expressed concern about injecting additional uncertainty into the privilege's application. . . .

. . .

C. Existing Checks on Abuse and Unwarranted Assertion of the Attorney–Client Privilege and the Work Product Doctrine

. . .

The crime-fraud exception protects against the most egregious class of abuses of the privilege: instances in which a client misuses legal advice to commit a crime or perpetrate a fraud. The Supreme Court has stated that "the purpose of the crime-fraud exception to the attorney-client privilege [is] to assure that the 'seal of secrecy' . . . between lawyer and client does not extend to communications 'made for the purpose of getting advice for the commission of a fraud' or a crime." The rationale for the exception is well established and follows from the policy goals that underlie recognition of the attorney-client privilege in the first instance: the attorney-client privilege is intended to promote the administration of justice, and any use of the privilege that is inconsistent with that end should not be permitted. The crime-fraud exception prevents use of the privilege to protect communications that do not further legitimate purposes and therefore do not promote the administration of justice. It is important to recognize, however, that the exception applies even if the attorney is completely innocent and unaware of the client's wrongdoing; it is the intent and actions of the client that determine whether or not the exception applies. Of course, the exception also applies if the attorney acts in furtherance of criminal or fraudulent activity.

Although the rationale for the crime-fraud exception is widely accepted, the application of the exception in actual cases poses difficulties. As one appellate court has explained, "the crime/fraud exception to the attorney-client privilege cannot be successfully invoked merely upon a showing that the client communicated with counsel while the client was engaged in criminal activity." . . .

The Supreme Court weighed in on the issues presented by application of the crime-fraud exception in 1989 with its decision in [*United States v.] Zolin*[.][155] . . . The focus of the Court's opinion in *Zolin* was not "the quantum of proof necessary ultimately to establish the applicability

155. 491 U.S. 554 (1989).

of the crime-fraud exception," but rather the showing required to obtain in camera judicial review of the privileged communications at issue so that a court can make the determination of whether or not the exception applies. . . . [T]he *Zolin* Court concluded that to obtain in camera review the party opposing the privilege "must present evidence sufficient to support a reasonable belief that in camera review [of the purportedly privileged communications (tape recordings in the *Zolin* case)] may yield evidence that establishes the exception's applicability." The *Zolin* Court also rejected the "independent evidence rule" that had been applied by the appellate court below, concluding that "evidence directly but incompletely reflecting the content of the contested communications" (partial transcripts of the tape recordings) could be used by a court to determine whether in camera review of the privilege communications themselves would be appropriate.

. . .

. . . The relatively low showing required by *Zolin* to obtain in camera review, coupled with *Zolin*'s rejection of an independent evidence rule, means that if law enforcement authorities have credible evidence that legal advice is being or has been misused, they can obtain judicial review to determine if the crime-fraud exception should be invoked. . . .

2. *The Law of Waiver*

The crime-fraud exception to the privilege is only one of several established doctrines that serve to prevent unfounded or abusive assertions of privilege. Another such limitation is provided by the extensive body of law regarding waiver of the privilege. . . . A client can waive the protection of the privilege by voluntary disclosure of the privileged communications or by other conduct, such as partial disclosure, that is inconsistent with subsequent invocation of the privilege. . . .

Several established categories of waiver serve to prevent governmental law enforcement agencies from being disadvantaged by assertions of privilege that are not entitled to confidentiality. For example, if the subject of a civil governmental enforcement proceeding or a criminal prosecution asserts reliance on advice of counsel as a defense, the privilege will be deemed to have been waived and the government will be permitted full access to the privileged communications in which the advice was conveyed. Similarly, if the subject of an enforcement proceeding seeks to make "offensive" use of privileged communications in presenting a defense, such use will be construed as a waiver and the communications will no longer be protected. The rationale for this rule is that "the attorney-client privilege cannot at once be used as a shield and a sword." . . .

. . .

3. *The Common Interest Doctrine*

Like the crime-fraud exception and the law of waiver, the "common interest privilege" or "joint defense privilege" also provides protections against unwarranted assertions of privilege. The common interest doctrine is an exception to the law of waiver in that sharing of privileged information that otherwise would constitute a waiver does not relinquish the protections of the privilege, so long as the parties maintain the confidentiality of the shared information. . . .

. . .

4. *Limits on Work Product Protection*

A final safeguard under existing law should be noted briefly. It is well settled that under [*Hickman v. Taylor**] and its progeny, as well as both Rule 26(b)(3) of the Federal Rules of Civil Procedure and Rule 16 of the Federal Rules of Criminal Procedure, work product protection is not absolute. In both civil and criminal proceedings, a party, including the government in a criminal prosecution or civil enforcement proceeding, can obtain otherwise protected work product by showing "substantial need" and that the information is not otherwise available without "undue hardship." If the government can make this showing to the satisfaction of a reviewing court, work product protection can be overcome. Although this exception to work product protection applies only to factual information and not to "opinion work product," it nonetheless provides another important "safety valve" limiting confidentiality protections for information that in the interests of efficient administration of justice should not be protected from disclosure. If law enforcement officials have a substantial need for factual information and cannot obtain that information from other sources without undue hardship, the present system allows them to obtain such information from opposing counsel after making that showing to a court.

. . .

A. *The Starr Investigations*

Perhaps the most widely publicized governmental attacks on the privilege in recent years have been the actions of the Office of Independent Counsel Kenneth W. Starr. Starr's office fought vigorously to overcome assertions of attorney-client privilege and work product protection on a number of occasions during the long course of its several investigations of President Clinton. . . .

. . .

Oddly enough, Starr's most conventional and least objectionable—by current standards of prosecutorial behavior—efforts to overcome the attorney-client privilege and the work product doctrine occurred in the

---

* [329 U.S. 495 (1947).]

context of what probably was the most widely criticized of the several separate and discrete investigations conducted by Starr's office during the course of its more than seven-year life: the Monica Lewinsky investigation. The major events leading up to that investigation are well-known, so it is unnecessary to review them here.

For purposes of this discussion, the key event in the Monica Lewinsky saga is her retention of Washington, D.C. attorney Francis D. Carter to represent her in connection with the Paula Jones lawsuit and to prepare an affidavit stating that she did not engage in a sexual relationship with President Clinton. In early 1998, shortly after Starr's office began investigating the Lewinsky matter, grand jury subpoenas were issued to Carter calling for him to provide testimony and produce documents relating to his representation of Lewinsky. Carter moved to quash the subpoenas, arguing, among other things, that the subpoenas improperly sought to pierce Lewinsky's attorney-client privilege and work product doctrine protection. Starr's office countered with the argument that the crime-fraud exception applied and therefore Carter should be compelled to produce the subpoenaed documents and testify before the grand jury.

Chief Judge Norma Holloway Johnson analyzed the application of the crime-fraud exception to Lewinsky's engagement of Carter to prepare the affidavit.[201] Based upon an in camera submission of evidence by Starr's office, Judge Johnson concluded that the crime-fraud exception was applicable and overruled the assertions of attorney-client privilege. The evidence contained in the in camera submission was sufficient to convince the court that "Lewinsky committed perjury when she signed her affidavit, procured as a result of Mr. Carter's legal advice, and used her false affidavit as part of a broader scheme to obstruct justice." Judge Johnson also concluded that the crime-fraud exception should overcome the assertion of work product doctrine protection because Lewinsky consulted Carter for the purpose of committing perjury and obstruction of justice, and used his work product for that purpose. Based upon those conclusions, the court ordered Carter to testify and to produce the subpoenaed documents.

. . .

In two cases, Starr's office convinced federal appeals courts to reject assertions of attorney-client privilege by government attorneys. . . .

. . .

[The first case] . . . arose out of a Whitewater investigation grand jury subpoena for handwritten notes taken by attorneys in the White House Counsel's office at two meetings with Hillary Clinton. Starr's office took the position that applying the attorney-client privilege to

---

201. In re Grand Jury Subpoena to Francis D. Carter, 1998 U.S. Dist. LEXIS 19497, at 28 (D.D.C. Apr. 28, 1998) (unpublished opinion), aff'd in part and rev'd in part sub nom., In re Sealed Case, 162 F.3d 670 (D.C.Cir.1998).

those meetings "would be tantamount to establishing a new privilege," while the White House took the position that under established privilege law the communications that took place at the meetings should be protected. The federal district court concluded that both the attorney-client privilege and the work product doctrine applied to the notes, and Starr's office appealed to the Eighth Circuit Court of Appeals.[219]

Finding little case law on point, the appeals court relied on "general principles," to analyze the privilege issue, and concluded that the governmental attorney-client privilege should not be available to thwart a federal grand jury subpoena because of the "important differences between the government and non-governmental organizations such as business corporations." The key differences identified by the court were that a business corporation may be subjected to criminal liability based upon the actions of its agents, while a governmental agency like the Office of the President cannot, and that a "general duty of public service" requires government employees, including White House attorneys, "to favor disclosure over concealment." These considerations were sufficient to cause the court to agree with Starr's office that the White House should not be able to rely upon the attorney-client privilege to withhold the notes from a grand jury conducting a criminal investigation.

Employing essentially the same reasoning, the court also concluded that the attorney work product doctrine did not apply to the attorneys' notes. Because the White House attorneys were not working in anticipation of litigation involving the White House, and because the White House as a governmental entity was not the subject or target of the grand jury investigation, the court concluded that the work product doctrine was inapplicable. In the court's view, the "essential element" necessary for attorney work product protection, preparation for an adversarial proceeding involving one's client, was not present because the White House lawyers did not represent Mrs. Clinton in her personal capacity; and, it was in that capacity that she was being investigated by Starr's office.

Finally, the court rejected applying the common interest doctrine based upon the presence of Mrs. Clinton's private counsel at the meetings at which the notes were taken. In what was perhaps the most remarkable assertion in the entire opinion, the court categorically declared: "The OIC's investigation can have no legal, factual, or even strategic effect on the White House as an institution." The court went on to reject demands upon the time of White House staff, vacancies in positions if staff members were indicted, and other "political concerns" as legitimate "common interests" between the White House and Mrs. Clinton in her personal capacity....

. . .

219.   In re Grand Jury Subpoena Duces Tecum, 112 F.3d 910 (8th Cir.1997).

Starr's office's second attempt to overcome assertions of governmental attorney-client privilege involved another White House attorney, Deputy White House Counsel Bruce Lindsey, and a different investigation, the Monica Lewinsky investigation. In seeking to compel Lindsey's testimony about discussions with President Clinton concerning Lewinsky, Starr's office took the position that permitting Lindsey to assert a governmental attorney-client privilege before the grand jury "would be inconsistent with the proper role of a government lawyer," and that President Clinton should be required to rely only upon "his private [attorneys] for fully confidential counsel." The district court concluded that the President does possess a governmental attorney-client privilege for official consultations with White House attorneys, but ruled that the privilege was qualified in the grand jury subpoena context and could be overcome by a showing of sufficient need and unavailability of the subpoenaed information from other sources. The district court concluded that Starr's office had made a sufficient showing to overcome the qualified governmental attorney-client privilege, and the parties appealed to the D.C. Circuit Court of Appeals.

The D.C. Circuit undertook its own analysis of the governmental attorney-client privilege issue,[235] and did not base its conclusions on the Eighth Circuit's prior opinion on that issue. After a detailed review of the relevant authorities, the D.C. Circuit concluded that a federal government attorney should not be permitted to assert the governmental attorney-client privilege in response to a federal grand jury subpoena:

> In sum, it would be contrary to tradition, common understanding, and our governmental system for the attorney-client privilege to attach to White House Counsel in the same manner as private counsel. When government attorneys learn, through communications with their clients, of information related to criminal misconduct, they may not rely on the government attorney-client privilege to shield such information from disclosure to a grand jury.

President Clinton also argued that Lindsey's interactions with the President's private counsel should be protected by the common interest doctrine. In analyzing the common interest doctrine issue, the D.C. Circuit, unlike the Eighth Circuit in the case involving Mrs. Clinton, seemed to accept the proposition that "the President in his private persona" may share some common interests with the Office of the President as an institution, such as concerns relating to impeachment. In the court's view, however, "the overarching duties of Lindsey in his role as a government attorney prevent him from withholding information about possible criminal misconduct from the grand jury." As a result, the D.C. Circuit, like the Eighth Circuit, refused to permit use of the common interest doctrine by government attorneys to frustrate a grand jury subpoena in a criminal investigation.

235. In re Lindsey, 158 F.3d 1263 (D.C.Cir.1998) (per curiam).

. . .

B. *The Marc Rich Pardon Investigation*

. . . On his last day in office in January 2001, President Clinton granted 177 presidential pardons and reprieves. The end-of-term pardons generated enormous controversy and widespread criticism and were the subject of a grand jury investigation conducted by the United States Attorney's Office for the Southern District of New York. The grand jury investigation focused on Clinton's pardons of fugitive international financiers Marc Rich and Pincus Green. Then-United States Attorney Rudolph Giuliani's office had obtained an indictment of Rich and Green in the Southern District of New York in September 1983 for alleged violations of federal income tax and oil price controls, but Rich and Green fled the country shortly before the indictment was returned and never returned to face trial. Because of the manner in which the court addressed the attorney-client privilege and work product issues that arose in the grand jury investigation of the Rich and Green pardons, it is helpful to review briefly the sequence of events that led up to investigation.

Between 1983 and 1999 various attorneys representing Rich and Green sought unsuccessfully to negotiate a resolution of the criminal case, but Justice Department attorneys refused to negotiate unless Rich and Green returned to the U.S. and surrendered themselves to the jurisdiction of the court, which they refused to do. In early 1999 Rich and Green and their legal advisers decided to explore the possibility of seeking a presidential pardon, and in July 1999 Rich retained former Clinton White House Counsel John Quinn, then a partner at the Washington law firm of Arnold & Porter, to represent him. The retainer agreement between Rich and the law firm stated that the firm was being retained "to provide legal services and in connection with Mr. Rich's potential negotiations with the Department of Justice."

Quinn met with Deputy Attorney General Eric H. Holder, Jr. and wrote to then-United States Attorney for the Southern District of New York Mary Jo White seeking to negotiate a resolution of the case against Rich, but, like his predecessors, he was unsuccessful in initiating negotiations with the Justice Department. In March 2000 efforts to negotiate with the Justice Department ceased, and Rich's attorneys and advisers began working on a presidential pardon request. On December 11, 2000, Quinn submitted a pardon petition and supporting memorandum to the White House. After the petition was submitted, Rich's ex-wife Denise Rich and others contacted President Clinton and other White House officials in support of the petition. On January 19, 2001, Quinn spoke directly with President Clinton about the petition, and in response to a request by Clinton subsequently provided a letter confirming that Rich and Green would waive the statute of limitations for any civil claims the government might pursue against them. After receiving the statute of limitations waiver for civil claims, Clinton granted Rich and Green full and unconditional pardons on January 20, 2001, his last day in office.

In February 2001 a grand jury in the Southern District of New York began investigating the circumstances surrounding the Rich and Green pardons. In the course of the grand jury investigation, subpoenas were issued to the attorneys representing Rich and Green for all documents relating to their efforts to resolve the Justice Department's criminal case and to obtain presidential pardons for Rich and Green. The attorneys withheld certain documents on grounds of attorney-client privilege and work product doctrine, and the Justice Department sought to compel production.[275] Two of the arguments advanced by the government are particularly relevant to this Article and merit examination here, because they represent extremely aggressive attacks on the privilege by Department of Justice prosecutors.

The first argument advanced by the government was that the "fugitive disentitlement" doctrine should be applied to deprive Rich and Green of the protection of the work product doctrine because they were fugitives and had no intention of returning to the United States to face the charges against them. Under the fugitive disentitlement doctrine, which originated in the nineteenth century, "the fugitive from justice may not seek relief from the judicial system whose authority he or she evades." The noteworthy aspect of the Justice Department's attempt to use this doctrine to deprive Rich and Green of work product protection is that the two federal courts that had previously considered the matter both held that fugitive status alone was not a sufficient reason to deny a party the right to invoke the attorney-client privilege. Moreover, no case had ever applied the doctrine (which, as noted above, had been in existence since the nineteenth century) to a party's effort to invoke the work product doctrine. Even though the court concluded that Rich and Green indeed were fugitives, the court wisely declined to apply the fugitive disentitlement doctrine because Rich and Green were not seeking affirmative relief and instead were merely asserting the work product doctrine defensively in response to the government's subpoenas.

. . .

The prosecutors' other [argument], . . . however, survived judicial scrutiny and was successful in overcoming the privilege. . . . [T]he prosecutors argued that the privilege and the work product doctrine should not apply because the lawyers for Rich and Green were acting primarily as lobbyists and not as lawyers providing traditional legal services. The court accepted this argument, based upon its conclusions that the pardon process was not adversarial, that the lawyers were acting primarily as lobbyists, and that the "litigation" of the criminal charges against Rich and Green "was over." . . .

275. In re Grand Jury Subpoenas Dated March 9, 2001, 179 F. Supp. 2d 270 (S.D.N.Y. 2001).

. . .

. . . The Corporate Sentencing Guidelines

One of the most significant governmental controls on organizational behavior in the United States is the Federal Sentencing Guidelines for Organizations (Corporate Sentencing Guidelines), which have been in effect since November 1, 1991. These Corporate Sentencing Guidelines govern the way in which corporations and other business entities are sentenced for criminal violations of federal law. A noteworthy characteristic of the Guidelines is the burden they place on business entities to self-police their activities and, as a practical matter, to self-report violations of law. Under the Guidelines, if a corporation pleads guilty to or is convicted of a federal crime, it is subject to much harsher fines and remedies if it has not implemented a compliance program and has not "fully cooperated" with the government's investigation of the criminal activity.

. . .

. . . Mitigation of Sentences Under the Corporate Sentencing Guidelines

Under the Corporate Sentencing Guidelines, . . . mitigating factors will result in a lower culpability score and, consequently, a lower range of potential fines for a convicted corporation. . . . [One] such factor is the extent to which the corporation took the following actions: (1) reported the violation prior to an imminent threat of disclosure or investigation; (2) fully cooperated in the investigation; and (3) clearly demonstrated recognition of the criminal conduct and affirmatively accepted responsibility. A corporation can benefit substantially from taking some or all of these actions. These provisions of the Guidelines obviously exert substantial pressure on a corporation to cooperate with a government investigation of possible criminal wrongdoing. In the years since the adoption of the Guidelines, federal prosecutors have become more and more demanding in their assessment of what constitutes "cooperation" by a corporate offender. The most noteworthy aspect of these heightened prosecutorial demands is the expectation that a corporation will waive its attorney-client privilege and work product doctrine protection, and reveal to the prosecution any information it has collected concerning criminal violations. The information may include attorney work product prepared by the corporation's counsel in an internal investigation and even records of counsel's interviews with potential witnesses.

. . .

. . . In other words, complying with the guidelines may require waiving privileges, which has significant potential adverse consequences for both employees and the corporation in subsequent criminal and civil proceedings involving the same conduct.

. . .

... The New Prison Inmate Attorney–Client Eavesdropping Policy

On October 31, 2001, in the immediate aftermath of the September 11 terrorist attacks, the Justice Department's Bureau of Prisons amended the federal regulations governing "special administrative measures" that can be imposed on federal prison inmates. Among other things, the amendments gave the Attorney General the power, in cases where "reasonable suspicion exists to believe that a particular inmate may use communications with attorneys or their agents to further or facilitate acts of terrorism," to order monitoring of communications between that inmate and his attorneys or attorneys' agents. The regulations apply to all persons in custody under the authority of the Attorney General, which includes both persons held by Department of Justice agencies other than the Bureau of Prisons, such as the Immigration and Naturalization Service, and "persons held as witnesses, detainees, or otherwise."

The regulations do provide important limitations on their use and availability. Most important, the regulations require that the Director of the Bureau of Prisons must "provide written notice to the inmate and to the attorneys involved, prior to the initiation of any monitoring." They also contain a set of safeguards that are intended to ensure that no inappropriate use is made of information obtained through the monitoring. The regulations require that the monitoring will be conducted by a "privilege team" that consists of persons who are not involved in the underlying investigation or prosecution of the monitored inmate. The regulations further require approval of a federal judge prior to disclosure of information obtained through the attorney-client monitoring "except in cases where the person in charge of the privilege team determines that acts of violence or terrorism are imminent." The regulations also provide that "any properly privileged materials (including, but not limited to, recordings of privileged communications) are not retained during the course of the monitoring." The Department of Justice views these restrictions as adequate to protect the interests served by the attorney-client privilege.

Despite the restrictions on availability, use, and retention, the monitoring provisions of the new regulations immediately provoked widespread criticism. Commentators noted that the Justice Department had put the new regulations into place on an emergency basis, without the usual waiting period for public comment. One law professor, who had previously represented a client in an espionage case in which the government sought to monitor his discussions with his client, professed to be "astonished" by the new regulations and predicted that "the chilling effect of this will be positively glacial." Another law professor observed that "monitoring, even with these qualifications, seriously undermines people's constitutionally guaranteed right to counsel of their choice when they are accused of a crime: only the most trusting prisoner will be willing to discuss defense strategy candidly with his lawyer if he knows that agents from the organization that is trying to convict him are listening." ...

. . .

The Department of Justice's defense of the monitoring regulations is essentially that the end (protecting against further terrorist attacks) justifies the means (an undeniable intrusion into the attorney-client relationship and interference with the constitutional right to counsel in criminal cases). Attorney General Ashcroft defended the regulations in congressional testimony by emphasizing the importance of the objectives of the monitoring policy: "None of the information that is protected by attorney-client privilege may be used for prosecution. Information will only be used to stop impending terrorist attacks and to save American lives." Another senior Justice Department official has sought to deflect criticism of the monitoring regulations and other Justice Department actions in response to the September 11 attacks by arguing that "the dichotomy between freedom and security is not new, but it is false." This clever argument seeks to justify intrusions into personal freedoms and infringements of constitutional rights, such as the monitoring regulations, as necessary to achieve the greater "freedom" of security of our persons and absence of fear.

. . . Concern about the extent of the discretion the regulations give to Justice Department officials is heightened by the fact that the regulations do not require or provide for judicial involvement in the decision to monitor attorney-client privileged communications. . . .

. . . [After all, t]he Supreme Court in *Zolin* was unwilling to accept an approach to the crime-fraud problem that would "permit opponents of the privilege to engage in groundless fishing expeditions. . . ." . . .

. . .

Department of Justice regulations provide that "prior approval of the Assistant Attorney General of the Criminal Division is required before a grand jury subpoena may be issued to an attorney for information relating to the representation of a client or the fees paid by such client." The Department's regulations acknowledge "the potential effects upon an attorney-client relationship that may result from the issuance of a subpoena to an attorney for information relating to the attorney's representation of a client" and for that reason require prior approval for all such subpoenas (for both criminal and civil matters). This approval requirement, much like the Attorney General approval requirement in the inmate monitoring regulations discussed above, reflects a judgment by the Department that despite the potential intrusion on the attorney-client relationship, attorney subpoenas are a legitimate investigative tool in appropriate cases. In other words, the law enforcement end justifies the investigative means, despite the risk posed to some of the most important values and policies of our legal system. Having made that judgment, the Department then seeks to prevent abuses and contain damage to the attorney-client relationship by adopting guidelines that limit the availability of attorney subpoenas as an investigative tool—

subject to the discretion of the Assistant Attorney General of the Criminal Division and with the express proviso that the publication of those guidelines do not create any substantive legal rights.

The Department's guidelines do impose significant limitations on the use of attorney subpoenas. They emphasize that (1) an attorney subpoena should not be used to obtain information that is protected by a valid claim of privilege; (2) all reasonable effort should be made to obtain the information from alternative sources; and (3) an attorney subpoena should only be used to obtain information that is "reasonably needed for the successful completion of the investigation or prosecution" and not to obtain "peripheral or speculative information." Most important for purposes of this Article, the guidelines state that:

> The need for the information must outweigh the potential adverse effects upon the attorney-client relationship. In particular, the need for the information must outweigh the risk that the attorney may be disqualified from representation of the client as a result of having to testify against the client.

... A recent survey of reported cases found that federal prosecutors' use of attorney subpoenas and the crime-fraud exception had "significantly increased" between 1995 and 1998....

Notes

1. In the corporate context, there are several limitations on the corporate attorney-client privilege other than those discussed by Cole. Most important, the privilege is controlled by current management (including a trustee in bankruptcy), who may decide to waive the privilege (even apart from the Corporate Sentencing Guidelines Cole discusses) to permit, e.g., prosecution of corporate employees (as happened in the SEC action Cole discusses), or of prior managers. In addition, shareholders bringing a derivative suit may be able to acquire confidential corporate communications with counsel under the *Garner* doctrine, see Garner v. Wolfinbarger, 430 F.2d 1093 (5th Cir.1970), on remand, 56 F.R.D. 499 (S.D. Ala. 1972). It is also important to bear in mind that the privilege does not protect the underlying facts relevant to corporate wrongdoing. The privilege does not relieve any corporate agent from having to answer—in discovery or at trial—questions about what he did or saw others do.

2. The Arthur Andersen case provides a particularly vivid example of the effects of the Corporate Sentencing Guidelines Cole describes. Andersen agreed to waive the privilege and any work product protection with respect to many internal documents and communications, including the now-infamous memo from its in-house counsel that referred its accountants to Andersen's policy on destroying and retaining documents. The government then used these documents to prosecute Andersen after settlement negotiations broke down. Does the Andersen experience suggest that the government should not be allowed to ask for a waiver? That Andersen was imprudent in giving the waiver? That the government should not have prosecuted Andersen after securing the waiver? Or is there some other

lesson to be drawn? Keep in mind that the courts might have held that many of the documents were not protected under the crime-fraud exception to the privilege and work product doctrine.

3. Cole's implicit criticism of Justice Department requests for waiver from corporations would probably have a strange ring to many law and economics scholars. In law and economics terminology, the privileges are just legal "defaults," which parties can "waive" just as they can contract around other defaults. See Painter, p. 58. Moreover, the privileges give "property rule" protection to the privilege holders, which means that the other side must bargain for the waiver and must offer enough of an inducement for the privilege holder to waive. Economists generally view such bargains as beneficial to both sides and, in the absence of third party effects (e.g., perhaps, the effects on corporate employees hung out to dry), beneficial to society. So where is the problem? Critics of the Guidelines point to "coercion" by the government, but how susceptible are large, public corporations—the proverbial "sophisticated actors"—to coercion? If the government's case is overwhelming, it would not need the waiver, but the corporation might want to provide one to demonstrate cooperation. If the government's case is weak, then the government would want the waiver, but the corporation might prefer to take its chances on litigation. Is a corporation reluctant to take such a gamble—perhaps quite prudently—being "coerced?"

4. Cole criticizes the fact that the Holder memorandum leaves open, in a footnote, the possibility that in "unusual circumstances" the government might seek a waiver with respect to communications and work product connected with the government's investigation. This scenario raises the advocacy/transactional distinction discussed in the Weinstein excerpt on *Kaye, Scholer,* see p. 137, and written into the new SEC lawyer rules, see 17 C.F.R. §§ 205.2(b)(3)(ii), 205.3(b)(6)(ii), 205.3(b)(7)(ii). Cole argues that the only cases in which waiver would be appropriate are those related to obstruction of justice, which are already taken care of by the crime-fraud exception. Of course, the crime-fraud exception may be costly to litigate and one of the purposes of negotiating a waiver is to avoid this expense. More important, what if an "advocate" lawyer uncovers evidence of continuing wrongdoing, as opposed to obstructing evidence of past wrongdoing? Would allowing the government to request a waiver in this situation chill legitimate advocacy? How?

5. Cole's discussion of some recent high profile cases involving government lawyers raises the question of whether government lawyers should be treated like other lawyers by the law of lawyering. With the exception of conflicts of interest and a few special rules designed for prosecutors, under the Model Rules of Professional Conduct, including Model Rule 1.13 on representing "entities," they are generally not differentiated from lawyers for private parties. Is that a mistake? Does the Koniak & Cohen critique of Model Rule 1.13 in the class action and small business context, see In Hell [Part II], p. 329, apply to government lawyers as well?

6. Is the Justice Department's terrorist-related policy on monitoring federal inmate conversations more or less defensible than the Corporate Sentencing Guidelines approach to waiver? For a discussion of the government's monitoring policy, see, e.g., Akhil Reed Amar & Vikram David Amar, The New Regulation Allowing Federal Agents to Monitor Attorney–Client Conversations: Why it Threatens Fourth Amendment Values, 34 Conn. L. Rev. 1163 (2002); Avidan Y. Cover, Note, A Rule Unfit for All Seasons: Monitoring Attorney–Client Communications Violates Privilege and the Sixth Amendment, 87 Cornell L. Rev. 1233 (2002).

7. In 2002, the Justice Department indicted attorney Lynne Stewart for providing material support to a terrorist group mainly through facilitating communications between her client, a convicted prisoner in federal custody for, among other acts, involvement in the planning and execution of the 1993 World Trade Center bombing. The indictment alleged that she had provided this support by telling the media that her client no longer supported a cease-fire that his group had supposedly been abiding by in its terrorist campaign and by distracting government eavesdroppers so that her client could communicate through an interpreter messages to be delivered to members of his terrorist group. The Justice Department also charged Attorney Stewart with making false statements to the government by signing affidavits promising to abide by the Special Administrative Measures (SAMs) that limited her client's prison privileges in an effort to prevent him from giving his group marching orders from prison, and promising to use interpreters only for the purpose of providing legal advice. Stewart challenged the indictment on a number of grounds, and in July 2003, a federal district court dismissed those counts of the indictment alleging that the lawyer provided (and conspired with others to provide) material support to a terrorist group on the ground that the statute as applied to the conduct in this case was unconstitutionally vague. The Government had argued that the law's prohibition against knowingly providing material support in the form of "communication equipment" included using one's phone to state the client's views to others. The Government had also argued that providing support through "personnel" could mean offering oneself as a lawyer, at least, according to the Government's oral argument, if the lawyer was "house counsel" as opposed to "independent counsel"—concepts not found in the statute. The court saw in these interpretations a vagueness that could allow prosecutorial abuse and which failed to give potential defendants adequate notice of the law's scope. On the other hand, the court upheld that part of the indictment, charging Attorney Stewart with making false statement to the government by signing the affidavit promising to abide by the SAMs. Stewart argued that the SAMs were unconstitutional and thus she had no duty to abide by them. Perhaps, said the court, but a law's unconstitutionality is irrelevant to the question of whether one lied to the government by promising to obey the law. The court suggested that as long as the government had a colorable (if unconstitutional) basis for asking one a question, one had to answer truthfully or refuse to answer. Lying was, however, not a lawful option.

Next, Stewart argued that her words to the government were a promise of future performance, i.e., a promise to abide by the SAMs, and thus not a matter about which there was a "true" or "false" answer. The court held that a promise to the government could constitute the basis of a criminal charge of making false statements to the Government, as long as the Government showed that the promisor had no intention of fulfilling the promise when the promise was made. Notice that that is a matter upon which proof might be ambiguous, to put it mildly. Does the court's ruling give juries too much discretion?

Finally, Stewart argued that the Government was estopped from prosecuting her for the "false" affidavit on SAMs because it had entered into a deal with Stewart's attorney that promised no criminal charges in exchange for some cooperation. Emphasizing that Stewart's attorney had submitted an affidavit attesting to this deal and the Government had failed to submit any evidence on the matter one way or the other, the judge ordered, as Stewart had requested, an evidentiary hearing to determine whether the Government had broken its word and therefore could not proceed with the prosecution. There is more than a little irony in this last part of the tale. Assuming Stewart can demonstrate the Government promised not to prosecute her, should she then be allowed to show that the Government lied to her and her attorney when it made its promise? If so, should the prosecutor and/or the Justice Department be sanctioned by the judge in some manner for a form of "lying" that they claim is criminal when engaged in by a private lawyer, i.e., making a promise one intends to break?

Chapter IV: Conflicts of Interest

An Economic Analysis of Conflict of Interest Regulation*

JONATHAN R. MACEY AND **GEOFFREY P. MILLER**

. . .

An Economic Analysis of Conflict of Interest Regulation

. . .

A superficial application of economic principles might suggest that ethics rules are likely to be uniformly inefficient. For the most part, these rules are promulgated by the organized bar without substantial input from other interests. In particular, clients (other than large organizations with in-house attorneys) are not strongly represented in the councils which formulate bar rules. One might argue, therefore, that ethics rules represent a naked exercise of guild power, serving the interests of lawyers at the expense of clients or the general public. But this would be an oversimplification. The organized bar, which has principal responsibility for drafting the rules of legal ethics, can enhance its profits in at least two ways: first, by limiting the supply of legal services available in the marketplace (mainly by restricting entry into the practice of law); and second, by adopting economically efficient rules that reduce costs (in part, by lowering the contracting costs between lawyers and clients). Either a reduction in costs or a decrease in supply

* © 1997 Iowa Law Review. Reprinted by permission from 82 Iowa L. Rev. 965 (1997).

will increase the profitability of legal services, and by engaging in both techniques simultaneously, the bar can enhance profits still more and do so over the long run.

The efficiency implications of the supply-restricting and cost-reducing strategies utilized by the organized bar are complex and require careful case-by-case analysis. As a broad generalization, however, it would appear that while supply-reducing rules are likely to be inefficient on balance (because the welfare loss associated with the reduction in supply is greater than the welfare benefit that might be achieved by providing quality assurance), cost-reducing rules are likely, in many cases, to be efficient (because the bar's interest in reducing the cost of providing legal services aligns well with the public's interest in efficient contracting). Thus, while some ethics rules can indeed be understood as serving the interest of the organized bar at the expense of social wealth, other rules, arguably, can be justified on economic grounds. Efficient ethics rules are those that reduce contracting costs between lawyers and their clients by supplying reasonable terms to which lawyer and client would agree, in most cases, if they were to bargain over the issue.

The codes of professional responsibility, in other words, contain a number of "gap-filling" or "default" rules that supply terms to an attorney-client contract. Among the most important of such rules are those related to conflicts of interest.

In part, our purpose is to identify an efficiency rationale for certain rules that have heretofore generally been analyzed from other, principally moral and ethical, perspectives. We believe that economic analysis can provide a satisfactory and coherent explanation for the structure of rules that we observe in the legal ethics area. Through the economic lens the rules in question can be seen as supplying reasonable implied terms to the attorney-client contract in an environment characterized by information asymmetries, agency costs, dangers of ex post opportunism, and associated costs of monitoring and enforcement.

A second purpose of this paper is to suggest an economic framework for interpreting the gap-filling rules in cases of ambiguity. Once the economic function of these gap-filling rules is clarified, they can be interpreted in a fashion that is likely to enhance the efficiency of the provision of legal services. Efficiency-based interpretations turn out to be generally consistent with reasonable moral intuitions, but they are, in some cases, at variance with the constructions that courts or commentators have adopted. Thus, economic analysis of the gap-filling rules of attorney ethics may provide guidance for the interpretation of the rules of legal ethics in hard cases.

. . .

The Economic Analysis of Legal Representation

A. *Legal Representation as an Agency Relationship*

Lawyers function as agents for their clients. . . .

All agency relationships carry the possibility that the agent will be unfaithful. The legal profession is no exception. . . .

The attorney-client relationship is also an agency relationship in economic theory. Every time one person (the agent) acts on behalf of another person (the principal), the agent has an incentive to shirk or serve his own interests, simply because the agent does not capture the full benefit of his labor. In legal representation, as in other areas, the only way to truly eliminate the agency problem is to eliminate the agency: if the client elects to represent himself in a legal matter, the client will capture all the benefits of the representation. But eliminating the agency problem by self-representation often creates greater costs than it saves, because the client is unlikely to be as skilled or knowledgeable at law as the attorney. Furthermore, even if the client possesses the requisite skills, the client may suffer from distorted judgment because his or her own self-interest is involved. No matter how loyal a person engaged in self-representation may be to his or her own interests, he or she will not be better off if the process generates a fool for a client.

Rather than eliminating the agency arrangement, private actors attempt to minimize these inevitable costs of agency by reducing the agent's incentives to act in ways that conflict with the principal's interests. Incentives can be changed in three principal ways, with varied effectiveness and associated costs. The most direct method to change the agent's incentives is for the principal to monitor the agent's behavior and to intervene with an appropriate sanction in the event of shirking or other disloyal behavior. With perfect monitoring, the sanction for misbehavior is set at a level that removes the incentive that the agent would otherwise have to shirk. Moreover, because the agent understands that he is being perfectly monitored and will suffer the sanction if he shirks, it will rarely, if ever, be necessary for the principal to actually administer the sanction. The mere presence of the sanction will be enough to deter the agent from shirking in the first place. In the real world, of course, monitoring is never perfect and incentives can never be set at the precise level necessary to deter shirking; as a result, agents do shirk and intervention is required from time to time.

The second method of controlling agency costs is for the principal to alter the agent's incentives without ongoing monitoring. The principal selects an objective measure of output and rewards (or punishes) the agent depending on performance. Under very restrictive conditions—the principal perfectly defines the desired objective, the agent completely controls whether or not the defined result is obtained, and the structure of rewards and punishments is set so that the agent never has an incentive to shirk, even though the agent is not being watched—the parties could, in theory, perfectly control agency costs without any monitoring of the agent's actual behavior. Again, however, in the real world it is impossible to establish a perfect structure of incentives based on output: there will inevitably be overdeterrence or underdeterrence; it will be difficult, in most cases, to define the desired performance objective with precision; and the agent will have incentives to shirk when the agent believes he can get away with it.

The final method for controlling agency costs uses the sanctioning apparatus of the state. State intervention can reduce the agent's incentives to shirk by threatening the agent with penalties for doing so and by establishing norms that discourage shirking even if the parties have not explicitly specified terms in their contracts that anticipate the agency problem. State intervention can reduce transaction costs by relieving the parties of the need to negotiate their individual contracts; it also might have a valuable in terrorem effect by threatening the agent with an extreme sanction for noncompliance. However, state intervention is subject to drawbacks equally or even more serious than the private mechanisms discussed above: the state may overdeter or underdeter by threatening a sanction that is too harsh or too lenient under the circumstances; it may fail to detect violations or may punish behavior which is, in fact, appropriate; and it may impose inefficient conditions on the parties which they might not have agreed to through private bargaining.

All forms of altering the agent's incentives to overcome the agency problem are, therefore, problematic and costly. The problem for economic theory is to devise an approach that minimizes the sum of all the costs—including the residual costs of shirking by the agent.

Although the attorney-client relationship has the same structure as other agency relationships, it differs from some other agency relationships in the degree to which it is resistant to many of the incentive-altering techniques that reduce (but never eliminate) the agency problem in other settings. The main source of this resistance in the attorney-client relationship is the severe informational asymmetry between the parties. The lawyer possesses a store of specialized knowledge, skill, and judgment that the client lacks. Because clients often cannot distinguish good legal work from bad, the client will rarely be an effective monitor of the attorney's behavior (unless the client is a sophisticated party, such as a firm that employs its own in-house counsel). The client will have only a vague idea of how many hours the attorney should spend on a project under an hourly fee arrangement, whether the attorney has conducted the legal research well or poorly, and whether the attorney is making good arguments or bad ones. Furthermore, when the client has only a small stake in the controversy, as in some class action or shareholders' derivative litigation, any potential monitoring role the client may have becomes vestigial at best.

Agency costs in the attorney-client relationship are also, in most settings, resistant to the use of direct incentives based on performance. Except in cases where results can be obtained reliably and with certainty—for example, a simple incorporation or a name change—it will ordinarily be impossible to specify an objective performance measure that the attorney must achieve in order to obtain a given reward or to avoid a given sanction. Even good attorneys lose cases, and bad ones win them. Moreover, any measure of attorney compensation based on outcomes creates a form of reverse agency problem, in that the attorney's ability to predict whether he or she will achieve a given result depends crucially on the accuracy of the information that the client provides. Just as informational problems hamstring the client in judging the attorney's skills and competence, the attorney's inability to get complete and reliable information from the client about the nature and background of the representation may impede his or her ability to provide effective representation. Incentive problems can be mitigated through contingent fee arrangements, which are a partial sale of the claim to the attorney, but such problems inevitably may remain as long as the attorney has no more than a partial interest in the litigation.

These difficulties with private mechanisms for controlling agency costs suggest the possible utility of government regulation. The government may be able to act as a more accurate monitor or to impose more effective penalties than would be available under a regime of private contract. The government, moreover, may be able to respond to the externalities (if any) that are created as a consequence of the attorney-client relationship. However, government intervention in the attorney-client context is also problematic for a number of reasons. Because of the inevitably fact-specific and individualized nature of most legal representation, the government, as a disinterested third party, is unlikely to be an effective monitor of the parties' conduct. To the extent that the government actually influences the terms of the attorney-client relationship by direct regulation (for example, by prohibiting or limiting certain contingent arrangements), rather than merely enforcing the parties' private agreement, the government may impose conditions that may not reflect the parties' best interests. Government agencies are often subject to budget constraints that may hamper their ability to function as effective regulators. And, government intervention in the attorney-client relationship is especially problematic because the assistance of counsel is a right which the citizen enjoys in order, in part, to obtain protection against government abuse. Thus, government control over the attorney-client relationship is fraught with as many (or possibly more) difficulties as private control through contract.

. . .

C. Complete and Incomplete Contracts in the Attorney–Client Relationship

In this section, we consider the implications of agency problems in legal representation as they relate to conflicts of interest. We present the conflicts of interest rules as gap-fillers applicable when the attorney-client contract lacks express agreements on the question in point.[20]

For starters, it is easy to see why an attorney's conflict of interest represents a form of agency problem. Two main agency problems can arise as a result of an attorney representing clients with conflicting interests either consecutively or concurrently. First, in consecutive representations, the attorney (A) may learn confidential information about a client ($C1$) during the course of the representation that he can then use to $C1$'s disadvantage when representing another party with competing interests ($C2$, $C3$, etc.). Ordinarily, clients do not want their secrets revealed, and, if A discloses $C1$'s secrets to $C2$ in order to enhance A's own stature or increase his fees in the second representation, $C1$ obviously has legitimate concern. Second, in concurrent conflict situations, the attorney who takes on $C2$ may reduce the vigor of representation of his current client $C1$. Because the attorney favors his own interest over those of $C1$, a form of agency cost results.[21] ... But if A gains more from the $C2$ representation than $C1$ loses, a positive joint product results from the undertaking, and the parties (A and $C1$) may be able to share the gains from that product, thus making themselves both better off.

. . .

1. Perfect Contracting Environment

Consider the following hypothetical scenario. A and $C1$ are negotiating for a retainer agreement at time t. A has no conflicting representation at this time. At some point in the future, t1, however, there is ... [a] chance that A will have the opportunity to undertake a conflicting representation for either $C2$ or $C3$, thus imposing costs on $C1$ which would not be imposed if the first representation had never occurred.... These potential losses to $C1$ are due to the following factors: A's prior familiarity with $C1$'s case, which may make him a more informed or effective advocate than other attorneys; A's willingness to use attorney-client confidences obtained in the initial representation to the detriment of $C1$; or, if the representation of $C1$ is ongoing, the reduced vigor of A's representation of $C1$ that results from the existence of divided loyalties.

---

20. We exclude from the analysis here, and throughout the paper, the possibility that the attorney-client relationship will have external effects on third parties that cannot be controlled entirely by means of a contract between attorney and client, even if the contract is perfect and complete. This exclusion is intended to simplify the analysis, which, even excluding externalities, turns out to be surprisingly complex. A more complete theory of the conflicts of interest would have to deal with what are undoubtedly significant third party effects in the attorney-client relationship.

21. Clients may also have an interest in maintaining the integrity of the work-product which their attorneys generate. For example, clients may legitimately expect that an attorney who drafts a contractual term for them will not turn around and seek to nullify the force of the same term during representation of a subsequent party.

Faced with these possibilities, A and C1 have the option of either barring all conflicting representation or permitting all.

It might seem from this scenario that A should be absolutely precluded from the subsequent representations of C2 and C3. After all, the existence of the first representation might be used to the detriment of C1. Why should attorneys, unlike other agents, be allowed to behave in a disloyal way that imposes real costs on their clients—costs, moreover, that presumably benefit a party with whom C1 has an adversarial relationship? It does not require much thought to realize that this intuition is false.... If it were possible to specify a complete contract with respect to the possible future states of the world, A would be able to compensate C1 by paying some amount for the right to engage in a conflicting representation, an offer which would be in C1's interest to accept.

. . .

But what if A's ability to earn profits in the second matter is, in fact, the direct result of his willingness to pass on to C2 or C3 sensitive information obtained from C1 on a confidential basis? The possibility that such conduct will occur does not make it irrational for C1 to consent ex ante to the subsequent representation. Effectively, C1 consents to the appropriation and adverse use of his proprietary information, because C1 receives, in exchange, a greater value than that which she is relinquishing. C1 essentially sells information to A. Social welfare would be served by permitting A to use C1's confidences adversely to C1 in this situation: because both C1 and A are better off, and because no one else is worse off, social wealth is increased.

. . .

2. Imperfect Contracting Environment

... In the real world, ... contracting is neither complete nor costless, and several practical difficulties might affect the nature of the terms of an attorney-client contract that deals with conflicts of interest in a world of second-best. First is the problem of complexity. It is often impossible to specify in advance how different future states of the world should be handled, or even to predict with any degree of certainty what those future states would be. This does not mean that specificity is impossible; in some cases, A and C1 can foresee a possible subsequent representation and, having foreseen it, can determine how it is to be handled. But in the vast majority of cases, future events are not foreseeable. As a result, the attorney-client contract will inevitably be incomplete. The best course of action is for the parties to specify in broad terms what they view as the most important factors; however, such terms are often so uncertain as to be subject to difficulties of future interpretation.

·

Complexity is particularly problematic in light of the danger of opportunism inherent in these types of contracts. In the right circumstances, either A or $C1$ can act opportunistically—by seeking an unbargained-for-consideration ex post. For example, in the case of an attorney, A may seek out representations that are adverse to $C1$ in cases where A and $C1$ would not have agreed to allow the new representation ex ante. Clients, too, might behave opportunistically by attempting to prevent attorneys from representing new clients in situations where A and $C1$ would have agreed to allow the representation ex ante. Because it is impossible to specify all future states of the world in which opportunistic behavior is an option, it will be difficult for A and $C1$ to control all future opportunism by detailed contractual provisions.

A problem related to complexity is that of quantification. In actual representation settings, A and $C1$ may not be able to quantify, with even a pretense of precision, either the amount of their respective gains and losses in the event of a future representation by A of a client with a conflicting interest or the probability of the attorney undertaking such a representation if allowed to do so. It may, accordingly, be exceedingly difficult to settle on an amount of compensation that would cover $C1$'s expected losses from such representation. . . .

Finally, contracts between A and $C1$ regarding A's future behavior suffer from difficulties in monitoring and enforcement. $C1$ does not watch A on a day-to-day basis, especially after the relationship ends. $C1$ will thus often have very limited ability to determine whether or not A is keeping his promises regarding subsequent representation. Even in litigation, where A's subsequent behavior is likely to be most easily observable, A may have opportunities to provide advice behind the scenes, without publicly disclosing his involvement. $C1$ might also seek to make enforcement difficult; particularly, $C1$ might claim that her ex ante agreement to permit subsequent conflicting representation was obtained without full disclosure, and thus is unenforceable. Some courts are likely to view this argument favorably given the differences in sophistication on matters of law that ordinarily exist in the attorney-client relationship.

Accordingly, despite the fact that, in theory, there may be a substantial number of cases in which A and $C1$ would agree, ex ante, to allow A to represent conflicting interests, the difficulties in creating a complete contract make it unlikely that the parties will, in fact, be able to set forth an agreement with clear application to all, or even most, future states of the world. In general, parties do not bargain with their attorneys about the scope of future conflicts of interest. This is not always the case, however, especially when the client is sophisticated in legal matters.

. . .

. . . As we have shown, the principal harm to *C1* from *A*'s representation of *C2* is the danger that *A* will share with *C2* confidences or secrets of *C1*. Thus, one can imagine a rule that simply prohibits (or allows) *A* from disclosing to *C2* confidential information obtained in the *C1* representation. A rule restricted to confidences, however, has several problems in the real world setting. First, in concurrent representation situations the danger of conflicting representation is not limited to the chance that A will share *C1*'s confidences with *C2*, but includes the possibility that *A* will reduce the vigor of his representation of *C1* because of his conflicting loyalties to *C2* (*C2* faces the same danger as regards *A*'s loyalty to *C1*). A rule restricted to confidences and secrets would not cope with this vigor of representation problem. A second problem with a rule restricted to the disclosure of confidential information is that, as a practical matter, A can use *C1*'s confidences or secrets to *C1*'s disadvantage even if *A* tells *C2* nothing about *C1*. For example, *A* might adopt a litigation strategy in the *C2* representation based on *A*'s knowledge of *C1*'s confidences, without informing *C2* of the substance of those confidences. One might imagine a rule requiring *A* to act as if *A* had no confidences or secrets from the *C1* representation, but such a rule would impose an unrealistic, and probably impossible, burden on *A* to act as if he does not know something that, in fact, he does. A third problem with a rule restricted to *A*'s disclosure of information is that it would be extremely difficult to enforce, because *C1* would not be privy to *A*'s conversations with *C2*. In many cases *A* will have the ability to inform *C2* of *C1*'s confidences and secrets without *C1* ever discovering the disclosure.

Given these problems with a rule restricted to information disclosure by *A*, the parties might consider, in addition to an explicit rule on information disclosure, a broader rule that would bar (or, in the alternative, allow) *A* from representing *C2*. If *A* is prohibited from any representation of *C2*, then *A* will not display reduced vigor in the *C1* representation as a result of conflicting loyalties to *C2*; *A* will not have the opportunity to use information gained in the *C1* representation to the disadvantage of *C1* in a subsequent representation; and *A* will have less of an incentive to reveal *C1*'s confidences to third parties.

These two types of rules—disclosure rules and representation rules—can exist separately. For example, one can imagine that, in some cases, *A* would be barred from disclosing *C1*'s confidences or secrets to *C2*, but that *A* would not be barred from representing *C2* as long as he does not reveal confidences. A variety of other permutations are possible. For the most part, however, it turns out that the analyses of disclosure and representation rules are quite similar. We will, therefore, consider disclosure and representation rules together, although on occasion we will distinguish them.

. . .

III.   Some Modifications

So far, we have concluded that, in general, the best default rule for attorney conflicts of interest is one that gives *C1* the right to bar subsequent conflicting representation, subject to ex post renegotiation between attorney and client. In this section, we explore several modifications of this basic rule that might improve its operation as a default rule. It turns out that the existing rules on conflicts of interest, for the most part, operate in a way consistent with the economic analysis.

A.   *Threshold Exception*

One problem with a contractual clause that gives *C1* a right to bar subsequent representation of conflicting interests by *A* is that it will be costly for *A* to contract and negotiate with *C1* for permission and costly for *C1* to consider the matter. In cases where the costs to *C1* from the subsequent representation can be assumed to be negligible, it may be more efficient to allow *A* to proceed with the representation, even though doing so may impose a slight cost on *C1*. For example, if it costs *A* $1 to seek permission from *C1* for a representation that will cost *C1* only $.50, then it would be socially inefficient to require A to seek *C1*'s permission. Neither *A* nor *C1* would prefer a rule ex ante that required consultation and consent in this situation, given that such a rule reduces the joint product of the parties. This analysis suggests that the general rule ought to be qualified by a term that allows *A* to proceed with representation of *C2* in cases where the harm to *C1* from the representation is likely to be slight.

While the parties would probably agree, ex ante, to allow *A* to proceed with representation when the harm to *C1* is slight, this rule would create potential problems as it would be up to *A* to determine whether or not the harm to *C1* is in fact "slight." *A* may not have full information about *C1*'s affairs and so may decide in good faith that *C1* would only be slightly harmed by the *C2* representation, when in fact *C1* might be significantly harmed by the representation. In addition, *A* will not always act in good faith. If *A* wants to represent *C2* without having to seek *C1*'s permission (and, potentially, having to pay *C1* for the right to engage in the subsequent representation), *A* may decide to proceed as if the harm to *C1* is slight, even though *A* knows that it is not slight.

These problems will tend to arise only in marginal cases. In many cases, it will be perfectly clear that either the harm to *C1* from the *C2* representation is, in fact, slight, or that the harm to *C1* is substantial. When A represents *C2*, even though A knows or reasonably should know that the harm to *C1* is substantial, A should not be able to take advantage of a threshold exception to the property rule; by the same token, where it is clear that the harm to *C1* is indeed slight, *C1* should not be able to interpose an objection to the *A–C2* representation. In close cases, however, the uncertainty as to when the threshold rule should come into play can pose problems. There is no easy solution to these difficulties.[33] However, that there may be difficulties in close cases does not in itself rule out a threshold rule allowing *A* to proceed with the *C2* representation when the harm to *C1* is slight.

A more difficult question is whether there should also be a threshold exception to disclosure. One can imagine a default rule that permits *A* to proceed with the *C2* representation when the harm to *C1* is slight, but that nevertheless bars *A* from disclosing *C1*'s confidences or secrets during the course of this representation, even when *A* believes that the harm to *C1* from disclosure would also be slight. There could be several reasons for this distinction. First, because *A* will often lack information about the importance to *C1* of information *A* has obtained in the *C1* representation, *A* may often be in error as to whether or not the harm to *C1* of divulging the information is slight. Because *A* will tend to shade his judgment in favor of the conclusion that the harm to *C1* is in fact slight, it may be better simply to bar any disclosure of attorney-client information in the absence of *C1*'s consent. Additionally, the *A*–*C2* representation reflects the input of *A*'s labor and experience plus the value added by the prior representation of *C1*. In contrast, if *A* discloses a confidence or secret of *C1*, the only value from the disclosure is the value that *C1* has created in generating the information. Thus, there would appear to be less social harm in preventing *A* from divulging *C1*'s confidences or secrets in situations where *C1* has not consented than in preventing *A* from working on the matter altogether.

Another value of an absolute rule against disclosure, coupled with a threshold rule on representation, is that disclosure is potentially more dangerous and harder to prevent. Disclosure can happen very quickly, and once a secret is out, it cannot be taken back. Representation, on the other hand, occurs over time and, if the representation is inappropriate, can be stopped. Thus, a more stringent rule on disclosure, as compared with the rule on representation, may be warranted.

Finally, recall that if *A* fully complies with a rule banning disclosure, there will be little harm to *C1* from the *C2* representation (except in concurrent representation situations where the vigor of representation may be an issue). As we have seen, however, it will be difficult to police the rule prohibiting disclosure if *A* represents *C2*, and, when the harm to *C1* from the *C2* representation is likely to be substantial; thus, a prophylactic rule on representation is warranted. When the harm to *C1* from the *C2* representation is not likely to be substantial, however, it may not be necessary to bar subsequent representation provided that the attorney continues to operate under an obligation not to reveal *C1*'s confidences and secrets without permission. We may assume that due to

33. One approach might be to require A to inform *C1* of the *C2* representation in all close cases, without giving *C1* the power to veto the representation; *C1* would then have the burden of convincing A that the harm to *C1* is more than slight or of seeking judicial relief if A continues with the representation.

monitoring and enforcement problems, A will often disclose *C1*'s confidences or use *C1*'s confidences to her disadvantage in the *C2* representation. If the harm from the *C2* representation is only slight, however, the danger that A will disobey the injunction against disclosure may be sufficiently low as to remove the need for a prophylactic rule on representation in this setting.

In conclusion, the analysis is again not straightforward and is subject to competing inferences. It appears most reasonable that there should be a threshold exception to the property rule on representation— A should be allowed to represent *C2* without *C1*'s permission when the harm to *C1* from the *C2* representation is slight. However, a property rule should apply across the board on the question of disclosure, so that A cannot disclose *C1*'s confidences or secrets to *C2* without *C1*'s consent, even when the harm to *C1* from the disclosure is only slight.

B. *Rules to Combat Opportunism*

Another modification to the rule prohibiting A from representing *C2* without *C1*'s consent might take account of the danger of opportunism. As previously noted, there are two dangers here. First, ... [o]ne could imagine a rule that would allow A to go forward with the *C2* representation when A has incurred significant sunk costs in investigating the *C2* matter, but this would be subject to the serious drawback that it would give A an incentive to incur sunk costs in order to strip *C1* of her property right.

A less sweeping rule would allow A to go forward only if the harm to *C1* from the *C2* representation is slight ... This rule appears well crafted to deal with the sunk cost problem ..., because, in most cases in which A has expended significant sunk costs on the *C2* matter before discovering a conflict with *C1*, the harm to *C1* from the *C2* representation is likely to be slight (otherwise A likely would have identified the existence of a conflict earlier).[35] We conclude, therefore, that a threshold exception to a liability rule can be of help in addressing the sunk cost problem as well.

The second case to consider is one where *C1* has notice of A's representation but sits on her rights until A has incurred significant sunk costs and then interposes an objection to the *C2* representation. *C1*'s delay in this situation is quite clearly for opportunistic motives because, by waiting until A has incurred large sunk costs, *C1* can obtain greater bargaining leverage in the negotiations over consent to the *C2* representation. There would be good reason for the parties to stipulate ex ante that *C1*'s failure to act constitutes a waiver. Ex ante, both *C1* and A would agree to prohibit such behavior because it represents a

---

35. This is not necessarily true, of course; ... attorneys are sometimes sloppy, and even if they do exercise due diligence beforehand, they may not fully understand the conflict rules or the harm against which they protect the former client....

negative joint product, or at least a lower than optimal joint product, that can easily be avoided if *C1* does not sit on her rights.

C. *Additional Sanction for Noncompliance*

A third modification of the simple property rule would be for the law to specify penalties for *A*'s violation of the default rule, above and beyond the availability of an order disqualifying *A* from continuing to represent *C2*. There are at least two reasons why additional sanctions might be advisable. First, if *A* has disclosed *C1*'s confidences or secrets to *C2*, a judicial order of disqualification will do little to help *C1* and may not deter *A* because *A* may have already been paid for the information. Unless *A* fears a sanction in addition to disqualification, A will have an incentive to disclose *C1*'s confidences and secrets early in order to receive compensation before being required to leave the case. Second, as we have seen, rules regulating *A*'s representation or disclosure of information to *C2* are hard to enforce as *C1* does not directly monitor *A*'s conduct. The probability of detection is not high, especially because *A* can disguise his participation in a case by acting as a consultant whose name does not appear on court papers or other documents. If A believes there is a substantial probability that he will be able to represent *C2* or disclose *C1*'s information without being detected, A will likely do so, notwithstanding the presence of rules prohibiting such representation or disclosure, unless the state supplies an additional sanction for *A*'s misconduct.

These considerations suggest that in addition to disqualification, A should fear an additional sanction. What form this sanction should take is a different question. It could take the form of greater-than compensatory money damages in cases where disqualification alone will not make *C1* whole. The sanction could take the form of a fine or other penalty imposed by the state, the benefits of which, if any, would not go to *C1*. Perhaps even more effectively, the sanction could be in the form of reputation loss (and thus the resultant loss of business) to an attorney who engages in an inappropriate conflict of interest representation under the existing rules. If *A* and *C1* had the ability to do so, they would probably agree ex ante to the establishment of such an additional sanctioning regime.

IV. The Model Rules and the Model Code

The analysis of the appropriate background rule so far suggests that, in general, the attorney and client would ordinarily agree—subject to reasonable terms designed to deal with threshold situations, client opportunism, and sanctions for violations—that (i) A will not undertake a conflicting representation without the consent of *C1*, and (ii) A will not disclose or use adversely to *C1* information obtained during the representation. This represents the general pattern observed in the Model Rules of Professional Conduct and the Model Code of Professional

Responsibility, both of which were drafted by the American Bar Association, which impose upon the attorney a strict duty of confidentiality, and generally prohibit the representation of conflicting interests without the consent of the client. It appears that in broad pattern the Model Rules and the Model Code are quite consistent with reasonable inferences about economic efficiency.

What about the conclusions reached in this paper, that the background rule allowing $C1$ to prohibit A from conflicting representation should apply only beyond a certain threshold of harm to $C1$ in order to economize on transaction costs and to police against opportunistic behavior by $C1$? The ethics rules do not contain an explicit threshold exception of this sort, but they can be interpreted according to a rule of reason that permits representation to go forward without $C1$'s consent when the harm to $C1$ is not substantial. Thus, if the differences between $C1$ and $C2$ are not sufficiently concrete to rise to the level of a conflict, the rules do not apply. . . .

On the other hand, parallel to the default term which we have argued is optimal, the Model Rules and the Model Code do not appear to contain any threshold exception for disclosure (as opposed to representation). The attorney is barred from disclosing confidences or secrets of his client (or former client) even if the representation in which the attorney is engaged does not rise to the level of a conflict. If A's disclosure of a client confidence or secret is truly de minimis, it may be unlikely to constitute grounds for formal disciplinary proceedings, but it is nevertheless a violation of the disciplinary rules.

Similarly, the comments to the Model Code and the Model Rules also distinguish rather sharply between litigation and negotiation settings. This distinction makes sense from the standpoint of default rule analysis. In the negotiation setting, both clients are attempting to create value through a process of bargaining which they hope will generate substantial benefits for each of them. Their interests are aligned in that each wants to increase the size of the overall pie, even though they also have a conflict of interest in that each wants as big a share as possible of the wealth so created. Because of the substantial alignment of interests in the negotiation setting, the dangers of harm to $C1$ from the attorney who is also representing $C2$, a party in negotiation with $C1$, may not be as great as would be the case in a litigation setting in which the parties are fighting over the division of a fixed (or shrinking) pie with little or no alignment of interests. Thus, negotiations are more likely to fall below the consent threshold than is litigation.

Another factor of importance in the negotiation setting is the role assigned to the attorney. If A is functioning essentially as a scrivener, recording in proper legal form an agreement being negotiated by the parties on their own, there is little danger of harm to $C1$ from joint representation. By contrast, if A was charged by one or both parties with substantive authority for conducting the negotiation or with providing business advice on the terms of the deal, the risk of harm to *C1* increases. To the degree that the lawyer's role becomes merely technical, there is a reduced danger of harm to the clients from multiple representation and an increased likelihood that a given case will fall below the consent threshold.

The rules on conflicts within law firms also appear to be generally consistent with economic theory. With respect to concurrent conflicts, the rule is one of absolute imputed disqualification: disqualification of any attorney in a firm disqualifies the entire firm. This rule makes a great deal of sense for a small law office, with four or five lawyers. It makes less sense for a very large law firm, especially one with offices in different cities or countries and sophisticated procedures in place for maintaining confidentiality within the firm as well as between the firm and the outside world. At some point, the damage to *C1* from a firm representing *C2* may become attenuated when the firm is very large in size, the attorney who is working for *C2* is different from the attorney working for *C1*, and proper procedures for maintaining confidentiality of information in the two representations are followed. However, it does not appear unreasonable to maintain a rule of imputed disqualification even in large firm cases, given the absence of efficiency losses and the difficulty of identifying situations where the danger to *C1* is sufficiently attenuated as to fall below the relevant threshold. In this context, it is also relevant that, in the large, multi-office law firm, the efficiency gains from allowing *A*'s firm to represent *C2* are often nonexistent. Specifically, when the attorney working on *C2*'s matter is physically separated from the attorney in the firm who worked on *C1*'s matter then any generic legal skills that the firm acquired in representing *C1* will not benefit *C2*. In particular, in the large, multioffice law-firm context, there will be no cost savings to *C2* from the fact that another lawyer in the same firm previously represented *C1*. Because, obviously, if the lawyers are in different offices and are not working together, the human capital skills that were developed in one office are not going to be transferred to the lawyers in the other office. One implication of this is that as the damages to *C1* from the subsequent representation of *C2* becomes more attenuated, so too do the gains to *A* from such subsequent representations.

The ethics codes also adopt what appears to be a rather sensible default rule in such situations. If *A*'s representation of *C1* has terminated, and *A* subsequently considers a representation of *C2*, whose interests conflict with *C1*, there is clearly a danger that the second representation will harm *C1*'s interests. Thus, some rule of disqualification should apply. However, the dangers of conflict are considerably lower in this situation than in the simultaneous representation context because the information A has about *C1* is going to become quickly outdated. The rules capture this effect fairly well by providing that "a lawyer who has formerly represented a client in a matter shall not thereafter represent another person in the same or a substantially related matter in which that person's interests are materially adverse to the interests of the former client unless the former client consents after consultation." The comments to the rule make clear that the term "substantially related" refers to the specific facts of the former representation, not to general similarities in fact or law. Although the rule is not explicitly tied to the fact that the quality of information deteriorates over time, this is its practical effect, as, over time, circumstances are likely to change sufficiently as to make the subsequent representation not substantially related to the former representation.

When it comes to the movement of attorneys from firm to firm, the rules regarding conflicting representations are sensibly less stringent than the rule of absolute imputed disqualification that applies in the single-firm context. As a practical matter, if one attorney from a large firm carried all the firm's conflicts with him when he moved to a different firm, the costs to the second firm of hiring that attorney would be enormous because the second firm would have to turn away much more work on conflicts grounds. A rule of absolute disqualification would thus greatly impair the market for lateral hiring of attorneys. Not only would the rule impose a significant cost on the attorney, but it would also reduce the efficiency of the legal services market as a whole. Moreover, in most cases, $C1$ has little to fear if the attorney in question has not, while at the first law firm, personally worked on any issue involving $C1$. Under the imputed disqualification rule, A would be barred from representing $C2$ while at the first firm, whereas there is no significant danger to $C1$ if the new firm represents $C2$—even if A himself is assigned to work on the new representation. If A had no involvement with $C1$'s affairs while at the former firm, there is little danger that he will carry with him information damaging to $C1$ when he changes firms. The parties, therefore, would not agree ex ante to the application of an imputed disqualification rule in the case of A moving between firms because A has much more to lose from such a rule than $C1$ has to gain.

On the other hand, $C1$ does risk incurring significant costs if A has worked on $C1$'s matters, or otherwise gained actual knowledge about $C1$'s affairs, while working at the former firm and then moves to a firm that represents $C2$. In such a case, it may be presumed that A does carry information potentially damaging to $C1$ when he moves, and the parties, ex ante, would likely agree that $C1$ should have veto power over the new firm's continuing to represent $C2$ in such circumstances. However, because A will no longer have access to $C1$'s files, and because the value of information in A's hands deteriorates over time, the risks associated with subsequent representation are less when the attorney has moved than when he remains at his former firm. One might legitimately question the efficiency of the rule of absolute disqualification of the second firm in this case. If A's new firm implements procedures to control the transfer of confidential information about the *C1* representation between *A* and other attorneys at the firm, and, if *A* is barred from any participation in the *C2* representation at the new firm, it might be more efficient to allow the new firm to represent *C2*, subject to the creation of adequate firewalls to control the risk to *C1* due to A's prior representation.

The Model Rules adjust these competing considerations in a sensible fashion....

We also concluded that, as a theoretical matter, *C1* should not be able to assert the right to bar an attorney from a case if *C1* has deliberately delayed interposing an objection in order to achieve economic leverage against the attorney (or, more realistically in most cases, against the attorney's current client). This appears to be consonant with current practice, under which courts facing disqualification motions in litigation are increasingly skeptical about the bona fides of the parties seeking disqualification and increasingly attuned to the possibility that the disqualification motion is being used for strategic purposes, rather than to protect the former client against a real and substantial risk of harm.

Finally, we concluded that an optimal system of default rules would include sanctions in addition to disqualifying *A* if he inappropriately represents *C2* without *C1*'s consent. The rules of legal ethics do in fact impose such an additional level of sanctions, as the attorney found to have engaged in an impermissible conflict of interest is subject to serious penalties, including loss of reputation, license suspension, or even disbarment—sanctions sufficient to make attorneys think twice about engaging in inappropriate conflicts of interest or disclosing client secrets or confidences to third parties.

In general, therefore, economic analysis suggests that the current rules of attorney ethics are efficient rules to which the parties would agree if they were to bargain ex ante. However, there are two respects in which the conflicts of interest rules, or the overall regime in which the rules are understood, might be critiqued from an economic perspective. First, the professional codes are to some extent in conflict with the economic analysis in their treatment of consent. Nothing in the rules suggests that *C1* and *A* are expected to engage in negotiation for consent to subsequent representations. The implicit model is one in which *A* approaches *C1* and asks for permission. One might wonder, however, why *C1* would grant this permission, thereby giving up a potentially valuable asset (the right to bar *A* from representing *C2*) without receiving something of value in return. The relationship between lawyer and client is, in many cases, strictly a matter of business, often big business—the lawyer or law firm may bill the client for millions of dollars a year. It would appear unrealistic to expect that clients dealing at arm's length with lawyers—especially, as will often be the case in conflict of interest situations, lawyers who no longer represent them—will simply give away this valuable asset very often.

The idea that attorneys should be allowed to pay clients for the right to engage in conflicting representation might seem grossly inappropriate from the standpoint of traditional conceptions of the lawyer's role. The fact of the matter, however, is that if the attorney is not allowed to pay directly, one of two inefficient events is likely to happen: either A will pay indirectly, for example, by acknowledging to $C1$ that he "owes him one" and by performing favors or below-cost services for $C1$ in the future, or A will not seek $C1$'s permission and simply conduct the subsequent representation, on the theory that $C1$ would probably deny it. Neither of these outcomes is particularly desirable, especially because an efficient outcome can be achieved with a market approach. One of our recommendations for reform is to more explicitly recognize the utility of a market-based solution to the conflict of interest problem. It should be considered appropriate for attorneys to compensate their clients or former clients for the right to engage in conflicting representation of other clients.

A second aspect of the current rules that might be challenged from an economic perspective is their implication that some conflicts of interest are so severe that even a fully informed, rational, and sophisticated client could never effectively consent to them.... If the parties have made a full, free and voluntary choice to allow a subsequent representation, notwithstanding the presence of a conflict of interest, it should be conclusively presumed that the representation can proceed, at least in the absence of significant third-party effects.

... It is difficult to justify ... [restrictions on consent found in the ethics rules] in economic terms, however, especially given the fruitful opportunities it seems to offer for ex post opportunism on the part of unscrupulous clients.

Conclusion

In the conflicts of interest area, the applicable ethics rules adopt a remarkably sensible system of background rules to govern the attorney client relationship, subject only to a number of quibbles which, while not insignificant, are relatively minor in the scheme of things. Why would the bar—a group of attorneys—promote and enforce a system of regulation so apparently consonant with the public interest? Simply because, in this matter, the bar's interests are generally aligned with the interests of the public at large. We may assume that very few attorneys have an interest in systematically harming clients by engaging in conflict of interest representations to which the clients would not agree ex ante. There is little constituency in the bar in favor of a system of conflicts regulations that deviate systematically from the optimal default rules. Quite to the contrary, most lawyers would prefer a regulatory system that adopted reasonable default rules in the area of conflicts of interest, as such rules increase the joint product of the attorney-client relationship—an increase in wealth in which attorneys as well as clients can share. Effectively, the existing conflict of interest rules reduce the costs of attorney-client contracting by supplying reasonably efficient default rules that apply in case the parties have not specified the terms of their agreement on the point.

Where the rules deviate most clearly from economic efficiency, we may speculate that the bar gains more in public relations than it loses in revenues. It is doubtful that these rules have much real-world impact; there are very few cases where a representation was found to be inappropriate notwithstanding the client's informed consent. On the other hand, having these paternalistic-sounding rules in place reflects the bar's concern for the public welfare, and thus provides some defense to the widespread public belief that attorneys routinely take undue advantage of their clients.

What remains somewhat mysterious to us is why we do not seem to observe more instances of market transactions in which attorneys pay clients for the privilege of engaging in a conflicting regulation. Although such a market would face obstacles to effective operation—negotiating a price may be difficult, and it may be awkward for an attorney and client to bargain with each other in a situation in which their interests have become adversarial—these difficulties do not appear insurmountable. For example, the parties could agree ex ante to appoint a trusted neutral party who would be charged with determining the price, if any, that the client would charge for granting permission to engage in the representation. We imagine that deals of this type are sometimes struck (perhaps, with $C2$, rather than A, performing the bargaining), but that when they are reached, the parties do not publicize them. These deals probably take the form of an implicit promise for a return of a favor, rather than an explicit market transaction with cash compensation. Alternatively, $C2$ may agree to give up or settle claims against $C1$ in exchange for $C1$'s permission to the representation. Exploring the frequency with which such transactions occur and the terms negotiated by the parties might be a fruitful avenue for future research.

Notes

1. Macey & Miller draw a distinction at the outset between "supply-reducing" ethics rules, which are likely to be inefficient, and "cost-reducing" ethics rules, which are likely to be efficient. How easy is it to tell these apart? More important, don't many ethics rules have both effects?

2. The authors ask what harm could be caused by strictly enforcing the conflicts rules, given that clients can always substitute a lawyer without a conflict. Their answer is that the conflicted lawyer, for reasons independent of the conflict, might be more valuable to the client than substitute lawyers.

Another, complementary, explanation is that if the conflicts rules were strictly enforced, finding an unconflicted lawyer might not be so easy, at least not for the biggest of corporate clients or those trying to take on major corporate entities.

3. Calabresi & Melamed put forth a framework for analyzing disputes between property owners involving use by one that interferes with use by another. See Guido Calabresi & A. Douglas Melamed, Property Rules, Liability Rules, and Inalienability: One View of the Cathedral, 85 Harv. L.Rev. 1089 (1972). Under that framework, in pollution cases, for example, the questions are whether the polluter or the victim has the entitlement to a scarce resource, such as air, and how that entitlement is to be protected. In the full version of their article, Macey & Miller use this framework to analyze lawyer conflicts. But in the lawyer-conflict situation, the analogous question is whether A (the lawyer) or C1 has the entitlement to use C1's information in the representation of C2, and how that entitlement is to be protected. Unlike the pollution case, however, there is really no controversy about who owns C1's information. So shouldn't the possibility of A being given the entitlement be dismissed out of hand?

4. The remaining choice is between protecting C1's entitlement with a property rule (as in a disqualification motion) or a liability rule (a damage remedy). But again, unlike the pollution case, the court is generally not faced with a choice between these remedies. C1 (or C2's opponent in litigation) may decide to bring a disqualification motion. The court will rule on that motion, without regard to whether a damage claim might be made at some later date (i.e., the court does not engage in a question analogous to the "adequate remedy at law" question raised when a party asks for injunctive relief). Are Macey & Miller suggesting that courts should take into account the possibility of a subsequent damage action in ruling on disqualification motions?

5. Macey & Miller's analysis views C1's information as a valuable, and tradeable, asset and contemplates A as a potential buyer of, or broker for, that information. Yet we do not typically see clients "selling" their information in this way. Of course, clients do waive conflicts, but generally when they perceive the risks that they will be harmed as low or nonexistent. We do not see them negotiating lower prices for the use of their confidences against them. In the waivers we do see, the "price" is essentially zero. Yet Macey & Miller argue: "It would appear unrealistic to expect that clients dealing at arm's length with lawyers ... will simply give away [a] valuable asset [the right to bar A from representing C2] very often." Can you explain why clients do what the authors think they will not do?

6. Macey & Miller state: "When A represents C2, even though A knows or reasonably should know that the harm to C1 is substantial. . . . " But the prohibition in the ethics rules does not impose a "know or reasonably should know" limitation; that is, the rule is a strict liability rule. Does Macey & Miller's analysis call into question the strict liability formulation of the conflicts rules? Consider the following language in the conflicts rules: "materially limited," "adversely affected" (a term not in the ABA's latest version

of Model Rule 1.7, but which remains in the rules of most states) and "substantially related." All those terms function as "threshold exceptions," to use Macey & Miller's terminology. Notice too that Model Rule 1.9(c)(1) exempts "generally known" information from the confidences of a former client that a lawyer must keep, providing an exception for disclosures not likely to cause any substantial harm.

7.   Macey & Miller justify the substantial relationship test governing successive conflicts on the ground that over time the quality of information that A has about C1 will deteriorate, and "circumstances are likely to change sufficiently as to make the subsequent representation not substantially related to the former representation." Is that correct? Note that neither Model Rule 1.9(a), nor Model Rule 1.6 has an expiration date. If C2 asks A to represent him in a suit against C1 on a substantially related matter to A's former representation of C1, how often will it matter that the subsequent representation is one year, or five years, or twenty years later? Of course, courts as a practical matter may take the time lapse into account in various ways, but that's different from saying that the rule itself makes or should make lapse of time an important factor.

8.   In discussing imputation, the authors say "obviously, if the lawyers are in different offices [within one large firm] and are not working together, the human capital skills that were developed in one office are not going to be transferred to the lawyers in the other office." Are you convinced? In today's cyberworld does the distance between offices matter? What is Macey & Miller's position on imputing conflicts within large firms? Others have argued that the conflicts rules impose artificial, inefficient limits on the size of law firms, see e.g., Larry E. Ribstein, Ethical Rules, Law Firm Structure and Choice of Law, 69 U.Cin. L. Rev. 1161 (2001). Law firms nonetheless seem to have grown quite large.

9.   At the end of their article, Macey & Miller express the view that conflicts should generally be waivable, and argue that to the extent the ethics rules suggest to the contrary they should be changed. Cf. Painter, p. 58. Is this position consistent with the difficulties in bargaining over conflicts that they identify in the earlier part of the paper?

Triangular Lawyer Relationships: An Exploratory Analysis*

GEOFFREY C. HAZARD, JR.

I. Introduction

This article examines the nature of a lawyer's responsibilities where the lawyer's client has a special legal relationship with another party that modifies the lawyer's "normal" professional responsibilities. This legal relationship is termed "triangular," denoting the coexistence of a linkage of legal responsibility between the lawyer's client and a third person along with a linkage of professional responsibility between the lawyer and the client. The combination results in a special legal relationship between the lawyer and the third person.

This exploration focuses on two types of triangular relationships. The first involves a client in a fiduciary relationship to a third party. The classic example is that of a lawyer representing a guardian in matters relating to the guardian's responsibilities to a ward. In that relationship, the client-guardian has a set of strong and well defined legal obligations. Given these obligations, what are the legal obligations of the lawyer to the ward?

The lawyer-guardian-ward triangular relationship can be diagrammed:

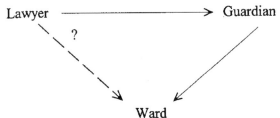

The second type of triangular relationship involves a third party who owes fiduciary duties to the lawyer's client, and the third party rather than the client is the one with whom the lawyer deals ordinarily. The classic situation is that of a lawyer who represents a corporation but who, in the ordinary course of professional service, deals with the corporation's officers, directors, and employees. To simplify terminology, we can treat the corporate officers, directors, and employees as a single category, even though important differences exist in their legal relationships to the corporation. Thus simplified, the corporate lawyer triangular relationship can be designated as lawyer-corporation-officer.

* Reprinted with permission of the publisher, Georgetown Journal of Legal Ethics © 1987, 1 Geo. J. Legal Ethics 15 (1987).

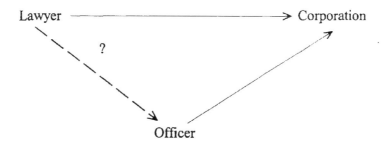

The difference in the vectors of obligation in these two triangular relationships is important. In the lawyer-guardian-ward triangular relationship, the ward is the dependent person and the obligee of the guardian, but the guardian is the dependent person and the primary obligee of the lawyer. In the lawyer-corporation-officer triangular relationship, the corporation is the dependent entity and the obligee of both the lawyer and the corporate officer. This structural difference in obligations can help identify and define the lawyer's role in the two triangular relationships. . . .

Other triangular relationships can be classified into the two basic types:

I.
Classic
Lawyer→Corporation→Ward
Others
Lawyer→General Partner→Partnership
Lawyer→Govt. Employee→Govt.
Lawyer→Union Officer→Union
Lawyer→Director→Corp.

II.
Classic
Lawyer→Corporation→Officer
Others
Lawyer→Partnership→General Partner
Lawyer→Govt.→Govt. Employee
Lawyer→Union→Union Officer
Lawyer→Ward→Guardian

As the foregoing chart depicts, whether a triangular relationship falls into one or the other of the two basic categories depends on which party is the lawyer's client. If the lawyer represents the guardian, for example, the relationship is lawyer-guardian-ward and is of the first basic type. On the other hand, if the lawyer represents the ward, the relationship is lawyer-ward-guardian and is of the second basic type. Similarly, a lawyer retained to represent a corporate office or director rather than the corporation falls under the first basic type, whereas the normal corporate lawyer relationship is lawyer-corporation-director and falls under the second basic type.

. . .

III.   Traditional Concepts for Defining a Lawyer's Responsibilities

A.   *Three Possible Relationships*

Part of the difficulty posed by triangular lawyer relationships lies in the traditional limitations in the definition of a lawyer's responsibilities.

Generally, those responsibilities recognize only three relationships that a lawyer may have. One is with a client; the second is with the court; and the third is with a third party. In substance and orientation, these relationships differ from each other radically. In moral and existential quality, they are strangely alike in their radical simplicity. They characterize the lawyer's "relevant other" respectively as something like friend, father, and foe.

1. Clients

[Hazard describes the lawyer's relationship with a client as legally both amorphous and secret. The lawyer's primary duty to the client is loyalty and the relationship may be analogized to that of limited-purpose "friendship."[1] Beyond the duty of loyalty, however, the lawyer-client relationship is largely unstructured, the only real limit being the "bounds of the law."]

2. Courts

[Starting with the basic proposition that "a lawyer is an officer of the court," Hazard suggests a lawyer owes the court only a minimal duty of diligence and candor. But while the lawyer's substantive responsibility to the court is minimal, the formal aspects of that relationship—the law of procedure and the rules of evidence—are highly detailed and exacting. Thus, where the lawyer's relationship with a client is legally unstructured and secret, the lawyer's relationship with the court is legally structured and visible.]

3. Third Party

The third kind of lawyer's relationship is that with a third party. In general, a third party is entitled to very little from the lawyer. If Brougham's dictum about the duty of the advocate is taken as the measure of the lawyer's legal duty to anyone but the client, a lawyer owes a third party nothing. The law concerning a lawyer's obligations to others is hard indeed, but not quite that hard. Against a lawyer, a third party is entitled to the protection of the criminal law and the law of fraud. . . . Rules against abusive litigation, such as rule 11 of the Federal Rules of Civil Procedure are essentially corollaries of the rule against fraud.

B. Inadequacy of Conceptual Premises

The established conceptual system thus allows for only three parties with whom the lawyer may have a professional relationship: client, court, third party. As we shall see, the most difficult problems in triangular relationships are those in which the lawyer is performing a counseling function as distinct from the function of advocate. In counsel-

---

1. Charles Fried, The Lawyer as Friend: The Moral Foundations of the Lawyer–Client Relationship, 85 Yale L.J. 1060 (1976).

ing situations one thing is clear: none of the relevant others is a judge. Under the established scheme, that reduces the conceptual possibilities from three to two. The lawyer's relationship to the other person—the ward or the corporate officer—must be characterized as either that between lawyer and client or that between lawyer and third party.

This is a stark choice. If the relationship is characterized as that with a client, then the duties of loyalty, zealous partisanship, and confidentiality are fully engaged. To say that when the lawyer represents a guardian he or she thereby also represents the ward, or that when a lawyer represents a corporation he or she also represents its corporate officers, is to implicate very serious practical and conceptual difficulties, indeed contradictions.

[Hazard describes three problems that would arise if we were to accept that guardian and ward were co-clients or that corporation and corporate officer were co-clients: (1) because potential conflict between the two clients (guardian and ward or corporation and corporate officer) is always present, concurrent representation of both would involve an impermissible conflict of interest; (2) similarly, the rules prohibiting representation adverse to a former client in the "same or a substantially related" matter would prevent a lawyer who was deemed to represent both from representing either the guardian or the ward if a subsequent dispute arose; and (3) confidential communications between the joint clients would not be protected either by professional rules or by the attorney-client privilege.]

. . .

The courts have rightly hesitated to embrace the foregoing implications. They have been confused, however, in knowing where to stop or even where to start. They evidently recognize that the lawyer in these triangular relationships has special protective responsibilities to the person who is not the client, but they do not wish to say that these responsibilities include the whole package owed to a client. Under the conventional conceptual system, the alternative is to say that the lawyer's relationship to the other person is that of lawyer and third party. In the guardian-ward situation, this would mean that the ward is merely a stranger. The same would be true of the corporate lawyer's responsibility to a corporate director, officer, or employee.

To treat the ward or the corporate officer as a mere stranger is unappealing and incoherent. It is unappealing because it affords the ward or the corporate employee, insofar as the lawyer is concerned, only the cold comfort provided by the laws of crime and fraud. It is incoherent in the guardianship situation because it calls for the lawyer as agent of the guardian to have an arm's length relationship with one to whom the guardian has an intimate and exacting fiduciary duty. That makes no sense under basic principles of the law of agency. Under the law of agency, the duty of an agent of the principal (i.e., the lawyer representing the guardian) to a third person (i.e., the ward) is a function of the duty of the principal (i.e., the guardian) to that person. To treat the ward as a stranger vis-à-vis the lawyer disregards that interconnection.

In the corporate situation an even more complicated set of difficulties is presented if the corporate officer is treated as a mere stranger. For one thing, the corporate officer is effectively the personification of the corporate client for most ordinary legal purposes. Corporate counsel and the corporate officer must maintain an intimacy that substantially replicates that between counsel and a flesh and blood client. It is simply impossible to hold that a person who is, in fact, a confidential intimate shall nevertheless be regarded in law as a total stranger. Moreover, under the law of agency, some kind of protective responsibility is owed by the principal to the agent in matters within the scope of the agency. A corporation owes a responsibility to its employees, sometimes something like that of guardian to ward. Thus, whatever the relationship between an corporation and its director, officer, or employee, it is not that of one stranger to another.

[Hazard argues that the unmodulated and polarized character of the alternative relationships (lawyer-client and lawyer-third party) are inappropriate when one of the two persons the lawyer is dealing with owes fiduciary duties to the other. The polar notions of friend or foe—the client as friend and the third party as foe—do not reflect the accommodation of competing values required by the situation. "The complex interdependencies in the[se] ... situations do not lend themselves to analysis in terms of friend or foe."]

The inadequacy of these premises no doubt explains why the responses of courts and scholars to lawyer triangular relationships have been so baffled and baffling. Lacking an adequate conceptual system to address the problem, the courts have done what courts always do in such circumstances: They adhere to bad concepts and get poor results, or, as in the *Fickett** and *Yablonski*** cases, they reach what may be good results but improvise on concepts. A variation of this technique is to marshal miscellaneous "factors," factors found in all the problematic situations, and then to maintain that the correct solution depends on "all the factors." ... [See, e.g., the list of factors to be considered in deciding whether shareholders may gain access to the corporation's confidential communications with counsel. *Garner v. Wolfinbarger*.]***

IV. Toward Better Conceptualizations

. . .

Neither the concept of "client" nor that of "third party" appropriately engages the complexities of triangular relationships, even a simple

* [Fickett v. Superior Court, 27 Ariz.App. 793, 588 P.2d 988 (1976).]

** [Yablonski v. United Mine Workers, 448 F.2d 1175 (D.C. Cir. 1971).]

*** [430 F.2d 1093 (5th Cir. 1970), cert. denied, 401 U.S. 974 (1971).]

one such as that of guardian and ward involved in *Fickett v. Superior Court*. The client in such a triangular situation is not a person alone— the A of classical legal hypotheticals, where "A, the owner of Blackacre" does something to or is done something by B. One who has become another's guardian is no longer A but has become "A encumbered by duties to B." So long as the relationship between A and B exists, and for some purposes even after it ends, A is not a legal monad. Rather A is a member of an "institution," (as said in *Yablonski v. United Mine Workers*), that has a "whole purpose," (as said in *Fickett*). In legal terms, a guardian as such is an officeholder constituted by law, by court appointment as in the *Fickett* case or by private contractual designation. So also, and more obviously, the corporate director, officer, or employee is an officeholder constituted by legally sanctioned private ordering, and is a member of an "institution" that has a "whole purpose." As a matter of law, both guardian and corporate officer are not persons but personages, individuals who act in legal capacities.

. . .

The vocabulary and metaphorical geometry used in analyzing the "normal" lawyer-client relationship contemplate an intimate dyad of lawyer and client, facing outward toward an alien and presumptively hostile world of third parties. That vocabulary and geometry misdescribes relationships between a lawyer, a client who is a legal personage, and a third person whose very existence defines that personage. The problem is to develop concepts and vocabulary that intelligibly address relationships where the lawyer must care about two parties.

. . .

A. Client Openly Adverse to the "Other"

There are cases where a lawyer in a triangular situation has the same "arm's length" position vis-à-vis the "relevant other" as a lawyer "normally" should have on behalf of a client. The clearest is where the lawyer, not having been involved previously, is retained to represent a guardian or a corporate officer in litigation concerning that person's performance of duties [such as a proceeding initiated by the ward against the guardian to surcharge or remove the guardian].

. . .

There should be no equivocation or confusion about the nature of lawyer-client relationship and the lawyer's duties in this situation. An action for surcharge is a legal claim against the guardian in his or her individual capacity for alleged wrong committed in the course of an official capacity. The potential financial loss, moral obloquy, and civic disgrace faced by the guardian are real individual interests. Persons with that kind of exposure are entitled to legal representation, which means full service advocacy. The lawyer is obliged to make zealous efforts on the guardian's behalf; hold in confidence information garnered for the representation; and abstain from conflicting representation in the matter.

The same analysis applies where a lawyer, not previously involved, is retained to represent a corporate director, officer, or employee. Ordinarily, that kind of representation is arranged only when there is a significant possibility that the interests of the director, officer, or employee may diverge from the corporation's interests. When this possibility exists, there is also a risk that there will be legal or informal recrimination on behalf of the corporation. Persons with that kind of exposure are likewise entitled to full service advocacy.

The same analysis again applies where a lawyer, not previously involved, is retained to represent the corporation against a corporate director, officer, or employee to redress malfeasance in office. That was the situation in *Yablonski*, where the derivative suit sought to redress the officer's misspending of organization funds. The holding in *Yablonski* that the organization is entitled to the zeal of an uncompromised advocate is correct. . . .

. . .

[Other cases of "arm's length" relationships arise when a lawyer is retained to represent someone nominated as guardian or corporate officer in negotiating the terms of the office and when a lawyer with no prior involvement is brought into negotiations for termination or reformation of the special relationship. In both instances the lawyer is not involved in the conduct of the relationship, but only in negotiations concerning the creation, reformation, or termination of the relationship. In both cases the fiduciary is dealing at arm's length with a beneficiary, and the role of the lawyer becomes the typical one of negotiation or advocacy on behalf of the fiduciary-client.]

B. Normal Protective Relationship

While the positions of the fiduciary and the "relevant other" are openly adverse in some situations, normally the fiduciary's protective responsibility is unambiguous. In the normal legal relationship between guardian and ward, or between corporation and corporate director, officer, or employee, the legal purpose of the relationship is being fulfilled and the fiduciary is conforming his or her conduct to legal requirements.

The lawyer's task in this normal situation is to assist the fiduciary in meeting his or her legal obligations, and to help minimize legal risks to the relationship from outside forces, such as persons with competing claims on the assets or the tax collector. Toward these ends the lawyer supplies advice and employs legally recognized techniques that further the undertaking. Thus, the lawyer provides the forms and procedures for board action in the corporation, for the proprieties where a director has a conflict of interest that disqualifies him or her from voting on a corporate matter, etc. In the guardianship, the lawyer similarly safe-guards the proprieties. The lawyer represents the guardian in taking care of the ward—the "whole purpose of the relationship," to use the phrase from *Fickett*. In the corporate situation, the corporate counsel works with the corporate director, officer, or employee *in taking care* of the corporation's "institutional interests," to use the phrase from *Yablonski*. Neither a "guardianship" nor a "corporation" has material existence or autonomous identity. They are legal events, artifacts of the lawyer's endeavors in the representation. The relationship itself is an evolving legal event that the lawyer's services continuously create.

. . .

[T]he lawyer's responsibilities may well be analogized to multiple representation. The key rules are those of confidentiality and loyalty. In multiple representation, the rule of confidentiality includes all within the group and excludes all outside it. In the corporate situation, the rule of confidentiality applies to information the corporate lawyer obtains from corporate "constituents" in the course of the representation, as does the corresponding rule of attorney-client privilege.[51] The same principle would apply to information provided to a lawyer for a partnership and ought to apply to information received from a ward by a lawyer or a guardian.

Concerning the principle of loyalty, a lawyer may serve two or more clients in the same matter if they do not have adverse interests. In a triangular relationship in the normal state, the interests of the nonlawyer participants are not adverse; both, therefore, may be considered to be clients.

Conceptualizing both the "relevant others" as clients, and the lawyer as engaged in multiple representation, seems entirely natural when the triangular relationship is in its normal state. The question is whether there are reasons for refusing to conceptualize it in this way. Only one reason exists for such hesitancy: the implications that follow if the triangular relationship ceases to be normal and instead becomes antagonistic.

. . . Under standard doctrine, in multiple representation each client has the full rights of a client, including the power over confidentiality and the right to enforce the conflict of interest rules against the lawyer. Thus, if the corporate officer is treated in all respects as a client, then confidences he or she has imparted to the lawyer would not be usable against him or her after the normal triangular relationship has collapsed and the corporation and its officers become legal antagonists.[54] If the

51. Upjohn Co. v. United States, 449 U.S. 383 (1981) (attorney-client privilege covers employee responses to questionnaires and interview notes of counsel).

54. The corporate officer does not have that right. E.g., Lane v. Chowning, 610 F.2d 1385 (8th Cir.1979) (defendant bank's attorney has no obligation to plaintiff-officer to refrain from using information acquired in representing bank).

corporate officer is treated as a client in all respects, upon the collapse of his or her relationship with the corporation, the officer could then insist that the corporate lawyer not represent the corporation against him or her.[55] These are undesirable corollaries and their specter is a weighty objection.

This weighty objection indicates that the multiple representation concept should not operate fully once the triangular relationship has collapsed; indeed, that is the recognized rule. Ordinarily upon collapse of the relationship, the lawyer may continue to represent the person or entity that was his client in the full and formal sense, even though representation entails a position adverse to the other member of the triangle.[56] If both were treated as clients in the strict sense, that option would not be available.[57] The law should continue to recognize the lawyer's authority to continue representation of a guardian or a corporation after the relationship with the other party becomes antagonistic. On the other hand, the possibility that a triangular relationship might collapse into antagonism is an insufficient reason for rejecting the multiple representation analogy while the triangular relationship is still intact. It is also insufficient reason for denying the "relevant other" some of the rights of a full-fledged former client if the relationship does collapse, particularly where the lawyer had not made the ground rules clear earlier.[59]

C. *Ambivalent and Unstable Situations*

A triangular relationship may, then, be analyzed in two ways regarding the lawyer. One of the parties can be regarded as the client and the other as the third party, or both can be regarded as clients. Each

55. The corporate officer does not have that right either. E.g., Meehan v. Hopps, 144 Cal.App.2d 284, 301 P.2d 10 (1956) (attorney not precluded from representing client-corporation against officer where no prior attorney-client relationship existed between counsel and officer).

56. E.g., Commodity Futures Trading Comm'n v. Weintraub, 471 U.S. (1985) (trustee of corporation in bankruptcy has power to waive corporation's attorney-client privilege with respect to communications that took place before filing petition in bankruptcy); Lane v. Chowning, 610 F.2d 1385 (8th Cir.1979); Meehan v. Hopps, 144 Cal.App.2d 284, 301 P.2d 10 (1956).

57. E.g., Opdyke v. Kent Liquor Market, Inc., 40 Del.Ch. 316, 181 A.2d 579 (1962) (attorney who organized and was retained by three man corporation owed fiduciary duty to stockholders, breached fiduciary duty to minority stockholder by buying majority stock to which minority shareholder had claim, and held stock as constructive trustee for minority stockholder).

59. Compare Model Rule Rule 1.13 (Organization as Client) ... with E.F. Hutton & Co. v. Brown, 305 F.Supp. 371 (S.D.Tex.1969) (in-house counsel who had represented corporate officer in his individual capacity in prior separate litigation disqualified from representing corporation in negligence action against officer); see G. Hazard & W. Hodes, THE LAW OF LAWYERING 243–244, 262–264 (1985) (discussing fairness to nonclients within an organization and the Miranda-type warning reqired by rule 1.13(d)); but cf. W.T. Grant Co. v. Haines, 531 F.2d 671 (2d Cir.1976) (court has discretion to allow outside counsel to represent corporation in antitrust action against former employee even if counsel has had allegedly improper communication with employee unrepresented by counsel).

interpretation fits traditional concepts and terminology, and each implies a firm set of legal consequences. While both interpretations are plausible, they result in radically different definitions of the lawyer's responsibilities. Under one interpretation the "relevant other" is like a friend, under the second the "relevant other" is like a foe.

. . .

The difference between a "normal" triangular relationship and one contaminated by antagonism does not lie in the *structure* of the relationship. Until finally resolved or dissolved, the structure is ambiguously triangular, with the nonlawyer parties being fellow clients, or antipodal, with the non-lawyer parties being antagonists. The proper interpretation depends not on structure but on process—what has happened within the relationship. The relevant set of happenings include, above all, what the lawyer has done in the relationship.

In *Fickett*, the lawyer had done nothing when he should have been doing something. The "something" he should have been doing was neither mysterious nor extraordinary. If he had adhered to normal lawyer practice followed in a normal guardian representation, he would have satisfied himself that the guardian had at least some idea of the responsibilities concerning investments and of the requirements for periodic accounting, and would have activated the procedure for submitting such accounts. If the guardian had approached him to confide that some of the investments were irregular, normal lawyer practice would suggest that the lawyer should have said something like, "That could involve very serious difficulties." The lawyer would thereby not commit himself to representing the guardian versus the ward, or vice versa; the lawyer would only be suggesting the urgent need for redefinition of the relationship between the guardian and the ward. He or she should do nothing to further or conceal the guardian's misfeasance, because the law provides that doing so would constitute fraudulent conduct on the lawyer's part. If the guardian persisted in misconduct, under accepted standards of practice the lawyer could withdraw and advise the ward of the fact of withdrawal.

In *Yablonski*, the organization's lawyer did things when the situation was such that "the role of . . . counsel . . . becomes usually a passive one."[61] The lawyer should not have assisted the president in defending colorable claims of malfeasance toward the organization. If the lawyer had adhered to proper practice in this abnormal situation, he or she would have advised the president to get independent legal representation and perhaps have advised the board to get other independent representation for the organization. Indeed, as the law has now evolved, any other course by the lawyer could be regarded as furthering or concealing the president's malfeasance.

61. *Yablonski*, 448 F.2d at 1179.

V. Conclusion

The critical problem the lawyer faces in triangular relationships is that his or her professional responsibilities depend unavoidably on what the other two parties do for and to each other. The lawyer's duty cannot adequately be defined, as it normally is, by specifying ex ante the identity of "the client." Neither of the "relevant others" is a legally freestanding person in the standard conceptual sense of "client." The guardian is not an individual alone but a person whose legal identity is expressed in terms of legal responsibilities ex officio. The corporation is not an individual at all, but exists only in law and through personification by others who act ex officio. If the other parties to the relationship conduct themselves as the law contemplates they should, then all the "relevant others" collectively can be considered "the client." That principle is already well established for corporations, and there seems to be no reason not to think of guardianships and other triangular relationships in the same way. On the other hand, if the dominant party is guilty of misconduct toward the dependent one and if the lawyer behaves as though everything were still normal, the lawyer would then have at least an ethical problem and quite possibly legal liability.

. . .

The lawyer can see and act. Depending on what he or she sees and does, the dominant actor may have to be treated as something less than a client simplicitor and the lawyer himself or herself as something different from one who "knows no other duty." That definition of role entails being an active, visible participant in the transaction and exercising independent judgment. Such deportment does not fit the conventional mold.

Notes

1. Hazard rejects categorizing the object of the third leg of the triangular relationship (the ward when the lawyer represents the guardian and the corporate officers when the lawyer represents the corporation) as a full-fledged client, calling that idea unworkable. Moore, on the other hand, see p. 344, argues that it may make more sense for the law to treat a nonclient as a client when the nonclient's expectation that the lawyer would treat her as a client was reasonable. What accounts for the difference? Hazard is more concerned with the problems involved in applying the confidentiality and conflicts rules if the "others" are treated as clients. Moore is more concerned with the absence of a duty of competence if the "others" are not treated as clients. Is there a way to put their approaches together? Hazard seems to be addressing lawyers and talking about how they should think about their responsibilities. Does Moore have a different audience in mind or a different purpose in writing?

2. Hazard argues that under the law of agency, the agent's duty to third parties is a function of the duty of the principal to third parties. The

Restatement of Agency's general position on agent's liabilities to third parties is that an agent cannot justify committing torts, or assisting in the principal's torts, against third parties simply because the agent is acting on behalf of the principal. See Restatement (Second) Agency §§ 343–351. Also, a third party generally has no cause of action an agent for pecuniary harm to the third party caused by the agent's breach of a duty to the principal. See id. §§ 352, 357. Does any of that affect the power of Hazard's argument?

3. Hazard argues that lawyers in a triangular situation may treat the "nonclient" as an ordinary third party, to whom the lawyer owes few obligations, in cases where the lawyer is retained to advocate or negotiate for a client and the lawyer has not previously been involved in the situation. Consider first the qualification "not previously involved." Why should previous involvement be so critical a factor? In fact it is quite common for lawyers, or at least their firms, to act as advocates (and negotiators) concerning matters in which they have been involved previously as facilitators or planners of the actions now being challenged. For example, Vinson & Elkins agreed to conduct a "preliminary" investigation for Enron into the charges of misconduct raised by "whistleblower" Sherron Watkins, although the law firm had lawyered some of the transactions and practices about which Watkins had complained. When, if ever, should lawyers act as advocates, negotiators or investigators concerning activities that the lawyers had planned or implemented? Second, consider the "advocacy" line that Hazard employs. As the *Kaye, Scholer* case, see Weinstein excerpt, p. 137, demonstrates, the line between advocacy and transactional lawyering may not always be easy to discern. Similarly, although advocacy about past acts poses few difficulties, advocacy that occurs while wrongdoing continues creates risks for the lawyer.

4. In the summer of 2003, the ABA made some changes to its Model Rules that included limited responsibilities of lawyer "advocates." Under the ABA's new version of Model Rule 1.13, lawyers are allowed to report corporate wrongdoing outside of the organization when their attempts to get a corporation's officers and directors to stop (or to rectify) serious wrongdoing have been unsuccessful. But the rule denies the report-out option to lawyers hired to "defend the organization or an officer, employee or other constituent associated with the organization against a claim arising out of an alleged violation of law." The rule, however, holds advocates to the same reporting requirements as other lawyers when it comes to reporting wrongdoing *within* the corporation. Is the ABA exemption for "advocates" broader than it should be? Should there be any exception at all? The SEC rules create an even broader exemption for advocates than that included in the new Model Rule 1.13. The SEC rule relieves lawyers hired to investigate or advocate a company's position regarding corporate wrongdoing from any duty to report any discovered wrongdoing to corporate management, officers or anyone else. See 17 CFR §§ 205.3(b)(6)(ii), 205.3(b)(7)(ii). It seems that to qualify for the SEC exemption, the investigating or advocating lawyer must have been hired by the company's board of directors. But why should that relieve a lawyer from having to report evidence of ongoing fraud to the board? Should it relieve a lawyer from demanding, at a minimum, that any

ongoing fraud be stopped? Should it relieve a lawyer from a duty to resign if the board fails to take appropriate action on, at least, any reports by the lawyer of wrongdoing other than the alleged wrongdoing the lawyer was hired to defend? Do those accused of wrongdoing have immunity to continue with other wrongs? If not, aren't the advocate exceptions all too broad?

5.   Hazard analyzes the lawyer's responsibilities within the triangular relationship in its "normal" state as well as in its ruptured state. He gives less attention to the formation of such relationships, what economists would call the ex ante position. How do the conceptions of triangular relationships and the rights of the "others" affect the willingness of the parties to form such relationships? The willingness of lawyers to serve in such relationships? The ways in which lawyers structure such relationships? See Cohen, When Law and Economics Met Professional Responsibility, p. 44 (viewing rules on disqualification in failed joint representation as a kind of "bonding device" that encourages lawyers to be more careful in entering into such representations).

6.   Advocates of a strong confidentiality rule rarely take issue with cases like *Weintraub*, cited by Hazard, which allow a corporation's new management to waive the attorney-client privilege as to communications between its old management and the company's lawyers or other cases that allow the corporation to use confidential information against corporate officers. Yet one would think that if any rules would have the chilling effect on communications that confidentiality proponents so fear, these rules would be the ones. Why are these rules not challenged more often? Is Hazard correct to view them (as well as the rules allowing the corporation's lawyer to continue to represent the corporation in a dispute with corporate officers) as so obviously desirable?

7.   Hazard concludes by arguing that lawyers in triangular relationships may have a greater obligation to be "active" and "visible" participants in the transactions between the full-fledged client and the other. Yet proponents of limited lawyer obligations to nonclients might respond that imposing such obligations could have exactly the opposite effect: lawyers will be more aloof and reluctant to get involved. Do you think that is a serious risk? If it is, is the solution to limit obligations to nonclients?

8.   In understanding the ethical and legal problems that pervade law practice, Hazard's triangle metaphor may be more powerful than he suggests. Hazard's point may be boiled down to this: A lawyer must keep her eye on the line that represents the client's legal duties to third parties and her duties to the client. When the line is straight, the lawyer need not worry about which corner of the triangle is the real "client." But for lawyers, at least when they are not acting as advocates, when the line gets wavy, it is the lawyer's first job to make the line straight again. When the client is acting within the law, the lawyer can proceed with unmitigated devotion and zeal. But isn't that true for all lawyers, whether or not they are in a triangular relationship?

Mass Lawsuits and the Aggregate Settlement Rule*
CHARLES SILVER AND LYNN A. BAKER

> *"You'll all have to agree that you will act as one unit. There'll be no talk about this is for Toomey and not for Robbins or Zona, no talk about whose claim is more viable than someone else's claim."*
>
> *Schlichtmann paused to gauge his clients' reaction. They looked expectantly at him. No one said anything.*
>
> *"If the eight families can't do that," Schlichtmann said, "then we're in real trouble. If there's a problem between families, then I won't know who I'm representing. If there's a problem, it means that each family will have to get its own attorney."*
>
> *Thirty seconds of silence ensued. Schlichtmann waited for a response. People looked cautiously at each other, wondering who would speak first.*
>
> *Richard Toomey, whose dead son, Patrick, had the strongest of the remaining claims, sat directly across the table from where Schlichtmann stood.... He was the first to break the silence, in a voice clear and strong. "We're all in this together," he said. "That's how we started, and that's how we'll stay."*
>
> *Anne Anderson smiled in sudden relief, and everyone began to say, as if in chorus, "We're unanimous, we're together."*

Jonathan Harr, A Civil Action

Introduction

Rule 1.8(g) of the Model Rules of Professional Conduct is known as the aggregate settlement rule.... On its face and as interpreted in the few pertinent decisions to date, the Rule imposes three requirements on lawyers seeking to settle lawsuits in which they represent multiple clients: (1) disclosure of all settlement terms to all clients, including disclosure to each of what other plaintiffs are to receive or other defendants are to pay; (2) unanimous consent by all clients to all settlement terms; and (3) a prohibition on agreements to waive requirements (1) or (2) even with the clients' unanimous consent.

These requirements have been on the books for years. Model Rule 1.8(g) carries forward Disciplinary Rule (DR) 5–106 of the Model Code of Professional Responsibility "almost verbatim." ...

... The thesis we will advance is that clients and their lawyers should be permitted to agree on alternatives to the disclosure and consent requirements set out in the Rule....

... [First, here is some information on what happens in the real world.] Some plaintiffs' attorneys make lump-sum demands on behalf of groups of clients without telling defendants how the money will be distributed. Others present a series of individual demands showing what

* © 1997 Wake Forest Law Review Ass'n. Reprinted by permission from 32 Wake Forest L. Rev. 733 (1997).

each client is to receive. Some plaintiffs' attorneys obtain settlement authority from all their clients before making demands. Others get authority only after defendants indicate their willingness to pay. Some defendants make settlement offers that all plaintiffs or a specified number of plaintiffs must accept before any plaintiff is paid. Others make offers that individual plaintiffs can accept or reject without limitation. Some plaintiffs' attorneys feel comfortable helping their clients divide a gross settlement recovery among themselves. Others feel awkward doing this and let the clients handle the task or bring in third parties to recommend allocations. Some lawyers feel comfortable with majority rule arrangements which allow groups of claimants to settle over the objection of minority plaintiffs. Others take a dim view of such arrangements, fearing that they give defendants strategic advantages and may deny the clients with the most at stake the power to control their fates.

. . .

I.   The Economic Structure of Mass Actions

A.   *Mass Actions Distinguished from Class Actions and Consolidations*

. . .

Class actions are involuntary group lawsuits. They are permitted only when transaction costs prevent plaintiffs from forming groups on their own, even though they would be better off acting collectively. Class action rules facilitate collective action by allowing some plaintiffs to draw others into groups without their consent, thereby eliminating any need to transact with other plaintiffs. A single named plaintiff can conscript any number of absent plaintiffs by filing a complaint alleging classwide harm and by having the class certified. The absent plaintiffs may never have heard of the named plaintiff, need not have filed lawsuits of their own, and may have no opportunity to exclude themselves from the class.

. . . The right of the named plaintiff and class counsel to act on behalf of the absent plaintiffs is bestowed by class action law, which performs all the functions an engagement agreement ordinarily serves. Class action law creates the group, determines its members, appoints its leader-representatives, fixes the scope of the representation, regulates compensation, and establishes criteria to govern settlement. . . .

Consolidations are more consensual than class actions. Consolidations bring together plaintiffs with pending lawsuits, so one can at least be confident that each member of these groups wants to sue. But consolidations are also involuntary because they bring together plaintiffs who originally chose to sue separately rather than as a group. It therefore seems appropriate to presume that group litigation is likely to make consolidated plaintiffs worse off. If collective action improved their expected payoffs, judges probably would not have to order them to join forces. Of course, this is not a hard and fast rule. Plaintiffs sometimes initiate consolidation motions or join motions filed by others, thereby expressing support for group proceedings. Also, consolidation may facilitate the formation of some desirable groups whose creation is impeded by transaction costs or perverse incentives. . . .

After consolidation is ordered, a governance structure must be created for the joint undertaking. . . . Usually, the lawyers who represent the individual consolidated plaintiffs decide among themselves how power, responsibility, fees, and costs will be shared, building a governance structure which the court rubber stamps. The process is often acrimonious, with only the threat of a judicially imposed solution ensuring that an agreement is ultimately reached.

Because they eliminate the need to actually organize litigation groups, class actions and consolidations are powerful means of processing claims in volume. For the same reason, they are also dangerous and challenging. . . . [T]here is wide agreement that defective incentive systems and monitoring arrangements create real risks of inadequate representation. . . .

Mass lawsuits differ from class actions and consolidations by being fully consensual. They come to exist when numerous plaintiffs with legally or factually related claims against common defendants are jointly represented by the same attorneys. Sometimes lawyers assemble mass actions by soliciting or recruiting clients directly. This can occur via targeted mailings, other advertising campaigns, and lay referrals. Open air meetings can also be effective recruiting tools. At these gatherings, lawyers and civic leaders speak to large numbers of potential plaintiffs about matters affecting them generally, and clients are signed up after the speeches conclude. Unions, churches, homeowners and renters associations, and other voluntary membership groups are also potential sources of clients. Lawyers may approach leaders of these organizations to discuss the possibility of screening and representing their members.

Referral networks also help create client groups. Referrals move cases from generalist lawyers who are good at recruiting clients to lawyers who, because they specialize in particular kinds of lawsuits or possess other attributes, are better able to maximize the value of clients' claims. Many lawyers who handle mass actions receive large numbers of cases by referral. Texas asbestos lawyers are a good case in point. They have represented tens of thousands of nonresident plaintiffs who were enlisted by lawyers in other states. . . .

. . .

B. *The Basic Structure of Mass Actions*

Whether created by direct solicitation, referrals, or a combination of the two, all mass lawsuits involve a nexus of contracts that connect each plaintiff to the lawyers for the group. . . .

Mass actions are natural products of market forces that encourage claimant groups to form. They are spontaneous collective actions organized by lawyer-entrepreneurs who use retainer contracts to establish governance structures. In these respects, mass actions resemble corporations, partnerships, and voluntary membership organizations, whose shareholders, partners, and members decide whether to participate and on what terms. Plaintiffs contribute assets—their claims—to the joint undertaking. In a few of the cases, they also contribute money or time. They engage lawyer-managers to run the enterprise and give these individuals incentives to maximize their gains. The primary forms of lawyer-manager compensation are stock in the enterprise (the right to a contingent percentage of the recovery) plus a priority claim to repayment of monies advanced on behalf of the enterprise.

The lawyer-manager's job is to sell the assets of the enterprise to the defendant at the highest possible price. One way to effect the transaction is by trying the group lawsuit. A trial forces the defendant to pay, and the plaintiffs to accept, a price set by a jury or a judge. Plaintiffs' attorneys can also sell claims by negotiating consensual transactions called settlements. Because settlements occur in all but a tiny fraction of disputes, trial preparation is largely an effort in salesmanship and is often seen by the participants as such. Its purpose, from the plaintiffs' perspective, is to persuade a reluctant defendant-purchaser that a trial would yield a high forced-sale price so that settlement at a still high, but slightly lower, price would be a good deal.

Absent an indication that claimants are systematically likely to act irrationally or that markets consistently fail for other reasons, it is reasonable to presume that mass actions form because they are advantageous for their members. When a pattern of consensual group litigation emerges, as has occurred in the asbestos context, the inference that claimants are better off in groups than they would be suing alone seems especially strong.... [Of course,] when [deciding on joint representation] ... plaintiffs and defendants usually rely heavily on lawyers for advice.

Plaintiffs can gain several important advantages by suing collectively. These include (1) economies of scale in litigation costs, (2) increased leverage in settlement negotiations, (3) equalization of plaintiffs' and defendants' risks, and (4) conservation of defendants' assets.

1. *Economies of scale*

Group lawsuits can enable plaintiffs to reduce per capita litigation costs by taking advantage of ...: jointness of supply. A good or service is joint (or nonrival) if an additional person can use it without diminishing its availability to others....

Many litigation resources display the property of jointness across a broad range of consumption. These include: information produced by investigations of common legal and factual questions, such as whether asbestos causes certain diseases, whether a defendant knew asbestos dust to be hazardous, what law governs plaintiffs' claims, and what the standard of care is under the applicable state law; representation at trial, especially when so-called "bellwether" trials are employed; representation in settlement negotiations; document preparation, such as drafting a complaint or a response to a motion; expert witness testimony on common issues; and computer simulations. By sharing these goods and services after paying for them once, plaintiffs can substantially reduce their per capita litigation costs.

. . .

2. *Increased leverage in settlement negotiations*

Most group lawsuits settle [, as do most individual suits.] ... In theory, plaintiffs can often gain leverage in settlement negotiations with a common defendant by joining forces. This happens in large part because plaintiff groups often find it rational to litigate more intensively than plaintiffs who sue individually.

The impact of economies of scale on bargaining power is clearest when individual claims are too small to justify the expense of litigation.... [Small] claims pressed by individual plaintiffs have little settlement value because plaintiffs cannot make credible threats to take their cases to trial. By comparison, the threat value, and therefore the settlement value, of groups of small claims may be relatively great, due to the feasibility of trying small claims en masse.

Reduced litigation costs per capita are predicted to increase the settlement value of large claims as well. On the standard economic model of the decision to settle or sue, a plaintiff's minimum settlement demand falls as litigation costs rise. Because aggregation reduces plaintiffs' per capita litigation costs, it should increase their minimum settlement demands and, therefore, the settlement value of their claims.

Aggregation can also increase plaintiffs' demands by increasing the expected value of their claims at trial. A claim's expected value is partly a function of the probability that a plaintiff will prevail in a trial against a defendant.... If members of plaintiff groups save money by sharing ... [costs], they can afford to purchase more [or better] services ... than plaintiffs who sue by themselves. One should therefore expect plaintiff groups to be better represented than individual plaintiffs, and better representation can be predicted to yield ... more favorable settlements.

Cooperation among plaintiffs also helps equalize the stakes between plaintiffs and defendants, resulting in more nearly balanced litigation investments and more equal bargaining power. When plaintiffs with related claims sue separately, a defendant typically enjoys a bargaining advantage because the defendant, as a repeat player confronting a one-time player, can credibly threaten to out-spend any individual plaintiff's attorney. . . .

. . .

Aggregation brings the plaintiffs' and defendants' incentives to invest in litigation more nearly into balance, although defendants are still likely to enjoy an edge. When all plaintiffs join in a single lawsuit, the defendant's liability exposure is the sum of the expected values of the plaintiffs' claims at trial (or the defendant's total assets, whichever is less). As a group, the plaintiffs' expected gain is the same amount. The investment incentives are still unequal, however, because it is the attorneys representing the plaintiffs . . . who decide how much to invest. And the plaintiffs' attorneys stand to earn only a fraction of the amount their clients recover. Nonetheless, . . . [attorneys representing groups] can certainly commit to spending far greater resources than any individual plaintiff's claim would warrant. . . .

3. *Equalizing plaintiffs' and defendants' risks*

A defendant facing a group lawsuit is often concerned about the prospect of facing a single trial in which its entire liability will be adjudged. In this respect, a defendant opposing a plaintiff group differs from a defendant who is opposing the same number of plaintiffs one by one. . . .

. . .

4. *Conservation of defendants' assets*

When a defendant's assets (including insurance) are insufficient to cover all plaintiffs' claims, a group lawsuit can benefit plaintiffs by conserving the defendant's resources and preserving the going concern value of the defendant's operations. When claims are litigated in separate forums, defendants must retain local counsel in each venue, pay experts to testify . . . at each trial, suffer the expense of repetitive depositions of managerial personnel, and bear other duplicative costs. These expenditures, which can be avoided when plaintiffs sue in a single proceeding, diminish the pool of resources ultimately available to satisfy the plaintiffs' claims.

. . .

II.   Settlement Allocation and Monitoring Problems in Group Lawsuits

Group litigation is not for every client. The . . . advantages that may flow from group lawsuits, . . . [may not always materialize.]

A.   *The Problems Conceptualized*

. . . [A]ssume[] that X and Y expect to recover $50,000 and $100,000, respectively, for a total of $150,000. . . . [This] will be referred to as each client's security level, because it is the amount each client can guarantee himself or herself without cooperating with the other.

By joining forces, X and Y[, plaintiffs with related claims,] can recover more ... [Assume the expected aggregate recovery is, for example, $600,000.] ... By cooperating, X and Y can make themselves jointly better off, by an expected $450,000. They can also make themselves individually better off by dividing the cooperative surplus in a manner that gives each some amount more than his or her security level.

Group litigation can [, however,] make X or Y individually worse off because by suing together X and Y put their security level payoffs at risk. The expected aggregate return from joint litigation can be divided between X and Y in amounts ranging from ($600,000, $0) to ($0, $600,000). Some of these allocations ... give X or Y less than his or her security level. Any of these extreme allocations would make X or Y worse off. . . .

Even if extreme allocations are ruled out, it is important to see that X and Y also have divergent preferences. . . . [Each would prefer to keep the lion-share of the surplus.] [In g]roup lawsuits ... plaintiffs' interests [both] align and conflict. Plaintiffs share an interest in maximizing their aggregate recovery, but can be expected to have different preferences with respect to the settlement fund's allocation.

. . . [Also, note that t]he expected outcome from group litigation ... is the payoff predicted to be realized if the group lawsuit is conducted in a collectively rational manner, i.e., a manner that maximizes the expected joint return. . . . [However, that might not happen,] for example, if the plaintiffs' attorney operates under defective incentives[,] ... shirk[s,] or ... [engages in] other opportunistic behavior.

In both single-client and multiple-client representations, plaintiffs' attorneys are customarily compensated by ... contingent percentage fees that encourage them to maximize their clients' recoveries. . . . [T]his fee arrangement does not[, however,] prevent plaintiffs' attorneys from engaging in opportunistic behavior. For example, ... before much time has been invested in a case, a defendant may effectively "bribe" a plaintiffs' attorney by offering a relatively cheap settlement that would nonetheless pay the attorney a handsome premium on his or her hourly rate. An attorney may accept the offer, even though it fails to maximize the client's recovery, because the marginally greater fee to be earned if the offer is declined is too small to induce the attorney to incur added risk of continued litigation. An offer of this sort is especially likely to succeed when a defendant makes a credible threat to litigate aggressively if the offer is declined.

The danger of attorney opportunism is predictably greater in mass actions than in conventional lawsuits ... [because there is more] to be gained by [that behavior] ... in mass actions ... than in a conventional lawsuit. Aggregation enables a defendant to offer a plaintiffs' attorney a huge premium for settling early and cheaply. Effective hourly rates in the hundreds of thousands of dollars are possible, making such offers especially difficult to resist. . . .

Although individual group members can discourage opportunism by closely monitoring their lawyers, no individual plaintiff is likely to do so at a level that is efficient for the group. . . . [E]ach [plaintiff,] hoping to enjoy the benefits of another's labor without bearing any portion of the cost, will rationally decline to perform monitoring activities that are cost-justified from the perspective of the group. Free-riding of this sort is especially likely . . . in large groups that bring together plaintiffs who do not otherwise know . . . one another.

. . . [The potential for attorney opportunism thus] creates a serious risk that . . . group members . . . [will not reap all, or any, of the benefits of group litigation] and [may end up] . . . worse off than they would have been suing alone. . . . [But, assuming mass suits generate substantially higher settlements than the sum of individual lawsuits, a little attorney opportunism may not be sufficient to wipe out the entire cooperative surplus.] Group lawsuits can [thus] work less than ideally yet still be better for plaintiffs than individual suits.

B. The Aggregate Settlement Rule as a Means of Handling Allocation Conflicts and Monitoring Failures

Attorney opportunism and allocation conflicts among the plaintiffs create a need for governance structures that will encourage the plaintiffs' agents to act appropriately. The aggregate settlement rule is one such structure. . . . [T]he purpose of Rule 1.8(g) [seems to be] . . . to enable each plaintiff to police allocation conflicts by vetoing a proposed settlement. A veto is most likely to be exercised whenever a plaintiff considers his or her share of a settlement to be too small, either in absolute terms or in relation to the payments other plaintiffs are to receive.

. . .

. . . [We doubt that giving individual clients a veto is necessary to ensure a fair split of the cooperative surplus among clients; the interest of each in cooperating with the others to enlarge the aggregate settlement . . . should suffice to prevent grossly unfair allocations among group members. . . . On the other hand,] empowering group members to reject settlements they dislike . . . [may work to] discourage . . . lawyers from acting opportunistically. . . .

. . .

The effectiveness of each client's right to reject an offer in . . . [controlling attorney opportunism and guaranteeing a fair allocation among plaintiffs] depends partly on the voting rule that governs a litigation group. Any of three rules could govern. . . . First, affirmative votes by [all] ... clients could be required as a condition of settlement by either client.... Second, the rule could allow [any] ... client to settle individually even if the [an]other client votes against the offer.... Third, the rule could allow the affirmative vote of a single client to bind the group....

Clearly, different voting regimes can have different ... effects. Under the third regime, a dissenter has little power to challenge misallocations and attorney opportunism because a single supporting vote can seal the fate of the entire plaintiff group. Under the first regime, a dissenter has great power because a single negative vote can prevent everyone from settling. The second regime seems to give a dissenter a middling degree of power, enough to protect himself or herself from an inadequate settlement, but too little to prevent others from taking advantage of offers they want to accept.... [I]t is the second regime that appears to be codified in the [aggregate settlement r]ule.... [T]he Rule appears to allow any client to settle his or her own claim while authorizing no client to determine whether another's claim will be settled or not.... [Should this regime be mandatory or] a waivable default[?]

III. Problems Caused by the Aggregate Settlement Rule

... [W]e believe the Rule complicates the settlement process: by invading plaintiffs' privacy; by preventing plaintiffs from offering defendants finality; by generating expense and delay; and by encouraging strategic behavior within plaintiff groups that frustrates global settlements.

A. *Privacy Concerns*

The aggregate settlement rule requires attorneys engaged in multiple-client representations to disclose to each client "the existence and nature of all the claims ... involved and of the participation of each person in the settlement" in the course of obtaining each client's consent to a settlement.... In mass actions ... the emotional and other costs to the plaintiffs of these invasions of privacy may well exceed any benefits of having information about other group members' claims and anticipated settlement payments. Consider two recent Texas cases....

In 1992, a large volume of natural gas escaped from an underground storage facility near Brenham, Texas. When a truck ignited the gas cloud, the resulting explosion caused several deaths and numerous personal injuries, and damaged scores of buildings. Through referrals and solicitations, a single law firm came to represent more than 900 people whose homes or businesses were affected by the explosion. When the defendants showed an interest in settling all pending claims for an amount in excess of $40 million, the plaintiffs' attorneys became concerned about ... the Texas equivalent of Model Rule 1.8(g). The lawyers knew they could not comply with the Rule because many of their clients refused to allow them to tell other clients how much they would receive under the proposed settlement. To settle the lawsuit en masse, the lawyers had to find a way around ... [the rule] by devising a means of settling 900–plus claims that was not an "aggregate settlement."

A similar problem arose in a mass asbestos action handled by lawyers in Beaumont, Texas. The defendants, all companies that operated plants where workers were exposed to asbestos, wanted to settle three separate lawsuits brought by injured employees. The settlement was to exceed $140 million and would resolve the claims of approximately 1700 families, all of whom were named parties on at least one of the petitions. Again, the plaintiffs' lawyers were worried about ... [the aggregate settlement rule]. They feared that their clients would be hounded by reporters, stock brokers, con men, and long-lost family members if information about their recoveries became public, so they looked for a way to settle the case without distributing (even to other plaintiffs) a list of the amount each plaintiff was to be paid.

Brenham, Texas, the site of the natural gas explosion, is a small town where everyone knows everyone else. Telling all 900–plus plaintiffs what every plaintiff was to receive would have been the equivalent of publishing the information in the local newspaper....

...

Consider the ambiguity in the disclosure requirement that the Beaumont lawyers exploited. By its terms, [the] Texas Rule ... mandates "disclosure ... of the participation of each person in the settlement." ... [T]he Rule does not expressly state that each person must be identified by name.... [That] omission [in the Rule, which also appears in the Model Rule,] allowed the Beaumont lawyers to reveal only proposed payments by disease categories and the number of persons with each disease.... To protect themselves from the charge of having violated the Rule, the lawyers also told their clients that a list containing complete information for each plaintiff was available for inspection in their offices....

The Brenham lawyers exploited a different ambiguity in the Rule— the meaning of the phrase "aggregate settlement." The Texas Rule, like the Model Rule, states that "[a] lawyer who represents two or more clients shall not participate in making an aggregate settlement of the claims of or against the clients...." It does not say that a lawyer must refrain from making a nonaggregate settlement of multiple clients' claims. Several cases take the position that a series of individual settlement demands for jointly represented clients does not constitute an aggregate settlement. The Brenham lawyers therefore structured their settlement as 900–plus independent demands, each of which had prior authorization from the client on whose behalf it was made and each of which could be accepted or rejected by the defendants without limitation.

... Although the conduct of these Texas attorneys seems perfectly reasonable to us, there is little question that the risk-averse course [for the lawyers] would have been to disclose the details of each plaintiff's claim and settlement payment to all other plaintiffs.

The magnitude of the risk a lawyer incurs by experimenting with the rule was recently made clear. In *Arce v. Burrow*,[88] plaintiffs sued their former attorneys alleging a violation of the aggregate settlement rule. The court of appeals held that in the event of a violation, plaintiffs can recover the entire attorney's fee without a showing of harm....

... [Could] infringement of clients' privacy ... be avoided by telling clients at the time the attorney is engaged that the[clients'] names and settlement payments will ... be disclosed to other members of the plaintiff group[?] ... [T]hat would force [clients] to either join with other plaintiffs and compromise their privacy or sue alone and lose the advantages of litigating as part of a group....

B. Finality

. . .

A potential advantage of group-wide settlements stems from the fact that defendants who settle these lawsuits want finality and are willing to pay for it. The desire for finality accounts for a variety of common settlement features, including mandatory classes from which plaintiffs cannot opt-out and ceilings on the number of plaintiffs who can reject an offer in a mass action without causing a settlement to explode.

Why do defendants value finality? ... First, defendants may face a risk of adverse selection. When plaintiffs can opt-out of settlements, there is a danger that those with the strongest claims will do so, leaving a defendant with a settlement dominated by weak claims. The danger is clearest when a defendant offers to make level payments for entire claim categories. For example, the schedule shown below was used in a lawsuit involving 153 asbestos plaintiffs.

DISEASE	PAYMENT
Mesothelioma	$25,000
Lung Cancer	$13,000
Other Cancers	$9,600
Pulmonary Asbestosis	$8,000
Pleural Disease	$4,800

In each disease category, this arrangement likely overcompensated plaintiffs with weak claims and undercompensated plaintiffs with strong claims.... If this figure reflected the value of the average lung cancer claim, then victims with relatively weak claims (smokers) did marginally

88. Arce v. Burrow, 1997 WL 665541 (Tex.App.1997).

better than they should have, and victims with relatively strong claims (nonsmokers) fared marginally worse. Victims with strong claims therefore had the greatest incentive to opt-out.... [A] defendant's settlement offer may [thus] reasonably be conditioned on its acceptance by a high percentage of the plaintiff group.

Defendants also prefer broader settlements to narrower ones because broad settlements give them better returns on their sunk transaction costs, the money they spend negotiating deals....

. . .

C. *Expense and Delay*

... Ordinarily, the information required to be communicated [to clients under the aggregate settlement rule] cannot be known until [settlement] negotiations occur. The Rule clearly contemplates that a lawyer will confer with his or her clients before closing a deal whose details have already been hammered out.

. . .

Expense and delay [resulting from this requirement of communication with each member of the group] can be real concerns when clients number in the hundreds or thousands.... A lawsuit involving approximately 25,000 farm workers is an extreme example, but a good one. The plaintiffs, who resided in twelve foreign countries, alleged that exposure to a pesticide reduced their fertility and prevented them from having children. They sought compensation from the manufacturer of the pesticide and from growers who used it on their crops. After their claims were dismissed on forum non conveniens grounds, the plaintiffs appealed to the Fifth Circuit. While the appeal was pending, the manufacturer offered to settle all 25,000 claims. The plaintiffs' attorneys regarded the offer as a great opportunity. They wanted to settle immediately, but the aggregate settlement rule prevented them from doing so. They had to confer with and poll their clients before agreeing to the deal.

The difficulty of contacting 25,000 agricultural workers in twelve foreign countries is hard to exaggerate. Few claimants had telephones or permanent addresses.... The plaintiffs' attorneys therefore wanted to make only one contact, at which the settlement would be described and checks would be distributed to those ... who accepted the manufacturer's offer.

The defendant manufacturer had grave concerns about this procedure.... [It had] no assurance in advance as to the number of plaintiffs who would approve the settlement [and was worried that most settlers would have relatively weak claims, leaving the strong claims still unresolved.] If a large number ... rejected the offer or if mainly plaintiffs, with weak claims accepted it, the settlement would turn out to be an expensive proposition that would do the manufacturer little good. The

manufacturer was also concerned that [while the plaintiffs were considering it's offer,] ... the Fifth Circuit would decide the pending appeal.... If the Fifth Circuit affirmed the forum non conveniens dismissal, the vast majority of the farm workers would accept the proposed
settlement and the manufacturer would lose its money. But, if the Fifth
Circuit reversed, the plaintiffs would have live claims and their lawyers
might encourage many of them to reject the deal....

These problems could have been solved if the plaintiffs' attorneys
had been able to bind the farm workers without polling them. Such
settlement authority might have been conferred in several ways. At the
extreme, the clients could have authorized the lawyers in advance to
accept any deal within the reasonable exercise of their discretion. Short
of this, the farm workers could have agreed to be bound by the decision
of ... a ... committee ... of [claimants] ... who could be consulted
easily. A third alternative would have been to authorize a lawyer in each
country to settle on behalf of all workers living there....

...

If fewer than all plaintiffs are to participate in a settlement, a
defendant will want to limit the size and composition of the opt-out
group.... If [too many or too many with strong claims reject a group
offer] ..., a defendant may prefer ... [to settle none of the claims.
Thus,] mass settlements usually contain walk-away provisions. For example, in one asbestos settlement, the defendants reserved the right to
kill the deal unless one-hundred percent of the mesothelioma victims and
claimants representing eighty-five percent of the total settlement fund
accepted the deal.

Walk-away provisions are sources of transaction costs. To set the
thresholds in the asbestos settlement, the lawyers had to bargain in the
face of uncertainty about the number of plaintiffs who would approve
the deal. They walked a fine line, protecting the settling defendants from
future litigation to the greatest possible extent without imposing participation requirements so high that a few disgruntled or strategic plaintiffs
could scotch a nearly global deal. The defendants also had to take care to
give the plaintiffs' attorneys an incentive to maximize the number of
plaintiffs who would accept the deal. Although only claimants representing eighty-five percent of the settlement fund were required to join in,
the defendants wanted one hundred percent to accept. Because only the
plaintiffs' attorneys could convince their clients to participate, the defendants required assurances that they would use their best efforts to
minimize the plaintiffs' opt-out rate.

Another matter of great concern to defendants is who will represent
nonsettling claimants in future litigation. Many defendants refuse to
proceed with partial settlements unless the attorneys representing the
original group agree not to represent nonsettling claimants in the future.
This desire is understandable. Throughout the settlement process, defen-

dants ... give plaintiffs' attorneys valuable information that can be used against them in future litigation. To protect themselves, defendants must either settle all claims, thereby avoiding future litigation, or must preclude the plaintiffs' attorneys from representing opt-out claimants. Because the unanimity requirement all but eliminates the first option, it forces defendants to bargain for the second. ... [Binding the lawyers to a promise to withdraw from representing all nonsettlers] is problematic, however, even when the plaintiffs' attorneys want to go along. ... [The ethics rules in all states prohibit] a lawyer from agreeing to restrict his or her right to practice law in connection with the settlement of civil litigation.

    ... [I]n practice ... [that prohibition] frequently is ignored. ...

. . .

D. *Strategic Behavior*

The Rule's nonwaivable unanimous consent requirement is probably the most significant barrier to settlement in mass lawsuits. It is certainly a big obstacle to global deals that extinguish all plaintiffs' claims. Critically, this requirement enables a single plaintiff to block an all-encompassing group deal unless he or she receives a disproportionately large share of the available funds. A strategic plaintiff with little at stake in a lawsuit, such as a person who was exposed to asbestos but has no disease, can therefore make a credible threat to veto a desirable group deal unless paid a disproportionately large amount. ...

Under any less-than-unanimity rule, such as a simple majority rule, a small-claim plaintiff inclined toward strategic settlement behavior will have less bargaining power. As the percentage of plaintiffs needed to bind a group declines, the difficulty of extortion by any one member increases. ...

Not surprisingly, some plaintiffs have anticipated the holdout problem endemic to group decision-making under a unanimity rule, and have agreed ex ante that majority rule will govern their settlement negotiations. In *Hayes v. Eagle–Picher Industries, Inc.*,[118] eighteen plaintiffs retained a single lawyer to act on their behalf against the common defendant. In addition to addressing the usual matters like fees and costs, the plaintiffs' retainer agreement established that the decision to settle as a group would be made by majority rule. Initially, the decision to include this provision appeared to be wise because the defendant made a group-level offer and the plaintiffs were divided over whether to accept it: thirteen plaintiffs voted to accept the offer and five voted to decline it. Collective action was possible only because the plaintiffs agreed in advance to be bound by majority rule. Even so, the will of the majority was defeated. After the group's attorney had the trial court enter the settlement on behalf of all eighteen plaintiffs, two of the dissenters

---

118. 513 F.2d 892 (10th Cir.1975).

appealed. The Tenth Circuit sided with them, holding that the Rule's requirement that each plaintiff consent to the settlement after being informed of its terms could not be waived.

. . .

IV.   The Case for Waivability

. . .

Under many circumstances, American law permits individuals to waive procedural protections established for their benefit. . . .

Consider, as well, that voluntary membership organizations, including social, political, economic, religious, and charitable groups, rarely make decisions under a unanimity rule. . . . Because plaintiffs join litigation groups voluntarily, it seems natural that they should also have the option of using less-than-unanimity rules for making group decisions.

. . . In class actions and consolidations, the wishes of individual plaintiffs are regularly ignored for the sake of some larger good. Plaintiffs who may not want to sue at all are forced to sue, and plaintiffs who may prefer to sue individually are forced to sue as members of a group. In addition, plaintiffs in class actions and consolidations are required to accept representation by court-selected counsel and to pay court-ordered attorneys' fees. Their claims are settled without their consent and often even over their objections. . . .

. . .

A.   *Waivability of the Unanimity Requirement*

. . .

1.   *Agency law permits the use of less-than-unanimity rules*

The simplest argument against waivability is that deeply embedded principles of law require the use of unanimity rules. . . . Agency law . . . however, . . . [expresses a] strong [bias for] allow[ing] principals to structure relationships as they wish. . . .

. . . [I]n Hayes[, however,] the Tenth Circuit . . . [said] that th[e] agreement to waive the Rule's unanimous consent requirement ran

> contrary to the plain duties owed by an attorney to a client. An agreement . . . which allows a case to be settled contrary to the wishes of the client and without his approving the terms of the settlement is opposed to the basic fundamentals of the attorney-client relationship. Inasmuch as the attorney is merely an agent for the client in negotiation and settlement, the approval of the client is an all important essential to a settlement which is to be binding, and if this approval is not present the court is placed in a most unfavorable position in enforcing it.

. . .

... [But t]he Restatement (Second) of Agency states that "[a] number of persons, such as the members of a partnership, may act jointly in the authorization of an agent." ... [A]gency law leaves co-principals free to use any decision rule they please.

...

b.   In search of a few good lawyers....

Attorneys' character, integrity, and attitude toward risk are crucial determinants of outcomes for plaintiffs. It is therefore important to put diligent, honest, and risk-neutral lawyers in charge of mass lawsuits. Such lawyers are likely to wind up at the helm much of the time because ... the referral market plays an active role in selecting lawyers to lead client groups.

When clients are referred, forwarding lawyers retain fee interests in the cases, usually in the form of a percentage of the percent age fee charged to the successful client. The connection between the size of the referral fee and the amount recovered by the clients gives forwarding lawyers incentives to select lead attorneys who are likely to recover larger rather than smaller amounts....

...

c.   *Malpractice threats.* Malpractice liability ... [also] discourages lead lawyers from acting arbitrarily or opportunistically, although its strength as a deterrent may vary greatly from case to case. By agreeing to an allocation formula that significantly undervalues some plaintiffs' claims relative to others, a lead attorney risks being sued for malpractice by the plaintiffs who are harmed....

d.   *Sophisticated versions of majority rule.* Certain kinds of attorney opportunism can also be policed by voting rules that, like majority rule, facilitate collective action, but may be less subject to abuse. Under simple majority rule, for example, an attorney could get a cheap settlement accepted by allocating all of it to fifty-one percent of the clients. The remaining forty-nine percent of the client group would then be sold out. Likewise, a defendant could potentially exploit plaintiffs who agreed to be governed by simple majority rule by offering a settlement attractive to the fifty-percent-plus-one members of the plaintiff group with the smallest claims....

Some other less-than-unanimity rules are less easily manipulated than simple majority rule. Requiring eighty or ninety percent of the client group to vote for a proposal is the most obvious way of reducing the number of clients in danger of being sold out....

...

Notes

1.   Silver & Baker view "mass lawsuits" as "fully consensual." Are they? Doesn't that depend on how much the lawyer tells the client who signs

up for such representation, and how much real choice the client has in using this lawyer as opposed to another? Suppose the lawyer simply says to a prospective client, "By the way, we are representing others with claims like yours and that gives us extra clout with the defendant." Under the conflict of interest rules, would that count as informed consent? What should the lawyer have to disclose to the client for us to describe the "mass" representation as "fully consensual?" The requirements of Model Rule 1.8(g)? How the lawyer plans to resolve conflicts among the claims of various clients? The pros and cons of individual versus group representation?

2. Silver & Baker compare mass lawsuits to class actions and consolidations. But the aggregate settlement rule was originally devised to deal with relatively small numbers of co-clients. Does Silver & Baker's critique of the rule apply with equal force to smaller groups? If the critique applies only to larger groups, are there reasons to insist that such aggregations be brought as class actions? Silver & Baker argue that mass lawsuits would be appropriate for small value claims. But isn't the small claims case with lots of plaintiffs the paradigm for class actions? Class actions involve a variety of requirements (e.g., similarity of claims) and procedural protections (notice, judicial review of settlement and often opt out rights). If the claims are, for example, too dissimilar to justify class action treatment, should we be enthusiastic about one lawyer or firm handling them all with not even nominal court review of how conflicts between clients were handled? Silver & Baker also argue that mass lawsuits are appropriate for situations in which the defendant's assets might be exhausted. Again, isn't that an appropriate case for using a class action (the so-called "limited fund" class action), or perhaps more appropriately, bankruptcy? Both of these provide, at least on paper, greater rights and protections for clients.

3. Class action requirements are often overlooked and the protections for the class often do little to protect class members. Does the abuse present in many class action cases and the emptiness of many of the procedural protections designed to protect class members somehow warrant a relaxation of the aggregate settlement rule? Due to the laxity of judicial oversight of class action settlements and the anything-goes attitude that still persists in most courts as to class counsel's conflicts, as a practical matter class members with strong claims have little protection from settlements that transfer money that might be available to pay them to class members with weak or nonexistent claims. If that is how things actually work, is there really any justification for insisting that "mass" clients be treated with more care, as Model Rule 1.8(g) directs? Or does it make more sense to insist that class action notices conform to Model Rule 1.8(g), i.e., use that rule as an argument to improve class action representation instead of using class action practice as an excuse to weaken 1.8(g)?

4. Silver & Baker draw an analogy between mass lawsuits and other organizational forms, such as partnerships and corporations. Recall the Koniak & Cohen argument, p. 329, that other organizational forms enjoy much more developed law than class actions. That is equally true, if not more true, of mass suits that are less "formal" than class actions. Are there other problems with the analogy?

5.   In most business organizations, the absolute and relative value of what the investors contribute is usually fairly clear; the return on that investment is uncertain. In most voluntary membership organizations that people join, their main purpose is not to make a financial investment in the hope of a monetary return. In lawsuits, by contrast, determining the absolute and relative value of the "investments" is the primary purpose of the enterprise (there are, of course, other reasons people litigate, but monetary recovery is usually the predominant one). Perhaps a lawyer with mass clients is more analogous to an agent who collects patents from various inventors who are unsure of their worth, and who then agrees to sell the patents as a package to a company that seeks to use the patents together. Does shifting the analogy help in deciding what the law should require of the agent? There are important differences between organizational forms, which Silver & Baker ignore. See generally Henry Hansmann, THE OWNERSHIP OF ENTERPRISE (1996). Owners in partnerships (partners) generally have a greater role in managing the enterprise than owners of corporations (shareholders). Why? Are some mass clients more like partners and others more like shareholders? If so, should the two kinds of mass clients be treated differently?

6.   Silver & Baker argue that economies of scale are an important reason for mass lawsuits. How important are economies of scale likely to be? First, consider the activities listed by Silver & Baker as "joint." Can we determine how much "jointness" exists without knowing how similar, both legally and factually, the plaintiffs' claims are? Second, some economies of scale for plaintiffs, such as those involving researching legal issues and some factual ones, might be achieved by sequential suits just as well as simultaneous suits. Sequential suits pose financing problems for individual lawyers because the recoupment of their fixed investments may take years (e.g., asbestos or tobacco litigation). But that problem might be more directly addressed by improving financing devices.

7.   Most plaintiffs involved in mass actions pay their lawyers under a contingency fee arrangement. That means the cost savings in mass suits must come either from lawyers taking a smaller percentage contingency fee or obtaining a larger settlement. Silver & Baker do not present evidence that lawyers offer clients who participate in mass lawsuits lower contingency fee percentages than clients represented individually, and we do not believe there is evidence that shows that lawyers lower their rates for mass clients. If mass clients do better, it must therefore be from either a substantial reduction in costs (e.g., travel, copying) that are not lawyer fees or because defendants pay a premium for settling en masse. Consider again Silver & Baker's list of "joint" costs. How many are costs not associated with lawyer time or effort? It may well be that lawyers reap most of the benefits of jointness by not reducing fees for mass clients. Why don't lawyers representing mass clients compete on the basis of lower percentage fees? Put another way, why no Wal–Marts?

8.   If cost savings to clients are not likely to be substantial, the boon to clients (as opposed to plaintiffs lawyers) in mass settlements must come from some premium paid by defendants. No one knows (and we know of no

objective way to establish) whether such premiums are actually paid. Defendants, of course, would have no reason to increase settlement offers to reflect the savings to *plaintiffs* of suing en masse. Outside of litigation, buying in bulk is generally cheaper. Thus, defendants who buy in bulk would similarly be expected to pay less, not more. Any premium, then, would have to be be a function, not of savings to plaintiffs, but of savings to the defendant occasioned by the mass suit. But given the greater risk to defendants posed by mass suits, can we be confident that aggregation yields substantial savings to the defendants?

9. Silver & Baker argue that the greater risk to defendants posed by mass lawsuits increases the leverage of plaintiffs in settlement negotiations. Defendants, however, need not agree to try cases en masse just because one lawyer handles many clients. Just as defendants have many ways to resist certification of a class suit, they have many ways to resist less formal consolidations that do not further the defendants' interests. If lawyers can keep (by not lowering the percentage charged as fees) most of the gain from "jointness," and the defendant's cooperation (agreement not to resist consolidation or mass settlement) is necessary for the plaintiff's lawyer to reap that surplus, we would expect collusion between defendants and plaintiffs' lawyers, resulting in lower settlements for clients, not higher ones. Silver & Baker argue that the plaintiffs get leverage from the fact that the group lawyer can offer the defendant lower costs associated with litigation. But might not the defendant also benefit from the group lawyer's ability to sell out some of his clients?

10. Another argument Silver & Baker make for concluding that mass lawsuits give plaintiffs increased leverage is that litigating in a group enables individuals to buy superior service and a higher expected value for their claim. Defendants may, however, have more power than Silver & Baker acknowledge to influence which law firms end up as big players in the mass lawsuit market. A market that tends to be dominated by lawyer cartels, by the way. What might a defendant do to further the business of one plaintiffs' firm over another?

11. Are juries more likely to give higher damage awards to groups than to individuals? Why should that matter?

12. Silver & Baker question the desirability of a unanimity rule as a way of dealing with the risk of attorney misbehavior and unfair allocations. In other contexts, the unanimity rule for group decisionmaking has a long list of defenders, perhaps most notably James M. Buchanan & Gordon Tullock, THE CALCULUS OF CONSENT (1962). Moreover, we find unanimity requirements in various areas of the law, such as criminal juries and partnership (partnership law requires extraordinary matters or matters in contravention of the partnership agreement to be decided by unanimous vote unless the partners agree otherwise). We tend to depart from unanimity rules when the likelihood of a group's failure to agree and the costs of that failure are particularly high or when it is more important for the group to make some decision rather than the best possible decision. Do either of these states inhere in the settlement of mass lawsuits? (Recall that the unanimity

rule regarding mass lawsuits does not apply to the conduct of litigation, but only to settlement agreements.) Silver & Baker argue that "the interest of each [plaintiff] in cooperating with the others to enlarge the aggregate settlement ... should suffice to prevent grossly unfair allocations among group members," making unanimity an unnecessary protection. Why wouldn't the same interests cause each plaintiff to avoid most unreasonable vetoes under a unanimity rule? In fact, the anthropological literature on stateless societies suggests that people in those communities tend to exercise self-restraint because they know that fully pursuing self-interest is likely to bring recrimination and retaliation. Elizabeth Carlson, TRADITION AND CONTRACT (1974).

13.   What do you think of the solutions devised by the Texas lawyers to the "privacy concerns" raised by the aggregate settlement rule? Would the "risk averse" solution have been to disclose all information to all clients? If privacy is a serious concern, why isn't the better solution not to have a mass action at all, assuming the information that would allow clients to assess their settlement in comparison with others could not be provided without violating client privacy? Note that one of the legal protections of privacy, the attorney-client privilege, does not protect attorney-client conversations with one of several "joint clients" from later discovery from another joint client in a subsequent dispute with the lawyer or other clients. Finally, participating in any civil litigation involves sacrificing privacy to some degree. Should that matter to the analysis?

14.   The adverse selection problem identified by Silver & Baker suggests that the main concern of defendants is the ability to award average claims within categories rather than more individualized amounts. This is arguably a different kind of "cost saving" than negotiation costs, legal and factual research, and document drafting. For one thing, it guarantees, as Silver & Baker acknowledge, that some plaintiffs will do worse than they would do if they got paid the full value of their claims. Why should those people join the settlement? If the other cost savings are great enough so that the payout to the high-valued plaintiffs still exceeds the amount they would receive in a separate lawsuit, they would have a strong incentive to stay in the settlement. So why would the defendants fear that they would opt out in that case? Doesn't the mere existence of this concern signal that the defendant thinks that the high-valued plaintiffs are in fact getting a bad deal in the group settlement?

15.   Silver & Baker do not advocate that any individual client be forced to give a majority or super-majority the right to accept a settlement for that client. They argue that each client should be asked to agree to a less-than-unanimous voting rule in the event an aggregate settlement is negotiated. One could say, then, that their real objection is not so much to unanimity as to timing. That is, they are essentially arguing for an advance conflict waiver. Cf. Painter, p. 58 and Macey & Miller, p. 179. This perspective may help explain why Silver & Baker view the waiver of the aggregate settlement rule as consistent with agency law. Does viewing the problem in this way shed any light on it? Note that the law in many jurisdictions is that lawyers for individual clients may not contract away the client's right to decide to

accept a settlement. See Restatement 3rd Law Governing Lawyers § 22 cmt. c (section "prohibits an irrevocable contract that the lawyer will decide on the terms of the settlement"; rather a lawyer's "settlement authority ... is revocable before a settlement is reached"). Would Silver & Baker argue that the rules for individual clients should be changed as well?

16. Silver & Baker argue that defendants often seek restrictions on future practice, despite the prohibition on such restrictions in the ethics rules, because they seek to protect the disclosure of information. There is an alternative explanation. The restrictions create a strong incentive for the group lawyer to discourage any plaintiffs from opting out of the settlement, because the lawyer would not be able to represent those plaintiffs in a subsequent suit. Cf. Painter's discussion of Rule 5.6(b), p. 55 and the notes following Painter's article.

17. For further discussion of the aggregate settlement problem, see Nancy J. Moore, The Case Against Changing the Aggregate Settlement Rule in Mass Tort Lawsuits, 41 S.Tex.L.Rev. 149 (1999); Charles Silver & Lynn Baker, I Cut, You Choose: The Role of Plaintiffs' Counsel in Allocating Settlement Proceeds, 84 Va.L.Rev. 1465 (1998); John C. Coffee, Jr., Conflicts, Consent, and Allocation After Amchem Products—Or, Why Attorneys Still Need Consent to Give Away Their Clients' Money, 84 Va.L.Rev. 1541 (1998), Lewis A. Kornhauser, Fair Division of Settlements: A Comment on Silver and Baker, 84 Va.L.Rev. 1561 (1998).

Chapter V: Competence

Legal Malpractice and Professional Responsibility[*]
JOHN LEUBSDORF

. . .

The time has come to consider legal malpractice law as part of the system of lawyer regulation. . . .

This article will demonstrate how legal malpractice law relates to three important functions of the law of lawyers, namely, delineating the duties of lawyers, creating appropriate incentives and disincentives for lawyers in their dealings with clients and others, and providing access to remedies for those injured by improper lawyer behavior. . . .

I. Specifying Lawyers' Duties

One of the most striking ways in which medical and legal malpractice differ concerns the role of the courts in outlining standards for practice. Although courts properly fashion medical malpractice rules protecting patient rights, such as the informed consent doctrine, no sensible person wants courts to decide how doctors should practice medicine. . . .

Courts hearing legal malpractice cases should pursue a very different course. Judges are lawyers and usually have practiced law although their experience may be limited to litigation or another specialty. Moreover, judges themselves are the main authors of the changes affecting the law of lawyering. They promulgate professional rules, albeit drawing

[*] © 1995 Rutgers University, The State Univ. of New Jersey. Reprinted by permission from 48 Rutgers L. Rev. 101 (1995).

heavily on the proposals of the bar. They construe those rules, in disciplinary proceedings and otherwise, and resolve constitutional challenges to them. Judges frequently decide issues arising in litigation, such as motions to disqualify counsel, invocations of the attorney-client privilege, and attorney fee disputes. They have been responsible for the demolition of the bar's bans on advertising, unhindered price competition, and group practice. In most states, judges wield the inherent power to regulate the bar.

. . .

Lawyers read malpractice decisions, and will heed the possibility of personal liability. Indeed, the evidence indicates that medical malpractice law has a substantial impact on the conduct of physicians, who are less likely than lawyers to learn of and follow legal precedents.

Nevertheless, courts have often failed to recognize the relevance of the judicial role in regulating the legal profession to basic, recurring issues of legal malpractice law.

A. What is Malpractice?

Courts seeking to define the care that lawyers owe clients typically rely on combinations of reasonableness and norms of professional practice. Each of these definitions has its strengths; yet neither is sufficient alone or in combination.

1. Reasonableness. Reasonableness is the usual standard for negligence, either in its traditional "reasonable person" form or under the Learned Hand formula that calls on the judge or jury to balance the cost of precaution against the risk averted multiplied by its probability. . . .

The reasonableness test in either form can resolve many malpractice claims including the very common variety in which a client alleges that a lawyer has failed to meet a statute of limitations or similar deadline. A reasonable lawyer, except in the most extraordinary circumstances, ascertains the limitations period for a client's claim and files before it expires. The cost of doing so by establishing a calendaring system, for example, is less than the cost to clients of losing their claims multiplied by the substantial likelihood that neglect will cause that result.

Reasonableness provides less adequate guidance to resolving other types of malpractice claims. These include claims that a lawyer failed to follow a client's instructions, to inform a client of a conflict of interest, or to exercise sound professional judgment. Some of these claims implicate duties in addition to the duty of care. Other claims call for an assessment of a lawyer's choices, which is difficult to reconcile with the concept of reasonableness embodied in the Learned Hand test: What is the cost of thinking before acting? What is the cost of foregoing a trial on the merits for a client who prefers it to a potentially more favorable settlement? . . .

2. *Professional practice.* Courts decide medical malpractice cases under a standard based on sound professional practice. Some courts have applied a similar standard to legal malpractice cases. 48 In medical cases, this standard reflects the obvious superiority of medical knowledge over legal insight as a guide for physicians.

Whatever its merits in medical malpractice cases, a professional practice test simply will not work for legal malpractice except in a very few areas where procedures are standardized as in real estate closings. Otherwise, we have no information about how most lawyers deal with most of the problems that arise in malpractice cases. A lawyer called as an expert witness will know of the practice in his or her firm and possibly also that of a few other firms. He or she cannot possibly know how most of the thousands of lawyers who practice in a typical jurisdiction handle a specific problem. Even were such knowledge available, it is unclear whose practice would set the standard. . . .

Setting a standard requires considering what lawyers should do, not merely looking to what they actually do. Of course, the standard must be one that ordinary lawyers can meet. . . .

Legal malpractice . . . should be defined as failure to provide a client the services that a lawyer of ordinary knowledge, skill and diligence reasonably should provide. Both reasonableness and professional practice count importantly in this standard. The ultimate question, however, is whether the lawyer in question has done what a lawyer should do in light of all relevant concerns and authorities.

B. Breach of Fiduciary Duty

. . .

There can be no question, of course, that lawyers are fiduciaries. Regardless of whether the ground for this classification is the importance of the matters confided to lawyers, the trust that clients are encouraged to place in them, or the difficulty of monitoring their performance, lawyers are and should be subject to special rules for the protection of their clients. . . .

Courts have said extraordinarily little, and commentators still less, about the relationship between a lawyer's liability for breach of fiduciary duty and legal malpractice liability. . . .

Must a client claiming breach of fiduciary duty prove that the lawyer acted negligently or intentionally, as would be required for a claim of legal malpractice in the narrow sense (that is, a claim limited to lack of due care), or are there acts that render a lawyer strictly liable? Is contributory negligence a defense, as it is for malpractice in the narrow sense? Do the burden-shifting rules that courts have invoked against other fiduciaries apply to lawyers as well? If so, do they apply in suits for malpractice in the narrow sense? Courts and commentators do not seem to have noticed these issues.

Nor have courts and commentators discussed just what fiduciary duties lawyers have....

The fiduciary duties of lawyers raise some serious, but undiscussed, issues. Is there, for example, something akin to a corporate opportunity doctrine for lawyers, analogous to the rule that prevents corporate officers and directors from pursuing business opportunities that might be of interest to their corporation but have not been presented to it? To what extent, if any, can lawyers "contract out" of their fiduciary duties, if they are forbidden to contract out of malpractice liability while agency law duties usually can be varied by contract? When can one obtain from lawyers the equitable remedies traditionally available from other fiduciaries? ...

Fiduciary duties are like traditional malpractice law in that they are enforced through civil actions by injured parties: the beneficiaries of the fiduciary relationship. They are like the obligations to clients set forth in disciplinary rules in that they articulate a relatively detailed regulatory scheme, based on the vulnerability of clients. At the same time, the invocation of fiduciary duty summons up the law and scholarship that deals with the duties of fiduciaries other than lawyers, such as trustees, corporate officers and directors, and agents. Ultimately, legal malpractice in the narrow sense should be considered just one form of actionable breach of fiduciary duty; breach of fiduciary duty should not be viewed as a peripheral subject area that must somehow be squeezed into legal malpractice....

C. The Relevance of Professional Rules

...

Because courts and scholars have given so much attention to professional rules, the role of those rules in malpractice actions has been litigated and discussed with desirable results. Courts have generally approved the use of professional rules as evidence of what the standard of care requires of a lawyer, with some holding that rules define that standard as a matter of law. Commentators likewise support use of the rules either as evidence of the standard or the standard per se. On the other hand, courts have rejected assertions that violation of a professional rule by itself gives rise to a cause of action, particularly in cases where a non-client sues a lawyer.

Using the professional rules makes sense. Not only do these rules reflect a broad consensus among courts and bar committees about how lawyers should behave, they also constitute law that lawyers must obey....

When, for example, the disciplinary rules require a lawyer to withdraw from a representation, it would be intolerable to hold the lawyer liable in damages for abandoning a client. This result would be equally intolerable even if the rules permitted withdrawal, because such permission is usually based on important grounds of public policy. Similarly, when the rules forbid the lawyer to withdraw but the lawyer nevertheless does so, it is hard to imagine a situation in which the lawyer should be able to avoid malpractice liability by claiming that withdrawal was consistent with the duties a lawyer owes a client.

The argument for ignoring the rules in devising malpractice standards is based almost entirely on assertions by the American Bar Association, in the preambles to the Model Rules and Model Code, that the Rules and Code do not augment damage liability. Some state supreme courts did not include these disclaimers when they promulgated versions of the Rules or Code in their states. In any event, courts do not authorize the use of professional rules as evidence of professional standards because the rules themselves so provide, but because of the need for consistent, knowable principles for lawyers to follow. These, of course, are the same concerns underlying the traditional use by courts of criminal and other statutes to fill in the negligence standard, often by treating violations as negligent per se. Nor will using professional rules in malpractice suits discourage rule-makers from raising lawyer standards. Those who draft the rules already proceed on the assumption that they will inevitably affect civil suits, and indeed sometimes shape them for that purpose. And civil liability decisions in turn influence the drafting of rules.

Disciplinary rules cannot be a complete or infallible guide in malpractice actions. Some rules are too vague to provide much help. Other rules seek to protect non-clients and do not prescribe the duties that a lawyer owes to a client....

Most importantly, professional rules are not the only source of legal malpractice law. They must be harmonized with existing law on the civil liabilities of lawyers and other relevant law and should be considered in light of overall regulatory goals....

D. *The Role of Expert Witnesses*

Lawyers and courts have used expert witnesses to fill the gaps left by the courts' failure to define with sufficient specificity what duties a legal malpractice action enforces. Courts have ordinarily required malpractice plaintiffs to produce an expert witness in order to go to the jury, except in the rare case in which it is plain that the acts alleged constitute malpractice. When the plaintiff introduces the testimony of one or more experts, the defendant usually replies in kind. Some of the more celebrated professional responsibility scholars often appear as experts, and have become like the Roman jurisconsults: private persons authorized to give legal opinions.[96]

On what are the experts expert? Typically, on just the matters that I have been contending should be the responsibility of courts: how lawyers should act in various circumstances. The experts rely on professional rules, malpractice and other disciplinary caselaw, practice guides, ethics opinions, scholarship, and principles derived from such sources. Of course, the experts rely also on their own experiences and on what they know of the practice of other lawyers. But so little is known of the behavior of lawyers, and so great is the importance of the circumstances in a malpractice claim, that few opinions, if any, could be given based exclusively on such knowledge. . . .

It follows that much of the role now undertaken by malpractice experts could appropriately be replaced by more detailed instructions from the court. . . .

Several reasons reinforce the desirability of instructions. The cost of access to courts would be reduced were plaintiffs to be less frequently required to produce experts. Cynics might suggest that lawyers advocating mandatory production of expert witnesses are aware that its cost discourages actions, and indeed the protection of those lawyers who have acted properly is one plausible argument for the requirement. More detailed court instructions might also clarify the issues for juries, obviating the need for them to choose between comparable experts with contrary views. Such instructions would also make it easier to coordinate legal malpractice law with other lawyer regulation. The judge's instructions could rely on existing legal authority and would be subject to review on appeal.

These are, of course, some reasons why courts decide issues of law and why expert testimony on such issues is usually inadmissible. In effect, this article has argued that a lawyer's duties, unlike those of a physician, should often be treated as an issue of law. This does not mean that the judge should decide all legal malpractice cases. As in other cases, there will often be instances in which evidence conflicts, or in which advocates properly may make competing arguments. Jurors in malpractice cases, as in others, have a legitimate role in bringing community judgment to bear.

Under this proposal, expert evidence would often continue to be useful, and hence admissible under the broad standards that are currently applicable. Even if courts define lawyer norms with greater specificity, applying these norms to particular situations will often be a matter of professional judgment and not simply one of grasping the meaning of a

---

96. *See* Bruce W. Frier, The Rise of the Roman Jurists 139–96 (1985) (discussing the advisory role and influence of private lawyers); Tony Honoré, Emperors and Lawyers 4–5, 11 (1981) (discussing the influential role played by private lawyers, authorized by the roman emperors to give official opinions).

judge's instruction. Experts can provide insight into whether a lawyer exercised professional judgment within acceptable limits. Experts can communicate what they know of actual professional practice. Experts can sometimes explain the background and reasons for a norm or the context in which a problem arises in ways that would be inappropriate for a court. They can even educate judges. Sometimes, a lawyer will have acted on expert advice, which may be relevant to the propriety of the act in question. . . .

Nevertheless, courts should assume responsibility for the development of legal malpractice law. To the extent possible and appropriate, courts should strive to define malpractice with greater specificity in their instructions. . . . [T]he most important advantage is that [this would] facilitate[] coordinating malpractice law with other kinds of law governing lawyers, making them all more effective and consistent.

II. Adjusting Lawyer Incentives

. . .

To what extent are lawyers privileged to pursue the interests of clients at the expense of others? Another problem concerns lawyer independence from a client. To what extent may or must a lawyer act or advise on the basis of the lawyer's own values, even if a client might prefer a different course? A third group of problems, just beginning to be considered, involves law firms, house counsel offices, and other professional settings in which lawyers practice. To what extent should a lawyer be responsible for the conduct, or subject to the decisions, of colleagues?

Although these problems reappear in the law of legal malpractice, they fail to be recognized as familiar problems of professional responsibility. Instead, they are usually handled with the ungainly tools of negligence law. . . .

Every cause of action encourages the prospective defendant to act to avoid liability. This is often desirable and is indeed a major reason for imposing liability. The incentive, however, may be too great or unfocused, leading to undesirable behavior. Such misincentives are particularly likely to arise from lawyer liabilities because a lawyer's acts often affect people with conflicting interests. Holding lawyers liable to clients increases the incentive to abuse non-clients; holding lawyers liable to non-clients increases the incentive to laxity in representing clients.

In this respect, medical malpractice differs from legal malpractice. Physicians may affect the lives of non-patients. The ethical problem of curing a murderer, for example, has long been recognized. Nonetheless, physicians do and should disregard these effects, receiving a privilege even broader than that of a lawyer to consider the well-being of one person alone. The exceptions are few and strictly limited.[108] . . .

***

108.   See N.J. Stat. Ann. section 26:4-15 (West 1987) (requiring physicians to report communicable diseases of patients to authorities); Tarasoff v. Regents of the Univ. of Cal.,

A. *Lawyer Liability to Nonclients*

The traditional tort battleground of privity furnishes poor terrain to determine when lawyers should be liable to non-clients.... In actions against lawyers, it has often been foreseeable that negligence by a lawyer could harm non-clients. Rendering lawyers liable to non-clients, however, may improperly hamper their efforts to look out for clients. This problem is distinct from the fears of unlimited liability and subjective claims of damage that have led many courts to restrict negligence liability in other situations.

Courts, when determining whether a non-client has a cause of action against a lawyer, should balance the possible incentive to lawyers not to serve their own clients properly and the need of the non-client for protection from lawyer misconduct. This calls for particularized inquiries, with an emphasis on such factors as whether the nonclient is represented by counsel or otherwise protected. Some examples follow.

1. Recovery by opposing litigant. The arguments against allowing recovery by a non-client are strongest when a litigant sues opposing counsel. The adversary system, the judge, and the litigant's own counsel furnish considerable (albeit incomplete) protection against opposing counsel's misconduct....

The tort law of lawyer liability is generally in accord with this conclusion. Courts have held that a lawyer owes no duty of care to an opposing litigant, that a lawyer, like a client, is absolutely privileged against defamation claims arising out of statements in the litigation, and that almost insuperable barriers protect lawyers against suits by opposing parties for abuse of civil proceedings and the like. The main exceptions in tort law to the rule of lawyer nonliability to opposing litigants are intentional misrepresentation 119 and the use of inappropriate process for an improper purpose.

Turning to the law of civil procedure, however, we often find courts holding lawyers liable under Federal Rule of Civil Procedure 11 and similar provisions in ways that are inconsistent with the tort rules. Before the 1993 amendments, an opposing litigant could institute Rule 11 proceedings against a lawyer with prospects (at least in some Circuits) of obtaining a substantial monetary award, even though courts insisted that the award was deterrence rather than compensation. The grounds for recovery—asserting a claim or defense without reasonable factual investigation or reasonable legal foundation—were hard to distinguish from negligence. Since it is unthinkable to recognize a tort duty of due care running between a lawyer and an opposing litigant, it is difficult to justify attorney liability under former Rule 11. In my opinion,

551 P.2d 334, 347 (Cal.1976) (imposing psychotherapist's duty to act when patient threatens to injure another); cf. Molien v. Kaiser Found. Hosps., 616 P.2d 813, 817 (Cal.1980) (holding that physician owes to patient's spouse a duty to exercise due care in diagnosing patient with syphilis).

it could not be justified even though Rule 11 claims were decided by judges with liberal discretion as to the appropriate sanction. Proposals to restore Rule 11 to its pre–1993 form should hence be resisted.

Whether the 1993 amendments have sufficiently defanged Rule 11 remains to be seen. Litigation excesses by lawyers nevertheless consti- tute a real ill, for which other remedies must be found if proceedings for damages are unavailable. Rule 11 could be an appropriate remedy if it were revised further to reduce its potential for adversarial abuse. One possibility would be to provide monetary sanctions assessed at a relative- ly modest rate, say, ten times the lawyer's fee for one hour for a first offense, with a prohibition against reimbursement from the client. An- other remedy would be to induce more frequent disciplinary proceedings by directing judges to report all instances of apparent lawyer misconduct to the authorities for investigation. A national data base for lawyers' disciplinary records could help the public to select ethical counsel and discourage unethical conduct by lawyers. . . .

2. Actions by will beneficiaries. At the opposite extreme from a litigant's suit against opposing counsel is one by a frustrated will beneficiary against a lawyer who drafted the will for a client and supervised its execution, but negligently failed to make it valid. Here, allowing the suit gives lawyers an added incentive to comply with the directives of their clients. Indeed, because the defect only appears after the client's death, the prospect of a suit by the beneficiary probably is the only civil damage incentive available.

Not surprisingly, therefore, courts have increasingly allowed suits by beneficiaries in such circumstances. These courts, however, have often relied on the inadequate theory that the plaintiff is a third party beneficiary of the agreement between the client and the lawyer. It is implausible as a matter of contractual theory to speak of a third party beneficiary having the right to sue a contracting party for failing to fulfill a duty of due care not stated in the agreement, and on which the beneficiary could not reasonably have relied. Such a claim would not be allowed in other contractual situations, or in other situations in which a client intends a lawyer's services to benefit a non-client.[128]

Even in will cases, some courts have disallowed suits brought by one claiming that a testator intended to benefit her, but that the lawyer negligently failed to set forth the testator's intent in the will. The third party beneficiary theory seems at least as applicable to this situation as

---

128. See Raritan River Steel Co. v. Cherry, Bekaert & Holland, 407 S.E.2d 178 (N.C.1991) (explaining that a third party beneficiary must prove that he was an explicitly intended beneficiary to bring suit on the contract); Department of Gen. Servs. v. Celli- Flynn, 540 A.2d 1365, 1368 (Pa.Commw.Ct.1988) (holding that the contract must explicitly express the intention of the parties to make third party a beneficiary, with legal malprac- tice suits by intended beneficiaries of wills forming a narrow exception). But see 3 E. Allan Farnsworth, FARNSWORTH ON CONTRACTS section 10.3, at 16 n.19 (1990) (approvingly citing a number of will cases employing the third party beneficiary theory).

to the defective will problem. The objection that allowing recovery would undermine the evidentiary requirements of the law of wills applies to both situations....

When there is strong evidence of the testator's intent—and often lawyers can help the testator create such evidence—a lawyer need not fear that complying with that intent will subject the lawyer to liability at the hands of frustrated beneficiaries. On the contrary, if beneficiaries are allowed to sue, it is failing to comply with the client's wishes that puts the lawyer in jeopardy.... Courts should carefully consider the good and bad incentives to be created in the circumstances of the cases before them when deciding whether to allow such actions.

3. *Claims by a beneficiary against lawyers who represent trustees and executors.* It is not surprising that courts disagree whether the lawyer for a trustee or executor owes a duty of care to the beneficiaries under the trust or will. Often it is unclear how such lawyers should act and what incentives are appropriate. Because the clients are themselves fiduciaries, they must act in the best interests of others. That limits the proper behavior of their lawyers, who may assist their clients only toward those clients' lawful ends. Beneficiaries are often the logical persons to enforce those limits. Yet in many situations trustees and executors may properly disagree with one or more beneficiaries, and in doing so they are entitled to the assistance of counsel, which should not be hindered by their lawyers' fear of suits by non-clients.

The need of beneficiaries for protection also varies. Many beneficiaries are vulnerable to exploitation. That is one reason trustees and executors are treated as fiduciaries. Some beneficiaries, however, are wealthy, sophisticated adults with their own lawyers. Such beneficiaries might use the right to sue to wrest undue advantage. And sometimes the fiduciary is sufficiently controllable by direct actions. This, for instance, is ordinarily the situation of corporate directors subject to derivative actions.

The issue should thus not be whether the lawyers for trustees and executors owe beneficiaries an enforceable duty of care, but rather what kinds of duties they owe and in what circumstances....

4. *Claims by parties to commercial transactions encouraged to rely on another party's lawyer....*

Courts ... have permitted suit for negligence when a lawyer or party has encouraged the opposing party to rely on the lawyer's words or acts. For example, a plaintiff may have insisted on the lawyer's opinion letter as a condition of the transaction. In other cases, a lawyer has volunteered advice or help to an unrepresented person at a real estate closing.

Recognizing non-client claims in such limited situations does not undermine services a client can properly expect from a lawyer. The client benefits from the non-client's reliance on the client's lawyer because that reliance facilitates the consummation of the transaction. Looking at the situation ex ante, the client benefits from the non-client's right to sue the lawyer for negligence because the existence of that right encourages nonclients to rely on lawyers in similar situations. No doubt some clients would benefit even more if they could use the reliance of a non-client without their lawyers' following through; but clients have no right to that benefit.

B. Lawyers and Clients

Legal malpractice law should give lawyers an incentive to pursue the best interests of clients. That seems simple enough, but courts have not always recognized it. Moreover, liability should sometimes be limited to protect the proper independence of the bar, among other reasons. Here, as elsewhere, courts should shape malpractice law to meet the concerns of professional responsibility law, not through unthinking application of tort law norms.

1. Damages for emotional distress. Although some courts routinely allow emotional distress damages in malpractice actions, other courts either regard them as a kind of punitive damages, granted only to punish egregious lawyer misconduct, or take intermediate positions. The hesitation to award such damages probably results from comparing malpractice claims arising from economic disputes to contract claims, in which emotional distress damages are rarely allowed. It also reflects fear of padded claims.

At a minimum, a party should be entitled to emotional distress damages upon a proper evidentiary showing when other damages are normally unavailable. Otherwise, lawyers would have a diminished incentive to exercise care in such situations. . . .

2. Malpractice in criminal defense. A number of courts have allowed a convicted criminal defendant to recover for malpractice only on a showing, not just that he or she would have been acquitted but for malpractice, but also that he or she was in fact innocent, or has received post-conviction relief setting aside the conviction. Such holdings reflect a fear of overstimulated defense lawyers 143 or overlitigious convicts.

In my opinion, there is more reason to fear that defense lawyers will do too little than too much. Most defense lawyers practice under fee arrangements—a lump sum fee paid in advance, or a modest salary from a public defender's office—that provide smaller incentives to diligence than hourly or contingent fees. Criminal defense work is demoralizing. Criminal defendants, except for the organized and white collar crime elites, lack the money, status or power that makes some lawyers listen to clients. Institutional pressures encourage guilty pleas and quick trials. Moreover, malpractice juries will be reluctant to award damages to clients who are also convicted criminals. With great respect for the many dedicated and able criminal defense lawyers who continue to strive in difficult circumstances to make defendants' rights a reality, and with regrets for making their lives still harder, there is no reason to exempt the defense bar from the malpractice remedy considered salutary for other lawyers.

3. *A lawyer independence defense.* One way to deal with the possibility that malpractice liability will push lawyers, whatever their field of practice, into abusively adversarial behavior is to recognize as a defense to malpractice claims a lawyer's refusal to perform an act reasonably believed to be unlawful or immoral.

Some authority supports this lawyer independence defense. Were courts and commentators to enunciate the defense more explicitly, they would make it more effective in reinforcing the willingness of lawyers to resist pressures to pursue a client's interest beyond proper limits.

. . .

C. *Lawyers in Firms: Vicarious Liability*

When lawyers practice in groups, legal malpractice law should seek to provide at least two further incentives. First, the law should spur lawyers to monitor and improve each other's practice. Second, it should encourage lawyers to resist peer pressure to behave improperly.

Although civil liability has important roles in providing these incentives, the relevant liability is usually not for legal malpractice. Giving lawyers causes of action against their firms or (in the case of house counsel) against their employers can help them resist attempts to induce unprofessional behavior and discourage potential defendants from resorting to such pressures. Malpractice liability may have the same impact or a contrary one, depending on whether the unprofessional behavior in question hurts or helps clients.

The essential impact of malpractice law on behavior within firms stems from the vicarious liability of the firm itself and its partners, which gives all of them the incentive to make sure that other lawyers in the firm do not commit malpractice. When a firm is organized as a partnership, partnership law provides this vicarious liability. Liability, however, also implements the professional principle that the firm and each of its partners take responsibility for the practice of every lawyer in the firm. Thus, vicarious liability has sometimes been recognized for professional corporations.

Unfortunately, the growth of law firms and the multiplication of malpractice suits against them 163 has led to efforts to limit vicarious liability. Lawyers have persuaded state legislatures to allow them to create professional corporations (or limited liability partnerships or limited liability companies) in which the shareholder-lawyers are not liable for torts of their fellows in which they did not actually participate.

Reportedly, some firms are seeking to produce similar results by turning themselves into limited partnerships or by entering into other types of contract. Lawyers understandably shy away from liability for the negligence of hundreds of other lawyers, some of whom are scattered around the world and unknown to them. Because most law firms are thinly capitalized, their partners face a real threat of personal liability. The multimillion dollar settlements accepted by Kaye, Scholer and other firms, and the financial collapse of Finley, Kumble naturally caused prudent lawyers to seek protection. So many firms have taken advantage of professional corporation and similar statutes, that little may soon remain of vicarious liability in practice.

The growth of law firms, however, makes vicarious liability more important than ever. Each of a firm's lawyers, no matter how lowly or distant from the main office, wields the prestige of the firm. Clients rely on the firm as a whole, expect it to live up to its reputation, and can be gravely harmed if it does not. To the extent that the partners boost the associate-partner ratio by hiring many inexperienced lawyers with fewer experienced ones to supervise them, they increase the likelihood of negligence. Partners of large firms, moreover, reap benefits sufficient to compensate them for the risks of vicarious liability and are not distant investors who cannot reasonably be expected to supervise the corporation. The thin capitalization of many firms makes vicarious liability important to ensure internalization of the full costs of malpractice.

Most importantly, the measures that control malpractice are institutional measures such as data bases that track conflicts of interest, committees to screen new clients, computerized calendaring systems, proper accounting systems, supervisory arrangements, internal peer review of professional conduct, hiring and training procedures, and review of opinion letters. Vicarious liability ensures that partners will institute such measures. Considering the propensity of lawyers to act independently and to bend rules, it is also important to ensure that measures, once instituted, will receive more than lip service. Indeed, vicarious liability benefits the firm and its lawyers by promoting mutual efforts to raise standards, and by discouraging efforts by sued lawyers to shift the blame to their partners.

These professional concerns, rather than those of business organization or agency law, should be used to distinguish between acceptable and unacceptable limitations of law firm liability. When it comes to a firm's commercial transactions, such as signing a lease for its office, shareholders of a professional corporation should enjoy the same freedom to limit liability that people in other businesses do. Landlords are accustomed to dealing with limited liability corporations. If dissatisfied with the firm's credit, they can ask individual lawyers to sign the lease or guaranty their firm's performance under it. Likewise, there need be no partner liability for a partner's private business venture even if carried out from the partner's office, provided that the partner was not also acting as a lawyer in the matter. But there should be no surrender of the principle that lawyers stand behind their fellows in a firm's practice of law.

III.   Access to Remedies

. . .

A. *Some Current Problems*

. . .

1. Statutes of limitations. As many courts have recognized, the characteristics of legal malpractice litigation call for at least four specialized rules affecting statutes of limitations. First, because of a lawyer's duty to inform a client of any malpractice claim and a client's right to rely on a lawyer, the statute should not run until the client discovers, or should have discovered, facts indicating the presence of a malpractice claim. Second, while a representation continues, a client is entitled to assume that a lawyer will correct any mistakes. Therefore, the statute should not run until the representation for the matter in question comes to an end. Third, because some errors by lawyers do not harm a client until discovered and exploited by others, as in contract drafting, and because a client should not have to draw the attention of others to the error by filing suit, the statute should not run until the client has suffered significant harm. Fourth, because bringing a malpractice action during another action out of which it arose could trip up the client in that underlying action, the statute should not run until the underlying action ends and all appeals are decided.

As in California, these rules should be embodied in a special legal malpractice statute of limitations. Probably more legal malpractice precedents deal with the statute of limitations than with any other issue. It is deplorable that time and money have been wasted in litigating what should have been a threshold issue. Courts in each state should not have to work out, case by case, principles recognized elsewhere.

A legal malpractice statute of limitations could also set its own time period, which might well be shorter than that of other statutes of limitations. Once all the events required by the special malpractice rules have occurred, it should not require more than two years for a client to find a new lawyer, seek a settlement, and file suit when necessary. . . .

2. The case within a case. Much of the expense of legal malpractice litigation results from the "case within a case" doctrine. This doctrine requires a client claiming malpractice in the conduct of another action to relitigate that other action to prove that the client would have prevailed but for the lawyer's malpractice. Aside from its expense, the doctrine gives a client the task of litigating a former case against the client's own former lawyer, who knows the strengths and weaknesses of the case, perhaps from the client's own confidences. Furthermore, the doctrine puts a lawyer in the unseemly position of contending that a case he or she agreed to bring was hopeless.

One plausible substitute for trying the case within a case would be the loss-of-a-chance approach, which has been adopted in England and France, and in medical malpractice actions in the United States. Under this approach, the plaintiff obtains compensation for losing the chance of recovery, whose value is measured by the probability of prevailing and the likely damages. This approach may call for less precision than the case within a case approach and may be less costly. Courts, however, have not accepted it in the rare instances in which litigants proposed it in legal malpractice cases. Perhaps judges find it easier to accept the unpredictability of medical matters than that of litigation.

A related approach would grant plaintiffs relief based on the settlement value of their claims. Most civil claims are settled and settlement occurs even after trial begins. Courts have allowed clients to recover from their former lawyers for failure to settle and for negligently making inadequate settlements. Because settlement is always probable, courts should extend these rulings by presuming that when a lawyer commits malpractice and loses the case, it would otherwise have been settled. . . .

The damages under this approach would be the case's settlement value, a figure that tort lawyers are accustomed to specifying, and that is roughly equivalent to that allowed under the "loss of a chance" approach. . . .

3. *Collectibility of previous judgment.* Not content with requiring a client to show that he or she would have prevailed in a previous civil action but for a lawyer's malpractice, most courts have also placed on the client the burden of showing that the resulting judgment would have been collectible.

This burden is unjustifiable. It ill befits a lawyer who has agreed to bring an action to contend later that the litigation was pointless. It is hardly credible that most judgments are uncollectible; if they are, litigation is a cruel hoax. When a judgment really is uncollectible, the defendant, as a trial lawyer, should not find that hard to prove. When the judgment is collectible, requiring the client to prove collectibility is inefficient and obstructs access to court.

Here, and perhaps in other instances, courts should follow the traditional reversal of the burden of proof for appropriate issues arising in actions by beneficiaries against fiduciaries. The lawyer should bear the burden of persuading the jury that any judgment would have been uncollectible, or at a minimum should bear the burden of coming forward with evidence demonstrating that uncollectibility was a real possibility.

4. *Deducting phantom attorney fees from recovery; attorney fee recovery.* Another issue that arises when a lawyer has negligently failed

to succeed in a civil action is whether the client should recover the full amount of the judgment that would have been obtained but for the lawyer's malpractice, or whether the lawyer may deduct the attorney fee that the client would have paid in the event of success. Most decisions allow full recovery. . . .

Refusal to deduct the attorney fee can be supported as a regulatory sanction, analogous to the doctrine under which a misbehaving lawyer may forfeit the right to payment even for valuable services. . . .

Another argument that supports the majority view denying fee deduction is that the client should not have to deduct two attorney fees from a single recovery, one for the negligent lawyer's services or phantom services in the original action, and one for the client's lawyer in the malpractice action itself. Such a double deduction would discourage malpractice claims. Indeed, it would make them virtually impossible to bring whenever the original claim was not large enough to pay both fees. The lawyer defendant, after all, in effect represented that his or her services would suffice to resolve the client's problem. By failing to do so, and by then declining to recompense the client without a suit, the lawyer multiplied the client's legal expenses, or rather, will have done so if the court deducts phantom legal expenses from the malpractice judgment. When the court declines to deduct legal fees, the client receives not a windfall, but rather what the lawyer originally agreed to provide.

. . .

Notes

1. One of Leubsdorf's big themes is that the law of legal malpractice should be oriented more toward "professional responsibility" goals than tied to the doctrinal requirements of tort, contract, agency, or organizational law. Is he right? What does he mean by professional responsibility goals? Note that as a matter of tort law, legal malpractice is relatively unique because it allows recovery of economic loss for negligent, nonphysical harm, which tort law's "economic loss doctrine" generally precludes. This might help explain, for example, the reluctance of courts to impose damages for emotional harm—something Leubsdorf criticizes. To say it "explains" the reluctance, does not mean the reluctance is justified. Would awarding damages for emotional harm in legal malpractice cases be a good idea?

2. Early in the article, Leubsdorf states: "Lawyers read malpractice decisions, and will heed the possibility of personal liability." Do lawyers in fact read malpractice decisions? Perhaps in large firms, which can afford to employ lawyers to keep up with malpractice law and distribute updates to firm members. Or legal malpractice insurers may keep firms abreast of important developments. See Cohen, Legal Malpractice Insurance, p. 253. That aside, it is interesting to consider how malpractice liability is underemphasized in legal culture in comparison to the ethics rules, at least in the rhetoric of practicing lawyers and in law schools. Most law schools have no course on legal malpractice and many professional responsibility courses give

scant attention to the subject. Many state bars have special continuing legal education requirements for ethics, but courses focusing on malpractice liability may not "count." In our experience, state bar authorities are not inclined to treat malpractice courses as satisfying the ethics requirement.

3. Leubsdorf's proposed "lawyer independence defense" is an attempt to respond to lawyers who argue that they have no choice but to follow the client's wishes because if they do not the client will sue them. Another way to think about this issue is through the tort law doctrine of duty. A lawyer does not have a duty to break the ethics rules or other law to further the client's cause. Is Leubsdorf's defense a better idea? Note also that although there is scant case law supporting Leubsdorf's proposed defense, there is also scant (to put it mildly) case law holding a lawyer liable for refusing to act unethically (or otherwise illegally) to further a client's cause. Nonetheless, lawyers continually argue that following some ethics rules (or other law) might leave them vulnerable to malpractice suits, particularly those ethics rules or other law designed to protect third parties or prevent cut throat litigation practices. They seem to imagine (conveniently) a body of case law that does not exist.

4. Leubsdorf argues that the standard of care for lawyers should be based on what lawyers should do (that is, a normative standard) rather than simply what they actually do (a custom-based standard). Are there problems with having judges set those norms? How should they (or anyone else for that matter) decide on the correct norm? How are they (or we) to know what the "average" lawyer can and cannot do, at "reasonable" cost? Is Leubsdorf really only arguing that a normative standard be substituted for a custom-based standard where custom is not easily ascertained? Or when custom is demonstrably wrong? Demonstrably wrong in what sense?

5. Leubsdorf asks whether an analogy to the corporate opportunity doctrine applies to lawyers. As a matter of the ethics rules, the answer appears to be yes. Under Model Rules of Professional Conduct Rule 1.8(b) (2003), a lawyer may not use information relating to the representation to the client's disadvantage without the client's consent. One of the new comments approved by the ABA as part of the Ethics 2000 revisions gives an example of conduct that would violate the rule: a lawyer who learns that a client intends to buy and develop several parcels of land and uses that information to buy one of the parcels for himself or another client. And as Leubsdorf points out in an omitted footnote, the answer under the Restatement (Third) of the Law Governing Lawyers also appears to be yes.

6. Leubsdorf refers to the controversy over whether courts should look to ethics rules as establishing the standard of care in legal malpractice actions. As he states, often they do, despite the ABA's attempts to forestall such usage. In the Scope Section of the newest version of the Model Rules, the ABA repeats its position that the rules "are not designed to be a basis of civil liability," but concedes that violation of a rule may be evidence that the applicable standard of conduct was breached. Why is the bar so concerned about the use of ethics rules to establish civil liability, especially given that its position encourages the multiplication of norms and hence risks confus-

ing lawyers? Is it that the ethical prohibitions or requirements are so arduous or (as Leubsdorf suggests) vague that the average lawyer cannot be expected to follow them? Or is the bar's commitment to keep the ethics rules separate from civil law a means of preserving the rules as territory from which civil law may be challenged, critiqued or resisted, as Koniak suggests in The Law Between the Bar and the State, p. 23? Is the preservation of such territory a good thing, given that the state's law, as Koniak calls it, might well be wrong? Notice that even Leubsdorf does not advocate an approach that would call every violation of an ethics rule per se negligence. Why doesn't he?

7. Leubsdorf argues that judges should take over more responsibility from expert witnesses in the form of detailed jury instructions. Since the publication of Leubsdorf's article, courts have tightened up the rules on expert testimony, particularly "scientific" testimony, but thus far those rulings have had little effect on the use of "ethics" experts. But see Cicero v. Borg–Warner Automotive, Inc. (ED Mich 9/24/01) (law professor's qualification to testify as expert in legal ethics cannot be established simply by pointing to non-peer-reviewed law review articles, service as a TV commentator, awards, and appointments to professionalism and discipline committees). For some recent thinking on the ethical responsibilities of ethics experts, see Carl M. Selinger, The Problematic Role of the Legal Ethics Expert Witness, 13 Geo. J. Legal Ethics 405 (2000); and Nancy J. Moore, The Ethical Role and Responsibilities of a Lawyer–Ethicist: The Case of the Independent Counsel's Independent Counsel, 68 Fordham L. Rev. 771 (1999).

8. Leubsdorf endorses the results in the will beneficiary cases allowing suits by nonclient beneficiaries against the lawyers on the ground that this increases the incentives for lawyer competence when the client could not bring the suit. Not all states, however, allow such suits, even when some allow some other nonclients to sue. See, e.g, Glover v. Southard, 894 P.2d 21 (Colo. App. 1994); Noble v. Bruce, 709 A.2d 1264 (Md.1998); cf. Davis v. Somers, 915 P.2d 1047 (Ore.1996) (holding that 10 year statute of repose started to run from date of drafting of will rather than death of testator, and so suit by beneficiaries was time-barred). One might ask why the executor could not bring such suits, as trustees in bankruptcy sometimes do. One answer is the executor may be the lawyer who drafted the will; another is that the executor may not have sufficient incentive to bring the suit because he would not get anything from it.

9. Leubsdorf is also critical of the contract beneficiary theory. But in the badly-drawn will case, unlike the typical contract case (where the original contracting parties are often still available or if not, substitutes are available via assignment), the intended beneficiary may be the only person available to enforce the contractual obligations. Would the adoption of a third party beneficiary theory mean that the lawyer and will client could contract out of liability to the beneficiaries in return for a lower fee? Would this run afoul of the ethics rule prohibiting lawyers from limiting malpractice liability? In a state that recognizes the privity limitation, could the lawyer and client contract around that, by designating beneficiaries as

contractual third party beneficiaries? If so, would a lawyer's failure to suggest that option to the client itself be malpractice? Enforceable by the beneficiaries?

10.   Leubsdorf refers to the possibility of contracting to avoid fiduciary duties. See Painter, p. 58, for a discussion of contracting around ethics rules; and Wolfram, p. 402 for a discussion of the rule against contracting out of malpractice liability and the inconsistency of limited liability partnerships with that prohibition. There is also an extensive literature in organizational law about how broad the ability to contract out of fiduciary duties should be, pitting the "contractarians" against advocates of more immutable fiduciary obligations. E.g., Frank H. Easterbrook & Daniel R. Fischel, Contract and Fiduciary Duty, 36 J.L. & Econ. 425 (1993); Symposium, Contractual Freedom in Corporate Law, 89 Colum. L. Rev. 1395 (1989). Note that with respect to the ethics rules, lawyers need to consider the applicability of Model Rule 1.2(c), which allows lawyers to contract with clients to limit the scope of the representation as long as the limitation is reasonable and the client gives informed consent. See generally Zacharias, Hyman & Silver; Leonard E. Gross, Contractual Limitations on Attorney Malpractice Liability: An Economic Approach, 75 Ky. L.J. 793 (1987).

Legal Malpractice Insurance and Loss Prevention: a Comparative Analysis of Economic Institutions*
GEORGE M. COHEN

. . .

I. A Brief History of Legal Malpractice Insurance

Although the first policy for lawyers' professional liability written through a United States company was issued in 1945, the history of legal malpractice insurance in this country is usually traced to the 1960s, when it first gained prominence. Legal malpractice insurance was offered by property and casualty insurers as an ancillary service to their main business. . . .

In the 1970s malpractice claims against lawyers increased substantially. In some jurisdictions, such as California, insurers started dropping out of the of the legal malpractice insurance market and focusing on more profitable and stable areas. In other jurisdictions, the availability of insurance increased. . . . By the end of the 1970s, premiums were increasing sharply. . . . On the insurance side, in 1978 Oregon adopted mandatory malpractice insurance for lawyers, and North Carolina and California formed the first "bar-related," mutual (owned by the lawyers) insurance companies. The following year saw the arrival of the Attorneys' Liability Assurance Society (ALAS), a non-bar-related mutual that limited membership to large (at the time, 40 or more lawyers) law firms outside of New York.

. . .

In the 1980s the insurance crisis hit legal malpractice insurance, as it did other areas. Premiums increased between 400% and 1500%, coverage decreased, and availability declined. These premium increases were driven in part by lower interest rates and in part by an increase in the frequency and severity of malpractice claims being made against lawyers. Some of these claims were securities actions spurred on by *National Student Marketing*,* liability for which insurance companies were unable to avoid completely because of their broad duty to defend. Other claims stemmed from the collapse of the real estate market, and a crackdown on tax shelters by the IRS and SEC. According to one source: "Between 1982 and 1984, estimated losses nationwide, including adjustment expenses, roughly doubled. Between 1982 and 1986, no other area of professional liability insurance experienced anywhere near this rate of severe increase for a similar period." Some insurers responded by dropping out of the market; others restricted coverage and limited the

---

* © 1997 Connecticut Insurance Law Journal Ass'n. Reprinted by permission from 4 Conn. Ins. L. J. 305 (1997).

* [See discussion of this case by Koniak, pp. 32–35.]

availability of excess insurance. Premiums remained high through the end of the decade, as claims frequency remained high. Lawyers again responded by forming more bar-related mutuals, in part spurred on by the 1986 Liability Risk Retention Act.[23] Most notable among the new mutuals were the Association of Trial Lawyers Assurance (ATLA) for members of the trial lawyers' group that has the same acronym, and the Attorneys Liability Protection Society (ALPS), both of which started in 1988.

In the 1990s, the biggest developments so far have not been in malpractice insurance, where rates seem to have stabilized and mutuals continue to grow and thrive, but in the law of lawyering and the law of law firms. Cases arising out of the savings and loan crisis, including the famous *Kaye, Scholer* case,* led to huge payouts by malpractice insurers. . . .

II.   The Economic Institutions of Legal Malpractice Insurance

A.   *What Is Legal Malpractice Insurance?*

Legal malpractice insurance is one of many economic institutions that regulate lawyer behavior. It does so indirectly and often incidentally. Like other third-party liability insurance, legal malpractice insurance regulates indirectly in the sense that legal liability—in this case, legal malpractice—provides the primary form of regulation. Legal liability sets the regulatory standard; liability insurance responds to that standard. Legal liability is of course not the only form of regulation. Ethics rules, for example, also serve to regulate lawyer behavior. But in this article, I take legal malpractice liability as the relevant regulatory mechanism. I also take the standard of legal malpractice as given, though recognizing how it has changed.

Liability insurance can either help or hinder the regulatory goals of the liability system, in addition to simply serving the interests of the insured.[25] To understand the regulatory function of legal malpractice insurance, then, we must understand the goals of legal malpractice. Recognizing that other legitimate goals of legal malpractice exist, I . . . focus in this paper on deterrence. . . . Liability insurance serves the

---

23.   The purpose of the act was to encourage the formation of Risk Retention Groups (RRGs), which are special purpose insurance companies wholly owned by the policyholders. The major advantage of RRG status is that "after meeting the regulatory requirements of the state in which it is chartered, an RRG can provide insurance to members in other states without first having to meet their individual licensing requirements." [ISSUES IN FORMING A BAR-RELATED PROFESSIONAL LIABILITY INSURANCE CO. (American Bar Ass'n., Standing Committee on Lawyers' Professional Liability ed., 1989)] at 7.

* [See discussion of this case by Weinstein, p. 137].

25.   It is common to think of liability insurance as providing the link between ignorance of the law and deterrence. Even if a person doesn't know the rules of negligence, the deterrence theorist argues, his insurance company does, and will force him to conform his conduct to these rules. *See, e.g.,* William M. Landes & Richard A. Posner, THE ECONOMIC STRUCTURE OF TORT LAW 11 (1987) (arguing that one way tort law deters is "by forcing up liability insurance rates to the point where people are priced out of driving").

deterrence goal of the liability system when it reduces the sum of the costs of prevention and expected harm below what would exist in the absence of insurance. Liability insurance disserves the deterrence goal of the liability system when it reduces costs to the insured merely at the expense of increasing costs to the victims of harm. . . .

. . . I define liability insurance broadly as any institution whose purpose is to reduce for some person (the insured) any cost associated with liability risk to that person. We tend not to think of liability insurance as any institution designed to reduce costs associated with the risk of liability, and to think of liability insurance so broadly is perhaps confusing. But thinking of it more narrowly is also somewhat confusing, or at least confining. The narrow conception of liability insurance views insurance as "loss spreading" services offered by a commercial entity designed primarily to offer such services. Economists, however, have tried to get us to think of insurance more broadly than that to show how other institutions perform the same functions. But even economists seem not to want to adopt the broadest definition. Nor do they seem to agree on how to delimit liability insurance.

For example, one way to think of liability insurance is as a particular method of risk reduction, namely risk pooling or diversification. This definition ties the concept of insurance to risk aversion. Risk aversion . . . represents a willingness to pay more than the expected value of some risk (the probability of harm times the size of the loss) to avoid bearing that risk. The amount in excess of the expected value that a risk-bearer would be willing to pay is called the "risk premium." . . . Risk pooling eliminates the costs of risk aversion to the insured by substituting the certain costs of pooling for the uncertain risks of harmful conduct and its attendant liability. Defining insurance in terms of risk pooling narrows the concept of insurance in two ways. First, risk pooling does not reduce other costs associated with the risk of liability, such as the costs of preventing harmful conduct (precautions) and the loss associated with the harmful conduct. Second, risk pooling is not the only means of reducing the costs associated with risk aversion. One could also reduce the costs of risk aversion by reducing the magnitude of losses associated with harmful conduct, or by increasing wealth.

For these reasons, economists have sometimes espoused broader definitions of liability insurance. Judge Posner in his treatise seems to define insurance as any effort, not just pooling, to reduce the costs associated with risk aversion as opposed to expected accident costs. Thus, he distinguishes "insurance" from "prevention"[.] . . . For example, if expected losses from an accident are $100, then any expenditure up to $100 to eliminate those expected losses is "prevention." Any (rational) expenditure above $100, however, is not "prevention" but rather "insurance" because the only purpose it serves is to reduce the costs associated with risk aversion. The reason for this somewhat strained definition is to emphasize the idea that if more than $100 is spent on prevention, there is, in some meaningful sense, "too much" prevention, a point I shall return to....

... Professors Ehrlich and Becker, in their classic article,* define insurance as any attempt to reduce the size of the loss associated with harmful conduct. They distinguish insurance from "protection," which they define as any attempt to reduce the likelihood of harm. Thus, in the above example, if the expected losses of $100 are the product of a $100,000 harm and a likelihood of .001, then any expenditure designed to reduce the $100,000 (as opposed to reducing the .001) is "insurance," whether such expenditure is more or less than the $100 expected harm, and whether or not it involves pooling....

The reason Ehrlich and Becker define insurance in the way they do is to emphasize that self-insurance, which they define as any attempt by an individual to reduce the size of his potential losses without resorting to the market, can be viewed as a substitute for insurance purchased on the market. This focus on self-insurance distinguishes the Ehrlich and Becker definition from another definition of insurance, used by Shavell and Arrow, which involves any shifting of risk from one party to another. The risk-shifting definition is useful because it leads one to recognize that many contracts, whether with insurance companies, the potential victims of harm, or with other loss reduction entities such as law firms, provide a form of insurance against the risks associated with legal liability. I will use the term "contract insurance" to refer to any contract with a party other than an insurance company that serves to shift liability risks.

I have elaborated on these definitions of insurance to make several points. Definitions depend on the purposes to be served. If we want to engage in comparative institutional analysis, then it makes sense to define insurance more broadly than economists have so far done. Thus, I shall use legal malpractice insurance to refer ... to any institution designed to reduce any of the costs associated with the risk of legal liability. That means that self-insurance, contract insurance, and market insurance are all possible forms of insurance. It also means that insurance is not necessarily tied to risk pooling, risk aversion, or size-of-loss reduction. In particular, insurance may involve loss prevention. And to return to the earlier notion of insurance as what insurance companies do, insurance companies do sometimes provide loss prevention services. In fact, sometimes this is the main thing insurance companies do.... But to preserve the common and regulatory notion of insurance companies, I will reserve the term "market insurance" for firms that provide at least risk pooling services and may also provide loss prevention services....

---

* See Isaac Ehrlich & Gary S. Becker, Market Insurance, Self–Insurance, and Self–Protection, J. Pol. Econ. 623, 633 (1972).

B. *Self–Insurance*

Self-insurance is the simplest form of insurance. It is also an extremely common one among lawyers, especially among sole practitioners. To isolate the incentives on lawyers created by self-insurance, let us assume for the moment that clients can neither take precautions nor buy market insurance to reduce the risks associated with legal malpractice.

Lawyers have a variety of risk reduction measures at their disposal. First, lawyers can take steps ex ante to reduce the likelihood that malpractice liability will occur. These steps include precautions, such as an improved calendaring or conflicts-checking system. They also include reducing the activity level of various forms of practice, such as restricting areas of practice or screening for and refusing to service high-risk clients. Second, lawyers can take steps to reduce the size of any loss to them from malpractice liability that does occur. These steps include ex ante precautions, such as . . . improving one's system for handling and accounting for client funds. They also include ex post mitigation, such as refiling a claim barred by the statute of limitations in another jurisdiction, or ex post loss reduction.

Not all methods of risk reduction by lawyers are socially beneficial. Some forms of risk reduction by lawyers will increase risk to their clients. In particular, a lawyer could reduce his losses from malpractice liability by making himself more judgment proof, say by maintaining minimal assets or sheltering assets in a way that would make them more costly for a plaintiff to reach. . . . Expenditures that do not increase accuracy are socially wasteful; expenditures that improve accuracy may be socially beneficial, but only if they reduce error costs more than the amount of the expenditures. Legal defense expenditures decrease the likelihood that the lawyer will be wrongfully convicted of malpractice, but they also increase the likelihood that the lawyer will be wrongfully exonerated of malpractice. . . .

Finally, self-insured lawyers may be able to diversify their risks, that is, to reduce their risk premium associated with risk aversion. Diversification reduces the risk to the lawyer, but leaves the risk to the client unchanged. Diversification may be difficult for sole practitioners, however. They can perhaps diversify by expanding their client base, but diversification requires that risks be uncorrelated, and because the risk of malpractice is generally lawyer-controlled rather than client-controlled, it is possible that the risk of malpractice could increase from having more clients. . . .

A lawyer who bears the full cost of his legal malpractice as a result of liability will be led to minimize the sum of his risk reduction (precaution) costs, expected malpractice costs (represented by the probability of malpractice times the loss, or PL), and risk premium. What this means is that the rational lawyer will allocate risk reduction dollars among the different techniques—pay for insurance services—until the marginal cost of the last act of cost reduction equals the marginal benefit to him in terms of reduced costs. This result differs slightly, but significantly, from the result usually presented in the law and economics literature, which is that the tortfeasor will take precautions until the marginal benefit of those precautions in reduced expected liability equals the marginal cost of the precautions. The difference is that there may be some situations in which it will be desirable for the lawyer to spend $1 on risk reduction even if that $1 is greater than the marginal reduction in expected malpractice costs (PL). The reason for the difference is that the typical economic model, for reasons of analytical convenience as well as the model's focus on the choice of liability rule rather than insurance institution, assumes the risk premium is 0 (the actors are risk neutral), or at least defines the social optimum with reference to that assumption. The justification for the assumption is either the lawyer or the client can diversify the risk at no cost, or equivalently, can purchase market insurance at an "actuarially fair" premium equal to the expected malpractice costs....

The final part of the economic analysis of self-insurance asks how lawyers respond to exogenous changes in risk, or what economists call comparative statics.... Let us consider how that increased risk has probably affected self-insurance. An increase in risk can be caused by an increase in the probability of malpractice liability or an increase in the size of the losses associated with malpractice, as well as by an increase in the risk premium of lawyers or clients. The source of this increased risk can be a change in the legal, economic, or social environment, or more likely a combination of all three.

For example, one plausible explanation of increased risk of malpractice liability is increased competition among lawyers. Although increased competition could reduce malpractice by making lawyers more responsive to their clients' needs, there are other possibilities. One is that if clients cannot distinguish careful lawyering from bad lawyering, competition might lead lawyers to become more neglectful of their clients because lawyers choose to spend more time "competing" for new clients and less time servicing existing clients, or more time engaging in competitive activity that clients can identify, but may not be related to quality, such as price competition or advertising. In economists' terms, the opportunity costs of risk prevention techniques (namely, the time spent on them) have increased. One would predict increased competition to increase the probability of malpractice liability arising from, for example, calendaring problems. The increased liability would in turn lead lawyers over time to adjust their behavior by substituting other, now relatively cheaper, methods of risk reduction. Perhaps lawyers would be led to hire a law office administrator, which seemed extravagant before the change in circumstances....

The same analysis applies if the source of the increased risk is a change in the liability regime and the nature of the increased risk is an increase in the size of malpractice losses. For example, courts have become more willing to allow punitive damages and damages for emotional distress in legal malpractice cases. These changes not only increase expected malpractice liability, but to the extent they put a greater percentage of the lawyer's wealth at risk, they increase the lawyer's risk premium as well. The lawyer will again be led to undertake new risk reduction techniques, such as improving client communications or reducing the number of clients he takes on.

This last example is important because it implicates the assumption of the now-traditional economic model discussed earlier. If the change in legal regime increases the lawyer's risk premium, that is, makes him more risk averse, and the lawyer takes extra precautions to reduce that increased risk, is this a bad thing? The traditional law and economics answer is yes, if the additional expenditure on the new precautions exceeds the additional expected malpractice cost (PL) savings. The increased expenditure on precautions is now "excessive." But that analysis depends on the assumption that there is available an alternative insurance institution that can bear the new risk at lower cost, for example, market insurance available at an actuarially fair premium. If, however, there is no such alternative institution, then the extra precautions are excessive only with respect to a nonexistent ideal. One could of course argue that there is an available institution that imposes lower costs, namely the prior liability rules. That is possible, but it depends again on the assumption that perfect insurance was available to clients to eliminate the residual risks they bore under the prior rules. Absent such an institution, evaluating whether the change in legal rule was a good one requires analyzing difficult questions of whether clients or lawyers have lower risk premiums, that is, an evaluation of relative risk aversion. But this brings us to the reason for the rule change. Courts do not just change the liability rules willy nilly. Judges do not just wake up one morning and decide after breakfast, to use an overworked metaphor, that it might be nice to adopt punitive damages today. They respond to some perceived need, some perceived inadequacy in the current regime. That does not mean they always respond correctly, but it does mean that it is foolish to ignore the perceived need and what is driving it....

C. *Client Contract Insurance*

The existence of a contractual relationship between a lawyer and the client victim of malpractice affects the lawyer's choice of risk reduction methods. At the very least, clients bear the costs of lawyers' risk reduction choices in the fees the clients wind up paying, in the costs to them of enforcing their malpractice rights, and in the failure of the legal system to compensate them fully for their malpractice losses. I want to focus here, however, on the voluntary transfer of malpractice risks from the lawyer to the client.

Contracting parties can use ordinary contracts to provide insurance to each other by transferring risks to the party better able to reduce those risks, the least cost insurer. But in lawyer-client contracts, the ethics rules severely limit the ability of lawyers to shift malpractice risks to their clients. . . .

Let us consider the various risk reduction methods. As for reducing the probability of malpractice liability, if this liability is sensibly applied with some kind of contributory negligence defense, then usually there is little the client can reasonably do that would warrant a contractual shifting of malpractice risks. One possibility that the ethics rules permit is a lawyer's limiting the scope of his representation to areas within his expertise. For example, a lawyer might say to a client, "I am not an expert in tax matters. Before you consummate this transaction, I urge you to consult with a tax attorney." This could be viewed as effectively shifting the risk of the lawyer's "malpractice" (inexpertness in necessary tax advice) to the client, who must now hire a second lawyer. In addition, a client might be willing to waive malpractice liability with its attendant costs if the client's long-term relationship with his lawyer gives the client alternative responses to lawyer malpractice, or if the client is sufficiently knowledgeable about the lawyer's quality that he believes that likelihood of the lawyer's committing malpractice is extremely small. . . . [A]s for diversification, if clients have a continual need for legal services, they might be able to diversify by hiring multiple lawyers,[57] or perhaps by maintaining a portfolio of transactions with uncorrelated risks.

But even if clients might seem to be superior insurers, the restrictions against the shifting of malpractice risk may be justified on the basis of transaction cost problems that would often make contract insurance undesirable if such risk shifting were allowed. Transaction costs is a tricky term, but I will use it here in the institutional economics sense of "costs that are most likely to differ under alternative institutional arrangements." . . .

. . . The first type of transaction cost arises out of the fact that in a client-lawyer relationship, as in any principal-agent relationship but in particular in contracts involving professionals and their clients, the parties have asymmetric information about the agent's riskiness and ability to engage in risk reduction. . . . Asymmetric information causes the twin problems of moral hazard and adverse selection. . . . Moral hazard means that a lawyer who transfers malpractice risk to his client contractually will have an incentive after signing the contract not to engage in reasonable risk reduction, that is, to act opportunistically by

---

57. To see how hiring multiple law firms could of course increase the likelihood of malpractice, as Charles Keating's Lincoln Savings & Loan experience might suggest, see In re American Continental Corp./Lincoln Sav. & Loan Sec. Litig., 794 F.Supp. 1424 (D.Ariz. 1992), though it also might have increased the likelihood of malpractice recovery for Lincoln and its successors-in-interest.

increasing risk to the client-insurer.... [A]n insured lawyer might pursue a higher risk strategy than his client would prefer, might favor other clients' or his own pecuniary interests to the detriment of this client, or might increase enforcement costs to the client ex post in the event of malpractice. Adverse selection means that lawyers more prone to malpractice will not candidly disclose their true risk to their clients, and so would be more likely to "purchase" contract insurance if they could. Clients will find it difficult to do sufficient "underwriting" to separate out the good lawyers from the bad....

Aside from moral hazard and adverse selection, other transaction costs [exist].... Insurance contracts are contingent claims contracts. Drafting such contracts is costly—in particular it might necessitate an additional lawyer to represent the client in negotiating with the first lawyer—and may not be worthwhile, especially if the "claims" are too infrequent, or the losses are too small to be worth contracting over. A related point is that lawyers and clients both may have insufficient information about the relevant risks to be able to determine a "price" (fee reduction) for the insurance or client risk reduction measures.

The concept of transaction costs can help us compare the institutions of insurance on which I have so far focused, self-insurance and contract insurance.... To go back to our prior hypothesis about increased competition among lawyers leading to more client neglect, it seems unlikely that this source of increased malpractice risk would lead to more contract insurance. We might expect just the reverse. Increased competition among lawyers could lead clients to be more suspicious of lawyer requests for malpractice waivers and in a better bargaining position to reject such requests.

Increased competition among lawyers has led, however, to an increase in an important class of malpractice against which we might expect clients to be willing to provide more contract insurance to lawyers. I refer to the extraordinary rise in malpractice claims by "non-clients" or "ambiguous clients." Lawyer competition has contributed to this type of malpractice by encouraging lawyers to seek out more marginal clients and engage in more marginal activity on behalf of clients to keep them satisfied.... The "client" may be perfectly happy to "waive" malpractice rights against the lawyer because the client may be benefited, not harmed, by the lawyer's actions. Thus, although clients might want contract insurance in these cases, contract insurance is not socially desirable. Contract insurance in these cases may increase moral hazard by allowing lawyers and their clients to increase risks to third parties....

D. Market Insurance

... A lawyer may purchase insurance services from a commercial provider either because the lawyer unilaterally decides that such insurance is desirable, because the client insists on such insurance as part of the contract, or because the law requires it. . . .

1. *Methods of Risk Reduction*

Legal malpractice insurers make use of all the methods of risk reduction I have discussed so far. The primary method is, of course, diversification, which is generally thought to be the main advantage market insurance offers over self-insurance and contract insurance. Diversification is made possible by economies of scale and gains from specialization leading to superior information about risk. To provide diversification, the market insurer must be able to amass a sufficient pool of similar, but sufficiently uncorrelated, risks and to compute the expected losses associated with that pool. Thus, the insurer needs a broad customer base and accurate information. The cost of attracting lawyers and acquiring information about their riskiness must be sufficiently low and the risk to lawyers sufficiently great that market insurance is an attractive option to lawyers compared to alternative insurance institutions. Legal malpractice insurance developed later than other liability insurance, and has been a less stable market, in large part because these requirements have not always been met. . . .

After diversification, the risk reduction method most used by legal malpractice insurers, as well as by other liability insurers, is ex post loss reduction. In insurance jargon, this method goes under the names of claims management and claims repair. Claims management largely refers to the legal defense services provided by the insurer. All legal malpractice insurance policies impose a duty to defend against malpractice claims. It may not be obvious why this is so, especially when one considers the other insurance institutions we have already looked at. . . . [T]he duty to defend in most market insurance contracts can be explained on transaction cost grounds. By defending numerous claims, the commercial insurer gains an informational advantage over insureds, and is able to enjoy the contracting advantage of a long-term relationship with legal defense firms, as well as the expertise to monitor lawyer performance. But these advantages seem far smaller for lawyer-insureds, many of whom would be well aware of good lawyers to represent them and would be able to monitor any lawyer chosen by the insurance company fairly closely. Thus, although most legal malpractice policies allow the insurance company the right to choose defense counsel, in practice, most legal malpractice insurers probably allow substantial input from their insureds.

Insurers do, of course, need to worry about the moral hazard problem of an insured insisting on an exorbitantly priced legal defense. Lawyers have a keen interest in protecting their reputations, and so would often insist on the best defense possible. As a result, most legal malpractice insurance policies now have "eroding policy limits," that is, they include legal defense costs in the limits of the policy. Eroding policy limits put the burden on the insured lawyers to monitor their defense counsel.... They also encourage early settlement by malpractice plaintiffs who are reluctant to seek more than the policy limits in damages....

In addition to claims management, legal malpractice insurers also try to reduce losses ex post through claims repair, which is essentially a form of mitigation that occurs before a claim is filed. Unlike claims management provisions, however, claims repair provisions in legal malpractice policies do not seem to raise any issues unique to legal malpractice insurance. Notification requirements, such as the requirement to notify the carrier as soon as he or she becomes aware of an act or omission that could be the basis of a suit, may facilitate mitigation. In addition, some carriers maintain a consultation "hotline" for insured lawyers who need help resolving a problem. Other carriers ... offer discounts on deductibles for early notice. These provisions and services suggest that mitigation may be a more realistic possibility in many cases than one might think.

Finally, many legal malpractice insurers take steps to try to reduce the probability of legal malpractice loss ex ante.[78] Insurers refer to these steps as loss prevention. Types of loss prevention range from general educational services, such as newsletters, seminars, and speeches, to more individually tailored consulting services, such as firm audits. These services may be provided by in-house insurance personnel, such as a "loss prevention counsel," or by outside lawyers retained by the insurance company. The services include identifying and seeking to reform "troubled" lawyers or firms, as well as risky practices. As with claims management services, why a legal malpractice insurer would provide loss prevention services to lawyers is something of a puzzle. Legal malpractice insurance protects lawyers against risks for which they are, in theory, expert at avoiding. Loss prevention often involves essentially legal advice. This makes legal malpractice insurance akin to fire insurance purchased by fire safety equipment manufacturers (such as First Alert), whom we might not expect to seek loss prevention services from their insurers. In fact, though, lawyers are not as expert in legal malpractice as many think they are; in particular, they tend not to fully appreciate the extent to which they owe duties to people other than their clients.

Finally, it is important to note that not all "loss prevention" to the insurance company results in loss prevention to society. In particular, the insurance company will engage in underwriting (assessing the risk of

---

78. Of the 50 legal malpractice insurance carriers listed by Long & Levit in their survey, 32 reported having some kind of loss prevention program, 11 reported having no such program, and 7 did not respond. Of the 32 reporting the existence of a loss prevention program, 20 listed either on-site review or audits as part of the available package. *See* Long & Levit, LEGAL MALPRACTICE: THE LAW OFFICE GUIDE TO PURCHASING LEGAL MALPRACTICE INSURANCE 39 (Ronald E. Mallen, ed. 1995–96), at 159–69.

a potential insured) before deciding whether to take on a new insured and will reject an applicant it deems too risky. Similarly, the company could fail to renew an existing insured with a bad enough track record. If these lawyers go on simply to commit malpractice elsewhere, then the insurance company has not reduced social loss. . . .

2. *The Effect of an Increase in Risk on the Demand for Market Insurance*

. . .

The first effect of an increase in risk is the substitution effect. . . . In the insurance context, an increase in expected malpractice liability risk (PL) will increase the price of malpractice insurance (i.e., premiums), which must be at least sufficient to cover the extra payouts, and therefore will tend to decrease the amount of malpractice insurance purchased. Insureds who previously bought market insurance will now be diverted to substitute activities, such as self-insurance.

The second effect of an increase in risk is the income effect. . . . In the insurance context, . . . the income effect works in the opposite direction from the substitution effect. If the increase in risk is due to the fact that the magnitude of malpractice losses is increasing, then the potential losses are a larger proportion of wealth. That means the risk premium is likely to increase, which will increase the demand for diversification services and hence the demand for market insurance. . . .

But—and this is the key point for our purposes—there is yet a third effect, which results from the fact that, as we have defined it (hence the importance of the definition), insurance is not only diversification. The third effect is that the higher risk premium could lead the insured to demand more risk reduction in addition to, or instead of, diversification services. This effect could either increase or decrease the demand for market insurance, depending on whether market insurers or other insurance institutions could provide risk reduction services more cheaply. Thus, the effects of an increase in liability risk on the demand for market insurance are highly ambiguous.

3. *The Demand for Legal Malpractice Insurance and the Insurer's Transaction Cost Advantage*

Given the ambiguity of the effects of increased risk on the demand for market insurance, I turn in this section to a transaction cost comparison to try to sort out which effects might predominate. . . .

Under the standard law and economics analysis of insurance, market insurance creates a moral hazard problem. Unless the insurance company can perfectly observe the behavior of its insureds and adjust its premiums based on these observations, then insureds will engage in too much inefficient behavior. In our context, malpractice insurance will give lawyers too much incentive to commit malpractice. The institutional economics approach is different. Whereas under the traditional approach moral hazard makes market insurance costly, under the institutional approach moral hazard may make market insurance necessary. The key point is that the moral hazard problem exists no matter what insurance institution governs behavior. If a lawyer seeks contract insurance, he is still subject to a moral hazard problem. Even if the lawyer self-insures, he may still be subject to a moral hazard problem stemming from the temptation to engage in activities that do not reduce the social cost of malpractice, such as making himself more judgment proof. Thus, market insurance might reduce moral hazard rather than increase it. As a result, the absence of perfect monitoring by a market insurer does by itself not tell us whether market insurance is an inefficient institution.

The difference between the approaches is the relevant baseline. Under the traditional approach, the baseline is perfection; under the institutional approach, the baseline is the next best available institution. Thus, the relevant moral hazard question in the institutional approach is not which institution is the perfect monitor of lawyer behavior, but rather which institution is the best monitor....

... When legal malpractice insurers are better monitors of lawyer performance—and hence moral hazard than other insurance institutions, lawyers will buy more malpractice insurance. The reduction in moral hazard will lead insurers to reduce premiums and expand coverage. It will also lead clients to insist that their lawyers purchase malpractice insurance, or buy it at higher levels, as a bonding device to guarantee lawyer performance.

A similar argument applies to adverse selection. The traditional adverse selection argument is that if an insured has better information about his riskiness than an insurer, too many poor risks will end up buying insurance and at the extreme the insurance will not be available. Again, adverse selection is viewed as a cost of market insurance. But under the institutional approach, market insurance may reduce the adverse selection problems of alternative insurance institutions. Recall that because clients may be poor underwriters of the riskiness of their lawyers, they would be reluctant to offer contract insurance to their lawyers, even if it were allowed by the ethics rules. But if malpractice insurers are better underwriters than clients, clients have another reason to insist that their lawyers buy malpractice insurance: the lawyers' ability to procure malpractice insurance will provide a signal of lawyer quality.[91] As for self-insurance, the ability of lawyers to make themselves judgment proof may mean that too many high risk lawyers will choose this insurance institution. Thus, the institutional perspective leads to the complete opposite of the traditional adverse selection story: the good risks will buy market insurance. On the other hand, if the

91. The signaling function would, of course, be significantly curtailed if insurance were mandatory.

client is better at judging lawyer quality than the market insurer, the client would view the lawyer's purchase of market insurance as a signal of poor quality; the traditional adverse selection story would then apply.

This last example suggests that the transaction cost story is not yet complete. The fact that malpractice insurers might be better monitors of lawyer moral hazard or adverse selection does not mean that they are. Thus, we cannot necessarily infer from the fact that lawyers purchase malpractice insurance that malpractice insurers have transaction cost advantages over other insurance institutions in controlling moral hazard and adverse selection. Unlike the case with corporate insurance, where diversification is not available as an explanation, diversification might explain a fair amount of the motivation for lawyers purchasing market insurance against legal malpractice.... The short answer to this objection is that legal malpractice insurers have increased their loss prevention services over the last twenty years.... [D]iversification ... cannot explain the rise in loss prevention services offered by legal malpractice insurers. But not all legal malpractice insurers offer loss prevention services, and it is possible that these services are largely public relations and window-dressing....

4. *The Demand for Loss Prevention Services from Malpractice Insurers*

. . .

a. *The Incentive Problem*

The first hurdle that an insurer offering loss prevention services must overcome is ... what might be termed ... the paradox of loss prevention.... If the insurer adjusts premiums based on riskiness, then the insured has an incentive to engage in loss prevention to enjoy lower premiums, but the insurer has no incentive to provide it, because "any reduction in its eventual payouts is offset by a reduction in its premium income." On the other hand, if the insurer does not adjust premiums based on riskiness, the insurer has an incentive to offer loss prevention, but the insured gets no benefit from following the advice. The first of these propositions is theoretically unsound; the second is factually inaccurate.

... If an insurer can charge lower premiums to its insureds because they follow the insurer's loss prevention techniques and so are better risks, the insurer might very well increase the demand for its services, as insureds substitute more market insurance for other insurance institutions. And if the demand for these services is elastic, the total revenue for the insurer will increase.

The second proposition, that "flat" insurance premiums will give an incentive to the insurer to offer, but not to the insured to adopt, loss prevention measures, is based on the unrealistic assumption that perfectly flat insurance exists, or more precisely that lawyer insureds bear no residual risk of malpractice liability. Even if a market insurer charged perfectly flat premiums, lawyers would bear risk associated with reputational harm, the threat of nonrenewal by the insurer, and the possibility of professional discipline or court sanctions.... Legal malpractice insurers impose deductibles, caps on payments, 100 and exclusions from coverage for certain activities they view as too risky. Finally, and most significant, legal malpractice insurers are more and more taking into account the riskiness of individual insureds in setting premiums.

b. Information about Loss Prevention

The resolution of the loss prevention paradox does not of course, guarantee that the market insurer will offer loss prevention services. A second factor is whether the market insurer has better information about loss prevention than lawyers do. Although it might seem that lawyers should have better information than their malpractice insurers about how to avoid malpractice, in fact this is not necessarily true. As Professor Abraham argues:

> In its capacity as a risk pooler the insurer may acquire useful information more efficiently than individual insureds.... [103]

The relevant legal regime may also affect who is better able to acquire loss prevention information. The more liability is based on custom, as negligence usually—but not always—is, the more likely the insured will have superior information. But when custom is rejected as a standard of liability, as in a strict liability system, the insurer may be in a better position to acquire information about cost-effective loss prevention techniques. Liability not based on custom may be becoming more common in legal malpractice cases, as many involve duties to nonclients, conflicts of interest, or other breaches of fiduciary duties. Market insurers may also have an informational advantage when liability rules are simply changing or new cases are rapidly accumulating.

Finally, apart from economies of scale and changes in legal regime, there may simply be psychological reasons associated with cognitive dissonance that may make it difficult for a lawyer to process and assimilate, rather than discount and discard, information that suggests he should change his established method of practice.

c. Free Rider Problems

Even if the market insurer has better information about loss prevention, free rider problems may discourage the insurer from providing this information to its insureds....

It is important not to exaggerate the extent of free rider problems in the context of legal malpractice insurance, however. As for general information, many lawyers make a good living providing loss prevention advice that is to a large extent publicly available. The reason is that the

---

103. *See* Kenneth S. Abraham, Distributing Risk 1 (1986) at 16.

information is costly to collect, organize, and digest in a useful way. Moreover, although insurance companies often do not broadly circulate their loss prevention materials, legal malpractice insurers may find it worthwhile to publicize loss prevention information, rather than hoard it, to encourage other institutions, such as law schools, law firms, or bar associations to do the loss prevention work in the future.[111]

. . .

d. The Nature of Precautions

Information is not all there is to loss prevention. Loss prevention involves taking precautions. The nature of these precautions will also influence whether insurance companies are better situated than alternative institutions to provide loss prevention services. In particular, loss prevention may be less useful when malpractice is caused by inattention rather than a failure to invest in some durable precautionary device or structure. It will be easier for the insurer to monitor durable precautions than attentiveness. This distinction may explain why loss prevention is not an important part of homeowner and car insurance, which cover many accidents caused by momentary inattentiveness. Although some legal malpractice certainly results from momentary inattentiveness, such as a calculation error made in the last-minute rush before a transactional deadline, or a missed objection opportunity in the heat of trial, much malpractice can be prevented by some durable precaution. Examples include improved systems for checking conflicts, calendaring, preserving confidentiality, staffing, maintaining accurate billing records, and evaluating client riskiness. Standardized procedures in all these areas could make even malpractice due to inattentiveness less likely.

Loss prevention may also be difficult when malpractice results from poorly exercised discretion in a particular situation, both because it will be difficult to put in place a corrective mechanism that solves the problem and because it will be difficult to monitor such behavior. But difficult does not necessarily mean impossible. Ex ante, practice manuals

---

111. ALAS, for example, makes available a fair amount of general loss prevention information. An example is the charts found in most Professional Responsibility supplements noting state variations in the ethics rules on client fraud and imputed disqualification. Moreover, Robert O'Malley, ALAS's chief loss prevention counsel, has written several publicly available articles on loss prevention. *See* Robert E. O'Malley, Loss Prevention, in ISSUES IN FORMING A BAR-RELATED PROFESSIONAL LIABILITY INSURANCE COMPANY 118–19 (1989) . . .; Robert E. O'Malley, Preventing Legal Malpractice in Large Law Firms, 20 Toledo L. Rev. 325, 332 (1989). . . . A more ambiguous example is the fact that the St. Paul Fire and Marine Insurance Company, one of the largest legal malpractice insurers in the country, published the Legal Malpractice Review from 1977 until 1984. The insurer's explanation for stopping publication was:

. . . The legal community has become much more aware of legal malpractice exposure and the adverse professional liability climate . . .

Legal Malpractice Rev., Winter 1984, at 1. Putting aside the delicious irony of this explanation coming in the midst of the largest liability insurance crisis in history, one might surmise that St. Paul was tired of having others free ride and anxious to free ride itself. . . .

could provide guidance, at the time of decision, an ethics hotline could backstop discretionary judgments or random audits could regulate others, and ex post, a review and critique of prior decisions could improve future performance....

e. Monitoring by Insureds: Mutual Insurance Companies

... One way to mitigate many of the problems already discussed is to have insureds monitor each other. That is essentially what mutual insurance companies, which are owned by their policyholders, do. In fact, many, though not all, legal malpractice insurers that offer loss prevention services are mutuals. Mutuals trade off the costs of reduced diversification against the benefits of improved loss prevention. Mutuals can reduce moral hazard and adverse selection problems, and enhance compliance with loss prevention measures by having their members monitor each other. For example, Robert O'Malley, chief loss prevention counsel for ALAS, the largest mutual legal malpractice insurer, recommends that "when possible, seminars should be held at the [insurance] company's Annual Meeting." The reason is obvious. It would be hard to think of a more effective informal enforcement mechanism than having representatives from an insurer's member law firms present to discuss the claims from the prior year. Having a legal autopsy done on one of your malpractice cases by top lawyers in your field who have a financial stake in your future behavior is probably a very sobering experience.[123] Such a meeting would also serve to establish a kind of group solidarity that would deter free rider problems, and would improve information by fostering the sharing of relevant experiences among insured members.

f. The Problem of Solvency Risk

Not all roads lead to loss prevention. There is a class of lawyers who have a strong incentive to resist loss prevention by insurers. These are lawyers who would face a severe risk of insolvency in the absence of insurance.... [W]e should not be surprised if insolvent lawyers purchase

---

123. For a fascinating discussion of the goings-on at one such annual meeting of ALAS in Bermuda, see Rita Henley Jensen, Malpractice Rates May Level Off: ALAS Confab Looked at Future Costs, Past Law Firm Mistakes, NAT'L L.J., July 19, 1993, at 1. Jensen reports that "the most well-attended seminars, to the surprise of some ALAS officials, were the 'Monday morning quarterbacking-confessionals' of six firms hit recently by sizable malpractice verdicts or settlements, and a workshop on conflicts." She describes these sessions further:

Some ALAS law firms that are involved in litigation must each year face their toughest audience available: their colleagues who help pick up the tab. For each case, a presenter summarized the facts and the legal arguments, and noted what lessons might be learned from both.

This year the crowd seemed to pay little heed to the arguments made on behalf of two firms caught in highly publicized and controversial malpractice cases. Many who had sat through the presentations said later they thought the firms had made serious mistakes, despite the opinions of the panelists.

Id.

. . .

a disproportionate amount of malpractice insurance that does not offer loss prevention services. If the insolvency problem is serious enough, and if the other factors discussed in this section suggest that loss prevention by insurers would be effective, then legislatively mandated legal malpractice insurance that includes a mandatory loss prevention component and an opt-out provision for those who can demonstrate sufficient asset reserves may be the best solution.

. . .

6. Is More Liability Insurance Good?

The preceding discussion can help inform the recent debate that has occurred over whether liability insurance is socially desirable. . . . Under what might be termed the diversification externality, insureds might inefficiently substitute more diversification for less expected loss reduction (the classic moral hazard problem). This makes insurers and insureds better off at the expense of victims, with the result that there will be too much liability insurance.

But as I have discussed, several features of the insurance market tend to mitigate the diversification externality. First, market insurers will not offer insurance if the moral hazard problem (the absence of loss reduction activity) is too severe; the price of market insurance will be so high that insureds will turn to substitutes, as they did during the liability insurance crisis. Second, when tort victims are in contractual relationships with tortfeasors, as clients are with their lawyers, the potential for the lawyer and insurer to combine to impose "external" costs on the client is reduced, at least for sophisticated, repeat clients. Third, clients might rationally decide that having their lawyers buy malpractice insurance is better than extra deterrence; thus, the diversification externality story seems especially implausible when clients demand malpractice insurance. The reason clients might be willing to trade off insurance for loss prevention is that to the extent that the tort system undercompensates them, by for example denying attorneys' fees or damages for emotional harm, clients face a higher risk premium than they would if the tort system fully "insured" them. There may be some cases in which $1 spent on diversification may yield greater social benefit, by reducing the client's risk premium, than $1 spent on prevention, despite the fact that expected malpractice losses will be somewhat greater. This argument forms the basis for the support of no-fault insurance regimes; that is, there may be times when efforts to improve compensation may be more cost-effective than efforts to reduce expected losses. Fourth, and most important for our purposes, to the extent that the insurer provides loss prevention services, the diversification externality argument is weaker. The strongest case for the diversification externality is where otherwise judgment proof lawyers are able to obtain the insurance and neither the insurer nor the client is a good monitor of lawyer behavior.

A variant on the externality argument is that liability insurance leads to more lawsuits. Although this is undoubtedly true, it is also true of any procedural reform that reduces the cost of bringing a suit. Yet no one argues that all such reforms are bad. The question is whether the extra lawsuits are more likely to be meritorious ones that would not be brought without liability insurance, or frivolous ones that would not be brought without liability insurance (essentially client moral hazard). This in turn depends on how effective insurers and lawyers are at deterring or resolving malpractice suits that lack merit. . . .

III.   Clients and Lawyers as Entities

. . .

A.   *Complex Clients as Insurers*

When lawyers' clients are entities rather than individuals, one might think that market malpractice insurance should be less important. . . .

The problem is that entity clients have agency problems within themselves. As a result, the "client" faces the risk that he may have not one unfaithful agent—the lawyer, but two—the lawyer and management. To the extent that the lawyer is likely to side with the managing agent, even when that agent's action is not in the client's best interest, the client might be quite interested in having the lawyer monitored by an active insurer and quite reluctant to have the managing agent offer contract insurance to the lawyer.

. . .

B.   *Law Firm Insurance*

An important insurance institution remains, namely the law firm. Traditionally, law firms have been organized as partnerships. Partners in general partnerships are subject to vicarious liability for torts and breaches of fiduciary obligation committed by fellow partners, as well as associate lawyers. The combination of vicarious liability and the general failure to seek indemnity from the lawyer who commits malpractice means that the firm provides the equivalent of a malpractice insurance policy to its lawyers.

Partnerships engage in all of the risk reduction methods that market insurers do, including diversification. Although market insurers may provide more diversification, large law partnerships are close to, if not greater than, the size of some mutual malpractice insurers. Partnerships also engage in extensive underwriting and monitoring of their lawyers to minimize adverse selection and moral hazard problems. They have elaborate screening methods for hiring. They put their associate lawyers on lengthy and highly scrutinized "partnership tracks" before allowing admission to partnership. And they are more frequently creating "ethics committees" to supervise and ameliorate difficulties that arise in day-to-day practice. In fact, a strong argument could be made that partnerships are better situated than market insurers to perform these tasks. Partners have more continual contact with lawyers in their firm than an insurer with even an extensive loss prevention program probably has. Partners may also have better information about the strengths and weaknesses of the lawyers in the firm. Thus, one could make a plausible argument that at least large partnerships are superior insurers.

But if partnerships are superior insurers, then one might reasonably ask why they purchase as much market insurance as they do, and why they often favor malpractice insurance that offers loss prevention services. Law firms seem to be getting less enthusiastic about providing partnership malpractice insurance. The latest evidence of this fact is the current rush to pass Limited Liability Company (LLC) and Limited Liability Partnership (LLP) legislation and allow law firms to take advantage of these new organizational forms. In general, vicarious liability of LLCs and LLPs for the torts of members or partners is limited to the assets of the firm and does not reach the assets of the individual members or partners. But individual members or partners are subject to personal liability for torts they commit, and for the torts of others over whom they had supervisory responsibility, or torts of which they have notice. Several LLC and LLP statutes require firms wishing to take advantage of these entities to maintain a minimum amount of liability insurance. These statutes certainly encourage the substitution of market insurance for partnership insurance. Because active monitoring of one's colleagues exposes a member of an LLC or LLP to personal liability, such monitoring may well be discouraged, though how significant this effect will be remains to be seen.

But these statutes may simply represent a legislative approval of a trend that was already taking place. One of the most striking features of the last two decades of lawyer regulation is the decline of the partnership as a regulatory institution. As law partnerships have approached mutual insurance companies in size, they have distanced themselves in spirit. Why?

Superior diversification of market insurers is probably part of the answer, because the costs of some types of monitoring have increased. But it seems unlikely that the rise of mutuals such as ALAS can be fully explained by their superior diversification abilities compared to commercial insurers such as CNA or imperfections in the commercial insurance market. That leaves superior loss prevention services. But why, given the partnership's apparent advantages in this area, should we ever expect market insurers ever to do better?

The theory developed above suggests several possible reasons. First, the character of law partnerships has changed, largely as a result of increased competition, in ways that may increase agency costs within the firm. A particularly important example of how large firms have changed is the fact that the locus of power in partnerships seems to have shifted away from centralized control to individual autonomy. If central authority declines generally, that will increase the ability of individual lawyers to pursue their own agendas at the expense of the firm's welfare, and thereby hinder the firm's ability to monitor malpractice. If the managing partner cannot control the rainmaker's salary, he probably cannot control the rainmaker's behavior either. A mutual insurer may be able to exert leverage over firms that the firm's management cannot on its own.

Another feature of the changing character of law partnerships is increased mobility of lawyers between firms. The more mobile lawyers are, the harder they are to control because they can threaten to leave and take their clients with them. Insurers like ALAS may effectively reduce the mobility of lawyers by making it more likely that lawyers will face similar constraints on their behavior at their new firm, which may also be insured by ALAS or a similar market insurer.

Relatedly, the combination of competition for clients and increased third party liability may make it necessary for the partnership to have some "outside authority" to refer to as a way of maintaining independence from their clients. Third party liability means that malpractice is not only failing to do what your client wants when you should, but also doing what your client wants when you should not. A lawyer may not be able, however, to "just say no" to his client's desires, especially when the client can threaten to go elsewhere. But if the lawyer can rely on the authority of his malpractice insurer, he might be able to convince the client not to do something risky or wrong. . . .

Notes

1. Why does Cohen want to "expand" the definition of insurance? Is his conception of insurance more confusing than illuminating? Or does it help us to see relationships we might otherwise miss?

2. Cohen supports rules restricting the ability of lawyers to shift the risk of malpractice to clients, that is to buy "client contract insurance." Why? Are you convinced? Are the principal-agent problems more severe in lawyer-client relationships than in other agent-principal relationships? What about sophisticated clients (see discussion of "complex clients" in Part III)?

3. Cohen mentions the possibility of mandatory legal malpractice insurance in two places. First, n.91 argues that mandatory insurance would eliminate the ability of lawyers to signal responsibility or competence to clients by maintaining malpractice insurance. Second, and in contrast, he argues that mandatory legal malpractice insurance may be necessary for "insolvent" lawyers who have an insufficient incentive to engage in loss prevention. Can you think of other arguments for or against mandatory legal malpractice insurance? Note that many lawyers—a majority by some estimates—carry no malpractice insurance at all. We believe only one state, Oregon, mandates legal malpractice insurance, although as Cohen mentions

in the last section, some states have mandatory malpractice insurance requirements as a condition of adopting limited liability status. Does Cohen's analysis have any bearing (aside from the above-mentioned points) on whether or not legal malpractice insurance should be made mandatory? See Theodore J. Schneyer, Mandatory Malpractice Insurance for Lawyers in Wisconsin—And Elsewhere, 1979 Wis. L. Rev. 1019. Why might we not see more states requiring malpractice insurance?

4. Cohen's comparative institutional analysis in some ways parallels Wilkins' comparative institutional approach to lawyer regulation, see p. 4, but with a focus on different institutions (note that Wilkins does not mention legal malpractice insurance as a form of lawyer regulation). Does Cohen's analysis help illuminate the choice among different institutions for regulating lawyers?

5. Is Cohen's primary thesis, that lawyers may look to malpractice insurers for loss prevention services, convincing? After all, as Cohen admits, it is somewhat surprising that lawyers, who are experts in the law, would seek guidance in this area from outsiders. Why should we expect lawyers to be convinced that there are transaction cost advantages to letting their malpractice insurance companies do loss prevention? In fact, law firms often resist loss prevention efforts, whether by malpractice insurers or firms, for a variety of reasons (e.g., they think loss prevention is a waste of billable time, interferes with their autonomy, or is necessary only for the "other guy"). Or they give lip service to loss prevention measures but lack any commitment to it (in the Cover–Koniak model, the measures do not act as "law"). Does the fact of lawyer resistance or lack of commitment to loss prevention undercut Cohen's model? Even if lawyers don't resist loss prevention, how effective is loss prevention likely to be? As Cohen notes, for many forms of malpractice, such as inattentiveness, loss prevention may not work (and focusing on root causes of inattentiveness, such as addiction or long hours, may raise issues of discrimination or interfere too much with the firm's profit motives). Other types of malpractice involve discretionary activities (such as drafting a brief or opinion letter) that may be difficult to monitor. Some loss prevention activities, such as screening out high-risk clients, might not be beneficial from the perspective of society as a whole because the result might be that the high-risk clients get inadequate representation. See David A. Hyman, Professional Responsibility, Legal Malpractice, and the Eternal Triangle: Will Lawyers or Insurers Call the Shots?, 4 Conn. Ins. L.J. 353 (1997).

6. Cohen argues that changing standards of lawyer liability may contribute to an increased demand for loss prevention. Might it be instead that the uncertainty caused by rapidly changing standards would actually lead to less loss prevention and more traditional insurance because the value of loss prevention will be difficult to predict?

7. One of the difficulties with the insurer as regulator is that lawyers have the choice whether to insure or not, or whether to insure with a particular carrier or not. The more choices lawyers have, the harder for any particular insurer to "enforce" regulations that the lawyers do not want.

One alternative to malpractice insurer regulation of lawyer behavior is law firm peer review. Peer review has apparently not worked very well to regulate accounting firms. Is it more promising as a regulator of lawyers? For a discussion of this alternative, see Susan Saab Fortney, Am I My Partner's Keeper? Peer Review in Law Firms, 66 U. Colo. L. Rev. 329 (1995); Susan Saab Fortney, Are Law Firm Partners Islands Unto Themselves? An Empirical Study of Law Firm Peer Review, 10 Geo. J. Legal Ethics 271. Other articles on legal malpractice insurance as a form of lawyer regulation include Anthony E. Davis, Professional Liability Insurers as Regulators of Law Practice, 65 Fordham L. Rev. 209 (1996); Charles Silver, Professional Liability Insurance as Insurance and as Lawyer Regulation: Response to Davis, 65 Fordham L. Rev. 233 (1996); and Kent D. Syverud, What Professional Responsibility Scholars Should Know about Insurance, 4 Conn. Ins. L. J. 17 (1997).

The Practice of Law as Confidence Game: Organizational Cooptation of a Profession*
ABRAHAM S. BLUMBERG

. . .

Court Structure Defines Role of Defense Lawyer

The overwhelming majority of convictions in criminal cases (usually over 90 per cent) are not the product of a combative, trial-by-jury process at all, but instead merely involve the sentencing of the individual after a negotiated, bargained-for plea of guilty has been entered. . . .

The institutional setting of the court defines a role for the defense counsel in a criminal case radically different from the one traditionally depicted. . . . Largely overlooked is the variable of the court organization itself, which possesses a thrust, purpose, and direction of its own. It is grounded in pragmatic values, bureaucratic priorities, and administrative instruments. These exalt maximum production and the particularistic career designs of organizational incumbents, whose occupational and career commitments tend to generate a set of priorities. These priorities exert a higher claim than the stated ideological goals of "due process of law," and are often inconsistent with them.

Organizational goals and discipline impose a set of demands and conditions of practice on the respective professions in the criminal court, to which they respond by abandoning their ideological and professional commitments to the accused client, in the service of these higher claims of the court organization. All court personnel, including the accused redefine his situation and restructure his perceptions concomitant with a plea of guilty.

Of all the occupational roles in the court the only private individual who is officially recognized as having a special status and concomitant obligations is the lawyer. His legal status is that of "an officer of the court" and he is held to a standard of ethical performance and duty to his client as well as to the court. This obligation is thought to be far higher than that expected of ordinary individuals occupying the various occupational statuses in the court community. However, lawyers, whether privately retained or of the legal-aid, public defender variety, have close and continuing relations with the prosecuting office and the court itself though discreet relations with the judges via their law secretaries or "confidential" assistants. Indeed, lines of communication, influence and contact with those offices, as well as with the Office of the Clerk of the court, Probation Division, and with the press, are essential to present and prospective requirements of criminal law practice. Similarly,

* © Law and Society Ass'n. 1967. Reprinted with permission by Blackwell Publishing on behalf of the Law and Society Review. Originally printed at 1 L. & Soc. Rev. 15 (1967).

the subtle involvement of the press and other mass media in the court's organizational network is not readily discernible to the casual observer. Accused persons come and go in the court system schema, but the structure and its occupational incumbents remain to carry on their respective career, occupational and organizational enterprises. The individual stridencies, tensions, and conflicts a given accused person's case may present to all the participants are overcome, because the formal and informal relations of all the groups in the court setting require it. The probability of continued future relations and interaction must be preserved at all costs.

This is particularly true of the "lawyer regulars" i.e., those defense lawyers, who by virtue of their continuous appearances in behalf of defendants, tend to represent the bulk of a criminal court's non-indigent case workload, and those lawyers who are not "regulars," who appear almost casually in behalf of an occasional client. Some of the "lawyer regulars" are highly visible as one moves about the major urban centers of the nation, their offices line the back streets of the courthouses, at times sharing space with bondsmen. Their political "visibility" in terms of local club house ties, reaching into the judge's chambers and prosecutor's office, are also deemed essential to successful practitioners. Previous research has indicated that the "lawyer regulars" make no effort to conceal their dependence upon police, bondsmen, jail personnel. Nor do they conceal the necessity for maintaining intimate relations with all levels of personnel in the court setting as a means of obtaining, maintaining, and building their practice. These informal relations are the *sine qua non* not only of retaining a practice, but also in the negotiation of pleas and sentences.

The client, then, is a secondary figure in the court system as in certain other bureaucratic settings. He becomes a means to other ends of the organization's incumbents. He may present doubts, contingencies, and pressures which challenge existing informal arrangements or disrupt them; but these tend to be resolved in favor of the continuance of the organization and its relations as before. There is a greater community of interest among all the principal organizational structures and their incumbents than exists elsewhere in other settings. The accused's lawyer has far greater professional, economic, intellectual and other ties to the various elements of the court system than he does to his own client. In short, the court is a closed community.

. . . Rather than any view of the matter in terms of some variation of a "conspiracy" hypothesis, the simple explanation is one of an ongoing system handling delicate tensions, managing the trauma produced by law enforcement and administration, and requiring almost pathological distrust of "outsiders" bordering on group paranoia.

The hostile attitude toward "outsiders" is in large measure engendered by a defensiveness itself produced by the inherent deficiencies of assembly line justice, so characteristic of our major criminal courts. Intolerably large caseloads of defendants which must be disposed of in an organizational context of limited resources and personnel, potentially subject the participants in the court community to harsh scrutiny from appellate courts, and other public and private sources of condemnation. As a consequence, an almost irreconcilable conflict is posed in terms of intense pressures to process large numbers of cases on the one hand, and the stringent ideological and legal requirements of "due process of law," on the other hand. A rather tenuous resolution of the dilemma has emerged in the shape of a large variety of bureaucratically ordained and controlled "work crimes," short cuts, deviations, and outright rule violations adopted as court practice in order to meet production norms. Fearfully anticipating criticism on ethical as well as legal grounds, all the significant participants in the court's social structure are bound into an organized system of complicity. This consists of a work arrangement in which the patterned, covert, informal breaches, and evasions of "due process" are institutionalized, but are, nevertheless, denied to exist.

These institutionalized evasions will be found to occur to some degree, in all criminal courts. Their nature, scope and complexity are largely determined by the size of the court, and the character of the community in which it is located, e.g., whether it is a large, urban institution, or a relatively small rural county court. In addition, idiosyn-cratic, local conditions may contribute to a unique flavor in the character and quality of the criminal law's administration in a particular commu-nity. However, in most instances a variety of stratagems are employed—some subtle, some crude, in effectively disposing of what are often too large caseloads. A wide variety of coercive devices employed against an accused-client, couched in a depersonalized, instrumental, bureaucratic version of due process of law, and which are in reality a perfunctory obeisance to the ideology of due process. These include some very explicit pressures which are exerted in some manner by all court personnel, including judges, to plead guilty and trial. In many instances the sanc-tion of a potentially harsh sentence is utilized as the visible alternative to pleading guilty, in the case of recalcitrants. Probation and psychiatric reports are "tailored" to organizational needs, or are at least responsive to the court organization's requirements for the refurbishment of a defendant's social biography, consonant with his new status. A resource-ful judge can, through his subtle domination of the proceedings, impose his will on the final outcome of a trial. . . .

The defense attorneys, therefore, whether of the legal-aid, public defender variety, or privately retained, although operating in terms of pressures specific to their respective role and organizational obligations, ultimately are concerned with strategies which tend to lead to a plea. It is the rational, impersonal elements involving economies of time, labor, expense and a superior commitment of the defense counsel to these rationalistic values of maximum production is of court organization that prevail, in his relationship with a client. The lawyer "regulars" are frequently former staff members of the prosecutor's office and utilize the prestige, know-how and contacts of their former affiliation as part of their stock in trade. Close and continuing relations between the lawyer "regular" and his former colleagues in the prosecutor's office generally overshadow the relationship between the regular and his client. The continuing colleague ship of supposedly adversary counsel rests on real professional and organizational needs of a *quid pro quo*, which goes beyond the limits of an accommodation or *modus vivendi* one might ordinarily expect under the circumstances of an otherwise seemingly adversary relationship. Indeed, the adversary features which are manifest are for the most part muted and exist even in their attenuated form largely for external consumption. The principals, lawyer and assistant district attorney, rely upon one another's cooperation for their continued professional existence, and so the bargaining between them tends usually to be "reasonable" rather than fierce.

Fee Collection and Fixing

The real key to understanding the role of defense counsel in a criminal case is to be found in the area of the fixing of the fee to be charged and its collection. The problem of fixing and collecting the fee tends to influence to a significant degree the criminal court process itself, and not just the relationship of the lawyer and his client. In essence, a lawyer-client "confidence game" is played. A true confidence game is unlike the case of the emperor's new clothes wherein that monarch's nakedness was a result of inordinate gullibility and credulity. In a genuine confidence game, the perpetrator manipulates the basic dishonesty of his partner, the victim or mark, toward his own (the confidence operator's) ends. Thus, "the victim of a con scheme must have some larceny in his heart."

Legal service lends itself particularly well to confidence games. Usually, a plumber will be able to demonstrate empirically that he performed a service by clearing up the stuffed drain, repairing the leaky faucet or pipe—and therefore merits his fee. He has rendered, summoned, a visible, tangible boon for his client in return for the requested fee....

In the practice of law there is a special problem in this regard, no matter what the level of the practitioner or his place in the hierarchy of prestige. Much legal work is intangible either because it is simply a few words of advice, some preventive action, a telephone call, negotiation of some kind, a form filled out and filed, a hurried conference with another attorney or an official of a government agency, a letter or opinion written, or a countless variety of seemingly innocuous, and even prosaic procedures and actions. These are the basic activities, apart from any possible court appearance, of almost all lawyers, at all levels of practice. Much of the activity is not in the nature of the exercise of the traditional, precise professional skills of the attorney such as library research and oral argument in connection with appellate briefs, court motions, trial work, drafting of opinions, memoranda, contracts, and other complex documents and agreements. Instead, much legal activity, whether it is at the lowest or highest "white shoe" law firm levels, is of the brokerage, agent, sales representative, lobbyist type of activity, in which the lawyer acts for someone else in pursuing the latter's interests and designs. The service is intangible.

The large scale law firm may not speak as openly of their "contacts," their "fixing" abilities, as does the lower level lawyer. They trade instead upon a facade of thick carpeting, walnut paneling, genteel low pressure, and superficialities of traditional legal professionalism. There are occasions when even the large firm is on the defensive in connection with the fees they charge because the services rendered or results obtained do not appear to merit the fee asked. Therefore, there is a recurrent problem in the legal profession in fixing the amount of fee, and in justifying the basis for the requested fee.

Although the fee at times amounts to what the traffic and the conscience of the lawyer will bear, one further observation must be made with regard to the size of the fee and its collection. The defendant in a criminal case and the material gain he may have acquired during the course of his illicit activities are soon parted. Not infrequently the ill gotten fruits of the various modes of larceny are sequestered by a defense lawyer in payment of his fee. Inexorably, the amount of the fee is a function of the dollar value of the crime committed, and is frequently set with meticulous precision at a sum which bears an uncanny relationship to that of the net proceeds of the particular offense involved. On occasion, defendants have been known to commit additional offenses while at liberty on bail, in order to secure the requisite funds with which to meet their obligations for payment of legal fees. Defense lawyers condition even the most obtuse clients to recognize that there is a firm interconnection between fee payment and the zealous exercise of professional expertise, secret knowledge, and organizational "connections" in their behalf. Lawyers, therefore, seek to keep their clients in a proper state of tension, and to arouse in them the precise edge of anxiety which is calculated to encourage prompt fee payment. Consequently, the client attitude in the relationship between defense counsel and an accused is in many instances a precarious admixture of hostility, mistrust, dependence, and sycophancy. By keeping his client's anxieties aroused to the proper pitch, and establishing a seemingly causal relationship between a requested fee and the accused's ultimate extrication from his onerous difficulties,. the lawyer will have established the necessary preliminary groundwork to assure a minimum of haggling over the fee and its eventual payment.

In varying degrees, as a consequence, all law practice involves a manipulation of the client and a stage management of the lawyer-client relationship so that at least an *appearance* of help and service will be forthcoming. This is accomplished in a variety of ways, often exercised in combination with each other. At the outset, the lawyer-professional employs with suitable variation a measure of sales-puff which may range from an air of unbounding self confidence, adequacy, and dominion over events, to that of complete arrogance. This will be supplemented by the affectation of a studied, faultless mode of personal attire. In the larger firms, the furnishings and office trappings will serve as the backdrop to help in impression management and client intimidation. In all firms, solo or large scale, an access to secret knowledge, and to the seats of power and influence is inferred, or presumed to a varying degree as the basic vendible commodity of the practitioners.

The lack of visible end product offers a special complication in the course of the professional life of the criminal court lawyer with respect to his fee and in his relations with his client. The plain fact is that an accused in a criminal case always "loses" even when he has been exonerated by an acquittal, discharge, or dismissal of his case. The hostility of an accused which follows as a consequence of his arrest, incarceration, possible loss of job, expense and other traumas connected with his case is directed, by means of displacement; toward his lawyer. It is in this sense that it may be said that a criminal lawyer never really "wins" a case. The really satisfied client is rare, since in the very nature of the situation even an accused's vindication leaves him with some degree of dissatisfaction and hostility. It is this state of affairs that makes for a lawyer-client relationship in the criminal court which tends to be a somewhat exaggerated version of the usual lawyer-client confidence game.

At the outset, because there are great risks of nonpayment of the fee, due to the impecuniousness of his clients, and the fact that a man who is sentenced to jail may be a singularly unappreciative client, the criminal lawyer collects his fee *in advance*. Often, because the lawyer and the accused both have questionable designs of their own upon each other, the confidence game can be played. The criminal lawyer must serve three major functions, or stated another way, he must solve three problems. First, he must arrange for his fee; second, he must prepare and then, if necessary, "cool out" his client in case of defeat (a highly likely contingency); third, he must satisfy the court organization that he has performed adequately in the process of negotiating the plea, so as to preclude the possibility of any sort of embarrassing incident which may serve to invite "outside" scrutiny.

In assuring the attainment of one of his primary objectives, his fee, the criminal lawyer will very often enter into negotiations with the accused's kin, including collateral relatives. In many instances, the accused himself is unable to pay any sort of fee or anything more than a token fee. It then becomes important to involve as many of the accused's kin as possible in the situation. This is especially so if the attorney hopes to collect a significant part of a proposed substantial fee. It is not uncommon for several relatives to contribute toward the fee. The larger the group, the greater the possibility that the lawyer will collect a sizable fee by getting contributions from each.

... [T]he larger the fee the lawyer wishes to exact, the more impressive his performance must be, in terms of his stage managed image as a personage of great influence and power in the court organization. Court personnel are keenly aware of the extent to which a lawyer's stock in trade involves the precarious stage management of an image which goes beyond the usual professional flamboyance, and for this reason alone the lawyer is "bound in" to the authority system of the court's organizational discipline. Therefore, to some extent, court personnel will aid the lawyer in the creation and maintenance of that impression. There is a tacit commitment to the lawyer by the court organization, apart from formal etiquette, to aid him in this. Such augmentation of the lawyer's stage managed image as this affords, is the partial basis for the *quid pro quo* which exists between the lawyer and the court organization. It tends to serve as the continuing basis for the higher loyalty of the lawyer to the organization; his relationship with his client, in contrast, is transient, ephemeral and often superficial.

Defense Lawyer as Double Agent

. . .

[T]he criminal lawyer ... enlists the aid of relatives not only to assure payment of his fee, but he will also rely on these persons to help him in his agent-mediator role of convincing the accused to plead guilty, and ultimately to help in "cooling out" the accused if necessary.

. . .

The fee is often collected in stages, each installment usually payable prior to a necessary court appearance required during the course of an accused's career journey. At each stage, in his interviews and communications with the accused, or in addition, with members of his family, if they are helping with the fee payment, the lawyer employs an air of professional confidence and "inside-dopesterism" in order to assuage anxieties on all sides. He makes the necessary bland assurances, and in effect manipulates his client, who is usually willing to do and say the things, true or not, which will help his attorney extricate him. Since the dimensions of what he is essentially selling, organizational influence and expertise; are not technically and precisely measurable, the lawyer can make extravagant claims of influence and secret knowledge with impunity. Thus, lawyers frequently claim to have inside knowledge in connection with information in the hands of the D.A., police, probation officials or to have access to these functionaries. Factually, they often do, and need only to exaggerate the nature of their relationships with them to obtain the desired effective impression upon the client. But, as in the genuine confidence game, the victim who has participated is loathe to do anything which will upset the lesser plea which his lawyer has "conned" him into accepting.

In effect, in his role as double agent, the criminal lawyer performs an extremely vital and delicate mission for the court organization and the accused. Both principals are anxious to terminate the litigation with a minimum of expense and damage to each other. There is no other personage or role incumbent in the total court structure more strategically located, who by training and in terms of his own requirements, is more ideally suited to do so than the lawyer. In recognition of this, judges will cooperate with attorneys in many important ways. For example, they will adjourn the case of an accused in jail awaiting plea or sentence if the attorney requests such action. While explicitly this may be done for some innocuous and seemingly valid reason, the tacit purpose is that pressure is being applied by the attorney for the collection of his fee, which he knows will probably not be forthcoming if the case is concluded. Judges are aware of this tactic on the part of lawyers, who, by requesting an adjournment, keep an accused incarcerated awhile longer as a not too subtle method of dunning a client for payment. However, the judges will go along with this, on the ground that important ends are being served. Often, the only end served is to protect a lawyer's fee.

The judge will help an accused's lawyer in still another way. He will lend the official aura of his office and courtroom so that a lawyer can stage manage an impression of an "all out" performance for the accused in justification of his fee. The judge and other court personnel will serve as a backdrop for a scene charged with dramatic fire, in which the accused's lawyer makes a stirring appeal in his behalf. With a show of restrained passion, the lawyer will intone the virtues of the accused and recite the social deprivations which have reduced him to his present state. The speech varies somewhat, depending on whether the accused has been convicted after trial or has pleaded guilty. In the main, however, the incongruity, superficiality, and ritualistic character of the total performance is underscored by a visibly impassive, almost bored reaction on the part of the judge and other members of the court retinue.

Afterward, there is a hearty exchange of pleasantries between the lawyer and district attorney, wholly out of context in terms of the supposed adversary nature of the preceding events. The fiery passion in defense of his client is gone, and the lawyers for both sides resume their offstage relations, chatting amiably and perhaps including the judge in their restrained banter. No other aspect of their visible conduct so effectively serves to put even a casual observer on notice, that these individuals have claims upon each other. These seemingly innocuous actions are indicative of continuing organizational and informal relations, which, in their intricacy and depth, range far beyond any priorities or claims a particular defendant may have.

Criminal law practice is a unique form of private law practice since it really only appears to be private practice. Actually it is bureaucratic practice, because of the legal practitioner's enmeshment in the authority, discipline, and perspectives of the court organization. Private practice, supposedly, in a professional sense, involves the maintenance of an organized, disciplined body of knowledge and learning; the individual practitioners are imbued with a spirit of autonomy and service, the earning of a livelihood being incidental. In the sense that the lawyer in the criminal court serves as a double agent, serving higher organizational rather than professional ends, he may be deemed to be engaged in bureaucratic rather than private practice. To some extent the lawyer-client "confidence game," in addition to its other functions, serves to conceal this fact.

The Client's Perception

The "cop-out" ceremony, in which the court process culminates, is not only invaluable for redefining the accused's perspectives of himself, but also in reiterating publicly in a formally structured ritual the accused person's guilt for the benefit of significant "others" who are observing. The accused not only is made to assert publicly his guilt of a specific crime, but also a complete recital of its details. He is further made to indicate that he is entering his plea of guilt freely, willingly, and voluntarily, and that he is not doing so because of any promises or in consideration of any commitments that may have been made to him by anyone. This last is intended as a blanket statement to shield the participants from any possible charges of "coercion" or undue influence that may have been exerted in violation of due process requirements. Its function is to preclude any later review by an appellate court on these grounds, and also to obviate any second thoughts an accused may develop in connection with his plea.

However, for the accused, the conception of self as a guilty person is in large measure a temporary role adaptation. His career socialization as an accused, if it is successful, eventuates in his acceptance and redefinition of himself as a guilty person. However, the transformation is ephemeral, in that he will, in private, quickly reassert his innocence. Of importance is that he accept his defeat, publicly proclaim it, and find some measure of pacification in it. Almost immediately after his plea, a defendant will generally be interviewed by a representative of the probation division in connection with a presentence report which is to be prepared. The very first question to be asked of him by the probation officer is: "Are you guilty of the crime to which you pleaded?" This is by way of double affirmation of the defendant's guilt. Should the defendant now begin to make bold assertions of his innocence, despite his plea of guilty, he will be asked to withdraw his plea and stand trial on the original charges. Such a threatened possibility is, in most instances, sufficient to cause an accused to let the plea stand and to request the probation officer to overlook his exclamations of innocence. . . .

. . .

It is popularly assumed that the police, through forced confessions, and the district attorney, employing still other pressures, are most instrumental in the inducement of an accused to plead guilty. . . . [I]t is actually the defendant's own counsel who is most effective in this role. Further, this phenomenon tends to reinforce the extremely rational nature of criminal law administration, for an organization could not rely upon the sort of idiosyncratic measures employed by the police to induce confessions and maintain its efficiency, high production and overall rational-legal character. The defense counsel becomes the ideal agent-mediator since, as "officer of the court" and confidant of the accused and his kin, he lives astride both worlds and can serve the ends of the two as well as his own.

. . .

. . . Of all the agent-mediators, it is the lawyer who is most effective in manipulating an accused's perspectives, notwithstanding pressures that may have been previously applied by police, district attorney, judge or any of the agent-mediators that may have been activated by them. Legal-aid and assigned counsel would apparently be more likely to suggest a possible plea at the point of initial interview as response to pressures of time. In the case of the assigned counsel, the strong possibility that there is no fee involved, may be an added impetus to such a suggestion at the first contact.

. . . There is little real effort to individualize, and the lawyer's role as agent-mediator may be seen as unique in that he is in effect a double agent. Although, as "officer of the court" he mediates between the court organization and the defendant, his roles with respect to each are rent by conflicts of interest. Too often these must be resolved in favor of the organization which provides him with the means for his professional existence. Consequently, in order to reduce the strains and conflicts imposed in what is ultimately an over-demanding role obligation for him, the lawyer engages in the lawyer-client "confidence game" so as to structure more favorably an otherwise onerous role system.

Conclusion

. . . [D]ecisions of the Supreme Court, in the area of criminal law administration and defendant's rights, fail to take into account three crucial aspects of social structure which may tend to render the more libertarian rules as nugatory. The decisions overlook (1) the nature of courts as formal organization; (2) the relationship that the lawyer-regular *actually* has with the court organization; and (3) the character of the lawyer-client relationship in the criminal court (the routine relationships, not those unusual ones that are described in "heroic" terms in novels, movies, and TV).

Courts, like many other modern large-scale organizations possess a monstrous appetite for the cooptation of entire professional groups as well as individuals. Almost all those who come within the ambit of organizational authority, find that their definitions, perceptions and values have been refurbished, largely in terms favorable to the particular organization and its goals. As a result, ... libertarian rules will tend to produce the rather ironic end result of augmenting the *existing* organizational arrangements, enriching court organizations with more personnel and elaborate structure, which in turn will maximize organizational goals of "efficiency" and production. Thus, many defendants will find that courts will possess an even more sophisticated apparatus for processing them toward a guilty plea!

Notes

1. Imagine a criminal defense lawyer with the purest motives and sufficient financial backing. Would he act any differently than the lawyers Blumberg describes? How would a true adversarial lawyer act?

2. Blumberg is critical of expanded "rights" of criminal defendants on the grounds that these often wind up enhancing the power of the court system to pressure defendants into pleading guilty. Does that mean that criminal defendants would be better off without these rights, or simply that the pressure would surface elsewhere in the system? For criticism of Blumberg position, see Skolnick, Social Control in the Adversary System, 11 J. Conflict Resolution 52, 59–68 (1967).

3. A number of doctrines make it very difficult to bring a successful malpractice action against a criminal defense lawyer. See generally Koniak, Through the Looking Glass of Ethics, excerpted at p. 287. If criminal defendants could bring malpractice actions as easily as clients in civil matters, would that change the world Blumberg describes? What else could or should be done?

4. In his article on delivery of legal services, see p. 460, Cramton argues that in civil cases poor people should be represented, not by staff lawyers in legal services offices, but by private lawyers reimbursed by the state—Judicare akin to Medicare. Would that risk replicating in the civil arena the problems Blumberg describes in the criminal defense system? What could be done to avoid that?

Through the Looking Glass of Ethics and the Wrong with Rights We Find There*
SUSAN P. KONIAK

Introduction

An ethic that imposes strong obligations to protect those who are most powerful and capable of protecting themselves and weak obligations to protect the powerless and most vulnerable is wrong. I take it this first proposition is self-evident, at least for those of us who still feel comfortable speaking of right and wrong....

Where do I perceive such an ethic? In the law's willingness to impose stronger obligations of competence on lawyers who represent paying clients in civil matters than it imposes on lawyers who represent indigent criminal defendants. In the law's willingness to impose stronger obligations of loyalty and diligence on lawyers who are voluntarily selected by clients and who are subject to summary dismissal by those clients than on lawyers who represent huge groups of people in class actions, clients who do not select their own lawyers and are incapable of monitoring their lawyers' diligence or loyalty. These are my examples of looking glass ethics.

... The looking glass ethics I criticize in this piece are embedded in the ethical obligations articulated and imposed by courts. It is the ethical obligations imposed by the state that I criticize here, not those affirmed by the practicing bar....

Looking glass ethics lead us away from any sensible notion of where our obligations should lie. A looking glass path appears to lead one way, but leads instead in the opposite direction.... Looking glass ethics ... concerns me greatly and provides much of the impetus for this paper. But I have a larger concern as well: how our law is able to construct such paths. I contend that these paths are a product of a fundamental weakness in our understanding of law, our obsession with rights. By taking the law of obligation, ethics, seriously we have much to gain, not merely in the situations I discuss, but in our larger search for a more just world.

I.   On the Right Side of the Mirror

Before stepping through the looking glass, let us remain for a moment on the right side. The law governing lawyers is not all a mirror image of what it should be. Take for example the obligation imposed on lawyers not to charge excessive fees. Quite sensibly, the law takes this obligation most seriously when the client is most vulnerable. At the other extreme, the courts do not scrutinize for excessiveness the fees

* Reprinted with permission of the publisher, Georgetown Journal of Legal Ethics © 1995, 9 Geo. J. Legal Ethics 1 (1995).

lawyers charge large corporations, which are capable of monitoring attorney fees for themselves.

. . .

If we think of legal ethics as obligations imposed on the profession by the courts, . . . there is no ethical obligation to refrain from charging excessive fees to sophisticated corporate players. . . .

. . . I find the result eminently sensible. The point is to demonstrate that while the language of the ethics rules in force in most states suggests an obligation on lawyers to refrain from charging excessive fees to anyone, the absence of commitment to this norm when the client is a sophisticated corporate player means the law is not what the ethics rules suggest on their face.

On the other hand, the obligation not to charge excessive fees is taken quite seriously when it comes to clients who are more likely to be bilked. . . . [This] approach is also eminently sensible.

Having suggested what a normatively sensible world looks like and having demonstrated the ability of the law to encode such a world, it is time to portray a normatively backward world and to show how the law encodes that.

II.   Through the Looking Glass

A.   *Demeaning the Criminal Defense Lawyer's Obligation of Competence*

A criminal defendant not only has a lot more at stake than a civil plaintiff or defendant, but is also much less likely to have chosen his own counsel. Most criminal defendants cannot afford to retain private counsel. They must settle for whomever the state appoints, which means lawyers paid bargain basement wages and burdened with extraordinarily heavy caseloads. For these reasons, if we were on the right side of the mirror, one would expect that the obligation to provide competent representation would be most strongly reinforced in the criminal context. Instead, we find an obligation of competence without credible reinforcement. In fact, the case law generally demonstrates so little commitment to the obligation to provide competent representation in the criminal context that it is difficult to describe legal ethics as including such an obligation.

There is in the ethical rules, as espoused by all courts, an obligation to provide competent representation to all clients, including criminal defendants. But as we have seen with the obligation not to charge excessive fees, a court may have a rule and not enforce it as law in a particular context, rendering the "obligation" in that context something rather less than an obligation. So it is with the obligation to provide competent representation to criminal defendants.

Disciplining lawyers is not the primary method of enforcing the obligation to provide competent representation. Discipline for incompetence is rare and is generally reserved for the most egregious conduct—cases involving either multiple instances of incompetence or incompetence combined with other misconduct. Court decisions and ethics opinions proclaim alike that discipline should not be used to enforce the obligation to render reasonably competent representation: that is the domain of malpractice. Nowhere is there a suggestion that discipline for mere negligence might be appropriate for lawyers representing criminal defendants, a principle we might expect to find if the ethical obligation was perceived as strongest in that context. On the other hand, the case law on disciplining lawyers provides no overt evidence of the looking glass effect. In other words, one finds no assertion that criminal lawyers should somehow be provided special immunity from discipline. For the looking glass effect to become apparent we must move from the discipline system to the primary method relied on by courts to enforce the duty of competence: malpractice actions.

Here, we do find what amounts to special immunity for criminal defense lawyers to perform incompetently. Most state courts make it significantly more difficult for criminal defendants to bring malpractice actions against their lawyers than for civil plaintiffs or defendants to do so. The state courts are all but unanimous in holding that a criminal defendant, who challenges his conviction based on ineffective assistance of counsel and whose claim is denied, is collaterally estopped from suing for malpractice. Assuming that the standards for demonstrating ineffective assistance of counsel are similar enough to the malpractice standards to justify the conclusion that the issues litigated were the same, what is the problem?

As others have noted, the collateral estoppel rule threatens the criminal defendant's right to effective assistance of counsel. As a practical matter, an ineffective assistance of counsel claim is unlikely to succeed if the criminal defense lawyer vigorously contests the allegations of ineffectiveness. Conversely, the cooperation of the criminal defense lawyer greatly increases the chances that such a claim will succeed. As the Supreme Court stated in *Strickland v. Washington*,* the case articulating the standard for effective assistance of counsel under the Sixth Amendment, counsel's performance must be judged in light of what the defendant told counsel about the case and, therefore, "inquiry into counsel's conversations with the defendant may be critical to a proper assessment of counsel's litigation decisions." The two parties competent to testify as to those conversations are the defendant and counsel. But the collateral estoppel rule provides counsel with a powerful incentive to oppose actively the ineffectiveness challenge to the conviction because if the challenge is rejected, the lawyer is immunized from malpractice liability. By creating this incentive for lawyers to oppose ineffectiveness claims, the courts threaten the right to effective assistance of counsel

* [466 U.S. 668 (1984).]

supposedly guaranteed by the Constitution, making its vindication less likely in some worthy cases. That problem is a serious one and enough of a reason for courts to rethink the collateral estoppel rule, but it is not the focus here.

The focus in this piece is not on rights but on obligations. It is on how the courts express commitment to the obligations lawyers have to protect their clients. From this perspective, the collateral estoppel rule is by and large neutral, assuming all it does is prevent criminal defendants from bringing malpractice cases that clients, civil or criminal, would lose anyway. On the other hand, if the burden on the criminal defendant is greater in an ineffectiveness proceeding than it would be in a malpractice action, then the collateral estoppel rule does show that courts are more willing to impose obligations of competence in civil cases than they are in criminal cases, and that seems backwards. The important question then is whether the standards set forth in *Strickland* for ineffectiveness claims are more onerous than those imposed in an ordinary civil malpractice case.

The argument that the standards are equivalent goes like this: *Strickland* requires that the defendant show that counsel's performance fell below that of a reasonably competent lawyer under prevailing professional norms. That is no different than the standard for assessing whether counsel acted negligently in a malpractice suit. True. Second, *Strickland* requires that the defendant show that he was prejudiced by the lawyer's actions. A malpractice plaintiff must show damages. Prejudice and damages are substantially equivalent concepts. This proposition is questionable, but for now let us concede it. The equivalency argument still fails. It fails because it omits critical information. *Strickland* sets out presumptions that make it much harder for a petitioner to meet his burden of showing substandard lawyer performance/negligence and prejudice/damages—presumptions that are nowhere to be found in malpractice law.

According to *Strickland*, "judicial scrutiny of counsel's performance must be highly deferential." The Supreme Court continued, "a court must indulge a strong presumption that counsel's conduct falls within the wide range of reasonable professional assistance; that is, the defendant must overcome the presumption that, under the circumstances, the challenged action 'might be considered sound trial strategy.'" On the off chance that some lower court might miss the import of these words, the Court emphasized the point yet again: "The court should recognize that counsel is strongly presumed to have rendered adequate assistance and made all significant decisions in the exercise of reasonable professional judgment." In malpractice cases the lawyer's actions are not viewed through any prism of extreme deference. No presumptions of competence apply.

Similarly, the prejudice finding in *Strickland* is weighted against the defendant through the imposition of a presumption. In assessing whether there is a reasonable probability that the outcome of the proceeding would have been different but for the errors of counsel, the prejudice inquiry under *Strickland*, the court is to indulge a "strong presumption" that the outcome is reliable. In other words, that it was not affected by the errors. Again, no similar hurdle must be overcome by the malpractice plaintiff seeking to establish damages by a showing that the result of a civil proceeding would have been different but for the errors of counsel. In short, the *Strickland* presumptions make it much harder to establish ineffective assistance of counsel than it is to establish malpractice.

Thus, the general rule that collaterally estops a malpractice claim where a *Strickland* claim has failed, renders a criminal defense lawyer less likely to be held liable for malpractice than a civil counterpart. However troubling this result is from a rights-based perspective, it would not demonstrate a lackadaisical attitude on the part of courts toward the obligations of criminal defense lawyers, if the courts had adopted some alternate method of demonstrating commitment to the criminal defense lawyer's obligation of competence. For example, having adopted the collateral estoppel rule for criminal defense malpractice, the courts could have chosen to reinforce the obligation of competence through the disciplinary system. They could have held that mere negligence in criminal cases would be grounds for discipline and that collateral estoppel would not be a defense in those proceedings because in discipline cases, unlike malpractice actions and ineffective assistance claims, prejudice to the client need not be shown, which is the general rule in discipline actions. If the courts had taken that route, I would make no claim of a looking glass ethic. But having adopted the collateral estoppel rule for malpractice actions, not one court has made the slightest move to find some other method of demonstrating commitment to the obligation that lawyers provide competent representation to criminal defendants. They have set a lower standard of competence in cases when the client is most vulnerable and has the most at stake. That is what is backward.

The collateral estoppel rule is, moreover, only the first backward step. It gets worse. Assuming the criminal defendant succeeds in securing a new trial, having shown that the lawyer was so negligent that even *Strickland*'s presumptions could not whitewash the incompetence, how do the courts deal with the lawyer? Is malpractice presumed? Is the lawyer automatically subject to some disciplinary action? Is the attorney required to undergo continuing peer review and supervision? Is the lawyer barred from handling criminal cases or required to attend classes? Anything? No. The lawyer may experience some degree of humiliation, assuming peers read the court decision reversing the defendant's conviction. But that is it. As for any subsequent malpractice action, it may still be barred. True, the criminal defendant is not now collaterally estopped from bringing such an action, but in a growing number of states, the defendant faces an additional hurdle.

The defendant must establish innocence of the criminal charge. Please note that this is quite different from the ordinary requirement in malpractice cases that a plaintiff must show damages. After all, a defendant who has committed a crime can be damaged by a lawyer's negligence: by a lawyer's failure to move for the exclusion of damaging evidence or a confession that should have been excluded; by a lawyer's failure to communicate a plea offer made by the state; by a lawyer's drunkenness during trial; or by a lawyer's failure to investigate or present a defense. A corporate civil defendant found liable, whose lawyer failed in any of these ways, need not establish that it did not in fact cause the wrongful death of the child to prevail in a malpractice suit, but merely that the result in the case would more likely than not have been different but for the errors. The innocence hurdle immunizes from malpractice liability very serious, *Strickland*-qualifying negligence in every case where it is more likely than not that the plaintiff committed a crime—a crime for which the plaintiff would have been found legally innocent but for the lawyer's error. With this move, the malpractice threat is effectively removed for criminal defense lawyers.

On the off chance that some criminal defense lawyer might still fear being held accountable for malpractice, some courts have gone even further. For example, Alaska not only applies the collateral estoppel rule and makes "actual" as opposed to "legal" guilt an affirmative defense, it also requires that a defendant first successfully file a *Strickland* challenge to the conviction before suing for malpractice. Pennsylvania goes the furthest, requiring not only post-conviction relief and proof of innocence, but also a showing of reckless or wanton disregard of the plaintiff's interest before the former criminal defendant can recover against the lawyer.

According to most courts, a rights-based perspective justifies the innocence hurdle. The argument is of the following form: it is unjust to let someone who is actually guilty of a crime benefit even indirectly from criminal conduct, and that is what awarding malpractice damages would do.[34] Out of a respect for the defendant's rights, the state is prevented from punishing the legally innocent but actually guilty person. Having protected the defendant's right to liberty at some considerable cost to the state, it is deemed just to deny the former criminal defendant some

---

34. For the concept of "actual guilt" to abide in a legal system that supposedly cherishes due process is more than a little strange. The concept suggests that the legal system can break free of the procedural blindfolds of justice and see what actually happened, unimpeded by legal constructs or niceties. More remarkable, the concept suggests that the legal system, unencumbered by procedural restraints, can mark what actually happened with a legal stamp, guilt, as if that concept existed as a natural construct instead of as a product of law itself. The concept of "actual guilt" demonstrates legal meaning at its most complex, paradoxical and grotesque. It is a fascinating monstrosity that reveals the wonder and the horror of law.

lesser right, such as the right to sue the lawyer for malpractice, on the ground that the former criminal defendant is a bad actor. But defendants who are legally guilty, as well as those who are found innocent but who may have "done it," do not lose the right to sue and collect damages for other wrongs experienced in the criminal justice system, like police brutality. Why should lawyer misconduct be treated differently? The implicit answer is that deterring lawyer incompetence is not important enough a goal to trump the unseemliness of bad actors collecting money. In other words, enforcing a criminal defense lawyer's obligation of competence is just not important enough. If courts saw this goal as important, the unseemliness of enriching bad people would be weighed against the good that courts saw in deterring lawyer incompetence. If the goal were important and courts could not stomach awarding monetary damages, another method of deterring criminal defense incompetence would be put in place. But no alternatives have been discussed or adopted by the courts and so the obligation of competence for criminal defense lawyers is reduced to insignificance.

The fear of frivolous malpractice suits may be driving the adoption of these hurdles for criminal defendants, but to the extent this is a legitimate concern, the collateral estoppel rule by itself would allow courts to summarily dismiss most frivolous suits and then some. The innocence hurdle and the other innovations would appear to be overkill. More important, the frivolous malpractice suit problem does not explain why alternate means of enforcing the obligation of competence, like imposing discipline for "mere" negligence, have not been pursued by the courts.

Some courts have argued that limits on a criminal defendant's right to bring a malpractice action are justified by the need to encourage lawyers to work for the low fees that are generally paid to counsel appointed to represent the indigent. In short, this argument boils down to nothing more than an admission that we do not pay these lawyers enough to demand that they be competent. That surely explains why criminal defense lawyers are generally held to a lesser obligation of competence, but explanation is not justification. Normative principle, whether called ethics or law, is a path from the world as it is to the world as it should be. The path of law just described does not lead to a better world. It demands nothing of criminal defense lawyers, accepting almost all actual performance as adequate performance. It demands nothing of the rest of us, allowing us to continue to pride ourselves on guaranteeing the right of counsel in criminal cases, while not paying enough to ensure that indigent criminal defendants receive competent representation.

B.   Demeaning Class Counsel's Obligations to the Class

If any client is more vulnerable to abuses by a lawyer than the criminal defendant, it is the unidentified plaintiff in a huge class action lawsuit. By unidentified I mean class members who are not provided individual notice that they are parties to the suit and are left to discover that their rights are being adjudicated by seeing and understanding a ten-second television announcement or reading and understanding an advertisement placed in a newspaper or magazine. By definition, this person is represented by a lawyer she never met and over whom she has no means of exercising control. At the outset of the litigation and perhaps through to its conclusion, the class member may be unaware that a court is adjudicating her legal rights. If all that was at stake for individual class members was some nominal compensation for having been charged an extra five cents on a bag of potato chips, one might not be too concerned with how the courts enforced class counsel's duties to these people. But often much more is at stake, such as whether a plaintiff will recover for a fatal illness caused by a defective product, and if so, how much. Today, such a person may have her rights adjudicated by a court without actual notice of the action and before she even knows she has been injured. Fantastic as this may seem to those readers who have not been keeping up with the most recent innovations in mass tort/class action case law, it is true.

From a rights-perspective, the very existence of such fantastic procedural options is troubling, but again that is not my concern here. My question is how courts enforce the lawyers' duties of loyalty and diligence in such cases. Do courts take special care to protect vulnerable class members, identifiable and unidentifiable members of a huge class who have no control over the selection, retention or performance of their lawyer? No. Class counsel, like their criminal defense colleagues, are relieved of obligations the courts impose on lawyers representing less vulnerable clients. We are in looking glass land again.

When the class is large and, particularly, when the class is composed of plaintiffs who do not have actual notice that their rights are being adjudicated, the lawyer is in a perfect position to settle the class claims for less than they are worth in exchange for a large payoff in attorneys' fees (less work for class counsel, less recovery for the class and a promise from the defendants not to oppose the application for attorneys' fees). Every court acknowledges this danger. It is the reason Federal Rule of Civil Procedure 23(e) insists that no class action be settled without court approval. But, as we shall see, that Rule as applied serves to gut the obligations of lawyers, not to enforce them.

First, some preliminaries. As in the criminal defense situation, discipline is not used to enforce the obligations of class counsel.[44] As for malpractice liability, no case has held class counsel liable for malpractice....

---

44. Disciplinary proceedings against class counsel are virtually nonexistent. Of course, courts retain inherent power to sanction lawyers appearing before them without waiting for bar counsel to bring formal disciplinary charges, but courts almost never use this power against class counsel.

For a class action to be certified and resolved, a court must determine that class counsel adequately represented the class.... [Some courts have held that] the existence of such a finding collaterally estops all malpractice actions against class counsel, but it came awfully close.... Thus, the class action court's responsibility under Federal Rule of Civil Procedure 23 to assess the adequacy of class counsel makes it unlikely that the courts will use malpractice actions as a means of enforcing class counsels' obligations.

With no discipline and no serious malpractice threat, the courts are left with Rule 23 as the vehicle to demonstrate that they are serious about class counsel fulfilling their obligations to the class. First, the good news: Rule 23, unlike the rule in *Strickland*, has the potential to send a clear and strong message that the courts are serious about holding class counsel to their obligations. The *Strickland* rule does not have this potential because a finding under *Strickland* that criminal defense counsel was ineffective does not directly affect the lawyer, aside from possible embarrassment. On the other hand, a finding under Rule 23 that class counsel is not an adequate representative of the class means counsel will not collect class counsel fees. Visiting that consequence on lawyers who fail to meet their obligations would do much to ensure that such failures were infrequent. Rule 23 has bite, or, more precisely, it has the potential to bite.

Now the bad news. In a Rule 23 proceeding the standard used by courts is not only lower than the malpractice standard ordinary lawyers are held to, the standard is nonexistent. In ordinary malpractice actions (and even in *Strickland* proceedings) the ethics rules are used as guidelines to establish what constitutes a breach of a lawyer's duty to the client. However in assessing the adequacy of representation under Rule 23, the ethics rules are eschewed as unreliable guides. The argument is that the ethics rules were not written with class counsel in mind. By and large, this is a true claim. Class actions would be effectively precluded, a result inconsistent with the Rules of Civil Procedure, if some of the ethics rules were applied literally because some of the rules impose obligations that cannot be met when the client is a huge class. For example, on its face Model Rule 1.7 ... requires that a lawyer fully inform the client of potential conflicts of interest that might adversely affect the representation that client receives and prohibits the lawyer from proceeding with the representation unless, *inter alia*, the client consents after being fully informed. If this rule were applied literally to class counsel, almost no class action could be maintained. In most class actions, the membership of the class is simply too numerous to make consultation with each person, no less the assent of each, a realistic goal. In a large number of class actions, many class members cannot even be identified by name. Thus, it seems irrefutable that at least some of the ethics rules cannot be applied literally to class counsel.

To acknowledge that a rule like Model Rule 1.7 ..., which is designed to ensure that lawyers are loyal to their clients' interests, cannot be applied literally in the class action context does not, however, imply that no standards of loyalty should be imposed. But having abandoned the ethics rules, courts have not articulated alternate rules of obligation designed to guarantee reasonable loyalty and diligence on the part of class counsel. They adopt instead an "anything goes" attitude. As long as class counsel has any experience in the area of law covered by the class action or some experience in other class actions, he is presumed to be adequate. Experience is, however, no guarantee of either diligence or loyalty. The idea that evidence of experience could serve as a substitute for ethics rules designed to impose these obligations is ridiculous. The courts would say they require more than just experience, but, as we shall see, what little more they do require is as tangential to the obligations of diligence and loyalty as experience is.

To make matters worse, the presumption of adequacy created by experience is rendered virtually irrefutable by class counsel's presentation to the court of a settlement of the class action suit that the court finds to be fair and reasonable. Moreover, the court relies heavily on counsel's representations about the settlement in assessing whether it is fair. This reliance creates the following absurd situation: the court finds counsel is adequate relying to a significant degree on counsel's own representations that the deal is fair and reasonable and that counsel is experienced. Apart from the circular reasoning, what is wrong with judging class counsel's adequacy by assessing whether the settlement is fair?

If the range of settlements that could be considered fair in any case were narrow, then assessing diligence and loyalty by whether the lawyer had managed to achieve a fair result might make some sense. One could then argue that any lawyer who was not reasonably diligent or loyal would not have been able to achieve a result within the narrow range. But in every case the range of fair settlements is very wide. Laziness, selfishness, incompetence and corruption have considerable room to influence the outcome without being revealed by the result because in every case there is such a wide range of results that could be called fair. Thus, to say, as the courts are fond of saying, that the proof of the pudding is in the eating, is simply false. A poisoned or tainted pudding may taste okay, if not delicious. When okay is enough, there is a lot of room for the abdication of obligation.

Lawyers who represent ordinary civil plaintiffs and defendants are not automatically relieved of their obligations of loyalty and diligence on the ground that the judgment or settlement is reasonable. In many states, if conflicting interests or a lack of diligence cause a settlement to be lower than it might otherwise have been, the lawyer may be liable for malpractice, notwithstanding the client's acceptance of the settlement or how the pudding tastes to the court. The lawyer for an ordinary client is thereby obligated to do more than recommend a reasonable deal. Lawyers for ordinary clients cannot so easily escape the obligation to put the clients' interests first in negotiating settlements nor the obligation to advocate diligently their clients' causes. But class counsel, whose clients are vulnerable, is effectively immunized from malpractice liability by the presentation of a reasonable deal, even by the presentation of the worst possible deal that can be called reasonable with a straight face.

In addition to requiring experience and tasting the pudding, courts impose two further obligations on class lawyers. Class attorneys must not name themselves or their partners as plaintiffs in the class suit, and class counsel must not commit fraud against the class in the course of the representation. To the extent the rule ... is designed to protect vulnerable class members from their lawyers' self-serving conduct, it could do this only if class lawyers were obligated to consult with the named representatives, so that class representatives could monitor class counsel's performance. However, courts do not treat class representatives as serious monitors of lawyer performance. Courts neither require class counsel to keep the named representatives up to speed on the status of the case, nor require that the lawyers seek the named representatives' consent to any particular course of action. Therefore, the courts might as well let lawyers serve as class representatives for all the good the rule does the class.

As to the second requirement, that class counsel not defraud the class, the courts affirm this requirement at every turn by stating in absolute language that a lawyer who colludes with the defendants would not be certified as adequate. The very articulation of such a standard proves my case. A stranger is not legally entitled to defraud you. One should hope that one's lawyer is held to the same standard. Of course, a lawyer who defrauds the class should not be affirmed as an adequate class lawyer. Indeed, one would hope that such a lawyer is treated to more severe sanctions than mere disqualification. There is no evidence that any harsher penalties are visited on such a lawyer, but that claim is somewhat empty because, according to the courts, there are virtually no class lawyers who collude. One can scarcely find a case where disqualification is imposed for collusive conduct. After all, accusing a lawyer of what is tantamount to criminal behavior is not something a court is likely to do in a civil proceeding under Rule 23. The no-collusion standard is thus meaningless as a source of obligation. The courts never find collusion, and if they did, insisting that lawyers not commit crimes against the class can scarcely be called a rigorous ethic.

As to the claim that Rule 23 proceedings are not the appropriate place to worry about lawyers fulfilling their obligations, the first response is the one I made to the similar claim about *Strickland* proceedings: So where is the place? As with the criminal defense situation, courts have not encouraged the use of tort actions as an alternate method of enforcing obligations; nor have they used disciplinary proceedings for this purpose. Moreover, the claim that hearings under Rule 23(e) are not the place to worry about obligations is less coherent than the similar argument about *Strickland* proceedings. In assessing the adequacy of a class settlement and the representation provided the class, the court is supposed to sit as a guardian to protect the class' interests. This role makes the justifications offered in *Strickland* for not interfering with the lawyer's independence inapplicable. In *Strickland* the independence of counsel and, thus, implicitly the Court's role as umpire—as opposed to guardian—were used to explain why it would be inappropriate for the courts to get specific about what counsel was required to do and were used to justify strong deference in reviewing counsel's performance. But counsel is not trusted to be independent by Rule 23 because with no concrete client, there is no way to ensure that counsel's independence will not be misused. The court is thus charged with standing in for the client, as guardian. It is, therefore, appropriate to ask what obligations the role of guardian entails.

A guardian is charged with seeing to it that third parties, like lawyers, fulfill their obligations to the ward. Imagine a guardian for a semi-comatose man behaving toward that man's lawyer as the courts behave toward class counsel. Would a guardian concerned about the lawyer fulfilling obligations to the ward allow the corporation that had injured the man to select the man's lawyer? Courts sitting as guardians allow just that. Would such a guardian hire the first lawyer who nominated himself or herself, foregoing the opportunity to shop for quality and price? Courts sitting as guardians do that too. Given the understanding that under Rule 23 courts have special responsibilities toward class members, there is nothing inherently awkward about using that rule as a vehicle for articulating and enforcing the obligations of lawyers. Courts simply choose not to.

III.   Taking Rights Too Seriously and the Looking Glass Effect

Why is it that the courts demand so little of criminal defense lawyers and class counsel? It is not enough to answer that law generally serves the powerful at the expense of the powerless because, sometimes, it does not. Even in this small corner of the legal world, legal ethics, we find the excessive fee cases, which show that it is possible to have law run in favor of the vulnerable. Yes, the typical criminal defendant, like the typical class action plaintiff, is a relatively powerless player, but something more is going on here. The courts say that, because these clients are so vulnerable, they deserve more protection, not less. How we get from that statement of principle to the actuality that fewer obligations are placed on lawyers who represent classes or criminal defendants is the interesting and important question.

The basic process, as I see it, goes like this. Recognizing precisely how vulnerable both groups are, the legal system grants them the greatest protection our legal system has to offer: they are granted rights.

The criminal defendant is granted the right to effective assistance of counsel and the class action plaintiff is effectively granted the same right, although it is called "adequate representation," and is found in the Due Process Clause and Rule 23, instead of in the Sixth Amendment. Ordinary clients in civil matters have no similar rights. All that those people have are lawyers with obligations, enforceable in tort or contract actions, and, in cases of extreme breach, in disciplinary proceedings.

Armed with rights—the trump cards of our legal system—how can it be that criminal defendants and class action plaintiffs are legally entitled to less from their lawyers than those without corresponding rights? The answer is that a jurisprudence of rights does some things better than others. Precious as they are, rights are not always what we need.[73]

In our legal culture, there is no more fundamental concept than the concept of right. The story that gives rights such power is our central story, the story of social contract, the myth that underlies our legal and social order. In this story the starting point is the individual, and he comes complete with rights. To obtain security, some of these rights are traded in and, thus, the state is formed. Other rights are retained. It is a story that defines rights as the basic good: they are traded only to preserve the possibility of rights. This story, with its implicit yearning for the return of what was given up—the return of all rights—reveals the normative significance of granting rights in our culture. Every demand for justice that aspires to be taken seriously in our order speaks in terms of rights: the right to life, the right to choose, the right to an education, the right to effective representation. When we want to convey that a demand is fundamental, we each understand enough about our normative order to place our demands in terms of rights. This takes no conscious reflection. Just as we know how to negotiate our way in the physical world without conscious reflection, we understand the topography of our normative world without conscious reflection too. In this sense, the normative world in which we live is no less real to us than the physical world around us, and we learn to consider our normative world as no less natural.

Rights jurisprudence provides a story that justifies both the state and resistance to it. It is therefore not surprising that such a jurisprudence has flourished in a world dominated by powerful nation states, providing as it does both an apology and a check on state power. The natural concern and domain of rights theory is the freedom of the individual against the collective that is the state, and in guaranteeing that freedom, it excels. That is not to say that it does so perfectly, but rather that it speaks to this concern directly and powerfully. By doing so, it provides, or at least carries the ability to provide, as much protection

---

73. These thoughts and the discussion that follows were inspired by and draw heavily upon an essay by my dear friend and teacher, Bob Cover. Robert M. Cover, Obligation: A Jewish Jurisprudence of the Social Order, 5 J. Law & Relig. 65 (1987) hereinafter Cover, Obligation.

from state power as principle may ever provide. This is its strength. It has, however, its weakness too.

It is weak at providing for needs, as opposed to restraining state power. The story that provides rights theory with its power to check (and justify) the state begins with the individual (and his rights) surrounded by a world of hostile (or at best indifferent) others. The collective is formed because each individual, concerned with his own rights and the threat to them and him posed by others, has no recourse but to cede something valued so that a state may be created to protect him and his own interests. He is not bound to his fellows by anything but a desire to protect his own interests. He has no brothers. He is obligated to no one but himself, and, after he makes his contract, to the state (at least so far as one who contracts assumes a duty to fulfill the terms of the bargain). This does not mean that a normative world based on rights cannot justify collective solutions that tend to the needs of individuals. But it does mean that rights theory does so awkwardly and without the rhetorical punch provided when it attends to struggles over freedom. Rhetoric is serious business in the normative world, which seeks to affect the material world by appeal to principle—by commitment—which is mustered by the power of words.

. . .

Supplying a principle of obligation is what rights theory does awkwardly. It is rhetorically difficult to explain how the state (an arms-length contract partner), composed as it is of hostile or indifferent others, is obligated to do anything other than place "no obstacles—absolute or otherwise—in the individual's path" when she seeks to exercise a right. My claim is not that rights theory is inherently incapable of providing for needs, but that it is inherently ill-suited to doing so. It is disabled, if you will, or needs challenged. When rights theory reaches an unnatural result—the fulfillment of needs—it must do so by the following move: a claim that the right cannot be realized at all, is effectively voided by the state, without imposing an obligation upon the state to do something affirmative toward its realization. The rhetorical emphasis, however, remains on the importance of the right; the obligation is a byproduct, an afterthought, and rarely receives much attention or elaboration. So Gideon v. Wainwright is described in our world, and aptly so, as the case that establishes the right to counsel in all felony cases, not the case that establishes the state's obligation to pay lawyers to represent poor people charged with felonies. The obligation imposed by Gideon and its progeny is nowhere elaborated. The state must provide some lawyer. How the state does that, who it provides, how much, if anything, it pays that lawyer, are not matters of constitutional concern. At center stage is the right and what is clear is that the exercise of state power will be denied, if the right is denied. Obligation is not the focus. The focus is the right.

And so we arrive at how the right to effective counsel fails in both the criminal defense and the class action context. While one might imagine the right is addressed at counsel, it is not. It is a right given to the clients to check the exercise of state power, whether in the form of a criminal conviction or the form of a court order issued in a class suit. At the heart of both a *Strickland* hearing and a hearing on whether to approve a class action settlement is the question of whether an exercise of state force is legitimate. What the state must do, if the right has been violated, is refrain from acting against the person, nothing more. Of counsel, nothing in particular is required. Rights analysis has trouble enough obligating the state. Founded as it is in a story that posits the individual and the state, third-party obligations are as difficult a matter to introduce as one can imagine.

Indeed in *Strickland* the Court went out of its way to emphasize that the rights story it told was not intended to impede the actions or discretion of lawyers, the third parties in the drama. Courts were to be "highly deferential" in judging the actions of lawyers. While defendants have a right not to be prejudiced by performance of counsel that falls "below an objective standard of reasonableness," the Court explicitly refused to impose any specific obligations on counsel or the state or the judge to see to it that the right was realized.

> More specific guidelines rather than overall objective reasonableness are not appropriate. The Sixth Amendment refers simply to "counsel" not specifying particular requirements of effective assistance. It relies instead on the legal profession's maintenance of standards sufficient to justify the law's presumption that counsel will fulfill the role in the adversary process that the Amendment envisions. Any set of detailed rules would interfere with the constitutionally protected independence of counsel. Indeed, the existence of detailed guidelines could distract counsel from the overriding mission of vigorous advocacy of the defendant's cause. Moreover, the purpose of the effective assistance guarantee of the Sixth Amendment is not to improve the quality of legal representation, although that is a goal of considerable importance to the legal system. The purpose is simply to ensure that criminal defendants receive a fair trial.

The Court's language emphasizes that the right is not addressed to counsel or directed at guaranteeing that obligations are fulfilled, and the same emphasis appears in the Court's definition of prejudice. The prejudice inquiry focuses on whether an imposition of state force would be appropriate, defective performance notwithstanding.

The goal of improving "the quality of legal representation may be of considerable importance," but in a normative world where rights are primary, it is of secondary importance. Seeing to it that needs are met is not at the center of our normative world. It is difficult to keep obligations on center stage, once we start speaking of rights.

. . .

... A system of obligation has its inherent weaknesses and strengths, just as a system of rights does. Obligation jurisprudence deals awkwardly with the oppression of individuals. Matters of freedom, to which rights theory speaks directly, can be addressed only through indirection in obligation jurisprudence. The rhetoric is cumbersome, awkward, and, thus, loses some of its power to compel. Try on "I or we are obligated to let you choose what to do." There is an implicit paradox in such a statement, the flipside of the paradox implicit in "my right to obligate you." To resolve these seeming paradoxes each system must strain against its own logic. The reasoning, thus, becomes attenuated, and the resulting statement of principle seems weak and is inherently vulnerable. A system built on obligation can handle problems of freedom, just as a system built on rights can handle providing for needs, but the fact remains that both systems tend to stumble outside their natural domains and pull away from moving onto uncertain ground.

. . .

American law, with rights as its central category, does manage to dole out responsibilities. We have taxes and tort law, for example. States have regulations that set up public defender offices or provide that counsel appointed by the court will be paid X dollars an hour, where X is some meager amount. Rule 23(e) of the Federal Rules of Civil Procedure requires courts to approve the settlement of a class action. But, as Professor Cover explained in discussing similar fiscal and administrative provisions for public schools, these laws "neither move nor dignify in themselves." They do not compel us toward a goal in the same way that talk of rights does, and in a competition with rights rhetoric these devices are easily overshadowed and trumped.

When we try to control the definition of rights by relying on our laws of obligation, we seem ridiculous, as if we were advocating that the tail wag the dog. The ethical obligations of lawyers, whether they be those articulated by the courts in ethics rules or enforced by the courts in tort actions, are simply too weak to drive the definition of right. The idea that a constitutional right should be contoured to reinforce the obligations set forth in secondary (obligation) law, like the rules of legal ethics, seems absurd and is rejected easily both by the Supreme Court in *Strickland* and by the federal courts deciding whether due process has been satisfied in a class action proceeding through the provision of adequate representation.

Rights law is not only strong enough to overshadow obligation law, it is strong enough to stop obligation law altogether. The right having been satisfied, making state action appropriate, it seems at once unseemly and unnecessary to question whether obligations have been met. This attitude accounts for the legal obstacles that prevent tort actions and the absence of disciplinary proceedings in both the class action and the criminal defense context.

Unlike tax law, tort law or other sources of legal obligation in our normative world, ethics is not merely a source of obligation but the place where obligation is understood as dignifying and ennobling. Our normative structure thus allows for the possibility that obligation can be understood as something more akin to a blessing than a burden. But the fact that this idea is so central to ethics may account for the secondary status that ethics occupies in our world, culturally and legally. The idea basic to ethics—dignifying and ennobling obligation—is an idea adrift in an alien universe. It does not resonate with our basic normative structures and, thus, we cannot quite take the enterprise seriously. Our thought tends to get stuck in this circle: if the obligation were meant to be mandatory or binding in some strong sense, it would be legal; on the other hand, if the obligation were designed to be ennobling, it would not be a legal obligation, which we understand to be a burden visited on us by the state, not a gift.

Legal obligations in our world are not worthy of the name of ethics. By making that move we make ethics not just something more than law, more ennobling, but something also much less, less compelling. Ultimately, we conceive of ethics in terms of rights. We have the right to be ethical or not, which in terms of an ethic makes no sense at all. The inconsistency in our world between law and ennobling obligation is apparent when we start speaking of legal ethics, which claims to be both law and ethics, both mandatory and dignifying. It claims to occupy a place in our normative world that seems like it cannot exist, a place where rain falls up instead of down.

Despite these problems, courts sometimes, however reluctantly, take the responsibilities of lawyers seriously, although not often and never with the passion that courts speak of rights. Blinded by rights rhetoric in the case of vulnerable clients, courts are easily persuaded that their job is done, that obligation will somehow take care of itself, that the petty matter of lawyer obligation cannot dictate the outcome of the struggle between individual and state or even be allowed to speak after the outcome of that struggle has been determined. That is how we get looking glass ethics.

The solution is not to get rid of the rights the law provides these vulnerable clients. In our world, with its understanding of rights, such a move would signal precisely the wrong thing. The answer is to understand that rights are not a substitute for obligations, to reinstate the tort remedies, to enliven the disciplinary process, and to express commitment to obligations by using them to contour rights. For any of this to happen, we first need to realize how nonsensical a law our rights jurisprudence has created. It is a law that imposes fewer obligations where the need is greatest, that guarantees the least protection for the most vulnerable of clients. That end is inconsistent with what we set out to do when we confer a right and, thus, the result may be critiqued from within the rights framework itself.

An internal critique is, however, not enough. The inherent weakness of rights theory is an important and pervasive problem, not only in the little corner of concern that has served as the vehicle for this discussion, but also everywhere where basic needs remain unmet. For all those who believe that a just society provides more than freedom, the inherent weakness of rights theory presents a formidable obstacle to achieving justice. To address this weakness, we need more than an internal critique. We need a serious jurisprudence of obligation.

Ethics, legal ethics and judicial ethics in particular, is the natural starting point for such an effort. In legal and judicial ethics we find the possibility of dignifying obligations that are enforceable as law. Adrift in a legal world obsessed with rights, these areas of study have long been and remain the step-children of American legal thought. They are considered soft, secondary subjects not worthy of the attention of our most serious scholars. They are law that is not quite law because how could dignifying obligation be mandatory like law? And ethics that is not quite ethics because how could mandatory obligation like law be worthy of the name of ethics? These subjects posit a possibility not found elsewhere in law, a possible normative understanding we need to nurture and explore, not ignore or mock. By treating legal obligations that dignify as important features in our jurisprudential vision, we may not only be able to walk back through the looking glass. We may be able to bring with us new possibilities of achieving a more just world.

. . .

Notes

1. Does Koniak's conception of "looking-glass ethics" apply across the board? Under Learned Hand's standard for judging negligence, a higher degree of care is required if more is at stake. In the criminal context, high stakes may correlate inversely with wealth because indigent people may commit (or are more likely to be prosecuted for) crimes punishable by long terms of imprisonment or execution. But in the civil context, high stakes may correlate directly with wealth. If so, those with the most at stake are entitled to stronger obligations of care and we can assume are most able to get that level of care that they deserve. But is it true that in the civil context the poor generally have little at stake? Cf. Cramton's article, p. 460.

2. In her discussion of the competence obligations of criminal defense lawyers, Koniak focuses on the weak obligations of such lawyers in general. In addition, there might be incentives for those lawyers to differentiate among their clients. In particular, to minimize their chances of whatever malpractice liability exists, criminal defense lawyers would have an incentive to exert a greater effort on behalf of clients they judge (or believe the legal system will judge) to be innocent. What, if anything, would be wrong with that? Is it realistic to think lawyers would allocate their energy and other resources based on such reasoning?

3. Koniak suggests that alternatives to malpractice liability, such as discipline or court sanctions, might be used to bolster the state's commitment to competent legal representation in the criminal defense and class action contexts. This suggestion relates to Wilkins' analysis of different ways of regulating lawyers p. 4. How would the Wilkins analysis apply to the problems Koniak is addressing? For a recent discussion of the problem of malpractice as a means of regulating criminal defense lawyers, see Meredith J. Duncan, Criminal Malpractice: A Lawyer's Holiday, 37 Ga. L. Rev. 1251 (2003).

4. Do you find Koniak's explanation of why we get looking glass ethics—our law's focus on rights rather than obligations—convincing? Our legal system's concern with negative liberties as opposed to positive liberties (in Isaiah Berlin's terms) can certainly help explain the courts' reluctance to use state resources to ensure lawyer competence in the indigent criminal defense and class action areas. But does it explain the courts' reluctance to support the malpractice remedy in these areas, which relies primarily on private resources? Can you think of any alternative explanations?

5. Compare the Koniak discussion of a jurisprudence of obligation as the foundation for ethics, based on the writings of Professor Cover, with the more common discussion of "norms" and "ethics" in the legal literature, which typically views these concepts as somehow separate from and beyond law. For Koniak, ethical obligation and legal obligation are often complementary, not substitutes. Moreover, legal obligation can be ennobling, rather than burdensome or demeaning. Are lawyers capable of seeing legal obligation as ennobling? Are they any less or more capable of seeing law this way than anyone else in our society? Cf. Gordon's discussion of purposive lawyering, p. 362.

6. For a further discussion of the role malpractice actions might play in regulating class lawyers, see Koniak & Cohen, Under Cloak of Settlement, 82 Va. L. Rev. 1051 (1996).

Chapter VI: Lawyer-Client Relationship

The Ideology of Advocacy: Procedural Justice and Professional Ethics*
WILLIAM H. SIMON

The Lawyer as Champion (The War of All Against All)

. . .

The fullest justification of the Ideology of Advocacy rests on Positivist legal theory. The term Positivist is used here to refer to the kind of theory which emphasizes the separation of law from personal and social norms, the connection of law with the authoritative application of force, and the systematic, objective character of law. Positivism was the basis of the profession's conception of advocacy in the late 19th and early 20th centuries, and it is still an important component of the professional self-image of some lawyers, despite its repudiation in most areas by the intellectual leaders of the bar. Even lawyers who reject Positivism as a general jurisprudential theory are sometimes prone to fall back on it when justifying their professional roles.

. . .

A. Positivist Advocacy

The Positivist theory is constructed on the philosophical foundation laid by Thomas Hobbes. In the Positivist view, society is an aggregate of

* © 2002 by the Board of Regents of the University of Wisconsin, reprinted by permission of the Wisconsin Law Review, 1978 Wis. L. Rev. 30.

egoistic individuals each pursuing his own ends. Government is an artificial creation, the basic function of which is to remedy the disorder which would result if the natural centrifugal tendencies of society went unchecked. . . .

Ends are natural, individual, subjective, and arbitrary. Social norms result from the random convergence of individual ends. By contrast, it is possible to construct a system of rules which is artificial, impersonal, objective, and rational. The best way to provide order is to create a sovereign (e.g., monarch, legislature, party) which is neutral toward the various ends of the citizens and which acts through rules. Rules will give a regularity to social life and thus eliminate uncertainty. Oppression will be eliminated once power is concentrated in the hands of a neutral ruler. An obstacle remains. The legitimacy of the sovereign rests solely on the unique end of order which all share. Yet, from the point of view of each citizen, this end extends only to the orderly behavior of the others. People will constantly be tempted to violate the rules in order to pursue their own individual ends. No one will be willing to pay the price of resisting such temptation without some assurance that the others will also obey. The solution is to have the rules provide for the administration of rewards and punishments in a manner calculated to insure general obedience.

The rules will define for each citizen a private sphere of autonomy. Within this sphere, he need not account to anyone for his actions. So long as he remains within his sphere, he need not fear coercion by the sovereign. The sovereign's enforcement of the rules against the other citizens will insure that they do not trespass within his sphere. Where disputes arise, they must be resolved in accordance with the rules. Since the sovereign cannot itself apply the rules to every particular dispute, it must appoint judges to act on its behalf. It is important that the judges apply the rules with impersonal regularity. They must not refer to their own personal ends. . . . The system enables the judge to reason from the general prescriptions of the rules to particular results. The judge applies the rules to the factual premises of the given situation. The disposition of the case is dictated by the system. The judge has no discretion; he is bound by the system.

The need for lawyers in the Positivist theory arises from the strangeness of the law. Since the legal system is independent of personal ends and social norms, its prescriptions often appear alien. They may be very complicated, and the sovereign may find it convenient to express them in an esoteric language. Thus, the rules are not easily apprehensible. But the individual needs to know how he can further his ends without causing the sovereign to intervene with sanctions. Otherwise, he will be in the very state of uncertainty that government was supposed to remedy. Moreover, if other citizens can gain a superior understanding of the rules, they can use this knowledge to oppress him by maneuvering him into situations where sovereign power will operate to his disadvantage. The solution is to create a class of legal specialists and to require its members to serve every citizen regardless of his ends.

The function of the lawyer is to explain how, and under what circumstances, the sovereign will intervene in his client's life. The lawyer enables his client to pursue his ends effectively by predicting the likelihood of assistance or sanction which attaches to alternative courses of action. He does so by the same type of systematic reasoning which the judge uses to decide cases. From another perspective, this function can be described as informing the client of his rights. A right is an opportunity to invoke or resist the force of the sovereign in a certain way. Rights are defined by the rules of the legal system.

. . .

B. The Critique of Positivist Advocacy

. . .

. . . Positivism fails to show that the lawyer can enhance his client's autonomy. Rather, it appears from Positivism's own premises that the lawyer who adheres to the Positivist version of the Ideology of Advocacy must end by subverting his client's autonomy. . . .

The Positivist version of the Ideology of Advocacy focuses on the person for whom the law is a mystery. Such a person, even if conscious of and articulate about his ends, would not know which aspects of them the lawyer would need to understand in order to gauge the impact of the legal system on his life. In order to isolate these aspects, he would need the legal knowledge for which he relies on his lawyer. The lawyer, on the other hand, has no reliable way of learning the client's ends on his own. . . . [An underlying assumption of Positivism is that the client's] ends are subjective, individual, and arbitrary, [and that therefore] the lawyer has no access to them. . . . [It then follows that] any attempt to [ask] . . . the client [about] . . . his ends or to interpret the client's ambiguous replies will necessarily involve the intrusion of the lawyer's own ends. Thus, consciously or not, the Positivist lawyer is faced with a dilemma: On the one hand, he cannot give intelligible advice to his client without referring to [what the client wants, i.e., the client's] ends; on the other hand, he cannot refer to ends without endangering the client's autonomy, and thus, undermining the basic purpose of his role.

. . .

. . . [The Positivist Lawyer resolves this dilemma by imputing ends to the client.] The ends which Positivism imputes are derived from the basic Positivist premise of egoism, but they go beyond this initial premise to emphasize characteristics of extreme selfishness. The specific ends most often imputed are the maximization of freedom of movement and the accumulation of wealth.

. . .

... The client of whom Positivism is most solicitous is the naive person, face to face with the alien force of the state, threatened with a massive disruption of his life. Confronted with the need to act in this strange situation, the client must make sense of it as best he can. The lawyer puts himself forth quite plausibly as the client's best hope of mastering his predicament. If he is to avoid being overwhelmed by chaos, he must acquiesce in his lawyer's definition of the situation. He must think in a manner which gives coherence to the advice he is given. He may begin to do this quite unconsciously. If he is at all aware of the change, he is likely to see it as a defensive posture forced on him by the hostile intentions of opposing parties ... His only strategy of survival requires that he see himself as the lawyers and the officials see him, as an abstraction, a hypothetical person with only a few crude, discrete ends. He must assume that his subtler ends, his long-range plans, and his social relationships are irrelevant to the situation at hand. This is the profound and unintended meaning of Holmes's remark:

> If you want to know the law and nothing else, you must look at it as a bad man, who cares only for the material consequences which such knowledge enables him to predict, not as a good one, who finds his reasons for conduct, whether inside the law or outside of it, in the vaguer sanctions of conscience.*

The role of the bad man, conceived as an analytical device for the lawyer, becomes, under pressure of circumstances, a psychological reality for the client.

Despite its complete irrationality, this Positivist strategy [of imposing ends on the client] has become so widely accepted that many lawyers have come to equate the manipulation of the client ... with neutral advice to the client on his rights. For instance, lawyers constantly express astonishment at the willingness of intelligent laymen, aware of their rights, to make inculpatory statements to the authorities. They can think of no other explanation for this phenomenon besides confusion or pressure from the interrogators, and they thus conclude that no one can be expected to make an "informed decision" on such matters without the assistance of counsel. But the lawyer's assistance does not take the form of neutral information or the alleviation of pressure. Along with his knowledge of the law, the lawyer brings his own prejudices and his own psychological pressures. These derive from the conception of the roles of lawyer and client which is implicit in Positivism generally and in the strategy of imputed ends. As Justice Jackson put it, "[A]ny lawyer worth his salt will tell the suspect in no uncertain terms to make no statement to the police under any circumstances."[66] The Positivist lawyer is not an advisor, but a lobbyist for a peculiar theory of human nature.

---

* [O.W. Holmes, THE PATH OF THE LAW, 10 Harv. L. Rev. 457 (1897).]

66. Watts v. Indiana, 338 U.S. 49, 59 (1949).

Notes

1. In the portion of this article that we print, Simon does not address why lawyers might adopt a Positivist approach to advocacy. What might motivate them to do so? Self interest? See Cohen, When Law and Economics Met Professional Responsibility, p. 44. The "law" of the bar (which might just push the question back to why the bar has such an ethos)? See Koniak, The Law Between the Bar and the State, p. 23. Is the positivist viewpoint merely a function of our larger mythos, see the discussion of the Social Contract story in Koniak, Through the Looking Glass, p. 287. If so, is there any escape from it?

2. Autonomy theories necessarily struggle with certain "boundary" questions, several of which have particular relevance to lawyers. In particular, autonomy theories must define when someone counts as an "autonomous" actor rather than someone whose vulnerabilities makes him less than autonomous and therefore requiring some kind of protection (children, mentally impaired people, physically disabled, etc.). An adult otherwise "abled" client can be "disabled" in at least three ways. First, the client may be at serious risk of loss of property, liberty, or even life. Given these vulnerable states, lawyers may have a hard time knowing whether the disability resulting from exposure to legal risk is preventing the client from acting "autonomously." Second, a client might be considered "disabled" in that the client does not fully understand the law. Unlike other disabilities, however, clients may be able to learn the law and overcome this disability. Third, and related to the second, a client might be viewed as "disabled" because the client is dependent on a lawyer who has greater expertise and experience, and who may have his or her own agenda (what economists call "agency problems"). Simon's view is that although overcoming these disabilities is theoretically possible, in practice it is difficult to know when or whether the client has sufficient understanding (can give "informed consent" to use the ethics rule jargon) to be an autonomous actor. Are the problems Simon sees equally severe for all these types of client disability?

3. Simon draws a connection between a particular view, or theory, of law (i.e., Positivism) and a particular approach to ethics. Is there a necessary connection? Would a natural law perspective lead to a different ethical stance? Or a legal realist perspective? See David B. Wilkins, Legal Realism for Lawyers, 104 Harv. L. Rev. 469 (1990); cf. Koniak & Cohen, In Hell, Part I (noting tension between view of law as malleable and requirement that lawyers act within the bounds of the law), p. 76. Or critical legal studies? What happens to the Positivist story if law and courts in fact take morality into account in making rulings?

4. Simon uses Holmes's "bad man" metaphor to argue that lawyers may in fact wind up advising clients as if they were "bad men" even if they, in fact, are not. An alternative view of clients is that they, in fact, want their lawyers to act as "bad men," while they preserve a more genteel image for themselves. One might view this as the "Picture of Dorian Gray" view of clienthood. In this view, lawyers are "the technically powerful embodiments of the public's own worst but often necessary instincts." See Edward A.

Dauer & Arthur Allen Leff, Correspondence: The Lawyer as Friend, 86 Yale L.J. 573, 573–84 (1977) (response to Charles Fried, The Lawyer as Friend: The Moral Foundations of the Lawyer–Client Relation, 85 Yale L. J. 1060 (1976)); and Charles Fried, Author's Reply, 86 Yale L.J. 584 (1977). Is this "picture" more realistic than Simon's? In certain contexts, such as litigation? Why is Simon so sure that clients (some clients? most clients?) do not want a "bad man" lawyer?

5. How does Simon's approach apply to entity clients? Does it matter whether the entity is a for-profit corporation, nonprofit organization, or a government agency?

Lying to Clients*
LISA G. LERMAN

. . .

Introduction

Lawyers are not supposed to lie to their clients. Ever. The disciplinary rules prohibit all conduct involving "dishonesty, fraud, deceit or misrepresentation." A lawyer must "keep a client reasonably informed about the status of a matter" and must "render candid advice." Loyalty and zealous representation are paramount values within the bar. These values presume both a close relationship between lawyer and client and total openness in the lawyer's dealings with clients.

Real life is not so simple. . . .

. . .

IV.   What Lawyers Lie about

. . .

B.   *The Lawyer Interviews*

I interviewed twenty lawyers to identify examples of lawyers deceiving clients. Most of these attorneys are in private practice, though a few work for the government or for other public service institutions. I spoke with people in various practices, including small firms, large firms, local practice, and national practice. The focus is on civil practice. The purpose of the study was not to expose egregious deception, but to probe the fabric of daily law practice to identify common types of deception.

. . .

1.   *Billing*

Nearly all of the lawyers interviewed reported some amount of deception in practices relating to billing clients. In many instances the lawyers often failed to keep a running log of their time and estimated the number of hours they worked for their clients. Some attorneys reported that they were too busy to keep detailed records. As long as any amounts added were trivial, most lawyers felt that there was nothing wrong with making good faith estimates of hours or with rounding off hours. Some believed that keeping accurate track of hours would result in more time billed to the clients. . . .

a.   *Doing Nonessential Work—Running the Meter*

Several lawyers reported performing unnecessary work and then billing for it. This practice is deceptive if the lawyer conceals from the

* © 1990 The Trustees of the University of Pennsylvania. Reprinted by permission from 138 U. Pa. L. Rev. 659 (1990).

client what work is being done, or if the lawyer informs the client about the work but leads the client to believe that it is essential.

Madeline Stein[196] characterized the practice this way:

> [L]egal research can be more or less thorough, depending on the amount of money at stake in the litigation. Where the clients have been willing to pay and where the stakes are high, my experience is that the firm will leave no stone unturned and engage in perhaps unnecessary legal background work.

. . .

Winston Hall reported similar practices. "The most common [type of deception], by far, is makework that the client pays for but that didn't lead very directly to the result. That describes an enormous percentage of the activity that I think goes on in law firms." He described one conversation with a partner in his law firm, in which the partner explained that "law practice is somewhat supply-side driven. You can decide how heavily you are going to bill on a matter. There is a wide range of acceptability. If you've got the people, you do more work; if you don't have the people, then you don't." Hall contends that the problem with this phenomenon is twofold. First, the lawyer has too much discretion. "A business acquisition can cost anywhere between $20,000 and $100,000," depending on the lawyer's decisions about how to approach the work. Second, "the client can't even evaluate how [the lawyer] exercised that discretion after the fact."

Hall offered as an example one situation in which a company hired his firm and another firm to work on two very similar matters. His firm "did an exhaustive $100,000 job and produced a two-inch binder filled with memos.... [T]he other firm did a fifteen page memo that cost about $5,000." The client was "initially kind of horrified at the difference."

. . .

If clients understood the broad scope of the lawyer's discretion, they might exercise more control over what work was to be done. Hall elaborates:

> The worst clients from the point of view of a lawyer are the ex-partners from the firm ... who know damn well ... [that lawyers do work to run the meter]. One lawyer ... who [left to become general counsel of a client bank] would say, "I don't want a single memo written about this" ... because he knew exactly what happens.

. . .

... Madeline Stein, who worked in two firms in which most of the clients paid on an hourly basis, said: "From my experience it was more

---

196. I have assigned fictitious names to the interviewees for purposes of reference. The pseudonyms accurately denote the sex of the speakers. If necessary to protect a speaker's identity, more than one fictitious name has been used.

likely that a lawyer would attempt to deceive a client into continued litigation, including trial, by inflating the client's chances of success."

b.   Padding Bills and Double Billing

One of the most significant types of billing deception reported was inflating or padding the bills of wealthy clients. Several different techniques were reported.

Some attorneys reported that the work performed did not always correspond to the hours billed. Michael Williams, characterizing a widespread attitude in his firm toward wealthy clients, said "some people in the firm feel like, 'well they are a rich client, they can pay, we can put a couple more hours down than we worked' " . . .

As to his own billing practices, he explained: "my billing is certainly influenced by the size and ability of the client to pay. There's pressure to bill . . . at least eight hours a day and I generally bill as much as I can to the richest client [and underbill] clients who can't afford standard rates. . . . It's rough justice." He also reported that:

> There are rough premiums and discounts that are put into the bills without being disclosed to the client. Not large ones—not like the New York firms. But when I settled a case I threw down another six hours to a small client, thinking that I under-billed them at other times because they didn't have much money, but I got a good settlement for them. That isn't disclosed.

. . .

Martin Richards, a former paralegal at a large law firm, reported that he had been ordered by a partner in the law firm to double-bill his time: [Billing client A for travel time to a deposition and Client B for reading material on its case, while on the plane traveling for client A.]

> . . . [L]ater, in similar situations, the senior paralegal in charge of assignments let it be known that this is how billing was to be handled.

. . .

Winston Hall reported pervasive dishonesty about billing at his firm. "I'm sure people were making up hours, because the totals were so high. . . . Like lots of people [were billing] over 2000 hours. And people weren't at work that often after seven o'clock. . . ." He offered two specific stories about lawyers with whom he worked at two different law firms who were overtly dishonest about billing. One of these, whom Hall calls "the fraud,"

> would brag about how a client asked him a question, and he knew the answer, so he wrote the answer in a letter and billed ten hours for research time. . . .

> He had his own gauge. If he gave an answer that he knew, he would think about how much research time . . . [the answer] represented [having done no actual research] and bill for it.

Hall's second story reinforces the impression that lawyers sometimes overbill rich clients. Hall explains:

> I worked on a project for a very rich [Asian].... to set up a very simple trust. We billed way over the amount that was indicated on the billing sheet.... The partner came into my office and said 'This guy, Mr. so and so, is bitching about the bill. I hate when they do that.' And I said, 'well, what did you bill him?' and he told me the amount, ... and I said, 'that does sound like a lot for the little bit of work we did on this, It's just a little trust.' And he said, 'yeah, but these people are so rich, and besides, so and so at whatever investment bank wants to send them a big bill too, so I couldn't send them a small bill.'
>
> That's outright fraud.... and it's not racism, but ... [The attitude is] they've got so much money in these countries where there is nothing to buy, they might as well give it to me.

When asked why the lawyer cared about keeping the bills high to avoid a dispute with the bank, Hall explained that it was "Because we wanted that investment bank to send us more business. We couldn't piss them off by charging too little to their clients."

Another lawyer listed several reasons why padding of wealthy clients' bills is so common: (1) they can afford it, (2) one does so much work for them that it is easy to lose track, (3) padding is unlikely to be noticed because the bills are so large, (4) small clients have no money, and to keep hours up lawyers must bill the time to someone (which seems fair from a "Robin Hood" perspective), and (6) eventually the work done for one client is used for another.

David Larsen said he pads his bills to his clients to cover some related pro bono work. He does work for some states and for a non-profit group to which the state agencies belong. The state agency representatives have agreed (but have not told their superiors) that he should "fluff" his bills to the states to cover the work for the organization, thus subsidizing the organization. The "client" deceived by this practice is not the official who deals directly with the attorney, but the agency that employs the representative. The lawyer thinks that this practice is justifiable both because "the state benefits by it," and because he feels that his "client" is the person he is dealing with rather than the agency.

. . .

c. Meeting Minimum Firm Hours Requirements

Attorneys in many large, urban law firms are expected to bill up to 2500 hours a year....

. . .

Deborah Greenberg said that at her firm "the minimum for associates is 1700–1800 per year, or about 35 hours a week, not including administrative time and pro bono time. 1700–1800 used to be a target. Now it is a minimum." ... Alison Price, who works for a smaller firm, reported that she did not have enough work to bill the requisite number of hours. "The problem is that they want these many hours, and you're looking for work to do, and there is no work to do. You have to fudge."

d. *Premium Billing and Itemization*

Winston Hall explained that ... "premium billing"—adding substantial sums to the bills based on a subjective determination of the value of the work—is the latest innovation....

> The trend now in law firms is this concept of premium billing. Lawyers are on a feeding frenzy, and they are trying to figure out new ways to make money. So they pump up the hours of associates. There's got to be a limit to that; ... When [lawyers] do a specially good job they want to bill extra money. sometimes they tell clients that, and sometimes they don't.... It started in New York; Wachtel and Skadden invented it, and it has caught on in a big way.... Our firm tries to do it to the extent that they can....
>
> Because that system [premium billing] has no apparent limits on money, it gets them tremendously excited, ... this is how the firm is going to average, instead of half a million dollars a year, a million dollars a year per partner, by this premium billing. And then they point to investment bankers and say, investment bankers bill this way, why shouldn't we, we are smarter and we work harder....
>
> This is using hours as a minimum, and taking further advantage of the information imbalances.... What it is moving toward is a vague notion of taking a larger share of the profits you earn for a client, but it is really taking advantage of the information unfairness.

Lawyers may be less than precise in billing practices with relative confidence that no one will ask too many embarrassing questions because the content of bills sent to clients offers little information on which to base questions. The lawyers know little or nothing about the actual billing.... [B]illing paralegal Gordon Foster spent all his time writing bills to clients. The bills ... (which ranged from $50,000 to $120,000 per month) generally began with the line "for professional services rendered, including ..." and then included between several paragraphs and three pages of "cryptic narrative".... The narratives came directly from the lawyers' and paralegals' billing sheets and were separated by semicolons.... This was followed by an itemized list of charges for copying, word processing, overtime, postage, travel, and production of documents.

The bills usually did not specify who performed each task, how long it took, or at what rate paralegals and attorneys were billing. In addition, Foster explained, the bills concealed the firm's multiplier: the firm multiplied every subtotal (lawyers' hourly rate X number of hours worked) by about 1.5.... [C]lients who asked for explanations of their bills were given the lawyer's rate including the multiplier....

Foster reported that partners told new lawyers and paralegals to keep complete records of their hours and ... that if, in reviewing the bills, the partners thought the time was excessive they would cut the bills. Partners, however, "never cut the time. . . .

. . .

e. Estimating Hours—Non–Contemporaneous Records

Failure to keep precise records of work time was perhaps the most prevalent deceptive billing practice among the lawyers whom I interviewed. Only one lawyer reported that he meticulously records his hours as he works, making a note each time he moves from one matter to the next. . . .

[Lawyers reported that] "small amounts of time often get fudged" . . . [One said:] "I feel guilty about not keeping much more accurate time. . . . If I were a client I wouldn't like it." . . .

f. Explaining the Bills

When a client challenges a bill that is not entirely accurate, the lawyer often buttresses one lie with another. Alison Price said . . . :

> The client calls up and . . . ask[s] about [the] bill, and you are saying, "Oh, yeah, on 1/26/88 I spend x amount of time," and you go through as if you had kept to the minute time records when in fact each week you've been fudging on them and padding them because you were required to have eighteen to twenty-two hundred billable hours [per year]. . . .

g. Charging Clients for Perks, Leisure, and Administrative Time

Some lawyers indicated that they billed clients for time spent on nonlegal activities, or for expenses that were not necessary to the particular client's matter. . . . Generally, each attorney resolved doubts about what to bill alone, without consulting supervisors or clients. . . .

Alison Price reported that while working for a firm, "I took a cab home every night and it was charged to the client. If I worked a minute after eight, they bought me dinner. . . . I don't think the clients were advised of [this practice]."

. . . Madeline Stein . . . [said]:

> After days of working nearly non-stop on a large case for a large corporate client, the . . . entire office becomes inundated with documents, drafts of pleadings, xeroxed cases, and notes. Cleaning up becomes imperative, and most of it involves sorting, filing and throwing away, with no more thought involved than the discretion of one who is intimately involved with the case. An hour passes, and the job is done. Where did the hour go? Is it billable? If so, does one write "straighten office" on the billing sheet?
>
> I would most normally bill the time, perhaps discounting it a bit for sorting other client's papers and for the nature of the work. But I would not let the client or the billing partner know I was billing for cleaning my office—it just doesn't sound right. And besides, it is necessary work that must be done for proper case management . . . by the person who created

the mess. . . . So I bill it to "case management" or "legal research" or "draft pleadings," depending on the occupation that created the mess in the first place. . . . If billing in this way is either padding or deceptive, I never thought of it as such.

.   .   .

h. The Impact of Client Confrontation

Most clients do not ask for detailed explanations of their bills. . . .

Lawyer billing practices might be more precise if clients scrutinized bills and questioned them more frequently. Arthur Katz recalled . . .:

> I went to a client's office at 8:30 this morning. . . . I had lunch with [a client's] in-house counsel and he asked, "By the way, what are your billing rates?", and I told him [$125 per hour] and he said "Oh my God—you better not bill me for this lunch". . . . I said "I won't bill you for lunch and I won't even bill you for the ride home" and he said "Oh you can bill me for the drive home. . . ." He was saying it jokingly . . . [but] I'm sure he doesn't want me to.

Katz implied that if the client had not asked, he would have billed him for all the time he spent with the client, including lunch and transportation time. He suggested that direct confrontation about his rate and about whether he would bill for lunch caused him to promise the client that the bill would include only time spent doing legal work.

2. Bringing in Business

a. Exaggeration of Expertise

Several interviewees reported instances in which they or others overstated the experience or expertise of the firm in a particular area of law. Many lawyers do not consider what they characterize as "puffing" to be lying; they espouse a "macho philosophy" that they "can learn anything in a week," and therefore, that any representations they make about expertise will be true in a negligible amount of time. Puffing does not harm clients, they argue, because usually they do not bill clients for time spent learning new law, or "study time."

Whether a lawyer actually bills the client for study time, however, often "depends on the file." Claude Adams explained that, "[for a] big client, we would [bill for study time]. [For] other clients we would write it off for a while, and maybe if it expands into a bigger client, bill it progressively later on."

Lawyers also engage in puffing by being intentionally vague about their actual experience. Adams explained:

> I would regard [it] as routine practice of business development, if you have . . . any experience in an area, to call it expertise. . . . I tend to think that standards have broken down a lot in that area. . . .

Andy Baird reported that lawyers in his firm ... do not fully disclose the limits of their experience. They might fail to mention, for example, that the firm has never been involved in the type of hearing that a client is facing. . . .

Some lawyers deceive clients about the extent of their professional contacts or access to influential people. Claude Adams, for example, said:

> I have exaggerated and other ... [administrative] lawyers have exaggerated ... the extent to which we know certain ... heads of agencies. I talked once or maybe twice to the head of ... [one branch of a federal agency], but as far as any client knows, he is my best friend and nobody [would] dare call him directly without going through me.

. . .

b. Business Development

Numerous examples of deception emerged in the area of business development, specifically, in situations in which lawyers were giving advice about what additional legal work their clients needed. . . . The attorneys interviewed reported that lawyers sometimes recommend work that will benefit clients only marginally, but which promises significant pecuniary gains for the lawyers.

Alison Price, for example, recounted that other lawyers in her firm were often heard saying to clients: "Listen, I think you ought to get involved with this." (Suggesting that the client hire the firm to intervene in a case or file comments in an administrative proceeding.) Price thought that this was good advice about half of the time.

Explaining that her firm represents numerous clients with similar interests, she reported one incident in which an agency had requested comments on a proposed rule. One lawyer in the firm said "Let's see if we can get [them all] ... involved in this. We can charge them each $1000, we can file one comment, and everybody concurs." She noted one recent proceeding in which 5000 comments were filed, and speculated that much of what is filed is never even read by any government officials.

Claude Adams discussed pressures within his firm to encourage clients to authorize the firm to file comments on proposed agency rules, even when client interest was tenuous. As to one such incident, he explained:

> It seemed a waste of my client's time [to file comments on this rule] ... but I had enormous pressure from the partner to put together a letter to them [proposing that we do the work]. . . .

Adams acknowledged that the practice was deceptive, but ... felt that in-house counsel are quite sophisticated and realize that firms are always trying to get more business. . . .

3. Covering Up Mistakes

One of the most common reasons that lawyers deceive clients is to avoid having to disclose their mistakes....

. . .

Many lawyers felt that it is all right to deceive clients about their progress on work as long as they finish in a timely fashion and the clients do not suffer any harm.

Carol Morgan voiced the commonly expressed opinion that if you assure a client that you are almost finished with a task "then you will do it." She qualified her statement, however, by saying, "I won't make that representation unless I can deliver in a short time." ... She asserted that the client feels better if deceived than if he or she knew that the piece of work was at the bottom of the in-box....

. . .

The more serious the error or oversight, the greater the incentive to conceal it. Andrew Carpenter, who was in-house counsel to a corporation, had to review some advertising [for the corporation] prior to [its] publication. One of the ads stated the results of empirical research in a manner that arguably was deceptive. The lawyer explained: "They were in my in-box and I looked at them and I said, 'Oh shit, I can't do this, I can't approve it, I can't deal with it.' ... I never approved it or disapproved it. When somebody asked had I reviewed it, I said 'no.' " The lawyer was seriously troubled by the whole situation, and by his own response to it:

> It just seems normal in a corporation that when the shit hits the fan everybody ducks.... When something goes wrong, nobody ever saw the document and nobody ever approved it.
>
> I think it was wrong because it was not assuming responsibility. What I am having trouble with is would I do it again under those circumstances? ... Maybe yes.

. . .

... Carol Morgan ... [had a case dismissed because she was late for a status conference.] She wrote a letter to the judge apologizing, and ... planned to file a motion to vacate the dismissal. So far, she has not reported any of these events to the client and will do so only if she loses the motion. Morgan explained: "If I told the client, the client would get hysterical. I am reasonably confident that I will get it straightened out."

. . .

4. Impressing Clients

Lawyers' efforts to cover up mistakes are partly motivated by their desire to gain clients' respect, confidence, and admiration. This goal leads some lawyers to exaggerate what they have done for their clients, or what they think they can do for future clients.

a. Who Did the Work

In law firms, partners usually bring in most of the business. Many clients feel that they have hired the partner ... rather than a firm of lawyers. Many partners, in turn, feel they must give each client the impression that they, the partners, have personally attended to every aspect of the client's matter....

...

The most common way that law firms deceive clients about who does work is by precluding associates who did the work from signing documents sent to clients. Beth Forrester said that her memos to a partner often become memos from the partner to the client. Andy Baird reported that for "every pleading that I worked on with a partner, the partner usually signs ... and I don't.... The argument they make is that the partnership is ultimately liable [and therefore a member of the partnership should sign]."

Alison Price said that her firm sends many opinion letters to clients that associates write but only partners sign. She thought this deceptive practice went too far:

... He doesn't like his clients talking to me.

Andy Baird reported an incident in which an associate at his firm investigated a situation, talked to a law enforcement official, and reported the relevant information to the partner for whom he was working. The partner then wrote a letter reporting this information to the client, and stated that he (the partner) had spoken to the law enforcement official....

...

If the lawyer who writes the document is not identified, it hurts the lawyer more than the client, because she feels disrespected, and doesn't perform as well. If the junior lawyer is invisible to the client, the senior lawyer is less likely to listen to the junior lawyer's advice.

...

b. Making the Work Look Easier or Harder

Some lawyers deceive their clients about their availability or about the amount of work required to accomplish certain tasks. Deborah Greenberg reported that sometimes she would tell a client she was not too busy to take on another matter when in fact she was swamped....

On the other hand, attorneys sometimes try to impress a client by making the work look harder than it is. Many of the lawyers interviewed reported that, when telling clients about settlement negotiations, they exaggerate their achievements or the level of effort required. In some instances the lawyer is merely trying to look good; in other cases the lawyer intends to make the settlement look advantageous to persuade the client to accept it. One lawyer noted that in describing to a client his dealings with opposing counsel, he might say, "I had to do some fast talking," when he really did not. Another lawyer indicated that he might say to a client that in dealing with his adversary, "we've gone round and round on this," when in fact they had not.

Michael Williams admitted: "I am not sure I always accurately portray the negotiations [with opposing counsel] to the client. I always portray that I had to fight for it. I have never called a client and said, 'My God, he just gave in—I didn't have to do anything.'"

c. Deception About What the Law Is

If a lawyer lies to a client about what the law says, one ordinarily would assume that the lawyer has deceived the client. But what if the client knows what the law really says and wants the lawyer to misinterpret the law so that the client can do something that is illegal? In such circumstances, the lawyer may have lied, but the client is not deceived. Madeline Stein offered a[n] ... example ...:

> I think misstatements of the intent of the law is [sic] one of the most prevalent and odious forms of deception in the legal business. There are certain corporate practices perceived by certain industries to be necessary to survival, and many of them are clearly illegal.... Clients will shop around until they find a law firm that will sanction in an "opinion letter" the doing of an illegal act. The letters are usually written with a thousand escape hatches: "if the facts are as you have presented them, blah, blah," but the bottom line message is, "yes you can do it even though the law is intended not to permit it." The firm writes the letter to keep the faith of the large client and to keep the business coming.

. . .

f. Strategic Deception

In some cases lawyers withhold information from their clients as part of the strategy of a courtroom presentation. George Brenner described a personal injury case in which a woman had been severely injured by a piece of machinery at the factory where she worked:

> When she talked about this thing she got very upset.... We [her lawyers] made a conscious decision that we were not going to have her talk about it any more ... we wanted the same thing to happen in front of the jury.... She broke down on the stand.... [T]here were members of the jury who were openly crying.

The lawyers did not explain to their client that they wanted her to emote in the courtroom and therefore had decided to avoid rehearsal of the testimony. Brenner said he felt uncomfortable with this strategy, even though "very clearly this was to her advantage." He pointed out that this approach was to the lawyers' advantage also, because of the contingent fee arrangement.

. . .

5. Convenience and Control of Work Time

. . .

c. Impact of Workload on Advice

Some lawyers reported that their need to control their workloads affected the substance of the legal advice they gave. The classic example is the lawyer who presents a settlement offer in a manner designed to induce the client to accept it because the lawyer, for one reason or another, does not want to litigate the case.

. . .

6. Deceiving Clients to Impress the Boss

Some of the lawyers I interviewed reported deceiving clients to make a good impression in the law firm, to increase their chances for promotion, to avoid disapproval, or to avoid conflict. The most dramatic examples of this pressure came from Andrew Carpenter. He described the dynamics within the General Counsel's office of the corporation where he works:

. . .

He mentioned an incident in which one of the officers of the corporation came to consult him about a proposal which he thought was of questionable legality: "I was tired late one night and somebody came up and said 'can we do it?' I was just fed up with how many possible violations of the law I had approved that day. . . . I said 'No. That's it. No more.' " Carpenter later had to defend his position to the General Counsel, his immediate supervisor. Realizing that the corporation did not want to take "no" for an answer, Carpenter "very rationally explained the risks and benefits [to the General Counsel] . . . and said there is no actual legal prohibition." What he had said the night before (and what he believed to be accurate advice) was, "No, don't do it, it is probably illegal."

Carpenter . . . [said] an attorney who had recently joined the office . . . "hasn't been sleeping nights because of the tension of being told to say 'yes'—to be pro-business, regardless."

None of the lawyers I interviewed reported this degree of pressure in their law firms . . .

. . .

D.   Recommendations for Change in Regulation of Deception of Clients

[What follows are drafts of new rules that might address the deception described above.]

1.   Fee Questions

. . . [Proposal:]

RULE 1.5 Fees

(f) *Billing*

1) *Hourly Billing Requirements.* If a lawyer agrees to bill a client on an hourly basis, the written fee agreement and each bill sent to the client shall specify:

a) each lawyer's hourly rate;

b) the hourly rates of paralegals, secretaries, or other staff whose time will be billed to the client on an hourly basis;

c) all other charges that will be billed to the client, such as court costs, telephone, photocopy, postage, messengers, etc.; and

d) a detailed statement of any other factors that will affect the amount of the bill.

2) *Estimates.* If a lawyer has provided a client with an estimate of the likely total charges, that estimate should be recorded in writing.

3) *Contemporaneous Recording of Time.* If a lawyer or other firm employees are billing on an hourly basis, those billing for their time must keep contemporaneous time records, recording their time at least twice each day. If work is performed for more than one client during each day, billing time must be recorded each time the person billing begins a task for a different client.

4) *Accuracy.* Records shall be accurate within one quarter of an hour. Rounding is permitted if the actual time worked is half or more of the number of minutes in the billing unit. (A task which takes nine minutes may be recorded as one quarter of an hour; a task which takes six minutes may not.)

5) *Recording Requirements.* Time records shall include precise and accurate records of the work done during each time block. The records must be included with each bill sent to a client, and must note:

a) the client for whom the work is done, and the person doing the work; and

b) the specific task in which the person billing is engaged, such as legal research, drafting a document, making a telephone call, meeting with identified individuals, or review of discovery documents. Each of these tasks must be described with particularity. For example, it is not sufficient merely to record "legal research;" the question being researched must be noted. If a particular task benefits two or more clients, the records kept must indicate the percentage of the total time for the task that is being billed to each client.

6) Explaining Bills. Each bill sent to a client shall include the following notice, printed on the front page of the bill in type the same size as the numerals used to communicate charges:

> You are entitled by law to precise and accurate records of the time for which you are being billed and the work done during that time. If you have questions about the information provided in this bill, please call at . If, after discussing the bill with him/her, you still have concerns about this bill, you may call the (State Bar Grievance Committee) at . If you dispute the amount of a bill, your lawyer may not withdraw the disputed amount from a client trust account until the dispute is resolved.

7) *Billable activities.* Unless parties contract otherwise in writing,

a) Lawyers may bill clients for time spent:

(1) on work that calls for the professional judgment of a lawyer;

(2) conferring with other lawyers about a matter;

(3) traveling to and from a meeting or proceeding;

(4) administrative tasks such as filing which require familiarity with the legal issues in a case.

b) Lawyers shall not bill clients for time spent:

(1) taking breaks from work, eating meals, or sleeping;

(2) socializing with a client in person or on the telephone;

(3) keeping time records or explaining a bill to a client;

(4) correcting errors made by firm personnel;

(5) soliciting new business from existing clients or advising existing clients of new areas of possible work, unless or until the lawyer is retained to do work on the matter discussed;

8) Splitting time between two clients. If a piece of work is done which benefits more than one client, the time shall be allocated between the clients' bills based on the degree of benefit to each, unless the clients have agreed to some other method of allocating time. If a task is to be billed to more than one client, that fact, and the percentage billed to each client, shall be explained in each bill.

Many lawyers will object that these rules are too onerous.... [L]awyers' hourly rates are so high that clients are entitled to a detailed accounting. Given ... the technology ... available ..., sloppy time-keeping is inexcusable.

Some lawyers might object that greater disclosure will multiply the number of questions and objections to bills made by clients. That ... is part of the purpose of these rules. ...

2. *Lawyers' Representations Regarding Expertise*

... Some states have imposed certification requirements for lawyers who wish to hold themselves out as specialists in particular fields. These rules do not explicitly require lawyers to be accurate in telling clients about their knowledge and experience. ... [Proposal:]

RULE 7.4 Communication of Fields of Practice

(b) *Expertise*

1) *Disclosure.* In discussing prospective work, a lawyer shall inform each client of the precise extent of his or her expertise in the area in which the work is to be performed. The lawyer shall offer information regarding the extent of his or her knowledge, or the knowledge of others in his or her firm, of the laws and regulations that bear on the issue, of the procedural rules that govern the proposed action, and of any technical knowledge (e.g., medical, scientific, or economic) required. The lawyer shall provide accurate information concerning the number and type of related cases that the individual lawyer has handled, and that the firm has handled. If known, the lawyer shall provide information about whether other firms have had more experience in the area in question.

2) *Acquisition of expertise.* A lawyer shall explain to each client what aspects of the relevant law are familiar to the lawyer and what aspects must be researched. A lawyer shall explain at the outset that clients will be billed for any research required.

3. Advising Clients About Possible Additional Work

... [Proposal:]

RULE 7.35 Solicitation of New Business From Existing Clients

a) A lawyer shall not suggest to a present client legal action additional to that already undertaken unless the lawyer is personally convinced that retaining the lawyer to undertake such additional action would be so beneficial that the cost of the services would be an appropriate investment. The lawyer must disclose all factors that might reduce the benefit of the proposed work to the client.

b) In making compensation and promotion decisions, a law firm may not sanction a lawyer for advising a client that a particular action probably will not be beneficial.

4. *Communicating With the Client*

... Model Rule 1.4 might be amended as follows ...:

RULE 1.4 Communication

(c) A lawyer shall respond to a client call within two business days after receiving it, or shall make arrangements for a partner or an employee to respond to the call within that time period.

(d) A lawyer shall inform a client of all matters relating to representation which, if known to the client, might cause the client to alter his or her course of conduct.

(e) In discussing progress on a matter with a client, a lawyer shall disclose any errors made by the law firm or the lawyer, and shall disclose any failure to progress on work and the reasons for the delay. A lawyer shall not represent to a client that the lawyer has done work that the lawyer has in fact not done.

(f) A lawyer shall not withhold information from client to serve the lawyer's own interest or convenience.

5. *Duty to Confront Lawyers Violating Disciplinary Rules*

... Instead of requiring lawyers to report violations to the bar grievance committee, the Model Rules should require a lawyer who learns of an ethical violation to confront the violator. The Rules should require a lawyer to report a violator ..., only if the violator fails to take adequate corrective measures. A similar duty of confrontation is part of the ethical code used in the field of clinical psychology.... [Proposal:]

RULE 8.3 Confronting and Reporting Professional Misconduct

(a) A lawyer who becomes aware of a violation of a disciplinary rule by another lawyer shall confront the other lawyer, inform her of the alleged violation, and suggest measures that might correct or mitigate the violation. If the lawyer in violation is in a supervisory position over the confronting lawyer, the latter may elect to inform another senior lawyer in the firm of the violation. In this case, the reporting lawyer may pass the duty of confrontation to the more senior lawyer. If the violator fails to take adequate steps to correct or mitigate the damage that the violation of the disciplinary rule has caused, the confronting lawyer shall report the violation to the bar grievance committee.

Conclusion

... Almost every time I talk with a practicing lawyer or a law student about this Article, the person tells me another story about lawyer deception of clients. Occasionally I talk with a lawyer who reacts instead by getting angry with me for writing this Article....

... I look back over my notes from the interviews and see many stories that I did not include because they were almost identical to stories already in the text. ...

...

Many of the lawyers I talked with told me stories about other lawyers that were truly outrageous. Most of the large firm lawyers I talked to were associates; the most frightening stories are the ones of major fraud and conversion perpetrated by partners in large firms, and the stories of pervasive overbilling in an effort to meet the firm minimums. ...

...

New disciplinary rules alone will not correct the institutional problems that erode lawyers' ability to value truthfulness. ... Law firms need to reevaluate the work environments that they create for their lawyers. ... In a field in which the touchstone is self-regulation, externally imposed rules can solve only some of the problems.

Notes

1.   Lerman lumps together lies of various sorts, sizes and effects. Does that weaken her analysis? Should some of the lies she describes bother us a lot more than others? Which ones and why? Are any of the lies she discusses justifiable to you? On what ground? Are you telling the truth about the lies that you are willing to tolerate either when you tell them or when others do? Think of the times you lie, including the times you lie when there is really little to be gained by doing so. For example, the times you have added a few points when asked your LSAT score by a friend, deducted a pound or two from your weight or fudged how much you paid for your car or house? What makes us do that? Do those little lies teach us anything about the big lies we tell or might be tempted to tell?

2.   Lerman writes that "the difficulty of enforcement should not dampen efforts to write principled standards of conduct." But is law that is not enforced really "law?" Cf. Koniak's, discussion of commitment as a necessary component of law, p. 23; Pepper, p. 109. Do you think writing more detailed and specific rules will reduce the incidence of lawyers lying to clients? Consider the tax code's detail and reaction to it.

3.   Lerman focuses her reform suggestions on the ethics codes. Does Wilkins' analysis, p. 4, suggest that a different route to reform would work better?

4.   The recently completed Ethics 2000 revisions to the Model Rules did not adopt *any* of Professor Lerman's suggestions. Why might lawyers resist these changes? Can you suggest any changes to Lerman's proposals that might make them stronger? More likely to be adopted?

Essay: In Hell There Will Be Lawyers Without Clients or Law [Part II]

SUSAN P. KONIAK AND **GEORGE M. COHEN***

I. Introduction

. . .

Class action abuse is a particularly interesting area in which to explore both when and why law might fail to affect lawyer conduct and the complexity of the lawyer-entity relationship. By class action abuse, we have in mind three related problems: collusive settlements, inadequate representation of class interests, and payoffs to objectors and their counsel. The law condemns collusive settlements and the lawyers who make them. It demands that class counsel adequately represent the class. Paying objectors and their counsel to drop their challenges to class settlements is, at best, legally questionable behavior and, at worst, evidence of collusion and inadequate representation. If, as we contend, these practices have become commonplace, the law has proved a poor regulator of lawyer conduct. Why?

As to the complexity of the lawyer-entity relationship, class-clients differ significantly from partnership-clients and corporation-clients, to name just a few of the possible varieties of entity-clients. For example, class counsel plays an important, and sometimes exclusive, role in selecting and controlling the class representatives and shaping the size and purpose of the enterprise. By contrast, lawyers representing other entities typically do not select or control the managing agents, nor do they define the nature of the firm. Other entities typically have chains of command, and they have agents authorized to hire and monitor the entity's lawyers; classes typically have neither. With respect to the scope of the lawyer's representation, the law generally presumes that corporate counsel represents the corporation and not its officers, but class counsel necessarily represents both the class and its named representatives.

III. The Complexities of the Lawyer–Entity Relationship

Undoubtedly, much of the work that lawyers do involves the representation of entities, as opposed to individuals, though quantifying how much is difficult. The representation of corporations alone represents a significant percentage of the work of all lawyers, and if one adds to that all the work lawyers do representing partnerships (and, more recently, limited liability companies), labor unions, formal and informal associations, governments and classes, there can be little question that the representation of entities is at the heart of what many, if not most, lawyers do. Although the Model Rules of Professional Conduct repre-

* © 2001 Hofstra Law Review. Reprinted by permission from 30 Hofstra L. Rev. 129 (2001). Originally published in ETHICS IN PRACTICE, edited by Deborah Rhode. © 2000 by Oxford University Press, Inc. Used by permission of Oxford University Press, Inc.

sents an improvement over its predecessor Model Code of Professional Responsibility in addressing the relationship between lawyers and their entity-clients, the Model Rules are woefully inadequate to the complexity of the task at hand. Policymakers and legal ethics scholars have similarly neglected the problems of entity representation. How does the representation of entity-clients in general differ from the representation of individual clients? How do entity-clients differ from one another? Do the ethics rules adequately deal with the representation of partnerships, or associations, or classes? These questions have received too little attention. . . .

The less one's entity-client resembles a large, publicly held corporation, the less sense the ethics rules make. The only rule specifically applicable to entity representation, Model Rule 1.13, addresses a particular crisis in the lawyer's relationship to an entity-client: what a lawyer should do when she discovers that a constituent of the organization is violating duties to the organization or violating the law in a manner that might be imputed to the organization. In the representation of large, publicly held corporations this is the crisis: the rogue manager or, worse yet, the rogue officers or directors. With its singular focus on this crisis, Rule 1.13 implies that in other situations, representing an entity is not much different from representing a person or at least so simple a matter that no particular guidance is required. When the client is a corporation, this position is at least tenable, because in the absence of lawless management, it is reasonable for a lawyer to defer to directions from management or the board just as the lawyer would defer to directions from an individual client. Such a stance is consistent with and, indeed vindicates, the corporate form—a form that presumes that shareholders invest management and the board with the power to direct corporate activities, and insists that managers and directors act as faithful fiduciaries in exercising that power. The ethics rule on entity representation presupposes, and depends upon, the checks and balances that have evolved as a matter of corporate and agency law. To take an important example, corporate law is fuzziest when the corporation is on the verge of bankruptcy. With no clear answer in law on who speaks for the corporation in this situation, Rule 1.13 is of little use, as lawyers representing failing savings and loans discovered to their detriment. In general, however, the comprehensive legal backdrop makes it tenable to posit that only when management breaches its fiduciary duties must the lawyer cease to treat the decisions of managers as if they were comparable to the decisions of an individual client.

Not all entity-clients are corporations, however. They do not all share the same central crisis and, when an analogous crisis does present itself, lawyers for other entity-clients may find that the remedial measures dictated by Rule 1.13 make little sense, despite the bold insistence of the rule's comment that the lawyer's duties "apply equally to unincorporated associations."

Let's start with partnerships. Two of the central crises in the representation of partnerships involve seemingly analogous situations to the crisis most likely to occur in corporate representation. When a majority of the general partners breach fiduciary duties owed the minority of general partners and when general partners breach fiduciary duties to limited partners, the lawyer for the partnership is in an analogous position to that of the corporate lawyer who discovers a manager engaged in illegal conduct. Rule 1.13, however, provides much more guidance to the corporate lawyer and is relatively unhelpful to her partnership-lawyer counterpart. The Rule presumes a formal hierarchy of control within the entity-client, which the lawyer may use to help protect the entity from the lawlessness of its agents. In plain language, the Rule tells a lawyer to make her way up the entity's chain of command, bringing the misconduct to ever-higher levels of authority in an effort to bring the lawless agent into line. When general partners act in breach of fiduciary duties to limited partners or to a minority of their peers, to whom should the lawyer appeal? The partnership lawyer is likely to begin at the place Rule 1.13 marks as an end: advising the highest authority designated to act on behalf of the entity typically all general partners—to abide by the law, and in all likelihood meeting resistance.

. . .

More troublesome, the crises central to the representation of other entity-clients, like classes, are simply not analogous to those that plague corporations. In class actions, the big problem is not that those designated to represent the class as typical plaintiffs or defendants (the named representatives) are likely to act lawlessly and thereby harm the class; the problem is that class lawyers will subordinate the class's interest to their own. In fact, the class is entirely a creation of the lawyer: class counsel control its beginning, its end, its shape, and its conduct. Rule 1.13 assumes that a well-defined entity exists with a hierarchical structure protected by legal checks and balances, and that an agent other than the lawyer is available to monitor the lawyer and direct the lawyer's effort. The Rule, therefore, simply does not speak to the problem of lawyer domination of the entity-client, which is at the core of all the difficult situations that confront class counsel.

Class actions are merely an extreme example of a more general point about the lawyer-entity relationship. That relationship depends on the law that structures or fails to structure the entity-client. The more that internal and external rules structure an entity, for example, by designating the agents authorized to speak, listen, and act on behalf of that entity, the easier it is for lawyers, authors of ethics rules, commentators, and courts to conceptualize how lawyers should act in representing those entities, and to envision and address the crises likely to plague particular entities. On the other hand, the more formless the entity—the less defined it is by internal or external law—the more difficult it is to speak coherently about what lawyers should and should not do . . . .

IV. Class Action Abuse

The world of class action practice we see is one in which abuse flourishes. It is a world in which lawyers make fabulous fees for achieving very little, if anything, on behalf of their clients; defendant-corporations make sweetheart deals to dispose of serious liability at bargain-basement rates; and absent class members end up with useless coupons or pennies on the dollar as compensation for their alleged injuries. While we believe abuse is rampant, others believe it is relatively rare: the exception, not the rule. There is no way to establish to a certainty which belief more accurately reflects the current state of class actions. There is no common definition of abuse. Many, although no one knows how many, court opinions in class action cases are not published. In those cases in which detailed court opinions are available, information critical to the determination of whether the settlement is abusive may not appear on the surface of the opinion, and the underlying record is likely to be either unavailable, skimpy, or, at the other extreme, too voluminous to make an assessment of many cases a practical undertaking. Despite these difficulties, we need to begin by setting out the reasons for our conviction that abuse in class actions is pervasive. We have two: the incentives built into the present system, and available empirical and anecdotal evidence.

. . .

In ordinary lawyer-client relationships, clients can deal with the agency problem [that is inherent in the lawyer-client relationship] in two ways: by a contract between the lawyer and client that limits the lawyer's fee or ties it to the client's recovery, or by monitoring the lawyer's performance carefully as the representation proceeds. These solutions, imperfect enough in the ordinary client setting (especially when clients are unsophisticated individuals), are even more ineffective in the class action setting: "The reason is that absent class members, by definition the majority of the class, neither contract with the lawyer, nor . . . monitor the lawyers' actions." Class representatives, chosen and controlled by class counsel, are in no position to make restrictive fee contracts with class counsel. Nor have courts in general insisted that the class representatives be consulted about the progress of the suit. Indeed, they regularly approve class settlements even though the class representative has only the vaguest idea of what the settlement provides. Thus, client monitoring of lawyer performance is effectively unavailable in almost all class actions.

Defendants and their lawyers in class action suits understand the agency problem just discussed and have every incentive to exploit it. Defendants have a strong interest in minimizing their liability exposure through a settlement. They "care only about the total amount they must pay out in settlement, not how the payoff is distributed between class members and the class lawyer." Thus, defendants have a strong incentive to offer class counsel a deal in which the defendants accede to increased class counsel fees in return for the class counsel's agreeing to a lower recovery for class members. There is every reason to believe that many class action settlements involve the trade of a smaller recovery pie for a larger fee slice. We call this a collusive deal.

Of course, honorable class counsel could try to resist the collusive settlement offers of defendants and their lawyers. But if class counsel "balk at the prospect of selling out their clients," the defendant can try auctioning off the right to bargain on behalf of the class to lawyers more willing to cooperate. The fact that defendants have effective control over which lawyers represent the class may seem surprising. Defendants get that control because they have a very important bargaining chip: the ability to challenge class certification. In most mass tort cases, the defendant's agreement not to fight class certification is crucial, because the heterogeneity of the class would prevent certification if the defendant decided to challenge it. Even in class suits not involving mass torts, the threat to challenge certification and impose high costs on uncooperative class counsel gives defendants great leverage. A lawyer who wages an expensive fight to get a class certified for trial and loses gets no fees.

The collusion between class counsel and defendants can and does take a variety of forms. One strategy is to make the class as big and undivided as possible, which means bigger fees for class counsel, greater finality for defendants, and fewer competing plaintiffs' lawyers to muck things up. This strategy can disadvantage some members of the class—for example, those few with relatively strong claims relative to others. But dividing the class into subgroups of people, known as subclasses, is not in the interest of class counsel or defendants.

Another strategy is to find methods to lock class members into settlements, thereby defeating the ordinary right of absent class members to "opt out." Transforming opt-out classes into non-opt-out classes is another way of ensuring as much finality as possible for defendants.... [T]he defendant can, [for example,] get class counsel to tack a request for an injunction onto a class complaint for money damages. When a class action is brought to ask for an injunction to help the whole class, the rule does not give class members the right to opt out. The defendant tells the class lawyer that the defendant would settle the class's claims for money damages on the condition that class counsel include a request for a makeweight injunction—for example, one ordering the defendant to put up a plaque to commemorate those who died as a result of the defendant's product. That ensures that no one in the class can refuse to accept what the class settlement offered her in money damages (or coupons) and elect to sue as an individual.

. . .

Courts in class actions are supposed to thwart collusive efforts . . . by fulfilling the monitoring role that the client cannot. Rule 23(e) of the Federal Rules of Civil Procedure requires district court approval of class action settlements:

> Ostensibly, the court stands in for the client as a fiduciary to ensure that the settlement is fair to the client and does not merely serve the lawyer's interest. But this arrangement simply replaces one imperfect agent (class counsel) with another (the court). Although the court has no monetary interest in the settlement, its interests are not perfectly aligned with the interests of class members.

Courts generally favor settlements because they clear crowded dockets. The alternatives—trying the class action or, worse yet, trying the multitude of suits that make up the class action individually—are particularly burdensome, taking up significant court time and resources. Judge Henry Friendly observed that "all the dynamics conduce to judicial approval of [the] settlement[]" once the adversaries have agreed. Although the case law may require full and elaborate judicial review before a settlement is approved, it is doubtful that courts have much incentive to be very demanding. Their deferential attitude is probably best expressed by one recent decision which acknowledged that "in deciding whether to approve [a] settlement proposal, the court starts from the familiar axiom that a bad settlement is almost always better than a good trial." Even if courts did not face these incentives, they may lack the information necessary to make an informed evaluation of the settlement. Moreover, the court's institutional role as neutral arbiter limits its ability to serve as an effective fiduciary. Courts are not and cannot be advocates for the class. Although courts provide some constraint on collusive behavior, for the reasons just given it is predictable that courts would be generally unreliable monitors of class counsel's performance and ineffective protectors of class members' interests. . . .

Judges do have "an interest in promoting their reputation for fairness," which at least "should encourage them to safeguard the interests of absent class members." However, individual judges are unlikely to suffer negative reputational effects among the general public from approving bad class deals. The press and academia have imperfect access to class settlements, and even when settlement documents are readily accessible, they are likely to be so complex that sorting out what happened is very difficult.

> Class settlements are, if nothing else, heavily lawyered affairs, and discerning fraud through reams of legalese drafted to conceal any such activity requires effort few reporters . . . and few academics have thus far made. To the extent the general public, media or academics blame anyone for the abuse they perceive, albeit find difficult to document, that blame tends to

land on the doorstep of lawyers, not the judiciary.... And ... judges understand all of this....[132]

More important, courts worry not only about their reputation among the general public, but also about their reputation among other judges and lawyers. Rejecting a settlement that clears not only one's own docket but the dockets of colleagues is not apt to win a judge the praise of fellow judges. Nor should a judge expect to win praise from the bar for rejecting the efforts of lawyers and firms. The judge who has to work with these lawyers on a continual basis would be understandably reluctant to reject a settlement on the grounds that those lawyers colluded. Moreover, state judges who must stand for election may depend on lawyers for campaign contributions, and all judges, whether elected or appointed, may depend on the bar for endorsements. Judges may be wary of academic criticism, but this has far less practical impact. Indeed, academic criticism can be—and often is in the class action area dismissed as idealistic musing by people not sufficiently grounded in the "real world." More important, many legal academics are hesitant to criticize at least federal judges, perhaps because they hope someday to join their ranks, or for whatever reason. Legal academics have also developed something of a stake in the class action system by, for example, serving as special masters in evaluating settlements, who get paid only if a settlement is approved.

It is possible that trial courts' enthusiasm for settlement could be tempered by the possibility of reversal on appeal ... "But being one step removed also means that appellate judges are to a large extent necessarily dependent on the findings of the trial judge as to the fairness of the terms, the adequacy of the representation and the appropriateness of the request for attorney's fees."[139] That distance explains why appellate courts review such matters under the abuse of discretion standard, which seems appropriate but which also will never lead to a high rejection rate....

The available empirical evidence supports the claim that courts are extremely reluctant to reject proposed class action settlements. A recent empirical study conducted by the Federal Judicial Center of class action practice in four federal district courts finds that of the 117 proposed class action settlements, around 90% were approved without changes. The percentage of approved settlements jumps to 98% if one includes settlements in which the judge conditioned approval on some change, however minor. As for attorneys' fees, although the study found that objections were made in 21 (18%) of the cases, in 19 of those cases the court awarded the full fee requested. Thus, not only are proposed settlements routinely approved without change, but so are the proposed

---

132. [Susan P. Koniak & George M. Cohen, Under Cloak of Settlement, 82 Va. L. Rev. 1051,] at 1126 [(1996)].

139. Id. [at 1124].

attorneys' fees. Of the settlements approved in the study, only three were appealed, and only one of those three—the only appeal filed by objectors—was reversed.

Moreover, if judges had no bias in favor of accepting class settlements and the standard on appeal were much more stringent, it is reasonable to believe that the vast majority of class settlements would still be approved no matter how dirty the conduct was that surrounded the settlement. The reason: most hearings on the fairness of class settlements are not adversarial proceedings. The Federal Judicial Center study found that in the four districts studied 42% to 64% of the fairness hearings were concluded without any presentation of objections to the proposed settlement by "class members and other objectors." The study provides no information on whether, in the cases where objectors made written objections or appeared at the hearing, they were represented by counsel or appeared pro se, but it is probably safe to assume that many of those objections were raised pro se. In the absence of a trained advocate to present problems with a proposed settlement, the likelihood that a judge could ferret out corruption or illegality surrounding a settlement that is presented jointly by class counsel and defendant's counsel as fair, legal, and just is quite small.

The current system provides little incentive for lawyers to seek out corruption or illegality in proposed settlements. Objecting lawyers stand little chance of receiving fees or even reimbursement of expenses incurred in mounting a challenge. When a court rejects a settlement, there is by definition no common fund from which to award attorneys' fees to objecting counsel. To award counsel fees to objecting counsel who exposed a settlement as the product of collusion and thus unworthy of approval would require the courts to find some other source of funds from which to pay those fees. Thus far, no court has taken that step. Lawyers are sometimes motivated to challenge proposed settlements in the hope of reaping some later economic benefit, such as success in one's own bid to be class counsel in a later suit or continued income from individual suits, which would be more lucrative than processing people through a claims procedure set up for class members under a proposed settlement. However, because the chances of convincing a trial judge to reject a settlement are so slim, and the chances on appeal are not much greater and entail added expenses, the expected benefit of derailing the settlement would have to be enormous to make it rational to launch a serious challenge. Even when objectors and their lawyers have sufficient incentive and funding to challenge the class settlement, however, they are often motivated not by the chance to protect the class from a sellout settlement but by the prospect of being paid off by class counsel and/or the defendant to drop their objections and walk away.

The situation is thus ripe for abuse. It is in the interest of all the participants in the class action—save the absent members of the class—to settle class actions by collusively transferring money from the class to class counsel. As long as some plaintiffs' lawyers are willing to act in a self-interested way, they will be rewarded by defendants with extraordinary fees funded at the expense of the class. Courts will not effectively monitor the abuse because of their interest in seeing cases settled. Because abuse—by which we mean fraud and negligence as to the class's interest—is in the interest of the participants, it is reasonable to expect abuse to be pervasive. Combined with our experience and the available evidence of class action practice, our understanding of the incentives built into the present system sustains our conviction that collusion and inadequate representation are everyday features of the class action world—a scandalous state of affairs.

V. No There, There

... [The] law condemns both collusion and inadequate representation; at least that's what the court opinions say....

... But a court (or, for that matter, any institution or individual) may say something is law and treat it as if it were not. To be law, as opposed to a string of words, the phrases courts repeat must "mean" something. For words to mean something, two things must be true about them: they must divide actions that occur in the world into valid and void, lawful and unlawful; and they must entail real consequences. If any and all conduct meets a particular "standard," or if the violation of the standard never results in tangible consequences to the violator, we put it to you that the "standard" is no "standard" and certainly not a rule of law. It is at most a mantra, something that is repeated no matter what the circumstances. It is mumbo-jumbo, not law.

"Class counsel has adequately represented the class" is a mantra. Some form of that phrase can be found in virtually every class action settlement opinion, seemingly without regard to what class counsel has actually done. In most cases, the court does not even bother to construct a story describing class counsel's activities. Instead, courts content themselves by summarizing class counsel's resume in the most laudatory terms and by making conclusory statements about how well-respected, talented and above reproach class counsel is. In most cases, in other words, courts are too busy heaping praise on class counsel to describe what they have done to represent the class, to elaborate on what the rule of adequacy demands of class counsel or to explain why it makes sense to hold that what class counsel did satisfies the law. It is true that some courts discuss class counsel's actions at length. But this is almost always to respond to an objector who has a lawyer to present a case challenging what class counsel has done, and that is a rare occurrence for reasons we explained earlier. More important, even in those cases, the courts manage not to create any law of adequacy, leaping as they do from the actions of counsel to the conclusion that those actions are adequate without pausing to explain the content of the standard they purport to be applying.

Conduct described by class action lawyers and stamped as adequate has included the following: negotiating a class settlement that leaves some members of the class paying more in attorneys' fees than they receive in recovery; negotiating a deal for the class that is worse than the deal simultaneously negotiated by the same lawyers for identically situated people outside the class; negotiating a deal that gives members of the class with no viable claims as good a recovery as those with viable, even strong, claims; negotiating a deal without conducting any discovery; and devising settlement notices that the average citizen could not hope to understand.

... The extant "law" prohibiting collusion is as illusory as that guaranteeing adequacy. One must search high and low for a court decision rejecting a class settlement on the ground that it was collusive. Unlike adequacy, collusion is sometimes defined by the courts. Nevertheless, the definition sets such a high bar for "collusive" conduct, equating it with acts that would constitute criminal fraud, that the definition itself seems to guarantee the "no collusion" result. After all, most judges would be highly unlikely to accuse class counsel and the defendant of the equivalent of criminal conduct on the basis of the scanty information likely to be available to the court on what these lawyers actually did in negotiating a class settlement and what their intent was in doing what they did. Whether the high bar for collusion is primarily responsible or not, the fact is that the collusion standard does not work any better than the adequacy standard to mark conduct as lawful or unlawful. Put another way, when nothing is collusive, the collusion prohibition is not functioning as law.

This state of class action law is, of course, not lost on class counsel and other lawyers in the class action world. Once again, their dilemma is not that they are tempted to act within the bounds of the law, yet immorally. Nor is their dilemma simply that class action law is uncertain, and so lawyers are tempted to go beyond the bounds they convince themselves do not exist (or at least do not exist for them). Rather, their ethical problem is that in a very real sense they are operating in a world without law as we generally understand it. Their representation knows no bounds.

The absence of law to control lawyer conduct in class action cases extends much further than we have thus far suggested. Class action "law" imposes little structure on the entity of the class, and to the extent it fails to do so, it leaves class counsel with what amounts in practice to virtually unlimited discretion to create, control, and manipulate her client: the class. A class is a unique entity in our legal system. Its true "owners," the class members, do not voluntarily form the entity. In fact, unlike any other legal entity, there is no law of class formation, save for the skimpy requirements of Rule 23. Only recently did the Supreme Court suggest that these requirements could not be bargained away as part of a compromise settlement. Nor, unlike any other legal entity, is there any law of "authority"—that is, decision-making power—within the class. Without this structural law as a foundation, ethics has nothing on which to build.

Let us be concrete. While class action law demands that each class have named representatives, the law nowhere defines what the responsibilities of those representatives are either in relation to the rest of the class or in relation to class counsel. The little courts do say about the responsibilities of the named representatives suggests that these "responsibilities" are nonexistent. For example, as we have already discussed, courts have said that named representatives may be adequate despite the fact that they know little, if anything, about the claims asserted on the class's behalf, the settlement negotiated by counsel, or the actions or conflicts of interests of counsel for the class. Moreover, courts have held that class counsel may advocate and a court may approve a settlement of a class action despite the objections of some or even all of the named representatives.

In *Amchem Products, Inc. v. Windsor,** the Supreme Court referred to the "representational responsibilities" of the named representatives and insisted that separate named representatives be appointed for subgroups within the class with differing interests ostensibly so that the named representatives could fulfill their "responsibilities" to those subgroups without being burdened by the need to advocate (or do whatever named representatives are supposed to do) on behalf of groups with widely divergent interests. But the Supreme Court never said what those representational responsibilities were. What point is there in insisting that separate named representatives be appointed for subgroups within a class, if class counsel need not follow the direction of the named representatives or even keep the named representatives informed of the case's progress? The Supreme Court's decision is coherent if one assumes, as the Court has since held in *Ortiz,*** that the Court meant that separate lawyers would be necessary to represent subgroups with divergent interests within a larger class—as long, that is, as the courts take seriously the notion that adequate counsel must advocate for the interests of the class or subclass that she represents. But the Court's decision is incoherent if read against the backdrop of "law" that demands nothing of the named representatives and gives those people no power to affect what happens to the class.

Not only does class action law fail to structure the responsibilities or powers of the named representatives, it says virtually nothing about the relation of objectors to the class or to class counsel.... Objectors are technically still members of the class, but the case law is silent on whether that means that objectors continue to be clients of class counsel, despite their representation by others (in the rare case when objectors

* [521 U.S. 591 (1997)].

** [Ortiz v. Fibreboard Corp., 527 U.S. 815 (1997).]

appear through counsel), and is equally silent on what class counsel's duties, if any, are to objectors, whether one imagines them to be clients or not. Must class counsel give some Miranda-like warning to unrepresented objectors, who all would have received notice that class counsel will represent their interests? There is no answer in law. May class counsel help objectors to get a different and better deal from the defendant to encourage the objectors to remain mute in court on the problems the objectors have with the settlement offered to the class? May class counsel help objectors to opt out of the class action after the opt-out period has passed? Although both of these practices occur, we believe, with some regularity, no law speaks to their propriety, as far as we have been able to ascertain.

The emptiness of the legal concepts of adequacy and collusion, together with the law's failure to define the rights and responsibilities of class counsel and the various constituent members of the class (named representatives, objectors, opt-outs and absent members), combine to create a free-zone of activity in which class lawyers can essentially do what they please. If one understands that in class action practice, defense counsel and plaintiffs' counsel have much to gain by cooperating to ensure that class counsel has wide discretion to dispose of the claims of the absent class, it is fairly easy to understand how this lawless state of affairs might result. Put simply, no subgroup within the bar has a strong interest in seeing any other subgroup involved in this area of practice constrained by the rule of law. With no subgroups within the bar to argue for or construct law constraining lawyer conduct in this field, we find no such law.

A better understanding of the relationship of lawyers to the law and the complexity of the lawyer-client relationship is helpful not only in illuminating what is happening in the world, but in identifying solutions that might have a chance at working as well as sifting out those that seem less promising. Expecting courts to develop the law of class actions in a manner sufficiently protective of the class would, for example, seem quite optimistic. Courts, even more than legislatures, are dependent on the assistance of lawyers in the construction of sensible law. Courts construct law, as we discussed earlier, largely by relying on the arguments of lawyers. With lawyers dedicated to preserving a lawless environment in which to operate, it is not surprising that class action law has developed in so anemic a fashion. Similarly, the Advisory Committee on the Rules of Civil Procedure, a committee of the Federal Judicial Center, would seem to be ill-suited to constructing class action law because it is too dependent on input from class action lawyers in framing its class action rules and too sensitive to the concerns of those lawyers. Indeed, the Advisory Committee's class action "reform" proposals have been aimed at increasing, not decreasing, the free-zone of activity now enjoyed by lawyers in this field. Legislatures, although also dependent on lawyers, are in a relatively more independent position. Not all legislators are lawyers and the legislature is more accessible than the courts or the Advisory Committee to nonlawyers and their concerns. If anything is to be done about class action abuse, the legislature is, in short, most likely to do it.

. . .

. . . [U]nderstanding that a lawyer's responsibilities to her entity-client will inevitably be a function of that entity's structure helps provide some direction. To decide what a class lawyer is supposed to do—what constitutes adequate representation—the relationship of the various components of a class to one another and then to the lawyer must be fleshed out. The more ephemeral the client, the more abstract and ultimately empty the lawyer's duty to that client will be. In short, class action abuse will thrive as long as the components of a class are as ill-defined as they are now. When one's client is unknowable or incoherent, one's duty will always be unclear. The law needs to make the class client coherent by explicating how its parts fit together and how they are designed to interact with the lawyer. With meaningless law and shapeless clients, the lawyer's self-interest is her only guide. The unchecked self-interest of lawyers drives class action practice today. That needs to change, and asking the right questions is the first step.

In hell there will be lawyers without clients or law.[222] It is time legal ethics scholars talked about that.

Notes

1. Koniak & Cohen argue that in the context of entity representation, lawyers' ethical obligations are only as strong as the underlying legal structure governing the entity. This position contrasts with the more conventional view of the relationship between ethics and law: ethics begins where law leaves off. See Koniak, Law Between the Bar and the State, p. 23. Do the authors paint an unfairly cynical picture of lawyers and an unfairly bleak view of ethics? Under the authors' view, would more reliance on law and less reliance on ethics always be better? Isn't that the "Hell" Gilmore warned of (see the last footnote to this excerpt)?

2. In Triangular Relationships, p. 200, Hazard argues that lawyer's obligations in triangular relationships depend in part on the legal responsibilities of the "client" and the "other" to each other, which is consistent with the Koniak & Cohen view on the importance of the legal structure governing the entity. But Hazard also places weight on the lawyer's role in the organization, and on the conduct leading up to the "crisis" at hand. The greater the lawyer's role, the greater the lawyer's obligations. Does that suggest that class counsel's obligations should be *greater* than those of other

---

222. This warning (repeated in the title of this Essay) is inspired by Grant Gilmore's famous closing to his book, THE AGES OF AMERICAN LAW: "In Heaven there will be no law, and the lion will lie down with the lamb. . . . In Hell there will be nothing but law, and due process will be meticulously observed." Grant Gilmore, THE AGES OF AMERICAN LAW 111 (1977).

lawyers because of the extent of their involvement in the "organization?" Or that the law of class actions should be *more* developed than the law of other organizations?

3. Organizational law, regardless of the organization, must grapple with a common set of problems: formation of the organization, obligations of the organization's members to each other (fiduciary duties), obligations of the organization's members to third parties (creditors, customers, tort victims), change in membership, and termination of the organization. Does Koniak & Cohen's analysis suggest we should have different ethics rules for each of these problems?

4. Class actions create more problems for lawyers than those discussed by Koniak & Cohen in this excerpt. Consider, for example, problems that arise post-settlement. Mass tort class action settlements often resemble complex administrative schemes in which individual claims get resolved according to an agreed-upon procedure. What happens if disputes arise concerning this procedure? What role, if any, may class counsel play in resolving these disputes? Note that fair treatment for class members may conflict with the interests of the class as a whole. How does this problem compare with the problem of objectors discussed by Koniak & Cohen? With the derivative suit problem discussed in Hazard, Triangular Relationships, p. 200? With the aggregate settlement problem discussed by Silver & Baker, p. 213? For an excellent overview of the problems in modern mass tort class action practice, see John C. Coffee, Jr., Class Wars: The Dilemma of the Mass Tort Class Action, 95 Colum. L. Rev. 1343 (1995).

5. Consider the debate between Hazard, Triangular Relationships, p. 200, and Moore, p. 344, about whether and when certain "others" should have the status of clients. How would their analyses apply to the question of whether class members should be viewed as clients of class counsel? For another interesting take on the class as client, see David L. Shapiro, Class Actions: The Class as Party and Client, 73 Notre Dame L. Rev. 913 (1998).

6. Koniak & Cohen argue that any solution to the class action problem is more likely to come from the legislature than from courts or lawyers. So far, however, the prospects are not encouraging. Repeated efforts to address the asbestos problem (the subject of several significant class action attempts) have failed. And recent legislative proposals introduced in Congress to "reform" class actions aimed ostensibly at "protecting" class members would do little more than shift more class actions from state courts into federal courts. Moreover, the political debate tends to get bogged down in the desire of "conservatives" to clamp down on plaintiff lawyer excesses, and the desire of "liberals" to ensure an effective deterrent to corporate wrongdoing. There seems to be no strong political constituency for reforming the system as a whole.

7. In their article, Under Cloak of Settlement (cited in the excerpt), Koniak & Cohen argue that one potential avenue for improving class action practice is a subsequent class action for malpractice against class counsel. So far, courts have been lukewarm to this possibility, raising a number of procedural hurdles. If courts were to do more to encourage these suits, would

they deter the kinds of practices Koniak & Cohen criticize? Or would they just exacerbate the existing problems?

8. Another important set of class action problems that Koniak & Cohen do not discuss in this excerpt concerns the market for class lawyers. One problem in this set is how lawyers get to become class counsel. Current practice involves largely a first-come, first-serve system. Sometimes overlapping class actions are filed, creating collusive as well as competitive possibilities. See Wasserman, Dueling Class Actions, 80 B.U. L.Rev. 461 (2000). Some have worried about the potential for "bid rotation" among class action lawyers and the antitrust problems created by such practices. Koniak & Cohen, Under Cloak of Settlement. Others have focused on the possibility of auctioning off the right to be class counsel. See e.g., Macey & Miller, The Plaintiffs' Attorney's Role in Class Action and Derivative Litigation: Economic Analysis and Recommendations for Reform, 58 U.Chi. L. Rev. 1 (1991); Jill Fisch, Lawyers on the Auction Block: Evaluating the Selection of Class Counsel by Auction, 102 Colum. L. Rev. 650 (2002) Others have criticized the restrictions on practice that are often written into class action settlements, raising problems under Model Rule 5.6(a), and raised questions about the conflicts presented by class counsel's role as lawyers for individuals in the post settlement claims resolution process. See Koniak, Feasting While the Widow Weeps: Georgine v. Amchem Products, Inc., 80 Cornell L. Rev. 1045 (1995) (raising those and other questions about class counsel's role).

9. A number of recent commentators have advanced a variety of proposals to deal with various problems of class actions. See, e.g., John C. Coffee, Jr., Class Action Accountability: Reconciling Exit, Voice and Loyalty in Representative Litigation, 100 Colum. L. Rev. 370 (2000); Bruce L. Hay and David Rosenberg, "Sweetheart" and "Blackmail" Settlements in Class Actions: Reality and Remedy, 75 Notre Dame L. Rev. 1377 (2000); Samuel Issacharoff, Preclusion, Due Process and the Right to Opt Out of Class Actions, 77 Notre Dame L. Rev. 1057 (2002); Richard A. Nagareda, Autonomy, Peace and Put Options in the Mass Tort Class Action, 115 Harv. L. Rev. 747 (2002).

Expanding Duties of Attorneys to "Non-clients": Reconceptualizing the Attorney–Client Relationship in Entity Representation and Other Inherently Ambiguous Situations*

NANCY J. MOORE

I. Introduction

Under the traditional approach to legal malpractice, an attorney is liable for negligence only to a client, with whom the attorney is in a privity relationship. Thus, an attorney's duties to non-clients are limited primarily to the avoidance of intentional wrongs. Recently, courts have expanded duties owed by attorneys to third-party non-clients; however, considerable confusion and disagreement exists regarding both the parameters and the rationales for such extensions....

. . .

Despite the concern with potential conflicts of interest, a growing number of cases have expanded the lawyer's duty to third-party non-clients who rely on the lawyer, in factual situations that go beyond the early will-drafting cases. Many of these cases involve a lawyer dealing with multiple persons or entities where there is some ambiguity regarding the proper identification of the client or clients.... This claim frequently arises in cases involving a lawyer who represents an entity such as a closely held corporation or partnership and deals directly with individual constituents of the entity such as the officers, directors, shareholders, or partners.

... [D]espite the difficulties in treating closely held corporations and small partnerships as entities distinct from their individual constituents, courts have resisted claims of individual representation (at least in the absence of an express agreement) because they realize that the interests of entities and their constituents are often diametrically opposed.

. . .

Entity representation is a good example of a situation where there is inherent, or at least frequent, ambiguity regarding the identification of the client both by the parties themselves, at the time of the relevant events, and by the courts, which must reconstruct the significance of these same events at a later time. The purpose of this article is to explore the possibility that the difficulties posed by entity representation and similar situations are better dealt with by reconceptualizing the attorney-client relationship, rather than by extending the attorney's duty to third-party non-clients.

. . .

II.   Viewing the Problem in the Context of Entity Representation

A quick survey of several recent decisions in the entity representation area reveals considerable confusion regarding not only the potential liability of an entity lawyer to individual constituents, but also the proper role of the lawyer in dealing with such individuals. Some of the decisions reflect the traditional restrictive approach where courts refuse to find either an attorney-client relationship or any third-party liability, regardless of the extent to which the individuals may have reasonably relied on the attorney to protect their interests. Other decisions indicate increasing discomfort with the inflexibility of the traditional approach and a willingness to examine the facts of each case. . . .

The traditional restrictive approach to entity representation is illustrated by *Torres v. Divis*, a recent decision by the Illinois Appellate Court. Torres was one of several investors and incorporators of a business formed to purchase and manage a restaurant. After Torres and his co-investors took over the restaurant, they became aware of numerous debts that had been previously incurred by the business. Unable to rescind the purchase agreement, Torres brought a malpractice action against the defendant lawyer who had incorporated and represented the corporation. While Torres did not deal directly with the lawyer, Torres stated he believed the lawyer was representing him, just as the lawyer represented one of Torres's co-investors, Powers. Without even exploring the reasonableness of this belief, the court held that no attorney-client relationship existed between Torres and the lawyer because that "relationship is consensual and arises only when both the attorney and client have consented to its formation," and no evidence suggested that the lawyer had expressly agreed to represent Torres.

The court also held that Torres could not recover under a third-party liability theory because the facts did not demonstrate that the primary purpose of the attorney-client relationship (between either the lawyer and Powers or the lawyer and the corporation) was to benefit Torres. The court emphasized that its reluctance to find that the defendant lawyer owed any duty to Torres stemmed from its concern for potential conflicts between the individual investors:

> The interests of the incorporators of a closely-held business are not always the same, and they are often adverse. Each incorporator may seek to maximize his personal return and to minimize his personal contributions. . . . It would be unwise to impose on an attorney, retained by only one of several incorporators for the purpose of organizing a corporation, a duty to act on behalf of all of the incorporators in the absence of an agreement that he do so. Recognition of such a duty would create an unacceptably wide range of potential conflicts of interest.

The court, however, failed to address both the obvious potential for conflict between the two clients the lawyer *did* expressly agree to represent—the corporation and Powers—and the fact that lawyers frequently do represent groups of individuals forming an entity such as a partnership or corporation. If the defendant lawyer could reasonably have foreseen that Torres and the other investors would rely on him as their attorney, then surely that fact ought to have had some bearing on the determination of whether the lawyer owed them any duty.

In *Torres* the court invoked the contractual nature of the attorney-client relationship as a barrier to . . . [holding the lawyer liable.] Other courts have raised as a barrier a narrow, unrealistic view of the proper role of a lawyer retained by a corporation or other similar entity. For example, in *Egan v. McNamara* the estate of Rohrich, the majority shareholder of a small, closely held corporation, sought to rescind a buy-sell agreement between the shareholders and the corporation, alleging a breach of fiduciary duty on the part of the lawyer for the corporation who was himself a director and a shareholder, as well as a party to the agreement. The estate claimed that the defendant lawyer also represented Rohrich, and indeed the lawyer had previously represented Rohrich both prior to the lawyer's association with the corporation and subsequently, during a "period of extensive estate and corporate planning" in which Rohrich and the lawyer initiated a series of transactions which ultimately led to the buy-sell agreement. This series of transactions was initiated to achieve various personal goals established by Rohrich.

Despite this extensive history of prior dealings, the District of Columbia Court of Appeals summarily rejected the possibility of any attorney-client relationship between the defendant lawyer and Rohrich. Citing Ethical Consideration 5–18 of the District of Columbia Code of Professional Responsibility, the court held that because a lawyer employed by a corporation "represents the entity, not its individual shareholders, officers and directors," the lawyer's sole duty in the transaction was to protect the corporation's "primary concerns." The court, however, failed to address the possibility that Rohrich might have continued to view the defendant as *his* lawyer, especially in light of the fact that the corporation itself had no real interest in the particular transaction.

In *Egan* Rohrich's estate also alleged that, apart from any attorney-client relationship, the lawyer owed Rohrich a fiduciary duty based on the trust relationship between shareholders and participants in a close corporation. The court also rejected this claim. However, in *Fassihi v. Sommers, Schwartz, Silver, Schwartz & Tyler, P.C.*, the Michigan Court of Appeals accepted a similar claim in a lawsuit brought by a fifty percent shareholder against the corporation's lawyer. In *Fassihi* the defendant lawyer drafted the agreements pertaining to membership in a professional corporation in which physicians Fassihi and Lopez were equal shareholders. Eighteen months later, the lawyer assisted Lopez in ousting Fassihi from the corporation while Lopez simultaneously exercised the authority he had under prior agreements with the hospital to oust Fassihi from the staff of the radiology department. In his subsequent lawsuit against the lawyer, Fassihi alleged that the lawyer breached his fiduciary duty to Fassihi by failing to inform him either that the lawyer was representing Lopez individually or that he was aware of Lopez's prior agreements with the hospital.

Like Rohrich's estate in *Egan,* Fassihi alleged a breach of fiduciary duty based on both an attorney-client relationship and a separate trust relationship. Not surprisingly, the court in *Fassihi* quickly disposed of the claim that an attorney-client relationship existed between the lawyer and Fassihi, citing the same narrow view of the role of a corporate attorney taken in *Egan* ...

Although the court rejected any possibility that the lawyer had assumed an attorney-client relationship with *Fassihi* when he agreed to help form the professional corporation, the *Fassihi* court nonetheless was disturbed that the lawyer had sided with Lopez against Fassihi from the very outset. The court sympathetically noted Fassihi's claim that "he reposed in [the defendant lawyer] his trust and confidence and believed that, as a 50% shareholder ..., defendant would treat him with the same degree of loyalty and impartiality extended to the other shareholder, Dr. Lopez." Moreover, although the court distinguished corporate veil piercing cases, it agreed that those cases were instructive in pointing out "the difficulties in treating a closely held corporation with few shareholders as an entity distinct from the shareholders."

These "difficulties" did not persuade the court to re-examine its summary rejection of an attorney-client relationship between the defendant and Fassihi.... But, the court did not explain the significance, *in this context,* of distinguishing between a fiduciary duty based on a relationship of trust and an ordinary attorney-client relationship. In *Fassihi* the defendant lawyer allegedly breached a duty of loyalty, but it could just as easily have been a question of incompetence. If, for example, the lawyer had negligently failed to create a valid corporation, it would be hard to understand how the court could hold that Lopez, but not Fassihi, could recover damages; and if Fassihi could have recovered damages based on negligent incorporation, then the court clearly would have created the functional equivalent of a full-scale attorney-client relationship.

A similar result was reached in *Kelly v. Kruse, Landa, Zimmerman & Maycock,* a case decided by the Tenth Circuit Court of Appeals under Utah law. Plaintiff Kelly was an officer and director of Earth Energy Resources (EER), which hired the defendant law firm to represent it in several securities transactions. EER sold some limited partnerships in violation of state securities laws and the purchasers of the partnerships sued Kelly and others individually. Kelly in turn sued the law firm for failure to inform her of her potential liability.

As in *Egan* and *Fassihi,* Kelly alleged that an attorney-client relationship existed between herself and the law firm. Indeed, even under the traditional tests, fairly strong support for such a relationship existed because the retention agreement specifically stated that the law firm "agreed to provide '[a]dvice with respect to liabilities ... [of] officers, directors and others in connection with ... the offering.' " Nonetheless, the *Kelly* court summarily rejected this claim ... The court, however, did acknowledge that the agreement created an intended third-party beneficiary relationship and that the law firm had breached its duty of care to Kelly. Given the specific language of the retention agreement, this result is not surprising; however, it *is* surprising that the court failed even to consider whether the agreement created an attorney-client relationship based on the law firm's express promise to render legal advice to Kelly and the other officers and directors of the corporation.

As decisions like *Fassihi* and *Kelly* demonstrate, courts are beginning to recognize that in some entity cases the nature of the relationship between an entity's lawyer and its individual constituents may be such that the lawyer owes a duty to the constituents. But what type of duty is owed, and how will it be established from case to case? To call it a "fiduciary duty" as the *Fassihi* court did ignores situations where an individual's interest in competent representation may be just as compelling as her interest in loyalty. Calling it "third-party liability," as the *Kelly* court did, solves the competency problem; however, under this approach it would not be clear whether or when a duty of loyalty or confidentiality will be imposed, because third-party liability traditionally has not included an attorney's fiduciary duties.

Perhaps the better approach is to recognize that given the frequent ambiguity of the relationship between an entity's lawyer and its individual constituents, entity lawyers who fail to clarify their role may be held to have entered into an attorney-client relationship with individual constituents, even though they had no intention of doing so....

III. The Misuse of Ethics Code Provisions in Entity Representation Cases

As in *Egan*, ... courts that refuse to find an attorney-client relationship between an entity lawyer and an individual constituent often rely on attorney codes of conduct. These ethics codes typically provide that "[a] lawyer employed or retained by a corporation or similar entity owes his allegiance to the entity and not to a stockholder, director, officer, employee, representative, or other person connected with the entity." Reliance on such provisions raises several problems, including ... the strong possibility in particular cases that the lawyer is representing *both* the entity itself and one or more of its individual constituents.

The concept of entity representation has been generally accepted for large, publicly held corporations. However, there is increasing dissatisfaction with its usefulness in the context of smaller organizations, particularly in regard to such intra-organizational matters as choice of an organizational form, questions of capital structure, finance or control mechanisms, and disputes among constituents. According to one view, a small organization like a closely held corporation may well be a separate legal entity for purposes of its dealing with outsiders; however, with respect to intra-organizational relations, the fictional "entity" has no interests to represent and the only relevant interests are those of the individuals themselves.

This view, although not widely held, was adopted for at least some situations by the Oregon Supreme Court in a series of attorney disciplinary cases. In the first case, *In re Banks,* the accused lawyers, Thompson and his law partner Banks, represented a family corporation owned by R. S. Michel, his wife, and his two daughters, each of whom was also a director of the corporation. Michel was the company's "creator, organizer, founder, chief executive, and driving force" and completely dominated the business, running it "as his private fief." The lawyers conducted estate planning, will drafting, and other private business for Michel and his wife and represented the corporation in both its business and litigation matters. Thompson drafted a ten-year employment contract with the corporation whereby Michel received a percentage of the gross income of the corporation and was thus "in a position to assure himself of substantially all immediate benefits from the operation of the corporation." The wife and daughters subsequently gained control of the corporation and Thompson took various actions against Michel, including rendering an opinion to the board that Michel had breached his employment contract.

In defending against disciplinary charges brought by the Oregon State Bar, the lawyers claimed that in drafting the employment agreement Thompson represented the corporation and not Michel. The court, however, refused to apply the general rule of entity representation "to a closely held family corporation which is substantially controlled and operated by one person and where the corporation's attorneys have been that person's personal attorneys as well." The court stated that "[a]t the time of the drawing of the contract *Michel was the corporation*[,]" and "[i]n such a situation ... common sense dictates that the corporate entity should be ignored." The court acknowledged the entity theory underlying the ethics code provisions, but viewed this situation as a "logical exception" necessitated by the reasonable expectations of Michel.

One year later, in *In re Brownstein,* the Oregon Supreme Court reaffirmed and extended its willingness to ignore the entity representation rule in some cases. The accused lawyer, Brownstein, represented a close corporation comprised of three approximately equal owners, including Woods, whom Brownstein represented in other matters as well.

The disciplinary action arose out of Brownstein's role in structuring a transaction in which a third party (who was also a client of Brownstein) made a loan to the corporation and received stock in the corporation and a corporate note personally guaranteed by Woods and another owner. The business subsequently faltered and Brownstein was dismissed as counsel for the corporation. Brownstein then represented the third party in an effort to collect from Woods on his personal guaranty of the corporate note.

In response to Brownstein's defense that he represented the corporation and not Woods personally, the court cited *Banks* for the proposition that "in a small, closely held corporation the rights of the individual stockholders who control the corporation and of the corporation are virtually identical and inseparable." In addition, although Woods did not testify unequivocally that he thought Brownstein was representing him, the court expressed concern that Brownstein never even discussed with Woods whom he represented or the possibility of conflicting interests. This concern led the court to state broadly that the attorney representing a close corporation may not undertake representation adverse to the stockholders because "[i]n actuality, the attorney in such a situation represents the corporate owners in their individual capacities as well as the corporation unless other arrangements are clearly made."

After *Brownstein,* however, the Oregon Supreme Court retreated from the extreme view that absent a clear understanding to the contrary, lawyers representing small, closely held corporations *necessarily* represent the interests of the individual owners. In a subsequent disciplinary case, *In re Kinsey,* the court limited *Banks* to situations "where the controlling stockholder *was* the corporation." Thus, the *Kinsey* court held that a corporate lawyer could not side with the controlling shareholder-directors against the corporation, because loyalty to the corporate entity was necessary to protect the interests of a minority shareholder....

... Nevertheless, even if the standard ethics rule insists on recognizing the separate existence of the entity in all circumstances, including intra-organizational relations, the basic purpose of such rules is not to exclude the possibility that the entity lawyer might *also* represent one or more individuals, but rather to clarify that a lawyer who represents an entity "does *not* thereby (and without more) become the lawyer for any of the entity's members, agents, [or] officers."

... Even the highest officials in large publicly held corporations "often consider themselves to be indistinguishable from the entity." As a result, the Model Rules of Professional Conduct provide that "[i]n dealing with an organization's directors, officers, employees, members, shareholders or other constituents, a lawyer shall explain the identity of the client when it is apparent that the organization's interests are adverse to those of the constituents with whom the lawyer is dealing."

The problem is[, however,] most acute in closely held corporations and small partnerships where, as the *Banks* court recognized, distinguishing between representation of the entity and its individual members is more difficult. This difficulty exists because, unlike the publicly held corporation, the ownership and management are substantially identical. As a result, even entities in which a single dominant shareholder does not exist, counsel "typically will have regular contact with [the owners] and may well have personal relationships with some or all of them, each of whom is likely to have a significant financial stake in the enterprise." In this context, it is difficult, if not impossible, to determine who speaks on behalf of the entity. Rather, "counsel is more likely to find individual participants attempting to realize their personal goals through the enterprise." Because these individuals often have the legal authority to direct the affairs of the business, neither counsel nor the individuals are likely to distinguish between advising the entity and advising the individual constituents.

. . .

. . . [Many commentators explain that the best reading of the ethics rules] is that there is a presumption that entity lawyers represent only the entity itself and not the individuals unless the specific circumstances show otherwise. Unfortunately, it is not at all clear what circumstances suffice to demonstrate individual representation in a particular case. According to the ABA Standing Committee on Ethics and Professional Responsibility,

> [w]hether such a relationship has been created almost always will depend on an analysis of the specific facts involved. The analysis may include such factors as whether the lawyer affirmatively assumed a duty of representation to the individual . . ., whether the [individual] was separately represented by other counsel when the [organization] was created or in connection with its affairs, whether the lawyer had represented an individual . . . before undertaking to represent the [entity], and whether there was evidence of reliance by the individual . . . on the lawyer as his or her separate counsel, or evidence of the [individual's] expectation of personal representation.

One or more of these factors is commonly present in entity representation, especially in representation of those involving small, closely held corporations or partnerships. Yet, it is extremely rare for courts to find an attorney-client relationship between an entity lawyer and an individual constituent. . . .

IV.   From a Contracts to a Tort-based Standard for Determining the Attorney-client Relationship

Part of the difficulty of articulating standards for the formation of the attorney-client relationship in the entity representation cases is that courts continue to emphasize the contractual nature of the relationship even when the action is brought in tort. . . .

The strict contract-based approach has little to justify it, at least in the many jurisdictions in which malpractice actions can be brought in tort. After all, the courts began abandoning the privity of contract requirement in negligence actions as early as 1916 in favor of tests that emphasize the foreseeability of harm as the most important factor in establishing the existence and scope of the duty owed by one person to another. . . .

Assuming tort theory is preferable to contract, an appropriate tort-based approach to the formation of an attorney-client relationship must still be determined. The "balance of factors" approach has the advantage of explicitly acknowledging that the question is one of policy and not form; however, it provides almost no guidance on how particular cases will be resolved. As a result, the test is unsatisfactory in determining whether an attorney-client relationship has been formed, just as it has proved unsatisfactory in determining the scope of an attorney's duty to third parties.

In negligence cases generally, courts typically emphasize foreseeability . . . While foreseeability of harm has been rejected as too broad a test for determining the existence of a lawyer's duty to third parties, because it casts too wide a net and dilutes lawyers' loyalty to their clients, foreseeability might still play a significant role in determining the existence of an attorney-client relationship in cases of entity representation. For example, because there is inherent, or at least frequent, ambiguity regarding the question of client identification in entity representation cases, a foreseeable risk exists that absent an affirmative effort by lawyers to clarify their role, individual constituents will reasonably believe that lawyers represent them. . . . The reasonable expectations of a would-be client have not yet been recognized as a basis for establishing an attorney-client relationship in legal malpractice cases. However, there is considerable support in another line of entity representation cases—those involving attorney disqualification from litigation adverse to a former "client"—for the proposition that an attorney-client relationship (or its functional equivalent) may be found whenever there is a foreseeable risk that the individual constituents will act under the reasonable belief that the entity lawyer represents them as well as the entity itself.

. . .

In *E.F. Hutton [v. Brown]* a federal district court found that an attorney-client relationship was established when an attorney representing E.F. Hutton & Co. appeared on behalf of Brown (then an E.F. Hutton regional vice-president) in SEC and bankruptcy hearings. Although the court acknowledged that the lawyer was representing the corporation at the hearings, it held that he was also representing Brown individually. Taking "judicial notice that it is not uncommon for corporate counsel to represent an individual corporate officer when he is sued as a result of actions he has taken within the ambit of his official duties," the court stated that "[a]n attorney's appearance in a judicial or semi-judicial proceeding creates a presumption that an attorney-client relationship exists between the attorney and the person with whom he appears." While this narrow holding will seldom be applicable in other cases involving entities and their constituents, the court went on to address another factor on which it relied—"Brown's reasonable under-standing of his relation with the attorneys"—which the court deemed to be "the controlling factor here." Given that Brown was aware that evidence developed at the hearings could be used against him as well as against the company, the court found that "[i]n this atmosphere it would seem reasonable and natural for Brown to have assumed that [the lawyer] represented him as well as Hutton when the [lawyer] accompanied him to the hearing[s]." Thus, the court granted Brown's motion to disqualify the law firm from representing Hutton in an action against Brown for alleged negligence and breach of fiduciary duty to the corporation.

Subsequent to *E.F. Hutton,* some courts continue to rely on the "reasonable expectations" of a moving party in attorney disqualification cases. However, beginning with *Westinghouse Electric Corp. v. Kerr–McGee Corp.,* courts have shifted from using such expectations as a basis for determining whether an attorney-client relationship has been formed, focusing instead on the existence of a separate fiduciary duty. In *Westinghouse* the law firm of Kirkland and Ellis (Kirkland) had been retained by the American Petroleum Institute (API) to assist it in resisting legislative proposals to break up the oil companies. Kirkland was asked to conduct surveys and interviews of API member companies (of which there were at least fifty-nine). API told Kirkland to keep this information " 'in strict confidence, not to be disclosed to any other company, or even to API, except in aggregated or such other form as will preclude identifying the source company with its data.' " Further, the individual companies were told that Kirkland was acting as independent special counsel for API and would hold any company information in strict confidence, as set forth above. Subsequently, three member companies were among the defendants sued in an action brought by Westinghouse—which was represented by Kirkland—seeking to establish an illegal conspiracy in restraint of trade in the uranium industry. The three companies moved to disqualify Kirkland from representing Westinghouse, claiming that Kirkland had represented them when it obtained confidential information from them related to the API matter.

. . . [T]he Seventh Circuit Court of Appeals appeared to be willing to adopt a more flexible test in recognition of the fact that an attorney " 'is dealing in an area in which he is expert and the client is not and as to which the client must necessarily rely on the attorney.' " However, apparently reluctant to decide whether each of the fifty-nine members of the unincorporated association was an actual client of Kirkland, the court found instead that the case "c[ould] and should be decided on a much more narrow ground." Examining a number of situations in which a fiduciary obligation had been recognized despite the lack of an attorney-client relationship—including the obligation to maintain confidences of a prospective client and of criminal codefendants who exchange information regarding a common defense—the court noted that what these situations have in common is " 'the client's belief that he is consulting a lawyer in that capacity and his manifested intention to seek professional legal advice.' " Thus, the court concluded that because the three member companies in *Westinghouse* "each entertained a reasonable belief that it was submitting confidential information regarding its involvement in the uranium industry to a law firm which had solicited the information upon a representation that the firm was acting in the undivided interest of each company," Kirkland had a fiduciary duty not to disclose this information and should thereby be disqualified from representing Westinghouse in the pending litigation.

After *Westinghouse*, courts deciding disqualification motions typically view the relevant issue as not whether the lawyer's relationship to the party seeking disqualification "is in all respects that of attorney and client, but whether there exist sufficient aspects of an attorney-client relationship 'for purposes of triggering inquiry into the potential conflict involved' " in the lawyer's representation in the pending litigation....

. . .

If the primary test for attorney disqualification in the entity representation context is a constituent's reasonable expectations of *confidentiality*, then the "reasonable expectations" test is of limited use in the legal malpractice cases.... [C]onstituents will rarely disclose information regarding entity affairs which they will not assume will be shared with other constituents. Other cases, however, ... more broadly consider the importance of loyalty in the attorney-client relationship. For example, in *Rosman v. Shapiro* the court held that the corporation's attorney could not represent one fifty percent shareholder in an action by the other. The court found no reasonable expectation of confidentiality, because the two shareholders jointly consulted the attorney and thus neither could expect information to be withheld from the other. Nevertheless, the court agreed that Rosman, the moving party, reasonably believed that the lawyer represented him as well as Shapiro....

... If a constituent's "reasonable expectations" that an entity lawyer is representing the constituent individually are sufficient to protect the constituent's interest in both confidentiality and loyalty, then it is perhaps a fairly small leap to recognize of a full-scale attorney-client relationship, for purposes of both disqualification and legal malpractice.

V. Refining and Applying a "Reasonable Expectations" Test to Malpractice Cases Involving Entity Representation

Extending the logic of attorney disqualification cases, an appropriate tort-based test for determining the formation of an attorney-client relationship in legal malpractice cases would focus on the reasonable expectations of the would-be client. In a strict sense, the test in the entity representation cases would be whether individual constituents reasonably believed that the entity lawyer was representing them as well as the entity, regardless of the lawyer's intent or belief, under circumstances in which such reliance was reasonably foreseeable. In most cases, satisfying this test will require not only evidence of the plaintiff's subjective belief, but also circumstances sufficient to make that belief a reasonable one. . . .

VI.   Reconceptualization Versus Functionalism

We may want to assume that entity constituents like Torres, Fassihi, and Kelly should recover damages from an entity lawyer because there was a foreseeable risk that they would reasonably rely on the lawyer to protect their interests, and they suffered harm as a result. However, perhaps the better solution is to craft liability rules which do not rely on an expansion or reconceptualization of the attorney-client relationship. After all, not all problems can be solved by "specifying *ex ante* the identity of 'the client.' " Indeed, there is much to be said in favor of a more functional approach, in which the purpose of examining the relationship is taken into account (e.g., malpractice, disqualification, evidentiary privilege) and in which additional categories are recognized (e.g., prospective client and "quasi-client").

One alternative which has been proposed is to recognize a special status for corporate constituents as "quasi" or "derivative" clients of an entity lawyer. This suggestion—which apparently would apply regardless of whether or not constituents reasonably believe they are being represented by the lawyers—was initially developed to meet the special concerns of a lawyer representing a fiduciary, such as a trustee or a guardian. Because the lawyer is engaged to represent the fiduciary, "and the fiduciary is legally required to serve the beneficiary, the lawyer should be deemed employed to further that service."

There are several problems with using the "derivative" client approach in the entity representation cases. First, it is the *constituents* who typically owe fiduciary duties to the *corporation,* and not vice versa, and so the original premise of the fiduciary-beneficiary relationship breaks down. Second, and equally important, the precise nature and scope of a lawyer's duty to a derivative client remains unclear. Thus far, the recognized duties appear to be limited to a duty of loyalty (e.g., a heightened obligation to avoid participating in a fraud) and perhaps a duty of disclosure (e.g., when the lawyer discovers wrongful conduct on the part of the primary client toward the derivative client). As so limited, these duties might not be sufficient to protect even constituents like Fassihi, who alleged a breach of fiduciary duty but whose ouster may not have been the result of unlawful conduct. They are certainly insufficient to protect constituents like Kelly, who reasonably relied on the lawyer to exercise reasonable care to protect her interests. . . .

The relative simplicity of the proposed alternative—reconceptualizing the attorney-client relationship—is one of its several advantages.

Another advantage is that unlike third-party liability, modifying the attorney-client relationship to take account of the reasonable expectations of putative clients is unlikely to result in any vast or indeterminate liability. . . .

One reason courts have resisted extending the attorney-client relationship is fear that it would result in the unethical representation of conflicting interests. . . . [But] lawyers can easily minimize that danger by carefully attending to existing ethics rules which expressly caution them to clarify the nature and scope of the representation whenever their role might be misunderstood. In the context of entity representation, current rules require that "[i]n dealing with an organization's directors, officers, employees, members, shareholders or other constituents, a lawyer shall explain the identity of the client when it is apparent that the organization's interests are adverse to those of the constituents with whom the lawyer is dealing." Aside from entity representation, current rules also provide that

> [i]n dealing on behalf of a client with a person who is not represented by counsel, a lawyer shall not state or imply that the lawyer is disinterested. When the lawyer knows or reasonably should know that the unrepresented person misunderstands the lawyer's role in the matter, the lawyer shall make reasonable efforts to correct the misunderstanding.

Thus, numerous authorities have urged lawyers dealing with groups (including unincorporated associations) to clarify whether the lawyer represents the group as an entity, as individuals, or both, particularly in the context of entity employees and individuals who may not understand the lawyer's role and may not have reason to appreciate the significance of any formal designation of that role.

VII. Reconceptualizing the Attorney-client Relationship in Other Inherently Ambiguous Situations

Aside from entity representation, a number of recurring situations are fraught with potential ambiguity regarding the identity of the client. . . . [I]t is probable that reconceptualizing the attorney-client relationship will result in better, more coherent decisions in these areas, as well as in the entity representation area.

A. *Family Representation*

When a lawyer represents a family member, particularly in matters relating to the family, there is often confusion regarding who it is the lawyer represents. Indeed, the dangers in this context may be even greater than in entity representation. Unlike corporate lawyers, who frequently are clear in their own mind that they are lawyers for the corporations and not the constituents, "lawyers faced with requests for . . . family representation are often unable unequivocally to identify 'the client.' " Perhaps this inability is because a family, unlike a business, is not ordinarily viewed as an entity (even by lawyers), but rather as a collection of individuals whose goals are sometimes shared and sometimes in conflict.

Not surprisingly, this potential for ambiguity results in outcomes in legal malpractice cases which are strikingly similar to the entity representation cases. Absent evidence of an agreement or a mutual understanding that the lawyer will represent more than one person, courts typically reject any finding of dual representation, despite obvious indications that one family member has relied on a lawyer retained by another family member (typically a spouse) for legal representation affecting the interests of both. . . . In some cases, the result is patently absurd. For example, in *Makela v. Roach,* an Illinois appellate court refused to find that a lawyer engaged by the wife for estate planning purposes also represented her husband, even though as a direct result of the lawyer's advice to the wife, the husband voluntarily transferred his interest in jointly held property to the wife. The court also noted that the lawyer could not have owed the husband a duty of care, since part of the plan was for the lawyer to represent the wife in a dissolution of marriage action, "thus making [the husband] the opposing party in an adversarial process," even though the purpose of dissolving the marriage was to protect the family's assets from the husband's medical creditors.

The court in *Makela* also rejected liability under a third-party beneficiary theory, in part because of the perceived conflict of interest between the husband and wife in the dissolution action. However, as in the entity representation cases, other courts have recently indicated an increased willingness to afford redress to a family member, usually under some theory of third-party liability. Moreover, as in the entity representation cases, the primary rationale for extending liability is that there was a foreseeable risk that the "non-clients" would reasonably rely on the attorney to protect their interests. For example, in *Jordan v. Lipsig, Sullivan, Mollen & Liapakis, P.C.* a federal district court permitted the husband to sue the wife's lawyer for failing to advise the husband of a loss of consortium claim stating, "A spouse should reasonably be able to rely on the representation afforded to the injured spouse to inform him or her of his or her potential derivative claims for loss of consortium." Similarly, in *Parker v. Carnahan* a Texas appellate court permitted the wife to sue the husband's criminal defense lawyer for failing to advise her of the dangers of filing jointly as part of a strategy to reduce the husband's sentence for income tax evasion. The court expressly acknowledged the likelihood that the lawyer's conduct had reasonably led the wife to believe she was represented by the lawyer, but the court used this conduct as a basis for extending third-party liability rather than reformulating the standard for determining whether an attorney-client relationship had been formed.

. . .

B.   Buyer/Seller and Borrower/Lender

Another area involving potential ambiguities in client identification involves transactions between buyers and sellers or borrowers and lenders in which there is only one attorney. Unlike entity or family representation, the parties may have no prior or continuing relationship with each other or the lawyer. However, in many of these transactions it is customary for only one lawyer to participate. Moreover, even though the lawyer may have been formally selected by one party for the purpose of representing that party alone, it is not unusual for the non-client party to pay the lawyer's fee as part of the underlying transaction. Given the lawyer's usual role in drafting the relevant documents, explaining their terms, and overseeing their execution, clearly a foreseeable risk exists that some unsophisticated parties will believe that the lawyer is there to protect the interests of both parties.

Here, courts have also been reluctant to find an attorney-client relationship absent sufficient evidence of either an agreement or a mutual understanding, but somewhat less reluctant to extend third-party liability when the "non-client" reasonably relies on the lawyer. As early as 1897, the Supreme Court of Pennsylvania held that a lawyer who represented a borrower could be held liable to the lender, even absent an attorney-client relationship. There, the court justified liability on the ground that the lawyer "undertook certain duties" for the lender (examining title and mistakenly advising the plaintiff that she had a first mortgage when in fact she held a third lien) "knowing that the plaintiff was relying on him, in his professional capacity, to see that her mortgage was the first lien." This theory, embraced by some but not all courts, is known as the "gratuitous undertaking" theory of third-party liability. It is most prevalent in these types of transactions, especially where the lawyer for one party offers to file or record a document for another.

There are several problems with the gratuitous undertaking theory. First, it may cover only acts of misfeasance and not nonfeasance. Thus, in *Nelson v. Nationwide Mortgage Corp.* a federal district court permitted the borrower to recover from the lender's attorney because the lawyer affirmatively gave her certain legal advice regarding the transaction. The nub of her complaint, however, was not the affirmative advice she had been given, but rather the lawyer's failure to explain adequately her rights and the nature of the documents she was signing. Given her allegation that the lawyer held himself out as " 'the' settlement attorney and purported to act on behalf of all parties," it is at least arguable that her right to recover should not have rested on the court's willingness to acknowledge an affirmative undertaking to give her advice. Rather, the fact that he volunteered to provide a legal explanation of the documents and affirmatively responded to questions she raised should have been relevant primarily in determining whether the circumstances were such that it was foreseeable that she would reasonably believe that he was acting as her attorney.

. . .

C. *Trustee/Beneficiary*

Lawyers for a trust are generally considered to be representing the trustee, an individual with fiduciary obligations to the beneficiaries of the trust. As in the other areas of representation, the traditional rule is that absent fraud or another malicious act, an injured beneficiary may not sue the lawyer directly because there is no privity of contract. Of course, the earliest cases departing from the strict rule of privity were estate planning cases. However, the cases involving trusts and other fiduciaries have been distinguished from the early will drafting cases on the ground that there are conflicts of interest between trustees and trust beneficiaries which are not typically present between testators and beneficiaries under a will. Nevertheless, as in other areas, there has been significant movement away from the strict rule of privity in a number of recent cases involving fiduciaries.

Some of these cases involve issues of public policy unrelated to any confusion regarding client identification on the part of the beneficiaries. For example, in *Fickett v. Superior Court* an Arizona appellate court held that a lawyer for a guardian owed duties to both the guardian and the ward. Because the ward was incompetent, there was no possibility that he had relied on the attorney to protect his interests. However, this incompetence (and resulting inability to protect his interests) was in itself a compelling reason to impose additional duties on the attorney as a matter of public policy.

It may be true that cases like *Fickett* can only be explained by recognizing some type of functional approach to legal representation in which a lawyer's duties are divided between "primary" and "derivative" clients. However, there are other cases in which the lawyer for a trustee or other fiduciary has engaged in direct dealings with a beneficiary, causing considerable confusion regarding the lawyer's role. For example, in *Baer v. Broder* a widow who was both the executrix and the beneficiary of her late husband's estate hired a lawyer to prosecute a wrongful death action on behalf of the estate. When she later sued the lawyer in her individual capacity for malpractice, a New York appellate court permitted a rare departure from that state's strict privity rule, on the ground that "plaintiff and defendant were engaged in a face-to-face relationship" and "[i]n a real sense, the plaintiff in this action was also one of the real parties in interest in the wrongful death action." The case is typically viewed as an example of "special circumstances" in which attorneys incur liability to third-party non-clients. However, given that the widow certainly did not distinguish between the lawyer's representation of her in her institutional and her individual capacities, the case could just as easily and perhaps more suitably be described in terms of an attorney-client relationship. . . .

The difficulty with the "derivative" client doctrine is that the nature and scope of the lawyer's duties to such clients are unclear, particularly when the relationship between a primary and a derivative client becomes antagonistic. It may well be that like "gratuitous undertakings," there are some fiduciary cases, such as *Fickett,* in which a separate doctrine of third-party liability is necessary. This is particularly true where the lawyer's duty will be limited to something less than the full panoply of duties owed an actual client. Nevertheless, if the primary reason for extending liability is the lawyer's failure to clarify her role, as in *Baer* and *Pizel,* then basing liability on an extended and reconceptualized attorney-client relationship is almost certainly a better approach.

Notes

1. Moore's approach to the ambiguities of entity representation involves what economists sometimes call an "information-forcing default rule." See generally, Painter's article, p. 58. The idea is to put liability on the party with superior information (in this case, the lawyer) to encourage that person or entity to reveal the information to another (in this case, the person who may be in doubt about whom the lawyer represents). M.R. 1.13(d) (the so-called corporate Miranda warning) contains a similar rule, but it's limited to situations where the lawyer "knows or reasonably should know that the organization's interests are adverse to those of the constituent with whom the lawyer is dealing." Note that that rule could discourage two types of misconduct: negligently failing to clarify the relationship and intentionally misleading the constituent. Should it matter for any purposes (e.g., damages, burden of proof, causation) which of the two types of conduct occurred?

2. The problem of a lawyer clarifying whom he represents in the entity representation context raises questions of timing similar to those encountered in discussions of advance waivers of conflicts of interests. If, at the outset of the representation, the warning may be too general to be fully understood by the constituent, and may not sufficiently take account of changed circumstances, must repeated clarifications be given? Excessive repetition may dull the constituent's attentiveness to the issue. Insufficient repetition risks the message not getting through.

3. Why does Moore favor a tort-based approach to lawyer liability in the entity context over a contract-based approach? Isn't "reasonable expectations of a client" consistent with a contract-based approach?

4. Assuming courts adopted Moore's "reasonable expectations" approach, it would not mean that they would treat all constituents as clients for all intents and purposes. When might constituents be treated as nonclients under Moore's approach? Courts also might expand the "accommodation client" doctrine (which treats certain tag-along co-clients as less than full clients of the lawyer) to prevent disqualifying a lawyer from continuing to represent the "primary client" (i.e., the entity) in the event of a subsequent conflict. See e.g., In re Rite Aid Corp. Securities Litigation, 139 F.Supp.2d 649, 655–60 (ED Pa 2001). They might in some cases adopt a

procedural exhaustion requirement for suits constituents sought to bring against entity lawyers, requiring the constituent to show that the entity client would not satisfactorily protect his rights by going after the lawyer before allowing the constituent to proceed. They might adopt a lesser standard of care in constituent-sues-entity-lawyer cases because of the "gratuitous" nature of the relationship. They might limit the constituent to the entity's statute of limitations. If courts reacted in any of these ways, would it weaken Moore's argument?

5. Moore focuses on the benefits from treating entity constituents as full-fledged clients when they reasonably expected that the lawyer was representing them individually. What benefits does Moore see in this approach? Are there any costs to this "reconceptualization?"

6. Is Moore's "reasonable expectations" approach easier to apply than a "balancing of factors" approach or a "foreseeability" approach? How will lawyers and courts know what is reasonable? Is this an issue on which expert testimony would be appropriate? By whom? See Leubsdorf, p. 234. One possibility of fleshing out the concept of "reasonable expectation" is to focus on the size of the organization or the number of constituents. Another possibility is to focus on the type of task being performed. Or one could focus on whether the particular activity involves a matter between the organization and one of its constituents, between two constituents of the organization, or between a constituent and/or the organization and a third party. Would combining these approaches be any improvement over tests Moore criticizes as too open-ended?

7. Moore argues that the "reasonable expectations" approach she advocates will not "result in any vast or indeterminate liability." But isn't the likely result of adopting this approach the expansion of liability? Isn't the primary practical difference between her approach and the alternatives the fact that under her approach lawyers will owe constituents (at least, some constituents) a duty of care, not just duties of loyalty?

8. Another area where the question of who the client is leads to difficulties involves a lawyer hired by an insurance company to represent the insured. The question is whether the lawyer also represents the insurance company. This issue has generated a fair amount of controversy. For some of the literature in this area, see Ellen S. Pryor, & Charles Silver, Defense Lawyers' Professional Responsibilities: Part II–Contested Coverage Cases, 15 Geo. J. Legal Ethics 29 (2001); Ellen S. Pryor & Charles Silver, Defense Lawyers' Professional Responsibilities: Part I—Excess Exposure Cases, 78 Tex. L. Rev. 599 (2000); Symposium, Liability Insurance Conflicts and Professional Responsibility, 4 Conn. Ins. L.J. 1 (1997–1998); Charles Silver & Kent Syverud, The Professional Responsibilities of Insurance Defense Lawyers, 45 Duke L.J. 255 (1995); Charles Silver, Does Insurance Defense Counsel Represent the Company or the Insured?, 72 Tex. L. Rev. 1583 (1994); Douglas R. Richmond, Walking a Tightrope: The Tripartite Relationship Between Insurer, Insured, and Insurance Defense Counsel, 73 Neb. L. Rev. 265 (1994); Robert E. O'Malley, Ethics Principles for the Insurer, the Insured, and Defense Counsel: The Eternal Triangle Reformed, 66 Tulane L. Rev. 511 (1991).

Chapter VII: Structure of Practice

The Independence of Lawyers*
ROBERT W. GORDON

. . .

C. Political Independence: Lawyers as a Separate Estate or Autonomous Social Force

. . .

1. The Ideal of Liberal Advocacy: Independence from the State

Within a normative framework of liberal advocacy, the vindication of individual rights, especially as against the state, requires that lawyers be able to assert and pursue client interests free of external controls, especially controls imposed by state officials. In its usual formulations, this argument tends toward vacuity. Everyone concedes that even the most zealous advocate must remain within the framework of professional ethical rules and the "law." Thus disputes over the advocate's proper role cannot really be disputes over freedom versus regulation, but rather over what the form and content of regulation should be.

. . .

. . . [Our] system is often contrasted with that of totalitarian polities that recruit the defense lawyer to the cause of the state. The most extreme embodiment of this and most other horrors was probably found

* © Robert W. Gordon, 68 B.U.L.Rev. 1 (1988). Reprinted with permission.

in Nazi Germany, where judges would treat the defense's procedural objections as a form of obstructionist sabotage and where defense attorneys were sometimes tortured to obtain clients' confessions.

2. *The Ideal of Law as a Public Profession, or Lawyers as a Universal Class: Independence from Clienteles*

. . .

Proponents of the Advocacy Ideal emphasize lawyers' nonsubordination to the officers and purposes of the state. Believers in the ideal of lawyers as engaged in a public profession, on the other hand, stress that lawyers should remain independent of all the particular factional interests of civil society, including those of their clients. . . .

I know perfectly well that when lawyers start talking this way about their public duties, being officers of the court and so on, most of us understand that we have left ordinary life far behind for the hazy aspirational world of the Law Day sermon and Bar Association after dinner speech— inspirational, boozily solemn, anything but real. But try for a moment to suspend disbelief. The vision of lawyering as a public profession has real historical content, even if the "republican" tradition that gave it content happens for the moment to be in recession. It even has a real current content, meaning . . .

(a) *The Republican Tradition. . . .* This view ascribes to lawyers both negative and positive roles. The negative role is that of resolutely obstructing, out of their instinctive conservativism, any attempted domination of the legal apparatus by executive tyrants, populist mobs, or powerful private factions. Lawyers were to be the guardians, in the face of threats posed by transitory political and economic powers, of the long-term values of legalism. Performing their positive functions entails the assumption of a special responsibility beyond that of ordinary citizens. They are to repair defects in the framework of legality, to serve as a policy intelligentsia, recommending improvements in the law to adapt it to changing conditions, and to use the authority and influence deriving from their public prominence and professional skill to create and disseminate, both within and without the context of advising clients, a culture of respect for and compliance with the purposes of the laws.

In the republican vocabulary, independence from the dominant factions of civil society was the essential precondition to the "civic virtue" or "patriot capacity" that lawyers needed to perform these functions.

. . .

(b) *The Tradition Modernized.* The ideology of professional independence originated with a legal elite anxious to play the role of the "Few," the aristocratic component of society, in classical political theory. Over the nineteenth century, the ideal shed its aristocratic origins and became the ideology of a middle class searching for a source of prestige other than landed wealth or success in business. The middle class discovered such a source in "professionalism."

As one sector of the middle class, lawyers espoused the ideology of professional independence . . .

(c) *Current Views of the Ideal* . . . . Even someone committed to the most thoroughly reductionist versions of modern liberal theory—that there is no public interest, save that in fair rules for the free competition of private interests in the market, the provision of public goods, and the correction of market failures—must still imagine some mechanism for maintaining the basic framework of legal rules that constitute and support the market. To provide such a mechanism, it turns out that it is very difficult to manage without some notion that lawyers must be committed to helping to maintain the legal framework. The system of adversary representation can only work, can only be justified, if it's carried on within a framework of law and regulation that assures approximately just outcomes, at least in the aggregate. At a minimum, lawyers must be independent enough from their clients to support the rules and institutions of the framework, even when doing so hurts their clients.

. . .

. . . Law, in secular modern societies, is one of the most important sources of universal norms. One function of lawyers, therefore, in addition to pursuing their clients' particular interests, is to give advice that will help align those interests with the set of general social norms.

There is also a narrower functionalist argument in favor of the lawyer's independence. . . . [M]arkets cannot operate on purely self-seeking opportunism and strategic behavior; rather, they require an underlying substratum of moral conventions—norms of trust, loyalty, honesty, and reciprocity of dealing. As a method of settling commercial disputes, for example, untempered adversarial advocacy of the kind that exploits every opportunity offered by formal legalism may have long-run corrosive effects on this infrastructure of conventions, and thus should be avoided where possible. On this view, one purpose of legal advice is to remind clients who may be tempted to ignore the infrastructure for the sake of short-term profits of the usefulness of underlying business conventions (e.g., to tell a client who is either about to break a contract or sue a trading partner that the client is being "unreasonable" in a way that will hurt the client's reputation and invite retaliation) as well as of the explicit rules of the legal framework. In other words, lawyers are sometimes in the best position to know when some of the strategic tools of law—formalism, proceduralism, an adversarial attitude—will defeat their clients' overall goals by poisoning the cultural environment in which the clients operate.

A final argument that lawyers have made for their independence is one that seems powerful today without any translation: a country lacking a tradition and a prospect of a strong civil service needs a cadre of competent professionals to staff the upper political posts in the bureaucracies and, in or out of office, to give policy advice. Because lawyers more often than any other occupational group are called upon for such service, it would be better for everyone if their perspective were broader than that of their factional clienteles.

(d) *Implications of the Ideal for Practice*....

. . .

For one thing, many business executives want their lawyers to exercise political judgment, to serve as the "corporate conscience," to monitor middle-managers tempted to cut legal corners to meet profit targets, to follow the spirit as well as the letter of the law in order to preserve employee morale as well as a public image of civic leadership. Even if the client calls for no such advice, the lawyer might still plausibly assume, unless expressly told otherwise, that the client's "over-all" or "long-term" interest lies in following the spirit as well as the bare letter of the laws, and so feel obliged as a fiduciary to give advice based on that assumption. The lawyer could further assume that regardless of what the company's managers say they want, the lawyer-client contract, like every other contractual relation, implies a host of standard duties appropriate to the social roles of the parties. Indeed, lawyers might consider certain professional duties so important for the protection of the parties or potentially affected outsiders that they should be nondis-claimable. The contractual regime could require the lawyer to give "purposive" advice, just as the doctor must warn the patient of risks in seeking consent to the operation, regardless of whether the client waives the benefit of such advice....

My point, however, is a broader one: political judgments are virtual-ly inescapable. Take one of the most routine contexts of business law practice, compliance counseling. The client hopes to seize a profitable opportunity. The plan is routed through the lawyer's office and is seen to pose a potential problem: some legal doctrine or regulation arguably prohibits the plan. What can the lawyer do? Here is a simple, nonex-haustive array of the types of advice a lawyer can give in the context of compliance counseling. The lawyer might advise that:

a) The plan in its current form is prohibited;

b) The plan is clearly prohibited, but the risk of detection is slight or, if significant, expected profits will still exceed the likely penal-ties;

c) Same as (b) except that the lawyer advises that there is a non-negligible risk of getting caught and being exposed to later liabili-ties, so that prudence dictates forbearance;

d) The form of the plan is clearly prohibited, but can be cosmetically recast in another form that will accomplish its essential purposes;

e) The substance of the plan is clearly prohibited, but can be made legal if altered in some substantive particulars;

f) The plan contravenes the regulations' basic purposes, but it technically complies with the regulations, and is legal;

g) Same as (f), except that the lawyer advises that the plan is illegal;

h) Same as (f), except that the lawyer advises that the plan is only technically legal, and that there is some risk that the regulators or courts will be interested in substance rather than form;

i) Same as (f), except that the lawyer advises that although adoption of the plan is technically legal, outsiders may perceive it as immoral or unscrupulous, so that for the sake of appearances or morale the plan should be altered or abandoned;

j) Same as (f), except that the lawyer advises that the plan, though it may survive technical review, is wrong—violative of general norms of responsible social conduct expressed in existing or emergent legal tendencies—and should not be adopted;

k) Same as (f), except that the lawyer recommends an alternative business plan that accomplishes most of the purposes of the original while also promoting the underlying spirit of the law;

l) Though the plan conforms to the underlying purposes of the law, some regulator may disapprove it on technical grounds, and the company should not (or may not want to) take the risk of sanctions;

m) Because the plan complies in spirit, sanctions would be an unfair form of harassment by narrow-minded, overly-zealous regulators or opportunistic adversaries; as such, the plan should be adopted and sanction aggressively resisted;

n) The plan does not comply with the law, but because the law is an unfair and misguided interference with business judgments, the lawyer will work for legal reform through the lawyer's bar association, suggest changes to the trade association's lobbyists in the capital, recommend nonenforcement strategies to or seek exemptions from influential administrators, etc.

And so on.

Suppose the lawyer expresses opposition to the plan in deliberations, but is overruled. Once again, several courses of action are available to the lawyer, who might:

a) acquiesce in the adverse decision at the first sign of opposition;

b) press the point, using the techniques of advocacy to try to induce a change of mind;

c) continue to oppose the plan, carrying objections to a higher level of management or the Board;

d) acquiesce, and zealously help to execute the plan;

e) seek discreetly to modify the obnoxious features of the plan, perhaps by influencing middle-managers to execute it cautiously;

f) insist upon recording objections, reservations, or adverse-risk assessments in Board minutes, opinion letters, or formal memos to the file;

g) refuse to participate further in implementing the plan, but agree to represent the client if an adversary proceeding results;

h) withdraw from the representation of that client entirely;

i) whether or not the lawyer withdraws, warn that if the client goes ahead with the plan the lawyer will disclose;

j) continue to represent the client, but work through writings, bar associations, political pressure groups, public interest lobbies, advice to political candidates, influence with officials, etc., to tighten regulation of the conduct called for by the plan.

. . .

Obviously most lawyers, or at least lawyers for big, powerful companies, will avoid abrasive and unnecessary confrontations with their clients. They will phrase negative advice as prudential rather than moralistic, supporting their recommendations with reasons that sound much more like statements of technical rules or empirical predictions of risks and results than political or moral judgments. But even such tactful and delicate counseling involves discretion, and every exercise of that discretion entails making "political" decisions. For even if the lawyer wanted to, the lawyer simply could not neutrally, objectively, inform the client what the probable legal implications would be if the client followed its proposed plan. The "law" of the situation is always ambiguous. . . . Moreover, the law is alterable by the interpretive spin, the degree of avoidance or resistance, and the political manipulations that the lawyer and others can persuade the client to bring to bear upon it. The life of the law, as the Legal Realists and Law and Society movement keep reminding us, is in interpretations and applications, where the practices of clients amplify, alter, and nullify formal rules. The very language and tone in which lawyers speak of the law to their clients is a local political action that subtly reinforces or subverts the legitimacy of the regulatory state. When they speak of the law deferentially, they imply that it is a set of authoritative norms with which everyone will want to comply. When their tone is cynical and contemptuous, they implicitly portray law as harassment by petty bureaucrats enforcing the legislation of populist demagogues. And when they adopt a neutral attitude toward the law, they convey an idea of law as a set of external nuisances and hurdles completely divorced from their own and their clients' membership in a common political community.

I am not arguing that lawyers should speak of every rule of law with reverence and deference. On the contrary, it is entirely appropriate to treat different types of legal rules differently, and lawyers habitually do so. Few lawyers asked for advice by clients contemplating murder, for instance, would respond simply that no penalty will be imposed so long as the client takes care not to leave behind proof beyond a reasonable doubt. Some tax lawyers, on the other hand, are quite willing to phrase advice in the "neutral" form that the penalties-discounted-by-audit-risks of their proposed illegal scheme are lower than its expected profits. But other attorneys consider such advice highly improper.... Though the form and content of advice may vary, the choice of how to characterize the law to the client inevitably implicates political judgment.

The client's "interest" is as malleable a concept as the "law"— never infinitely manipulable, of course, but material that can be shaped in a number of ways. The interest—and the "client," the different levels and divisions of the company—does not arrive on the lawyer's desk in a fixed and objective form, but is something that the lawyer molds and influences through advice. Lawyers plainly influence the compliance culture of corporate clients. Attorneys can submit to what seem to be the prevailing company norms. They can side with one department or set of managers against another.... Lawyers who say they just provide technical input and lay out the options while leaving the decisions and methods of implementing them up to their clients are kidding themselves by failing to recognize or admit that clients will process their advice differently depending on the form and manner and setting in which they give it.

Lawyers, then, do influence their clients to some extent, whether they want to or not. Their advice communicates by implication many political judgments about the legitimacy of legal norms and regulations and about the normative value of complying with them, whether they want it to or not. They can't choose not to be influential; they can only decide not to care or think about their influence and whether they should exercise it differently. The ideal of independence reflected in the model of purposive lawyering, however, requires lawyers to reflect and deliberate about the nature and results of their influence, as well as to act prudently, either within or without the context of representation, to change whatever results of that influence they think are bad ones.

II. Conditions of Political Independence

. . .

B. *The Declension Thesis*

. . .

. . . Evidence relating to independent counseling is particularly hard to come by, for such counseling occurs in confidential lawyer-client interactions seldom set down on paper. Even where records are available, independent counseling is most likely to take covert prudential forms. That is, lawyers may inform their clients that "the risks of exposure attendant on following Plan A may be minimized by restructuring the Plan as follows" or ... they may just state that the client's impulse to litigate or to ignore some new regulation, though understandable, probably should be suppressed given the costs and risks involved. There is just no way to tell whether such advice incorporates a calculated judgment about the social consequences of the client's action or the purposes of the law involved. I can therefore only examine the degree to which the social conditions favoring influential counseling have prevailed, and uncover contemporary lawyers' assessments of their professional cultures.

... There are particularly good reasons for skepticism about the ..., the old fellow complaining about how much better it was in the old days. For one thing, the rhetoric of decline is so continuous.... Can things really have been declining for so long? Also, laudators sometimes compare the expressed rhetorical ideals of the earlier age to what they perceive to be the actual practices of their own. (OK, so we all concede that lawyers of an earlier age talked up a public service storm, but how did they really act?) Or they compare the greatest lawyer-statesmen of the earlier age to the average practitioner of today. (OK, so we don't have a bar full of Hamiltons and Brandeises, but neither did they.) Or they compare public service contributions of the bar during great national crises that drove all available talent into public service—the Revolution, the Confederation period, the Great Depression, World War II—with periods of business as usual. Furthermore, it often turns out, upon closer inspection, that the speaker's lofty conception of professional ideals conceals a narrow or unattractive factional interest. When speakers complain that law has turned from a profession to a business, their real complaint is that accountants and title insurance companies are stealing lawyers' work, or (if they represent defendants) that lawyers take cases on contingent fees and are overaggressive in discovery tactics, or that new immigrant ethnic groups are beginning to compete with their own, or just that ungrateful clients are beginning to ask for some cost-accounting instead of unquestioningly paying bills "For Professional Services."

. . .

All of the concerns just raised must be kept in mind ... Nevertheless, I think that the rhetoric of decline has captured something real. Analysis of changes in the social conditions arguably facilitating political independence can lend fairly strong support to the view that, at the level of elite private practice, such conditions have indeed eroded in this century, and perhaps eroded most rapidly during the revolution in the organization of large firm practice that has occurred in the last ten years....

1. Conditions of Independence in the Course of Representation

(a) *Autonomous Authoritative Knowledge and Norms.* If lawyers' advice is to come from a perspective independent of their clientele's, that perspective must be cultivated. Lawyers have to find some community given to theorizing (however loosely and informally) about legal practices, fitting them into some vision of what a better society might look like, reflecting in practical ways on consequences, and imparting rough guidelines and working methods for conduct. The usual candidate for such a community is the law school. But as the case method began to predominate, legal educators gave up trying to teach about law's relation to political, social, economic, and moral life.... In the last fifteen years the situation has actually improved considerably—how nice to be able to note some progress!—as law teachers have revived interest in fitting their technical subjects into general perspectives on law, society, and economy, thereby exposing students to a real diversity of political views.

But school is school, and practice practice; students leaving the academy experience a terrific shock of discontinuity. Nothing has prepared them for the professional culture they now inhabit....

The rise of modern corporate law practice, ... changed the nature of the commercial law. Courtroom practice of any kind became increasingly rare. With the gradual demise of judicial review of economic regulation, constitutional law faded out as a source of norms and interest for corporate lawyers. Above all, the new practice became so technical and specialized that its ethical and political significance was often utterly obscure—not nonexistent, for every social practice implicates a larger set of meanings, but buried under mountains of detail....

. . .

(b) *Knowledge of and Trust Relations With Clients....* [I]t has [also] become much harder for outside counsel to acquire the intimate knowledge of the client's business plans and the trust relations with members of the client's organization that would facilitate both an understanding of how the counselor's advice will be used and the framing of alternatives that would serve the client's long-term interests. House counsel now spreads specialized fragments of the company's legal business around to many different firms. Thus the business that law firms receive from corporations increasingly tends to consist of one-shot transactions—an initial public offering, a big lawsuit, a takeover contest. Clients are highly mobile, no longer loyal to particular firms....

(c) *Comparative Advantage in Special Knowledge and Contacts.* Here the trends are more mixed. Now more than ever, lawyers operate on specialized turf. On the other hand, corporate clients have many more in-house resources for learning about the world than they did in the early twentieth century, when tycoons had to rely on their lawyers to interpret the mysteries of government or to communicate with bankers and financiers. Now political affairs specialists, trade association lobbyists, financial managers—all of whom are frequently far more cosmopolitan than technically specialized lawyers—perform these roles....

(d) *Market Position*. Compare opportunities for independence under two different regimes. In the first, typical of many big firm corporate law markets before the 1970s, a sort of bilateral-monopoly relation developed, in which the corporate client hired one outside firm to handle virtually all its legal work.... The second regime, in which various outside firms compete vigorously for pieces of corporate legal business, is typical of the present day. If clients don't like the advice they get, they feel free to shop around for the most permissive advice, the most favorable opinion letter, or the most hardball attitude toward regulators or adversaries....

(e) *Professional Identity Separate from Clientele's*....

... [T]he American bar began to specialize by clienteles quite early in its history. Moving up the ladder meant representing creditors rather than debtors. Later in the century, lawyers on regular retainers, especially railroad lawyers, came to be completely identified with, and indeed seen as extensions of, their clients....

In this century the client base of elite law firms has become even less diverse. Tort, antitrust, corporate, and securities litigation split into a plaintiffs' and a defendants' bar, labor relations between a labor and a management bar. Social barriers of class background and ethnicity as well as ideology, outlook, and professional styles contributed to this segregation (the plaintiff's bar sees itself as the populist champions of the little person against the corporate system, the defendant's bar as the preservers of corporate stability and prosperity). Heinz and Laumann's exhaustive study of the Chicago bar of the 1970s found that the place of lawyers in professionally established hierarchies of prestige derived mainly from who their clients were. Nothing else, not even how much money they made, and certainly not how many important public questions they argued, was nearly as important. Lawyers representing individuals in trouble had the lowest prestige. Lawyers doing technically complex work (tax, securities) for very large corporations had the highest.

(f) *Desire for Autonomy from Clienteles*....

. . .

It does seem to be true, and is certainly not surprising, that lawyers who begin practice with an anticorporate animus and a feeling that they are betraying their social commitments, tend to soften those feelings over time. Life gradually comes to seem much more morally ambiguous, and one's early reservations appear rather feeble in the face of the surrounding culture's aggressive certainties. The clients seem often to be decent people, not monsters in human shape. . . .

This explanation, however, is incomplete. . . . Lawyers tend to be somewhat more liberal, to be somewhat more favorable to regulation, to identify (sometimes due to early service with an agency) somewhat more with the purposes of regulation, than their clients. Indeed it is not uncommon for lawyers to despise some among their clients as boorish, greedy, amoral social menaces. But such antagonism does not necessarily, or even usually, mean that lawyers who have chosen practices that expose them to such clients will construct an alternative set of objectives, or a counterculture of values, or will translate their criticisms into political action. The much more common response to dissonance is to withdraw into technique, into the professional cult of craftsmanship and competence for its own sake, or just into the cynicism that seems to be our profession's main defense mechanism. . . .

. . .

Whatever the explanation for the relative passivity of corporate lawyers, it has produced a dramatic paradox: we belong to a profession in which higher status correlates with diminished autonomy. Influence varies inversely, subservience directly, with professional standing. Lawyers for tort plaintiffs, small businesses, or divorcing spouses, exert considerable control in their relations with clients. Lawyers for big corporations exert relatively little. Even when top management would prefer that their lawyers serve as the corporate superego, there is a deliberate shrinking from that role.

(g) *Corporate Self–Regulation as an Autonomous Source of Practice Standards*. Toward the end of the nineteenth century, elite lawyers grew alarmed at their increasing public identification with and subservience to big business. In consequence, they formed bar associations with the hope of cartelizing practice standards that would protect them from their own temptations to dependency. This project has notoriously failed, at least in its original ambitious form. Even when still dominated by elites, bar association members could not agree on how to regulate or find the will to discipline lawyers like themselves. Their ethical codes focused on defining as misconduct practices such as ambulance chasing which were not exactly big temptations for the upper bar. As bar associations became more heterogeneous, they could no longer agree on much of anything except the need to control competition for legal services and to resist outside regulation.

Still, this picture is not quite as gloomy as it looks. The failure of self-regulation through bar association ethical codes and disciplinary machinery does not mean all self-regulation will fail. In all professions, informal conventions about what constitutes ethical, fastidious, and conscientious practice develop, thereby setting limits on how far one can go on a client's behalf without feeling one has crossed the frontiers of self-respect, sliding into sleaziness. A good example, once again, is the tax bar's attempts to define boundaries between avoidance and evasion, and to set standards for tax opinions. Sometimes a fastidious faction manages to capture a bar committee or law reform project and to codify its views as rules of practice or procedure, or at least as expressive norms. The issue then becomes how well can such weakly institutionalized norms stand up to increasing competition for clients' business and all the temptations to ignore such norms which that competition entails? An emerging, albeit very tentative and experimental, solution is to shift the main responsibility for declaring and enforcing practice norms from regular bar groups to the judiciary, new regulatory boards partially composed of lawyers, and regulatory agencies.

2. *Conditions of Independence Outside Representation*
    (a) *Time, Working Conditions, and Professional Culture....*

...

  To say that current conditions of large-firm practice are not very conducive to outside commitments would be an understatement. Only firms that have managed to preserve strong collegial cultures supporting engagement in politics and public service have resisted the trend. Elsewhere, the new interfirm mobility of lawyers, the breakdown of ethics of loyalty and collegiality within firms, as well as the increasing competition of firms for clients, of partners for a share of the take, of associates for partnerships, and of firms for new associates, all conspire to discourage the development of any values besides making money for the collective. The pressures to seek and take on new clients and to pile up billable hours wipe out most of the time and energy that lawyers might otherwise have for outside activities. Firms treat the partner engaged in politics and the associates who want to do pro bono work as parasites, free riders on the income-producing efforts of others. The lawyer at any level who risks offending a client is an Enemy of the People.

  The ... inflat[ion] of the salaries of first-year associates ... has been one of the most antisocial acts of the bar in recent history. It further devalues public service by widening the gulf—until recently not very large—between starting salaries in private practice and in government and public interest law. It drives impressionable young associates toward consumption patterns and expectations of opulence that will be hard to shake off if they want to change careers. It forces every lawyer in the firm, especially the associates who are its supposed beneficiaries, to pay heavily for it in extra billable hours and, insofar as high incomes for the partners depend upon low partner-associate ratios, in reduced prospects of reaching partnership.

  ... Other than greater job security (another vanishing feature of ... [law] practice), the comparative advantages that law used to offer folks with professional aspirations who had chosen law over business school—such as concern for collegiality in the organization of work, intellectual stimulation, opportunities for public service, association with older people who had seen such service themselves, and values besides profitability—are getting harder to find all the time.

Law firms commonly restrict the independence of their members in ways more direct than the creation of a set of working conditions and incentives that effectively preclude other involvements. Sometimes they explicitly prohibit other activities, such as pro bono activities or political causes or even just publishing law review articles, that might create a potential "business" conflict—that is, not a properly disqualifying conflict of interest, but merely the risk of loss of business from having a firm member be perceived to adopt a policy position that one of the firm's clients might not like. What is especially interesting about such prohibitions is not so much that partners impose them, but that the partners are so unembarrassed about doing so, even though the practice violates—in addition to the formal provisions of some codes of ethics— every conceivable traditional ideal of independence their profession has ever entertained....

   ... Why don't firms offer partners and associates a different mix of goods, such as lower profits and salaries in exchange for lower billable time quotas, flexible work, the privilege of exercising a fastidious preference for socially responsible clients, firm-sponsored public interest projects, a firm culture encouraging public interest, pro bono and political involvements in practice, as well as sabbaticals to pursue such projects? There are some such firms, why aren't there more? I ask this question of lawyers in big firm practice all the time.... The[] responses typically take the following forms: (a) We'd love that, but the partners who pull in most of the business for the firm would leave, and we can't afford that. (b) Big clients are attracted to firms with a reputation for giving 100 percent to their clients. They hate it if the lawyers assigned to their transactions are not constantly on call. (c) It's the partners who want 100 percent control over associates' time. They can't bear the idea of somebody not being instantly available when wanted. (d) Too many of the most talented associates we would like to attract to the firm only pay attention to the bottom line, so we have to match what other firms are paying. (e) Even in firms with a strong commitment to public interest work and political involvement, the associates can never be sure how their work for any but paying clients will affect their chances to become partners, and their unwillingness to take risks drives them out of the public interest and political arenas. (f) The lawyers committed to other values besides money-making, even if there are in fact a lot of them, tend to believe that they are unusual and that almost everyone else cares only about money. Thus firms end up being single-mindedly driven by values which many of their members would prefer not to adopt as exclusive ends.

... [O]ther explanations for the homogeneity and profit orientation of large law firms sound both less rationalistic and closer to the heart of the matter, explanations like: "... There's a hysteria out there. Some lawyers are making fortunes, while other firms are going under. People feel they have to grab everything they can.... *It's out of control.*"

(b) *Autonomous Norms....* "Rights" can be interpreted broadly or narrowly; they can stress vested property, sexual preferences, "social" goods like employment and housing and education, or welfare entitlements.... The notion that there might be some normative objectivity at the end of the rainbow, some apolitical way to choose sides in these battles, seems like a premodern fairy tale to many (though by no means all) of us.

... [Another] problem [interfering] with the maintenance of autonomous norms, which are conducive to maintaining independence from clients] ... is that one of the current heavyweight contenders among ideologies ... holds that lawyers perform their most socially desirable functions by aggressively promoting the interests and values of their business clienteles....

. . .

3. An Alternative Interpretation: No Decline, Just Relocation

Perhaps the Political Ideal has not eroded, but only shifted location into other more specialized segments of practice.... In America the private bar took on work for which bureaucracies were responsible in Europe—helping judges to articulate the basic frameworks of constitutional and common law, drafting legislation, staffing (often as unpaid volunteers) some of the first regulatory commissions. But America now has large public bureaucracies and public legal staffs to do these jobs....

... [Also,] new entities have emerged to represent points of view other than those of business constituencies. The legal world now includes a full-time labor bar, civil rights and civil liberties organizations such as the ACLU and NAACP Legal Defense Fund, the National Lawyers Guild, and the public interest organizations of the 1970s and 80s—the Legal Services Corporation, Nader's groups, environmental groups, and small firms that take employment discrimination and civil rights claims.

Proponents of the "relocation" thesis could also argue that the potential for an "independent counseling" role is still very much alive [within corporations, if not in outside law firms.] ... Some legal departments have ... organized themselves to mimic the forms of independent "firms" within the corporation. A house counsel's office with good connections to the CEO and Board of Directors can carry a lot of weight, at least against middle management ... [And because in-house counsel hire and direct outside law firms,] house counsel [may] only speak with an independent voice inside the organization, but can also order up as much outside independence as they need. . . .

Despite the increased independence of in-house counsel, the outside firms themselves have not lost all opportunities for influential counseling. They are still retained to extricate companies from major crises in their corporate existences—attempted takeovers, strikes, antitrust suits, massive citations for occupational health or environmental violations, class action suits for employment discrimination, mass tort litigation—and in those capacities have great potential influence to shape litigation and settlement strategies as well as the structures to prevent recurrences. Outside lawyers are already used, and could be used a lot more, to audit companies that have been caught committing major illegalities . . . to find out what went wrong and how to avoid it in the future.

Furthermore, as big law firms have lost more of their old Fortune 500 company business to inside counsel, they have picked up a lot of new legal business representing much smaller companies—high-technology start-up companies, for instance, or Health Maintenance Organizations. Such clients rarely have the experience and inside resources of huge corporations. For them, their lawyers are still sources of general business advice, contacts with financial institutions, and interpreters of the mysterious ways of government. It was in representing such businesses that Louis Brandeis was able to give content to his vision of socially responsible counsel "for the situation."

This alternative interpretation is encouraging but hardly justifies a Panglossian euphoric confidence . . . We have developed bureaucracies, but they are nothing like the prestigious and powerful civil services of Europe or Japan. Even the best government legal jobs are absurdly underpaid compared to private ones at the entry level. And most—though happily by no means all—of the ambitious and well-qualified lawyers who enter public service do so only as a stepping-stone to private practice. The legal resources of public agencies remain pitiful compared to those of their corporate adversaries, and are kept that way in part through the political activity of the lawyers for those adversaries. . . .

. . .

III.   Conclusion: Critiques and Defenses of Lawyers' Independence

. . .

A.   *The Quality-of-Services Critique*

Quality-of-services critics point out that lawyers' autonomy has a dark side: independence is not an unambiguous good. The dark side is revealed most clearly in the practices of lawyers who deal with clients less informed or of lower status than themselves—lawyers who preempt virtually all of the decision-making authority, keep information to themselves, don't spread a full range of choices before their clients or heavily bias the choices they do present, don't tell clients what is happening in their cases, patronize their clients and view them as overemotional and dumb laypeople who can't possibly know what legal options will serve them best, or presume that they know what's in their clients' best interests (criminals must want to get off as lightly as possible, rather than relieve their minds through confession or atone for their crimes; divorcing spouses must want to take their ex-partners for everything they can get) without even trying to explore the complexities of the clients' intentions and desires.

According to this critique, the lawyer who forsakes the unalloyed ideal of client loyalty to counsel "for the situation" may be particularly prone to confuse independence with self-interest. . . .

. . .

. . . These critics allege that taking an "independent" view of craft excellence could rationalize all sorts of undesirable practices: overlawyering every transaction, redrafting every document seventeen times with five layers of review, billing thousands of dollars for time spent drafting clauses concerning risks of remote or insignificant contingencies, pulling out all stops to litigate every case to the hilt, even though early settlement would result in greater net saving or gain after taking attorneys' fees into account, raising unhelpful conservative objections to clients' legitimate goals without suggesting any alternatives. . . .

. . .

These critiques, though valid as far as they go, are not entirely logical. "Independence" isn't like pureed baby food—you don't have to swallow all the ingredients if you only like some of them. Of course independent lawyers may abuse their discretion to serve their self-interest . . . but that's not an argument against autonomy, only against bad exercises of it. Besides, intense competition for and subservience to the wishes of clients foster pathologies of their own. When firm lawyers tell me that their litigation machine, now . . . retooled to run on the thin fuel of budget constraints imposed by corporate counsel, is more powerful and effective than . . . [before], I see no reason to disbelieve them. When the same lawyers . . ., tell me that they are now issuing tax opinions that ten years ago they would have classified as schlock-firm products bordering on the unethical, I believe them too. . . .

. . . Granted, the service ethic originated in the ideology of a privileged class, the Federalist gentry. It is also true that the public service ethic continued to justify the privileges of that class even when most of its members did little to live up to it. But public service is hardly the credo or aspiration of a particular class. . . .

. . . [Now] the lawyers who seek fulfillment in public service are the children of patricians, . . . union members, . . . members of victimized minority groups, graduates of elite and non-elite schools alike. The great political movements in which lawyers have played a big part in this century, from the New Deal to Civil Rights and Women's movements and beyond, have in fact drawn disproportionately from groups marginal to the dominant culture: Jews, blacks, women.

B.   *The Illegitimacy Critique*

Probably the most common critique of the independence ideal is that it either conflicts with the ideal of client loyalty or arrogates to lawyers an improper role in political decisionmaking, or both....

Underlying the illegitimacy critique is the central belief that lawyers' roles begin and end with vigorously pursuing their clients' interests within the limits of the law....

... Take any simple case of compliance counseling: suppose the legal rule is clear, yet the chance of detecting violations low, the penalties small in relation to the gains from noncompliance, or the terrorizing of regulators into settlement by a deluge of paper predictably easy. The mass of lawyers who advise and then assist with noncompliance in such a situation could, in the vigorous pursuit of their clients' interests, effectively nullify the laws.... Yes, lawyers must pursue clients' interests within the framework of the rules of the game. But the issue of lawyers' public responsibility is precisely that of what their position should be vis-a-vis those rules.

The principal fallacy implicit in the view of lawyering underlying the illegitimacy critique, is that lawyers must reconcile two sets of social purposes—clients' interests and the law's plain meaning—that arrive at their offices already fully formed and filled in with some definite determinate content. But in fact part of the lawyer's job is to interpret both sets of purposes....

But the critic then says: ... But in this capacity lawyers have no right to intrude their opinions, their influence, their political values. They are neither elected officials nor their agents; lawyers have no special authority to go around telling people how they should behave.

The traditional response to this is simple: lawyers do indeed have an official status as licensed fiduciaries for the public interest, charged with encouraging compliance with legal norms. In contexts like counseling, where there is no official third party like a judge to oversee the interaction between the client and the state, the lawyer is not only supposed to predict the empirical consequences of certain behavior, but also to represent the viewpoint of the legal system to the client.... The other and even better response to the critic is that even conceding that lawyers have no special authority to guide their clients, neither do they have any special immunity from responsibility for the things they help their clients do.

Critics may still want to defend their conception of the lawyer's role by arguing that the legitimacy of lawyers exercising independent judgment has been undermined by the vanishing of a broad consensus on the goals of law....

. . .

... [But i]t seems rather extreme to refrain from trying to develop and act on a commitment to a particular view of legal purposes simply because others may arrive at a different view. That may be a reason for caution, for avoiding dogmatism, for empathizing with and taking account of the views of opponents, but not for paralysis....

C. The Competence Critique

The position that lawyers have no special competence to bring to counseling, nor any special contribution to make to political life, makes sense as a critique of the most pompously inflated view of political independence....

Most of the arguments in favor of lawyers playing an independent role in counseling and politics, however, are much more modest.... Legal education is to some extent an education in applied political theory. Lawyers are articulate in one of the major media of public discourse, legal language. They often have diverse experience—government work, different kinds of clients, different kinds of corruption and evil, all the myriad ways in which plans can misfire and go askew. They are professionally capable of detachment, able to see different sides of a problem and analyze motivations. They know powerful people and something about what makes them tick and what will move them....

... Why should everybody else around the corporation—the engineers, the financial people, the safety and health division—be permitted to deliberate upon and engage in the internal politics of the corporation to promote their views of its best interests, but not the lawyers?

D. The Critiques of Consequences

. . .

1. The Critique from the Right

According to the critique from the Right ... much of the regulation the Progressive and New Deal lawyers favored (including all the licensing conditions they imposed on entry to the legal profession) was really just "rent-seeking" by regulated industries trying to set up government-coordinated cartels to protect them from competition. The critics from the Right also insist that a large part of the Progressive–New Deal–Great Society regulatory agenda was based on deficient economic analysis and irrational "populist" hostility to large corporations, a naive overconfidence in administrative command-and-control regulation, and a failure to appreciate that in this second-best world the attempt to correct even genuine market failure through regulation often imposes enforcement and compliance costs exceeding their benefits. If regulation is inefficient, the last thing society needs is lawyers using their strategic positions in society to get more of it, and more compliance with it.

. . .

. . . To the extent that regulation results from antisocial rent-seeking by corporations, lawyers do not promote the public interest by assisting their clients to get more of it. It would be better if, as politically independent citizens, they supported economic deregulation initiatives against their clients' immediate interests. To the extent that regulation addresses "real" market failures and produces "real" public goods, but is inefficient, lawyers should help to lower its costs by encouraging clients to voluntarily comply with its purposes instead of undertaking expensive adversary resistance, and should help design creative alternatives to ponderous, unwieldly regimes of command-and-control rulemaking. I cannot imagine any reasons at all why the intensity with which a corporation wanted to resist regulation would ever bear any but an arbitrary relation to the worth of the regulation, however defined. In fact, the relation may well be positive. The worst violators, the corporations producing far more than their "optimal" fair share of pollution and sick workers, are also likely to be the hardball adversaries. They have the most to lose from detection and enforcement, and the most to gain from barricading themselves behind lawyers to nullify the laws. It is even harder to understand why having lawyers simply pursue these worst violators' self-interest in a competitive market will produce advice that is optimal for either the client or the society. . . .

Ultimately, if you accept the premises of the rightwing critique, I think you end up having to argue for more rather than less independent political activity and political judgment in counseling. I cannot honestly argue, however, that the advice likely to be rendered by a more independent corporate bar would much please those conservatives who think lawyers should uncritically assist businesses do whatever they believe to be in their immediate interest. On the contrary, insofar as many laws express collective social purposes that conflict with or qualify those of short-term corporate profit-seeking, the right wing will disapprove of advice that seeks to promote conformity to such purposes.

2.   *The Critique from the Left*

Critics from the Left also rely on history when they contend that the policies recommended by elite lawyers in the name of independence have often been dubious or pernicious—not anything worth emulating. . . . On the whole, the left critics say, we might have been better off if elite lawyers had been completely demobilized politically, had thought of themselves as nothing more than functionaries of client interests.

... My own quick response is that, ... in at least some of these instances the intervention of conservative but public-minded legal elites probably produced results rather better from a leftist standpoint—relief for the most miserable casualties of market dislocations, moderation of the cruelest excesses of corporate power in labor relations, cautious support for expansion of Black civil rights, and due process protections for radicals—than unmediated pursuit of client interests would have done....

3. The Liberal Critique

Left-liberals sometimes offer an interesting variant of the critique of consequences which goes something like this ...: it might well have been true that socially concerned lawyering in the Progressive and New Deal and Civil Rights generations was more liberal than the conventional legal consensus, represented by the Supreme Court and the American Bar Association. But by now ... [whilte o]rdinary elite practitioners have no interest in dismantling Social Security, Medicare and Medicaid, affirmative action, environmental regulation, or government-funded legal services ..., the present day activist lawyer in corporate practice ... is likely to be a right wing radical. Check out the "public interest" law firms of the present day: they are overwhelmingly fronts for antiregulatory business groups.

I'm not sure the critique is empirically well-founded.... Moreover, it is hard to see how conservative corporate lawyers could do much more to further the political values and goals of business than they do already....

4. The Critique of Legalism

From many different points on the political spectrum comes the critique that lawyers' public projects, whatever their political thrust, have the vice of favoring the legalistic solutions familiar to lawyers and congenial to creating legal business: legislation, administrative rule making, cumbersome and expensive lawyer-driven due process machinery, and arcane and involuted legalistic reasoning. There is a general disenchantment with the legalism of the Progressive period. Conservatives hate the way due process rights undermine traditional authority in schools, hospitals, welfare administration, and prisons. Radicals hate the illusion of legitimacy that enshrines such rights even when they cost too much to vindicate. Almost everyone except the plaintiffs' bar is unhappy with current litigation practice as a mode of dispute settlement.

It's true that lawyers have a bias toward legalism. But they also know the pathologies of legalism better than most people, and in fact have taken the lead in many of the antilegalist reform movements of the present: deregulation, regulatory negotiations, alternative mechanisms of dispute resolution, reform of the tort system, and so forth....

5. *Refuting the Critiques of Consequences*

In the end, refuting the critiques of consequences requires only that we recognize that it is never a sufficient argument against committed and deliberate political action that such action has had, and may have, bad consequences. This is just as true of thoughtless and unreflective action, and for that matter of inaction. The viewpoint that everyone is best off if nobody thinks of anything but making money is indefensible. Moreover, it is incoherent even on its own terms, for the invisible hand only works to maximize welfare within a hypothesized framework of laws, institutions, and morals, which some people must be committed to defending against opportunists and rent-seekers.

E. *The Critique from Futility*

The last attitude toward lawyer's independence may be the most widely shared of all: What's the point? Corporate practice is the way it is, and not the place to be if you have any commitments to social change. There's nothing that can be done, nothing important anyway.

The best response to this lies in Galileo's reply to the Cardinal's contention that the world stands still: "And yet it moves!" Historically, lawyers have found legal practice not an obstacle to but a congenial platform for pursuing independent politics. Even the recent revolution in big firm practice, as we have seen, has created new opportunities for influence while removing others.... [L]awyers can be committed to changing that culture, and some of them are.

... [T]here are no privileged locations or levers for social change, and also no positions from which pressure for change, involving whatever tiny, modest risks the participants are willing to take, is not possible.... What is needed to produce the "independent life of society" is the will, reflection on how best to use it, collaboration with others, and action.

Notes

1. Think of the lawyers you have encountered. In describing them would "independent" be a word you would use? If so, in what sense do you see them as "independent?" In what sense do you see them as dependent? What other words would you use to describe the lawyers you have encountered? The lawyers you admire? Is "admire" a word you would use?

2. Consider the factors that Gordon says contribute to the lawyer's ability to be independent. Does he miss any? Cf. Dana, p. 128. What about alternative employment available to individual lawyers who face tough choices? What about the importance of individual matters to clients (i.e., clients may care relatively less about certain matters than others?) Complexity of law may allow lawyers to exert independence but may also allow lawyers, as Gordon notes, to bury themselves in detail.

3. In discussing the role of law schools in creating "professional culture," Gordon focuses on clinical courses. Do other courses or other aspects of law school affect the professional culture and the role of independence? Gordon also refers to the influence of "successful lawyers," who promote independence as an ideal. But isn't there a problem here? How do we know that the "successful" lawyers have really lived out this ideal in their practice? Part of the problem is confidentiality: it's a lot harder to find out about examples of heroic lawyers who stopped bad things from happening than it is to learn about lawyers who did bad things, although that too is not terribly easy. Cf. Gilson & Mnookin, p. 417, on the potential power of the lawyer-reputation market.

4. Consider Gordon's arguments that political judgments are unavoidable because the law and corporate client interests are always uncertain and to some extent malleable. If that's true, then how important are the structural "conditions" of independence he discusses in section II? Shouldn't the focus rather be on the type of law and type of client?

5. What does Luban's article, printed next, say about the bar's willingness to fight for the ideal of independence from the state that Gordon suggests is the form of independence that matters to lawyers? Cf. Blumberg's description of the representation of indigent defendants, p. 276.

Taking Out the Adversary: The Assault on Progressive Public–interest Lawyers*

DAVID LUBAN

Introduction

This Essay concerns laws and doctrines, some very recent, that undermine the capacity of progressive public-interest lawyers to bring cases. It asks a simple-sounding question: how just is the adversary system if one side is not adequately represented in it? And it defends a simple-sounding answer: It is not just at all. As we shall see, however, neither the question nor the answer is quite as simple as it sounds.

Like most issues implicating distributive justice, the question of who has access to lawyers and who does not has become a political football. Political partisans do not care about impartial justice. They care about rewarding their friends and defeating their enemies, and that means ensuring that their enemies receive as little money as possible, including money to pay for legal advocacy. Advocacy, after all, might be used to turn the tables. In the last few years, a disturbing pattern of legal attacks on public-interest lawyers has emerged, targeting every one of the principal sources of support for progressive public-interest law: the Legal Services Corporation ("LSC"), state Interest on Lawyers Trust Account ("IOLTA") programs, law school clinics, and civil rights attorney's fees. The attacks seek to win political disputes not by offering better arguments, but by defunding or otherwise hobbling the advocates who make the arguments for the other side. Suitable analogies might be found in a story about Lyndon Johnson defeating insurgents in the Texas Democratic Party by arranging to have the microphone unplugged when they got up to speak at the party convention, or Republican consultant Ed Rollins's boast (which he later recanted) that he had paid Black ministers to sit on their hands rather than telling their flocks to vote in the 1992 New Jersey gubernatorial race. Just as tactics like these are dirty politics, this Essay argues that taking out your adversary's lawyers is dirty law.

Law is a $100 billion per year industry. Of that $100 billion, however, less than $1 billion is dedicated to delivering legal services to low-income Americans. Put in terms of people rather than dollars, there is about one lawyer for every 240 nonpoor Americans, but only one lawyer for every 9,000 Americans whose low income would qualify them for legal aid. Forty-five million Americans qualify for civil legal aid, and they are served by a mere 4,000 legal-aid lawyers plus an estimated 1,000 to 2,000 additional poor people's lawyers. Although the myth persists that the very rich and the very poor have no trouble getting

* © 2003 by the California Law Review. Reprinted by permission of the University of California, Berkeley, from 91 Calif. L. Rev. 209 (2003).

lawyers (because the rich have money and the poor qualify for legal aid), and that only the middle class is squeezed, these numbers reveal the true scarcity of lawyers and services available to low-income people. In very real effect, low-income Americans are denied access to justice. The reason is simple: one lawyer per 9,000 clients. To put in perspective what those numbers mean, the American Bar Association's Comprehensive Legal Needs Study found that every year about half of low-income people face legal needs—that is, "situations, events, or difficulties any member of the household faced ... that raised legal issues." That amounts to 4,500 cases a year for each lawyer—90 a week, 18 a day. . . .

I. *Audi Alteram Partem* and the Adversary System

In his recent book Justice Is Conflict, the distinguished philosopher Stuart Hampshire sets out an argument that conflict is a component of justice, not an obstacle to achieving it. . . . According to Hampshire, human values arise not from the intellect (in which case everyone's values might converge) but from memory and imagination. These are primordial forces, and they are idiosyncratic to the core.

As a result, conceptions of the good are irreducibly diverse, and ideals are "polymorphous." Conflict flows from human plurality, and ultimately from human imagination. We might say that conflict is imagination's trace in the world. Human plurality implies the hopelessness of the philosophical quest to deduce some master principle of substantive justice. All such deductions are circular, because people will never agree on starting points. In place of substantive justice, Hampshire therefore offers a principle of bare-minimum procedural justice, "the single prescription *audi alteram partem* ('hear the other side')." Hampshire titles this maxim the "principle of adversary argument," and the label is an apt one. The common-law maxim audi alteram partem has long been recognized as a fundamental principle of adversary adjudication, reflecting the common lawyer's deep suspicion of ex parte decision making. . . .

Properly understood, ... *audi alteram partem* requires actually listening to the other side in good faith, even when the chance of changing the decision maker's mind is virtually nil. Hearing the other side in good faith requires setting one's prejudices aside, and that makes it a powerful, hard-to-live-up-to moral requirement, even though it is "merely" procedural.

. . .

... [P]hilosophers such as Hampshire and Lon Fuller, who view the adversary system only as a tool for the benign purpose of maximizing input and voice, are being naive about the operation of our adversary system. The closest approximation of their ideal is appellate argument. . . . The adversary system of evidence-taking is a far more mixed bag, in which efforts to inject input into the system mingle promiscuously with strategic manipulations to keep information out. In this system, even the selection of voices that gain a hearing is hostage to adversarial manipulation. But the point of this Essay is not to propose replacing our adversary system. My point is that an adversary system with only one adversary is an adversary system in name alone, and in that case, all justifications are simply beside the point. When judges and legislatures create doctrines that enable well-funded parties to take out the other side's lawyer, they undermine basic fairness and turn the adversary system into a system of procedural injustice.

II.   Silencing Doctrines

My specific topic, then, is the deliberate attempt to keep progressive voices out of the legal system by taking away their lawyers.... [The] legal weapons [used to achieve this] ... I call "silencing doctrines." ...

In recent years, a pattern of silencing doctrines has begun to emerge challenging—to greater or lesser extent—virtually every principal source of support for low-income public-interest lawyering: the LSC, state IOLTA programs, law school clinics, and fee awards in civil rights cases. Most of these doctrines are the handiwork of judicial and congressional conservatives, and one originates in lawsuits from a probusiness public-interest law firm that has made its mission defunding public-interest lawyers it dislikes. Of course it would be just as wrong if the doctrines came from the Left to silence the Right. Someday they may, and then the same criticisms would apply. For the criticism concerns procedural injustice, regardless of its political orientation.

A.   *The 1996 Legal Services Corporation Restrictions*

The single biggest source of funding for poor people's lawyers is the Legal Services Corporation, with a fiscal year 2001 budget of $330 million ($310 million for client representation). In 1998, this budget funded 3,590 attorneys at an average salary of just under $40,000, along with 4,637 paralegals. The pathetic numbers—one underpaid legal-services lawyer per 10,000 poor people—have not prevented decades of political assaults on the program, including the outright lie that poor people have no trouble finding a free lawyer.

Restrictions on the use of LSC funding have always existed. From the beginning of the program, Congress prohibited LSC recipients from using their federal funds on volatile political issues like abortion, school desegregation, and the military draft. Although this often frustrated progressives, it made a certain amount of sense to keep a controversial program such as LSC out of the most hot-button political issues of the day. Moreover, LSC lawyers could still advocate on these issues provided they did not use federal funds to do so. These restrictions could be weakly justified on grounds of liberal neutrality, inasmuch as they kept federal funds out of advocacy over divisive issues. So long as there were other funds and other advocates available, the restrictions were tolerable, and only minimally offended the principle audi alteram partem.

In 1996, however, Congress enacted restrictions on legal-services lawyers that went much further. Not only do they prohibit LSC recipients from taking on certain issues, but they also forbid them from representing entire classes of clients. These include whole classes of aliens, many of whom are legal. The new regulations likewise prohibit the representation of all incarcerated people, including those not convicted of a crime, and those whose cases have nothing to do with why they are in jail, as, for example, in parental-rights lawsuits. The restrictions also prevent LSC attorneys from using specific procedural devices or arguments. They cannot attempt to influence rulemaking or lawmaking, participate in class actions, request attorney's fees under applicable statutes, challenge any welfare reform, or defend anyone charged with a drug offense in a public-housing eviction proceeding. Furthermore, LSC grant recipients must file statements revealing the identity of their clients and stating the facts of the case, and these statements must be made available "to any Federal department or agency that is auditing or monitoring the activities of the Corporation or of the recipient."

Perhaps the most devastating regulation, however, is Congress's prohibition on LSC recipients using their nonfederal funds for these prohibited activities. This requirement had a drastic effect. A legal-aid office could no longer accept an LSC grant if it did any prohibited legal work. This provision forced legal-services providers to split into separate organizations with separate offices, one receiving federal funds and abiding by the restrictions, the other maintaining its freedom of action at the cost of its LSC grant. LSC enacted "program integrity" regulations to implement this restriction by ensuring that the two offspring organizations maintained physical and financial separation. The result was bifurcated organizations substantially weaker than the initial organization. Some organizations had to purchase duplicate computer systems and hire duplicate staff. Some locales could afford only a restricted office, so that clients with the "wrong" cases were forced to travel hundreds of miles to find counsel or, more realistically, do without. In hundreds of ongoing cases, restricted LSC lawyers had to withdraw.

The congressional restrictions are silencing doctrines, preventing attorneys from advocating for people who have no recourse to non-LSC advocates. . . .

Do these restrictions compel legal-services lawyers to practice law unethically? The American Bar Association ("ABA") Model Rules of Professional Conduct ("Model Rules") forbid lawyers from letting a nonclient who pays them interfere with their professional judgment on the client's behalf. Suppose a legal-aid lawyer wants to go after a revolving-credit scam that has bilked 1,000 poor people out of $20 each. She cannot very well litigate 1,000 individual cases, and her best professional judgment screams "class action!" But the restrictions forbid class actions. To take another example, the restrictions require legal-services lawyers to forego whatever negotiating leverage the possibility of statutory attorney's fees provides in settlement talks. That may hurt the lawyer's effectiveness as well as her office finances. Are such lawyers then violating the Model Rules by abiding by the regulations? The answer is no, because attorneys have an obvious recourse: they can simply decline to accept cases that are best pursued through forbidden means. Nothing prevents the legal-services lawyer from turning down the revolving-credit case that needs a class action, and to comply with both the congressional restrictions and the Model Rules, she may well turn down the case. The perverse result: the more poor people a legal problem affects, the less likely they are to find a lawyer to represent them. If the client is an inmate in a mental institution complaining of abusive treatment, then the legal-services lawyer has to warn the client that he may be in danger of having his identity revealed. If having such a frightening conversation with an emotionally fragile client poisons the client-lawyer relationship, then the lawyer cannot take the case. The ABA went so far as to say that legal-services lawyers must warn all their clients at the first interview that if they get jailed, the lawyers will have to drop them. . . .

While permitting legal-services lawyers to avoid violating the Model Rules of Professional Conduct, these results are deeply problematic from an ethical standpoint. Viewed in the most favorable light, the 1996 restrictions represent Congress's legitimate attempt to ensure that legal-services lawyers accept only cases that carry no tincture of political advocacy or social engineering: If class actions are proscribed, it is because class actions are a favorite device of structural reformers; if attorney's-fees cases are proscribed, it is because these tend to be awarded in environmental or civil rights cases; if aliens or prison inmates cannot be represented, it is because these are politically controversial groups. However, those poor enough to meet legal-aid eligibility criteria are extremely unlikely to have the money to hire a lawyer, and non-LSC-funded public-interest lawyers are rare. Thus, the overwhelming presumption must be that the vast majority of cases that legal-services lawyers turn down will never be brought by anyone. It follows, then, that the restrictions ensure that entire subgroups of low-income people will never be heard in the legal system, including many aliens, all prisoners (including those in jail for only a brief time and those whose incarceration has nothing to do with their legal-services case), public-housing residents accused (perhaps falsely) of drug offenses and facing eviction, and clients for whom a class action is the most effective means of representation.

. . .

Disappointingly, neither the Bar nor the legal-services establishment offered any organized protest when the 1996 restrictions were enacted—

unlike a similar assault in 1981, when law school deans and the organized bar united in protest against efforts to abolish the LSC. The reason was pure fear that Congress, in the heady days of Newt Gingrich's revolution and the Contract With America, would simply abolish the LSC. Even attempts to challenge the restrictions in court were discouraged by many people in the legal-services community. The ABA Ethics Committee's response was entirely typical: instead of writing a formal opinion insisting that the restrictions violate the ideals of the legal profession, it chose instead to write an opinion insisting that a legal-services grant recipient could practice law ethically by abandoning clients to keep its funding intact. The advice is undoubtedly accurate: declining cases is a sure-fire way to stay out of trouble. Nevertheless, ... [t]he ideals this violates are set out in the ABA's Model Code of Professional Responsibility ("Model Code"), the predecessor to the Model Rules of Professional Conduct. The Model Code states that "the objective of the bar [is] to make legal services fully available." ... A forthright statement by the ethics committee of the nation's largest organization of lawyers that the restrictions are inconsistent with professional ideals might have provided ammunition for legal challenges to the restrictions. One can only conclude that the ABA committee decided that, for the good of the legal-services lawyers, capitulation was the better part of valor.

Lawsuits eventually were brought challenging the LSC restrictions, although the results to date have been discouraging. An unconstitutional-conditions challenge to the restrictions failed in the Ninth Circuit, as did an equal-protection challenge.[59] A due process and First Amendment challenge in the Second Circuit also failed, except for one portion of it, directed against the ban on legal arguments against the validity of welfare laws.[60] The 1996 restrictions prohibited LSC lawyers from arguing that welfare laws are invalid but not from arguing that they are valid. The Second Circuit held—and the U.S. Supreme Court agreed— that this remarkable restriction on what legal-services lawyers may say in court was not viewpoint-neutral, and thus it violated the First Amendment.[61] Although the objection seems decisive, the victory affects only a small part of the regulation. The statute remains intact to silence legal-services lawyers in the other ways we have examined. Hear the other side—except when the other side is an indigent who is also a prisoner or alien, a member of a class, someone who objects to a rulemaking process, or someone who would be adversely affected by a lawyer who abides by the restrictions. In that case, defund his lawyer.

B. The Challenges to IOLTA Programs

IOLTA [Interest on Lawyers' Trust Accounts] programs provide the second biggest source of funds for legal-aid lawyers, after the LSC.

---

59. See Legal Aid Soc. of Haw. v. Legal Servs. Corp., 145 F.3d 1017 (9th Cir.1998).

60. Velazquez v. Legal Servs. Corp., 164 F.3d 757, 764–73 (2d Cir.1999).

61. See Legal Services Corp. v. Velazquez, 531 U.S. 533 (2001).

Lawyers are required to maintain trust accounts for client money that they hold. When the amount is large, or held for a significant time period, attorneys open an interest-bearing savings account in the client's behalf, but when the amount of money the lawyer holds for clients is small, or the money is held for a short period of time only, the administrative cost of getting the interest to clients would devour the interest and might actually cost the client money. In such cases, the attorney deposits client funds in a demand account, that is, an account from which funds may be obtained on demand. Until 1980, banking law prohibited interest payments on demand accounts. In 1980, Congress amended the law to permit interest-bearing demand accounts, but only for "funds in which the entire beneficial interest is held by one or more individuals or by an organization which is operated primarily for religious, philanthropic, charitable, educational, political, or other similar purposes and which is not operated for profit." States responded to the new law by creating IOLTA programs: nonprofit foundations to fund low-income legal services, financed by the interest on lawyer's demand trust accounts. Lawyers participating in IOLTA programs pool client funds that are too small or held for too short a time to generate collectible interest for the client in an IOLTA account, where the interest goes to the nonprofit foundation funding low-income legal services. Client funds that are capable of generating collectible interest for the client—that is, interest that would not be devoured by the transaction costs of getting it to the client—must still be deposited into a separate savings account for the client, not into the IOLTA account.

The idea was ingenious. The clients could not get the interest on small or short-term lawyer-held funds because transaction costs would gobble it up. Because no one else could get the interest either, it all went to the banks by default. As one Texas judge quipped, IOLTA takes from the banks and gives to the poor. IOLTA programs generated more than $125 million a year for indigent legal services in 2001. Almost all were enacted by the states' highest courts under their rulemaking authority. All fifty states and the District of Columbia have IOLTA plans, and half of them are mandatory.

Almost from the beginning, IOLTA faced constitutional challenges from disgruntled lawyers, clients, and activists who objected to the idea of helping legal-services lawyers. Generally based on the Takings Clause, the early challenges failed because IOLTA programs keep only interest that would not exist if the clients could get it back. However, the judicial and political climates have changed, and the U.S. Supreme Court is currently reconsidering whether IOLTA statutes violate the Takings Clause of the federal Constitution.

1. *IOLTA and the Takings Clause*

The Washington Legal Foundation ("WLF"), a conservative public-interest law foundation and ... a stalwart champion of silencing doctrines, challenged IOLTA statutes in Massachusetts, Texas, and Washington. The WLF lost in Massachusetts,[72] but soon won a major victory in its Texas litigation when the United States Supreme Court held in a five-to-four decision in Phillips v. Washington Legal Foundation that unrecoverable interest on client funds remains the property of the client.[73] The Court remanded the case to determine whether IOLTA amounts to an unconstitutional taking of that property without just compensation. On remand, the Texas district court found no taking, relying on the U.S. Supreme Court's observation that "the Fifth Amendment does not proscribe the taking of property; it proscribes taking without just compensation."[75] The court found no taking without just compensation because a client with money in an IOLTA account is "in as good a position as he would have enjoyed without the alleged taking." However, the Fifth Circuit Court of Appeals reversed this decision and held that the Texas Supreme Court's justices could be enjoined from disciplining attorneys who refuse to deposit client funds in IOLTA accounts.[77] . . .

Meanwhile, the WLF prevailed before a Ninth Circuit panel, which found an unconstitutional taking and remanded the case to determine just compensation.[81] However, the Ninth Circuit sitting en banc reversed the panel decision, holding that IOLTA plans do not constitute a taking, and that in any event, the just compensation would be zero.[82] The Ninth Circuit en banc opinion also remanded the case to the District Court to decide a First Amendment claim by the IOLTA protestors that their mandatory contributions to pooled accounts are unconstitutional compelled speech and association. The WLF appealed to the U.S. Supreme Court. [The Supreme Court held in a 5–4 opinion, that IOLTA plans could be a taking requiring just compensation but that no compensation was necessary here because only client funds that would have generated no net interest were to be deposited in IOLTA accounts under California law.]*

. . . The Ninth Circuit panel [had] recognized the dynamics of spite in Washington Legal Foundation v. Legal Foundation of Washington, its IOLTA decision. The court paraphrases the mentality of IOLTA chal-

72. See Washington Legal Foundation v. Massachusetts Bar Foundation, 993 F.2d 962 (1st Cir.1993).

73. 524 U.S. 156 (1998).

75. Washington Legal Found. v. Texas Equal Access to Justice Found., 86 F.Supp.2d 624, 637 (W.D.Tex.2000) (quoting Williamson County Reg'l Planning Comm'n v. Hamilton Bank of Johnson City, 473 U.S. 172, 194 (1985)).

77. Washington Legal Found. v. Texas Equal Access to Justice Found., 270 F.3d 180, 194–95 (5th Cir.2001).

81. Washington Legal Found. v. Legal Found. of Wash., 236 F.3d 1097 (9th Cir.2001).

82. Washington Legal Found. v. Legal Found. of Wash., 271 F.3d 835 (9th Cir.2001) (en banc). The decision provoked a spirited dissent from Judge Kozinski, joined by Judges Kleinfeld, Trott, and Silverman. See id. at 864 (Kozinski, J., dissenting).

* Brown v. Legal Foundation, 123 S.Ct. 1406 (2003).

lengers as, "it is not so much that I want the $20, though I do, as that I don't want the [IOLTA] donees to get it." ...

2. *The First Amendment*

... [T]he Ninth Circuit sitting en banc remanded *Washington Legal Foundation* to the district court to consider arguments that mandatory IOLTA contributions amount to compulsory speech and association, violating the First Amendment rights of protestors. [The Supreme Court case did not resolve this question in its 2003 IOLTA decision.] ... The Supreme Court has sustained such challenges to mandatory labor-union dues and mandatory bar-association dues, [but] it has done so only when the unions or bar associations were spending the money on contentious political activities rather than on their core functions. Providing legal representation to underserved populations should be regarded as a core function of the judicial system, not a partisan political act, and so courts should reject the First Amendment challenge to judicially mandated IOLTA participation.

Clearly IOLTA challengers do not see it that way: to them, poor people's lawyers are political adversaries. In the words of a WLF press release, "the use of the plaintiffs' funds violates their First Amendment rights by forcing them to finance ideological causes with which they disagree." But the compulsory speech argument is extraordinary. Contributors know only that IOLTA money goes to fund poor people's lawyers. They have no idea who the lawyers are, who their clients are (other than that they are poor), what issues the lawyers will argue, or what they will say. To assert that making them contribute IOLTA interest compels clients to fund speech that they abhor is tantamount to saying that they abhor anything that anyone might say on behalf of a poor person. It follows that what bothers the objectors is not the speech (about which they know nothing), but the speaker. Talk of compelled speech muddies the issue, which, if it is about anything, is about compelled association rather than compelled speech.

... Proponents of such arguments sometimes quote Thomas Jefferson's maxim "To compel a man to furnish funds for the propagation of ideas he disbelieves and abhors is sinful and tyrannical." But the ordinary business of government and commerce seldom takes this overblown rhetoric seriously. For example, federal tax dollars pay the salaries of senators whose words many constituents find hateful. Atheists fund plenty of God-talk by government officials, creationists subsidize federally funded research on evolutionary biology, and we all pay the salaries of public prosecutors and defenders who say things that occasionally make us seethe. For that matter, it seems likely that virtually every consumer purchase helps pay for corporate speech that the same consumers disagree with (and please do not reply that making purchases is optional rather than compelled behavior). All these examples of so-called compelled speech and association are in reality nothing more than necessary incidents to living in society.... The ... clients whose uncollectible interest goes to IOLTA are in the same boat as taxpayers and consumers: they are thinly and anonymously connected to any particular expenditure of their money....

It is not just the arguments in the IOLTA litigation that are extraordinary, however. The litigation presents the spectacle of a comfortably funded public-interest law firm—the WLF, which has an annual budget of $4 million, 32% of which comes from corporate contributions—trying to defund other public-interest lawyers because they have different politics.... [S]uch attacks on indigent lawyers by well-funded groups are not limited to attacks against IOLTA.

C. Law School Clinics and the Battle of New Orleans

Today, 182 American law schools offer clinics in more than 130 different subject areas, staffed by more than 1,400 clinical instructors. Counting salaries, fringe benefits, and overhead, law schools annually invest perhaps $280 million in clinical education. In return, clinics provide millions of hours each year of unpaid student legal work.

It should be noted that very little clinical work is "cause" lawyering, that is, lawyering "directed at altering some aspect of the social, economic, and political status quo." Civil and criminal litigation clinics form the backbone of clinical education in the United States, and they typically provide one-client-at-a-time, more-or-less routine, direct client representation. Clinical education also includes street-law programs, entrepreneurial clinics with business clients, and externships. It seems likely, however, that the overwhelming majority of clinical teachers would identify themselves as political progressives. While nothing in principle prevents conservatives from starting clinics devoted to issues they favor, for example, crime victims' rights or small business deregulation clinics, it has rarely come to pass, although the WLF started an Economic Freedom Law Clinic at George Mason Law School, which takes a "pro-free enterprise, limited government, and economic freedom perspective." The perception of a leftward tilt makes law school clinics a natural target for adversaries of progressive public-interest law. Although relatively infrequently, law school clinics have indeed been subjected to political attacks and silencing doctrines.

The principal lightning rod has been environmental-law clinics, which sometimes take anti-development stances that put them at odds with business interests. In the 1980s, under pressure from the timber industry, the University of Oregon School of Law's environmental-law clinic came under siege, and eventually had to leave the law school. Environmental-law clinics in the University of West Virginia College of Law and University of Wyoming College of Law have also been attacked by politicians and business interests. Most recently, the University of Pittsburgh School of Law's environmental law clinic infuriated the state legislature by filing suits delaying highway and logging projects in a national forest. The Pittsburgh Post–Gazette reported that under pressure from the legislature, the University of Pittsburgh law school took back $60,000 of the clinic's $100,000 annual budget, a move denounced by the university faculty's Tenure and Academic Freedom Committee as a violation of academic freedom.

The most notorious effort to silence an environmental-law clinic involves Tulane Law School, a private law school in New Orleans. After the Tulane environmental clinic successfully stopped a polyvinylchloride factory from locating in a low-income Black residential neighborhood, angry business groups complained to the Louisiana Supreme Court. In response, the court amended its student-practice rule, Rule XX, to make it harder for students to represent environmental groups.

Clinic supporters filed a federal law suit on academic freedom and free speech grounds.[119] The WLF and, ironically, the Economic Freedom Law Clinic at George Mason Law School weighed in on the opposite side with an amicus brief. Subsequently, the WLF also placed an anticlinic attack ad in the New York Times, explaining why it opposes law school clinics. The advertisement assails law school clinics for "suing property owners, representing criminals, filing appeals on behalf of convicted murderers, and tormenting small business with novel theories of legal liability." At one point the ad poses a question: "Why do law schools fear a level playing field?" This question is striking coming from an organization campaigning for a playing field with no opponent.

Currently, the anti-environmental-clinic rule, Rule XX, stands. The district court sided with the Louisiana Supreme Court and the Fifth Circuit Court of Appeals affirmed.[123] The heart of the Fifth Circuit's argument is that the Louisiana Supreme Court has no obligation to permit unlicensed law students to represent any clients at all. That means its new student-practice rule cannot violate the clinician's rights because they have no such rights. The court adds that it does not matter whether the Louisiana Supreme Court was responding to pressure from groups whose motivation was political and retaliatory. There is no viewpoint discrimination because Rule XX does not prevent anyone from speaking, it merely refuses to promote certain kinds of speech....

. . .

The Fifth Circuit writes as though permitting students to represent clients is an act of grace by the Louisiana justices, because it is an exception to the rule that only lawyers can practice law. But this argument gets matters completely upside down. In most walks of life, it is restrictions on the market for services that call for a special justifica-

119. Southern Christian Leadership Conference, La. Chapter v. Supreme Ct. of La., 61 F.Supp.2d 499 (E.D.La.1999).

123. See Southern Christian Leadership Conference, La. Chapter v. Supreme Ct. of La., 252 F.3d 781 (5th Cir.2001)....

tion and open access that is the preferred rule. To my knowledge, only two arguments are ever offered to justify the state-sanctioned professional monopoly: restricting the practice of law to trained, barred lawyers is supposed to protect consumers from incompetent representation and unethical representation.

However, no one was complaining about the competence or the ethics of the student lawyers at Tulane or any other Louisiana law school. The complaint was that they represented the wrong causes. The state supreme court had been lobbied by three powerful business associations to clamp down on the law students. The justices were up for re-election. The federal district judge thought this was irrelevant: dismissing the clinicians' lawsuit, he wrote, "in Louisiana, where state judges are elected, one cannot claim complete surprise when political pressure somehow manifests itself within the judiciary." No doubt; but such complacent cynicism seems wholly out of place in a legal opinion about whether a politically motivated rule is viewpoint discrimination. Of course it is viewpoint discrimination. . . .

The attacks on the environmental-law clinics at the University of Pittsburgh and Tulane failed to shut them down. . . . That is not the point, however If the attacks failed, they were near misses, and eventually some will succeed. Indeed, they may already have succeeded in one of their aims, because clinic directors will undoubtedly hesitate before taking on volatile cases that may provoke dangerous backlash against the clinics or their law schools. . . .

D. The Civil Rights Fee Cases

In more than half a dozen decisions over the past fifteen years, the U.S. Supreme Court has cut back on statutorily authorized attorneys' fees given to prevailing parties in civil rights and environmental cases. Because they create weapons that adversaries can use to attack the funding of civil rights and environmental lawyers, at least two of these decisions create silencing doctrines.

The first is the Court's 1986 decision *Evans v. Jeff D.*[137] Here, a civil rights defendant offered a settlement granting the plaintiff full relief, provided that the plaintiff waived statutory attorneys' fees. Legal-aid lawyers represented the plaintiff. Counsel concluded that they had no ethical alternative to accepting the offer, but later moved to have the fee-waiver set aside because the defendant had exploited their ethical obligation and undercut Congress's intention in enacting the fee-award statute. The Court, through Justice Stevens, disagreed. The Court admitted that a "sacrifice offer" (that is, "tell your client that we will give her everything she wants provided that you do not get paid") creates an instant tension between attorney and client; n140 the client wins only if the attorney loses. However the Court denied that this raises any

---

137.   475 U.S. 717 (1986).

genuine problem of legal ethics, because plaintiff's counsel can always fulfill their ethical obligations by sacrificing their statutorily authorized fees. The Court acknowledged but dismissed the possibility that the widespread practice of skillfully targeted sacrifice offers could put a public-interest firm out of business.

In practice, private civil rights lawyers have avoided the problem of sacrifice offers by writing retainer agreements that make clients responsible for the attorney's fees if they accept a sacrifice offer. But as Justice Brennan noted in his dissent in *Jeff D.*, public-interest lawyers who write such retainer agreements risk their tax-exempt status. . . .

The Court's reasoning in *Jeff D.* is hard to fathom. It says that having to choose between your client's interests and your own livelihood creates no ethical dilemmas, because you can always sacrifice yourself on the altar of duty. But on this planet, conflicts of interest are ethical dilemmas. While the written codes of ethics provide no express prohibition on lawyers representing clients whose cases would threaten the lawyer's financial interests, they rightly single these cases out as problem situations that deserve special scrutiny.

In his dissent in *Jeff D.*, Justice Brennan urged state bars to enact an ethics rule prohibiting defense lawyers from making sacrifice offers, and I have heard public-interest lawyers agree that this is the solution. However, this approach is unworkable. A legal-ethics rule cannot prohibit defendant clients from proposing a sacrifice settlement, and it should not prohibit their lawyers from presenting to the adversary the settlement their clients propose. . . . Nor can the rule forbid defense lawyers from counseling their clients to make the sacrifice offer, as that would be a gross interference with the lawyer's right to say what she wishes to her client. Perhaps other rules could be amended to permit public-interest lawyers to write fee agreements making their clients responsible for their fees if they accept a sacrifice offer. But public-interest lawyers might still be very reluctant to write such agreements, because given their clients' straitened finances, the agreement will inevitably seem exploitative and extortionate. Most likely, the only resolution to the silencing doctrines espoused in *Jeff D.* must come from Congress or the Supreme Court.

In addition to *Jeff D.*, the Court recently decided *Buckhannon v. West Virginia Department of Health and Human Services.*[148] The *Buckhannon* Court held, in a five-to-four decision, that if a defendant gives a plaintiff the sought-after relief before there has been a judicial decision or a judicially approved settlement, then the plaintiff does not count as a prevailing party and receives no statutory attorneys' fees. This elimi-

---

148. 532 U.S. 598 (2001). The fee-shifting statutes here are contained in the Fair Housing Amendments Act, 42 U.S.C. 3613(c)(2), and the Americans with Disabilities Act, 42 U.S.C. 12205. Although the WLF did not participate in this case, the Pacific Legal Foundation, another conservative public-interest law firm, filed an amicus brief on behalf of the respondent.

nates a so-called catalyst theory used by many courts, according to which plaintiffs were awarded attorney's fees if it was determined that their litigation efforts were the catalyst bringing about the relief or settlement, so that they deserve the fees that go to prevailing parties. After *Buckhannon*, a vindictive defendant can throw in the towel on the eve of judgment to stop the onset of fee shifting, after the plaintiff and plaintiff's counsel have accrued years of expenses. *Buckhannon* thus creates another silencing doctrine by discouraging plaintiffs lawyers from litigating expensive suits that previously held the allure of recouping costs through fee shifting.

The Court's opinion (written by Chief Justice Rehnquist) offers no satisfactory explanation for the decision. It does little more than review past decisions on the meaning of the term "prevailing party" and then refuse to extend the word "prevailing" to include a party gaining what it wants from its lawsuit without judicial involvement. But why not extend the word that far? If getting what one wants through an approved settlement counts as "prevailing," why should not gaining the identical relief through the identical lawsuit still count as "prevailing" even if there is no official settlement? The Court does not say, but Justice Scalia's concurrence tries to answer these questions. He argues that without some judicial involvement, there is no way of knowing whether the plaintiff's case was "phony." Maybe the plaintiff's lawyer is an "extortionist" who made the defendant cry uncle merely by manipulating the media, or by running up defendant's legal bills. ("Phony" and "extortionist" are Justice Scalia's words, not mine.)

However, high-profile media cases are rare; cases where the plaintiff rather than the defendant runs the adversary's legal-fee meter are rarer still. Why build a rule around rare exceptions? Why not presume that, if the defense capitulates, it is probably because the plaintiff had a credible case? Justice Scalia's hypotheticals seem to rest on little more than a visceral suspicion of plaintiffs' lawyers. In any event, his argument fails because judicial involvement provides no remedy to the evils he fears. Judges never disapprove settlements merely because the defendant settled to avoid bad publicity or attorney's fees. Judges think these are splendid reasons to settle. Therefore, cases where the defendant surrenders for these reasons are no different than cases where the defendant settles, except that in the latter the law grants statutory attorneys' fees.

One prominent public-interest lawyer described the effects of *Buckhannon*:

> ... The only word is "disastrous." There is now the lethal combination of *Jeff D.* and *Buckhannon. Jeff D.* was bad, and like everyone else we've suffered through more than our share of sacrifice offers. But *Buckhannon*'s significance can't be overstated. True example: We've been litigating fiercely a longstanding dispute with an agency. We have just received a letter—after years of litigation mind you—saying, in essence, "you're right, we're wrong, we will change our policy to address your concerns." No judicial order will or

now can be entered because the case will be moot.... I have no hope of getting fees here post-*Buckhannon*, though we have, even using [the statute's] low rates, probably $40,000 in fees in the case. That is a big chunk of my budget. We see this kind of pattern: lengthy litigation, and at some point, capitulation, time and again. Up until now, using a catalyst theory, we could often get fees in these cases (although at times we've encountered the Jeff D./sacrifice offer problem). Now we have no chance. I can't tell you how dispiriting this is for us.

Conclusion

Silencing doctrines raise the prospect of an adversary system in which one set of adversaries, the progressive public-interest lawyers and the clients they represent, is relentlessly squeezed by political opponents who would rather muzzle them than argue against them. Those who value procedural justice should find silencing doctrines deeply offensive.

    . . .

... Public-interest law has long been an active front in the larger culture wars that mark American politics. Surely no one should be shocked, shocked to learn that politics is going on here. But I am not shocked; I am merely disgusted. I believe that fair-minded individuals, regardless of their political orientation, should accept the principle of adversary argument, *audi alteram partem*. When politics impinges on the imperative to hear both sides, the adversary system threatens to dissolve into farce or fraud....

Political attacks require political responses. Obviously, the injustice of silencing doctrines is unlikely to become an electoral issue—the issues are too specialized and too remote. They are issues for the bar, not the voters, to take up. However, this is unlikely to happen so long as the bar perceives nothing more than partisan squabbles between the Left and the Right over relatively esoteric matters (the legal-services restrictions, IOLTA, environmental-law clinics, fee-shifting rules).... [But] combating silencing doctrines is not a partisan issue involving only the lawyers the doctrines harm. It is an issue for every lawyer who supports the minimum procedural justice embodied in the injunction to hear both sides....

Let me add one final thought. The private demon of all progressive public-interest lawyers is a sense of futility. Few lawyers who win so few cases and lose so many are immune from the gnawing sense that they are merely wasting their time. It sometimes seems as though their voices accomplish little beyond making a historical record of rejected arguments on behalf of vanquished causes. But they do win sometimes, and even when they fail, the alternative is not making a historical record, so that the very fact that they had a cause disappears without a trace. Without their voices, a kind of smug consensus—a lie, really—is the outcome. And the adversary system becomes little more than a field of lies. Even enemies of progressive public-interest lawyers should want something more than this.

Notes

1.   Do you agree with Luban that the adversary system is a component of procedural justice necessary to ensure that different voices are heard? Why isn't lobbying the legislature sufficient for that purpose? Or publicizing one's views in the media or academia? Is the adversary system a more necessary outlet for poor people than for others? Why? Does wealth have less effect on litigation than on other political exercise? Should we be doing more to subsidize lawsuits?

2.   Luban asserts that he would be just as critical if the Left were silencing the Right as he is of the reverse phenomenon. What about charges by conservatives that a liberal bias exists in the media and academia, and that conservative voices are often silenced in those settings? If true (there is, of course, disagreement about the existence and extent of such bias), are those situations distinguishable because no legal doctrines endorse or support such silencing?

3.   Defense lawyers for alleged enemy combatants are subject to numerous restrictions, not the least of which is the ease of monitoring lawyer-client communications, the security clearance procedures that these lawyers must undergo (according to some sources, at the lawyer's own expense) and the limited access to evidence in the possession of the government due to national security concerns. Is this another example of silencing or something else? See discussion of the Lynn E. Stewart case pp. 177–178.

4.   Cramton, p. 460, raises an issue that has long dogged the Legal Services Corporation: What types of cases should legal services lawyers handle in a world of scarce resources? Cramton describes a line between cases involving individual legal problems and those implicating more "structural" concerns. How does the ban on class actions fit into that dichotomy? Aren't class actions for damages more like the individual legal problems that conservatives have typically argued the legal services lawyers should focus on? On the other hand, one could argue that if the class action is for damages, a lawyer in the private sector should be willing to bring it. Why does Luban think this is unlikely to occur? If the relevant criterion should be whether or not a lawyer in the private sector would bring the suit, then why are class actions that seek only injunctive relief barred? Would it make sense to allow legal services lawyers to serve as objectors in class actions seeking damages as a check on the performance and legal fees of other lawyers? Should we be steering legal services lawyers into the least economically desirable suits? Will that result in more suits being brought whose economic justification is doubtful?

5.   Luban argues that in failing to challenge the restrictions on activities by legal services lawyers, the ABA Ethics Committee failed to live up to the Bar's stated ideal that lawyers have an obligation to make legal services fully available. Note that the ideal was dropped in the Model Rules. This may be another example of Koniak's argument in Through the Looking Glass, p. 287, that our legal system deals more effectively with rights than with obligations.

6. The excerpted part of Luban's article we have printed focuses on the recent constitutional challenges to IOLTA programs. There have also been challenges under the ethics rules. ABA Formal Op. 348 (1982) stated that lawyers who participate in IOLTA programs do not violate the ethics rules on the handling of client trust accounts because the interest is not client "property," a position with which the Supreme Court ultimately disagreed for purposes of determining whether or not the programs involve a "taking" of property in violation of the Fifth Amendment. Does the Supreme Court's decision in *Phillips* and its more recent decision in *Brown* (holding that a taking might have occurred but no compensation is required) now make it unethical for lawyers to participate in IOLTA programs? One case, decided after *Phillips* and before *Brown*, held no because the mere fact that the interest was client "property" does not necessarily mean that there has been a taking without just compensation; if there is no taking without just compensation, there are no "funds or other property that the client . . . is entitled to receive" under the ethics rules. Paulsen v. State Bar of Texas, 55 S.W.3d 39 (Tex. App. 2001).

7. Model Rules of Professional Conduct Rule 1.15(d) (2003) states:

Upon receiving funds or other property in which a client or third person has an interest, a lawyer shall promptly notify the client or third person. Except as stated in this rule or otherwise permitted by law or by agreement with the client, a lawyer shall promptly deliver to the client or third person any funds or other property that the client or third person is entitled to receive and upon request by the client or third person, shall promptly render a full accounting regarding such property.

Does this rule require lawyers to notify clients of IOLTA accounts?

8. Are IOLTA programs a good way to fund legal services for the poor? Are they the best use of the trust account interest that cannot feasibly be returned to clients? Would it be better to use the money to fund activities that benefit clients as a whole, such as creating an uninsured or underinsured lawyer compensation fund (which of course would provide no potential benefit to clients of adequately insured lawyers) or increasing funding for disciplinary authorities or drug rehabilitation programs for lawyers? Do you think any of these alternatives would satisfy those who object to IOLTA programs?

9. Model Rule 1.2(b) states: "A lawyer's representation of a client, including representation by appointment, does not constitute an endorsement of the client's political, economic, social or moral views or activities." The comment to that section states: "Legal representation should not be denied to people who are unable to afford legal services, or whose cause is controversial or the subject of popular disapproval. By the same token, representing a client does not constitute approval of the client's views or activities." This rule is unenforced, and is perhaps unenforceable, but are lawyers who are fighting for what Luban calls "silencing" policies acting in opposition to this rule? If the rule is unenforced (or unenforceable), does the last question make sense?

10. Do you think those who sponsored the advertisement opposing legal clinics would oppose family law clinics at law schools? Students in those

clinics sometimes represent deadbeat dads, child molesters, adulterers, and other unsavory types. They also sometimes represent abused children, battered women, and men denied parental rights by their divorced wives or unmarried partners.

11.   How do the silencing activities Luban discusses square with Model Rule 5.4(c), which states: "A lawyer shall not permit a person who ... pays the lawyer to render legal services for another to direct or regulate the lawyer's professional judgment in rendering such services." Similarly, Model Rule 1.8(f)(2) states: "A lawyer shall not accept compensation for representing a client from one other than the client unless ... there is no interference with the lawyer's independence or professional judgment or with the client-lawyer relationship." Are legal services lawyers, lawyers for the University of Pittsburgh's environmental clinic, and civil rights lawyers who agree to a defendant's demand of no-lawyer-fees in exchange for a fairly good settlement for the client violating those rules?

12.   Luban argues that sacrifice offers on the model that we have just described are a problem created by *Jeff D.*, a problem that only Congress or the Supreme Court, not ethics rules alone, can solve. The problem is one of a general class of problems that might be characterized as a lawyer (here, we mean the defense lawyer who offers the deal) assisting in client conduct that may be undesirable but is lawful. Most people see the same structure in settlement agreements to keep information about a defendant's wrongs secret, although there is reason to question just how lawful some of these agreements are. See Susan P. Koniak, Are Agreements to Keep Secret Information Learned in Discovery Legal, Illegal or Something in Between?, 30 Hofstra L. Rev. 783 (2002).

13.   What incentives do *Jeff D.* and *Buckhannon* create for plaintiff and defense lawyers, other than the one discussed by Luban? Why don't government defendants in civil rights cases always insist that the plaintiff's lawyer waive any fee? Are defendants making offers that implicitly subtract attorneys' fees from the settlement amount, so that essentially the clients are paying what amounts to a contingency fee on the recovery? With respect to *Buckhannon*, will defendants have an incentive to give in to the plaintiffs' settlement demands more often? Sooner? Will defendants protract litigation because they are indifferent to running up the plaintiff lawyer's fees, knowing that a last minute settlement means the defendant doesn't pay those fees? What effect will *Buckhannon* have on the market for plaintiffs' lawyers? Would limiting *Buckhannon* to settlement offers accepted by defendants early in the process make sense? Will plaintiffs' lawyers respond to *Buckhannon* by filing more class actions, which cannot be settled without a fairness hearing and judicial approval, thus effectively bypassing *Buckhannon*? Senator Feingold introduced a bill to overturn *Buckhannon* by redefining "prevailing party" to mean any plaintiff whose claim causes a policy shift by the defendant government entity, thus restoring the "catalyst" theory. Is the organized bar likely to support such legislation?

14.   Recall the Cole article, p. 163, and the notes after it. Which, if any, of the measures described there are silencing devices similar to those discussed by Luban?

Inherent Powers in the Crucible of Lawyer Self-Protection: Reflections on the LLP Campaign*

CHARLES W. WOLFRAM

I. Introduction

In the early part of this decade, law firms, and their allies-for-the-occasion—primarily accounting firms—mounted a successful and rapid campaign to gain the limited liability protection enjoyed by corporations. In the process, the law of client protection was transformed. Lawyers thereby eliminated what formerly had been collective lawyer exposure to threatened personal liability each year for hundreds of millions of dollars of legal malpractice settlements and judgments. Those awards are entered annually against law firms after successful suits by clients, primarily, and by non-clients to a much more modest extent. Some group, of course, lost in this classical zero-sum game. The group who will end up paying for the gains lawyers thereby achieved, of course, consists of their financially harmed clients and other claimants. They lost the right to look to the personal assets of each partner in a law partnership if necessary to satisfy a judgment entered against the firm based on the incompetence or breach of fiduciary duty of a lawyer within it.

All this happened by force ... legislative enactment.... [Now,] a law firm wishing to eliminate the vicarious liability of its owner-lawyers need only do the routine paperwork necessary to convert the firm into a "limited liability partnership"—an LLP—or, in some states, a differently named entity with the same feature of limited liability to clients. The client's agreement or consent—or, to the contrary, a client's outraged objection—is entirely irrelevant. In some few states, clients were provided some offsetting protection or advantage. But, in states like Texas, lawyers drove a very hard bargain with their clients. At least at the level of describing the sweep of legal pronouncement, it is difficult to imagine a change that more dramatically affects the client-lawyer relationship—and that affects it so markedly in favor of lawyers and unfavorably to their clients.

If the relationship between lawyers and their clients were that of the Darwinian-Hobbesian jungle of the business world, we would leave it at that. In an arena governed only by arm's length bargaining—including bargaining for narrow economic advantage before the state's legislature—the change in the relative position of client and lawyer wrought by the LLP legislation would be unremarkable, other than for its magnitude. But at least two central concepts of the law of client-lawyer relationship have also been discarded, or at least thus far ignored, in the rush to enact LLP legislation for lawyers and in the rush by many firms

* © 1998 South Texas Law Review, Inc. Reprinted by permission from 39 S. Tex. L. Rev. 359 (1998).

to invoke its protection. First, the client-lawyer relationship has in most other contexts been claimed to be one in which the lawyer emphatically does not have the right to deploy all the weapons of economic and political warfare to advance the lawyer's economic advantage to the direct disadvantage of clients. To the contrary, the law of client-lawyer relationships can accurately be characterized as client-centered, carefully and rigorously confining the extent to which lawyers may impose their economic will on them. Perhaps most obviously on point is the universally adopted provision of the lawyer codes prohibiting a lawyer from entering into an agreement with a client that would limit the lawyer's liability to the client. Second, judicial opinions in almost every state have insisted that only the state's highest court may regulate lawyers. That claim of exclusive "inherent powers" of courts is embodied in two principles. The milder version of the claim involves judicial assertion of a constitutional power to regulate lawyers even in the absence of legislation. Quite beyond that, most state supreme courts also claim the exclusive power to regulate lawyers as the court sees fit—even if the state's legislature has enacted legislation that on its face is applicable to lawyers. Under the latter claim, courts say they have both the power and the duty to strike down legislation interfering with the judicial power to regulate lawyers. Nor was the concept of inherent powers one forced on an unwilling profession. To the contrary, lawyers invented the concept and have been assiduous to assert it both to courts and to legislative and administrative pretenders who, in the view of the bar, would attempt to usurp the judicial power to regulate them.

. . .

II.   Origins of the LLP Movement

LLPs, ... began in Texas, and not by coincidence.... [Most commentators assert that] legal malpractice recoveries as a result of S & L "bank lawyer liability" litigation were the direct parent of the LLP reform movement.... As one who has been retained as an expert witness in some of the most grisly of those cases, I can certainly agree that ... the threat of personal liability of all members of the firm [was critical to the strategy of plaintiffs' lawyers.] A tactic I have heard described in more than one of those cases is for a lawyer, negotiating on behalf of the receiver of the failed S & L, to begin a settlement discussion session by flipping back a sheet of a large tablet on an easel, revealing a list of the names of each partner in the defendant law firm and what the plaintiff lawyers then understood to be his or her personal assets. This would be totaled together with what the lawyer claimed to be the limits of available insurance coverage. The strong implication, if not explicit demand, was that the grand total should be considered the amount of money on the table for purposes of further settlement discussions.

The threat to lump together all of the personal wealth of each partner—whether or not they personally played any part in the liability-producing events—was, of course, a threat with apparent teeth. At the time, most lawyers in private practice ... worked in law firms that were organized as general partnerships. That meant that each partner in the firm was vicariously liable, jointly and severally, for the malpractice of each other partner or lawyer-employee. "Vicarious" liability, of course, means that the plaintiff was not required to demonstrate any personal wrongdoing of a particular firm lawyer in order to hold the firm lawyer financially responsible for the claimed loss. Being a partner was as valid a basis for entire-wealth liability as was committing acts so wrongful that the lawyer had been sent to prison. Once the plaintiff had a judgment, the plaintiff was entitled to proceed to obtain execution by seizing assets until the judgment was satisfied. The assets of the partnership were, of course, the first thing exposed to liability and seizure, but, however prized and useful, a law library, desks, and personal computers are not very interesting objects out of which to satisfy a large judgment. All large firms, of course, carried legal malpractice liability insurance, but some firms were caught at the beginning of the S & L litigation wave with what proved to be limits of coverage that were improvidently lower than the dollar amount of claims asserted against the firm. It was quite natural in such an environment for firm lawyers to feel that they, and their families, were exposed to great personal risk for the malpractice of their colleagues. Beyond the large firms, malpractice insurance fell off steeply, both in the typically lower dollar limit of coverage and in the lower percentage of smaller lawyer groupings and solo practitioners who carried any insurance protection. For lawyers in such firms facing either an S & L lawsuit or any legal malpractice claim for a substantial sum, the apparent threat of personal financial ruin ... was stark. The answer to the threat was to enact limited liability legislation.

III. The LLP Revolution—and Its Dubious Theoretical and Empirical Bases

... By the mid–1990s the large majority of states had enacted something like the Texas LLP liability-limiting statute for lawyers. Many states adopted two or more of the limited liability forms, apparently offering lawyers a smorgasbord of structures by means of which to limit their liability to their clients. In part the revolution occurred on the merits, so to speak, of lawyers' claims for limited liability. In part it occurred because of appeals by lawyers for equal treatment. In most states, lawyers were among the very few professions or occupational groups that were prohibited from practicing in a liability-protected form. Other occupations, such as engineers, could practice in various corporate arrangements—at least one of the features of which was limited liability. Lawyers also argued that, with new lawyer code rules meaningfully enforced in a significantly enhanced disciplinary system, the threat of vicarious liability was no longer necessary to impel lawyers to practice competently and carefully. Conversely (and, of course, inconsistently) they could argue that modern-day practice in sprawling law factories with large lawyer populations and branch offices scattered about state, nation, and world made the concept of effective supervision of one's colleagues meaningless. The assertion typically ends there, without completing the thought with the obvious observation that large size was both a self-inflicted wound as far as supervision is concerned as well as a vehicle designed to maximize the profits of lawyer-owners of the firm (the same lawyers whose liability would be limited through LLP legislation). It was also unclear why supervision was, on the whole, less viable in a firm of four hundred lawyers than it was in a firm of forty.... [E]ffective supervision probably occurs only among very small subgroups of lawyers. But it can occur in those sub-groups in large firms just as well as in smaller ones. It was also argued that liability for the wrongs committed by other firm lawyers is no longer appropriate. There is, of course, the argument that vicarious liability is itself unjust, an argument that has fallen on deaf ears of common law judges for two centuries.... With respect to the fairness of vicarious financial liability, of course, one counterargument is that—as between innocent partner of a wrongdoing firm lawyer and innocent client who has been harmed—the innocent partner is in a much better position than most clients to ensure that a colleague complies with applicable norms. Moreover, unlike an injured client, a lawyer's partners have enjoyed the benefits of pooled resources and shared profits from the law firm's practice, and it is thus roughly just to require that they each bear part of the law firm's liabilities.

While the affirmative side of those points was often asserted in the lawyer campaign for LLP legislation, the basic point of the effort was naked self-interest—lawyers wanted to be protected from liability, period.... Very rarely was it pointed out that this protection would necessarily and inevitably be paid for from the pocketbooks of those to whom lawyers owe extensive duties, the breach of which is a precondition to liability in damages to a client. From ... much of the lawyer clamor, one would have gathered that legal malpractice was a form of judicial theft by clients.... [L]awyers never felt it necessary to demonstrate that abusive recoveries were widespread. Indeed, the entire legislative effort was characterized by lawyer empiricism—surmises from the armchair about the impact of legal malpractice liability, without any significant empirical support for the underlying claims and assumptions.

. . .

IV. The Ill Fit Between Client Protection in the Lawyer Codes and LLP Limited Liability

. . .

An obvious device by which lawyers in a general partnership could limit their vicarious liability to clients would be through explicit agreement with each client. For example, a law firm might think to provide in its standard initial agreement with clients that, in consideration of the firm's provision of legal services, the client agreed that the client would look solely to the firm's assets and those of lawyers who actually worked on the matter in the event of a legal malpractice recovery. Would such a provision protect other lawyers in the firm as intended?

Rather clearly, such an attempt to limit liability by agreement with a client would be in violation of the jurisdiction's lawyer code and . . . as a matter of public policy, [would likely be] unenforceable in a malpractice proceeding. . . . The lawyer code provision is explicit. Typical is the ABA's Model Rule 1.8(h): "A lawyer shall not make an agreement prospectively limiting the lawyer's liability to a client for malpractice unless permitted by law and the client is independently represented in making the agreement. . . ." To be sure, the rule does not explicitly prohibit the precise kind of waiver here—that of the vicarious liability of the law firm—and it could be argued that the rule is specifically addressed only to "the lawyer's liability." It could thus be argued that having a client sign an agreement expressly waiving the vicarious liability of the lawyer's partners would be acceptable under the rule. But such a reading would be at war with the evident rationale for the rule. First, it would tend to undermine competent and diligent legal representation. . . . [Aware of the contract limiting vicarious liability,] partners of the retained lawyer may be reluctant to assist in the representation because that would [trigger] personal liability. . . . Moreover, the incentives of other firm lawyers to supervise the lawyer retained by the client would be diminished. Second, many clients are unable to evaluate the desirability of such an agreement prior to the time when a dispute arises and at a time when they are represented by the lawyer seeking his law firm's exoneration. A client with a problem dire enough to search out a lawyer (a lawyer who will probably seek to induce the client to trust the lawyer's advice on all other matters) is in a poor position to exert skepticism or resistance when confronted with the lawyer's request for other-lawyer exoneration. For such reasons, a contractual undertaking to achieve limited liability for a lawyer's firm should subject the lawyer to discipline and the agreement to being avoided.

What, then, distinguishes LLP protection—which achieves much the same liability avoidance as would the prohibited contractual arrangement? If a contractual arrangement to which the client explicitly agrees is objectionable, isn't it a fortiori objectionable to achieve the same result without the client's agreement? In Formal Opinion 96–401, the ABA's ethics committee confronted the issue of the permissibility of assuming the mantle of LLP protection in light of Rule 1.8(h). In an opinion that was uncharacteristically weak on reasoned support, the committee gave the green light to LLP protection. At the time of its opinion, of course, the committee was confronted with a bar eager for only one answer to the question posed to it and flush with success in persuading almost all states to extend statutory LLP protection to lawyers. It would have taken unusual courage for the committee to reach a different result. The committee showed no such inclination. It held that conversion of a firm from a general partnership to an LLP was permissible, with mild conditions that any firm could readily satisfy.[40] In distinguishing Rule 1.8(h), the committee meekly noted only that LLP legislation did not insulate a lawyer from liability to the client for the lawyer's own act (as if that were the only concern of the rule), and that the LLP limitation on liability derived from state legislation and not from an individual contract (which would seem to make its impact more objectionable, not less).[41]

Rather clearly, no one but a lawyer eager for the protection afforded by the LLP form would believe that the protections for clients built into the lawyer codes of every state were at all consistent with that protection. But even were the point debatable, the apparently unyielding position of the ABA and many local bar associations over the years provided an even more straightforward ground of objection to the LLP legislation. In almost every state, the bar had successfully campaigned for rulings holding that only the state supreme court had the "inherent power" to regulate lawyers. Surely that would preclude legislation permitting LLPs. Or would it?

V. Inherent Powers in the Crucible

. . .

A. *The Theory of the Negative Aspect of Inherent Powers as Applied to LLP Legislation*

. . . At least for the last century or longer in the United States, courts have been the governmental body primarily responsible for regulating lawyers. . . . [L]awyer regulation, along with the more obvious judicial business of adjudicating cases . . . [became] one of the inherent functions of the state judiciary. . . . [T]he absence of specific empowering legislation [thus has] not prevent[ed] court[s] from . . . enacting . . . code[s] to regulate lawyers, setting up . . . [administrative structures] to [process complaints against lawyers] for violations [of these codes] . . . ,

40. See ABA Comm. on Ethics and Professional Responsibility, Formal Op. 96–401 (1996). . . . The only significant condition imposed by the committee was that "restrictions on liability as to other lawyers in the organization [must] be made apparent to the client." Id. A majority of the committee was of the view that the use of "LLP" or other appropriate abbreviation would do that. See id. The majority also held that such an abbreviation would cause the lawyer's advertising not to be "misleading" or "deceptive" within the meaning of ABA Model Rules 7.1 and 7.5(a). See id.

41. See id. The committee also noted that several local bar associations had already decided that adopting the LLP form was permissible. See id. (citing Comm. on Professional Ethics of the New York County Lawyers' Ass'n, Op. 703 (1994) and Ops. 235 (1993) and 254 (modifying Op. 235) (1995) of the Legal Ethics Comm. of the District of Columbia).

or [imposing discipline after that process].... [All that, however, is] ... merely an "affirmative" notion of judicial power under the judiciary article of ... [a] state's constitution.

But the "negative" form of the inherent powers concept has a much grander reach. Simplifying it only slightly, the negative aspect claims that, by force of the separation of powers clause of the state constitution, the judiciary's control over lawyer regulation is exclusive of that of other branches of state government. Thus, any attempt by the state legislature, for example, to enact a statute dealing with lawyer regulation is unconstitutional.... [T]he negative aspect of the inherent powers doctrine has been created and sustained with the strong support of the organized bar. The ABA in particular has frequently insisted that only courts may regulate law practice in a number of settings and on a number of issues.

... [One might object:] "There are all sorts of statutes and regulations that control lawyers." ... Lawyers are subject to the general criminal laws and to such general laws as those requiring all citizens to pay income, property, and similar taxes and to avoid discriminatory practices with respect to their law practice employees. To explain the coexistence of such legislation alongside the negative aspect of the inherent powers doctrine, one needs to understand two foils to the doctrine. One foil is to state that laws of general application may also apply to lawyers. Another foil is a trick of the doctrine. Many courts will accept statutes regulating lawyers as a matter of what the court declares to be "comity" with the legislative branch.

But it should not be imagined that the courts will frequently duck a possible run-in with a coordinate branch of government through one foil or the other. Indeed, on occasion, and at least in some jurisdictions, inherent powers decisions seem to bristle with aggressive assertions of judicial power. Take what admittedly may be an extreme case, the recent decision of the Pennsylvania Supreme Court in Commonwealth v. Stern.[50] In 1994, along with legislation outlawing insurance fraud, the Pennsylvania legislature enacted a section in the state's criminal code, making it a misdemeanor for a lawyer to give anything of value to a non-lawyer for recommending or securing the lawyer's employment by a client.... [A]s the Pennsylvania court readily conceded, the misdemeanor law precisely paralleled (indeed it was copied verbatim from) a prohibition of the court's own Rules of Professional Conduct. One might have thought, then, that the statute—far from challenging the court's power—was merely providing an additional, complementary remedy for violations of the court's own rules. Nonetheless, three lawyers ... challenged the constitutionality of the statute as violating the inherent powers of the Pennsylvania Supreme Court. That court agreed, holding that only a statute that prohibited all persons from paying another

50.   701 A.2d 568, 570 (Pa.1997).

person to solicit business would be constitutional, and rejected the argument that the parallelism between the court's rule and the rule of the statute saved the latter. The suggestion that the legislature might pass such a "general" criminal statute is patently absurd, for it would outlaw a great many widely accepted business practices. And note that, in the absence of such a statute (or the court's reversal of its own ruling), there is no method by which the state could apply criminal sanctions to a lawyer who pays a runner. . . .

Application of the robust form of the negative aspect to LLP legislation would rather clearly require that the legislation be held unconstitutional. The legislation clearly purports to regulate lawyers in the practice of law, and particularly the financial aspects of the client-lawyer relationship. Such legislation, although general in its reach, is similar to other general legislation that courts have struck down. Moreover, given the obvious clash between the policy of lawyer protection reflected in the LLP statutes and the policy of client protection reflected in the lawyer codes, it cannot be said that the court should accept the LLP legislation on some notion of comity. . . .

B. *The Inherent Powers Limitations on Existing LLP Statutes—the Decisions*

Limited liability for lawyers did not first become a possibility with the bold LLP legislation in Texas. . . . [M]any states in the 1960s and 1970s had enacted or amended professional corporation statutes to permit lawyers to practice in that form. To be sure, the motivation for the PC legislation was to permit lawyers to gain the tax advantages that were then uniquely available for certain kinds of pension arrangements and that required practicing in the form of a professional corporation. However, lawyers being the creative folks they are, it was soon (or perhaps even earlier than that) realized that professional corporation statutes also typically provided for limited liability for the shareholders of the corporation, just like a "real" corporation. Thus, it was inevitable that lawyers practicing in the PC form would begin to argue in response to legal malpractice claims by clients that the individual lawyer-shareholders of the PC who were not personally complicit in the wrong done the plaintiff were not personally responsible to pay any judgment against the PC. While the number of decisions on point is not great, the lineup of decisions should give no [great] comfort to lawyers who hope to gain limited liability from the PC form. By what seems only a logical extension, the same might also be true of practice in the form of an LLP.

[At least three courts rejected limited liability of lawyers practicing in PC. It appears that an equal number of courts accepted the limitation, but with some reservations.]

C. *Where Were the Lawyers—and Their Bar Associations?*

The inconsistency of the position of bar associations in the LLP campaign has been blatant. The organized bar has been a vigorous proponent of the extreme form of the negative inherent powers doctrine.... Nonetheless, the organized bar led the campaign for LLP legislation. Lawyers in large firms played a prominent role in drafting and lobbying for the legislation....

VI. Realism About the LLP Revolution

... [T]he ingenuity of plaintiff lawyers and the receptive attitudes of many courts will probably still leave many firm lawyers exposed to personal liability in many legal malpractice cases involving LLPs.... [Also,] it is by no means clear that practicing under an LLP umbrella is all that attractive for reasons having nothing directly to do with limiting liability....

A.   *LLP-Consistent Bases for Personal Liability*

First, individual lawyers in law firms can still—and quite consistently with the LLP statutes—be held personally responsible for the malpractice of their lawyer colleagues. That can happen in several ways....

1.   *First-Order Actors: Lawyers Actually Causing Harm*

Most obviously, notwithstanding that she practices in an LLP in a jurisdiction that fully accepts the lawyer-favoring legal consequences that flow from that, a lawyer whose own acts violated a duty of care and proximately caused the client harm remains personally liable....

But the situation of other lawyers within the LLP, besides the lawyer individually named as defendant along with the organization, remains somewhat problematical notwithstanding the apparently protective legislation.... [M]any firm agreements have indemnification clauses that, in all but the more outrageous of instances, require that the firm as a whole—or perhaps individual members of it—pick up all or part of the first-order actor's tab. Those clauses are encountered in LLP agreements, as well as in partnership agreements, and they are founded on the straightforward notion that one lawyer in the firm does not want to be left holding the bag for a mistake that might threaten massive personal liability (as well as liability of the LLP entity).... [A]lmost all states provide, typically by statute, that a tortfeasor may recover contribution from others whose own negligence or other fault has contributed to the harm. More generally, many states now provide for liability-sharing through allocation by comparative fault....

2.   *Second-Order Actors: Peripheral Participants, Negligent Supervisors, Idling Would-Be Rescuers and Possibly Others*

. . .

... One way of adding other firm members will involve situations in which other firm lawyers have some peripheral, but nonetheless substantial and personal involvement in the alleged first-order lawyer's wrongdoing....

A second basis for extending liability within an LLP, again beyond the main first-order actors, is either by force of specific provisions in several of the LLP statutes (as in Texas) or by common law elsewhere. Under those theories, an otherwise "innocent" firm lawyer may be liable on a theory that the lawyer negligently failed to supervise the activities of the first-order lawyer that caused harm, or that these second-order lawyers otherwise failed to act to prevent or limit the harm. That form of liability is known to the common law, although, given the general availability of vicarious-liability bases for recovery, it has been invoked primarily to extend liability to an enterprise for acts of agents that are otherwise outside the scope and course of the agent's employment....

The utility of a duty-to-supervise basis for a claim of breach has been greatly enhanced because of the presence in most of the post-1983 lawyer codes of specific disciplinary requirements that supervisory lawyers exercise that power reasonably to avoid harm to, most obviously among others, clients. Some case authority already exists. In a well-known but unreported decision, a federal court in Baltimore held that the two second-order partners in a three-lawyer firm could be held personally liable to an injured client on a theory that they had negligently failed to supervise the extent to which the third lawyer had been racking up huge totals of hours to clients—numbers that the evidence suggested they must have known to be contrived or at least suspicious.[102]

... The personal liability of the second-order lawyer is based on inaction—a failure to come to the aid of a firm client known to be at risk because of the negligence or other wrongful act of the primary-actor lawyer....

In the final analysis, it would appear that the LLP shield leaks.... [However,] the extent of liability will be less, and will certainly be less than automatic, as compared with the situation of lawyers in general partnerships, where personal liability is a constant. The plaintiff will find it more difficult, more expensive, and more time-consuming, to launch attacks on second-order actors within an LLP....

D. LLPs in the Real World

... There are decided downside risks, problems, and threats involved in adopting one of the LLP forms.... For one thing, it seems

---

102. See Dresser Indus., Inc. v. Digges, Civ. No. JH–89–485, 1989 WL 139240, at *1 (D. Md. Sept. 5, 1989) (granting summary judgment against individual lawyers on theory of failure to supervise co-partner); id. at *7–8 (mentioning supervisory theory of personal liability, but reserving ruling); see also, e.g., FDIC v. Nathan, 804 F.Supp. 888, 897–98 (S.D.Tex.1992) (pleading sufficiently alleged direct liability of lawyer to firm client "because he failed to supervise attorneys in his firm and to deter negligent and unethical conduct"); Gautam v. De Luca, 521 A.2d 1343, 1347 (N.J.Super.Ct.App.Div.1987) ("Although our research has disclosed no published opinion bearing on the precise issue, we are equally convinced that an attorney's failure to properly supervise the work of his associate may constitute negligence particularly where, as here, the associate is hindered or disabled by virtue of his illness.").

agreed that the various LLP forms impose a more inflexible form of structure on a law firm and a formal and less flexible pattern of interaction among lawyer-principals. Some indeed have wondered whether at least part of the burnout being reported from large law firms has not been contributed to by the excessively impersonal, detached, and ruthlessly profit-driven mentality that might waft into a firm when it converts to an LLP structure.

And even if we are reluctant to lift our eyes from the bottom line, there are ample reasons to think that adopting the LLP form is simply bad for business. In the first place, I wonder how many law firms, before they adopted an LLP form—all of which require identifying the firm on its stationery and elsewhere as "LLP" (or worse)—stopped to think how some clients would react to the implicit screen from personal liability that the form rather obviously throws up between a law firm and its clients. At least some clients undoubtedly think it's tacky at best, and highly suspicious at worst, that a firm is ducking personal firm-wide responsibility for the acts of whatever lawyer is assigned to the client. . . .

Lawyers in many firms, of course, are capable of ignoring the bottom line, particularly where its message is blurred. . . . [T]here is in many firms a philosophy of public service and an attitude of client service that would be severely compromised by adopting the LLP structure. . . .

1. The Mixed Blessing of LLP Limited Liability Protection—Another Look at Doomsday

In the final analysis, what does a law firm really gain by slipping on the arguably soiled mantle of LLP limited liability? Ultimately, LLP protection is relevant only in "doomsday" situations—situations in which a law firm has been reduced to dust and ashes. . . . [T]he LLP entity can be levied upon for the full amount of the judgment against it. So long as the claimant has taken all available procedural steps, each and every one of the firm's assets are exposed to levy and execution sale to satisfy the judgment. Without going into the wearying detail, it is obvious that the firm can thus be forced to cease to function—lacking law library, desks, computers, accounts receivable, or any other asset. . . . [B]y this point if not long before, the firm's lawyers will have been driven to abandon the firm and their practice. Then and only then do they begin to "enjoy" the limited liability protection of the LLP form.

2. Holding a Candle to the Crucible

The doomsday scenario is literally the only one in which LLP protection in fact protects individual firm lawyers. For a judgment that is less massive, some assets of the firm will survive—perhaps enough to keep the firm going as a law practice enterprise. . . . The going-business value of a law firm is its chief economic value to all firm principals, and this more than anything is what such insurance is designed to protect. Independent of the fact that it is very much in the self-interest of LLP members to maintain adequate malpractice insurance, note that a substantial number of LLP statutes or court rules also require maintenance of a minimal level of such insurance as a condition to adopting the LLP form (although some, like Texas,in ridiculously small amounts). Because of the doomsday scenario, it is only prudent for LLPs to carry a policy sufficiently large to fend off the stake-in-the-heart malpractice claim....

... [W]hy, if the law firm is going to continue to need a large malpractice policy and appropriate firm controls over poor practice, [does] it also needs to bear the risk of offending clients and perhaps cheapening itself in the eyes of the firm's own lawyers and those of its peer law firms by adopting the LLP label? ...

. . .

... In the final analysis, there is probably only one type of law firm in which the LLP form of practice makes dramatically clear economic sense.... [Although] it does not make sense for the firm that hopes to survive to a fine old age ..., it does make sense to a lawyer or group of lawyers who has little interest in longevity of the practice form....

Notes

1. The LLP movement for lawyers was part of a larger movement to limit liability in the waning years of the 20th century. Limited liability companies (LLCs), which first appeared on the scene in 1977, were created to offer the corporate advantage of limited liability combined with the partnership advantage of so-called pass-through taxation (income is not taxed at the entity level, but only when it is "passed through" to the owners) without the restrictions imposed on other forms of ownership such as limited partnerships (which require a general partner who manages the business and who is not protected by limited liability rules). After the IRS ruled in 1988 that an LLC indeed qualified for partnership tax treatment, states rushed to pass LLC statutes. The development of LLPs followed soon thereafter. And as Wolfram reports, lawyers (as well as accountants) played a big role in pushing for this legislation, in part as a response to liability arising out of the S & L crisis (such as the Kaye Scholer case discussed in the Weinstein article, p. 137). See generally Symposium: The Revolution of the Limited Liability Entity, 32 Wake Forest L. Rev. 1–192 (1997); Susan Pace Hamill, The Origins Behind the Limited Liability Company, 59 Ohio St. L.J. 1459–1522 (1998). See also Robert W. Hamilton, Registered Limited Liability Partnerships: Present at the Birth (Nearly), 66 U. Colo. L. Rev. 1065 (1995).

2. Consider the "equal treatment" argument advanced by lawyers in support of LLP legislation. This is a variation on a theme that runs through this volume: how different are lawyers from other professionals or business people. One reason corporations have been allowed limited liability status is to facilitate raising large amounts of capital from investors who contribute nothing more than money to the enterprise. Even in that context some have

criticized corporate limited liability for tort claims. See Henry Hansmann & Reiner Kraakman, Toward Unlimited Shareholder Liability for Corporate Torts, 100 Yale L.J. 1879 (1991). But currently ethics rules prohibit passive investors in law firms, although some have argued for changing that. See, e.g., Edward S. Adams & John H. Matheson, Law Firms on the Big Board?: A Proposal for Nonlawyer Investment in Law Firms, 86 Calif. L. Rev. 1 (1998). Should the absence of passive investors matter for purposes of evaluating lawyer LLPs? Instead of LLPs, should the limitation on passive ownership be lifted with limited liability available only to the passive owners but not the lawyers practicing in the entity?

3. Is there a relationship between firm size and the need for or desirability of limited liability? Leubsdorf in his article, p. 234, finds the LLP movement especially troubling because as firms get larger vicarious liability becomes more, rather than less, important. On the other hand, Ribstein has argued that the larger the law firm, the greater the "reputational bond" at stake for the firm and therefore the more likely the firm will behave responsibly even without liability or legal regulation. See Larry E. Ribstein, Ethical Rules, Agency Costs, and Law Firm Structure, 84 Va. L. Rev. 1707 (1998). For a critique of Ribstein's position, see Pamela S. Karlan, The Path of the Law Firm: A Comment on Ribstein's "Ethical Rules, Agency Costs, and Law Firm Structure," 84 Va. L. Rev. 1761 (1998); Ted Schneyer, Reputational Bonding, Ethics Rules, and Law Firm Structure: The Economist as Storyteller, 84 Va. L. Rev. 1777 (1998). One might think that the larger the firm, the greater the firm's ability to provide loss spreading insurance, eliminating the need for limited liability protection. See Cohen, Legal Malpractice Insurance, p. 253. One reason the large firms pushed for LLPs was that they saw the risks of liability as greater than in the past. The source of these larger risks, however, often involves not simple negligence, but facilitating (knowingly or not) client fraud and breach of fiduciary duty by management. Why should society through LLPs be making it easier for lawyers to take such risks? Wolfram focuses on yet another aspect of firm size, namely the relationship between firm size and the costs of monitoring lawyers. As Wolfram points out, increasing law firm size does not necessarily increase the difficulty of monitoring lawyers. For some activities, monitoring even in a two or three person partnership would be difficult. For other activities, such as client screening, conflicts checking, and evaluation for partnership, large firms may in fact do a better job than smaller firms. Should LLPs be available only to large firms? Small firms? Should there be a sliding scale of minimum insurance requirements as firms get larger?

4. Wolfram draws an analogy to a law firm contracting with a client for limited liability and asks why an LLP should be treated any differently. He also argues that LLPs are in a sense worse because they are statutory creations, which raises issues concerning the inherent authority of courts to regulate lawyers. Are there other ways in which LLPs are more troubling than contractual limitations on liability? For one thing, unlike contractual arrangements, LLP protection applies across the board to all types of firms for all types of claims by all types of clients. Moreover, LLPs provide a crucial form of protection that contract cannot (and that ethics rule, like

Model Rule 1.8(h), do not reach), namely protection against suits by non-client third parties. And contracting parties are often able to extract a quid pro quo for reductions in liability, whereas LLP statutes were passed with very little demanded of lawyers in return (few states required LLPs to carry malpractice insurance and those that did set minimums very low; no states set up a victim compensation fund to deal with clients left without recovery). Are there other differences between a contract regime and the LLP statutes?

5. Wolfram uses the "negative inherent judicial powers" doctrine mainly to point out the hypocrisy of the bar. But what about the doctrine itself? Is it sensible? Should it matter whether the state legislature adopts a regulation that parallels the existing ethics rule (as in the Pennsylvania example cited by Wolfram), prohibits something the ethics rules otherwise permit, or permits something the ethics rules otherwise prohibit? Please note that unlike state courts, the federal courts do not claim any exclusive jurisdiction over the regulation of lawyers practicing before them. In other words, federal statutes regulating lawyers are not considered encroachments on federal court power. How should state courts treat a federal statute regulating lawyers? If state courts must accept (under the Constitution's Supremacy Clause) a federal law, like the Sarbanes–Oxley reform legislation, that includes provisions regulating lawyers, does it make sense for them to deny state legislators a similar power to reach the conduct of lawyers?

6. Why doesn't Wolfram think LLP statutes are laws of general application, which would place them outside the inherent court power doctrine? Isn't that the point of the "equal treatment" argument lawyers made for LLPs? Does it matter whether a law of general application contains specific provisions dealing with lawyers?

7. Compare Wolfram's discussion of the arguments made by lawyers for LLPs and Schneyer's argument, p. 448, for law firm discipline. If Schneyer is right that many lawyering problems are not the result of individual rogue behavior but rather firm-wide practices and cultures, then is there any justification for limited liability? In fact, as Wolfram indirectly suggests, malpractice law could be interpreted so that every partner (or a broad range of partners) could be responsible as "primary" tortfeasors for certain firm-wide failures. See Model Rules of Professional Conduct Rule 5.1(a) (2003) (every partner is responsible for making "reasonable efforts to ensure that the firm has in effect measures giving reasonable assurance that all lawyers in the firm conform to the" ethics rules). Courts might, for example, expand the concept of causation in a manner that would not be necessary if all partners were vicariously liable. In addition, as Wolfram suggests, courts might expand theories of recovery under agency and employment law, such as negligent supervision, as well as negligent hiring and negligent retention. For a corollary development, consider that after private parties were barred from suing lawyers and others for aiding securities fraud in 1995, courts expanded the notion of "primary" wrongdoer under the securities laws. Before the limit on private suits, the distinction between primary and secondary liability was relatively unimportant and thus went largely unaddressed. Afterwards all pressure was on that line and the

perception, at least, was that the dividing line not only got articulated with more precision, it moved.

8.   In a part of the articles not excerpted here, Wolfram suggests that adopting LLP status might not make business sense for firms because clients would not be happy about it. That suggestion does not seem to be borne out by developments in the last several years, as firms have rushed to become LLPs with nary a peep from clients. Why do you suppose this might be? Perhaps any discount clients might have demanded in exchange for accepting limited malpractice coverage is more than offset by the greater risks lawyers are willing to take on behalf of clients and at the expense of third parties who not only have LLPs to deal with but other obstacles to suit, some relatively new like the bar on suing for aiding securities fraud. Other reasons?

9.   Wolfram closes by arguing that the LLP shield may not be all that useful, except in rare "doomsday" scenarios. What about his argument at the beginning of the article that the threat of personal liability was an important negotiating tool in many of the S & L cases and that many law firms are thinly capitalized? Of course, the less useful the LLP shield is, the less likely it will be to lead to adverse consequences. But that simply raises the question again: Why the big push to adopt these statutes?

10.   What incentives do LLPs create for individual members of firms? Will they isolate themselves more from fellow lawyers to reap the benefits of the limited liability shield? Will they bargain for indemnity provisions that, if given to all lawyers, might effectively wipe out any limited liability? Will they abandon ship as soon as the firm is sued for a significant amount? See Ted Schneyer, Reputational Bonding, Ethics Rules, and Law Firm Structure: The Economist as Storyteller, 84 Va. L. Rev. 1777 (1998) (describing one NY firm that declined to adopt the limited liability form for fear that this could happen).

11.   Other articles on LLPs include: Poonam Puri, Judgment Proofing the Profession, 15 Geo. J. Legal Ethics 1 (2001); Susan Saab Fortney, Professional Responsibility and Liability Issues Related to Limited Liability Law Partnerships, 39 S. Tex. L. Rev. 399 (1998).

Disputing Through Agents: Cooperation and Conflict Between Lawyers in Litigation*

RONALD J. GILSON AND **ROBERT H. MNOOKIN**

. . .

Introduction

Do lawyers facilitate dispute resolution or do they instead exacerbate conflict and pose a barrier to the efficient resolution of disputes?
. . .

. . .

. . . Today, the dominant popular view is that lawyers magnify the inherent divisiveness of dispute resolution. According to this vision, litigators rarely cooperate to resolve disputes efficiently. Instead, shielded by a professional ideology that is said to require zealous advocacy, they endlessly and wastefully fight in ways that enrich themselves but rarely advantage the clients.

. . .

Purveyor of needless conflict need not be the only vision of the lawyer's role in litigation. Over a century ago, Abraham Lincoln suggested that lawyers can play an extraordinarily constructive role in disputes—as peacemakers who facilitate efficient and fair resolution of conflict when their clients could not do so for themselves. From this perspective, a central characteristic of the formal legal system—that clients carry on their dispute through lawyers who are their agents—has the potential for damping rather than exacerbating the conflictual character of litigation. . . .

. . .

I.   Litigation as a Prisoner's Dilemma

The prisoner's dilemma provides a useful heuristic to illuminate a common characteristic of dispute settlement through litigation. In many disputes, each litigant may feel compelled to make a contentious move either to exploit, or to avoid exploitation by, the other side. Yet, the combination of contentious moves by both results in a less efficient outcome than if the litigants had been able to cooperate.

. . .

A.   *The Litigation Game: A One–Round Prisoner's Dilemma*

Consider the following "litigation game," a highly abstracted model of litigation possessing the attributes of a one-round prisoner's dilemma.

* © 1994 The Columbia Law Review. Reprinted by permission from 94 Colum. L. Rev. 509 (1994).

Able and Baker dispute the proper division of $100 according to some legal standard. For the moment, assume that litigation does not involve lawyers, but only the two parties and a judge. Each party holds information not known by the other side. Some of this information is favorable and some of it is unfavorable. Before the judge decides the case, there is a one-stage simultaneous disclosure process in which each party hands to the judge and the opposing party a sealed envelope containing information. Only two moves are possible, and neither player can know in advance what the other will do. One move is cooperation: a player voluntarily (and at no cost to the other side) discloses to the other side and to the judge all material information in her possession. The second option, defection, involves the adversarial use of the disclosure process to hide unfavorable information. As a consequence, the other side must spend $15 to force disclosure of some but not all of the information withheld. After the envelope exchange and the "purchase" of some of the withheld information, the judge resolves the dispute based on the information disclosed.

With the payoff structure indicated by the following matrix, this game poses a prisoner's dilemma. If both players cooperate, there are no discovery expenses for either side and we will assume the judge awards $50 to Able and $50 to Baker. If both players defect, each must spend $15 to pry out some but not all of the unfavorable information possessed by the other side. Although the judge lacks complete information, we assume that she divides the $100 in the same ratio; the net recovery to the parties is now $35 to Able and $35 to Baker. The third scenario, in which one player defects while the other cooperates, provides the defector with a higher payoff ($70) and hurts the "sucker" in two ways. First, because the cooperating player has disclosed all of its unfavorable information while the defecting party has only disclosed some of the information unfavorable to it, the Judge awards the sucker a gross recovery of only $30. Second, the sucker has spent $15 to get less than all of the information unfavorable to the other side before the judge (without which his recovery would be even lower). Thus, the sucker's net recovery is only $15.

PAYOFF MATRIX

Player One

		Cooperate	Defect
Player Two	Cooperate	50/50	15/70
	Defect	70/15	35/35

In this litigation game, Able's best response to whatever strategy Baker chooses is to defect. In other words, defection is Able's dominant strategy. The same, of course, is true for Baker. Defect–Defect, therefore, is a "dominant strategy equilibrium," even though this result guarantees each party only $35, rather than the $50 produced by a strategy of mutual cooperation. If there is no way for the disputants to bind each other to make a cooperative move, rational actors end up with less than "fools" who simply cooperate.

B. *Is the Prisoner's Dilemma an Appropriate Model for Litigation?*

To what extent does the prisoner's dilemma represent an appropriate, albeit highly simplified, model of the litigation process? ... [A] prisoner's dilemma, the best payoff for a player occurs when that player defects and the other player cooperates. The worst payoff results when a player cooperates while the other player defects. The other two outcomes fall between these extremes, with the reward for mutual cooperation better than the payoff for mutual defection. This means that a prisoner's dilemma cannot be a zero sum or purely distributive game: the total combined payoff from mutual cooperation must exceed the total combined payoff from mutual defection. Indeed, in a symmetric prisoner's dilemma, each player's payoff from mutual cooperation must be greater than each player's payoff from mutual defection.

How realistic is it to assume that in litigation the payoff structure takes this form? In many disputes, the assumption that mutual cooperation might benefit both sides seems entirely plausible. Mutual cooperation involves lower total litigation costs than mutual defection. Moreover, when parties share information, reveal their true underlying interests, and engage in collaborative problem-solving, they may sometimes develop new options that "create value" or "expand the pie" for both disputants in comparison to the result flowing from mutual defection. Both parties may sometimes gain from a negotiated resolution that takes a form a judge could not impose. For example, both parties may prefer exchanging a property that the plaintiff values more highly than the defendant over a judicially determined damage award. It also seems plausible that the best and worst individual outcomes will occur when one party cooperates and the other does not. In many disputes, because of the adversarial nature of litigation, cooperative moves by one litigant, if not reciprocated by the other, can lead to exploitation and something akin to a sucker's payoff. Unbalanced discovery, where only one side discloses unfavorable information, yields this result.

Not every legal dispute involves the sort of payoff structure required by the prisoner's dilemma, and, as we suggest later, this has important implications. In some disputes ... mutual defection may yield the best payoff for a defendant interested in delay because interest earned by putting off the damage payment may exceed any differential in transaction costs. This suggests the importance of exploring in particular legal contexts whether the payoff assumptions for the prisoner's dilemma are, in fact, appropriate.

The rules of the game for a prisoner's dilemma also require that each player remains ignorant of what the other player will do before making a move: enforceable commitments or contracts are not possible and thus the parties cannot credibly bind themselves to cooperate. At first glance, this restrictive assumption seems entirely inappropriate. Disputants in litigation can enter into enforceable agreements with respect to future conduct. The prisoner's dilemma disappears if the parties can, at reasonable cost, spell out the terms of an enforceable agreement to cooperate in the litigation, and thereby bind each other to exchange all relevant information so as to decrease litigation costs.

The problem is that in many cases, particularly complex ones, the parties may not be able to specify fully the terms of such an agreement in advance. Agreements with respect to certain aspects of litigation—for example, limiting the number of depositions, or adopting a particular discovery schedule—may be easy to write and enforce, but it may be very difficult or expensive to specify fully a contract to "conduct a lawsuit cooperatively" or "to disclose all material information." Moreover, even if the terms can be specified, it may be very difficult to determine whether a defection has occurred. Even where a breach of such a contract is observable by the parties, a violation may be difficult to verify to a judge, thus making enforcement problematic.

. . .

... [A] judge may be no more able to ensure cooperation by enforcing general rules of procedure than by enforcing a general contract between the parties. A vague or nonspecific rule ... is easy to write, but poses potentially severe enforcement difficulties.... [B]reaches of general rules of procedure—e.g., "do not engage in burdensome discovery"— are no easier to verify than are breaches of a contract of similar specificity. In other words, a judge may have grave difficulty verifying defection even when both parties know it has occurred.

In sum, the payoff structure specified for a prisoner's dilemma seems appropriate for many disputes. Moreover, verification problems make the adequate enforcement of binding general commitments to cooperate in litigation (whether imposed by contract or rule) highly problematic. . . .

C. *Litigation as a Multi–Round Prisoner's Dilemma Game*

At first glance, litigation between principals who are unlikely to sue each other again appears to be a one-round game. However, one can view a single lawsuit as consisting of a number of strategic encounters: each discovery request, the scheduling of depositions, and each motion might be seen as a separate game between the same parties. If each of these many tactical encounters during a lawsuit has the structure of a prisoner's dilemma, does the fact that the same parties play each other on multiple occasions over the course of a single lawsuit provide an opportunity for cooperation that is not available to players in a one-round game?

[S]o long as the prisoner's dilemma game is played a known finite number of times, rational players still have no incentive to cooperate. . . . In the last round, both players recognize that there is no incentive to cooperate because the final game is identical to the one-round game described above. Now consider the next-to-last round. Because the players know that both will defect in the last round, the next-to-last round is no different from the last. Reasoning backwards round by round, the multi-round game unravels all the way back to the first round.

More recent research, however, suggests that cooperative behavior can develop in a multi-round prisoner's dilemma under certain conditions. . . .

. . . [T]here may be circumstances under which the parties can escape the prisoner's dilemma if there are significantly high prospects that they will have a large number of future dealings with each other and that they care enough about the outcomes of those future dealings. Unfortunately, [this does not describe the posture of most litigants.]

. . . [B]ecause players can locate with reasonable precision the final round of a lawsuit, unraveling may begin. . . . [Also] the strategies that induce cooperation in repeated games require that each party know after each round whether an opponent cooperated or defected. In litigation, where even cooperative behavior occurs in the context of a competitive environment, the risk of misunderstanding an opponent's move is significant. In the prisoner's dilemma, each player has only two basic moves: cooperation or defection. In litigation, there are many gray tones. . . . Was the [opponent's] action . . . a defection? Mistakes and misunderstandings can lead to conflictual outcomes even when both parties seek to follow a cooperative strategy.

II.   The Role Lawyers Might Play in Overcoming the Prisoner's Dilemma

   ... Lawyers, acting as agents, have the potential to solve the game theoretic problem of mutual defection....

A.   *The Pre–Litigation Game: Choosing Lawyers*

   Assume that both clients must litigate through a lawyer (an assumption that, for a change, is descriptively accurate). Further suppose that there exists a class of sole practitioners who have reputations for cooperation which assure that, once retained, they will conduct the litigation in a cooperative fashion. Three final assumptions define our "pre-litigation game." First, clients disclose their choice of lawyer—and thus, whether they have chosen a cooperative lawyer— prior to the beginning of the litigation game. Second, if one client chooses a cooperative lawyer and her opponent does not, the client choosing a cooperative lawyer can change her mind without cost before the litigation game begins. Third, after the litigation game begins, clients cannot change lawyers.

   Under these assumptions, disputing through lawyers provides an escape from the prisoner's dilemma. As we have defined the pre-litigation game, each client's dominant strategy is to choose a cooperative lawyer because the choice of a cooperative lawyer binds each client to a cooperative strategy. If client A chooses a cooperative lawyer and client B also chooses a cooperative lawyer, both clients receive the higher cooperative payoff. Alternatively, if client B does not choose a cooperative lawyer, client A is no worse off having initially chosen to cooperate. In that event, client A replaces her cooperative lawyer with a gladiator and is in the same position as if she had chosen a gladiator in the first instance. Thus, her dominant strategy is to choose a cooperative lawyer and to switch if her opponent does not adopt a parallel strategy. Of course, client B ... has the same dominant strategy. The result is a cooperative equilibrium because the introduction of lawyers has transformed the prisoner's dilemma payoff structure into a game in which the only choices are mutual cooperation or mutual defection. Mutual cooperation obviously has the higher payoff for each party.

   This is the easy part. Designing a game in which the players can credibly commit is not difficult if one assumes the availability of commitment techniques. What makes the game interesting from a policy perspective is the extent to which its assumptions are consistent with institutional patterns. This consistency is what interests us about lawyers as sources of credible commitments: We believe the assumptions that define the pre-litigation game are roughly consistent with the way litigation occurs.

In the pre-litigation game, we first required clients to disclose their choice of lawyer before the game began. In real litigation, plaintiffs must typically disclose their choice of lawyer at the outset of litigation: the lawyer's name is, quite literally, the first thing that appears on the complaint. Similarly, the defendant must have a lawyer to respond to the complaint, and even to request an extension of the time in which to file an answer to the complaint. Again, this discloses the identity of the lawyer chosen.

We next assumed that a plaintiff choosing a cooperative lawyer could costlessly switch to a gladiator upon learning that her opponent had chosen a gladiator. In the real world, there are costs in switching lawyers, but these costs are likely to be low at the outset. A client will have expended little on her lawyer by the time the identity of her opponent's lawyer is revealed. Thus, for practical purposes, the game's assumption of a costless opportunity to switch lawyers on the disclosure of opposing counsel is roughly consistent with real litigation patterns.[40]

The third assumption—that clients cannot change lawyers during the litigation game —is more problematic. At first glance, the assumption seems patently false ... [, but] the presence of substantial switching costs may provide a reasonable proxy for a prohibition against discharging cooperative counsel once the litigation is well underway....

... [T]he price of firing the lawyer is the cost of bringing another lawyer up to speed in the litigation. While not a prohibition on changing lawyers, switching costs impose a substantial penalty on defection....

Thus, the special assumptions underlying our pre-litigation game are not implausible. What remains, however, is the most critical of the assumptions on which lawyers' potential to facilitate cooperation de-

40. Thomas Schelling has called our attention to a possible agency problem at this stage of the pre-litigation game: how does the plaintiff know whether the lawyer chosen by the defendant is a cooperator or a gladiator. If the plaintiff has sufficient experience to make this determination herself, the game is unaffected. However, if the plaintiff must rely on the cooperative lawyer initially chosen to identify the type of lawyer chosen by the defendant, a not unrealistic assumption in many cases, the plaintiff's lawyer confronts a conflict. If the defendant chooses a gladiator and the plaintiff's cooperative lawyer so reports, the plaintiff will switch to a gladiator and the cooperative lawyer will lose the work. Hence, the cooperative lawyer may have an incentive to misrepresent the defense lawyer's type to the client in order to keep the work.

The primary barrier to the cooperative lawyer acting on this conflict is the lawyer's reputation. The cooperative lawyer's special value—why the lawyer can charge a premium—depends on truthful revelation of the defense lawyer's type; otherwise the plaintiff gets the worst outcome: the sucker's payoff where the defendant has a gladiator but the plaintiff has a cooperator. The failure to reveal truthfully the defense lawyer's type would result in the loss of the returns on the cooperative lawyer's investment in reputation. See infra text accompanying notes 149–151.

To be sure, that reputation loss requires that misrepresentation of lawyer type in the pre-litigation game be detectable and communicated to clients. However, even clients may recognize the sucker's payoff, a result consistent only with misrepresentation in the pre-litigation game. Nonetheless, we believe institutional structure can influence the lawyer's incentive to reveal truthfully the defense lawyer's type. We consider institutional strategies to facilitate truthful revelation of lawyer type infra Part IV.

pends: the existence of lawyers with reputations for cooperation. How and why are such reputations created and sustained? How do clients learn which lawyers are cooperative?

B.   A Reputation Market for Cooperative Lawyers

The preceding discussion suggests why there might be a demand for cooperative lawyers[-the higher cooperative payoffs they might bring]. Clients should therefore be willing to pay a premium for such lawyers. . . .

Establishing the supply side is also straightforward. Lawyers would be willing to invest in achieving a reputation for cooperation because they would receive a return on that investment by virtue of the premium fees clients would be willing to pay. As in standard reputation models, the lawyer's investment in reputation serves two functions. First, it identifies the lawyer as one who possesses the desired, but otherwise unobservable, attribute; the client must be able to find a cooperative lawyer. Second, it represents the penalty that the market will impose if the lawyer treats his reputation as bait rather than as bond by turning into a gladiator at the request of an opportunistic client. Noncooperative behavior would forfeit the lawyer's investment in a cooperative reputation. Thus, so long as the lawyer's possible loss of investment in reputation exceeds the size of the bribe an opportunistic client would be willing to pay, cooperative lawyers will not be suborned and a market for cooperative lawyers should be available.

However, establishing that clients would demand demonstrably cooperative lawyers and that lawyers would want to supply that service is not sufficient to assure that the market operates. The key word in the previous sentence is "demonstrably." The linchpin of this model is that the lawyer's cooperative or noncooperative behavior be observable. What makes the client's commitment credible is that her lawyer will lose his investment in reputation if he behaves noncooperatively. But this penalty cannot be imposed if the noncooperative behavior cannot be observed. Thus, the structure fails if an erstwhile cooperative lawyer can behave noncooperatively and get away with it.

. . . That misconduct be observable requires only that the party suffering the affront know with confidence that it occurred. For misconduct to be verifiable, in contrast, the party suffering the affront must be able to demonstrate to an enforcement agency, such as a court, that the misconduct occurred. The difference is important. Verification requires formal proof of misconduct sufficient to meet judicial thresholds. It is commonplace that misconduct which is observable—known to the participants—nonetheless may not be verifiable either because there is no extrinsic proof and the misbehaving party can simply deny the allegations, because the cost of verifying the misconduct is too high, or because the difficulty of defining misconduct limits the legal standard to extreme cases.[47]

In our case, noncooperative conduct by one client's lawyer may not be verifiable, but may nonetheless be readily observable by the lawyer on the other side.... A trained litigator, himself pursuing a cooperative strategy and completely familiar with the facts of the case, should be able to detect a change in the behavior of opposing counsel. After all, in litigation, noncooperative behavior by one lawyer must operate initially through its impact on the other side's lawyer. The lawyer can then pass on to the client the fact of noncooperative conduct—the reputation violation—following which both lawyer and client can impose the penalty of lost reputation on the misbehaving lawyer by distributing the information to the legal community.[49]

Thus, the conditions necessary for the operation of a reputation market for cooperative lawyers are plausible, at least at this level of abstraction.

C. Agency Problems that May Subvert Cooperation

The employment of lawyers with identifiable reputations does have the potential to facilitate cooperation between clients in litigation. However, the use of agents to make credible the commitment to cooperate itself poses two potential agency problems. First, the two lawyer-agents may "conspire" to maximize their incomes at the expense of their clients through noncooperative behavior that prolongs the litigation and increases legal fees. When each lawyer stands as gatekeeper against the other lawyer's individual noncooperative misconduct, what protects both clients from the lawyers' joint determination to behave noncooperatively? Second, a client may subvert a lawyer with a reputation for cooperation. This second problem represents the converse of the first. For a lawyer with a limited number of clients, a particular client may be so important that the threat of withdrawn patronage may induce the

47. Indeed, efforts to combat noncooperative conduct in litigation by giving the wronged party a cause of action against the party who engaged in misconduct have foundered on precisely this point. The cause of action for malicious prosecution—for bringing purely strategic litigation—is defined so narrowly as to leave most misconduct outside its scope. That has left the professionalism of lawyers as the primary barrier against such conduct. Thus, for lawyers who need only decide privately to withhold their services, the misconduct need only be observable. See Ronald J. Gilson, The Devolution of the Legal Profession: A Demand Side Perspective, 49 Md. L. Rev. 869, 88586 (1990).

49. Given the way we have defined the pre-litigation game, the information concerning the misconduct of a previously cooperative lawyer need only circulate within the community of cooperative lawyers. Recall that after the clients disclose their selection of lawyers, any client that has selected a cooperative lawyer may change counsel if her opponent has selected a gladiator. If a "cooperative" lawyer later defects, knowledge of this misconduct within the community of cooperative lawyers would impose the necessary reputational penalty if that lawyer would no longer be considered cooperative. This outcome depends on the loyalty of the nondefecting cooperative lawyer to spread the word within the community.

lawyer to risk his cooperative reputation by behaving noncooperative-ly. . . .

1. *A Conspiracy of Agents.*—While we proffer lawyers as a means to allow clients to precommit to cooperation, it is only fair to acknowledge that this idea stands current conventional wisdom on its head. . . . Most cases are settled, but not until years of contention run up large legal fees "because lawyers, who benefit most from litigation, are in control—not the clients who pay the bill."

Our model leaves room for this type of collusive behavior. . . . Noncooperative conduct that might otherwise be observable to the client may be obscured when the client's lawyer actively participates in its camouflage.[52] Lawyer collusion thus reduces the observability of misconduct and thereby threatens the structure of lawyer-mediated cooperation between clients.

2. *Giving in to Client Threats.*—The second potential problem with using sole practitioners to allow clients to precommit to cooperate results not from the lawyers' collusion against their clients, but from an individual lawyer's willingness to collude with the client. . . . The larger and more complex the matter, presumably the greater is the opportunity that exists for gain through cooperation. However, the larger and more complex the matter, the greater the percentage of a lawyer's practice it represents, and the more intimidating is a client's threat to change counsel unless the lawyer breaches his reputation. Because the opposing client would anticipate the risk of defection, in this situation the pre-litigation game might not allow for a cooperative result.

D. Law Firms and Reputational Commitments

. . .

1. *How the Law Firm Might Bond Cooperation When an Individual Lawyer Cannot.*—Because a firm may provide a larger repository of reputational capital . . . using a law firm . . . has the potential to mitigate the problem of collusion between opposing counsel. In effect, the firm pledges its reputation behind the cooperative commitment of each of its lawyers. Defection by any single lawyer in any single case may damage the entire firm's reputation for cooperation. The size of the penalty imposed on the firm for noncooperation in any single case may therefore be larger than the penalty that can be imposed against a sole practitioner for a similar defection. [Increasing the penalty for defection reduces (and may eliminate) the expected payoff from defection, thus reducing its occurrence.]

---

52. One might question how likely it is that clients would fail to observe that a game the client thought would provide a mutual cooperation payoff had been secretly converted to a mutual defection payoff, or, even worse, the sucker's payoff.

Cooperation & Conflict Between Lawyers in Litigation   427

... [Also,] because the firm allows each lawyer to invoke its entire reputation, the firm has a substantial incentive to monitor the behavior of its own lawyers....

... [Moreover, t]he [litigation] clients [of law firms] are [often] large commercial concerns ... [with] full-time in-house general counsel.... As a result, large corporate clients are more capable of observing noncooperation by opposing counsel and, as a result, the corporate client may be far less dependent on its outside lawyers to monitor opposing counsel. The opportunity for collusion between competing counsel declines as a consequence.[60]

... Large law firms [also] often have a diversified client base, with no single client or matter representing a material percentage of total firm revenues. As a result, the size and credibility of the threat posed by a client even in a large matter is reduced and so, correspondingly, is this danger to a cooperative outcome in the pre-litigation game.

2. *Agency Problems with Precommitting to Cooperation through Law Firms.*— ... While reliance upon a firm may mitigate the agency conflicts between lawyer and client, it creates new agency conflicts between the law firm and its agents—the lawyers acting on behalf of the firm....

First, law firm income-sharing rules may increase the size of the client's threat....

It has become commonplace for a law firm to divide its profits among its lawyers based on some measure of the productivity of individual lawyers. It has also become commonplace for the revenue generated by a lawyer to be treated as a proxy for his productivity, because "real" productivity is unobservable.... If an individual lawyer's income is largely a function of the number of hours billed to that lawyer's clients,

60. To the extent that a sole practitioner's finite professional life presents a barrier to precommitment to cooperation, ... a law firm may avoid the problem because of its longer life.

Even a sole practitioner could avoid the problem if the lawyer could sell his practice on retirement for a price that reflected the value of his reputation for cooperation. There would be no final period because any pre-retirement noncooperative behavior by the lawyer would result in the reduction in the sale price of his practice.... The difficulty with this neat solution is that it is very hard to transfer so intangible an asset as personal reputation.

... [L]aw firms can be understood, in effect, as a means of facilitating the intergenerational transfer of such personal reputations. Suppose that the reputation for cooperation attaches to the firm rather than the individual lawyer. Then the lawyers in the firm earn a return on their contribution to that reputation during their productive lives from two sources—the extra income the firm earns during their active years, and the amounts paid by the young lawyers for the right to share in the future returns on the firm's reputation through a reduction in the amounts young lawyers receive for their labor in their early years with the firm. By retirement, a lawyer will have been paid for his interest in the firm's reputation for cooperation, essentially having sold it to the firm's next generation of lawyers. This intra-firm sale of reputation effectively mitigates the pressure on the cooperative solution to unravel caused by the fact that individual lawyers are short-lived.

we must again measure the power of a client's threat to withdraw business not at the firm level, but at the level of the individual lawyer. Even if a client's work is quite small in relation to the firm's total revenues, it nonetheless may loom quite large with respect to the income of the individual lawyer who makes the actual litigation decisions on the firing line.

... Productivity-based profit splitting increases the incentives for collusion between opposing counsel. If the lawyers on both sides of a case are members of firms that split profits in this way, each has an interest in increasing the total billable hours of work....

... [Thus,] the individual lawyer is in a position to gain—whether through an increased share of current profits or an increased probability of ... [making partner]—from actions that risk the firm's reputational capital. And in each, the lawyer gets the bulk of the return from risking the firm's reputation, but bears only part of the loss if that risk is realized. Th[is] ... agency cost of disputing through a multiple agent entity, threatens the potential for a firm-mediated solution to the prisoner's dilemma game.

Second, client preferences may deconstruct the law firm.... The catch phrase for large clients has become that they "hire lawyers, not law firms." ... Shifting the search for reputation back to the individual from the firm potentially offsets the increase in the size of the reputational capital achieved by moving from individual to firm representation. If it is only the individual lawyer's reputation upon which the client relies, then the aggregate of the reputational capital of the lawyers in the firms does not bond the conduct of the individual lawyers.

III.   Understanding the Landscape of Litigation

... Does the prisoner's dilemma heuristic help us better understand the clear public and professional perception that the conduct of large-scale commercial litigation has dramatically deteriorated? ... [What about] a practice area in which one can observe persistent pockets of cooperation—family law practice[?] ...

A.   *Understanding the Contentiousness of Commercial Litigation*

. . .

1.   *The Changing Payoff Structure in Litigation.*— ... Recent studies have documented a dramatic increase in the amount of commercial litigation after 1970....

Over the same period, commercial litigators attested to the increasingly uncivil conduct of civil litigation. The phenomenon of discovery abuse was the most obvious manifestation.... Motion and counter-motion, each accompanied by requests for sanctions, created multiple satellite litigation that pushed the merits into the background.

The prisoner's dilemma heuristic suggests a possible link between the empirical fact of increased commercial litigation and the subjective fact that litigation behavior has become significantly more contentious.... If some commercial litigation has payoffs in which one party does not gain from mutual cooperation, such litigation would suffer from defections and be more conflictual. One or both parties would choose gladiators in the pre-litigation game even if that party knew the result would be that the other party would respond in kind.

At least some of the increase in commercial litigation stems from lawsuits in which there were no gains from cooperation.... [C]onsider the payoff to a litigation game in which one player owes the other money. As the interest rate spread increases, it becomes more likely that the defendant's dominant strategy will be noncooperation because the gains from the spread outweigh the transaction costs of conflict: the more conflictual the litigation, the longer the process takes, and the longer the defendant earns the interest rate spread. Indeed, in this game the debtor's best outcome is not the "sucker's payoff" in which the debtor acts noncooperatively and the creditor cooperatively, but "thermonuclear war" in which both sides play noncooperatively—the more conflict, the longer the delay.

This example suggests that ... [c]hanges in economic conditions or the rules concerning prejudgment interest can affect the payoff structure of commercial litigation. Some jurisdictions now have rules imposing market-level prejudgment interest in some disputes, and ... as legal fees have increased and interest rates have fallen, there may be fewer disputes in which delay so clearly serves one party's interest. Thus, it may be no coincidence that large corporations became much more interested in Alternative Dispute Resolution (ADR) in the 1980s when interest rates were falling and legal costs were increasing.

... [But then there's strategic litigation.] ... [L]itigation is strategic when it seeks not to vindicate a substantive legal right, but when the client uses it as a device to secure a business advantage by imposing costs on the opposing party. Examples include litigation brought by a target company simply to delay a hostile takeover, or trade secret litigation brought against former employees of a high technology company who leave to form a start-up venture, with the goal of creating sufficient uncertainty that financing is unavailable and the venture fails. As with strategies exploiting a positive interest rate spread, ... for one party the dominant strategy is noncooperation.

. . .

2. *The Size of the Legal Community and Reputations for Cooperation.*—Central to the potential for lawyers to facilitate a cooperative solution to a prisoner's dilemma litigation game is an effective reputation market for lawyers. Lawyers must be able to earn and maintain observable reputations for cooperation, and lawyers must be able to

observe breaches of reputation by opposing counsel and have an interest in reporting these breaches. There is reason to believe that the enormous growth in size of the large law firms ... has undermined the effectiveness of the reputation market.

. . .

... Suppose that the primary vehicle of reputation formation is a lawyer's relations with other lawyers, who then communicate that reputation to the client community....

... [R]epeated experience with the same lawyers facilitates the formation of a cooperative reputation because competing lawyers are able to factor out the noise associated with the lawyer's conduct in any particular matter.... [T]he smaller the community [of lawyers], the easier it is for lawyers to learn about the predilections of their adversaries toward cooperation.

... [I]f a lawyer can not develop a reputation for cooperation, then the dominant career strategy is noncooperation—to be a gladiator....

... [M]ost ... lawyers ... describe their personal strategy as flexible, either cooperator or gladiator, depending on how the other side plays.... [T]he picture is of a population of tit-for-tat lawyers: each cooperates until the other side defects and then retaliates. Wrapping oneself in the cloak of tit-for-tat ... [places] blame for observed conflict ... on the other lawyer—retaliation comes only after the other side defects— ... [and] it also carries a strong claim of effectiveness....

... [T]he puzzle ... [:] If litigators generally claim that they always cooperate unless the other side defects, who is left to defect first? ...

... [T]he information structure of the litigation game can explain ... [this]. Litigation is quite "noisy." Clearly identifying whether the other side has cooperated or defected in a competitive environment where cooperation is defined as being not too conflictual, is often quite difficult. For example, not all objections to discovery requests are defections.

. . .

... [There are other problems with the reputation market.] If a large law firm represents clients both in litigation in which mutual cooperation is beneficial and in litigation in which the dominant strategy for one party is to compete, reputation formation becomes much more complicated. The observation of noncooperative behavior is then consistent either with a noncooperative lawyer or noncooperative litigation.

... [B]oth aspects of noise we have considered—a mixed environment of cooperative and noncooperative litigation, and the difficulty of evaluating whether a particular action by an opponent is cooperative when the standard for cooperation is being not too competitive—make[] observation of defection more difficult.

B. Understanding the Presence of Cooperation in Family Law Practice

. . .

1. *The Payoff Structure in Divorce.*—The first step in applying the prisoner's dilemma heuristic to family law practice is analysis of the payoff structure. If lawyers are to have the potential to credibly commit their clients to cooperate, there must be gains from cooperation (and the risk of loss if the other party defects). Put in context, divorce litigation must be more than a zero-sum game in which the couple's property and children are simply divided.

. . . Both the money issues and the custody issues do have distributive elements with zero-sum characteristics. . . . [I]f a father must transfer more of his paycheck to the mother's household by way of support, there are fewer funds available to spend on himself. . . . When a child spends more time in one household, this necessarily reduces the time potentially spent in the other.

But divorce bargaining is hardly a zero-sum game in its entirety: in many circumstances, cooperation can "create value" and improve the outcome from each party's point of view. First, and most fundamentally, not all of the father and mother's interests are at odds . . . [Generally,] . . . devising an arrangement that benefits the child . . . creates joint gains for both parents. . . . Reducing the costs of divorce—financial and emotional—once again may benefit both parties. . . . [Differences in personal preferences means] ". . . there can be gains—and value created—through trades." . . .

While it is obvious that divorcing parents can sometimes themselves devise arrangements that benefit both themselves and their children, . . . the strong emotions attending divorce may pose a formidable barrier to collaborative rational problem-solving.

. . .

When inexperience, inability, or a soured relationship prevent divorcing spouses from cooperating themselves, the payoff structure of divorce proceedings may frequently take the form of the prisoner's dilemma. Cooperative divorce lawyers may therefore provide an escape: by credibly committing their clients to cooperate, the lawyers as intermediaries may be able to create gains that the spouses could not realize alone.

The potential for the sucker's payoff is also present. In the divorce process, cooperative moves by one side—if not reciprocated by the other side—may lead to exploitation. Opportunities for strategic behavior likewise exist because the parties often will not know with certainty (1) the other side's true preferences regarding the allocation of assets; (2) the other spouse's preferences or attitudes toward risk; and (3) the likely outcome in court if they do not settle their disputes. Some matrimonial lawyers are known as "bombers," or Rambo types who will defect in a variety of ways: by contesting custody on behalf of a client who is really interested in simply paying less support; by vigorously resisting the disclosure of relevant financial information; and by generally using discovery requests and responses, depositions, and motions to wear down the other side in what amounts to a war of attrition.

2. *The Institutional Structure of the Divorce Bar.*— ... [T]he institutional structure of family law practice appears to allow lawyers, at least in some instances, to create and sustain reputations for cooperation (and noncooperation). Family law practice tends to be both localized and specialized. A divorcing husband and wife usually hire attorneys in the same legal community. Increasingly, some lawyers have tended to specialize in family practice, especially in metropolitan areas. Typically, over a period of time, these local specialists repeatedly deal with one another. Through this repeated exposure lawyers can develop and sustain their reputations.

Professional organizations for family law specialists appear to facilitate this process of reputation development and maintenance. For example, the American Academy of Matrimonial Lawyers, a self-anointed elite of the family law bar, seems to exist for the principal purpose of providing an efficient reputational network among family lawyers....

. . .

A final feature of matrimonial practice may also facilitate cooperation. Unlike a commercial litigator, a family law specialist is usually not unduly dependent upon a single client for his or her livelihood. This should make it easier for a cooperative problem-solver to resist client pressure to defect after the case is underway.

We do not mean for our analysis of family law practice to suggest that matrimonial practice is exclusively or even predominantly cooperative. Instead, we use matrimonial practice to illustrate that reputational markets presently exist that permit clients to commit to cooperative strategies in circumstances in which the clients themselves might have great difficulty doing so. Our informal survey of San Francisco matrimonial specialists strongly suggests that the relationship between lawyers known to each other to have cooperative, problem-solving orientations facilitates dispute resolution.

. . .

IV.   Facilitating Cooperation

. . .

A.   *Cooperation and the Norms of Professional Conduct*

. . .

... [T]he lawyer's effort to preserve his reputation poses issues of professional conduct.... [T]he client has a strong claim to the ultimate authority on issues of strategy[, and lawyers must preserve] client's confidences. [Thus, a] lawyer's ... disclosure [that a client has chosen to switch midstream from cooperatiion to combat would appear to] conflict[] with ... professional norms. ... That leaves the lawyer with but a single response in the face of client direction to defect— ... withdrawal. But it is not clear that the ethical norms allow withdrawal under these circumstances. ...

. . .

... The risk that the lawyer cannot withdraw to avoid defection presents a serious barrier to reputation formation and, ultimately, a threat to the stability of a pre-litigation game cooperative equilibrium. If the client's selection of a cooperative lawyer is not a credible commitment to cooperate, then the lawyer-mediated solution to the litigation prisoner's dilemma unravels.

. . .

... A clear statement that the Model Rules contemplate a client's selection of a cooperative strategy, supported by the client's agreement at the time of retention to an unrestricted right of withdrawal if the lawyer subsequently disagrees with the client's strategic choices, would eliminate ... [this problem]. ...

B. Can Law Firms Develop Reputations for Providing Cooperative Services?

A striking characteristic of large commercial litigation is the absence of reputational differentiation with respect to attitudes toward cooperation among the dominant law firms. ... Law firms may include both cooperators and gladiators, and have practices that include cases in which there might be gains from cooperation and other cases in which the dominant strategy is gladiatorial. ... The overall cacophony inhibits the development of cooperative reputations for a firm as a whole.

Our analysis suggests two strategies through which law firms might develop reputations for cooperation, each of which involves noise reduction through specialization. One strategy envisions creating a boutique that only furnishes cooperative representation. The second contemplates a specialized cooperative department within a large firm. The two strategies have different advantages and drawbacks; in the end, each may be best suited to different segments of the profession. The boutique strategy is designed for lawyers forming new firms; the specialized department strategy is directed at existing large firms.

. . .

C. Reducing Noise: The Role of Professional Organizations

A professional organization might facilitate cooperation among its members and have a dramatic effect on the development of a reputational market. Imagine an organization that limited its membership to attorneys who specialized in cooperative representation. Such an organization might promulgate standards defining cooperative conduct and defection in various contexts. The organization might then certify an attorney as cooperative, but only after intensive screening and review: a number of existing members might have to vouch for the fact that the nominee had consistently behaved appropriately over an extended period of time and had never defected. The organization might also stand ready to impose sanctions—including suspension or expulsion—in order to maintain cooperative norms.

If such an organization existed, it would obviously enhance the reputation of its members: clients and lawyers alike would be invited to rely on the organization's claim that its members would engage only in cooperative litigation, and the organization and its members would have a powerful incentive to maintain the quality of its "stamp of approval." Although no such organization presently exists, the hypothetical provides a useful benchmark for exploring how the activities of existing professional groups and organizations for lawyers might well facilitate cooperation through reputational markets.

. . .

. . . [O]rganizations can facilitate the operation of reputational markets. . . . [M]embership, with or without certification . . . may increase the opportunities for repeat play within the group; litigation styles thereby become more directly observable. It may also make it easier and cheaper to impose informal sanctions for defection through gossip and reputational damage than would be true in a more atomistic world.

A second very important way that professional organizations can facilitate cooperation is by clarifying norms. In a prisoner's dilemma model, the parties either cooperate or defect, and the meaning of each move is clear. The real world is noisy: it may not be at all clear what types of behavior entail cooperation, or what moves constitute defection. One useful role for professional organizations is to clarify what cooperation or defection means in the context of particular kinds of disputes. . . .

Notes

1.   Why do Gilson & Mnookin use the term "cooperative" instead of "truthful" or "honest?" Would anything in their analysis change if the latter terms were substituted? Note that the Prisoner's Dilemma analysis assumes a simple dichotomous choice between "confess" and "remain silent." But in the context Gilson & Mnookin are analyzing, aren't there other choices?

2.   Although the authors do not make this point, their argument can be extended to conclude that litigation itself (with or without lawyers) is an attempt to solve a prisoner's dilemma problem, namely the resort to private violence as a means of dealing with disputes. Note also that settlement,

which involves a legally binding contract, is another solution to the prisoner's dilemma problem within litigation. Lawyers are not necessary for settlement, though of course they are often used to negotiate a settlement. Their function in negotiation, however, may not necessarily be to signal cooperation, but rather to use their expertise about a claim's value to make sure the client's interests are protected.

3.   Gilson & Mnookin make and defend the crucial assumption that it's easy for the plaintiff to switch lawyers at the outset of litigation. Is that really plausible? Drafting a complaint, especially in complex litigation, can be a significant undertaking, and the first lawyer might have a significant quantum meruit claim against the firing client.

4.   The authors acknowledge that many lawyers describe themselves as flexible, i.e., a cooperator or a gladiator depending on the circumstances. Lawyers don't advertise as being at either extreme. Why not?

5.   The key to the analysis is reputation. Gilson & Mnookin argue that lawyers' reputations will be tarnished if they don't cooperate because opposing counsel will "distribut[e] the information to the legal community." Although the authors call this scenario "plausible," is it really? Opposing counsel will often have a self-serving motive to tarnish another lawyer's reputation or to exaggerate how tough the other lawyer was. Even when a lawyer wins a case, it may be in her interest to mislead others about the talents and gladiator-like tactics of the other side. And, if one lawyer claims noncooperative behavior by another, the other may well retaliate by claiming that his noncooperation resulted from his opponent's misbehavior. How well will lawyers and clients who were not involved in the litigation be able to sort all this out?

6.   Gilson & Mnookin discuss the problem of collusion between lawyers as upsetting the reputation market. The collusion problem is much more likely to appear in some settings than in others. In class actions, the collusion problem is huge. Why there? See Koniak & Cohen, In Hell [Part II], p. 329. Where else is it most likely to surface?

7.   In discussing the advantage of law firms over individual lawyers, the authors cite the fact that firms often have a diversified client base. Of course, many individual lawyers have a diversified client base as well. The percentage of a large law firm's business that comes from representing one multi-national corporation may be much larger than the percentage of business that any one client's business represents to a solo practitioner. Moreover, the reputation effects for a big firm of losing a major client may substantially increase the cost to the firm of such a loss.

8.   Consider the argument that cooperation has decreased in commercial litigation because the growth of law firms has hindered the reputation mechanism necessary for their solution to work. Larry Ribstein has argued that large size improves the reputational mechanism because it increases the size of the "reputational bond" that can be forfeited if the firm's reputation is hurt. Larry E. Ribstein, Ethical Rules, Agency Costs, and Law Firm Structure, 84 Va. L. Rev. 1707 (1998). Big firm or small, we have serious doubts that the lawyer-reputation market functions (or can ever function)

well enough to affect something so dependent on other forces as the conduct of civil litigation. How well do you think the reputation market works? What might improve it?

9. The authors argue that one feature of family law practice that makes lawyers more likely to cooperate is the fact that clients are not likely to represent significant portions of their business. Of course, there are exceptions, especially for family lawyers who represent wealthy clients and who handle (whether by themselves or through their partners) other types of legal practice. But if clients are not likely to represent repeat business for the lawyers, doesn't the danger arise that the "cooperating" lawyers might collude against the interests of their unsuspecting clients, e.g., by running up the tab, or by downplaying issues that are actually very important to the parties but costly for the lawyers to pursue?

10. Gilson & Mnookin suggest that if a lawyer faces defection by the other side, the lawyer might recommend to the client to hire a gladiator as a substitute or associated counsel. They offer a similar solution to the problem of boutique cooperative firms (or cooperative departments within firms) facing a midstream defection by opposing counsel who at first postured as a cooperative type. If cooperative lawyers can hire gladiators as associated counsel midstream upon a perceived other-side defection, does that undermine the whole solution?

11. Gilson & Mnookin, like Painter, see p. 58, assume that an "opt out" world in which some lawyers adhere to one set of standards and other lawyers adhere to a second set of standards is both possible and desirable. Compare that view to the existing professional "model" of uniformity in standards (at least in theory). Does uniformity have any advantages? Cf. Zacharias, p. 83, on the fictions that are built into the ethics rules.

12. Consider the "norm clarifying" role Gilson & Mnookin posit for professional organizations. Why might we not expect them, as political bodies, to be just as likely to adopt "norm muddying" standards so as to increase membership?

Moral Character as a Professional Credential*
DEBORAH L. RHODE

... In this country, every state bar currently makes certification of character a prerequisite for practice, and most other nations and licensed professions impose a similar mandate. Yet despite the pervasiveness of these requirements, their content and implementation have attracted remarkably little serious scholarly interest....

... Through interviews with bar examiners in all fifty states, surveys of reported cases and character application forms, and interviews with selected law school administrators, this study presents the first comprehensive profile of the certification process. In addition, analysis of disciplinary actions for misconduct occurring within and outside lawyer-client professional relationships offers some insight into prevailing double standards for aspiring and admitted attorneys....

By focusing in depth on the administration of bar character mandates, this study raises certain fundamental questions about the premises and practices of our licensing structures. Throughout its history, the moral fitness requirement has functioned primarily as a cultural showpiece. In that role, it has excommunicated a diverse and changing community, variously defined to include not only former felons, but women, minorities, adulterers, radicals, and bankrupts. Although the number of applicants formally denied admission has always been quite small, the number deterred, delayed, or harassed has been more substantial. In the absence of meaningful standards or professional consensus, the filtering process has proved inconsistent, idiosyncratic, and needlessly intrusive. We have developed neither a coherent concept of professional character nor effective procedures to predict it. Rather, we have maintained a licensing ritual that too often has debased the ideals it seeks to sustain.

. . .

III.   The Certification Process Reconsidered

A.   *The Central Premises of Character Review*

... [C]ourts and commentators have traditionally identified two prophylactic objectives for the certification process. The first is safeguarding clients [and the administration of justice] from potential abuses, such as misrepresentation, misappropriation of funds, or betrayal of confidences, ... subornation of perjury, misrepresentation, bribery, or the like....

A second, although less frequently articulated, rationale for character screening rests on the bar's own interest in maintaining a professional community and public image.... As sociologists since Durkheim have argued, the concept of a profession presupposes some sense of common

* © 1985 Yale Law Journal Co. Reprinted by permission from 94 Yale L. J. 491 (1985).

identity. Excluding certain candidates on character grounds serves to designate deviance, thus establishing the boundaries of a moral community....

[Moreover,] ... certification appears to be an integral part of the general effort to legitimate the profession's regulatory autonomy and economic monopoly. The appearance of moral oversight may help both to preempt the call for external involvement in bar governance processes, and to buttress justifications for banning unregulated (and hence potentially unethical) competitors....

Even as a theoretical matter, however, this rationale for character screening remains problematic. While these professional interests help explain, they fail adequately to justify the bar's attachment to character screening. To prevent or deter individuals from entering a profession in order to promote the reputation, autonomy, or monopoly of existing members is troubling on constitutional as well as public policy grounds. Taken to its logical extreme, this rationale would support exclusion of any applicant whose conduct the local bar deemed unbecoming or likely to taint its public image. Particularly in a profession charged with safeguarding the rights of the unpopular, the price of such unbounded licensing discretion could be substantial. And it is difficult to construe the bar's parochial concerns as the kind of legitimate state interest normally required to restrain vocational choice.

In any event, as an empirical matter, it is questionable whether the certification process as currently administered inspires public confidence, and whether the system defines a moral community consistent with the profession's most enlightened instincts and ideals....

B. Structural Problems in Current Procedures

Among surveyed bar examiners, the most commonly cited problem in the certification process is the inadequacy of time, resources, staff, and sources of information to conduct meaningful character inquiries....

An inherent inadequacy in the certification process stems from the point at which oversight occurs. In essence, the current process is both too early and too late. Screening takes place before most applicants have faced situational pressures comparable to those in practice, yet after candidates have made such a significant investment in legal training that denying admission becomes extremely problematic.... Once individuals have invested three years and thousands of dollars in their legal education, many examiners are reluctant to withhold certification. That reluctance undoubtedly helps account for the low incidence of applications denied on character grounds. In 1981, in the thirty-eight jurisdictions for which statistic were available, about 6.5% of all eligible candidates, approximately 1,931 individuals, were subject to non-routine character investigation....

In the 41 states that could supply 1982 information, bar examiners declined to certify the character of approximately .2% of all eligible applicants, an estimated fifty-odd individuals. The only other empirical data available suggest that this percentage has remained relatively constant over the last quarter century. . . .

These figures cannot, however, be taken as a measure of the screening process' overall effect. Statistics on denials afford no indication of the deterrent impact of licensing procedures, an impact compounded by other structural features of the certification process. . . .

. . . [A]s some examiners pointed out, a substantial group of individuals may be deterred from applying to law school or to a particular state bar out of concern that they will not be certified. This deterrent effect is enhanced by the general lack of information concerning certification criteria and administration. Only three states have published policies or guidelines on the specific types of conduct that prompt investigation, and no jurisdiction issues statistics on the number of character investigations or denials of certification. With relatively few exceptions, definitive advance rulings by character committees are also unavailable. . . .

C. Substantive Problems in Character Assessment

1. The Subjectivity of Admission Standards

As the most recent Bar Examiners' Handbook candidly concedes: 'No definition of what constitutes grounds for denial of admission on the basis of faulty character exists.' On the whole, judicial attempts to give content to the standard have been infrequent and unilluminating. . . . [For example] in *Konigsberg v. State Bar of California*, the [Supreme] Court focused on whether a "reasonable man could fairly find that there were substantial doubts about [the applicant's] honesty, fairness and respect for the rights of others and for the laws of the state and nation."[176] . . . The difficulty, of course, is that reasonable men can readily disagree about what conduct would raise substantial doubts, a point amply demonstrated by the divergence of views among judges, bar examiners, and law school administrators. . . .

2. The Idiosyncracies of Implementation

[Data from bar screening authorities demonstrated little consensus among the states as to what forms of conduct were most likely to prove disqualifying].

. . .

A threshold difficulty in applying character standards stems from the inclusiveness of 'disrespect for law' as a ground for excluding applicants. The conventional view has been that certain illegal acts— regardless of the likelihood of their repetition in a lawyer-client relation-

---

176. . . . 353 U.S. 252, 264 (1957) . . .

ship—evidence attitudes toward law that cannot be countenanced among its practitioners; to hold otherwise would demean the profession's reputation and reduce the character requirement to a meaningless pretense. The difficulty, of course, is that this logic licenses inquiry into any illegal activity, no matter how remote or minor, and could justify excluding individuals convicted of any offense that affronted the sensibilities of a particular court or character committee. In fact, bar inquiry frequently extends to juvenile offenses, ... parking violations, and [civil disobedience, while] conduct warranting exclusion has been thought to include traffic convictions and cohabitation.

... Violation of a fishing license statute ten years earlier was sufficient to cause one local Michigan committee to decline certification. But, in the same state, at about the same time, other examiners on the central board admitted individuals convicted of child molesting and conspiring to bomb a public building.

Decisions concerning drug and alcohol offenses have proven particularly inconsistent. Convictions for marijuana are taken seriously in some jurisdictions and overlooked in others; much may depend on whether the examiner has, as one put it, grown more 'mellow' towards 'kids smoking pot.' ...

Attitudes toward sexual conduct such as cohabitation or homosexuality reflect similar diversity. Some bar examiners do not regard that activity as "within their purview," unless it becomes a "public nuisance" or results in criminal charges.... In other jurisdictions ... cohabitation and homosexuality can trigger extensive inquiry and delay, and some slight possibility of denial. In the remaining states, examiners reported few applications presenting evidence of "living in sin" or homosexuality. According to one Board of Bar Examiners president, "Thank God we don't have much of that [in Missouri]." How these individuals would view such conduct if brought to their attention remains unclear....

Not only does the 'disrespect for law' standard invite inconsistencies in application, it permits a hierarchy of concerns that are at best tenuously related to the primary justification for character review—protecting the public. It bears note that the conduct generating the greatest likelihood of investigation was unauthorized practice of law: Eighty-four percent of all jurisdictions would inquire into such activity, and it was the second most likely offense to preempt admission. Yet as some examiners implicitly acknowledged, such misconduct, by definition, could not recur after certification. And it is doubtful that the general public would view most lay legal assistance as evidencing serious and generalizable moral deficiencies....

...

Other major areas of concern to courts and bar committees have been psychological instability, financial irresponsibility, and radical political involvement, although again attitudes vary widely as to the significance of particular conduct. For example, ... the bar applications of some jurisdictions make no inquiries as to mental health; others require a psychiatrist's certificate and in some cases an examination for candidates who have a history of treatment.... The Nevada Supreme Court does not consider mental illness a ground for denial, while Wyoming, Arizona, and Illinois have excluded applicants evidencing 'religious fanaticism,' personality disorders involving 'hypersensitivity, unwarranted suspicion, and excessive self-importance,' or a 'propensity to unreasonably react' to perceived opposition.

Financial mismanagement provokes comparable disagreement. Most jurisdictions (73%) make no inquiries concerning debts past due, while others demand detailed information ranging from parking fines to child support obligations....

. . .

A final context in which decisionmaking has proven [highly subjective] concerns candidates' apparent attitudes toward their prior conduct and committee oversight. Arrogance, 'argumentativeness,' 'rudeness,' 'excessive immatur[ity],' 'lackadaisical' responses, or intimations that a candidate is 'not interested in correcting himself' can significantly color character assessments.

. . .

... Invocations of a 'higher personal ethic' or protestations of innocence are generally inadvisable. Accordingly, Michigan's bomber was admitted to the bar, despite several years in a maximum security facility, while North Carolina's unconfessed 'peeping Tom' was thought too great a public threat to be certified....

... [Some] courts and committees appear to assume that 'a leopard never changes its spots'; neither civic involvements nor 'self-serving statements' of remorse will adequately atone for certain sins. But whichever position they adopt on this point, bar decisionmakers are all operating on one shared empirical premise. Their common assumption is that certain attitudes and actions are sufficiently predictive of subsequent misconduct to justify the costs of certification procedures. Yet as the following sections suggest, that premise is empirically unsupported and flatly at odds with the disciplinary process as currently administered.

IV.   The Disciplinary Process

[The public interest would seem to demand greater disciplinary oversight for abuses committed within a lawyer-client relationship than for offenses occurring prior to bar admission.] ... Yet the bar's administration of admission and disciplinary processes has yielded precisely [the reverse] ...; both substantive and procedural requirements are more solicitous of practitioners than applicants....

... Except in the most egregious cases, the bar has always been disinclined to cast out a colleague for abuses within a lawyer-client relationship....

...

The disparity between entry and exclusionary standards raises a number of awkward questions about the current scope of certification procedures. If certain nonprofessional conduct is sufficiently probative to withhold a license, why is it not also grounds for license revocation? As long as bar members are unwilling to monitor their colleagues' parking violations, psychiatric treatment, and alimony payments, what justifies their reliance on such evidence in screening applicants? Insofar as the profession is truly committed to public-rather than self-protection, the incongruity between disciplinary and certification procedures is untenable.

That is not, however, to imply that stricter proctoring of nonprofessional offenses by practitioners would be desirable....

V.   The Predictive Power of Prior Conduct

...

Over the past half century, a vast array of social science research has failed to find evidence of consistent character traits. Hartshorn and May's seminal STUDIES IN THE NATURE OF CHARACTER found so little relationship among conduct reflecting children's honesty, integrity, and self-control that the authors concluded that moral behavior was more a function of specific habits and contexts than of any general attributes. Lying and cheating were essentially uncorrelated, and even the slightest change in situational variables dramatically altered tendencies toward deceit; one could not predict cheating in one class on the basis of cheating in another.... While subsequent studies have not been entirely conclusive, most ... suggest that ... [someone] with a "truly generalized conscience ... is a statistical rarity." Although individuals clearly differ in their responses to temptation, contextual pressures have a substantial effect on moral conduct independent of any generalized predisposition....

Although empirical evidence on lawyers' ethics is fragmentary, it also suggests that situational pressures play a critical role in shaping normative commitments and conduct. As Jerome Carlin's study of the Manhattan bar and Joel Handler's research on small town practitioners make clear, an attorney's willingness to violate legal or professional rules depends heavily on the exposures to temptation, client pressures, and collegial attitudes in his practice setting.

...

The situational nature of moral conduct makes predictions of behavior uncertain under any circumstances, and the context of bar decision-making presents particular difficulties. A threshold problem springs from the inherent limitations of clinical predictive techniques, i.e., those based on non-statistical information. Even trained psychiatrists, psychologists, and mental health workers have been notably unsuccessful in projecting future deviance, dishonesty, or other misconduct on the basis of similar prior acts....

. . .

... [Moreover,] not only do examiners and judges generally lack clinical expertise, they are dealing with highly circumscribed data. Decisionmakers are frequently drawing inferences about how individuals will cope with the pressures and temptations of uncertain future practice contexts based on one or two prior acts committed under vastly different circumstances. Yet, as just noted, a half century of behavioral research underscores the variability and contextual nature of moral behavior: A single incident or small number of acts committed in dissimilar social settings affords no basis for reliable generalization. Neither common sense nor common experience suggest that those who have violated drug laws or avoided military service are likely to commit professional abuses, or that applicants who on occasion have mismanaged their own financial affairs are destined to become comminglers....

. . .

Thus, the inherent limitations in predicting moral behavior, coupled with the subjectivity of bar standards, leave substantial room for error....

VI.   The Costs of Moral Oversight

A.   *The Misdirection of Resources*

Taken as a whole, the current certification process is an extraordinarily expensive means of providing a dubious level of public protection.... For the vast majority of candidates, the certification process is a highly burdensome mechanism for identifying the tiny number of individuals with serious offenses.... [B]ar applications generally demand an extended array of personal information and supplemental documentary submissions, [and personal references]....

... Such requirements generate an enormous paper flow, which is time consuming for all concerned and ill-designed to generate useful information....

. . .

... A critical question ... is whether resources now directed toward predicting future misconduct would be better expended in identifying and responding to the abuses that actually occur. The merits of that alternative focus must also be evaluated in light of certain other costs of moral oversight. To the extent that prevailing certification procedures legitimate the bar's regulatory autonomy or deflect attention from its sorry record in policing practitioners, the system ill serves its primary prophylactic objectives. . . .

B. First Amendment Concerns

Throughout this century, the moral character requirement has placed a price on nonconformist political commitments. Conscientious objectors, religious 'fanatics,' suspected subversives, and student radicals have been exhaustively investigated, frequently delayed, and occasionally denied admission. . . .

. . .

By penalizing a show of character in proceedings nominally designed to detect it, the bar has enshrined a morality manqué. To view subservience to authority as a requisite for virtue is to ignore a history rich in counter-examples. American ideals of liberty, equality, and dignity have sometimes found their highest expression in peaceful defiance of legal mandates. Abolitionists, civil rights activists, suffragists and labor organizers—indeed, the architects of our constitutional framework—all were guilty of 'disrespect for law' in precisely the sense that bar examiners employ it. As long as that criterion remains an indice of moral merit, the certification process will exemplify a commitment to conformity that makes a mockery of the bar's highest traditions.

C. Due Process Values

As the Supreme Court has long recognized, pursuit of a chosen vocation is one of the core liberties protected by the due process clause of the Fifth and Fourteenth Amendments. Accordingly, certification and disciplinary procedures must satisfy the requirements of specificity and regularity that give content to those constitutional guarantees. In addition, the scope of bar inquiry into personal affairs implicates concerns of privacy and substantive rationality that are also subject to due process constraints. The significance of these constitutional issues cannot be assessed solely or even primarily in doctrinal terms. As a policy matter, the societal values from which due process mandates draw should inform any judgments about the legitimacy of current character proceedings.

1. Vagueness

. . .

On its face, the bar's character requirement is—in Justice Black's phrase—'unusually ambiguous,' and court and committee amplification have done little to refine analysis. Prevailing definitions of virtue are circular or conclusory, and there is broad disagreement regarding particular conduct within and across jurisdictions. . . . Given such inconsistencies in application, the standard scarcely affords adequate notice of 'conduct to avoid' or of the professional consequences of prior activities....

Moreover, current certification structures have proven largely unresponsive to those indeterminacies. Only a tiny percentage of disputed cases generate written opinions by either courts or bar examiners, and not all bar decisions are readily available. Only three states have published policies regarding the types of conduct that would prompt investigation; the general assumption, as the California Board candidly concedes, is that no 'meaningful guidelines can be stated.' ...

. . .

Most certification processes operate without any formal boundaries on their scope of inquiry. Only about a fifth of the sampled states apply rules of evidence or formal constraints on questions examiners are authorized to ask. In general, committee inquiry ranges as broadly as members wish, and hearings may last anywhere from fifteen minutes to ten days. In all but one sampled jurisdiction, these hearings are not necessarily restricted to the areas that triggered review.

[This] undisciplined scope of inquiry opens ... opportunities for capricious and prejudicial inferences from [information about highly private matters.] ...

VII. Alternatives

. . .

The current administration of moral character criteria is, in effect, a form of Kadi justice with a procedural overlay. Politically non-accountable decisionmakers render intuitive judgments, largely unconstrained by formal standards and uninformed by a vast array of research that controverts the premises on which such adjudication proceeds. This process is a costly as well as empirically dubious means of securing public protection. Substantial resources are consumed in vacuous formalities for routine applications, and non-routine cases yield intrusive, inconsistent, and idiosyncratic decisionmaking. Examiners generally lack the resources, information, and techniques to predict subsequent abuses with any degree of accuracy. Only a minimal number of applicants are permanently excluded from practice, and the rationale for many of those exclusions is highly questionable.

. . .

... As currently implemented, the moral fitness requirement both subverts and trivializes the professional ideals it purports to sustain. In seeking to express our aspirations, such rituals succeed only in exposing our pretenses. While hypocrisy is often the bow vice pays to virtue, better forms of tribute may be available.

Notes

1.   Did you know about the moral character evaluation before coming to law school? Rhode critiques the timing of the character assessment, noting that it does not occur until the applicant has made a substantial investment in legal education. Should law school applicants have to undergo character assessment before matriculating? That would certainly be costly, especially if the applicants had to be assessed again upon graduation from law school. Would the second evaluation be important? Should law schools have to warn matriculating students of the character assessment process and detail some of the activities that might raise concerns?

2.   At several points in this book, we and various authors have compared lawyers to other professionals. Why don't other professionals require their members to satisfy a moral character requirement as a condition of certification? Is character less important for, say, teachers, doctors, journalists, business executives, government officials?

3.   If the bar is going to evaluate character, why not focus on people of extraordinary character? Why not, for example, ask law schools to nominate some top percentage of virtuous students for special commendation? To what end?

4.   If character assessment comes too early in a young (or soon-to-be) lawyer's career, i.e., before she has had to face the pressures and temptations of practice, why not have a probationary period for all newly minted lawyers (or alternatively for lawyers whose backgrounds raise sufficient concerns), during which any lawyer or client (and perhaps others who come in close professional contact) could submit negative or positive character assessments to the relevant bar committee? Does this idea seem frightening? Why?

5.   This article was published before passage of the Americans with Disabilities Act. How might that Act (or should the law) affect the character assessments described by Rhode?

6.   Can you think of any reasons why applicants for the bar should (or do) face stricter scrutiny of their character than practitioners? Consider that courts often exclude character evidence (or evidence of prior bad acts) even though people often make predictive judgments such as hiring or investment decisions based on such evidence. Indeed, under the securities laws, withholding information of relevant bad acts by a controlling manager might well be securities fraud.

7.   Why don't law firms pay more attention to the moral character of their applicants (or do they)?

8.   In recent years, the most famous denial of bar admission based on character involves Matthew Hale, an advocate of white supremacy, who was denied admission to the Illinois state bar. In his bar application and hearings before the character committee Hale frankly admitted his racist and anti-Semitic views, his past activities in support of these views and his intention to work to reform the law to coincide with these views. He also said that he

would have no trouble taking the oath of admission to abide by and uphold the law and Constitution. Hale had some mostly minor run-ins with the law on his record all related to his activist role, but had not been convicted of any crime greater than violating a public ordinance. The character committee said it was not his "criminal" record that demanded denying his admission, noting that many have been admitted to the bar who have had more serious legal violations on their records. The character committee found that "Hale's active commitment to bigotry under 'any civilized standards of decency' demonstrated a 'gross deficiency in moral character, particularly for lawyers who have a special responsibility to uphold the rule of law for all persons.'" Hale v. Committee on Character & Fitness for Illinois, 335 F.3d 678 (7th Cir.2003) (describing the Illinois committee's decision and holding that federal district court had no jurisdiction to review the Illinois state court's decision upholding that standard).

Hale appealed to the Illinois Supreme Court, arguing, *inter alia*, that the denial on these grounds violated the First Amendment. The Illinois Supreme Court rejected the appeal. The United States Supreme Court denied Hale's petition for certiorari. Hale then sued, alleging his civil rights had been violated, but the Seventh Circuit in the opinion just cited held that for a district court to hear the case would amount to the federal courts hearing an appeal from a state court proceeding, something the federal courts do not have jurisdiction to do. Hale's remedy, if any, would have to come in state court, said the federal court of appeals. Is the active advocacy of racist views, as the Illinois committee believed, so antithetical to the commitment to equal protection, the Bill of Rights and the Constitution that it is proper to deny bar admission on these grounds? Is the nexus, in other words, between these beliefs and the job Hale was applying to do (lawyering) so close as to make it legitimate for the government to consider these views?

Matthew Hale was the leader of a group that called itself the World Church of the Creator. He and his church were sued for trademark infringement for using that name and the first encounter between the Seventh Circuit and Mr. Hale involved that suit. The Seventh Circuit ordered Hale to rename his group. As the Seventh Circuit noted in throwing out his civil rights challenge to the character committee, early in 2003, "Hale was arrested for conspiring to kill the district court judge presiding in the trademark infringement case." Hale was being held without bond on that charge when the federal court decided that it had no jurisdiction to hear his bar admission challenge.

Professional Discipline for Law Firms?*
TED SCHNEYER

. . .

Disciplinary agencies have always taken individual lawyers as their targets. They have never proceeded against law firms either directly, for breaching ethics rules addressed to them, or vicariously, for the wrongdoing of firm lawyers in the course of their work. The traditional focus on individuals has probably resulted from the system's jurisdictional tie to licensing, which the state requires only for individuals, and from the system's development at a time when solo practice was the norm.

Legal practice, however, has changed. While as late as 1951, sixty percent of the bar practiced alone, two-thirds now work in law firms and other organizations; in addition, more lawyers in private practice now work in firms than as sole practitioners. Law firms themselves have also changed. As a result of internal growth and mergers, the top 100 law firms now account for nearly twenty percent of all legal fees. While only thirty-eight American law firms had more than fifty lawyers in the late 1950s, by 1986 over 500 firms did so and over 250 had more than 100 lawyers. As of 1984, 95 of the 100 largest firms had at least one branch office. Branching has made intrafirm coordination both more difficult and more important. Firms have also become highly leveraged—that is, the ratio of relatively inexperienced associates to partners has risen as high as four-to-one. The proportionally larger number of inexperienced lawyers within firms has heightened the need for supervision.

As law firms have grown, firm governance has become more complex. A few large firms may still govern themselves the old-fashioned ways—either as a patriarchy ruled by a single senior partner or as a loose collection of nearly independent practitioners. But most firms now recognize the limits of individual partner control in the face of extensive personal liability for firm malpractice and have adopted a variety of bureaucratic controls to limit their exposure: policy manuals, formal rules, committees, specialized departments, and centralized management. . . .

. . .

Proceedings against lawyers in large or even medium-sized firms are very rare. In 1981–82, for example, more than eighty percent of the lawyers disciplined in California, Illinois, and the District of Columbia were sole practitioners, and none practiced in a firm with over seven lawyers. Yet, judging from the frequency with which larger firms and their lawyers are the targets of civil suits, motions to disqualify, and sanctions under the rules of civil procedure, disciplinable offenses occur with some regularity in those firms. Some observers attribute the

* © 1992 Cornell Law Review. Reprinted by permission from 77 Cornell L. Rev. 1 (1991).

paucity of disciplinary actions against larger-firm lawyers to an informal immunity from disciplinary scrutiny that those lawyers, as the most prestigious segment of the bar, supposedly enjoy. Others point out that the types of misconduct that most often generate grievances and disciplinary sanctions—neglect of cases and misappropriation of client property, respectively—occur much more often in small practices than in larger firms. Still others cite the reactive nature of disciplinary enforcement; the authorities do not normally investigate until clients (or, occasionally, nonclients) complain about a lawyer's conduct. On this theory, the businesses that predominate on the client lists of large firms rarely report complaints against their lawyers.... [R]egular business clients ... may instead rely on their ability to take their business elsewhere to protect them.[49]

These factors may help to explain the infrequency of disciplinary proceedings against large-firm lawyers, but additional explanations, so far neglected, have important implications for disciplinary policy. These explanations stem from the nature of group practice. First, even when a firm has clearly committed wrongdoing, courts may have difficulty, as an evidentiary matter, in assigning blame to particular lawyers, each of whom has an incentive to shift responsibility for an ethical breach onto others in the firm. Many, perhaps most, of the tasks performed in large firms are assigned to teams. Teaming not only encourages lawyers to take ethical risks they would not take individually, but also obscures responsibility, which makes it difficult for both complainants and disciplinary authorities to determine which lawyers committed a wrongful act.[52] ...

Second, even when courts and disciplinary agencies can link professional misconduct to one or more lawyers in a firm as an evidentiary matter, they may be reluctant to sanction those lawyers for fear of making them scapegoats for others in the firm who would have taken the same actions in order to further the firm's interests....

Third and most important, a law firm's organization, policies, and operating procedures constitute an "ethical infrastructure" that cuts across particular lawyers and tasks.... But who ... [is developing] the appropriate infrastructure? ... To varying degrees this remains every partner's business—and sometimes, as a result, no one's. In no aspect of law firm work is teaming, and thus collective responsibility, more important than in the development of firm structure, policy, and procedures.

... [Thus,] a disciplinary regime that targets only individual lawyers in an era of large law firms is no longer sufficient. Sanctions against firms are needed as well.

49. Large business clients may have so much leverage over their law firms that wrongdoing in large firms is more likely to victimize third parties than clients....

52. Disciplinary agencies, having no authority to proceed against law firms as such, sometimes insist that a complainant specify which lawyers in a firm committed the alleged wrongdoing before they will process a complaint....

. . .

I. The Emerging Status of Law Firms as Appropriate Disciplinary Targets

. . .

A. *Prophylactic Ethics Rules*

The chief reason to allow disciplinary authorities to proceed directly against law firms is prophylaxis—the promotion of firm practices that prevent wrongdoing by individual lawyers. Modern ethics rules already require lawyers to take certain prophylactic measures to prevent misconduct. For example, . . . the Model Rules forbid lawyers to commingle client funds with their own and require lawyers to place client funds in trust accounts. They do so not because commingling is itself an evil, but largely because commingling tempts lawyers to treat client funds as their own.

. . .

B. *Firm–Directed Ethical Norms*

A second and more curious point about modern ethics rules is that occasionally they directly address law firms. The Model Code of Professional Responsibility (CPR), adopted by the ABA in 1969 and still in effect in some states, contains several rules of this type.[87] . . . [Schneyer mentions DR2–102(A); DR3–102(A); DR7–107, and DR9–102(A).]

Since only licensed individuals are now subject to professional discipline, these rules . . . seem odd. . . . Yet the rules may not be mere slips of the professional tongue. They have a common theme: each rule deals with matters that in law firms require collective action or at least collective acquiescence. . . .

C. *Ethics Rules on Matters of Law Firm Governance*

. . . [The] ABA Model Rules of Professional Conduct, . . . also . . . regulate matters of law firm governance that bear on ethical compliance. These rules, themselves prophylactic in nature, so far are addressed only to individual lawyers. . . .

Of special interest here is Model Rule 5.1(a), which . . . requires [partners and other lawyers with managerial authority in a law firm] to "make reasonable efforts to ensure that the firm has in effect measures giving reasonable assurance that all lawyers in the firm conform to the

---

87. One also finds professional standards addressed to practice entities and not just to individual lawyers in the ABA STANDARDS FOR CRIMINAL JUSTICE. See, e.g., 1 ABA STANDARDS FOR CRIMINAL JUSTICE, Standard 5–4.3 (2d ed. 1980) (public defender organizations should reject added cases that will necessitate inadequate representation). While this Article focuses on bringing private law firms under the jurisdiction of disciplinary agencies, the rationale for doing so extends to other practice entities such as prosecutors' offices, legal services offices and corporate law departments.

rules of professional conduct." ... At least in large firms, partners might be expected under Model Rule 5.1(a) to adopt such structural arrangements as an ethics committee to which lawyers could confidentially refer ethics problems and a new-business committee to detect potential conflicts of interest. The partners might be expected to adopt such policies as a ban on accepting new matters without approval by the new-business committee. They might also be expected to use computer programs with sophisticated databases as a procedure for identifying both potential conflicts of interest and billing irregularities, as well as an office "tickler" system to keep track of court dates.

Although the importance of an ethical infrastructure would seem to vary directly with firm size, the prospects for using Model Rule 5.1(a) as an effective tool for promoting the appropriate infrastructure are likely to vary inversely with size. The prospects are best where small firms are involved....

With ... still larger firms, Model Rule 5.1(a) has so far been a disciplinary dead letter. So long as the rule's up-to-date recognition of the importance of firm infrastructure is tied to the horse-and-buggy of individual discipline, the rule seems likely to remain so....

... Disciplinary authorities may have difficulty pinning ... structural defect[s] on particular partners (even on a managing partner), and they may be reluctant to try, for fear of scapegoating some lawyers for sins shared by others. Thus, authorities probably would not proceed against L or any other individual partner, even if Hazard and Hodes's assertion that Model Rule 5.1(a) offers a theoretical basis for doing so is correct. Accordingly, if we are to use professional discipline to encourage L's firm to adopt a conflict-avoidance program, and, more generally, if we are to pursue the regulatory aims of Model Rule 5.1(a) in the very firms where such programs are most important, then we may have to give disciplinary authorities the options of fining or censuring the firm or putting it on probation.

D. The Growing Use of Firm–Appropriate Disciplinary Sanctions

Before 1970, many states used disbarment or suspension from practice as their chief disciplinary sanction. A system of law firm discipline could never rely heavily on analogous sanctions. Unless the violation reflected a chronic pattern of serious misconduct, dissolving a law firm or temporarily shutting its doors would be inappropriate. Not only would dissolution generally deal too harshly with a firm's entire legal and nonlegal staff, it might also be ineffective. The dissolved firm could simply open shop under a new name with slightly different personnel.

... [But] sanctions that are quite appropriate for law firms—private reprimand, public censure, probation, and restitution—are now common.

. . .

The post–1970 development of probation as a sanction illustrates the shift toward a disciplinary philosophy compatible with firmwide discipline.... Probation is used "to help lawyers who have violated the disciplinary rules, but whose conduct likely can be corrected so that they can continue to serve the public." It is often used in cases where attorneys have neglected files or maintained inadequate books and records. To minimize the disciplinary agency's burden in overseeing probations, supervising lawyers may be appointed to monitor a probationer's practice.... From this arrangement, it would take no great leap to impose conditional probation on a firm whose monitoring practices have been proven deficient within the meaning of Model Rule 5.1(a), as that rule might be extended to cover law firms.

. . .

II. The Analogy to Corporate Criminal Liability: the Uses of Institutional Responsibility

In recent years, society has come to rely heavily on collective criminal sanctions to shape the activity of private organizations, and especially business corporations.... Were it not for the common use of special disciplinary systems to regulate law practice and certain other professions, one suspects that the criminal law would be more widely used to regulate law firms and other professional entities.[138] ...

. . .

C. Two Categories of Corporate Criminal Liability

1. Firm–Directed Standards

Two varieties of corporate criminal liability are of particular note in evaluating whether to implement a system of law firm discipline. First, some penal statutes directly address corporations and impose liability for failure to discharge a "specific duty of affirmative performance," such as a duty to file reports with an administrative agency. Taking this approach, a system of law firm discipline might address to law firms those ethics rules that implicate centralized firm functions, such as rules dealing with the handling of client funds, files, and property. It might

---

138. A few penal statutes target law firms. Under the Insider Trading and Securities Fraud Enforcement Act of 1988, Pub. L. No. 100–704 § 1, 102 Stat. 4677 (1988), for example, law firms, as "controlling persons," can become civilly or criminally liable for insider trading violations by their employees. ... Law firms are advised to adopt written procedures and an ongoing monitoring system to avoid such liability. More characteristically, Congress has been reluctant to regulate law practice through criminal law, largely on the ground that lawyers are already regulated at the state level in a specialized disciplinary system. In 1983, Senator Arlen Specter introduced a bill to amend the federal Mail Fraud Act, 18 U.S.C. § 1341 to require lawyers to "blow the whistle" on clients who intend to commit economic crimes; this whistleblowing would have been inconsistent with the lawyer's duty of confidentiality under the then pending Model Rules of Professional Conduct. See S. 485, 98th Cong., 1st Sess., 129 Cong. Rec. 51219 (1983). After ABA leaders testified that lawyers should be regulated primarily at the state level and by courts, this bill died in committee....

also address directly to law firms prophylactic ethics rules dealing with matters of ethical infrastructure; these rules might include a provision such as Model Rule 5.1(a). The disciplinary system might go even further down this road and give specific content to the "reasonable efforts" standard of Model Rule 5.1(a) by, for example, requiring law firms over a certain size to have new-business and ethics committees.

. . .

On the other hand, . . . [g]iven the enormous range in law firm size, as well as the structural diversity that exists among firms of comparable size, few specific monitoring practices are likely to be worthwhile in all firms. Only when a monitoring practice is obviously worthwhile and could be imposed on a sufficiently uniform set of firms should it be crystallized into a disciplinary rule.

2.   Respondent Superior

The second relevant type of corporate criminal liability is respondeat superior. Under federal law, organizations are liable for crimes committed by agents who act within the scope of their employment and with the intention of serving organizational interests. These organizations are vicariously liable for their agents' job-related crimes, even when an agent acts without the knowledge or authorization of management and even if management has forbidden the conduct in question. Moreover, the government need not prove that any specific agent acted illegally, but only that some agent committed the underlying crime. Thus, when a corporation is prosecuted on this theory, no individual codefendants are needed. Even when they exist, if a jury convicts the corporation but acquits the individuals, the conviction will stand. Furthermore, a corporation is deemed to have acquired the collective knowledge of its employees; it cannot avoid a guilty verdict by showing that the relevant knowledge "was not acquired by any one individual employee who then would have comprehended its full import."

The case for vicarious corporate criminal liability extends to disciplinary liability for law firms. Authorizing vicarious discipline for law firms when someone in the firm has committed an ethical infraction would enable a court or agency to impose discipline even when it cannot practically determine who committed the underlying offense or it is reluctant to proceed against specific lawyers because such action would amount to scapegoating. If a disciplined firm then considered it important to assign individual blame for the underlying infraction, it could do so on the basis of its own internal investigation. . . .

Some commentators argue that blameworthiness should always be a prerequisite to criminal liability and that an entity cannot be blamed when it has taken reasonable steps to prevent wrongdoing by its agents. These commentators would allow a corporation to show as an affirmative

defense in criminal cases based on respondeat superior (though not in civil suits, where compensation is involved) that it had implemented "reasonable safeguards designed to prevent [the underlying] crimes."
. . .

. . . This defense avoids the overdeterrence that might result if sanctions were imposed on law firms which had already taken all cost-justified precautions to promote ethical behavior. . . .

. . . In the context of law firm discipline, a major drawback of the due diligence defense is that the decisionmaker would have to determine in each case whether a firm had exercised due diligence. These determinations may often be expensive and unreliable[.] . . . Although disciplinary agencies . . . might eventually become experts on law firm operations and the meaning of due diligence, it seems wiser for now to give the agencies the option of subjecting law firms to vicarious discipline for their lawyers' job-related ethical infractions and to give the firms the discretion to then decide whether to abandon a questionable policy or develop new monitoring programs. For example, if a firm was disciplined because an associate had padded her hours, the firm could decide for itself whether its policy of requiring associates to bill 2300 hours a year posed unacceptable ethical risks.

Alternatively, disciplinary agencies could allow a firm to show that it was exercising due diligence (even if it only began to do so after the underlying infraction occurred), not for purposes of exoneration, but in order to determine the appropriate sanction. . . .

D. Corporate Criminal Sanctions

The criminal sanctions that are recognized as appropriate for convicted corporations can easily be converted into a sensible scheme of disciplinary sanctions for law firms. . . .

1. Fines and Restitution

Convicted corporations must often make restitution to their victims, as must lawyers in the disciplinary process. Restitution, however, is sometimes not feasible; and in any event, restitution alone would insufficiently deter misconduct because it fails to reflect the fact that wrongdoing often goes undetected or unpunished. As a result, the vast majority of corporate sentences include fines. . . .

Fines have traditionally not been authorized as a disciplinary sanction for lawyers. The Standards for Lawyer Disciplinary and Disability Proceedings reject fines because they are "punitive and criminal in nature" and "would erroneously imply that [disciplinary] proceedings are criminal and require proof beyond a reasonable doubt, trial by jury, and other standards of criminal due process." This seems a very flimsy reason for rejecting fines as a disciplinary sanction. Lawyers, after all, are already subject to sanctions in the nature of fines for breaching the

Federal Rules of Civil Procedure or improperly preparing tax returns, and are not afforded criminal due process protections in either of these instances. Moreover, the Canadian and English legal professions, as well as the American nonlegal professions, use fines as disciplinary sanctions.

... Regardless of whether fines should be imposed on individual lawyers, they should play a role in the disciplining of law firms, which as a practical matter, cannot be disbarred or suspended, are more capable of paying fines, and are, like corporations, attentive to the bottom line. Fines could also help to defray any additional cost the disciplinary system incurred by taking jurisdiction over law firms.

2. Adverse Publicity

... Adverse publicity works as a sanction by tarnishing a company's reputation among customers and in the business community.... [C]orporate executives are often more concerned about the loss of corporate prestige from adverse publicity than about paying a fine....

One might argue that adverse corporate or law firm publicity is ... redundant ... when a corporate agent is also convicted of a crime or when an individual law firm member is publicly disciplined.... If, however, the convicted official or disciplined lawyer is regarded as simply a "bad apple," the opprobrium attached to that official may not tarnish her firm. Moreover, public reports of individual sanctions may not even link the individual to her organization.... With respect to lawyer wrongdoing, press reports may mention the wrongdoer's firm, but firm spokesmen often distance the firm from the wrongdoer and limit the reputational damage to the firm by claiming that the individual acted alone and in violation of firm procedures....

... [In addition] concerns have ... been expressed about [the use of social ridicule as a sanction and] the civil liberty implications of forcing organizations to adversely publicize themselves.

The concern about social ridicule is that adverse publicity, because it relies heavily on "shaming," smacks of the pillory and is thus at odds with modern sentencing philosophy....

As a disciplinary sanction for law firms, public censure, long used against individual lawyers, has all the attractions of adverse publicity as a criminal sanction and none of its drawbacks. On the upside, law firms would presumably be quite sensitive to the threat of public censure.... Law firms ... rely more heavily than sole practitioners on the "brand" loyalty of repeat clients who may be scared away by adverse publicity. In addition, "shaming" sanctions are most effective when imposed on offenders who belong to a reasonably well-defined ethical community. More so than the business world, the legal profession arguably is such a community, as evidenced by its specialized ethics codes.

As for the alleged drawbacks of adverse publicity as a sanction, law firms as artificial entities lack the dignitary interests that make us uncomfortable about imposing shaming sanctions on individuals. For just this reason, law firms and other entities have no Fifth Amendment privilege against self-incrimination. Moreover, there would be no need in a system of law firm discipline for adverse self-publicity. Public censure of individual lawyers traditionally has involved notices in court reports and in bar journals which the trade press or general circulation newspapers sometimes republish. A few jurisdictions also issue general press releases to publicize the names of disciplined attorneys and the nature and extent of their discipline. . . . The press might consider the censuring of law firms, in contrast to individual lawyers, especially newsworthy.

3. *Corporate Probation*

. . .

Disciplinary agencies already use probation to sanction individual lawyers. The courts' use of probation for corporations suggests that it could also be effective against law firms. In order to avoid the danger of overdeterrence, however, a disciplinary agency should only resort to probation after finding that the firm can institute cost-justified institutional reforms that would be likely to prevent a recurrence of the offenses involved. . . .

. . .

Conclusion

. . .

A number of questions remain concerning the implementation of a system of law firm discipline which this Article has not fully addressed—how to fund the system, how disciplinary bodies will gain jurisdiction over law firms, whether they should also take jurisdiction over other entities in which lawyers practice, and who should have jurisdiction over a firm with branches in several states. These matters are secondary. For now, debate should focus on the merits of the general proposal.

Notes

1. After publication of this article, New York and New Jersey changed their ethics rules to allow disciplinary actions against law firms. But the ABA's Ethics 2000 Commission, after flirting with the notion, abandoned it. The recently adopted SEC rules governing lawyers do not address law firm, as opposed to individual lawyer, sanctions or responsibilities. For examples of the New Jersey rule in action, see e.g., In re Rovner, Allen, Seiken, and Rovner, 754 A.2d 554 (N.J.2000); In re Ravich, 715 A.2d 216 (N.J.1998); and In re Jacoby & Meyers, 687 A.2d 1007 (N.J.1997). Schneyer tells us that he now believes the concept will be used against small and medium-sized firms, as in Ravich, as opposed to large law firms.

2. As Schneyer reports, most disciplinary actions are brought for neglect of cases and misappropriation of client funds. Why do you think that is? In a part of his article not reproduced here, Schneyer outlines the regulatory landscape, explaining how the existence of malpractice, court sanctions and administrative regulation does not obviate the need for disciplining law firms because discipline serves different functions and covers wrongs not handled by these other mechanisms. Recall the advantages and disadvantages of discipline as a means of regulation given by Wilkins, p. 4. Do they strengthen or weaken the arguments for disciplining law firms?

3. Schneyer does not explain why resistance to discipline of firms persists. He suggests that law firms should welcome discipline as a chance for them to demonstrate their commitment to an ethical firm culture. So why the continued resistance? The recent experience with the prosecution and conviction of Arthur Andersen may be relevant to some of the arguments Schneyer makes. First, many people voiced outrage at the fact that "innocent" people were being punished because of the misdeeds of a few. Another aspect of the Andersen case may be relevant as well. Schneyer refers to the respondeat superior rule that the government need not prove that any specific agent acted illegally as long as it proves that some agent committed the crime. In the Andersen case, the government had to prove that agents of Andersen "corruptly persuaded" others in the organization to destroy documents. During their deliberations, the jury asked whether they all had to agree on the same "corrupt persuader." The judge struggled with this legal question, but it was rendered moot when the jury was able to reach agreement on a single individual, a lawyer. If the law were interpreted to require jurors to agree on which individual agent was the wrongdoer, the effectiveness of respondeat superior liability could be impaired. Should a jury be required to agree? Juries don't have to agree on the theory of a murder to convict someone for murder. Why not?

4. If disciplinary rules were changed to include law firms, would such discipline cases be brought? Large law firms in particular have sufficient resources to mount a formidable defense to any proposed disciplinary action. Disciplinary offices with limited resources would be at a severe disadvantage, and so could be expected to focus their energy and efforts on other matters. Are there ways to address this problem? Would it be possible, for example, for disciplinary authorities to establish a "large firm task force," to which firms would have to contribute financial support as well as personnel? Even if such a system could work, would the firms be likely to support it? It's possible, however, that smaller partnerships could be meaningfully subject to discipline. And to the extent that disciplinary offices do engage in protracted battles with firms, even if they end up (as they typically do) with a negotiated settlement, their actions may still have some deterrent effect because, as Geoffrey Hazard put it in a letter to Schneyer (quoted in a footnote we have omitted), "the process is part of the punishment."

5. With respect to discipline for ethical violations in litigation, it is important to recognize that discipline is rarely imposed now for violations of Rule 3.1 by individual lawyers. (Model Rule 3.1 states: "A lawyer shall not bring or defend a proceeding, or assert or controvert an issue therein, unless

there is a basis in law and fact for doing so that is not frivolous, which includes a good faith argument for an extension, modification or reversal of existing law.") Is there any reason to think that discipline for violations of that rule would increase if discipline became available against firms? Although in the full article, Schneyer suggests that courts should be reluctant to tread on the regulation of law firm behavior in litigation, in fact courts are relatively willing to tread there. It is the disciplinary authorities who are reluctant to tread on the court's regulatory turf. To the degree courts are reluctant to impose sanctions for abuses in litigation, it appears to be based on the belief that the adversary system allows for sufficient lawyer retaliation (or threat of retaliation) as well as the difficulty in deciding when a violation has occurred. On both points, see Gilson & Mnookin, p. 417. Disciplinary agencies would (and should) share those concerns.

6. Schneyer argues: "Were it not for the common use of special disciplinary systems to regulate law practice and certain other professions, one suspects that the criminal law would be more widely used to regulate law firms and other professional entities." Schneyer thus seems to view the disciplinary and criminal forms of lawyer regulation as substitutes rather than complements. In fact, when he discusses the "analogy" to corporate criminal regulation to justify the adoption of firm discipline, as well as the regulatory landscape for lawyers in Part III, the possibility of criminal regulation of lawyers and law firms seems to disappear from consideration. Do you agree that in the absence of a disciplinary system there would in fact be more criminal prosecutions of lawyers? Isn't it likely that the bar would seek to resist the state's intrusion into the practice of law through criminal regulation just as much, if not more, than it would seek to resist disciplinary actions against firms? In fact, Schneyer's "choice" between regulatory systems is arguably a false one, because law firms may use the existence of the disciplinary system, knowing of the lax enforcement there, as a justification for resisting regulation under federal or state criminal or other law. See Koniak, The Law Between the Bar and the State, p. 23. On lawyer resistance to criminal regulation generally, see Bruce A. Green, The Criminal Regulation of Lawyers, 67 Fordham L. Rev. 327 (1998).

7. One of Schneyer's primary arguments for law firm discipline is the fact that it's often difficult to tell which individual lawyer(s) should be held responsible for some given act or inaction. A related concern, discussed briefly by Schneyer in his section on respondeat superior, concerns knowledge. Many rules of legal ethics depend on what the lawyer "knows." When knowledge is diffused throughout an organization, it is often difficult to show that any one individual had the requisite level of knowledge. Organizational law, such as the law of partnership, deals with this problem by "imputing" knowledge of one partner to all other partners, in part to encourage partners to keep each other informed about potential problems rather than in the dark. A similar doctrine exists in corporate law.

8. In discussing the administrative sanction alternative, Schneyer does not challenge the bar's opposition to regulation of lawyers by federal agencies, but sees state discipline of law firms as strengthening the bar's argument. But why should these forms of regulation be viewed as substitutes

rather than complements? In fact, if state disciplinary authorities are not likely to bring disciplinary actions against large law firms, for some of the reasons discussed above, then wouldn't the better argument be to argue that the federal and state systems should be complementary? Note that since the publication of Schneyer's article, Congress passed the Sarbanes–Oxley Act, which required the SEC to promulgate rules governing lawyers practicing before the agency, thus taking away one argument that the bar has used to challenge SEC jurisdiction over disciplining lawyers (but most likely not ending the bar's resistance, see Koniak, When the Hurlyburly's Done: The Bar's Struggle With the SEC, 103 Colum. L. Rev. 1236 (2003). The rules thus far promulgated by the SEC went into effect in August 2003. The SEC has stated it may issue additional rules regulating the conduct of lawyers, including a rule requiring lawyers to report client fraud to the SEC in some circumstances. We doubt the SEC will issue such a rule, given the bar's reaction to the prospect.

9.   Schneyer concludes his article by referring to "secondary" matters such as how to fund the disciplinary system, how disciplinary bodies should obtain jurisdiction over firms, whether practice entities other than private law firms (e.g., prosecutor's offices) should be covered, and how to resolve jurisdictional disputes when a firm has multiple offices in several states. Are all these issues really secondary?

10.   For recent articles on law firm discipline discussing Schneyer's proposal, see Elizabeth Chambliss & David B. Wilkins, A New Framework for Law Firm Discipline, 16 Geo. J. L. Ethics 335 (2003); Julie Rose O'Sullivan, Professional Discipline for Law Firms? A Response to Professor Schneyer's Proposal, 16 Geo. J. Leg. Ethics 1 (2002).

The Future of the Legal Profession: Delivery of Legal Services to Ordinary Americans*
ROGER C. CRAMTON

I. Introduction

. . .

B. "Two Hemispheres" of Lawyering

Traditional legal ethics and bar ideology present an image of a unified profession composed of professional equals. . . . Yet, the structure of contemporary law practice resembles two large hemispheres with modest overlap. . . .

The . . . two hemispheres [are]: lawyers who serve individuals and those who serve corporate clients. Corporate lawyers, who have fewer clients each year than those representing individuals, are often engaged in "symbol manipulation;" those who represent individuals are more often involved in "people persuasion." Because lawyers respond to the interests and demands of their clients, "the nature of the clients served . . . primarily determines the structure of social differentiation. . . ." Fields of practice that serve large corporate clients, such as securities, corporate tax, antitrust, and banking, are at the top of the profession's prestige structure, while those serving individual clients such as divorce, landlord and tenant, debt collection, and criminal defense are at the bottom. Lawyers who serve the core economic values of American society are accorded more prestige than those who are people-oriented or cause-oriented.

The structural divide between individual-client service and corporate representation affects the tasks that lawyers perform, the recruitment and retention of clients, and the fee arrangements. Because the pattern of lawyer-client relationships tends to vary along the hemispheric divide, ethical problems take a somewhat different form. A number of empirical studies conclude that large firm corporate lawyers wield relatively little influence over their powerful, informed, and wealthy clients. Lawyers in this sector of the profession tend to view themselves as technicians who do what their clients want.

On the other hand, studies of lawyers who deal with personal plight practice (representation of individuals who face a legal problem and who have had little or no prior experience with lawyers or the legal system) emphasize the power and authority that lawyers exercise over clients in those sectors of practice. Lower-status practitioners provide the vast majority of legal services needed by ordinary Americans. They also have the best socio-economic connections to the potential clients of moderate means. These practitioners also have the least margin of profit for providing charitable or semi-charitable services.

The juxtaposition of these differing findings suggests that rules of professional conduct should differentiate between sectors of practice. The rules should adopt a client-protective ethic for lawyers serving predominantly individuals and small businesses (unsophisticated clients) and a lawyer—and society—protecting ethic for lawyers serving large corporations and their managers. In one hemisphere of the profession, where lawyers are dealing with informed, experienced, and well-to-do clients, ethics rules would seek to protect lawyer autonomy so that lawyers would be permitted or required to be something other than the client's "mouthpiece" or "hired gun." Simultaneously, ethics rules in the personal-plight sector would seek to protect clients against lawyer overreaching. Differences in the context of practice suggest that different regulatory approaches and sanctions are required in different areas of legal practice to assure efficient compliance while protecting the independence of lawyers.

. . .

3. *Market Imperfections in Delivery of Legal Services*

Prohibitions against the unauthorized practice of law prevent those who are not admitted to the bar in each state from engaging in the "practice of law." . . . Both conservative economists and Marxist analysts view much of the profession's regulation of itself (usually through the instrumentality of the highest court of a state) as designed to enhance the incomes and status of lawyers. Milton Friedman, for example, argues that fears that consumers are incapable of making choices for themselves are paternalistic and unsound; registration or certification are adequate to meet information barriers. Friedman "find[s] it difficult to see any case for which licensure [e.g., exclusion of competitors] rather than certification can be justified." Restraints on competition have adverse effects on the quality, variety, and cost of services. Innovation is reduced and the flow of information impeded. And, almost inevitably, the producer group will dominate occupational licensing at the expense of the public.

Persistence of occupational licensing and continued public support for some types of regulation of legal and medical services have stimulated economic arguments in defense of at least some occupational regulation. The principal arguments . . . [are]:

[1.] Information imperfections in the legal services market may lead to consumer harm or a debasement of the quality of service.

- Some consumers of legal services may need to be protected against their own ignorance. They may be harmed as a result of information deficiencies that are costly or impossible to correct. Individuals who have no experience with lawyers and are involved in a personal plight, such as physical injury, matrimonial breakup, or a criminal charge, lack information about choosing or supervising a lawyer. The gap between the client's information and that of the lawyer requires the client to make a leap of faith, trusting that the lawyer is competent and honest. Professional regulation seeks to justify the client's trust by assuring a minimal level of integrity and performance.

• If consumers cannot differentiate between high-quality and low-quality legal services, producers will not be compensated for the higher cost of high-quality service. Information asymmetry may result in a "market for lemons" because producers are forced to make price and quality reductions that lead to the sale of only cheap products or low-quality service and the market shrinking. The problem may be overcome by certification, advertising, or other measures that remedy the typical consumer's information deficiencies. Alternatively, a regulatory regime may define performance standards and provide adequate incentives for lawyers to invest time, education, and resources in providing quality services.

[2.] Neighborhood effects (externalities) of sufficient size and frequency may justify governmental intervention. Even if it is paternalistic and undesirable to deny consumers the freedom to choose the type of service they want, costs to third persons or to the public generally may justify regulation. If an unlicensed and incompetent person builds a bridge or skyscraper that collapses, huge costs are imposed on others. After-the-fact remedies, such as negligence law, may not prevent a sufficient number of such incidents. In the context of legal services, externalities come into play most obviously when the issue is representation in litigation, which involves the interests of the court, opposing parties, and the public in just and efficient resolution of disputes. Regulation of advocates may serve those goals.

... [3.] Free rider.... Free riders are those who benefit from collective goods without contributing to their payment. In a sense, the public trust created by the profession's scheme of entry regulation and control of conduct is a collective good of the profession or the public. "[A]bsent effective regulatory structures, individual attorneys will have inadequate economic incentives to avoid cheating; they can benefit as free riders from the bar's general reputation without adhering to the standards that maintain it."

. . .

II. Legal Services for Ordinary Americans

A. *Pervasive and Recurring Problems*

. . .

1. Competence and Diligence

Preventive measures to ensure that clients receive competent legal services include bar admission requirements and continuing legal education obligations. . . .

Reactive measures, which are also intended to have a deterrent effect, include professional discipline, civil liability for negligence (legal malpractice), and sanctions administered by a tribunal in which a lawyer is litigating (e.g., Rule 11 sanctions, contempt).

. . .

2. Cost

During the 20th century, the cost of legal services has been affected by increased legal complexity, specialization, development of technology, and increasing entry costs [i.e., the increased cost of a legal education.]. Specialists command larger incomes and technology is expensive, but cost increases due to these factors are partially or totally offset by gains in efficiency. . . . [T]he increasing costs of becoming a lawyer . . . have added a substantial amount . . . to legal fees.

The ABA's efforts to assure the competence of new entrants have had the effect of increasing the cost as well as the quality of legal education. When the opportunity costs of foregone income are taken into account, the investment in human capital presently required to become a lawyer amounts to at least $100,000. This amount is less than is required to establish many small businesses, but does reflect a substantial investment on the part of the new lawyer. Because entry costs become part of the cost structure of the profession, average hourly fees or other charges reflect these costs.

A serious question, infrequently discussed, is whether the required preparation and its cost are essential in all areas of law practice. Some types of routine client service, such as sales of residences, simple wills, and uncontested divorces, may not require lawyers who are as thoroughly educated and as costly as lawyers are today. If these and other areas are opened to competition from other service providers, a market test of price and quality would be provided.

. . .

4. Trust, Loyalty and Integrity

a. Asymmetry of information and the "necessity-for-trust" argument

The linchpin of the arguments supporting the exclusive professional license is the claim that the lawyer-client relationship is an asymmetric one: Clients cannot adequately evaluate the quality of the service, and consequently they must trust those they consult. It is this theory, generally, that overcomes the strong presumption in economics that occupational licensing is a form of cartel activity that restrains trade to the disadvantage of consumers and the public.

Indeed, much of the specific content of former and current professional self-regulation falls neatly within the economist's catalog of anti-competitive practices: entry restrictions that protect incumbents against new competition; market-division strategies that limit the competition of lawyers with one another, and restraints on price and service. Minimum fee schedules and the total prohibition of advertising are examples of prior professional practices that are now viewed as unreasonably limiting price and service competition.

The necessity-for-trust claim involves ... a theoretical argument....

... the social desirability of encouraging high-quality producers ... may justify self-regulation, some degree of exclusive licensing, or other professional privileges. Special privileges are granted so that the average competence, trustworthiness, and public spiritedness of lawyers will be increased to approximately what they would be if the market imperfection did not exist, i.e., if clients were fully informed and could evaluate the quality of legal services.

Even if the theory is sound, however, its factual predicate must be demonstrated rather than taken for granted. Are clients able to evaluate reasonably well, even if not perfectly, the quality of legal services they want or require? The answer, in all probability, is not a global "yes" or "no," but a more qualified response based on the relative plausibility of the information-asymmetry argument in different practice contexts. The necessity-for-trust claim, I believe, is generally stronger in medicine than in law, partly because the information gap between doctor and patient is wider than it is in law and partly because patients are typically sick individuals who are less able to remedy their information deficiencies. In the practice of law, however, the strength of the necessity-for-trust claim is highly variable depending upon the context of practice.

...

... The legal profession repeatedly asserts that, because clients cannot evaluate what lawyers have to offer, clients should be protected against their own ignorance. Because of the tendencies of groups to delude themselves that something that is in their self-interest is also in the public interest, skepticism is warranted concerning the extent of the scope of necessity-to-trust argument.

The necessity-for-trust argument also raises difficult, perhaps unanswerable, questions of what we mean when we talk about "quality" in legal services. Clearly, outcomes cannot be the sole determinant, since in close cases someone must lose—the best advocacy may be on behalf of a cause that loses or achieves less than the client hoped. Similarly, efficiency criteria, although important, cannot be the sole arbiter of quality. Lawyers, like other professionals, tend to judge quality in terms of professional notions involving the intellectual or legal facet of a particular case (the quality of the advocacy given the state of available legal materials and arguments); consumers, on the other hand, give larger weight to other matters when their satisfaction with their lawyers is measured (e.g., "he didn't return my phone calls"). Lawyers as well as laymen have difficulty evaluating the quality of legal services. Possible differences in the norms each group would apply in determining quality must also be considered, lest the profession fall back solely on its own ideas of what is good for clients.

. . . [I believe] the necessity-for-trust claim is weaker than generally supposed. The argument has some continuing justification in some contexts of personal-plight practice, but it does not provide a strong, across-the-board justification for professional privileges.

. . .

B. A Taxonomy of Reform Proposals

A number of studies and surveys reveal that ordinary Americans encounter legal problems on which a lawyer would be useful and desired, but the individuals lack the information or means to pay the full cost of the desired legal services. Is meeting these unserved needs an important social objective? If so, how might the unserved needs be met?

. . .

1. Delegalization and Simplification

The simplification or modification of legal rules or processes so that individuals could handle their own problems offers the promise of allowing the solution of problems without the intervention of lawyers or legal proceedings, or in proceedings so simple that lay people can handle them on their own. This approach, often referred to as "delegalization," is favored by Derek Bok and other commentators because it reduces the need for legal intervention by substituting an alternative regime.

Drastic simplification of transactions or events that now require the use of lawyers, such as probate of wills, sale of houses, and divorces, might reduce the need for lawyers for millions of routine matters. Simpler statutes and regulations written in "plain English" might more readily be followed without resort to professional advice. Changes in substantive law would also eliminate the need for lawyers and lawsuits. An example of such a change is the substitution of national health care for most personal injury and accident losses. Examples can be multiplied endlessly.

All of these proposals are highly controversial. In each case the legal profession tends to resist substantive or procedural change, whether out of concern for the substantive or procedural rights that would be sacrificed or out of economic self-interest or both. . . .

. . .

2. *Substituting Simpler and Cheaper Procedures (ADR)*

A second set of reform proposals seeks to reduce the cost of legal services and court proceedings by handing them more efficiently. Alternative dispute resolution (ADR) is a favorite proposal. . . . Repetitive and routinized adjudicatory functions would be handled by procedures less cumbersome than normal adjudication. Most cases, even the complex ones, would be disposed of in arbitration or mediation stages that would precede the trial stage. Economies of scale in court-annexed disposition of disputes provides private and public benefits.

Skeptics respond that the efficiency gains will occur only if the parties waive constitutional rights or the procedures deal effectively with intractable procedural dilemmas. Others attack the fundamental premises of ADR. Owen Fiss, for example, argues that social values inherent in judicial declaration of public norms are sacrificed by substitution of more informal processes of private settlement. Richard Abel and others worry that compulsory ADR will be confined in practice primarily to poor people, resulting in second-class justice for those who are already deprived.

3. *Increased Competition*

Another way to reduce the cost of legal services, favored by a number of commentators, involves deregulation of the practice of law. Increased competition within the legal profession and with nonlawyer service providers, it is argued, would lower the cost of routine legal services and make them more available to the public at acceptable levels of quality. This approach would eliminate the professional monopoly and the remaining restrictions on form of practice. Nonlawyers would be able to compete with lawyers in the provision of legal services by delivering services directly to clients (with a possible exception for representation of criminal defendants) or by employing various combinations of lawyers and paralegals to perform legal tasks on a high-volume, low-cost basis. Judge Richard Posner also favors the deregulation of legal education: individuals should be able to sit for bar examinations without attending accredited law schools, a change that would require law schools to justify their costs in a free market—costs that now are built into the cost of legal services.

. . .

4. *Provision of Free or Reduced–Fee Service*

A fourth set of prescriptions is designed to expand the availability of free or subsidized legal services. What can be done to ensure that people who have legal needs but lack resources can obtain the services of a competent lawyer? The principal methods of providing poor people with needed legal services are voluntary or mandatory pro bono representation by lawyers and publicly-financed civil legal assistance. . . .

C. More Competition from Within and Without

. . .

1. Competition from Outside Providers: Scope of Professional Monopoly

In the United States many tasks of a more or less legal nature may be undertaken only by a lawyer. Statutes, court rules and judicial decisions restrict "the practice of law" to lawyers duly admitted in the jurisdiction. The only general exception to the professional monopoly of law practice is that persons who are directly affected may undertake to handle their own legal problems by arguing their own cases, writing their own wills or copying out their own deeds—a right of self-representation. . . .

Until the 20th century, the doctrine of unauthorized practice of law meant only that a nonlawyer could not appear in court to represent another person. . . . Outside the courthouse, nonlawyers freely performed tasks (e.g., title searches and will drafting) that today would be called the unauthorized practice of law. A vigorous and expansive doctrine of unauthorized practice can be seen in incipient form by the turn of the century but did not fully appear upon the American scene until sometime after the First World War. During the Depression, economic pressures on the bar and a social environment that was more hospitable to occupational licensing led to more vigorous enforcement of the expanded doctrine by unauthorized practice committees in virtually every state. During this period, the present scope of unauthorized practice became embodied in judicial decisions that also state the modern rationale of the doctrine: protection of consumers from their own ignorance.

After judicial decisions had established broad parameters of unauthorized practice, the organized bar, beginning in the 1930s, negotiated treaties with organized groups of competitors that had the effect of dividing the market for services in areas reserved for lawyers, on the one hand, and accountants, architects, claims adjusters, collection agencies, liability insurance companies, lawbook publishers, professional engineers, realtors, title companies, trust companies, and social workers, on the other. The growth of the consumer movement and the evolution of federal antitrust law brought an end to this market division strategy. The *Goldfarb* decision in 1975,[94] striking down the bar's suggested minimum fee schedules on federal antitrust law grounds, made it clear that anticompetitive activity by bar associations was subject to the federal antitrust laws. Subsequently, lower court decisions and the initiation of a federal challenge led to retrenchment and reorganization of unauthorized practice activity. The interprofessional treaties were

---

94. Goldfarb v. Virginia State Bar, 421 U.S. 773, 793 (1975).

abandoned because of fears of antitrust liability, a number of states disbanded their unauthorized practice committees, and, in other states, activity was narrowed and channeled through the state supreme court. The statutory and common-law prohibitions against unauthorized practice, however, continue in force.

Lay assistance in the provision of routine legal services (e.g., divorces, wills, and consumer bankruptcies) has been a major field of contest during recent decades. Earlier efforts to restrict the availability of self-help materials to members of the public foundered on first amendment grounds. The battle ground then shifted to lay assistance in filling out and filing legal forms....

Defining the activities which constitute the "practice of law," if the term is not limited to representation in formal proceedings before courts of general jurisdiction, quickly becomes a broad issue of public policy: ... Court decisions use ad hoc circular reasoning in defining "the practice of law." The most common formulation is the "professional judgment" test: Is the activity one in which a lawyer's presumed special training and skills are relevant? A matter has legal ramifications requiring a lawyer's involvement only when it involves "difficult or doubtful legal questions." The actual boundaries, however, appear to be more responsive to political and economic realities than to efforts at principled line-drawing under these vague tests.

The location of the boundaries is the product of the ebb and flow of interaction between the organized bar and competing service-providers, state law as formulated by state courts, constitutional law as formulated by the Supreme Court, inter-professional detente, and market forces. In Florida and Colorado, for example, the bar associations have been fairly aggressive, whereas in other jurisdictions they have been nearly dormant or, as in California, active but on the defensive. In general, state courts act only in response to bar association initiatives. When state courts have been asked to suppress activity as unauthorized practice of law, they have in general sided with the bar's position.

. . .

The American law of unauthorized practice goes well beyond that of the remainder of the common-law world in extending the prohibition to out-of-court legal services. Because law is such an omnipresent reality in today's world, it is impossible for individuals in hundreds of endeavors to carry on their work without dealing with "the law." Consider the police officer patrolling a neighborhood beat, the small business filing its tax return, the buyer or seller of a residential home, the consumer dealing with an aggressive finance company or collection agency, or the spouse considering a no-fault divorce. Each of these individuals may consult a lawyer, but many of them may seek or get advice from nonlawyers: The police officer from a nonlawyer supervisor, the small business from an accountant, the home buyer from a realtor, the consumer from a consumer group, and the spouse from a self-help kit. . . .

The current law of unauthorized practice goes too far in seeking to protect consumers from competitive services provided by nonlawyers. . . . The higher costs of limiting service to lawyers means that consumers forego any assistance for many ordinary, but troublesome problems.

. . .

2. Competition from Legal Assistants and Paralegals

Many law firms operate a high volume practice in such matters as divorce, real estate closings, workers' compensation claims, and bankruptcy. In these firms, and in legal services organizations representing the poor, intake and basic work is done by paralegals, with lawyers involved only as necessary. Nonlawyer competitors of lawyers frequently complain that law firms engaged in the same activities do so with extensive use of nonlawyers (legal secretaries, legal assistants and paralegals) who are given very limited supervision by lawyers. The bar's response is that professional codes require supervision and make the supervising lawyer responsible for an employee's breach of fiduciary or other obligations.

. . .

3. Form-of-Practice Restrictions

Model Rule 5.4 forbids a lawyer to "form a partnership with a nonlawyer if any of the activities of the partnership consist of the practice of law," forbids a lawyer to "share legal fees with a nonlawyer," and states that a "lawyer shall not practice with or in the form of a professional corporation or association . . . if . . . a nonlawyer owns any interest therein . . .; a nonlawyer is a corporate director or officer thereof; or . . . a nonlawyer has the right to direct or control the professional judgment of a lawyer." The comment states that "[t]hese limitations are to protect the lawyer's professional independence of judgment."

Should nonlawyers be prohibited from investing in, managing, and profiting from companies that provide legal services? Critics of form-of-practice restrictions argue that the legal services market would benefit from enlarged competition and increased investment. Allowing accounting firms, banks, insurance companies, or retailers to diversify into legal services would serve that purpose. On the other hand, especially when legal services are combined with another business activity, such as the provision of banking or insurance services, legal advice may be distorted by the desire to sell these other services. . . .

. . .

D. Mandatory Pro Bono

. . .

What is the scope of the problem? No one knows the proportion of the legal needs of the poor that are now going unmet. The federally-funded national legal services program meets a portion of the need, although funding cuts since 1981 have reduced ... [substantially the number of federally funded legal services lawyers.] ... Various studies show that most lawyers do participate in some pro bono work, but much of that time is directed toward activities that build relations with other lawyers, such as bar association work, or work that is designed to attract clients, such as free or reduced-fee work for local charities.

Poor people have many needs and the pursuit of legal claims with the help of lawyers may be less important than other needs, such as housing, education, and employment. Social resources are finite and other programs and benefits for poor people compete with the provision of lawyers. Moreover, legal services are different from other professional services in ... [at least one respect].... [T]he availability to one party of subsidized legal services imposes costs on other persons, who are forced to hire lawyers to defend their interests, and on the public.

... In Europe, where a right to civil legal assistance is generally recognized, its actual provision is restricted by mechanisms designed to screen out nonmeritorious claims and by severe restrictions on the fees lawyers earn in handling matters that survive the screening process.

. . .

1. A Constitutional Right to Civil Legal Assistance?

After the Warren Court held in the *Gideon* case that due process "cannot be realized if the poor man charged with crime has to face his accusers without a lawyer to assist him," it seemed possible that a similar right might be recognized for civil matters....

In *Lassiter [v. Department of Social Services]*[127] the Court held that a state's failure to appoint counsel for an indigent, imprisoned mother, before terminating her parental rights to custody of her minor child as an unfit parent, did not violate due process.... Four dissenting justices asserted that termination of parental rights involves a more important interest than is involved in many misdemeanor cases. They also argued that appointment of counsel is particularly important for a fair adjudication of cases of this type, which involve the application of an imprecise standard in formal adversarial proceedings in which the opposing party, the state, is represented. As the dissenters predicted, few situations under *Lassiter*'s balancing-of-interests approach turn out to require the appointment of counsel in civil cases. States are free to provide counsel

---

127. 452 U.S. 18 (1981).

to indigents in civil cases, either generally or in specific categories of cases, but with limited exceptions, have not done so.

. . .

In the absence of any constitutional entitlement, provision of counsel to indigents in civil matters depends upon the volunteered services of lawyers, judicial actions appointing lawyers for indigents, and legislative provision of subsidized legal services.

2. *Professional Obligation to Represent Poor People*

The bar has long recognized some kind of an obligation on the part of its members to represent persons who need legal services but cannot afford them. Various rationales are offered. One is that a lawyer, as an officer of the court, has a concern that justice be done, and that representing an indigent person who requires legal assistance is an obvious way to act upon this concern. Another rationale is that the bar has a monopoly of law practice, and as a monopolist, it should reallocate some of its monopoly profits to a manifest public need that is related to the monopoly. A third rationale is that representation of the poor is a special kind of continuing legal education that exposes the lawyer to the realities of justice as administered to the poor.

. . .

Lawyers have embodied their aspirations concerning access to justice in their codes of professional ethics, but have not stated them in mandatory terms. . . . Mandatory pro bono proposals have arisen in states and localities with increasing frequency since the 1980s, partly stimulated by cutbacks in federal funding of the Legal Services Corporation. Thus far, state-wide proposals have been defeated or tabled after extensive discussion.

Because supporters and critics of mandatory pro bono often agree on overall objectives, yet disagree vehemently about the details of implementation, consideration of a concrete proposal is desirable. . . .

The proposal, like mandatory pro bono plans elsewhere, divided the New York bar. Most bar associations opposed it, but individual lawyers and a few bar associations supported it. The Association of the Bar of the City of New York, which is representative of New York City's largest firms, " 'reluctantly' but forcefully endorsed the proposal as essential to meet a 'desperate' need." In light of this mixed reaction, Chief Judge Wachtler postponed action on the report in the hope that the stimulus it provided to voluntary pro bono would suffice to meet the problem.

. . .

The legal objections [to mandatory pro bono] rest on various constitutional provisions, including freedom of speech and association, the takings clause, equal protection, and involuntary servitude. The legal arguments have generally been rejected in the context in which they have the largest force: Court-appointment programs which require an appointed lawyer to devote a substantial amount of time to handling a particular matter.... If the lawyer is given a great deal of choice concerning how the required service is performed, as is the case in most mandatory proposals, a claim that free speech and associational rights are impaired is ... difficult to maintain....

The moral objections to mandatory pro bono are that mandated service intrudes on personal autonomy; that it converts a gift of volunteered services into the duty of a compelled exaction, thus depriving the actor of the moral significance of the gift of service; and that in application it tends to be regressive and inequitable, falling with a heavier hand on the less affluent and less successful lawyers.

The principal practical objections to mandatory pro bono rest on concerns about the quality and efficiency of mandated services ...; the burdensome problems of administration and enforcement; the discouragement of charitable and bar association work if they are excluded from the required pro bono category, ...; and, finally, a concern that, if adopted in only one jurisdiction, lawyers in that state will be adversely affected vis-a-vis their competitors in other states. A pro bono obligation imposed on New York lawyers, for example, will operate essentially as a tax on legal services....

The problem of feasibility asks whether, for example, an office lawyer engaged in bond debenture work may be an effective advocate for poor people. The law in which poor people typically become involved is a set of highly technical subjects with which most lawyers are unfamiliar. Most law schools do not teach these subjects, at least not in an integrated way.... From a political-economic viewpoint, most poor people exist in a semi-socialist regime in which their lives are continuously dependent on government regulation and discretion. Hence, in most localities, certainly in all major cities, a very sophisticated system would be required to provide that every lawyer be on call for whatever may be the legal needs of the poor. These difficulties would be less severe, however, if the law governing the poor were as central to the law school curriculum as is corporation law, constitutional law, or administrative law....

. . .

E. Publicly Funded Legal Services for Poor People

1. Development of Federal Legal Services Program

Legal Aid in various forms began around 1900, sometimes as self-help associations of worker and immigrant groups, sometimes as charities. Through the 1950s legal aid programs were funded almost entirely by charity and subscription of members of the bar. The programs usually had a small staff, often one person, assisted by volunteers and law students. The agencies were few in number, located almost exclusively in major cities, thinly funded, relatively passive, concentrating on individual cases and having the aura of a charity. In the 1960s, the Ford Foundation made legal aid a major undertaking and infused it with new money, new stature, and new assertiveness. In 1964, President Johnson's Office of Economic Opportunity initiated funding for a quantum leap in civil legal assistance. The federal legal services program, discussed more fully below, originated in the OEO initiative.

The visionaries and activists who started the legal services movement in the turbulent 1960s had three missions in mind: (1) the individual client-service mission of traditional legal aid, (2) law reform and institutional change, and (3) empowering poor people by creating organized groups that might engage in direct action such as boycotts, demonstrations and political activity. The activists in the legal services movement were committed to the last two objectives and were critical of emphasis on the first. They deprecated individual-client assistance as "band-aid" work that failed to get at fundamental problems. They sought to direct the program's resources into social advocacy and organizational activity. The provision of lawyers for otherwise represented persons in dealing with public or private institutions resulted in numerous decisions requiring more elaborate procedure or establishing new substantive law. The ultimate objective—a substantial redistribution of societal wealth and power—proved to be too large and too politically controversial to be accomplished by lawyers through the mechanism of the courts.

The social reform potential visualized in the 1960s, for the federal legal assistance program excited hopes of reformers and fears of conservatives, both probably exaggerated. The result was a political struggle for control of the program, involving the organized bar at various levels, political action groups, factions in Congress, and various agencies in the Government. Broadly speaking, the reformers sought to make legal aid programs a vehicle for structural legal reform through test cases, class actions, and legislative activity, in such areas as housing, civil rights, education, women's rights, and regulation of the workplace. The conservatives sought to maintain legal aid as a service program for needy individuals in such traditional matters as child support and custody, landlord-tenant disputes, debtor-creditor disputes, and securing welfare benefits.

In 1974, a detente of sorts was reached. The federal legal services program was established on a permanent basis through the Legal Services Corporation Act. The statutory objectives are stated in politically neutral terms of "equal access to justice" and "high-quality legal assistance" for the poor. Political and organizational activities on the part of legal services lawyers are largely excluded by specific restrictions: a ban on political activity by lawyers in the field, a prohibition on participation in organizational activity (as distinct from legal advice concerning it) and procedural constraints on the use of class actions. These restrictions suggest that individual-client service and test-case litigation arising out of it constitute the central statutory mission.

The structure of the national program involves the Legal Services Corporation (LSC) as a funding agency for local programs that actually represent clients and deliver legal services. The Corporation is forbidden from providing legal services to eligible poor persons, but it has an uncertain amount of regulatory authority over the operation of the local programs. Restrictions on the matters that could be undertaken by the local programs were included in the original Act (e.g., abortion and school desegregation cases). These restrictions have since been modified, elaborated, and fought over, each time in highly political battles. Parallel struggles have occurred over the level of funding.

President Reagan was strongly against any reformist tendency in legal aid and favored abolishing the Legal Services Corporation. Major bar associations, led by the American Bar Association, along with various civil rights and other activist groups, held out for continuing the program. In the 1980s, the program continued on funding diminished by budget cuts and inflation. The federal legal services program has emerged with modest funding and a relatively traditional program, but on a more or less permanent basis. Periodic disputes over restrictions on program activities as well as funding levels are likely to recur.

2. Recurring Policy Issues

a. Staff-attorney system vs. judicare

The United States is distinctive in that civil legal assistance to the poor is provided primarily by organizations that employ "poverty lawyers"—lawyers who are employed full time by local nonprofit organizations engaged in delivering legal services to eligible poor persons (generally defined as persons whose household incomes are below 125% of the federal "poverty line"). In other countries, eligible poor persons are referred to members of the private bar, who are then paid by the state at rates fixed by statute or regulation. The latter system, by analogy to Medicare, is referred to as "Judicare" in the United States.

The staff-attorney system, which is favored by most participants in the U.S. legal services movement, provides a cadre of lawyers who are intellectually and personally committed to serving the poor. The delivery of service may be organized so that clients are served by experienced specialists in various areas of poverty law, such as welfare, housing, or education. Further, the staff-attorney system permits more aggressive pursuit of institutional reform that benefits groups of poor people rather than merely an individual client.

Proponents of Judicare as a replacement of or an alternative to the staff-attorney system argue that the use of private lawyers permits a more normal lawyer-client relationship (the client chooses the lawyer and controls the objectives of the representation) and leads to greater client satisfaction. Some proponents favor Judicare ... [because it] is more likely to stick to individual-client service....

b. Who should be served?

The demand for free goods, even if their use involves time and inconvenience, is likely to exceed the available supply. The result is an inevitable rationing problem.... Local legal services programs are required to establish priorities after consultation with representatives of client groups, but it is generally recognized that staff lawyers play a large role in shaping and then administering priorities. The establishment of a priority in one area, such as public housing issues, may lead to refusing service in categories of other cases....

Defenders of current arrangements rely on utilitarian arguments of *triage*: Because funding is so limited, scarce resources must be devoted to the most serious problems that will do the most good for poor people as a whole. This argument places group interests above the right of individuals to obtain access to justice to defend or enforce their legal rights....

c. Standard of service

Ordinary people who desire a lawyer to prepare a will, get a divorce, or facilitate a transaction must pay the customary charge of lawyers for that service. Numerous studies indicate that many of them forego the use of legal services because of cost, inconvenience, or fear of becoming involved in the legal machinery. Those with little choice, who are cast as defendants in a proceeding brought by someone else, reluctantly hire lawyers, but generally push them to handle the matter as cheaply as possible. The result is a world in which most people "lump it" on many legal matters and get low-cost or minimal representation on many others....

The most ambitious vision of legal services for the poor, however, looks to the representation provided to wealthy individuals and large corporations in high-stakes matters as the appropriate analogy. Earl Johnson, who headed the OEO legal program in the 1960s, states that he learned what full-service lawyering for a client really meant from a partner at Covington & Burling who represented American Airlines in highstakes matters. Poor people, Johnson concluded, are entitled to the same quality and extent of legal service that is provided to a wealthy client in a high-stakes matter: aggressive advocacy at every stage, including appeals, representation in administrative and legislative proceedings, including lobbying, and use of representative or class actions when in the interest of the client....

The premises of Johnson's argument, however, are fallacious. Upper income people, let alone people of lesser means, do not employ a "full court press" in litigation except where it appears cost effective and often not even then. Such a commitment of legal services may be warranted where the existence of a wealthy organization is threatened, but it is not warranted, even with wealthy people, in a dispute over repairs on a Mercedes. . . .

. . .

One caution is warranted. The stakes involved in some test cases or class actions clearly justify full-service lawyering. The aggregation of small, related claims may collectively constitute a major claim that justifies a substantial commitment of legal resources whether the case is pursued by a legal services lawyer without fee or by a class-action lawyer who anticipates a fee award from a successful action.

. . .

IV.   Recommendations

. . .

. . . Lawyers should be required to report settlements or money judgments in malpractice cases to the relevant disciplinary agency. . . . The disciplinary agency's file of malpractice awards or judgments concerning a particular lawyer should be treated as a public file available to any person upon request.

. . .   .

The profession's resistance to treating disciplinary proceedings in the same manner as all other aspects of the justice system—as public proceedings open to public attendance, observation, and comment—has outlived its time. . . . The better position is that of Oregon, which treats any complaint against a lawyer the same as a complaint filed in a court of general jurisdiction as the beginning of a public proceeding. . . .

. . .

. . . State law should require a licensed attorney to purchase a minimum amount of malpractice insurance coverage (perhaps $100,000). Since some lawyers might not be able to obtain private insurance coverage, the state bar should arrange for fall-back coverage of these lawyers. . . .

. . .

Consumers would benefit from the provision of a variety of quasi-legal services by nonlawyers or by organizations composed only partly of lawyers. The statutes prohibiting the practice of law by unlicensed practitioners should be amended or interpreted to limit the professional monopoly to its historic core—the representation of clients before courts of general jurisdiction. . . .

. . .

Efforts by lawyers to obtain legal business should not be regulated, except that in-person solicitation of individual clients should be limited by time, place, and manner restrictions and by prohibitions against the use of false or misleading information in seeking legal business....

. . .

The current restrictions on ownership and control of organizations engaged in the practice of law (e.g., Model Rule 5.4) curtail investment and restrict competition in legal services markets to the detriment of consumers....

. . .

... Entrants to the legal profession are now generally required to complete seven years of higher education before becoming eligible for admission to the bar. These requirements become part of the cost structure of legal services, restricting the access of lower income people to routine legal services. Substantial educational requirements are appropriate for a learned profession, but a market test of these entry requirements should be introduced by reducing the required educational accomplishment to three years of university-level education and two years of study at an ABA-approved law school....

. . .

An infusion of able lawyers into legal services programs benefiting the poor (primarily legal aid and public defender organizations) would be stimulated by federal legislation mandating partial payment of a law graduate's accumulated student loans for periods devoted to low-income service in these organizations. For example, legislation might provide that 10% of a graduate's loan obligation or $10,000, whichever is smaller, be paid by the federal government for each year of low-income public service. An additional or alternative recommendation is that funds provided to public service lawyers by law school programs should not be treated as taxable income to the recipient.

Notes

1. As Cramton says, regulation of lawyers can occur upon entry into the profession as well as during practice. Wilkins, p. 4, focuses exclusively on regulation during practice. What justifies entry regulation? Cramton challenges the assumption that the asymmetry of information between lawyer and client justifies limiting those who may practice law. He also points out that ascertaining what counts as quality legal work is no easy task. Doesn't the latter problem make ex ante regulation (entry regulation) a more promising route (or at least as promising a route) to ensuring quality as ex post regulation? Put another way, if the outputs are hard to measure, shouldn't we focus on improving the inputs. That is essentially what entry regulation is designed to do. Whether it does so effectively and at reasonable cost is another question. For a famous critique, see Milton Friedman,

Capitalism and Freedom 136–60 (1962). How might entry regulation be improved?

2. By focusing on the entry stage rather than the performance stage, many advocates of deregulation of the profession ignore the difficulties of dealing with shoddy performance after the fact. The liability system (the law of agency and the like) would, of course, be available to people harmed by nonlawyers practicing law just as it is available to those harmed by lawyers. But a disciplinary system can handle the small claims that the liability system cannot handle. In fact, the disciplinary system is another manifestation of Cramton's two hemispheres: Rich clients sue; poor clients file disciplinary claims. But to have a disciplinary system, we need to decide who will be governed by it (its jurisdiction) and what rules will apply (substantively and procedurally). Once we do that, haven't we recreated the concept of a profession—now made up of lawyers and others who practice law? Our legal system does have means, other than a disciplinary system, for handling small claims, for example, class actions, small claims court, and reliance on reputation. If these methods were substituted for a disciplinary system, what, if anything, would be lost? Gained?

3. Putting aside litigation, many lawyering activities operate quite like insurance, i.e., insurance for clients against various kinds of legal risks. Contracts, wills, deeds, prenuptial agreements, etc., are all likely to be relied on only when serious disputes arise, or rare or singular events occur. Insurance is a heavily regulated industry in part because it involves significant stakes and rare events. Does this analogy have any bearing on the desirable forms of regulation for the provision of legal services?

4. Cramton mentions the treaties the bar created with various competitor service groups to divide up the market for the overlapping services performed by lawyers and these other groups. Although as he reports, the treaties were largely abandoned, some remnants of these arrangements remain within the ABA in the form of working groups or liaison arrangements, between the lawyer organization and trade groups maintained by competitor groups. Why?

5. Cramton mentions that in Europe, the right to civil legal assistance is generally recognized, but the provision is limited by screening cases for merit and by severely restricting fees. Might limiting the fees obtainable by poor folks' lawyers result in inferior service, particularly harming those with the most valuable claims. See generally Luban's article, p. 384.

6. Should law students be required to do pro bono work as a condition of graduating from law school? Should law professors be required to do pro bono work to model good behavior for students? To ensure they have some experience with law practice? What use would that experience be, given the two hemispheres of law practice that Cramton describes? See generally Deborah L. Rhode, The Pro Bono Responsibilities of Lawyers and Law Students, 27 Wm. Mitchell L. Rev. 1201 (2000).

7. Does legally mandating a moral duty necessarily demean it? Consider Koniak's discussion of "obligation law" in Through the Looking Glass of Ethics, p. 287.

8. Cramton's discussion of Judicare raises the question of how legal services compare to medical services. Leubsdorf, p. 234 also draws the parallel between the legal and medical professions with respect to malpractice. One could argue that, for the most part, the medical needs of poor people do not differ in any systematic way from the medical needs the rich: a tumor is a tumor, for example. There are, of course, some exceptions to that statement: some diseases or pathologies correlate with economic status. Nonetheless, in law, the problems of the poor and the rich are much less likely to overlap. In many cases the legal issues faced by the poor are unique to them, or involve specialized law that is not applicable to others, i.e., welfare regulations or public housing law. Does this suggest that staff legal services programs are superior to a Judicare approach (based on the Medicare model)? Perhaps Medicare should be abandoned in favor of clinics trained to deal with the poor and their medical problems. Does Blumberg's description of criminal defense practice, see p. 276, change your view of the Judicare model?

9. A second problem with the analogy to medicine concerns what economists call "externalities." If a legal services lawyer successfully challenges a burdensome term in a lease, then the benefits from that challenge (assuming the change is truly beneficial) could benefit many poor people in a way that a doctor's treatment of a patient is not likely to benefit others, at least not as directly. (There could be indirect benefits from, e.g., the doctor's getting more experience in performing a particular procedure.) But it is precisely that potential of law to affect others that raises a conflict for legal services lawyers. The lawyer may want to do that which benefits the greatest number of poor people, at least as the lawyer imagines the benefits. The client may want to settle cheaply rather than litigate (cf. the class action problem). This conflict (which Cramton discusses in the context of the legal service organization's approach to triage) is likely responsible at least in part for any reduced client satisfaction in the legal services regime compared to Judicare.

10. Cramton mentions simplification of the law as an alternative approach to providing legal services to poor people. Lawyers, of course, play an important role in law reform, but Cramton reports that they have often opposed simplification efforts. Why might this be so? The simple answer is that simplification is bad for business. But if the expense of lawyers is deterring many clients from seeking their advice and simplification would reduce the cost, might simplification be good for business? Maybe not. Perhaps, if the law were simplified, some people who currently seek legal advice would no longer do so. On the other hand, not everyone would find it advantageous to use simplified procedures (cf. short form 1040). Lawyers might be able to retain many clients simply by shifting their marketing focus (e.g., from "everyone needs a will" to "with your assets, a simple will won't work; you need a trust").

11. On allowing people to sit for the bar without attending law school and other proposals for reform, see Richard A. Posner, The Uncertain Future of Legal Education, Speech Before the Association of American Law Schools' Annual Meeting (Jan. 5, 1991), *in* Nat'l L.J. Jan. 21, 1991, at 4.

†